MANAGERIAL ECONOMICS

ANALYSIS AND STRATEGY

4th Edition

Evan J. Douglas

Bond University

with Empirical Cases by

Scott Callan

Bentley College

 Prentice Hall, Englewood Cliffs, New Jersey 07632

Library of Congress Cataloging-in-Publication Data

Douglas, Evan J.
  Managerial economics : analysis and strategy / Evan J. Douglas,
with empirical cases by Scott Callan. — 4th ed.
      p. cm.
  Includes bibliographical references (p.   ) and index.
  ISBN 0-13-554346-0
  1. Managerial economics. I. Callan, Scott. II. Title.
HD30.22.D68 1992
  658.4'03—dc20   91-42640
                                                             CIP

Acquisition Editor: Garret White
Production Editor: Joanne Palmer
Cover Design: Ben Santora
Prepress Buyer: Trudy Pisciotti
Manufacturing Buyer: Robert Anderson
Editorial Assistant: Diane DeCastro

 © 1992 by Prentice-Hall, Inc.
A Simon & Schuster Company
Englewood Cliffs, New Jersey 07632

Printed in the United States of America

10 9 8 7 6 5 4

0-13-554346-0

PRENTICE-HALL INTERNATIONAL (UK) LIMITED, *London*
PRENTICE-HALL OF AUSTRALIA PTY. LIMITED, *Sydney*
PRENTICE-HALL OF CANADA, INC., *Toronto*
PRENTICE-HALL HISPANOAMERICANA, S.A., *Mexico*
PRENTICE-HALL OF INDIA PRIVATE LIMITED, *New Delhi*
PRENTICE-HALL OF JAPAN, INC., *Tokyo*
SIMON & SCHUSTER ASIA PTE. LTD., *Singapore*
EDITORA PRENTICE-HALL DO BRASIL, LTDA., *Rio de Janeiro*

The rest of the team deserves credit, too.
Thank you Shelley, Meghan, and Andrew.

CONTENTS

PREFACE

Managerial Economics is concerned with the application of economic principles and methodologies to the decision-making process of the business firm operating under conditions of risk and uncertainty. My approach to managerial economics can be summarized by the following four points. First, I believe that economic theory establishes important principles for business practice. I have tried to include the economics that is more readily applicable in business situations and to exclude or subordinate the economics that is less applicable.

Second, business practice must be recognized and incorporated into the discipline of managerial economics. For example, if firms choose to use markup pricing policies rather than take the marginalist approach, then the task of the managerial economist is to assist the decision maker in finding the optimal level of the markup, rather than to harangue for marginalism.

Third, as the subtitle of the book suggests, managerial economics should be concerned with the firm's competitive strategy, rather than simply costs and revenues. Thus this book is concerned with not only cost and price decisions, but also quality and advertising/promotional decisions, and it integrates all these in the chapter on product quality and competitive strategy.

Finally, the concepts and issues involved in managerial economics must be put into the context of real-world business decision problems to demonstrate methods of identifying problems and finding solutions. Thus each chapter incorporates business examples and is followed by provocative discussion questions and case-study problems.

A NOTE TO THE STUDENT

Welcome to managerial economics! You are about to embark on what will be an interesting and rewarding learning experience. When you finish this book, and the course in which this book is used, you will have a much clearer view of the applicability and relevance of economics to decision making within the business firm. You will know a lot more economics and, just as importantly, will have developed your analytical skills to a higher level. You will also know more about how businesses operate and about the types of problems managers face. You will more readily identify the nature of a decision problem, and you will know where to start looking for the answers to that problem. You will be armed with analytical techniques and conceptual insights that will make you a better business decision maker.

Managerial economics is a serious course that will require a serious effort on your part if you want to achieve the benefits noted in the previous paragraph, not to mention a respectable grade in the course. You will have to read a lot of material, answer the end-of-chapter discussion questions, and work your way through the case-study problems assigned by your instructor. The rewards will be worth the effort. To assist you, I have written short answers to all the case-study problems; these appear in Appendix C at the back of the book. Unfortunately, space does not permit more detailed answers, but these brief answers will let you know if you are on the right track. Your instructor will have the more detailed answers in the *Instructor's Manual*.

There is a *Study Guide* available through your bookstore that some of you might really appreciate. In the study guide each chapter is broken down into section summaries, followed by self-test questions and their answers. Case-study problems are then worked through in steps before you are asked to work one through by yourself and compare your answers with mine. Potential midterm and final exam questions are provided for you to practice on. Also, if you have access to a personal computer and a spreadsheet package (Lotus or Excel), ask your instructor about the *Computer Courseware* that accompanies this text. This set of spreadsheet files (for Lotus or Excel or compatible spreadsheet programs) is designed to help with the solution of the problems and short cases found at the end of every chapter and appendix. They facilitate understanding of the problems and take away the drudgery of the repeated calculations that are necessary for sensitivity analysis. Details are found in the *Computer Courseware Manual* in the *Study Guide*. Ask your instructor how to get this important learning aid (details are in the *Instructor's Manual*).

I wish you good luck, in this course and in your future career. If you have any comments on this book, or on any of the supplementary learning aids, please write and share them with me.

A NOTE TO THE INSTRUCTOR

This book is designed for use in a one-semester or one-quarter course at the undergraduate or MBA level, in courses with names like "Managerial Economics," "Economics of the Firm," or "Microeconomics for Business."

The only prerequisite course assumed is a principles course in microeconomics, and even this is not necessary in MBA programs where students are typically more mature and more highly motivated. Each concept is developed from the basics, presuming that students will need refreshing on their micro principles in any case. If intermediate microeconomics is a prerequisite in the curriculum, Chapters 3, 4, 6, and 9 can be covered more quickly or bypassed altogether, but note that Chapter 3 includes the attribute approach to consumer behavior, which students may not yet have encountered.

A basic statistics course as a prerequisite may make students more secure initially, but its absence does not seem to materially affect grades in this course, in my experience. The same applies to basic mathematics and algebra. All statistics and mathematics used in this book are explained in basic terms at the point of first usage, and a more detailed review of functions, graphs, algebra, and differential calculus is provided in Appendix A at the end of this book. Some instructors may wish to cover this material in class, and others will prefer to assign it as initial reading and preserve class time for more applied material.

OUTLINE OF THIS BOOK

Part 1 of the book contains two chapters that lay the groundwork for decision making under risk and uncertainty. Chapter 1 introduces the student to the field of managerial economics and the use of models and other analytical concepts in the decision-making process. Then, the concept of value is addressed, involving both present-value and expected-value analysis. The firm's objective is then related to its planning period and time horizon. Chapter 2 introduces the concept of risk and uncertainty, measurement of risk, and the adjustment of decisions to reflect the decision maker's attitude toward risk.

Part 2 is concerned with consumer behavior and the demand side of the firm's business. Chapter 3 considers the utility-maximizing behavior of consumers in response to changes in prices, incomes, tastes and preferences, and perceptions of product quality. Attribute analysis is introduced at a basic level to allow the qualitative differences between products to be distinguished. Chapter 4 examines the determinants of market demand, the elasticities of demand with respect to price, income, other product prices, and so on. Chapter 5 is concerned with the estimation of the firm's demand and involves both marketing research and statistical (regression) techniques that are introduced and developed from basics.

Part 3 considers the production and cost side of the firm's business. Chapter 6 examines production and cost theory, linking them together for pedagogical effectiveness. Chapter 7 is concerned with cost concepts for decision making and considers accounting versus economic cost and profit concepts, stressing incremental or contribution analysis of decision problems. Chapter 8, which is concerned with cost estimation, uses the gradient method, regression analysis, and the engineering technique to ascertain both short- and long-run costs. The learning curve is also estimated here.

Part 4 looks at the firm's pricing decisions. Chapter 9 examines several relevant economic models of firm behavior, and Appendix 9A extends this to several more complex models. Chapter 10 looks at pricing in practice and examines markup pricing for its optimality in view of the firm's objectives, as well as other empirical pricing practices. Chapter 11 considers the pricing of new products and serves to reinforce many of the concepts introduced in Chapters 9 and 10. Chapter 12 analyzes competitive bid markets, and it also draws together elements from throughout the course in a pricing context that is observed in the markets for a wide variety of products.

Part 5 considers three topics that many instructors will strive to include in their course, despite the limitation of class time. Chapter 13 concerns advertising and promotional decisions faced by the firm, including the joint determination of price and advertising expenditures. Chapter 14 examines the firm's choice of product quality, as well as price and advertising strategy, in the context of its chosen competitive strategy. Finally, Chapter 15 considers capital budgeting, building on the expected-present-value concept that was introduced in Chapter 1 and used throughout the book.

CHANGES IN THE FOURTH EDITION

A major change to the book for its fourth edition is the addition of ten "Empirical Cases" which were contributed by Scott Callan, of Bentley College. These are found at the end of chapters 2, 4, 5, 6, 8, 13, and at the end of Appendix 5A. They differ from the Problems and Short Cases (found at the end of all chapters and appendices) in that they require analysis of a real business situation using real data that is in the public domain. The "Problems and Short Cases" frequently involve real situations but typically provide assumed data that is constructed to facilitate demonstration of particular points. The Empirical Cases also illustrate to the students that the data is *available* for managers to estimate demand curves, cost functions, elasticities, and so on. These cases might be assigned as take-home assignments, or used as models for projects where students are required to do a similar study for a different firm or industry, or an updated study of the same situation.

There are fifteen new Problems and Short Cases included in the fourth edition. These have been class tested and usually replace problems that were less realistic, too simplistic, or problematic in some other way. The total number of these problems is now 178, and their average quality is now higher.

There has been a substantial improvement to the readability of the book, particularly in the first six chapters, which were edited heavily for style and readability, and I think students will appreciate the difference. (The latter half of the book received much more attention in its revision for the 3rd edition.) There is "learning by doing" in textbook writing as well, and I welcomed the opportunity (greatly facilitated by word processing) to work through the book and polish up the prose and remove what I perceived to be stumbling blocks, roundabouts, and other obstacles to the clear communication of concepts.

There have been many other minor changes throughout the book in the form of additions, deletions, changes of emphasis, updates, and corrections. Many of these are in response to feedback received from users, and others just seemed like a better way to approach the topic or to sequence the material.

DISTINCTIVE FEATURES OF THIS TEXT

In my view this book has several distinctive features, as compared to other books available in this field, as follows:

1. Flexibility

Many of the chapters and all of the appendices can be included or excluded at the instructor's discretion. Whatever the prerequisites for your course, and whether your approach is predominantly quantitative, theoretical, or practical, there is likely to be a suitable combination of topics here, in short, self-contained chapters and appendices, that will facilitate coverage of the material you want to cover. (In the *Instructor's Manual* I suggest several sequences that might be chosen, based on input from a large number of instructors teaching this course.)

2. Currency

This text incorporates recent advances in economics that seem indispensible to the study of managerial economics. For example, Lancaster's attribute analysis is included for its profound implications for consumer behavior, pricing, the quality choice, advertising, and competitive strategy. The principal-agent problem, arising from the separation of ownership and control, is considered before assuming that managers will strive to maximize the firm's net worth. Learning by doing, and the impact of learning on costs, is incorporated into production and cost analysis. The consumer's cost of information, which influences the quality decision, the desirability of price competition, and the extent and type of advertising expenditures, is incorporated into these subjects in this book. The three generic strategies of competitive strategy analysis are considered in the context of the joint determination of the firm's quality, price, and advertising strategies.

3. Breadth and Depth of Coverage

In addition to the topics mentioned before, several other issues that are neglected or treated superficially in other books are covered in depth in this text. Pricing in practice is covered in more detail than in any competing book, and the discussion includes in-depth analysis of markup and other practical pricing strategies, new-product pricing, and competitive bid pricing. The economics of advertising and promotion decisions are afforded a complete chapter. In Chapter 14, the firm's quality decision is considered in the context of the firm's competitive strategy. Yet this text also covers the bases, including all of the topics that are found in the core of typical managerial economics curricula. It economizes on space (and class time) by combining production and cost theory into one chapter, concentrating on business firms, and treating some topics more concisely in chapters and appendices.

4. Capstone Chapters

Each of the last five chapters in the book can be regarded as a "capstone" chapter for the course. In Chapters 11, 12, 13, 14, and 15, material from earlier chapters is reiterated and consolidated in the context of another extension of managerial economics into new territory. At whatever point your course runs out of time, your students will have been able to revise and consolidate their understanding of earlier material and apply it in a new context, thus "rounding out" the course.

5. Case-Study Problems

Reviewers have said that one of the major strengths of this book is the case-study problems at the end of each chapter. In this edition some are new, some are revised, and others are carried over because they serve their purpose well. These problems are "not simply plug and chug," as one reviewer said, but require analysis, judgment, and sensitivity analysis. They are designed to reinforce the material and apply it in business contexts.

6. Empirical Case Studies

These cases utilize data from real business situations and ask the student to apply managerial economics concepts and methods to the analysis of a particular issue. Topics include estimating the joint probabilities of a recession based on an opinion survey of the National Association of Business Economists; shifts of versus movement along demand curves for the Suzuki Samurai; estimating the demand functions for gasoline, for domestic autos, and for air travel; estimating the production function for bus transportation; estimating cost functions for an electric utility and for freight trucking; estimating the learning curve for fax machines; and estimating the advertising-sales function for PepsiCo.

7. Learning and Teaching Aids

In the text, definitions and examples are highlighted to assist student comprehension and preparation for classes and exams. Short answers to all of the end-of-chapter Problems and Short Cases are provided in Appendix C at the end of the text, to provide immediate feedback and reinforcement to students working through these problems. A comprehensive *Study Guide*, which has been tested over two prior editions in a distance learning course, is available separately to help the student who is having difficulty with the course or with the problem solving. More than that, I believe that conscientious use of the *Study Guide* can lift any student's performance one grade higher than he or she would otherwise attain in exams and assignments that are based on the material covered in this text. A *Computer Courseware* package, derived from the author's own teaching experience in this course over many years, is available to all adopters. The publisher will supply a disk copy of the files to adopting professors, and they in turn can arrange copies for their students. The *Computer Courseware Manual,* and details about the courseware, are included in the *Instructor's Manual,* which also includes detailed answers to all Discussion Questions, Problems and Short Cases, and Empirical Cases, as well as chapter summaries, hints for instructors, sample exams and assignments, and suggested course sequences.

ACKNOWLEDGMENTS

I wish to thank, once more, all the people who were thanked, or who should have been thanked, for their contributions to the earlier editions of this book. There are now too many names to list individually, but I will mention my former teachers Cliff Lloyd, Peter Kennedy, Brian Johns, my former Concordia University colleagues Steve Robbins, Gary Johns, and Ken Reiner, and my former Bentley College colleagues Dale Kuntz, Andrew Stollar, Steve Grubaugh, and Scott Sumner, who were instrumental in the development of this book through its earlier editions. Particular thanks go to Scott Callan for his work on the ten Empirical Cases that are new to this edition. Many adopters and student-users of the book have written with helpful suggestions and corrections over the years, and I thank them again here too. The assistance of a legion of secretarial and clerical personnel has been fundamental to the completion of the book, more so in earlier editions, perhaps, before word processing became easy enough for me to handle. At Bond University I thank my new colleagues for their support in this and other ventures.

At Prentice Hall, I thank my editors for this edition, first Bill Webber and later Whitney Blake, for their continuing support and developmental assistance. Thanks also to Production Editors Barbara Grasso and Joanne Palmer and Editorial Assistant Diane DeCastro for their efforts in transforming this somewhat messy manuscript into the magnificent finished article as you will no doubt see it.

Last, but most, thanks to my family. To my wife Shelley, and children Meghan and Andrew, thanks for your continued support and tolerance when deadlines relating to this book and other work commitments kept me from getting home early and consumed weekends and evenings. And, as always, my father and mother remain a source of inspiration.

Evan J. Douglas
School of Business
Bond University, Gold Coast, Australia, 4229.

MANAGERIAL ECONOMICS

Chapter 1

INTRODUCTION TO
MANAGERIAL ECONOMICS

EXECUTIVE SUMMARY

What is managerial economics? This chapter introduces you to the subject and and then proceeds to build the foundation necessary for **decision making under uncertainty**, which is a central theme of managerial economics. In the first section we examine the definition and scope of managerial economics. This leads to a discussion of the use of "models" in managerial economics. We will see that verbal, graphical, and algebraic models depicting the behavior of consumers and business firms can be of substantial assistance in decision analysis.

Decisions made now typically have cost and revenue implications not only for the present period but also for future periods. In the second section we consider the multi-period nature of decision making and introduce **present-value analysis**, also known as discounted cash flow analysis, to allow the appropriate valuation of future profits for effective decision making.

In business the outcome of a decision is usually far from certain (at the time the decision is taken) because the decision maker has incomplete information and the outcome depends on the simultaneous behavior of rival firms and other factors influencing the underlying cost and demand conditions. When the outcome of a decision is not predictable with certainty, we say that the decision is made under conditions of risk or uncertainty. In the third section we introduce **expected-value analysis** to allow the proper evaluation of decisions that must be made under conditions of risk and uncertainty.

Business problems usually have several solutions. That is, there are usually several different decisions that might be taken to alleviate the firm's problem to a greater or lesser degree. Which decision is optimal? This will depend on the firm's objective—does it wish to maximize sales, market share, profit, net worth, management leisure, or what? In the fourth section of this chapter we consider **the firm's objective** and various **decision criteria** or rules that allow the optimal decision to be selected. Finally, there is a brief summary of the chapter.

1.1   DEFINITION AND SCOPE OF MANAGERIAL ECONOMICS

Managerial economics is concerned with the application of economic principles and methodologies to the decision-making process within the firm or organization. It seeks to establish rules and principles to facilitate the attainment of the desired economic goals of management. These goals relate to costs, revenues, and profit and are important within both the business and the nonbusiness institution.

Central to the study of managerial economics is the concept of profit. *Profit* is defined as the excess of revenues over costs. For a nonprofit institution, an excess of revenues over costs is called a surplus. If costs exceed revenues there is a loss, known as a deficit in the nonprofit sector. No firm or organization, not even the national government, can incur losses or deficits forever. The objective of a business firm usually requires profit maximization over its time horizon, which may be short term or long term depending on the firm and its circumstances. Nonprofit institutions typically do not seek to make a surplus but wish to spend their available funds to maximum effect. The decision problems facing business and nonbusiness institutions are therefore essentially similar, involving revenue enhancement if possible and cost control wherever possible. The attainment of a profit (or the avoidance of a deficit) is seen as a measure of managerial effectiveness.

Some people think that profit is a dirty word, associating profit making with "profiteering." In the normal course of economic activity, seeking profit is a thoroughly honorable activity. Without the promise of profit, there would be no private business firms and all business activity would have to be organized by the government. History has shown us that this approach is not a superior alternative. Competition for profits among private business firms leads to the ongoing availability of high-quality goods and services at reasonable prices, to increasing productivity, and to continuing economic growth and well-being for the nation's people. Profit should be seen as the reward for enterprise, the reward for risking capital, and the reward for superior insight and judgment concerning market conditions. Profiteering, or "gouging" the consumer when supply is limited, is typically not a good business strategy (whether or not it is immoral), because consumer illwill is likely to hurt the firm in the longer term.

Decision making in the areas of revenue enhancement and cost control are the two major concerns of the managerial economist. This theme continues throughout this text. Chapters 1 and 2 consider effective decision-making methods. Chapters 3, 4, and 5 are concerned with understanding consumer behavior; the reactions of consumers to changes in prices, advertising, promotion, and product quality; and the estimation and forecasting of demand. These issues are of critical importance for the practicing manager and his or her appreciation of the issues underlying revenue enhancement. Chapters 6, 7, and 8 are concerned with issues relating to costs. Effective cost control requires a clear understanding of cost behavior, the components of cost, the relevant costs for a particular decision, techniques to estimate costs, and cost forecasting.

Revenue enhancement requires a sound knowledge of pricing theory and strategies. Chapters 9, 10, 11, and 12 address issues relating to pricing theory, pricing under uncertainty, pricing new products, and pricing by competitive bids. Advertising and promotion decisions intended to enhance revenue are analyzed in Chapter 13. The quality of the firm's products and the competitive strategy of the firm (typically involving a distinct tradeoff between cost reduction and revenue enhancement) is the topic of Chapter 14. Decisions to increase or reduce plant capacity in order to control costs or enhance revenues are covered in Chapter 15.

This brief overview of the text indicates that managerial economics covers a range of topics of critical interest to the practicing manager. It also indicates that managerial economics is an interdisciplinary and integrative course in the business school curriculum, since it draws on elements of accounting, finance, marketing, statistics, and quantitative methods for many of its concepts and analytical tools. The economic content of managerial economics is derived largely from microeconomics, the branch of economics concerned with the behavior of individual consumers, producers, and suppliers of resources. In this text I assume that, while you may have taken courses in microeconomics, statistics, accounting, finance, marketing, and so on, you are probably pretty rusty on the specifics. Thus each concept is developed from basic principles, presenting little difficulty for those who have no prior experience in these areas and allowing a quick review for those who have.

Certainty versus Uncertainty

In simple microeconomics, economists assume full information, or certainty. That is, they assume they know the exact shape and location of demand and cost curves, such that they know exactly how much will be demanded at each price and exactly what the cost of production will be at the chosen output level. In the business world, however, firms typically operate under conditions of incomplete information, or uncertainty, and must estimate the quantity demanded and the costs of production based on the limited information they have at hand or can obtain by conducting information-search activity.

Managerial economics has evolved out of microeconomics to provide guidance for business decision making under uncertainty. Nonetheless, we examine several microeconomic models that assume full information as a prelude to the incorporation of uncertainty into the decision problem. In many cases we can effectively estimate the demand and cost data necessary to apply the microeconomic model, but in other cases the information-search cost is prohibitive and we must look for an alternative solution procedure.

Positive versus Normative Economics

In economics, the distinction is made between those areas that are positive and those that are normative. Positive economics is descriptive: It describes how economic agents or economics systems *do operate* within the economy or society. Normative economics, on the other hand, is prescriptive: It prescribes how economic agents or systems *should operate* to attain desired objectives.

Managerial economics is primarily normative, since it seeks to establish rules and principles to be applied in decision making to attain the desired objectives. But managerial economics must start from a positive perspective: We must always be mindful of the actual practices in the business or institutional environment. For example, if firms choose their price level by applying a markup to their direct costs rather than by equating marginal revenue and marginal costs as implied by microeconomic principles, managerial economists should seek the optimal level of the markup rather than making speeches to deaf ears about marginalist principles. The approach taken in this textbook is to integrate business practice with economics. By reference to the microeconomic principles, the business practice can be evaluated in terms of its efficiency in attaining the desired objectives.

The Use of Models in Managerial Economics

Throughout this text you will see hundreds of special words that comprise the jargon of economics, dozens of graphs, and more than a few algebraic equations. The jargon, graphs, and equations are used to model relationships that exist between and among variables and to facilitate analysis and decision making.

- DEFINITION: A *model* is a simplified representation of a complex system or situation. Models abstract from reality by ignoring the finer details which are not essential to the purpose at hand. They concentrate on the major variables and relationships without obscuring the picture with less important details.[1]

  Symbolic models use jargon and other symbols to represent reality. Managerial economics involves a lot of jargon. Even words like *costs, revenues, profit, labor, capital*, and *risk* have special, more precise meanings in the jargon of economics. Each of these jargon words, and many others, are formally defined at appropriate points in this book. Jargon words are only verbal models of things or phenomena. They allow us to communicate with each other more efficiently since they offer a concise and precise means of conveying the information we wish to convey. For example, "utility" is substantially quicker to say than is "the psychic satisfaction which a consumer expects to derive from the consumption of a product or service." And since jargon words are definitional terms, there should be no ambiguity about the precise meaning of these words. Thus communication between economists, between managers, or between you and me through the medium of these printed pages is facilitated and greatly enhanced by the use of jargon.

  Diagrams similarly model a situation by means of lines, shading, and other features, and they abstract from the finer details. Mathematical expressions also model relationships between and among variables, and are used in this text only when they are a more effective means of explaining something or proving a point. Diagrams and mathematical expressions are a very efficient means of representing reality; they are quicker to make and comprehend (once you understand them), and there is less ambiguity in such models as compared to descriptive speech. They state precisely and concisely the relationships assumed to exist

---

[1]There are three main types of models. *Scale* models look like reality but are scaled down or up for convenience. *Analog* models (like maps, wind tunnels, and fashion models) look different but behave in the same way as the thing they represent. *Symbolic* models use symbols to represent reality. See I. M. Grossack and D. D. Martin, *Managerial Economics* (Boston: Little Brown & Company, 1973) pp. 5–10.

among facts, observations, or variables. If these assumed relationships are inaccurate, the inaccuracies will be exposed by later testing the model against reality; and our model may be modified to reflect the feedback received from this testing.

The Purposes of Models.   There are three main purposes of models. First, models are used for *pedagogical* purposes: They are a useful device for teaching individuals about the operation of a complex system, since they allow the complexity of reality to be abstracted to a framework of manageable proportions. By excluding from consideration the minor details that do not affect the basic features or relationships that are at issue, the model allows us to deal with the central issues of the problem without the added complexity of relatively minor influences.

Second, models are used for *explanatory* purposes. They allow us to discover the causal relationships between and among events in a logical fashion. The assumed links between events may be tested for their authenticity by reference to real-world situations. If an observation contradicting an assumed relationship is made, then this model is refuted, while the model is supported (although not proven) by the repeated observation of supporting evidence.

Third, models are used for *predictive* purposes. The predictive value of a model is usually based on the ability of that model to explain the past behavior of a system, and it uses this past relationship to predict the future behavior. Suppose we have found that two events are causally related, such as low winter temperatures and high consumption of heating oil. The model should specify the extent to which heating oil consumption is related to the temperature so we may predict with some degree of accuracy the consumption of heating oil the next time we observe temperatures falling. This model will remain a good predictor as long as the relationships it represents stay constant. For example, if many households were to change to electric heating, the model will no longer represent reality as well as it did, and its predictions would be less accurate than before. A new or revised model would then be called for.

Friedman[2] has argued that it is not necessary that the assumptions underlying a predictive model be valid and testable. For example, spurious models of the behavior of the stock market have been based on the intensity of sunspot activity, the length of skirts, and so on. Such models, although spurious, have nevertheless served (briefly) as tolerably good predictors of stock prices. For predictive purposes such models could be quite useful, although for pedagogical and explanatory purposes they have no virtue. Even for predictive purposes, however, we may be somewhat cautious and skeptical about the model's ability to predict on its *next* test. If the relationship postulated is obviously false and the real determinants are unknown, the latter could change and our prediction would turn out to be wrong. Thus we need to be more cautious in using such a model to predict, since it may fail as a predictor at any time if the underlying (true) relationship changes without our knowledge or observation.

---

[2]Milton Friedman, "The Methodology of Positive Economics" in his *Essays in Positive Economics* (Chicago: The University of Chicago Press, 1953). See also L. A. Boland, "A Critique of Friedman's Critics," *Journal of Economic Literature*, 17 (June 1979), pp. 503–22.

How Do We Evaluate Models?   The preceding discussion suggests that a model must be evaluated with regard to its purpose. If a model is intended for pedagogical purposes, then it must be evaluated on this basis. For example, simple models of oligopoly (an oligopoly is a small group of competing firms) do not perfectly explain the actual behavior of real firms in the real world, yet they do teach students about the problems of mutual interdependence in business situations. Criticisms of such (pedagogical) models as being unable to *explain* or *predict* the behavior of firms are unwarranted to the extent that the purpose of the model is to introduce these concepts to the student.

Similarly, models designed for explanatory purposes must be evaluated on the basis of how well they explain reality. If an observation is generated that is at variance with the model, then that model is refuted as an explanatory device. If there are two or more separate models that purport to explain a sequence of events, the best model is the one that most accurately depicts the important variables and relationships between and among these variables.

Finally, models designed for predictive purposes must be judged by the accuracy of their predictions in subsequent tests. A predictive model is superior to an alternative predictive model if its predictions are more accurate more of the time. As the situation being depicted changes or evolves, we would expect existing models to become less accurate, since they must be modified to represent the evolving or changed situation.

It is important to keep in mind that models are abstractions from reality and thus represent the general features of reality rather than the specific features of a particular case. It follows that the predictive or explanatory power of a model will generally not be exact for any particular instance, because variables and relationships have been excluded from the model for the sake of simplicity or expedience. For example, a model may predict that firms will increase their inventories of raw materials when the prices of these are seasonally low. If such a model abstracts from the cash flow situation of the firm, it may imperfectly predict the behavior of firms that are facing a liquidity problem.

In this text, liberal use is made of graphs to model and analyze economic phenomena. Understanding graphs requires a basic knowledge of analytical geometry and calculus, and specifically an understanding of such concepts as slopes, intercepts, linear functions, curvilinear functions, convexity, concavity, maximums, and minimums, among others. If your analytical geometry and basic calculus is rusty, I suggest you take the time to read about functions, graphs, and derivatives in Appendix A at the back of this book. This may save you many hours later, since graphs are an efficient tool for both understanding and expressing managerial economics. Someone once said "a picture is worth a thousand words." A graph is worth at least as much.

1.2   PRESENT-VALUE ANALYSIS AND THE FIRM'S TIME HORIZON

Many decisions involve cash flows extending beyond the present period. When choosing among alternative decisions, it is important to distinguish between revenues that are received immediately and those that are received at some later date. A dollar received today is worth more than a dollar received next year, because a dollar held today may be deposited in a bank and at the end of one year it will be worth the original dollar plus the interest earned on that dollar. Hence, if the interest rate is, say, 10%, a dollar held today will be worth $1.10 one year from today. Looking at this from the reverse aspect, a dollar earned one year from today has *present value* of only about 91 cents because 91 cents would grow to a dollar (at 10% interest) within the year.

Both revenues to be received and costs to be incurred in the future must be reduced to present-value terms for proper evaluation of decision alternatives. *Net* present value is found by subtracting the present value of costs from the present value of revenues and can be expressed alternatively as the present value of profit. The major convention used for discounting future cash flows to their present value is to treat all flows as if they arrive, or are incurred, at the end of year one, year two, and so on. We look also at other cash flow patterns, such as the receipt of funds as an annuity, or on a daily, weekly, or monthly basis.

Present Value and Future Value

The *future value* in one year of $1.00 presently held is equal to $1.00 plus the annual rate of interest times $1.00. That is,

$$FV = PV + r(PV)$$
$$= PV(1 + r)$$

where FV denotes future value, PV denotes present value, and r is the rate of interest available. Suppose we start off with $1.00 (which we call the principal) and that the interest rate is 10%. The value of the principal plus interest in one year is

$$FV = \$1(1 + 0.1)$$
$$= \$1.10$$

Now suppose we could leave this money in the bank for a second year, also at 10% interest. The future value would be

$$FV = \$1.10(1 + 0.1)$$
$$= \$1.21$$

If a third year were possible, we would find

$$FV = \$1.21(1 + 0.1)$$
$$= \$1.331$$

and so on for future years. Note that the principal sum each year was simply multiplied by $(1 + r)$. In effect, the dollar was multiplied by $(1 + r)$ initially, then the resulting product was multiplied by $(1 + r)$, and then the product of that was multiplied by $(1 + r)$ again. That is, for the three-year deposit,

$$FV = PV(1 + r)(1 + r)(1 + r)$$
$$= PV (1 + r)^3$$

Generalizing for any number of periods into the future, we have

$$FV = PV (1 + r)^n \tag{1-1}$$

where n represents the number of years into the future that the principal sum plus interest will be returned.

- EXAMPLE: Suppose we lend \$2,500 for a period of five years at 8.5% interest. What is the future value of the presently held \$2,500? Substituting these values in equation (1-1) we have

$$FV = 2,500(1 + 0.085)^5$$
$$= 2,500(1.085)^5$$
$$= 2,500(1.5037)$$
$$= 3,759.15$$

This process is known as *compounding* the principal sum plus annual interest over the period of the loan. It tells us that \$2,500 held today grows to \$3,759.15 in five years if we can obtain 8.5% interest compounded annually. The *compound factor* which we used to multiply the \$2,500 to obtain \$3759.15 was 1.5037. This compound factor effectively says that \$1.00 today is worth \$1.5037 in five years if the interest rate is 8.5%.

Now let's do it in the reverse direction. The *present value* of a future value can be found by manipulating equation (1-1). Dividing both sides by $(1 + r)^n$, we find

$$PV = \frac{FV}{(1 + r)^n} \tag{1-2}$$

- EXAMPLE: Although we already know the answer, let's find the present value of \$3,759.15 available in five years during which the available interest rate is 8.5%.

$$PV = \frac{3759.15}{(1 + 0.085)^5}$$
$$= \frac{3759.15}{1.5037}$$
$$= 2,500.00$$

What we have just done is to *discount* $3,759.15 (the future value) back to present-value terms and demonstrate that the discounting process is simply the inverse of the compounding process. Whereas future value equals present value multiplied by the compound factor, present value equals future value divided by the compound factor. Alternatively, let us define the *discount factor* as the reciprocal of the compound factor, and say that the present value is equal to the future value multiplied by the discount factor. The reciprocal of the compound factor (1.5037) is 0.6650. Thus the discount factor, when the interest rate is 8.5%, is 0.6650. (Note that $3,759.15 multiplied by 0.6650 equals $2,500.00.)

Thus, the *present value* of a sum of money to be received or disbursed in the future is the value of that future sum when discounted at the appropriate discount rate. But what is the appropriate discount rate? The decision maker must choose the discount rate quite carefully, since use of an inappropriate discount factor could cause a poor decision to be made when the future profit streams of alternative decisions differ markedly.

The Opportunity Discount Rate

The appropriate discount rate is the opportunity discount rate, meaning the rate of interest or return available if the funds were to be lent to a bank or any other borrower at the highest interest rate available, subject to the proviso that the alternative investment opportunity is of similar risk. Economists like to say "other things being equal" when comparing things: In this case the riskiness of the future profit stream and the best alternative investment opportunity should be equal, so the rate of return involved in the future profit stream can be compared directly with the rate of return on the best alternative use of the funds without any further adjustments being necessary to account for differing degrees of risk.

- DEFINITION: The *opportunity discount rate* (ODR) is the rate of interest or return the decision maker could earn in the best alternative use of the funds at the same level of risk.

- EXAMPLE: Suppose that a firm intends to invest $10,000 in an expansion of its facilities but might otherwise invest the funds in a bond issue which is subject to about the same degree of risk. The bond issue promises 12% interest compounded annually. The opportunity discount rate to be used when evaluating the future returns from the project under consideration is, therefore, 12%.

How do we judge whether the alternative investment opportunities have similar risk? This issue is discussed in detail in Chapter 2. It is enough to say here that the risk in any decision lies in the dispersion of possible outcomes. Finding the equal-risk, best-alternative use of the funds, therefore, involves finding the alternative savings and investment opportunities which have the same or very similar dispersions of possible outcomes, and noting the highest rate of interest or rate of return on investment available within this subset. If the project or decision is risk free, the appropriate comparison would be Treasury bills or guaranteed bank deposits, which are also risk free. More likely, the project or decision does involve risk, and we must look around for other investment opportunities that involve similar risk and note the highest rate available among these investments in the same risk class. That highest-attainable-at-similar-risk rate of interest or return is the opportunity discount rate to be used when discounting the future cash flows associated with the decision under consideration.

It is important to understand that the discount factor is inversely related to both the length of the time period and the opportunity interest rate. In Table 1-1 we show the discount factors associated with several different opportunity interest rates and several different periods of time. Each discount factor is calculated using the expression $1/(1 + r)^n$ and effectively indicates the value of $1.00 at the end of a given period for any opportunity interest rate. Thus, at 10% opportunity interest rate, $1.00 is worth $0.9091 if received after one year; $0.6209 if received after five years; and $0.0923 if received after twenty-five years. Similarly, with a 20% opportunity interest rate, $1.00 is worth only $0.4019 if received after five years; $0.0649 after fifteen years; and only a fraction of one cent if received after twenty-five years!

TABLE 1-1. *Discount Factors for Various Opportunity Interest Rates and Time Periods*

Number of Years	OPPORTUNITY INTEREST RATES (%)			
	5	10	15	20
0	1.0000	1.0000	1.0000	1.0000
1	0.9524	0.9091	0.8696	0.8333
2	0.9070	0.8264	0.7561	0.6944
3	0.8638	0.7513	0.6575	0.5787
4	0.8227	0.6830	0.5718	0.4823
5	0.7835	0.6209	0.4972	0.4019
10	0.6139	0.3855	0.2472	0.1615
15	0.4810	0.2394	0.1229	0.0649
20	0.3769	0.1486	0.0611	0.0261
25	0.2953	0.0923	0.0304	0.0105

- EXAMPLE: Which would you prefer, $5,000 now, $20,000 in ten years, or $100,000 in twenty-five years? If the opportunity discount rate is 10%, the present values of these alternatives are $5,000, $7,710 (i.e., $20,000 × 0.3855), and $9,230 (i.e., $100,000 × 0.0923), respectively. Thus, you would prefer to take $100,000 in twenty-five years over the other opportunities. But if the opportunity discount rate is 15%, the present values become $5,000, $4,944 (i.e., $20,000 × 0.2472), and $3,040 (i.e., $100,000 × 0.0304), respectively. In the latter case it is preferable to take the $5,000 now. This demonstrates the powerful effect that higher discount rates have on future cash flows, and it also shows that the selection of the appropriate discount rate is critical for the effective evaluation of decision alternatives.

Table 1-1 is excerpted from Table B-1 in Appendix B, found at the end of this text, which shows the discount factors for all opportunity interest rates from 1% to 28% over periods from one year to twenty-five years. For discount rates involving fractions, such as 16.125%, you should use your calculator and the formula supplied by Eq. (1-2).[3]

Net-Present-Value Analysis

When a decision involves both revenues and costs in future periods, we net the costs of each year against the revenues of each year to find the present value of the net revenues, or net costs. Since profit is the excess of revenues over costs, and a loss is the excess of costs over revenues, this procedure amounts to finding the present value of the profit (or loss) associated with the decision in future years. Using symbols, we can write

$$\text{NPV} = \sum_{i=1}^{n} \frac{FV_i}{(1 + r)^i} - C_0$$

(1-3)

where NPV is the net present value, FV_i represents the future net revenue (profit) to be received in each of the $i = 1,2,3, \ldots n$ years over which cash flows are expected, C_0 is the initial (present period) cost of the project or decision, and the Σ (sigma) connotes the sum of the discounted future values from $i = 1$ (the first year) to $i = n$ (the last year).

• EXAMPLE: Suppose our firm is considering the installation of equipment to manufacture a new product, and we anticipate the cost and revenue streams shown in Table 1-2. The cost stream includes the initial capital cost and the annual operating costs of the equipment and associated labor and material costs. The revenue stream shows the revenue expected from sales of the product and includes the salvage value of the equipment in the last year, at which point we assume the market will become saturated and production will cease.

TABLE 1-2. *The Net Present Value of a Decision*

Year	Revenues ($000)	Costs ($000)	Profit ($000)	Discount Factor (@ 18%)	NPV ($000)
0	—	744.85	−744.85	1.0000	−744.85
1	400.00	224.62	175.38	0.8475	148.63
2	1,085.00	648.22	436.78	0.7182	313.70
3	872.50	456.98	415.52	0.6086	252.89
4	220.00	131.43	88.57	0.5158	45.68
5	380.00	58.35	321.65	0.4371	140.59
				Net present value	156.64

---

[3]An approximation can be found by a linear interpolation between the 16% and 17% values. That is, subtract 1/8 of the difference from the 16% discount factor. This is approximate because the relationship is curvilinear. Equation (1-2) is simple to apply and gives the accurate result.

Since there is some uncertainty about the future revenue and cost streams, we must identify the opportunity discount rate. Suppose we investigate and conclude that it is 18%. We can then calculate the present value of the profits from the project as shown in Table 1-2 using the discount factors from Table B-1 in Appendix B. Note that this example includes year 0, or the present period, in the calculations, since the capital expenditure on the equipment ($744,850) must be made in the present period. The appropriate discount factor for this expenditure is 1.000, since this sum is *already* in present-value terms. For each year in which there are both revenues and costs, the net revenues (profits) are discounted by the appropriate discount factor to find the present value of each year's profits from the proposed decision. Adding up the present values of each year's profits or losses results in a net present value of the decision of $156,640. If this is the best alternative open to the firm, we would certainly advise the firm to go ahead with it, since it represents $156,640 more than the firm could earn if it invested the funds elsewhere at 18%, the opportunity interest rate.[4]

Annuities. A simplification can be applied if the stream of cash flows is regular and uniform for a number of periods. Such a uniform cash flow over several consecutive time periods is known as an annuity. You are probably aware of the concept of annuities. Retirement savings can be used to purchase an annuity which pays the owner a given sum of money every year or every month for a prescribed number of years. Any regular and uniform stream of payments can be treated like an annuity. For example, a firm expecting to earn $50,000 each year for five years as the result of a particular decision is, in effect, expecting an annuity.

It can be shown that the present value of an annuity can be calculated as the amount to be received in each period times the sum of the discount factors for each period. That is,

$$PV = \frac{FV_1}{(1 + r)^1} + \frac{FV_2}{(1 + r)^2} + \frac{FV_3}{(1 + r)^3} + \ldots + \frac{FV_n}{(1 + r)^n}$$

$$= \sum_{i = 1}^{n} \frac{FV_i}{(1 + r)^i}$$

or,
$$PV = FV \sum_{i = 1}^{n} \frac{1}{(1 + r)^i} \tag{1-4}$$

since all the FVs have the same value.

---

[4]If the NPV is positive, it means that the project yields an *internal rate of return* (IRR) that is higher than the opportunity rate at which the profit stream was discounted. The IRR is the discount rate that would reduce the NPV to zero or, alternatively, it is the discount rate that would reduce the present value of the future stream of profit to equality with the initial cost of the project. Thus, the internal rate of return of the project in the example is substantially in excess of its discount rate of 18%, and is, in fact, 29.89%. A good financial calculator will calculate the IRR, and an iterative method is shown in Chapter 15. The spreadsheet templates ENPVA and ENPVB, available with this text, allow the calculation of IRR quickly and easily.

- EXAMPLE: A firm expects to receive $50,000 for each of five years as a result of a decision it is about to implement. What is the present value of this annuity if the firm's opportunity discount rate is 16%? In Table 1-3 we find the present value of the revenue stream of $50,000 each year for five years, given 16% discount factors. The sum of the present values of the annual payments is $163,720. Now notice that the sum of the discount factors is 3.2744 and that this figure multiplied by $50,000 equals $163,720. The sum of the discount factors is known as the *present-value factor* for an annuity over that period of time.

TABLE 1-3. The Present Value of an Annuity

Year	Revenues ($000)	Discount Factor (@16%)	NPV ($000)
1	50,000	0.8621	43,105
2	50,000	0.7432	37,160
3	50,000	0.6407	32,035
4	50,000	0.5523	27,615
5	50,000	0.4761	23,805
	Totals	3.2744	163,720

    Table B-2 in Appendix B shows the present-value factors for annuities up to periods of twenty-five years and for opportunity interest rates of 1% through 28%. It is certainly much quicker to find the present value of an annuity in a single calculation than it is to find the present value of each annual cash flow and then add these to find the present value of the revenue stream. If you refer to Table B-2, you will find that the present-value factor for ODR = 16% and Years = 5 is shown as 3.2743. (This is the more accurate figure: The discount factors in Table 1-3 are rounded off.) Thus, the present value of the annuity is 3.2743 times the periodic payment of $50,000, which is $163,715.

Discounting Using Daily Interest Rates.   Most of the cash flows paid and received by firms do not occur in lump sums at the end of the year, but instead occur at more frequent intervals. Cash receipts from customers may be received daily, wages may be paid weekly, and management salary, payments to suppliers, and other expenses usually occur monthly. It makes a significant difference to the present value if the payments and receipts are received and disbursed frequently during the year, rather than being delayed until the year end. Money received during the year can be put in the bank and will earn interest between now and the end of the year. Daily-interest savings and checking accounts are now common, and our analysis should reflect the greater present value of a sum if it is received at the end of the year as a lump sum. The end-of-year convention is a simplification that is often quite appropriate. In many cases, the cash flows do occur annually in lump sums. For example, the firm's cash flow may be highly seasonal (such as around Christmas), and the end-of-year assumption is a tolerable approximation. In other cases, however, the cash flows of a decision are expected to occur more or less evenly throughout the year, and it is more appropriate to use discount factors based on daily interest rates.

The present-value formula is easily modified to reflect higher frequencies of receipt or disbursement of funds. Let m be the number of times that the payment period fits into the year, that is $m = 365/d$ where d is the number of days in the payment period. For example, $m = 365$ for daily cash flows, $m = 52$ for weekly cash flows, $m = 12$ for monthly cash flows, and $m = 4$ for quarterly cash flows. The modified present-value formula would then read

$$PV = \frac{FV/m}{(1 + r/m)^1} + \frac{FV/m}{(1 + r/m)^2} + \frac{FV/m}{(1 + r/m)^3} + \dots + \frac{FV/m}{(1 + r/m)^n}$$

$$= \sum_{i=1}^{n} \frac{FV/m}{(1 + r/m)^i} \tag{1-5}$$

where FV again represents the future sum received during the year but is received in a series of payments, each equal to FV/m. In effect, the firm receives an annuity of $1/m$ of the FV every d days during the year. For the daily interest case, and assuming FV = $1, that dollar is presumed to arrive in 365 equal installments, each equal to 1/365 of one dollar. Note that equation (1-5) is also the formula for the daily interest rate discount factor when FV = $1.

Discount factors based on daily interest rates are provided in Table B-3 in Appendix B. We can see the impact of using daily interest discount factors if we repeat the NPV calculations of the cash flows shown in Table 1-2, this time assuming that the cash flows occur on a daily basis throughout each year rather than as lump sums at the end of each year.[5] The results are shown in Table 1-4.

TABLE 1-4. *Net Present Value Using Daily Discount Factors*

Year	Profit ($000)	Discount Factor (@18%)	NPV ($000)
0	−744.85	1.0000	−744.850
1	175.38	0.9150	160.473
2	436.78	0.7643	333.831
3	415.52	0.6384	265.268
4	88.57	0.5333	47.234
5	321.65	0.4454	143.263
		Net present value	205.219

[5]Strictly speaking, the salvage value of the equipment should be separated from the sales revenues of year 5. Since the salvage value is no doubt received at the end of the year, it should be discounted at year-end rates. The purpose here is simply to show that the difference in the cash flow conventions can make a substantial difference in the present-value calculation.

Note that each discount factor in Table 1-4 is slightly higher than the corresponding year-end discount factor in Table 1-3. Higher discount factors mean the cash flows are discounted less severely and reflect the greater value of a dollar received as a stream of payments during the year rather than a simple payment at the end of the year. Consequently, the NPV is higher (by $48,579) when we account for the daily cash flow pattern rather than assuming year-end payments and receipts. This could be a critical consideration in deciding between two decision alternatives. If they both have the same annual cash flows, but one series of cash flows occurs at the end of the year, while the other series occurs more or less evenly throughout each year, then the latter will be the preferred option. NPV analysis should use the cash flow assumption that most closely matches the actual pattern of cash flows expected. End-of-year discount factors will be more appropriate for some decision alternatives, whereas daily discount factors will be more appropriate for others.

The Firm's Planning Period and Time Horizon

- DEFINITION: The firm's *planning period* is the period of time over which the firm takes into account the cost and revenue implications of its decisions. The firm's *time horizon* is the point in the future at which the firm no longer considers the cost and revenue implications of its decisions. The time horizon is, therefore, the end of the firm's planning period.

- EXAMPLE: Suppose a firm plans to invest in a new building and calculates the present value of the initial cost and future maintenance costs for the next fifteen years and sets against these the present value of the revenues it expects to receive from the building over the same fifteen-year period. This firm's planning period is thus fifteen years, since it has taken into account the cost and revenue implications of its decision to buy the new building only up to the fifteenth year into the future. The sixteenth and subsequent years' costs and revenues are ignored. In effect, the firm considers them to occur so far into the future that they are insignificant to the decision.

A firm's time horizon, and, thus, the length of its planning period, is likely to vary among firms for various reasons. Firms involved in intense competition for their day-to-day survival are less likely to worry about the longer-term cost and revenue implications of their decision. Immediate or short-term costs and revenues may be given full weight in their decision making, to the complete exclusion of the longer-term profit implications of their actions. Conversely, a firm that is well established and secure in its market, without the constant pressure of day-to-day price competition, can afford the luxury of taking into consideration the future profit implications of its current decisions.

Another reason for differing planning periods among firms is the motivation of the manager. A manager who expects to retire in six months, or who is actively seeking a promotion within the year, may be expected to prefer actions that do more for short-term profit over those that promise greater longer-term profit. Conversely, managers who wish to make a career out of their position, or who prefer longer-term stability of employment and salary income, may be expected to take the longer view and take actions which promise greater profits over an extended planning period.

Finally, the firm's planning period may be inversely related to the general level of interest rates, because the present value of future profits declines as the opportunity discount rate increases. This presumes that the decision maker decides to suspend the search for information (concerning future costs and revenues associated with a particular decision) when the present value of $1.00 earned at the time horizon falls below some predetermined level.

- EXAMPLE: A firm that places its time horizon at fifteen years, when the opportunity discount rate is 10%, may shorten its planning period to ten years when the opportunity discount rate is 15%, since the present value of $1.00 falls below $0.25 at the time horizon in each case. (You may confirm this in Table 1-1.) The reason a firm may adopt a cutoff rule like this is related to the cost of obtaining information, or *search costs*, which we examine in Chapter 2. It will suffice to say here that if the firm expects to pay $0.25 now to find out that it will earn $1.00 in ten years, it is profit maximizing to suspend search activity at that point if the present value of the $1.00 is less than $0.25.

The firm's time horizon will occur either within the present period or in some future period. If it occurs in the present period, we can treat all cash flows at face value, since they will already be in present-value terms. If the firm's time horizon lies beyond the present period, we must discount future cash flows back to present-value terms to compare them properly with present-period costs and revenues.

How long is the present period? Strictly, it should be very short indeed and should end before the value of a dollar to be received next week is worth fractionally less than $1.00 to be received today, because a lesser sum could grow to $1.00 (in a daily-interest savings account) by next week. Realistically, however, there is a cost involved in converting every cash flow into its present-value equivalent, and it is not worth doing for most cash flows that will arrive or will be disbursed in the near future. For our purposes it is probably sufficient to treat cash flows that occur within the coming year in nominal terms, ignoring the fact that doing so will slightly overstate their present value. But when the dollar amounts are very large and the interest rates are relatively high, we should certainly discount the nominal values to present values for cash flows occurring within the present year.[6]

---

[6]To discount a cash flow received within the current or a future year, use equation (1-2) with n reflecting the time period in (fractional) years. Thus, lump sum payment in six months would mean $n = 0.5$, while a lump sum received in two years and nine months would mean $n = 2.75$.

1.3 EXPECTED-VALUE ANALYSIS OF UNCERTAIN OUTCOMES

In this section we consider risk and uncertainty, and we describe the method for evaluating decision alternatives when the decision maker faces risk and uncertainty. We first clarify what is meant by risk and uncertainty and note that the phrase implies a probability distribution of outcomes related to each decision alternative. Expected-present-value (EPV) analysis is then introduced to summarize each probability distribution of outcomes into a single number such that the decision alternatives may be compared and an optimal decision may be selected.

Certainty, Risk, and Uncertainty

The state of information under which a decision is made has important implications for the predictability of the outcome of that decision. If there is full information, the outcome of a decision will be foreseen clearly and unambiguously. In this situation (of certainty) the firm can accurately predict the outcome of each of its decisions. When there is less than full information, however, the decision maker may foresee several potential outcomes to a decision and, therefore, will be unable to predict consistently which outcome will actually occur. In this case we say that the individual or firm is operating under conditions of risk and uncertainty.

- DEFINITION: *Certainty* exists if the outcome of a decision is known in advance without a shadow of a doubt. Under conditions of certainty, a decision leads to a single possible outcome, which is perfectly foreseen. *Uncertainty* is involved when a decision might lead to one of several possible outcomes and the exact outcome is not known in advance. Instead, there will be a probability distribution of possible outcomes, which the decision maker must identify.

The Probability Distributions of Possible Outcomes

Risk can be regarded as a subcategory of uncertainty in which the probabilities of each outcome can be assigned on an objective basis. Risk is involved when one flips a coin, throws dice, or plays a hand of poker. The probability of flipping a coin and having it land "heads" is 1/2, since there are only two possible outcomes (ruling out the coin landing on its edges), and each is equally likely to occur, given an unbiased coin. Similarly, when one throws two dice, the probability that they will turn up "snake eyes" or any other pair of numbers, is $1/6 \times 1/6 = 1/36$. The probability of drawing a "royal flush" in poker, or any other combination of cards, can be likewise calculated.

In each of the preceding illustrations, the probability of each outcome is known *a priori*. That is, on the basis of known mathematical and physical principles, we can calculate the probable incidence (or proportion) of each possible outcome in the total number of outcomes associated with a number of trials. That is, if we toss a coin a number of times, we expect to observe "heads" about half the time. Although "heads" might appear three or even four times out of the first four tosses of the coin, given a sufficiently large number of trials, the proportions will converge on 1/2 for each of the two possible outcomes.

A second class of risk situations is that in which probabilities are assigned *a posteriori*, or on the basis of past experience under similar circumstances. The insurance business is based on this type of risk situation. The possible outcomes are known: for example, a particular vehicle will or will not be involved in an accident. Insurance companies keep extensive data on previous policies and claims and other pertinent data; from these they compile actuarial tables, which show the relative incidence of the various outcomes in past situations or trials. On the presumption that a particular driver and vehicle are similar in all important respects to those of the data base, the companies are able to form an expectation (or assign a probability) of the chances of that particular driver having an accident in that vehicle.

In perhaps the great majority of decision-making problems, the precise nature of the potential outcomes cannot be foreseen clearly in advance. Instead the decision maker must estimate a range of potential outcomes. Similarly, there is typically no data bank of past decisions that are sufficiently similar to the problem at hand to allow the assignment of probabilities based on past observations. In these situations, the decision maker must assign the probabilities subjectively, based on experience, intuition, and judgment.

The Expected Value of a Decision

Under conditions of risk and uncertainty the decision maker looks at each of the potential solutions to a problem and, for each of these possible decisions, foresees a probability distribution of outcomes. That is, several different levels of profit (or loss) are perceived as possible, and each of these is assigned a probability of occurring. How does the decision maker summarize all this data so they can be compared with other potential solutions to the same problem?

• DEFINITION: The *expected value* of an outcome is the value of that outcome multiplied by the probability of that outcome occurring. Since several outcomes are possible under risk and uncertainty, the expected value of a decision is the sum of the expected values of all the possible outcomes that may follow the decision.[7]

---

[7]Formally, we define the expected value of a decision as

$$EV = \sum_{i=1}^{n} R_i P_i$$

where Σ connotes "the sum of"; R_i is the return of the ith outcome; $i = 1, 2, 3, \ldots, n$ identifies each separate possible outcome; n is the total number of possible outcomes; and P_i is the probability of the ith outcome occurring.

TABLE 1-5. The Expected Value of a Decision

Possible Profit Levels ($)		Probability of Each Occurring (P)	Expected Value of Each Profit Level ($)
− 50,000		0.05	− 2,500
0		0.10	0
50,000		0.15	7,500
100,000		0.20	20,000
150,000		0.25	37,500
200,000		0.15	30,000
250,000		0.10	25,000
	Totals	1.00	117,500

The expected-value notion allows the probability distribution of the possible outcomes of a particular decision to be characterized by a single number, which can then be compared with the expected values of other potential solutions to the problem. In Table 1-5 we show a hypothetical probability distribution of profit levels that are expected to be possible outcomes of a decision to invest in a particular investment project.

The first column shows the possible profit levels, ranging from a loss of $50,000 to a profit of $250,000. The second column shows the probability of each profit (or loss) level, as assigned by the decision maker. Thus there is considered to be a 5% chance of losing $50,000, a 10% chance of only breaking even, a 15% chance of making $50,000 in profits, and so on. Note that the probabilities must total 1.00, since all possible outcomes are included and these outcomes are mutually exclusive. The third column in the table is the product of columns one and two. The expected value of each possible outcome is equal to the possible profit (or loss) associated with each outcome, multiplied by the probability of that outcome's occurring. The sum of the expected values of all the possible outcomes is $117,500. This is the expected value of the decision to invest in this particular investment opportunity.

Note that the *actual* outcome will not be known until after the investment is made and all the returns are in. The expected value is an *a priori* measure of the decision that allows the probability distribution of outcomes to be summarized as a single number. This expected value is actually a weighted average of the possible profit levels, with each possible outcome weighted by the probability that it will occur.[8]

Thus, if a firm is faced with a decision problem, the manager should investigate all potential solutions to that problem and evaluate the probability distribution of each potential solution in terms of its expected value. The firm should choose that alternative which

---

[8]The potential outcomes each represent a range of outcomes, and this (actual) outcome falls within one of those ranges. In this case the potential outcome of $50,000 represents the range from $25,000 to $75,000 in which the actual outcome fell. The probability distribution is continuous in reality, but we have summarized it using, in this case, seven points along the continuum.

promises the highest expected value, subject to adjustment for risk, which we consider in Chapter 2.

Assigning Probabilities in Practice

Suppose a firm wants to enter a market with a product that will compete with the existing products. The firm has designed a product that is qualitatively similar to, and plans to sell it at the same price as, the existing products. It needs to know how many units of the product it can expect to sell for decisions relating to production levels, employment of additional personnel, purchases of raw materials and components, and so on.

To establish the expected value of the sales volume, the firm will need to estimate the probabilities of sales at various levels. In the aforementioned situation there were six specified outcomes, but it is clear that these are simply six representative points on a spectrum of outcomes between some notional minimum and maximum outcomes. In practice it is typically sufficient to select three representative outcomes, which we might characterize as the low, medium, and high outcomes. To identify the values of these outcomes, we would begin with three scenarios: the worst case, the most likely case, and the best case. The worst-case scenario would be the minimum level expected, supposing virtually everything went wrong. The best-case scenario would assume that virtually everything, including luck, went your way. The most likely scenario is the decision maker's informed guess as to the peak of the probability distribution, that is, the most probable outcome. The probability of obtaining the most likely outcome then needs to be estimated on the basis of the decision maker's experience, intuition, and judgment. Given estimated values of the minimum, maximum, and modal (highest frequency) values of the sales level, and an estimate of the probability of attaining the modal value, you have effectively estimated the shape of the probability distribution. If the mode is in the middle of the range suggested by the minimum and maximum values, then you may expect the distribution to be more or less symmetric about the modal value, as in Figure 1-1a. Alternatively, if the mode is closer to either the minimum or maximum values, you expect the distribution to be skewed to the right or the left, as in Figure 1-2a.

Having estimated (via informed guesses) the range, height, and shape of the probability distribution, we are ready to reduce this to a few representative outcomes that will allow easy calculation of the expected value. A simple means of achieving this is to divide the range into three equal parts and choose the midpoint of these parts as the low, medium, and high outcomes. The probability of the actual outcome occurring in each third of the range is the sum of the probabilities (or the area under the curve) within each range. We can use the sum of the probabilities in each third as a summary probability to be attached to the outcome chosen to represent that third.

As a guide to estimating the sum of the probabilities in each of the low, medium, and high ranges, it is useful to begin with the properties of a normal distribution. As you may know, a normal distribution is symmetric about the modal (which is also the mean) outcome and has the following characteristics: 68% of the observations fall within plus or minus one standard deviation of the mean; 95% of the observations fall within plus or minus two standard deviations of the mean; and virtually all (99.7%) of the observations

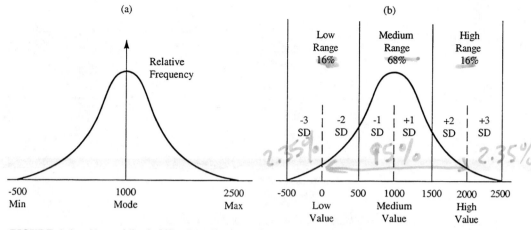

FIGURE 1-1. *Normal Probability Distributions of Possible Outcomes*

fall within plus or minus three standard deviations of the mean. Thus, 68% of the observations fall in the central third of the distribution, and 16% fall in each of the low and high ranges, since the distribution is symmetric. In Fig. 1-1b the low, medium, and high values are nominated as 0, 1000, and 2000, respectively, and the probabilities of each are nominated as 16%, 68%, and 16%, respectively.

From this starting point we can adjust the probabilities that we would attach to the low, medium, and high outcomes if we believe the probability distribution is skewed to one side or the other. For example, if we believe the distribution will be skewed in favor of higher outcomes, as in Figure 1-2, the probabilities might be, say, 10%, 40%, and 50% for the low, medium, and high outcomes of 450, 750, and 1050, respectively.[9]

1.4 THE OBJECTIVES OF THE FIRM

Any decision problem should be approached with the firm's objectives clearly in mind so the decision made will best serve the firm's objectives. What are the objectives of the business firm? Does the firm seek profit maximization, or would the firm sacrifice some current profitability for an enlarged market share? Does the firm wish to maximize its rate of growth, or is management content to attain profit, market share, and growth targets, while maximizing their own benefits and the quality of their lives?

At this point we confine ourselves to the assumption, which is well supported in the literature and the related disciplines of finance and accounting, that the decision maker's objective is to maximize the net worth of the firm over its time horizon, subject to

---

[9]Distributions have their "moments." The first moment is the mean, the second moment is the standard deviation, the third moment is the skewness, and the fourth moment is the kurtosis or peakedness of the distribution. Note that a symmetric distribution might be more peaked than a normal distribution (leptokurtic) or flatter than a normal distribution (platykurtic) and that we should adjust our estimates of the probabilities for each third of the range accordingly.

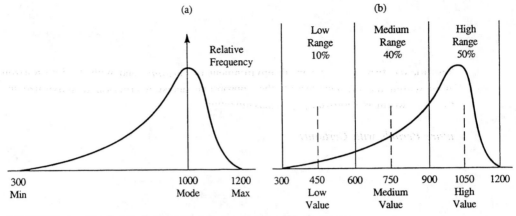

FIGURE 1-2.   Skewed Probability Distributions of Possible Outcomes

considerations of risk and uncertainty. The other aforementioned objectives will be incorporated into the analysis and reconciled with this objective in later chapters.[10]

• DEFINITION: *Net worth*, also known as owner's equity, is measured as the excess of the firm's assets (cash, securities, land, buildings, plant and equipment, and so on) over its liabilities (amounts owed to creditors, short-term and long-term loans, and so on). There are three groups of items on the firm's balance sheet, namely assets, liabilities, and owner's equity. Assets are equal to the sum of the other two. Thus, maximization of the net worth of the firm requires maximizing the difference between assets and liabilities, or, what amounts to the same thing, maximizing the owner's equity.

The preceding simple statement of the firm's objective function implies slightly different decision criteria for each of the different scenarios in which a firm may find itself. In the foregoing we have established two separate dichotomies, one referring to the time horizon (the present period versus future periods) and the second referring to the state of information (certainty versus uncertainty). There are four combinations and thus four rules which will allow the maximization of net worth under each scenario.

Different Rules for Different Scenarios

The Present Period with Certainty.   The most simple scenario is that in which the firm's horizon falls inside the present period and the firm enjoys full information, or certainty, about the outcome of all decisions. Thus there is no need for either present-value analysis or expected-value analysis. Rather, the firm may maximize its net worth by the pursuit of short-run profit maximization. Profits are calculated as the excess of total revenues over total costs. Total revenues add to asset accounts, such as cash and debtors, while total costs represent outflows of funds for materials, labor, and other ser-

---

[10]We shall see in Chapter 9 that sales, or market share maximization, growth maximization, managerial utility maximization, and even "satisficing" can be regarded as real-world approximations for the maximization of the expected present value of profits.

vices; and if these costs remain unpaid, there will be an increase in the liabilities. To the extent that profits are made, owner's equity, or net worth, therefore, rises by the same amount. Maximization of profits thus ensures the maximization of the firm's net worth. Thus, for the firm operating in an environment of *certainty* and with its time horizon falling within the *present period*, the appropriate decision criterion to maximize the firm's net worth is short-run profit maximization.

Future Periods with Certainty. If the firm has full information concerning revenues and costs but its time horizon falls in a future period, the firm must use present-value analysis to evaluate its decision alternatives properly. A decision that causes immediate profits and no future profits can be compared with another decision promising a stream of future profits only if both are expressed in present-value terms. The firm wishing to maximize its net worth in present-value terms, or its *net present worth*, should always choose the decision alternative that promises the greater net present value of profits. For the firm operating in an environment of *certainty*, and with its time horizon falling in a *future period*, the appropriate decision criterion to maximize the firm's net (present) worth is maximization of the present value of profits.

The Present Period with Uncertainty. Uncertainty means that decisions have more than one possible outcome that is foreseen, and that decisions must be made on the basis of the prior probability distribution of outcomes. Expected-value analysis is, therefore, required to summarize the probability distributions of the various decision alternatives and to allow the selection of that decision which will maximize the expected value of the firm's profits. If the firm always chooses the alternative that offers the greatest expected value of profits, it will sometimes receive less than the expected value and sometimes more, but after many decisions the firm will find its actual total profits to be greater than they would have been by following any other strategy. If the probability distributions are accurately estimated, the law of averages will ensure that after many decisions the probability distributions will be validated by the actual outcomes. For the firm operating in an environment of *uncertainty*, and with its time horizon falling within the *present period*, the appropriate decision criterion to maximize the firm's net (expected) worth is maximization of the expected value of profits.

Future Periods with Uncertainty. In the final scenario, the firm's time horizon falls in a future period, and the firm does not have full information about its potential costs and revenues. This is the predominant situation in business. Most firms consider the future cost and revenue implications of their decisions, and they face risk and uncertainty as to the possible outcomes of their decisions. Thus these firms should use both present-value analysis and expected-value analysis. First, all future cash flows must be discounted back to present-value terms, using the appropriate opportunity discount factor and the appropriate cash flow convention. Then the present value of each of the possible outcomes is weighted by the probability of its occurring, and the sum of these is the expected present value (EPV) of the decision. The decision maker then selects the decision alternative that promises the highest EPV of profits. (In Chapter 2 we present several examples of EPV analysis with the aid of "decision trees.") Thus, for the firm operating in an environment of *uncertainty* and with its time horizon falling in a *future period*, the appropriate decision criterion to maximize the firm's net (expected present) worth is maximization of the expected present value of profits. The decision rules for the four scenarios are summarized in Table 1-6.

TABLE 1-6.   The Decision Criteria for Maximization of Net Worth for the Four Scenarios

State of Information	THE FIRM'S TIME HORIZON FALLS WITHIN THE	
	Present Period	*Future Period*
Certainty	Maximize profit	Maximize present value of profit
Uncertainty	Maximize expected value of profit	Maximize expected present value of profit

The Principal-Agent Problem

We have stated that the objective of the firm is to maximize its net worth in expected-present-value terms. By *the firm* we really mean the owners or shareholders of the firm, whose interests presumably lie in the maximization of their personal net worth. However, in modern corporations that are owned jointly by thousands of stockholders, the owners of the firm are typically excluded from the day-to-day process of making decisions, having delegated the authority to trained managers whose job is to make these decisions. As absentee owners, shareholders are unable to observe whether or not the managers' decisions are always consistent with their objectives. Consequently, managers may pursue their own personal objectives, to some degree, rather than assiduously seek the maximization of net worth. Only in the case of owner-managed firms can we expect the objectives of the owners and the managers to coincide perfectly. This difficulty has been called the *principal-agent problem*.[11] The manager is an agent of the shareholders (the principals), making decisions on their behalf. Although the principals may monitor the agents' actions, monitoring involves information-search costs, and it will not be taken to the ultimate degree, with the result that there remains an asymmetry of information such that the actions of the agent are not perfectly observed by the principal. Thus managers may make decisions that do not best serve the firm's (owners') objectives.

---

[11]See A. A. Alchian and H. Demsetz, "Production, Information Costs, and Economic Organization," *American Economic Review*, 57 (December 1972), pp. 777–95; M. C. Jensen and W. H. Meckling, "Theory of the Firm: Managerial Behavior, Agency Costs, and Ownership Structure," *Journal of Financial Economics*, 3 (October 1976), pp. 305–60; E. F. Fama, "Agency Problems and the Theory of the Firm," *Journal of Political Economy*, 88 (April 1980), pp. 272–84; and G. M. MacDonald, "New Directions in the Theory of Agency," *Canadian Journal of Economics*, 17 (August 1984), pp. 415–40.

The manager may not select the decision alternative that maximizes the firm's net worth if another alternative better serves the manager's own objectives. These may include rapid promotion (served by highly visible decisions that make the decision maker look good), personal enrichment (served by allocating contracts to higher-cost suppliers who give kickbacks, or by channeling business to family members), aesthetics (served by choosing an alternative that has pleasant, rather than profit-maximizing, consequences), or avoidance of stress and competitive conflict both within the firm and in the firm's product markets (served by avoiding decision alternatives that may generate conflict or threaten job security).

A means of helping to ensure that the manager's efforts will serve the firm's objectives is to offer the manager an incentive contract that relates the manager's total compensation package to the profit performance of the firm. Thus the manager would be offered a bonus equal to some share of the firm's profits. To encourage decisions that best serve the expected present value of net worth, the current year's bonus is often related to profits over the past several years. Such incentive contracts do not guarantee the manager's unflagging pursuit of shareholder objectives, however, because the problem of asymmetric information remains. Managers may exert less than the maximum effort (known as "shirking") and take nonmonetary benefits (known as perquisites), with the result that net worth is not maximized. The shareholders may not be aware of these problems.

In this text we shall continue to speak of the firm's objective as the maximization of net worth, but keep in mind that managers' objectives may be at variance with those of the firm and that decisions may be made that do not maximize the firm's net worth, to the extent that shareholders remain unaware of the divergence, and/or are unable to discipline management effectively (through the board of directors), and/or are unable to induce cooperative behavior through an appropriate system of incentives.[12]

1.5 SUMMARY

In this chapter we have introduced the subject of managerial economics and proceeded to build a framework for business decision making. Managerial economics was defined as the application of economic principles and methodologies to the decision-making process within the firm or organization. It is a normative discipline, seeking to provide rules that allow the firm to best pursue its objective function. The use of models in managerial economics was examined, and we noted that the purpose of models may be either peda-

---

[12]See S. A. Ross, "The Economic Theory of Agency: The Principal's Problem," *American Economic Review*, 58 (May 1973), pp. 134–39; M. Harris and A. Raviv, "Some Results on Incentive Contracts with Applications to Education and Employment, Health Insurance, and Law Enforcement," *American Economic Review*, 68 (March 1978), pp. 20–30; S. Shavell, "Risk Sharing and Incentives in the Principal and Agent Relationship," *Bell Journal of Economics*, 10 (Spring 1979), pp. 55–73; and E. J. Douglas, "The Simple Analytics of the Principal-Agent Incentive Contract," *Journal of Economic Education*, 20 (Winter 1989), pp. 39–51.

gogical, explanatory, or predictive. In this course we will use symbolic models, including verbal, graphic, and some simple mathematical expressions.

Present-value analysis and expected-value analysis were introduced and examined in detail. The former involves the discounting of future cash flows so they may be properly compared with present cash flows for decision-making purposes. The appropriate rate of discount is the opportunity interest rate, defined as the best rate of return available elsewhere at similar risk.

Expected-value analysis allows the summary of a probability distribution of outcomes in a single number, which may then be compared with the expected values of other decision alternatives. The expected value of a decision is the weighted mean of the possible outcomes, where the weight for each outcome is the prior probability of its occurring. Expected-present-value analysis requires discounting the expected value of future profits back to present-value terms before aggregation to find the expected present value of each decision alternative.

If the firm's planning period is sufficiently short that its time horizon falls within the present period, the firm should maximize its profits within the present period (if it has the full information) or maximize the expected value of its profits (if it operates under uncertainty). If the firm's planning period is longer, so its time horizon falls in a future period, the firm should maximize the present value of its profits stream (under certainty) or the expected present value of its profit stream (under uncertainty).

DISCUSSION QUESTIONS

1-1. Distinguish between certainty, and risk and uncertainty.

1-2. Under what circumstances is it appropriate that a model be based on assumptions that are extremely simplistic? Could it, nevertheless, be a good model? Could a model be based on false assumptions and yet serve a purpose? Discuss.

1-3. What advantages are there in the graphical or algebraic representation of a model as compared with a verbal representation of the same phenomena?

1-4. What is the firm's time horizon? What kinds of considerations determine the firm's time horizon?

1-5. What determines the opportunity discount rate to be used when evaluating the present value of a multiperiod profit stream?

1-6. Which discounting formula should be used to calculate most accurately the present value of a stream of revenues received each week throughout the year? If, instead, you used daily discount factors, would this cause an overestimate or an underestimate of the true present value? Would the difference be important?

1-7. What is a decision problem? Is it necessarily a situation in which there is a crisis or in which remedial action is necessary? What has the firm's objective function to do with the existence (or nonexistence) of a decision problem?

1-8. Explain the notion of uncertainty in terms of the probability distribution of outcomes associated with each decision alternative.

1-9. Summarize the modifications necessary to the firm's objective function as the firm's time horizon shifts from the present to a future period and as we relax the assumption of full information.

1-10. Briefly outline the principal-agent problem and what it might mean for the achievement of the firm's objectives.

PROBLEMS AND SHORT CASES[13]

1-1. A large, internationally recognized manufacturer of soft drink products has announced it will establish a foundation to provide scholarships to business students at your university. The company acknowledges a slight cash flow problem at the present moment and gives your university's president two choices: Either take a once-and-for-all grant of $10 million immediately or $2.5 million immediately, $4 million more next year, and $5 million more in two years. Of course the president is euphoric and announces to the faculty that he intends to accept what he calls the "$11.5 million alternative." As an interested party, you are concerned that a complete analysis has not been made.

(a) Assuming that the opportunity discount rate is 14%, what is the present value of the second alternative?

(b) Explain to the president, in a memo of 200 words or less, what this revised estimate means and which alternative should be accepted.

(c) Would your decision change if the opportunity interest rate were 12%, or 16%, instead of the assumed 14%? Explain.

1-2. The Words-Are-Cheap Publishing Company is considering extending a contract offer to an author who has written a book entitled *How to Deal with High Interest Rates in the Mid-1980s*. This project would involve reviewing, editing, artwork, and composition costs of $80,000, payable in full at the end of year one, before a single book has been printed. The publisher expects to sell 20,000 copies in year two, 17,500 in year three, 12,500 in year four, and 2,500 in year five. It plans to sell the rights to another publisher at the end of year five for $10,000. Its production, distribution, and royalty costs will be constant at $1.50 per copy, and it will receive $3.50 per copy for every copy sold.

The finance vice-president advises that the funds involved could alternatively be invested in a corporate bond issue, considered no more or less risky than this book project, at an interest rate of 18%, the best rate available.

(a) Calculate the net present value of the book project, assuming that all cash flows are received or disbursed at the end of the year in which they occur.

(b) Advise the publisher whether or not to extend the contract offer to the author.

1-3. Your firm has called for bids for the fabrication and installation of a pollution-control system tailored specifically to meet the requirements applicable to your manufacturing process. The lowest bid is for $370,000, with delivery and installation in thirty-two months. Your firm plans to sign a contract with the supplier on the aforementioned terms, including a clause stating that the contract price of $370,000 is absolutely fixed (regardless of any cost overruns or production difficulties the supplier may encounter) and will be paid in full in thirty-two months' time, following the installation of the system. Between now and then your firm plans to invest its funds in the best available guaranteed, interest-bearing securities, which pay interest of 12% per annum.

(a) What is the present value of the cost of the pollution-control system to your firm?

(b) Why is 12% the appropriate discount rate?

---

[13]Short answers to all problems are provided in Appendix C at the back of this book.

1-4. Doreen Delights has invented a device that allows drinking drivers to self-test for excessive alcohol in their system. Rather than get into the business itself, the firm plans to license this device to the highest bidder. Company A has bid $40,000, payable $10,000 immediately, $15,000 after one year, $10,000 after two years, and $5,000 after three years. Company B has bid $42,500, payable $5,000 immediately, $10,000 after one year, $12,500 after two years, and $15,000 after three years. The management of Doreen Delights considers that their opportunity discount rate is 9%. You are concerned that this is a little low, in view of recent upward movements in interest rates and foreseeable trends, and you feel that 11% is the appropriate discount rate.

    (a) Calculate the present value of each proposal, using management's opportunity discount rate of 9%.

    (b) Would the decision be different if the 11% discount rate was applied?

    (c) Explain to the management which option you feel should be chosen and the impact of the time profile of the cash flows on the relative present values.

1-5. The owner of a restaurant approaches you and offers you the following deal: You would give up your $20,000 per annum job and manage his restaurant for two years while he goes back to his country to do his compulsory military service. He shows you all his records and you see the restaurant has annual sales revenues of $100,000 and operating costs of $60,000, each spread more or less evenly over each year. You expect the revenue and cost situations to remain stable for each of the next two years. The restaurant owner wants to sell you this opportunity on the following basis: You pay $30,000 initially to the owner but keep all the profits you make over the next two years. You know that you could, alternatively, invest your $30,000 in corporate bonds for a 20% rate of return, and you consider that alternative no more or less risky than the restaurant venture.

    (a) What is the present value of the opportunity to invest in the restaurant venture?

    (b) Which alternative should you choose, presuming these are the best opportunities available? Are there any other issues involved?

1-6. You are reading the "Businesses for Sale" advertisements and notice a corner-store business offered for sale. Its assets comprise inventory of $50,000, equipment and plant of $80,000, and land and buildings of $120,000 (all assets are current market value). There are no debtors or creditors. The store's profit stream is $30,000 per year, received more or less evenly throughout the year. Your time horizon is five years; your opportunity discount rate is 16% per annum; and you will resell the assets after five years for the same real value (you expect inflation to average 8% over the five years).

    (a) What is the net present cost of the assets of the business?

    (b) What is the present value of the profit stream over the five years?

    (c) What is the maximum you would offer for the business? Why?

    (d) If the present owner were asking $400,000, how would you explain your lower offer?

1-7. The Swiss Crest Embroidery Company is considering the installation of a computerized loom, which would be substantially more efficient than its existing equipment. The company has two options. Machine A would cost $100,000 initially; would earn net profits of $60,000, $80,000, $40,000, and $20,000 on a more or less continuous basis throughout years one to four, respectively; and would have salvage (resale) value of $20,000 at the end of the fourth year. Machine B costs $120,000, but payment for this machine can be deferred for twelve months. Machine B promises to earn net profits of $70,000, $60,000, $50,000, and $30,000 throughout the first, second, third, and fourth years, respectively, and it would have resale value of $30,000 at the end of the fourth year.

The firm is considering alternate areas for expansion, and the best of these other opportunities, which has the same degree of risk as the computerized loom project, promises to return 16% on the funds that might otherwise be invested.

(a) Evaluate the two machines in terms of the net present value of their cash flow streams.

(b) Advise the management about which machine they should select.

1-8. Your firm is considering diversification into a new product line. After an extensive investigation, the two most promising possibilities have been isolated. Product A is a line of personalized stationery, and Product B is a line of paper party decorations. Annual production and marketing costs for A will be $90,000 and those for B will be $115,000; in both cases these costs are incurred on a weekly basis throughout the year. Annual sales for A will be $100,000, received on a daily basis, and those for B will be $125,000 and will be seasonally biased, being heavily concentrated in December of each year.

For each product, the market research team has predicted a five-year stream of costs and revenues, constant at the aforementioned levels. Rather than embark on this diversification, the firm's next best alternative, at equal risk, is to invest the funds in an expansion of the market share for its existing products, which is expected to yield an 18% return on investment.

(a) What are the present values of the decision alternatives A and B over the five-year planning period?

(b) Which alternative should the firm choose?

(c) How would you rank the alternatives open to the firm? Explain.

1-9. The Oxford Equipment Company has decided that it will computerize its inventory, billing, payroll, and so on. It has two choices. First, it could buy a computer, several terminals, and a variety of software packages and have several of its employees trained to use the hardware and the software, and so do it all in house. The cost per annum of this alternative is uncertain, since the firm has not yet had experience with computers, and none of its executives knows much about either the hardware available or the software packages. The estimated probability distribution of costs for the coming year is as follows:

Possible Cost Level ($)	Probability (P)
20,000	0.15
30,000	0.20
40,000	0.30
50,000	0.25
60,000	0.10

Alternatively, it could contract with a specialist company that would keep contemporaneous records of inventory, handle the billing and payroll, and so on, at a fixed fee of $42,000 per annum. This fee would be payable at the end of the year, whereas the in-house alternative would involve cash outflows on a more or less daily basis throughout the year. Rather than invest the money in either alternative, Oxford could leave the money in bonds, where it is currently earning 15% interest per annum.

(a) Calculate the expected value of the in-house alternative.

(b) Calculate the expected present value of the in-house alternative.

(c) Calculate the expected present value of the outside contract alternative.

(d) Advise the management of Oxford Equipment which alternative you think they should select, making explicit any reservations that underlie your recommendation.

1-10. The manager of the Fearless Ambition Racing Team is faced with the following decision problem: There is one race left in the series, and his driver could win the championship with a win or a second placing in the final race. He is concerned that the engine of the race car may be a little "tired" and is considering either a complete rebuilding of the engine or the purchase of a new engine. There is uncertainty involved in both alternatives. In a complete rebuilding of the engine, the cost will vary depending on the mechanical components that must be replaced after inspection shows them to be worn beyond acceptable tolerances. Similarly, a new engine will be partially dismantled, examined, and subject to mechanical work and replacement of parts that are unlikely to withstand the rigors imposed by race conditions. Either option (to rebuild or to buy new) will result in an engine of the same power and durability. Based on past experience, the following probability distribution of costs associated with each option has been established:

REBUILD		BUY NEW	
Cost ($)	*Probability*	*Cost ($)*	*Probability*
25,000	0.05	35,000	0.05
30,000	0.15	36,000	0.10
35,000	0.40	37,000	0.30
40,000	0.25	38,000	0.35
45,000	0.10	39,000	0.15
50,000	0.05	40,000	0.05

If the team manager decides to rebuild the existing engine, the parts and labor expenses will be incurred more or less evenly throughout the year, because he will be able to keep suppliers waiting for their money for various lengths of time, up to a maximum of twelve months. If he purchases the new engine, the supplier will give the team a special deal in lieu of direct sponsorship: payment for the engine itself ($35,000) can be deferred twelve months. The opportunity interest rate is 14% per annum.

(a) What is the expected value of the costs for each option?

(b) What is the expected present value of the costs for each option?

(c) Which option should be selected? Explain.

SUGGESTED REFERENCES AND FURTHER READING

BAUMOL, W. J. "What Can Economic Theory Contribute to Managerial Economics?" *American Economic Review*, 51 (May 1961), pp. 142-46. Reprinted in T.J. Coyne, *Readings in Managerial Economics* (3rd ed.), chap. 1. Plano, Tex.: Business Publications, 1981.

CLAYTON, G. E., and C. B. SPIVEY. *The Time Value of Money*. Philadelphia: W. B. Saunders Company, 1978.

DOUGLAS, E. J. "The Simple Analytics of the Principle-Agent Incentive Contract," *Journal of Economic Education*, 20 (Winter, 1990), pp.39-51.

FAMA, E. F. "Agency Problems and the Theory of the Firm," *Journal of Political Economy*, 88 (April 1980), pp. 272-84.

GORDON, G., and I. PRESSMAN. *Quantitative Decision Making for Business*, chaps. 1, 2. Englewood Cliffs, N.J.: Prentice-Hall, Inc., 1978.

GROSSACK, I. M., and D. D. MARTIN. *Managerial Economics*, chap. 1. Boston: Little, Brown & Company, 1973.

HUBER, G. P. *Managerial Decision Making*, chaps. 1, 2, 3. Glenview, Ill.: Scott, Foresman & Company, 1980.

JENSEN, M. C., and W. H. MECKLING. "Theory of the Firm: Managerial Behavior, Agency Costs, and Ownership Structure," *Journal of Financial Economics*, 3 (October 1976), pp. 305-360.

KHOURY, S. J., and T. D. PARSONS. *Mathematical Methods in Finance and Economics*, chap. 2., New York: Elsevier North-Holland, Inc., 1981.

MACDONALD, G. M. "New Directions in the Theory of Agency," *Canadian Journal of Economics*, 17 (August 1984), pp. 415-40.

PAPPS, I., and W. HENDERSON. *Models and Economic Theory*. Philadelphia: W. B. Saunders Company, 1977.

RADFORD, K. J. *Modern Managerial Decision Making*, chaps. 1, 4. Reston, Va.: Reston Publishing Company, Inc., 1981.

SIMON, H. A. "Theory of Decision Making in Economics and Behavior Science," *American Economic Review*, 49 (June 1959), pp. 253-80. Reprinted in T. J. Coyne, *Readings in Managerial Economics* (3rd ed.), chap. 2. Plano, Tex.: Business Publications, 1981.

WILLIAMSON, O. E. "The Modern Corporation: Origins, Evolution, Attributes," *Journal of Economic Literature*, 19 (December 1981), pp. 1537-68.

Chapter 2

DECISION MAKING UNDER RISK AND UNCERTAINTY

EXECUTIVE SUMMARY

In this chapter we combine present-value (PV) analysis and expected-value (EV) analysis as **expected-present-value (EPV) analysis,** for cases where the decision to be made has future cash flows and is made in an uncertain environment. To facilitate multiperiod EPV analysis we introduce **decision trees,** which display the cost and revenue consequences of each decision like the branches of a tree, so all scenarios are accounted for and the EPV of the decision can be properly calculated.

We then consider the risk involved in each decision alternative, the measurement of this risk, and the **incorporation of risk analysis** into the decision-making process. Most business decision makers are risk *averse,* but they will bear risk if adequately compensated for so doing. Recognition of risk requires modifications to the decision criteria introduced in Chapter 1. Managers who are risk averters will want to incorporate some measure of risk into their decision rule, as well as considering the expected profitability. Thus, we introduce several decision criteria that incorporate risk. We also consider some noneconomic factors which may enter the decision-making process.

Next, we note that **the problem of incomplete information** can be at least partly rectified by information-search activity. Information-search costs should be incurred only if the decision maker expects that the value of the information acquired will exceed the search costs. If the information is expected to cost more than it is worth, the firm should proceed without seeking further information.

Finally, we ask the question "How do I know if I have just made a *good* decision?" We shall see that **decisions should be evaluated** as good or bad on the basis of whether or not sufficient search activity was undertaken, whether or not the information was fully and properly utilized, whether or not the appropriate decision criterion was applied, and whether or not the decision is highly sensitive to the validity of the assumptions on which it is based.

2.1 DECISION TREES AND EXPECTED-PRESENT-VALUE ANALYSIS

Expected-present-value (EPV) analysis is required whenever there are cost and revenue implications of the decision that fall in both the present period and at least one future period. The analysis is more complicated when there is also a probability distribution of outcomes in each period, because the outcomes in the second and subsequent periods will have *joint* probabilities of occurring. Decision trees facilitate EPV analysis because they spread out the consequences of the decision like the branches of a tree and allow easy calculation of the joint probabilities and the EPV of the decision.

Decision Trees and Joint Probabilities

Imagine looking at a tree and seeing that the trunk forks into two or three main branches, and then, at a higher level, each of these branches then forks into two or three smaller branches. A decision tree also has a trunk, which represents the decision maker's problem. The branches at the first fork represent the alternative decisions that might be made to solve the firm's problem. When there is uncertainty, and hence more than one scenario is possible, each of these branches has a fork in it with the higher branches representing each possible scenario. For decisions with profit outcomes in the second and subsequent years, each of these branches would then fork into higher branches representing the possible scenarios in the second year, with a new set of forks and branches to represent the third year, and so on. The uppermost branches on the tree represent the outcomes in the final period being considered (that is, at the time horizon.) These final branches are known as the terminal branches of the decision tree.[1]

We show in Table 2-1 the decision tree of a manager who wants to buy a new printing machine. She must now decide whether to buy a large machine or a smaller one. The decision tree shows the outcomes that are expected in the first and second years after the decision is made. The scenarios that are possible in each year reflect the market conditions that will affect demand for the firm's product. Suppose that market conditions next year will be either booming, unchanged, or depressed. These alternative states of nature are determined by factors outside the firm's control, and while one of them *will* be experienced by the firm in the following year, at the time the decision must be made the manager will not know *which* scenario will prevail. The three states of nature give rise to three demand situations, which are characterized as heavy, medium, and light demand. The profits associated with each demand situation, in nominal dollars, are shown in Table 2-1. You can see that with the large machine the expected profits for the first year are either $10,000, $4,000, or a loss of $1,000. In the second year, market conditions may change as compared with the first year, of course. For example, although demand may be

---

[1]A decision tree with m possible outcomes in each of n periods will have m^n jointly possible outcomes (terminal branches). The decision trees in this text are usually constrained to three states of nature in each of two years, to simplify calculations, although the analysis can be extended to any number of possible outcomes over any time horizon. Three states of nature are typically sufficient, however, since under uncertainty the firm will have enough difficulty specifying a high, medium, and low profit estimate. For practical application, the medium estimate might be the manager's best guess, or the most likely outcome. The low and high estimates would be a pessimistic and optimistic view, respectively.

TABLE 2-1.   The Decision Tree for the Printing Machine Decision

Machine Size	YEAR 1		YEAR 2	
	Demand	Profits ($)	Demand	Profits ($)
Large — Heavy	10,000	Heavy	12,500
			Medium	5,000
			Light	1,000
Large — Medium	4,000	Heavy	12,500
			Medium	5,000
			Light	1,000
Large — Light	−1,000	Heavy	12,500
			Medium	5,000
			Light	1,000
Small — Heavy	7,000	Heavy	8,000
			Medium	6,000
			Light	2,000
Small — Medium	5,000	Heavy	8,000
			Medium	6,000
			Light	2,000
Small — Light	1,000	Heavy	8,000
			Medium	6,000
			Light	2,000

light in the first year, it might be either heavy, medium, or light in the second year. Note that profits under each demand scenario in the second year, for each decision alternative, are shown in the final column of the table. Naturally these profit figures reflect the different cost situations of the large and small machines and the different prices that may be obtained under differing demand conditions.[2]

To decide which machine the firm should install, we evaluate the EPV of the profits promised by each alternative. It is first necessary to assign probabilities to the alternate demand scenarios in each of the two years. Suppose that market research indicates that in the first year the probabilities of demand being heavy, medium, or light are 20%, 30%, and 50%, respectively. In the second year the probabilities are estimated to be 40%, 40%, and 20%, respectively. Next, we must find the firm's opportunity discount rate (ODR.) Suppose we learn that the firm could have earned 10% per annum by investing the necessary financial outlay in other assets of comparable risk. Accordingly, we shall use a 10% ODR in evaluating the future profits from the enterprise. Finally, we need to seek information or make assumptions about the cash flow pattern, the time horizon, the initial costs of the machines, the residual value of the machines at the time horizon, and the tax deductability of depreciation. For simplicity here, we shall suppose

---

[2]When the states of nature in the second and subsequent periods are the same regardless of what happens in the preceding period, as in this case, we say that the probability distributions are *independent*. In other cases, the outcomes in the second period might depend on what happens in the first period, in which case we say that the probability distributions in subsequent periods are *conditional* on earlier outcomes.

that the profits are received in lump sum at the end of each year; that the time horizon is only two years; that the cost of the large machine is $2,000 while the cost of the small machine is $1,700; that neither machine has any scrap value after two years; and that depreciation expense is not tax deductible.[3]

The calculation of the EPV from each of the two machines is shown in Tables 2-2 and 2-3. In each table, column 1 indicates the size and initial cost of the alternatives. Column 2 shows the demand scenarios and their probabilities, and column 3 shows the profits expected under each demand scenario. Column 4 shows the present value of these profit levels, given the 10% ODR, which implies a discount factor of 0.909. The demand situations and profits in year two are listed in columns 5 and 6. Column 7 shows the present value of year-two profits. Column 8 shows the net present value of the profits of years one and two, minus the initial cost of the machine (which is already in present-value terms). Column 9 shows the probabilities that each of these sums will be achieved. Note that these are *joint* probabilities, since arriving at each terminal branch of the tree depends on both the probability of a particular scenario in the first year and the probability of another particular scenario in the second year. For example, the joint probability of the uppermost branch (0.8) is the product of the probability that demand will be heavy in the first year (0.2) and also heavy in the second year (0.4). In column 10 the Net PV data for each terminal branch is multiplied by the joint probability of its occurring (to weight it appropriately) and the EPV is calculated by summing the weighted PVs. Thus the large machine has an EPV of $6,401.50, while the small machine has an EPV of $6,346.60. Thus, in terms of the EPV, the large machine is preferred to the small machine.

2.2   RISK ANALYSIS OF DECISION ALTERNATIVES

Let us now consider the degree of risk involved in each decision and the appropriate measurement of that risk. This allows us to compare the risk of the decision alternatives and to incorporate risk into the decision process.

The Degree of Risk and Uncertainty

- DEFINITION: The *risk* associated with a particular decision is defined as the dispersion of the possible outcomes that might occur. In a simple sense, we could describe the dispersion of outcomes by the range of outcomes that are possible. Some decisions will exhibit a wider range of possible outcomes than will others, and we say that these are more risky decision alternatives. Look again at Tables 2-2 and 2-3 and note the dispersion of the possible profit (or loss) levels after two years under each decision alternative, which are evident in column 8 in each table. The range of possible outcomes is substantially greater for the large machine, which has a maximum outcome of $17,415 profit and

---

[3]The last two simplifying assumptions are made to avoid the complications associated with the tax deductibility of depreciation on the machine purchased. These issues are discussed in the context of capital budgeting in Chapter 15.

TABLE 2-2.   Calculation of Expected Present Value for the Large Machine

Machine (cost) [1]	Demand (probability) [2]	YEAR 1 Profits [3]	YEAR 1 PV (DF = 0.909) [4]	Demand (probability) [5]	YEAR 2 Profits [6]	YEAR 2 PV (DF = 0.826) [7]	CALCULATION OF EPV Total PV [8]	CALCULATION OF EPV Joint Probability [9]	CALCULATION OF EPV Weighted PV [10]
	Heavy (P = 0.2)	$10,000	$9,090	Heavy (P = 0.4)	$12,500	$10,325	$17,415	0.08	$1,393.20
				Medium (P = 0.4)	5,000	4,130	11,220	0.08	897.60
				Light (P = 0.2)	1,000	826	7,916	0.04	316.64
Large ($2,000)	Medium (P = 0.3)	4,000	3,636	Heavy (P = 0.4)	12,500	10,325	11,961	0.12	1,435.32
				Medium (P = 0.4)	5,000	4,130	5,766	0.12	691.92
				Light (P = 0.2)	1,000	826	2,462	0.06	147.72
	Light (P = 0.5)	−1,000	−909	Heavy (P = 0.4)	12,500	10,325	7,416	0.20	1,483.20
				Medium (P = 0.4)	5,000	4,130	1,221	0.20	244.20
				Light (P = 0.2)	1,000	826	−2,083	0.10	−208.30
								Expected present value	$6,401.50

TABLE 2-3. Calculation of Expected Present Value for the Small Machine

Machine (cost) [1]	Demand (probability) [2]	YEAR 1 Profits [3]	YEAR 1 PV (DF = 0.909) [4]	Demand (probability) [5]	YEAR 2 Profits [6]	YEAR 2 PV (DF = 0.826) [7]	Total PV [8]	CALCULATION OF EPV Joint Probability [9]	Weighted PV [10]
Small ($1,700)	Heavy (P = 0.2)	$7,000	$6,363	Heavy (P = 0.4)	$8,000	$6,608	$11,271	0.08	$ 901.68
				Medium (P = 0.4)	6,000	4,956	9,619	0.08	769.52
				Light (P = 0.2)	2,000	1,652	6,315	0.04	252.60
	Medium (P = 0.3)	5,000	4,545	Heavy (P = 0.4)	8,000	6,608	9,453	0.12	1,134.36
				Medium (P = 0.4)	6,000	4,956	7,801	0.12	936.12
				Light (P = 0.2)	2,000	1,652	4,497	0.06	269.82
	Light (P = 0.5)	1,000	909	Heavy (P = 0.4)	8,000	6,608	5,817	0.20	1,163.40
				Medium (P = 0.4)	6,000	4,956	4,165	0.20	833.00
				Light (P = 0.2)	2,000	1,652	861	0.10	86.10
								Expected present value	$6,346.60

a minimum outcome of $-2,083, as compared to the small machine's range of profits from $11,271 to $861.

But the range of outcomes is a crude measure of dispersion for a probability distribution, primarily because it ignores the probabilities. The extreme points on the probability distribution may only be remotely possible (for example, have probabilities of only 0.0001), yet the range will stay the same. A better measure of the dispersion of a probability distribution is the standard deviation of that probability distribution, because it incorporates the probabilities of all outcomes.

The Standard Deviation of a Probability Distribution

- DEFINITION: The *standard deviation of a probability distribution* shows the average absolute deviation of all possible outcomes from the expected value of that probability distribution. The deviation of each possible outcome from the expected value is weighted by the probability of each outcome occurring. We seek the absolute deviations—that is, without regard to whether they are positive deviations (above the expected value) or negative deviations (below the expected value)—because we do not want the negative deviations to offset the positive deviations. We eliminate the minus signs on the negative deviations by first squaring the deviations and later taking the square root of the sum of weighted deviations. In symbols,

$$\sigma = \sqrt{\sum_{i=1}^{n} (X_i - \text{EPV})^2 P_i}$$

(2-1)

where σ (lowercase sigma) is the conventional symbol used to denote standard deviation; Σ (uppercase sigma) denotes the sum of the series of squared and weighted deviations from $i = 1, 2, 3, \ldots, n$; X_i represents the ith possible outcome; P_i is the probability of that outcome; and EPV is the expected present value of the probability distribution.[4]

- EXAMPLE: Let us calculate the standard deviation for each of the probability distributions in the large-machine/small-machine problem introduced earlier. We show the full calculations in Table 2-4. Column 1 lists the possible outcomes for each decision alternative (repeated from column 8 in Tables 2-2 and 2-3), and column 2 shows the EPV that was calculated for each decision alternative. Column 3 shows the deviation of each possi-

---

[4]Note that equation (2-1) is different from the formula for the standard deviation of a simple series of numbers that are equally probable; namely

$$s = \sqrt{\sum_{i=1}^{n} (X_i - \bar{X})^2 / n}$$

where $\bar{X}$ is the simple arithmetic mean of the numbers $X_1, X_2, \ldots X_n$. Your calculator may be preprogrammed for this calculation. Do not make the fatal error of using it to calculate the standard deviation of a probability distribution where the outcomes are not equally likely.

ble outcome from the EPV, and column 4 shows the squares of these deviations. Column 5 repeats the joint probabilities of each outcome occurring (from column 9 in Tables 2-2 and 2-3), and column 6 shows the deviation weighted by the joint probabilities. The next step, as evident in the equation, is to sum these weighted squared deviations. This sum is known as the *variance* of the probability distribution. The final step is to calculate the square root of the variance to find the standard deviation.[5]

TABLE 2-4. **Calculation of the Standard Deviation for the Large and Small Machine Decision**

Large Machine

X_i ($000)	EPV ($000)	X_i − EPV ($000)	$(X_i$ − EPV$)^2$ ($000)	P_i	$(X_i$ − EPV$)^2 P_i$ ($000)
17.415	6.4015	11.0135	121.297	0.08	9.7038
11.220	6.4015	4.8185	23.218	0.08	1.8574
7.916	6.4015	1.5145	2.294	0.04	0.0917
11.961	6.4015	5.5595	30.908	0.12	3.7090
5.766	6.4015	− 0.6355	0.404	0.12	0.0485
2.462	6.4015	− 3.9395	15.520	0.06	0.9312
7.416	6.4015	1.0145	1.029	0.20	0.2058
1.221	6.4015	− 5.1805	26.838	0.20	5.3675
− 2.083	6.4015	− 8.4845	71.987	0.10	7.1987
				1.00	
				Variance =	29.1136

Standard deviation = $\sqrt{\text{Variance}}$ = 5.3957 or $5,395.70

Small Machine

X_i ($000)	EPV ($000)	X_i − EPV ($000)	$(X_i$ − EPV$)^2$ ($000)	P_i	$(X_i$ − EPV$)^2 P_i$ ($000)
11.271	6.3466	4.9244	24.250	0.08	1.9400
9.619	6.3466	3.2724	10.709	0.08	0.8567
6.315	6.3466	− 0.0316	0.001	0.04	0.0000
9.453	6.3466	3.1064	9.650	0.12	1.1580
7.801	6.3466	1.4544	2.115	0.12	0.2538
4.497	6.3466	− 1.8496	3.421	0.06	0.2053
5.817	6.3466	− 0.5296	0.281	0.20	0.0561
4.165	6.3466	− 2.1816	4.759	0.20	0.9519
0.861	6.3466	− 5.4856	30.092	0.10	3.0092
				1.00	
				Variance =	8.4310

Standard deviation = $\sqrt{\text{Variance}}$ = 2.9036 or $2,903.60

---

[5] Another fatal error is to attempt to calculate the standard deviation of a probability distribution without incorporating all m^n of the terminal outcomes of the decision tree, since the probabilities will not add to 1, meaning that some of the jointly possible outcomes will have been ignored.

Thus the standard deviation for the large machine's cash flow stream is $5,395.70, and it is $2,903.60 for the small machine. These numbers represent the average absolute deviation of the possible outcomes from the expected value in each case. Thus the decision to buy the larger machine is substantially more risky than is the decision to buy the smaller machine.

Risk Aversion, Risk Preference, and Risk Neutrality

- DEFINITION: *Risk aversion* is defined as the psychic dissatisfaction (or disutility) caused by uncertainty. That is, the dispersion of possible outcomes of an act causes the risk averter to feel uncomfortable, ill at ease, or anxious about the decision. Risk averters regard risk as a "bad" (an item which gives them disutility) as compared with a "good" (one which gives them utility, or psychic satisfaction). Risk averters will take on risk (and disutility) only if they, at the same time, expect to gain a sufficiently large amount of profit (and utility) associated with the proposed investment project. The greater the risk perceived, the greater the return the investor requires to offset the risk. Conversely, risk averters will accept lower expected returns if these are associated with lower degrees of risk. This willingness to trade off risk for return is characteristic of a risk averter: He or she *is* prepared to take risks, but only if there is sufficient compensation expected. In general, we expect business decision makers to be risk averse, by this definition.

We can depict a risk averter's preference structure between risk and return in terms of indifference-curve analysis. This method of analysis is examined in more detail in the context of consumer decision making in the following chapter. It will suffice to say here that indifference curves are lines joining combinations that give a person the same amount of utility. Thus the decision maker will be indifferent as to which of these combinations is chosen. Indifference curves showing combinations of two "goods" will be negatively sloping throughout, since more of one "good" must be combined with less of the other "good" for the consumer to remain indifferent between the combinations. But, since a risk averter gains utility from profits and disutility from risk, the indifference curves are *positively* sloping to reflect the fact that risk is a "bad" and that it generates disutility rather that utility.[6]

In Figure 2-1 we show risk (measured by the standard deviation of possible profit levels) on the horizontal axis, and we show return (measured by the expected present value of the possible profit levels) on the vertical axis. Three arbitrarily chosen indifference curves are shown as I_1, I_2, and I_3. The direction of preference, shown by the arrow, is upward and to the left: That is, any combination on I_1 is preferred to any on I_2, and any combination on I_2 is preferred to any on I_3.

---

[6]We show in Chapter 3 that higher indifference curves are preferred to lower indifference curves, that indifference curves do not meet or intersect, and that they are convex to the origin. These properties of indifference curves also apply to the positively sloped indifference curves of risk and return analysis.

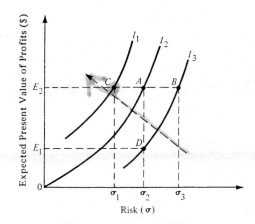

FIGURE 2-1. Indifference Curves for a Risk Averter in Risk-Return Space

- EXAMPLE: Suppose a manager is considering four alternative solutions to a problem, which we shall call projects A, B, C, and D. Point *A* in Figure 2-1 represents decision A, which has expected present value E_2 and the standard deviation σ_2 The decision maker is indifferent between this project and the status quo (with the funds invested in the best alternative investment), which is represented by the origin. You can see that the decision maker requires E_2 dollars of expected return to compensate for bearing σ_2 dollars of standard deviation, or risk. Note that decision A is preferred to decision B, which has the same expected value but higher risk, σ_3. It follows that the status quo (best alternative use of the funds) is also preferred to decision B, since decision A and the status quo are on the same indifference curve. Decision C is preferred to both A and B, since it has the same expected value but lower risk, σ_1. Finally, decision D is regarded as equally desirable to decision B, but it is inferior to both A and C, as well as to the status quo. Decision D has the same risk as A but lower expected profits, and it has both more risk and less return than decision C. In this case the decision maker's only desirable alternative is decision C.

- NOTE: The slopes of these indifference curves indicate the individual's degree of risk aversion. The slope of an indifference curve reflects the *marginal rate of substitution* (MRS) between the two variables under consideration. In this case, the decision maker's MRS is the amount of expected return he or she requires before accepting an extra unit of risk. You can see in Figure 2-1 that the person's MRS between risk and return is positive and increases as the level of risk and return increase, because the slope of each indifference curve becomes progressively steeper as the decision maker moves up the curve. Thus, a decision maker who is already bearing high levels of risk will require an even greater increment of expected profits before agreeing to accept any more risk. This reflects the implicit assumption of diminishing marginal utility of wealth and increasing marginal disutility of risk, which underlie the analysis and appear reasonable for most decision makers.

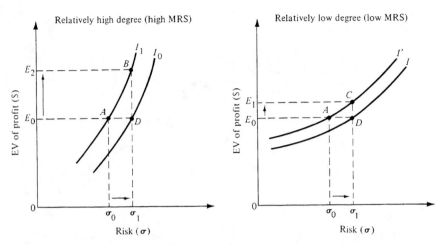

FIGURE 2-2.   *Different Degrees of Risk Aversion*

Differing Degrees of Risk Aversion.   Different people will have different degrees of risk aversion, because they have different marginal rates of substitution between risk and return. Graphically these differences are reflected in steeper or flatter indifference curves in risk-return space. In Figure 2-2 we show a person with a relatively high degree of risk aversion contrasted with someone with a relatively low degree of risk aversion. Note that points A and D are the same on both graphs. Project D is inferior to project A, since for the same expected return, E_0, it has the larger risk, σ_1. In both cases the person would accept the risk level σ_1 only if this is accompanied by an expected profit larger than that of project A. How much additional expected profit would it take to make each person indifferent between project A and a project containing σ_1 units of risk? The more risk-averse person in the left-hand graph requires an additional DB dollars to remain at the same level of utility and thus has a relatively high MRS of return for risk, measured by the ratio BD/AD. The less risk-averse person on the right-hand side requires only the smaller amount of extra expected profit, DC dollars, for the extra risk, $\sigma_1 - \sigma_0$, and thus exhibits a relatively low MRS of return for risk measured by the ratio CD/AD.

Risk Preference.   People show risk preference or neutrality in gambling, sporting, and recreational activities. Risk preference means that risk is viewed as a utility-producing good, and so the individual's indifference curves are negatively sloping as in the left-hand graph of Figure 2-3. Such an individual is prepared to give up expected profits for a larger amount of risk. For example, a gambler might prefer the thrill of a game in which the odds are poorer and the expected value of gains in lower, over a safer bet on another game in which the expected value is somewhat higher.

Risk Neutrality.   Risk neutrality means that the individual is indifferent to risk, receiving neither utility nor disutility from risk regardless of the amount of risk involved. Such an individual's indifference curves would be horizontal, as in the right-hand graph of

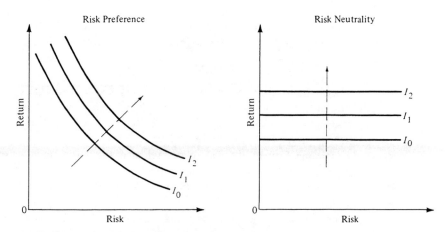

FIGURE 2-3.   Risk Preference and Risk Neutrality

Figure 2-3. The arrow shows the direction of preference: More expected profit is preferred to less, regardless of the risk. It should be noted that risk preference and risk neutrality are not common among business decision makers who are accountable to senior management and/or stockholders for their decisions.[7]

2.3   ADJUSTMENT FOR RISK IN DECISION MAKING

In this section we examine several methods by which the risk-averse decision maker can compare decision alternatives on a risk-adjusted basis to find the alternative that best serves the firm's objective function.

The Maximin Decision Criterion

- DEFINITION: *Maximin* is the term given to the largest (the maximum) of the smallest outcomes (the minimums) associated with each decision alternative. The maximin decision criterion is to select the alternative containing the maximin outcome.

- EXAMPLE: In the large versus small machine problem, there are nine possible outcomes after two years for each alternative, depending on whether demand over the first two years was heavy-heavy, heavy-medium, heavy-light, and so forth. The nine possible outcomes were shown in column 8 in Table 2-2 for the large machine and in Table 2-3 for

---

[7]Some would argue that there are indeed high-flying, entrepreneurial businesspeople who are risk preferring. Quite the contrary: These people take high risks only because they expect high returns, and they are more likely risk averters (although their degree of risk aversion might be relatively low). It is more likely that a firm or an individual can act like they are risk neutral if they are involved in a large number of projects that represent a diversified portfolio, and the present project is relatively small.

the small machine. The minimum outcomes in column 8 were $-2,083$ for the large machine and $861 for the small machine. The *maximin* outcome is, thus, $861, the larger of the smallest outcomes. Thus the maximin criterion selects the small machine in preference to the large machine.

In effect, the maximin criterion rules out every decision alternative except the one with the best of the worst outcomes. This is a risk averter's decision criterion in the sense that it avoids alternatives which contain worse "downside" outcomes. But note that it also ignores the probability distribution and would have chosen the small machine even if its worst outcome probability was very high and the large plant's worst outcome probability was very low. The maximin criterion also ignores all other outcomes. The large machine shows several relatively high outcomes, yet these don't enter into consideration at all.

So when would the maximin criterion be appropriate? For repeated decisions, where the law of averages should cause the EPV to be attained (on average) over many trials, it is clearly too pessimistic, since it always expects the worst to happen. For a one-shot deal, however, where the firm simply cannot afford to suffer the worst outcomes associated with some of the decision alternatives, the maximin criterion may be appropriate.

- EXAMPLE: In the large versus small machine decision, suppose that any loss over $1,000 would cause the firm to go bankrupt and be liquidated by its creditors. The decision maker might be unwilling to take the risk of the $2,083 loss associated with the large machine, and thus choose the small machine to avoid the possibility of a loss exceeding $1,000. Similarly, a decision maker looking for a promotion in the near future may think that a loss resulting from one of his or her decisions will most likely prevent that promotion and may want to use the maximin criterion. Thus, in particular situations, usually involving relatively short time horizons in which the law of averages cannot be relied on and in which the firm or decision maker cannot afford the outcomes associated with some of the decision alternatives, the maximin criterion may be appropriate.

The Coefficient-of-Variation Criterion

- DEFINITION: The *coefficient of variation* is defined here as the ratio of the standard deviation (σ) to the expected present value (EPV). The coefficient of variation for a probability distribution, σ/EPV, thus indicates the amount of risk per dollar of expected return. The risk-averse decision maker should choose the alternative with the lowest (but positive-valued) coefficient of variation.[8]

- EXAMPLE: In the large versus small machine example, we calculated both the EPV and the standard deviation for each decision alternative. For the large machine the standard

---

[8]Decision alternatives with negative coefficients of variation must also have negative EPVs, since the standard deviation cannot be negative. Such decisions must be inferior to the status quo (with the funds invested elsewhere at the opportunity rate of interest) and should not be considered further.

deviation was \$5,395.70 and the expected value was \$6,401.50. The ratio of these figures, or the coefficient of variation, is 0.8429. For the small machine the standard deviation was \$2,903.60 and the expected value was \$6,346.60. The coefficient of variation for the small machine is, thus, only 0.4575. In effect, these figures say that the large machine promises an average dispersion of about \$0.84 per \$1.00 of expected value, while the small machine offers about \$0.46 per \$1.00 average dispersion from the expected value.

The alternative with the least risk per dollar of return has the least return-adjusted risk. It follows that the reciprocal of the coefficient of variation namely EPV/σ, is a measure of risk-adjusted return. Choosing the alternative with the smaller coefficient of variation thus amounts to choosing the alternative with the larger risk-adjusted return.[9]

The EPV Criterion Using Different Discount Rates

An alternative method of adjusting the EPV criterion for risk is to use higher discount rates for the more risky decision alternatives. Recall that the opportunity discount rate (ODR) is defined as the best rate of interest that could be earned elsewhere at the same degree of risk. Thus, if one alternative has a dispersion of outcomes (and a resulting standard deviation value) similar to that of a corporate bond issue yielding 10%, while another alternative has a dispersion of outcomes similar to that of a 12% corporate bond issue, the appropriate ODRs are 10% and 12%, respectively.

• EXAMPLE: Looking back at the large versus small machine decision, we note that the dispersions (and the standard deviations) of the two alternatives are significantly different. Suppose 10% *is* the correct ODR for the small machine, but that the dispersion of the large machine's expected outcomes is similar to that of a 12% bond issue. In Table 2-5 we show the recalculation of the EPV of the large-machine decision using the 12% discount factors. As you can see, discounting the expected cash flows by the higher rate reduces the EPV to \$6,150.67. This is now somewhat less than the small machine's \$6,346.60. Thus the expected-present-value criterion using different ODRs (EPV-ODR for short) now favors the decision to purchase the small machine, just as the maximin and coefficient-of-variation criteria did.

You may be wondering why we didn't discount the two alternatives at different discount rates in the first instance. Essentially, there are two different ways to adjust the EPV criterion for risk. One is to discount both (or all) decision alternatives at the same discount rate and then use the coefficient of variation as the risk-adjusted EPV criterion. The second method is to foresee the different degrees of risk involved in the different decision alternatives and to discount each alternative at its appropriate ODR. One method

---

[9]It is important to note that the coefficient of variation may lead to a wrong decision in some instances, because it does not account for differing degrees of risk aversion. We shall return to this issue later in this section.

TABLE 2-5. Expected Present Value of the Large-Machine Decision Using 12% ODR

Initial Cost ($) [1]	YEAR 1			YEAR 2			CALCULATION OF EPV		
	Demand (probability) [2]	Profits ($) [3]	PV (DF = 0.8929) [4]	Demand (probability) [5]	Profits ($) [6]	PV (DF = 0.7972) [7]	Total PV ($) [8]	Joint Probability [9]	Weighted PV [10]
	Heavy (P = 0.2)	10,000	8,929	Heavy (P = 0.4)	12,500	9,965	16,894	0.08	1,351.52
				Medium (P = 0.4)	5,000	3,986	10,915	0.08	873.20
				Light (P = 0.2)	1,000	797	7,726	0.04	309.05
-2,000	Medium (P = 0.3)	4,000	3,572	Heavy (P = 0.4)	12,500	9,965	11,537	0.12	1,384.39
				Medium (P = 0.4)	5,000	3,986	5,558	0.12	666.91
				Light (P = 0.2)	1,000	797	2,369	0.06	142.13
	Light (P = 0.5)	-1,000	-893	Heavy (P = 0.4)	12,500	9,965	7,072	0.20	1,414.42
				Medium (P = 0.4)	5,000	3,986	1,093	0.20	218.62
				Light (P = 0.2)	1,000	797	-2,096	0.10	-209.57
							Expected present value		$6,150.67

or the other may be used but not a combination of the two. For example, if you discount two alternatives at different ODRs and then calculate the coefficient of variation, you will have doubly adjusted for risk and may subsequently choose the wrong alternative.

These two methods are basically similar and would normally rank decision alternatives in the same order. But which one is superior? In terms of data required to use the criterion, the coefficient-of-variation criterion can be used with much lower search costs, as compared to the proper implementation of the EPV-ODR criterion. The latter requires that a study be made of the dispersion of possible outcomes of a broad range of alternative investments, so the correct ODR may be ascertained for each decision alternative. The coefficient-of-variation criterion is usually implemented using the firm's *cost of capital* (the rate of interest which it pays to borrow funds) as the discount rate. Since the firm knows its cost of capital, the firm does not need an extensive search procedure each time it makes a decision.[10]

The Certainty-Equivalent Criterion

- DEFINITION: The *certainty equivalent* of a decision alternative is the sum of money, available with certainty, that would make the manager indifferent between taking that decision and accepting the certain sum of money. The certainty-equivalent criterion involves selecting the decision alternative which has the highest certainty equivalent.

- EXAMPLE: Suppose that I owe you $50 and I offer to give you back the $50 or "toss you" for double or nothing. If you choose the cash rather than the gamble, this means that you prefer the certain sum ($50) to the uncertain sum associated with the gamble (either $100 or nothing). To find your point of indifference I might now offer you the choice of $30 with certainty or the gamble for $100 or nothing. If you are now willing to take the gamble, this would mean that your certainty equivalent of the gamble lies somewhere between $30 and $50. Suppose that after several more offers I find that you are indifferent between accepting $45 with certainty and taking the gamble. Thus, your certainty equivalent (CE) for that gamble is $45. In effect, the CE is the sum of money that will almost bribe you to give up the gamble.

An individual's certainty equivalent incorporates that person's degree of risk aversion (or risk preference). The more risk-averse decision maker would exhibit a lower CE than a less risk-averse (or a risk-preferring) decision maker for the same gamble. Moreover, it can incorporate other considerations as well. If the gamble is to be repeated many times, we would expect the CE to be equal to the expected value (in this case $50). If the

---

[10]See Eugene F. Brigham, *Financial Management Theory and Practice*, 2nd ed. (Hinsdale, Ill.: The Dryden Press, 1979), pp. 555–93. Note that the firm's cost of capital (CC) may or may not be equal to the firm's ODR. The rate at which the firm borrows reflects the lender's assessment of the overall riskiness of the firm rather than the firm's assessment of the riskiness of the project under consideration. If the marginal project is more risky than the average risk of projects already undertaken by the firm, the CC will understate the ODR. Only when the marginal risk is equal to the average risk, or when the *marginal cost of capital* is used, is the CC an appropriate measure of the ODR.

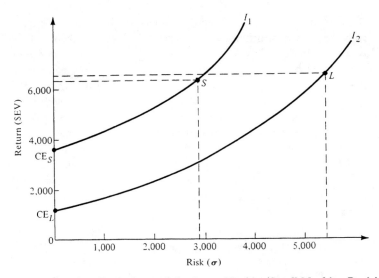

FIGURE 2-4. *Certainty Equivalents of the Large-Machine/Small-Machine Decision*

gamble is to be taken just once or a few times, we expect a risk averter's CE to be less than the EPV because, in effect, the risk averter would trade off expected return for removal of the risk. Conversely, a risk preferrer's CE is expected to exceed the EPV, since this person gets utility from risk and will require more than the gamble's EPV to be bribed into giving it up.

Expressed in terms of indifference-curve analysis, the certainty equivalent of a decision alternative can be shown as the point on the vertical axis joined by an indifference curve to the point representing the decision alternative under consideration. Note that since indifference curves neither meet nor intersect and since higher curves are preferred to lower curves, the certainty-equivalent criterion is entirely consistent with the maximization of the manager's utility.

• EXAMPLE: In Figure 2-4 we represent the large versus small machine problem once again. Note that we have shown the small machine as the preferred alternative, since it lies on the higher indifference curve. The point CE_S on the expected-value axis is the certainty equivalent of the combination of expected value and risk represented by point S. It is the certainty equivalent because risk, on the horizontal axis, has been reduced to zero and, thus, the decision maker is indifferent between $\$CE_S$ with certainty and $\$6,346.60$ with risk (standard deviation of $\$2,903.60$). Similarly, the certainty equivalent of the large machine, point L, is $\$CE_L$.

The Certainty-Equivalent Factor.   To find the certainty equivalent of an uncertain venture without involving indifference curves, decide what fraction of the EPV would make you indifferent between (1) the EPV of the uncertain venture and (2) that fraction of the EPV if it were available with certainty. One way to do this is to decide "how many cents

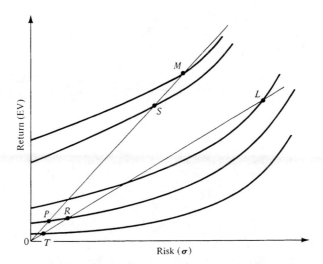

FIGURE 2-5. *Conflict between the Coefficient-of-Variation Criterion and the Certainty-Equivalent Criterion*

in the dollar'' you would consider to be equivalent if these were available with certainty. This fraction, say 0.75, is known as the certainty-equivalent factor (CEF). Multiplying the CEF by the EPV will give you the certainty equivalent of the gamble. Riskier ventures will have smaller CEFs, but the CE is the product of the CEF and the EPV, and thus the CE may be greater or smaller for the more risky venture. The decision rule remains the same: Choose the alternative with the greatest certainty equivalent.

Contradicting Criteria. Unfortunately, we are now in a position to see that the coefficient-of-variation and the EPV-ODR criteria may sometimes contradict the CE criterion, and thus indicate the choice of a decision alternative that would not be optimal in terms of the decision maker's utility. Consider Figure 2-5, in which the points S and L for the small and large machine alternatives are shown on rays emanating from the origin. The slopes of these rays reflect the ratio of expected value to standard deviation, or the reciprocal of the coefficient of variation. The steeper the ray, the lower is the coefficient of variation. As we saw earlier, the small machine, point S, is preferred to the large machine, point L, on the basis of both the coefficient-of-variation and the certainty-equivalent criteria.

But consider points M and P, which have the same value for their coefficient of variation as point S, yet are ranked differently in terms of their certainty equivalents: M is preferred to S, which in turn is preferred to P. The coefficient-of-variation criterion is unable to distinguish between M, S, and P and ranks them as equals. In effect, it says that the ray from the origin *OPSM* is an indifference curve; with all points on it giving equal utility to the decision maker. Similarly, it effectively says that the ray *OTRL* is a lower indifference curve, with all points on that ray regarded as equal but inferior to any

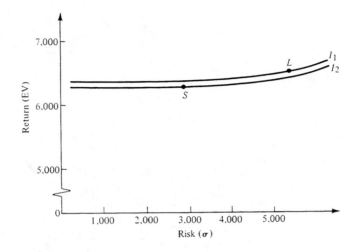

Figure 2-6. **Coefficient-of-Variation Criterion Refuted for a Slightly Risk-Averse Decision Maker**

point on the higher ray *OPSM*. The curvilinear indifference curves shown in Figure 2-5 indicate that this is untrue for the case presented: *L* is preferred to *T* and, moreover, *L* is preferred to *P*; and *R* is equivalent to *P*, despite *P*'s lower coefficient of variation.

Thus, although the coefficient-of-variation criterion correctly ranked points *S* and *L*, it incorrectly ranked most of the other points shown. Indeed, the coefficient-of-variation criterion may incorrectly rank *S* and *L* for some decision makers. In Figure 2-6 we show a manager who is only slightly risk averse (with very low marginal rate of substitution of expected return for risk) who prefers point *L* over point *S*. Point *L* lies on a higher indifference curve for this person and, accordingly, has a higher certainty equivalent. Note that the EV-ODR criterion also incorrectly ranked the small versus large machine alternatives for this person and would similarly make mistakes between other pairs of decision alternatives.

Why does this problem arise? Essentially, the coefficient-of-variation criterion and the EV-ODR criterion assume a linear and constant trade-off between risk and return. In fact, most risk averters exhibit a nonlinear risk-return trade-off. In economic terms we explain this as diminishing marginal utility of wealth and increasing marginal disutility of risk. The more wealth (expected return) one is offered, the less utility one receives from the marginal dollar, and the more risk one is offered, the greater the disutility one receives from the marginal unit of risk.

So should we throw away the coefficient-of-variation and the EV-ODR criteria and just use the certainty equivalent? No, the coefficient-of-variation criterion, and the EV-ODR criterion to a lesser extent, have value because they can be calculated and subjected to scrutiny, whereas certainty equivalents and utility are more cerebral and intuitive notions that are more difficult to defend quantitatively. Without doubt the certainty equivalent gives the better answers for maximizing the decision maker's utility function, but its

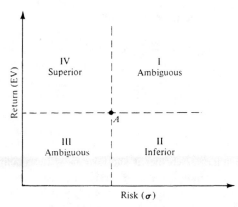

FIGURE 2-7. *Superior and Inferior Quadrants with Respect to a Particular Decision Alternative (Point A)*

calculation requires insight into the manager's preference patterns. (For oneself, a little introspection will provide CE values, but in the role of consultant or subordinate it is often impractical to discover the client's or boss's CE values.)

What to Do? The solution to this apparent impasse is to use all three methods with caution and with reservations. For example, one would say that the small machine appears to be preferable on a risk-adjusted basis, *unless the decision maker is only slightly risk averse*. As a consultant to the decision maker, one would pose the question, "Would you be willing to accept an additional $2,492.10 in risk (that is, the difference between the standard deviations) for an additional $54.90 expected return (that is, the difference in the EPVs)?" If the response is that the extra risk should be undertaken for the extra expected return (indicating in this case an extremely low degree of risk aversion), the simple risk-adjustment criterion is overturned. Alternatively, if the manager's preference is not to accept the extra risk for the extra return, the simple-risk-adjustment criterion is supported.

- NOTE: In many cases there will be no ambiguity about which decision alternative is preferred for a risk-averse decision maker or firm. Consider Figure 2-7, in which we show one of several possible outcomes, labeled point *A*. Relative to point *A*, we show quadrants I, II, III, and IV. Any point in quadrant IV is unambiguously superior to point *A* (for a risk averter) since it has either more return for the same or less risk, or less risk for the same return. Similarly, any point in quadrant II is unambiguously inferior to point *A*, having either less return for the same or more risk, or more risk for the same return. Quadrants I and III, relative to point *A*, do represent potential areas of conflict between the coefficient-of-variation and the EV-ODR criteria, on the one hand, and the certainty-equivalent criterion on the other. Points in quadrant I have both less risk and less return. When decision alternatives fall in quadrants I and III with respect to each other, one must use the "caution and reservation" approach.

Which Criterion Should Be Applied?

The choice among the various decision criteria available depends on three major considerations: the *frequency* with which one is confronted by decisions of this type, the *magnitude* of the gamble involved, and the decision maker's *attitude toward risk* and uncertainty.

- EXAMPLE: Suppose a firm has two major insurance contracts: one for collision damage to its fleet of automobiles and the other for fire damage to its plant and buildings. The firm is considering whether it should renew these contracts or carry the risk itself. The risk is known to the firm from insurance company data. The odds are 1 in 20 (probability 0.05) that each of the company's vehicles will be damaged to a mean value of $5,000. Hence, the expected value of the damage is $250 per vehicle. The insurance company, however, charges a premium of $275 per vehicle, since it wishes to contribute to its overhead expenses and profits. Also suppose that the odds are 1 in 1,000 that the company's plant will burn down. The value of the plant is $10 million, and thus the expected value of the possible loss is $10,000. The insurance company's premium for this policy is $11,000. Will the firm carry its own insurance?

    Concerning the frequency of the gamble, we must remember that risk involves the law of averages. If one runs the risk a large number of times, one might reasonably expect to win and lose in the same proportions as the general population. On the other hand, if one runs the risk only once, then one might be lucky and have neither an accident nor a fire; but, on the other hand, one might suffer all the bad luck all at once. In the case of the firm deciding to carry its own insurance, the automobiles represent a high frequency of taking the gamble. The company has, say, 100 vehicles, and it might expect the probability of any one being damaged to be similar to the population of vehicles at large. On the other hand, the firm has only one plant and the frequency of this gamble is only once. It does not have 100 plants; it does not take this gamble at a large number of locations; and, therefore, it should not expect the average incidence of fire damage.

    Concerning the magnitude of the gamble, the important point to consider here is whether or not the decision maker can afford the loss it would sustain if things turned out very badly. In the case of our company considering its insurance, it is possible that it could withstand the (unlikely) loss of all its vehicles for a total loss of $500,000. On the other hand, the loss of the plant and buildings to the tune of $10 million would probably represent a significant setback to that company. Thus the second factor would work in favor of the company renewing its insurance policy for fire damage to the plant and buildings, but not for the automobile fleet.

    The third issue is the individual's degree of risk preference or aversion. The crucial factor is the willingness of the decision maker to accept risk and its consequences. Thus, even though the first two considerations indicate that the firm should perhaps bear the risk on its motor vehicles, the decision maker might be sufficiently risk averse that the policy will be renewed. Alternatively, even though the first two aforementioned factors indicate that the firm should probably renew its insurance for fire damage for that plant, a risk-preferring decision maker might decide to cancel that policy.

TABLE 2-6. Plant and Buildings Insurance Problem

	INSURE			NOT INSURE		
	Cost	Probability	EV	Cost	Probability	EV
Fire	$-11,000	0.001	$- 11	$-10,000,000	0.001	$-10,000
No fire	-11,000	0.999	-10,989	0	0.999	0
Expected value			$-11,000			$-10,000
Standard deviation			0			316,701.75
Coefficient of variation			0			31.67

Table 2-6 shows the payoffs, expected values, standard deviations, and coefficients of variation for the firm's plant and buildings insurance problem. From this data we can choose the appropriate decision using each of the aforementioned criteria. Using the expected-value criterion, the decision maker would insure neither the fleet of automobiles nor the plant and buildings. Under the maximin and coefficient-of-variation criteria, the decision maker would insure both the fleet and the plant buildings. Under the certainty-equivalent criterion, we are unable to say, since this criterion depends on the decision maker's individual attitude toward bearing risk and uncertainty. On the basis of the three aforementioned factors, however, we may hazard a guess that under this criterion a risk-averse decision maker would choose to renew the insurance policy on the plant and buildings, and possibly to allow the collision policy on its fleet of cars to lapse. This information is summarized in Table 2-7.

Nonmonetary Factors in Decision Making. The objectives of the firm's owners and managers may include particular nonmonetary goals, such as concern for the environment, and philanthropic considerations relating to the impact of worker layoffs during periods of low demand. Similarly, managers may prefer decision alternatives that allow the avoidance of highly competitive markets and high-stress management situations. Concern for these nonmonetary issues may induce the managers to forego the decision alternative that would best serve the purely monetary objectives of the firm and, perhaps, its managers.[11]

TABLE 2-7. Comparing Decision Criteria

Criterion	Auto Fleet	Plant and Buildings
Expected value	Not insure	Not insure
Maximin	Insure	Insure
Coefficient of variation	Insure	Insure
Certainty equivalent	(Not insure?)	(Insure?)

[11]See A. R. Cohen, H. Gadon, and G. Miaoulis, "Decision Making in Firms: The Impact of Non-Economic Factors," *The Journal of Economic Issues*, 10 (June 1976), pp. 242–58.

2.4   SEARCH COSTS AND THE VALUE OF INFORMATION

In an environment of uncertainty, the firm lacks full information about the actual outcomes of its decision. It may choose to engage in search activity to improve its information. Information can be improved by various means, starting with simple surveys of potential customers and progressing all the way to complex computer modeling and simulation. Advice and information can be purchased from consultants, or the firm can engage its own personnel in search procedures. The information which decision makers often need will not simply be the raw data but will usually require adjustment in some way, such as finding the expected values and present values of the raw data. In addition, raw data will often need to be seasonally adjusted or deflated by a price index to be in the form most useful to the decision maker. Naturally, this search process costs money, and the costs of obtaining information are usually inversely related to the speed with which the information must be generated.

- DEFINITION: *Search costs* are defined as the costs of obtaining information in the form needed by the decision maker and within the time constraints required by the decision maker.

The Value of Information

The value of information is the difference between what you can earn with the information already held and what you could earn if you knew with certainty the outcome prior to making the decision. In cases where the search costs are expected to be greater than the value of the information, the decision maker should proceed on the basis of the information already held and should not incur the cost of obtaining any extra information, since that cost is expected to outweigh the benefits derived.

- EXAMPLE: Recall once more the large versus small machine problem. Now suppose that a consulting firm offers to undertake some intensive studies to tell the firm what the state of demand will be over the two-year period, before the firm has to make its decision. The consulting firm advises that its fee will be $1,000, including all expenses. Should the firm incur this search cost or not?

   If the decision maker could accurately predict, or know in advance, the exact state of demand over the next two years (for example, that it would be medium in year one and heavy in year two), he or she would simply choose the alternative that offers the greatest net present value under each of those circumstances. Similarly, for any other state of demand (if known in advance), it becomes a simple decision that can be made under conditions of certainty, since a single outcome follows each decision.

   In Table 2-8, we repeat the outcomes for each decision alternative under each of the nine jointly possible states of demand. Given the prior information concerning the actual state of demand, the firm would select the machine with the highest EPV of profits under that state of demand. The machine that should be chosen under each possible state of demand is indicated in column 4 of Table 2-8, with the resultant profits in column 5.

TABLE 2-8. *Expected Value of Choosing the Best Alternative Given Full Prior Information*

| State of Demand [1] | PRESENT VALUE OF PROFITS IF | | Choice with Certainty (machine) [4] | Present Value of Profits ($) [5] | Joint Probability [6] | Weighted PV ($) [7] |
	Large Machine ($) [2]	Small Machine ($) [3]				
Heavy-heavy	17,415	11,271	Large	17,415	0.08	1,393.20
Heavy-medium	11,220	9,619	Large	11,220	0.08	897.60
Heavy-light	7,916	6,315	Large	7,916	0.04	316.64
Medium-heavy	11,961	9,453	Large	11,961	0.12	1,435.32
Medium-medium	5,766	7,801	Small	7,801	0.12	936.12
Medium-light	2,462	4,497	Small	4,497	0.06	269.82
Light-heavy	7,416	5,817	Large	7,416	0.20	1,483.20
Light-medium	1,221	4,165	Small	4,165	0.20	833.00
Light-light	−2,083	861	Small	861	0.10	86.10
				Expected present value		$7,651.00

But what is the probability that the market researchers will advise the firm that the actual state of demand will be heavy-heavy, for example? Prior to receiving the additional information, the firm still has only its joint probability distribution shown in column 6. The firm's decision maker would weight each of the payoffs in column 5 by its probability of occurring and add these weighted payoffs to find the expected present value of the decision under conditions of certainty. As we can see, this sum is $7,651.00. The expected value of information is the difference between this sum and the expected value of the best alternative with the information already held. The large machine had the higher EPV of profits, namely $6,401.50, and the difference is, therefore, $7,651.00 − $6,401.50 = $1,249.50. Thus the expected value of information is $1,249.50. Since the cost of that information is only $1,000, the firm should go ahead and hire the consultants.[12]

2.5 EVALUATION OF THE DECISION MADE

How do we evaluate decisions? What is a good decision? Is a decision a bad one if the actual outcome is bad? For example, if the firm chooses the large machine and the actual outcome is $−2,083 (the worst possible outcome foreseen), should the manager be castigated for the quality of his or her decision? The answer is "not necessarily." The quality of the decision depends on five main considerations, discussed next.

---

[12]We are assuming that the consultant's predictions will be confirmed by the firm's later experience. Typically, a firm would require a substantial margin for error in case the "full information" supplied by the consultant turns out to be wrong.

Optimal Information Search?   First, was information-search activity undertaken to the point where it would not be marginally profitable to continue the search procedure? That is, in the best estimate of the decision maker, would additional search costs have exceeded the value of new information derived? Note that the time available plays a role in this. Sometimes there is insufficient time to conduct information search before a decision must be made. Or, equivalently, to obtain the information required within the time available might cost an inordinate amount, and in the decision maker's best estimate this would render the exercise uneconomic.

Accurate and Appropriate Data?   Second, was the data, or raw information that was obtained, accurate and used in the appropriate form? For example, was data on uncertain future cash flows transformed into expected-present-value terms? Was seasonal data deseasonalised? Were dollar figures considered in real terms (in constant purchasing power) or nominal terms, unadjusted for inflation? The decision maker must process the raw data into useful and usable information before making the decision.

Appropriate Decision Criterion?   Third, was the appropriate decision criterion used? Were the frequency of the gamble, the magnitude of the gamble, and the decision maker's attitude toward risk taken into consideration in the choice of the decision criterion that was ultimately given the most weight in discriminating among the decision alternatives?

Was the Decision Timely?   Since information tends to grow with the passage of time, decisions should not be made irrevocably before they *must* be made. A commitment made too early cannot easily be altered if new information comes along a little later. For example, if bids are solicited for a contract and the deadline for the submission of bids is at noon on the last day of the month, the firm should work all through the analysis and make a tentative decision (on the price of its bid), but it should delay submitting the bid until just before the deadline in case new information, such as a substantial increase in a major cost item or the bankruptcy of a major competitor, should come to light and cause the firm to want to change its commitment.

   Whether or not there is a specific deadline, the timing rule is to defer the decision until the expected value of deferring the decision further is equal to the expected profits foregone by not making the decision. This deferral is not the same as procrastination, but rather it means that the decision maker should consider and attempt to quantify the advantages of waiting and actually make the decision when it is apparent that more would be lost than gained by further waiting.

   What if important additional information does arrive after the decision is made? This happens all the time. When it does, a new decision problem occurs: that is, should the decision maker stick with the decision just made or make another decision? This new decision should be evaluated on the basis of the EPVs of each alternative, their relative risks, and so on. Even if the new decision is to change the earlier decision, this change does not make the earlier decision a bad one. If it was made on the basis of all information available at the time (after search had been carried to the optimal point), by the application of the appropriate decision criterion, and at a time when it appeared optimal to make the decision, then it was a good decision.

Sensitivity Analysis? *Sensitivity analysis* is defined as the examination of a decision to find the degree of inaccuracy in the underlying assumptions that can be tolerated without causing the decision to be inappropriate. The manager should consider the sensitivity of the decision to the assumptions on which it is based. All decisions are based on some assumptions: for example, that the data are accurate, that probability distributions will be validated by future events, that the discount rate used is appropriate, that fixed cost categories do not, in fact, vary with output levels, and so on.

Sensitivity analysis requires a systematic examination of the decision to see whether or not that decision would still be chosen under somewhat different assumptions concerning the cost and demand conditions and the opportunity discount rate. If the underlying assumptions can be varied over a relatively wide range but the selected decision still remains optimal, we can be confident that it is not very sensitive to the underlying assumptions. If, on the other hand, a slightly different set of assumptions causes another decision alternative to be the chosen one, then the choice under the initial assumptions is very sensitive to those assumptions.

To conduct sensitivity analysis, one proceeds systematically to vary one assumption at a time and note whether the changed assumption causes a change in the recommendation. You might start with the discount rate and recalculate the EPV assuming a discount rate that is, say, two points higher, and then assume a discount rate that is two points lower, to see if the optimal decision would change if interest rates were to rise or fall in the near future. Interest rates are potentially volatile and have been known to move dramatically in relatively short periods. The wise decision maker will be aware that significantly higher or lower interest rates either would or would not change the decision selected. If the decision is sensitive to the opportunity interest rate assumed, the decision maker should consider undertaking information-search activity to be assured which is the most likely interest rate scenario over the duration of the project.[13]

Similarly, you should be assured that your decision is not sensitive to the accuracy of the estimate of the initial costs. Since your initial costs are typically in present-value terms already, it is a simple matter to see how much of a cost overrun could be tolerated by looking at the EPV. If a small percentage variation in the initial costs would wipe out the EPV, then the decision is sensitive to the assumption that initial costs are estimated

---

[13]I can see you wincing at the thought of repeating all those calculations several more times! But with a personal computer and spreadsheet software like Lotus 1-2-3 and Excel, such recalculations are a simple matter. The *Computer Courseware Package and Manual* that is ancillary to this textbook contains a variety of templates, including EPV spreadsheets that allow you to enter the cost, demand, probability, and ODR data and instantly see the impact of any changes to that data. This "what if?" capability of spreadsheets greatly facilitates what we call sensitivity analysis. The *Courseware Manual* is included in the *Study Guide/Workbook* which is available through your bookstore, and which has full details on solving the problems as well as chapter summaries, self-tests, and answers to all of the Discussion Questions at the end of each chapter. Ask your instructor how to get a copy of the disk containing the spreadsheet templates (the details are in the *Instructor's Manual* or call the publisher).

accurately. Again, more information should be sought on the cost situation if the decision is sensitive to that assumption.

Finally, your estimated probability distributions relating to demand situations in future periods are assumed to be accurate. In case they are not, you should look at a more pessimistic set of demand probabilities as well as a more optimistic one. Here, you could either revise the profit figures downward (and later upward) using the same probabilities, or shift the weighting toward the lower outcomes (and later toward the high outcomes) to reflect a more pessimistic (and later more optimistic) demand scenario. If, under either the pessimistic or optimistic senario, the chosen decision becomes suboptimal, information should be sought to assure the decision maker of the most likely demand situations.

Thus, if these five issues have indeed been carefully considered, we can say that a decision *was* a good decision at the time it was taken, regardless of the actual outcome. Decision making under risk and uncertainty necessarily involves unsatisfactory outcomes from time to time. You win some and you lose some, but consistent application of the appropriate decision criterion, using as much good information as it seemed profitable to purchase, should ensure maximization of the firm's net worth, subject to risk considerations, over a series of decisions.

2.6 SUMMARY

In this chapter we have continued our examination of the basic foundations of economic decision making. The expected-present-value analysis of Chapter 1 was extended to incorporate risk analysis. Most business decision makers appear to be risk averse; that is, they derive disutility from risk and uncertainty. The degree of risk can be measured by the standard deviation of the probability distribution of outcomes, and the degree of risk aversion can be measured by the rate at which the decision maker is willing to trade off expected value (or profits) for reduced risk. For complex decision alternatives with probability distributions of outcomes in each year, there will be a joint probability distribution of outcomes at the end of the planning period. Such decision problems are best handled by using decision trees, which array the possible outcomes and joint probabilities in a manner that facilitates the understanding and the solution of the problem.

Four more decision criteria were introduced, each incorporating some method of adjustment for risk. The maximin decision criterion adjusts for risk in a crude way by avoiding the decision alternatives that have inferior "downside" outcomes. The coefficient-of-variation criterion effectively makes the decision on the basis of the least risk per dollar of expected value. The expected-value criterion can be adjusted for risk by the use of differing discount rates for alternatives with differing degrees of risk. The certainty-equivalent criterion is more comprehensive than the other two and adjusts for risk by choosing the decision alternative with the combination of risk or return that gives the decision maker the highest level of utility. The appropriate criterion for any particular decision depends on the firm's and the decision maker's objectives, the frequency and magnitude of the decision, and the firm's and the decision maker's attitude toward risk.

Decisions should be evaluated on an *ex ante* (before the event) basis, rather than on an *ex post* (after the event) basis. Good decisions are (1) based on properly adjusted EPV information; (2) obtained from a search procedure taken to the point where the value of additional information falls to equal costs of obtaining that information; (3) found by applying the appropriate decision criterion; (4) made at the optimal point in time; and (5) suitably qualified by a statement of the sensitivity of the decision to the assumption on which it is based.

DISCUSSION QUESTIONS

2-1. Define risk and uncertainty. How do we measure risk and uncertainty? Can you think of any other, more appropriate, measure of risk and uncertainty?

2-2. Define risk aversion. Does a risk averter refuse to take risks? Will a risk averter ever select the more risky alternative? Explain.

2-3. Explain why a risk preferrer might prefer a high-risk, low-stakes gamble to a low-risk, high-stakes gamble. Are you a risk averter, a risk preferrer, or are you risk indifferent? How do you know?

2-4. Demonstrate that the investor's *degree* of risk aversion (or preference) is an important element in determining his or her choice among investment alternatives.

2-5. Go through the thought process of determining your own certainty equivalent for a fifty-cent lottery ticket that is one of 100,000 sold for a $10,000 prize.
   (a) What is the expected value of the ticket?
   (b) Would you buy such a ticket? Why?
   (c) How much more or less expensive would the ticket need to be to *just* induce you to buy it?
   (d) Is that price your certainty equivalent for the gamble? Explain.

2-6. The product manager of a large company has had a series of disastrous new-product offerings. He fears that another failure will cost him his job. He is currently trying to make up his mind between two rather different new products for his next new-product launching. Product A has the greater expected value and has both a smaller minimum outcome and a larger maximum outcome as compared with Product B. Which product do you think the product manager will choose, and why?

2-7. In some cases the coefficient-of-variation criterion ranks decision alternatives in a different order, as compared to their ranking by the certainty-equivalent criterion. Explain.

2-8. Explain how the value of additional information is calculated.

2-9. Discuss the factors you would consider when evaluating a decision made by somebody else. Is it possible that you might conclude that it was a good decision even if the actual outcome was a disaster? Explain.

2-10. What is sensitivity analysis? How would you incorporate this into your recommendation to management concerning the choice between several decision alternatives?

PROBLEMS AND SHORT CASES

2-1. Sounds True, Inc., a small company producing stereo amplifiers, has found that its leading model has suffered substantial market share losses because of the competition from the other producers' newer models. The company is considering two alternatives for the coming year: either to give the existing product a minor facelift or to introduce a totally new model. The success or failure of these strategies will ultimately depend on the state of the economy, as is evident from the following payoff matrix. The payoffs shown represent thousands of dollars net profit. The company considers that the probabilities of a downturn, a constant economy, and of an upturn are 30%, 50% and 20%, respectively.

| State of | DECISION ALTERNATIVES | |
the Economy	Minor Facelift	New Model
Downturn	10	−20
Constant	30	20
Upturn	80	150

(a) Calculate the expected value, standard deviation, and coefficient of variation for each decision alternative.
(b) Apply the expected-value, coefficient-of-variation, and the maximin decision criteria to find which alternative is indicated under each criterion.
(c) Which alternative will have the greater certainty equivalent? Explain.

2-2. To help pay your way through college, you plan to operate either a hot dog stand or an ice cream stand at every home game of your local baseball team. The actual outcomes associated with each decision alternative depend to a large degree on the weather, since hot dogs will be in greater demand on cloudy or rainy days, whereas ice cream will be in greater demand on sunny days. The following payoff matrix shows the expected value of profits for each baseball game and for each decision alternative, under the three different states of nature considered possible. Your research at the local meteorological office indicates that over the past ten baseball seasons it was raining for 15% of the home games, cloudy for 55% of the games, and sunny for 30% of the games. You must decide which product to choose for the entire season, either hot dogs or ice cream.

| State of | DECISION ALTERNATIVES | |
Nature	Hot Dogs	Ice Cream
Rain	300	75
Cloud	250	150
Sun	100	400

(a) Calculate the expected value and the coefficient of variation of each decision alternative. Which alternative would you choose? Explain, including a statement about your certainty equivalent for each of the two alternatives.
(b) Suppose that you could purchase, for $50 per game, the right to choose between hot dogs and ice cream on the day of each game, so you could always have the appropriate product for the state of nature encountered each time. (Someone else would take the other product on each occasion.) What is the value of the information to be gained (about the weather) by delaying your decision until the day of the game?
(c) Assuming you must, before the season starts, decide among option A (to sell hot dogs), option B (to sell ice cream), or option C (buy the right to sell either hot dogs or ice

cream, depending on the weather for each game), which option would you choose? Explain.

2-3. Safeguard Stores is a relatively small chain operation in the retail supermarket industry. The area manager for Montreal, Nick Wolkowski, is considering opening a new store in a rapidly expanding suburb. Two store sizes have been suggested: the regular size of 27,000 square feet and the superstore of 40,000 square feet. The initial costs, expected-demand situation, profits, and probabilities are as follows:

Store Size	Initial Cost ($000)	Demand Situation	YEAR 1		YEAR 2	
			Profit ($000)	Probability	Profit ($000)	Probability
Regular	850	Low	300	0.2	500	0.2
		Medium	500	0.5	800	0.4
		High	800	0.3	1,000	0.4
Super	1,000	Low	300	0.6	600	0.4
		Medium	600	0.3	900	0.3
		High	1,000	0.1	1,200	0.3

Mr. Wolkowski is considering only a two-year horizon, since he hopes to be regional manager by then. He feels that the appropriate discount rate is 10%. (Treat the profits as though they are received in lump sum at the end of year one and year two. The costs are incurred immediately.)

(a) Which store promises the larger expected net present value?

(b) What do you think Mr. Wolkowski's decision will be, and why?

2-4. The Express Delivery Company operates a courier and parcel delivery service between the major cities in Southern California. Management is considering whether to lease or buy an additional truck it needs to extend its services. Careful analysis of costs and the potential demand situation has led to the following estimates of net cash flows (NCF) for each of the first two years:

Lease Option:

YEAR 1		YEAR 2	
NCF	Probability	NCF	Probability
−5,000	0.25	5,000	0.30
5,000	0.40	10,000	0.50
15,000	0.35	15,000	0.20

Buy Option:

YEAR 1		YEAR 2	
NCF	Probability	NCF	Probability
−10,000	0.20	10,000	0.30
0	0.50	15,000	0.50
10,000	0.30	20,000	0.20

The management considers that a two-year time horizon is appropriate, since it would replace this truck with a new one in two years whether it was leased or purchased. If purchased, the truck will have a salvage value of $5,000 at the end of the second year, and this value is included in the NCF figures. The lease agreement is for two years with no possibility of cancellation once signed. Management could alternatively invest the funds involved in corporate bonds, considered to be of similar risk to the strategy of expanding its services, and these bonds would yield 15% of current prices. Assume that all cash flows are spent or received at the end of each year in a single lump sum, and ignore any tax considerations.

(a) Using decision-tree analysis, find the expected net present value of each alternative.

(b) Calculate a measure of risk for each alternative.

(c) Apply several decision criteria and make your recommendation to management.

(d) State any qualifications and reservations you would wish to add to your recommendation.

2-5. The Keene Construction and Real Estate Development Company buys tracts of land, builds residential home units on the land, and sells them to home buyers. Keene is currently considering the development of Loon Swamp Estates, which is a tract of land it has owned and used as a dump for landfill for several years.

The potential development of Loon Swamp Estates has been narrowed to two alternatives. Project A is to build single-family houses, and project B is to build condominiums. In each case there would be immediate outlays to establish the streets, drainage, electrical and sewerage systems, and other amenities. For project A these initial costs will be $1 million, while for project B these costs will be $1.5 million because of the additional costs of a swimming pool, tennis courts, security services, and other features of the condominium project.

For either project there would be costs incurred throughout the following two years as the home units are constructed. Building would start at the main entrance and proceed in stages toward the back of the development. As units (either houses or condominiums) are completed, they will be sold at current market value. Keene faces uncertainty on the revenue side since market value might be high or low depending on various factors. This uncertainty is reflected in the following probability distributions of net cash flow (not including the initial costs) for each project:

PROJECT A NET CASH FLOWS				PROJECT B NET CASH FLOWS			
Year 1 (million dollars)	*Probability*	*Year 2 (million dollars)*	*Probability*	*Year 1 (million dollars)*	*Probability*	*Year 2 (million dollars)*	*Probability*
−1.5	0.30	2.0	0.20	−1.5	0.35	2	0.20
0.25	0.50	2.5	0.50	0.5	0.40	3	0.50
1.5	0.20	3.0	0.30	2.5	0.25	4	0.30

Rather than invest in either of these projects at all, Keene could alternatively invest in bonds being issued by another real estate developer in a nearby city, which promise 14% interest on funds being invested.

(a) Using decision-tree analysis, calculate the expected net present value and standard deviation of each project.

(b) Conduct sensitivity analysis with respect to your input data.

(c) Apply several decision criteria to this problem, and make your recommendation to Keene management.

(d) State explicitly any qualifications and assumptions which underlie your recommendation.

2-6. Your firm is considering the introduction of a new product, and you are required to set the price. You are considering three price strategies: high ($6), medium ($4), and low ($2.50). Your market research team has indicated that the probability distribution of sales at these prices is as follows:

HIGH PRICE		MEDIUM PRICE		LOW PRICE	
Sales	Probability	Sales	Probability	Sales	Probability
First year					
3,500	0.1	5,000	0.2	10,000	0.4
2,500	0.3	4,000	0.5	7,500	0.3
1,500	0.6	3,000	0.3	5,000	0.3
Second year					
5,000	0.2	8,000	0.3	12,000	0.3
4,000	0.3	6,500	0.4	9,000	0.5
3,000	0.5	5,000	0.3	7,500	0.2

The initial investment will be $22,000, and per-unit variable costs will be constant at $1 regardless of volume. You are advised by the finance department that the $22,000 could otherwise be invested (at comparable risk) in a forthcoming bond issue at 12.5% per annum.

(a) Using decision-tree analysis, find which pricing strategy promises the greatest net present value over the two-year period.

(b) Should the investment funds be used to buy the bonds instead? Why?

(c) Rank the strategies in order of their risk. Explain the basis for your ranking.

(d) Rank the strategies in order of their risk-adjusted expected value.

(e) Is the coefficient-of-variation criterion contradicted by the certainty-equivalent criterion in this case? Explain.

2-7. The Walgett Development Corporation has a tract of land that it is planning to develop, and has narrowed the options to the best two. Plan A is to seek city approval to subdivide the land into housing, install water, sewer, gas, and power lines, and offer the lots for sale to independent home builders. The initial cost of setting up this plan to the point of actually selling building lots is expected be $0.25 million. The initial set-up cost will be incurred immediately.

Estimated net cashflows (exclusive of the set-up cost) from sales during the first year of the project are estimated to be either "low" (namely, $0.25 million, with probability 0.4, or "medium" ($0.5 million, with probability 0.3), or "high" ($0.75 million, with probability 0.3). If sales are "low" in the first year, net cash flows in the second year are expected to be $0.5 million (probability 0.5), or $1.0 million (probability 0.35), or $1.5 million (probability 0.15). If sales are "medium" in the first year, net cash flows in the second year are expected to be $0.75 million (probability 0.4), or $1.25 million (probability 0.4), or $1.75 million (probability 0.2). Finally, if sales are "high" in the first year, net cash flows in the second year are expected to be $1.0 million (probability 0.3), or $1.5 million (probability 0.4), or $2.0 million (probability 0.3). Treat the net cashflows in each year as if they arrive in lump sum at the end of each year. The entire project will be finished at the end of the second year. The firm's cost of capital is currently 12%.

Plan B is to sell the land to a major home construction company that would develop the land into a new "executive suburb" with high-quality homes of relatively uniform appearance on large lots. This company, Stabole Quality Homes, has been trying to buy the land from WDC for several years and has just recently indicated they would be willing to offer $1.25 million dollars, payable $0.25 million now, $0.5 million after one year, and $0.5 million at the end of the second year.

(a) Calculate the expected present value of net cashflows for each plan, as well as the standard deviation of the potential outcomes for each plan.

(b) Apply several decision criteria to the problem, and indicate which plan is preferred under each criterion.

(c) Conduct sensitivity analysis to determine if the preferred alternative would change under other reasonable assumptions.

(d) Advise WDC which plan to pursue, in your considered opinion.

2-8. The Walwyn Widgets Company operates a thriving mail-order business and has achieved considerable success using television advertisements to promote new products, novelty items, record and tape collections of music, and so forth. The Director of New-Product Development, Charles van Winkle, has presented to the Executive Committee three new product suggestions, one of which will be the next product produced and sold. Because of limited availability of television time, sales personnel, and production facilities, only one of these projects can be implemented now. The other two will be set aside and will compete with any new possibilities that arise in the future.

Product A is an electronic message board that is programmed to roll a series of messages across the screen, including "Have a Nice Day!" and "God Loves You." This product is expected to encounter stiff competition after two years. The initial setup cost of Product A is $40,000. Product B is a collection of country music on a videotape album, initially costing $250,000 because of the permissions that must be purchased. Market research indicates that the market for this product will be saturated after two years. Product C, initially costing $30,000, is an antitheft alarm system for automobiles which is also expected to have only a two-year life because of rapid technological advances. Mr. van Winkle has obtained estimates of profits and probability distributions associated with each product.

	YEAR 1		YEAR 2	
Product	Profits	Probability	Profits	Probability
A	$30,000	0.60	$ 30,000	0.65
	80,000	0.30	60,000	0.25
	100,000	0.10	80,000	0.10
B	$100,000	0.30	$ 50,000	0.35
	300,000	0.50	100,000	0.40
	500,000	0.20	150,000	0.25
C	$ -25,000	0.20	$ 15,000	0.30
	50,000	0.40	50,000	0.40
	100,000	0.40	75.000	0.30

Assume that these profits are received at the end of the year and the Walwyn Widgets could otherwise invest the funds at 14% in a mutual fund, judged by Mr. van Winkle to be roughly equal in risk to the three proposals presented.

(a) Using decision-tree analysis, find the expected net present value of each proposal and calculate a measure of risk for each proposal.

(b) Apply several decision criteria to the problem and advise Mr. van Winkle which product he should choose.

(c) State any qualifications and reservations you would wish to add to your decision.

2-9. The Venture Startup Company (VESCO) solicits capital from investors and uses this capital to start new business ventures. It pays 14% on the capital it borrows and invests in new ventures that promise to make a return on investment higher than that. At the present time VESCO has $700,000 to invest and is considering two alternative ventures. Alternative A is a Christmas tree farm, already operating, and alternative B is a new fast-food restaurant chain, specializing in South American food. For each venture, VESCO has considered three demand scenarios for each of the first two years. VESCO typically sells its ventures after two years, presuming either a successful startup or rejuvenation of an existing business.

The initial cost of the Christmas tree farm is $550,000, and the profits in the first year are expected to be either $600,000, $400,000, or $200,000, with probabilities 0.25, 0.6, and 0.15, respectively. The profit in the second year will depend on what happened in the first year: It will be the same as the first year, with probability 0.4; 50% greater, with probability 0.4; or 50% less, with probability 0.2. This business is highly seasonal, of course, with the great bulk of the profits being generated at the end of each year. Assume that it is now January, and you would pay for the farm immediately.

The initial cost of the fast-food chain is $700,000, also payable immediately. First-year profits are expected to be $600,000, $500,000, or $400,000, with probabilities 0.3, 0.4, and 0.3, respectively. In the second year profits may be the same as they turn out to be in the first year, with probability 0.5, or $100,000 higher or lower, with probabilities 0.3 and 0.2, respectively. These profits flow in throughout each year in a more or less continuous stream.

(a) Calculate the EPV of each alternative.
(b) Using several decision criteria, advise VESCO as to which alternative it should choose.
(c) Qualify your recommendation with sensitivity analysis with regard to the discount rate used, VESCO's attitude toward risk, and the estimated demand scenarios.
(d) What other assumptions and qualifications underlie your recommendation?

2-10. Houston Homewares has suffered a declining market share over the past year, and management has considered various means of reversing the trend. Extensive analysis has narrowed the options to two. Plan A is to conduct a point-of-purchase promotion campaign involving the manufacture of special samples and the disbursement of these in shopping centers and on city streets. This plan would take a year to set up and would cost $100,000 during the first year. Implementation of this plan is expected to increase the firm's existing profits in the second year by $40,000, $60,000, or $80,000 (with probabilities of 0.2, 0.5, and 0.3, respectively), depending on whether the promotion is fairly, moderately, or highly successful, respectively. If fairly successful in year two, year-three profits will be increased by either $50,000, $100,000, or $150,000, with probabilities of 0.4, 0.3, and 0.3. If moderately successful in year two, year-three profits will be increased by either $80,000, $120,000, or $160,000, with probabilities of 0.3, 0.4, and 0.3. If highly successful in year two, year-three profits will be increased by either $100,000, $150,000, or $200,000, with probabilities of 0.2, 0.5, and 0.3. All cash flows under plan A will occur more or less continuously throughout each year.

Plan B is to contract out to an advertising agency that would prepare a series of campaigns for use predominately in the print media. This would cost $150,000 in the first year, and increase profits by $50,000, $100,000, or $150,000, with probabilities of 0.1, 0.5, and 0.4, depending upon whether the campaign is fairly successful, moderately successful, or highly successful. If year two is fairly successful, increased profits in year three will be $50,000, $100,000, or $150,000, with probabilities of 0.2, 0.4, and 0.4. If year two is moderately successful, year three's increased profits will be $100,000, $150,000, or $200,000, with probabilities of 0.2, 0.5, and 0.3. If year two is highly successful, profit in year three will be increased by $150,000, $200,000, or $250,000, with probabilities of 0.1, 0.5, and 0.4. Because of the financial arrangements associated with plan B, all cash flows will occur at the end of the each year. The firm's opportunity discount rate for both projects is 18%.

(a) Construct the decision tree for each decision alternative and calculate the expected present value of profits for each plan.

(b) Calculate the standard deviation of the outcome for each plan.

(c) Apply the expected-value, maximin, and coefficient-of-variation criteria to find the plan favored by each criterion.

(d) Discuss the application of the certainty-equivalent criterion to this problem, on the presumption that management is risk-averse.

SUGGESTED REFERENCES AND FURTHER READINGS

ARROW, K. J. "Risk Perception in Psychology and Economics," *Economic Inquiry,* 20 (January 1982), pp. 1–19.

BAUMOL, W. J. *Economic Theory and Operations Analysis* (4th ed.), chaps. 18, 19, 25. Englewood Cliffs, N.J.: Prentice-Hall, Inc., 1977.

BRIGHAM, E. F. *Financial Management Theory and Practice* (2nd ed.), chaps. 5, 12, 15. Hinsdale, Ill.: The Dryden Press, 1979.

DEAN, G., and A. HALTER. *Decisions Under Uncertainty.* Cincinnati. Ohio: South-Western Publishing, 1971.

FRIEDMAN, D. "Why There are No Risk Preferrers," *Journal of Political Economy,* 89 (June 1981), p. 600.

FRIEDMAN, M., and L. J. SAVAGE. "The Utility Analysis of Choices Involving Risk," *Journal of Political Economy,* 56 (August 1948), pp. 279–304.

GORDON, G., and I. PRESSMAN. *Quantitative Decision Making for Business,* chaps. 3, 4, 5. Englewood Cliffs, N.J.: Prentice-Hall, Inc., 1978.

HIRSHLEIFER, J. "Investment Decisions Under Uncertainty: Choice-Theoretic Approaches," *Quarterly Journal of Economics,* 79 (November 1965), pp. 509–36.

HOROWITZ, I. *Decision Making and the Theory of the Firm.* New York: Holt, Rinehart & Winston, 1970.

HUBER, G. P. *Managerial Decision Making.* Glenview, Ill.: Scott, Foresman Company, 1980.

LOOMES, G., and R. SUGDEN. "Regret Theory: An Alternate Theory of Rational Choice under Uncertainty," *Economic Journal,* 92 (December 1982), pp. 805–24.

MILLER, E. "Decision-Making under Uncertainty for Capital Budgeting and Hiring," *Managerial and Decision Economics,* 6 (March 1985), pp. 11–18.

RADFORD, K. J. *Modern Managerial Decision Making.* Reston, Va.: Reston Publishing Company, Inc., 1981.

RAIFFA, H. *Decision Analysis: Introductory Lectures on Choices under Uncertainty.* Reading, Mass.: Addison-Wesley Publishing Co., Inc., 1970.

Empirical Case 1

DECISION MAKING AND SUBJECTIVE PROBABILITY ESTIMATION

A regionally based company that produces a cyclical consumer good has asked you to decide if it should expand its distribution network to include the entire country. This increase in network size is estimated to have an initial cost of $2 million. In preparation for this possible expansion, internal research analysts have estimated that future sales are highly sensitive to the state of the economy. Specifically, if the economy is in a recession, profits are estimated to be $1 million per year. During nonrecessionary years, profits are expected to be $2 million. The company is interested in only a two-year time horizon.

On the surface, the problem appears to be a straightforward example of expected-net-present-value analysis. Note, however, that the probability of a recession has not been determined. It is precisely this lack of probability information that represents one of the major problems associated with decision making under risk.

To arrive at a decision, you must first estimate the likelihood of a recession during the two-year time horizon. Recall from introductory statistics that the probability of an event can be represented by the long-run relative frequency of the event occurring. You decide to rely on subjective probability estimates based on third-party opinions regarding the future state of the economy. Accordingly, you collect survey data from a random sample of members of the National Association of Business Economists. Your survey focuses on two questions:

1. In your opinion, do you believe the national economy will be in a recession next year? (yes or no)
2. If your answer to question 1 was no, do you believe the national economy will be in a recession the following year? (yes or no)

You realize that the response to question 2 is conditional on the response to question 1. As such, the relative frequencies of these two responses are generating estimates of conditional probabilities. Relying on introductory statistics, you know that the conditional probability of two events, A and B, can be represented by the following:

$$P(A/B) = P(A + B)/P(B)$$

where   P(A/B) = the probability of event A given that event B has already taken place,

P(A + B) = the joint probability of events A and B, and

P(B) = the unconditional probability of event B.

The survey results indicate that 50% of the economists believe the economy will be in a recession next year. Of those who feel the economy will not be in a recession next year, 70% believe a recession is likely for the following year. It is interesting to note that all economists stated that if a recession did occur, its duration would be longer than two years.

The percent responding yes to question 1 estimates the unconditional probability of a recession in year one. The percent responding yes to question two estimates the conditional probability of a recession for year two given no recession in year one. Finally, the fact that all respondents believe the recession will last at least two years indicates that the estimated probability of a recession in the first year and no recession in the second year is zero.

QUESTIONS

1. Calculate the appropriate joint probabilities for this case.
2. Using decision-tree analysis, what is your recommendation to the company? Assume a discount rate of 10% and end-of-year cash flows.
3. What are the assumptions you used to reach this conclusion? How realistic are these assumptions?
4. What are some other sources of subjective probability estimates you could have used in your analysis?

Chapter 3

CONSUMER BEHAVIOR

EXECUTIVE SUMMARY

In the first two chapters we spoke in general terms of costs, revenues, and profits. We now examine the **principles underlying consumer demand** and, hence, the firm's revenues. By understanding consumer behavior, we can predict consumers' responses to changes in variables that the firm can control, such as prices, product design, and promotional expenditures. We also examine the probable response of consumers to changes in variables that the firm cannot control, such as consumer incomes and the prices (and other competitive strategies) of other sellers. With this understanding, the manager is better able to explain and predict the behavior of the firm's revenues.

The first section of this chapter examines the traditional approach to consumer behavior, known as **indifference-curve analysis of consumer choice** between and among products. Consumers derive utility from products, and this utility, relative to the prices of these goods and services, determines which products are chosen within the consumer's income constraint.

We next examine the **attribute approach to consumer choice,** which assumes that consumers buy products because they like the benefits that the product delivers. Using a car as an example, the traditional view is that the consumer derives utility from the automobile itself, while the attribute approach is that utility is obtained from the benefits provided by the automobile, such as transportation, comfort, prestige, power, and fuel economy. The attribute approach has important implications for managers and, moreover, provides the bridge that links the economic analysis of consumer behavior with the marketing strategies of business firms, as we shall see in Chapters 10, 11, and 14. Since attributes generate value for consumers, the prices of products should be chosen with reference to the attributes embodied in the product. Similarly, products should be designed to include attributes that potential buyers want, and subsequently advertised to draw attention to the presence of desirable attributes.

3.1   INDIFFERENCE-CURVE ANALYSIS OF CONSUMER BEHAVIOR

The reasons people buy what they do, and react to changes in economic variables the way they do, are buried deep in their psyches, and we leave it to psychologists to investigate the actual thought processes that lead to the decision to purchase any particular product. Instead, we examine a model of consumer behavior that allows us to predict what the consumer will buy and how he or she will respond to changes in prices, income, availability of goods, advertising, and so on, without claiming that the model represents how people actually make their purchase decisions. Thus, the indifference-curve model of consumer behavior is a *predictive* model of consumer behavior rather than an *explanatory* model of consumer behavior. No consumers (that I know of) think of their indifference curves when deciding to buy something, but they usually act as if they do. In fact, the predictions of the indifference-curve model are remarkably accurate, and consequently this model is of great assistance to the manager.

Economists say that consumers gain *utility*, or psychic satisfaction, from the consumption of goods and services. Different products give different amounts of utility, and for any given product the consumer receives diminishing amounts of utility from each consecutive unit of the product or service consumed within a given period. For the purposes of the model we assume that utility is measurable, and we follow convention and call the unit of measurement a *util*. Now suppose a consumer, Louise, buys an ice cream and enjoys it immensely, receiving, say, 10 utils. A second ice cream then consumed would also be enjoyed, but probably not as much as the first one. Suppose she gets only 6 utils from the second ice cream. At this point Louise would have received *total* utility of 16 utils. The change in total utility for each additional ice cream is known as the *marginal* utility of those ice creams. Thus the marginal utility of the first ice cream is 10 utils, while it fell to only 6 utils for the second ice cream. Similarly, a third ice cream might give only 2 utils, since Louise would now be feeling quite full and her desire for ice cream would be largely satisfied.

- DEFINITIONS: *Utility* is the psychic satisfaction, or feeling of well-being, that a consumer derives from the consumption of goods and services. *Total utility* is the sum of all utility received from all goods and services consumed. The *marginal utility* of a good is equal to the change in total utility when the consumption of that good is changed by one unit.

The indifference-curve model is based on several assumptions. We assume diminishing marginal utility: that is, marginal utility declines as consumption increases during any given consumption period, as incorporated in the preceding ice cream example. We also assume that consumers are basically hedonists who wish to maximize their utility. Thus they choose products for consumption on the basis of the utility they expect to receive from each product. But since most goods and services cost money and since the budget of most consumers is limited, consumers must allocate their available funds among the goods and services, taking account of the differing prices and differing utility expected from different products, so their utility is maximized given the income constraint. A consumer who is pursuing the maximization of utility is said to be acting rationally. For the purposes of the analysis here, we assume that the consumer may consume any combination of two particular goods.[1]

Preference and Indifference

Since, by assumption, consumers want to maximize their utility, they will *prefer* combinations of goods and services that give them higher levels of total utility over combinations that give them lower levels of total utility. They will be *indifferent* among combinations that give exactly the same level of total utility. Now imagine all these combinations on a graph, with quantities of one product measured along the horizontal axis and quantities of the other product measured on the vertical axis. Through these combinations we can draw indifference curves.

- DEFINITION: An *indifference curve* is a line on a graph representing combinations of two products (or any two variables, such as risk and return) that give the same total utility to a particular person.

- EXAMPLE: Let us consider a particular consumer's demand for two particular products. Suppose Steve always buys hamburgers and cokes for lunch and we wish to know what combination of hamburgers and cokes, over a week, would maximize his utility from those two products. Figure 3-1 shows hamburgers on the vertical axis, measured in physical units, and cokes on the horizontal axis, also measured in physical units. The lines I_1 and I_2 are two of Steve's indifference curves. The combinations of hamburgers and cokes represented by the indifference curve I_1, such as point A (three burgers/two cokes) and point B (five burgers/one coke), give him the same level of expected utility. Combinations that lie to the right and above indifference curve I_1, such as on indifference curve I_2, promise a higher level of utility, and combinations that lie on indifference curves that lie below I_1 promise a lower level of utility. Thus the two indifference curves shown are simply indicative of the vast number of indifference curves that could be shown on the graph.

    For every point in Figure 3-1 there will be a series of other points among which Steve is indifferent. Consider point C on indifference curve I_2, which represents two burgers/four cokes. Starting from this point, we could find the other points on indifference curve I_2 by a process of questioning Steve about his preference or indifference between other combinations of burgers and cokes. Suppose we ask him which would he prefer: two burgers and four cokes (point C) or three burgers and three cokes (a point not marked in the graph). If he prefers the latter combination, it is evident that the extra burger in the latter combination more than compensates him in terms of utility for the coke that was taken away. If we then offer Steve the choice of the initial

---

[1]We restrict the analysis to combinations of only two goods so we can depict indifference curves on two dimensional graphs. This simplification does not limit our conclusions, however. Using mathematical techniques, the model can be extended to any number of goods and the major conclusions stay the same.

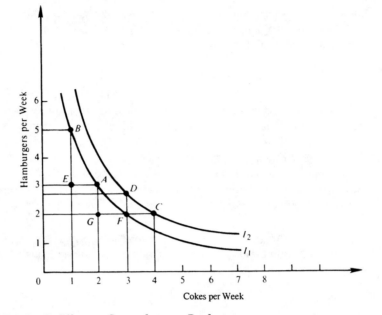

FIGURE 3-1.   Indifference Curves between Products

combination C, or of two and a half burgers and three cokes, and he chooses the initial combination, we know that the extra half burger does not compensate him for the loss of the one coke. Continuing this process, we would find a new combination of burgers and cokes for which Steve is indifferent when faced with a choice of that combination or with the combination represented by point C. Suppose this occurs at point D, which is two and three quarters burgers and three cokes. When given this choice, Steve says that he has no preference between the two combinations, that either one is as good as the other. Hence points D and C are on the same indifference curve. By the same process we could generate a multitude of other combinations that Steve feels are identical (in terms of utility derived) to points D and C and which, therefore, also lie on indifference curve I_2.

Since we could have started this process from *any* combination of hamburgers and cokes, it follows that there is an indifference curve passing through every point in the figure. We have shown simply two of the infinite number of indifference curves that represent this particular consumer's taste and preference pattern between the two products. To the right of the curves shown there will be curves that depict progressively higher levels of utility; and to the left and below indifference curve I_1 there will be curves that depict progressively lower levels of utility. Since there is an indifference curve passing through every point on the graph, a full map of the curves would totally black out the graph. For the purposes of analysis, we simply draw in those indifference curves that are relevant to the analysis, and ignore all the rest.

The Properties of Indifference Curves. Indifference curves showing combinations of goods have the following four properties. First, *higher curves are preferred to lower curves,* because we assume the consumer always prefers more to less. Second, indifference curves are *negatively sloped throughout,* for the same reason. To stay at the same level of total utility when the quantity of one good is increased necessarily requires a reduction in the quantity of the other good, if the consumer always prefers more of each good to less of each good, and other things remain equal. Thus the curve has a negative slope. Third, indifference curves *neither meet nor intersect,* because we assume that the consumer's preferences are consistent. If two curves did intersect, it would imply that there are some combinations that are equal but are simultaneously inferior (or superior) to each other. Finally, indifference curves are *convex from below,* because of the assumption of diminishing marginal utility for each product. This is best explained in terms of the marginal rate of substitution.

- DEFINITION: The *marginal rate of substitution* (MRS) is defined as the amount of one product that the consumer will be willing to give up for an additional unit of another product, while remaining at the same level of utility. The proviso that the consumer remains at the same level of utility makes it clear that the MRS refers to a movement along a particular indifference curve. By convention we define the MRS between two products for a movement down a particular indifference curve. Thus the MRS is the ratio of the amount given up of the product on the vertical axis, to the one-unit increment of the product on the horizontal axis. The MRS is thus equal to the *slope* of an indifference curve at any point on that curve, since it is defined in terms of the vertical rise (or fall) over the horizontal run. Symbolically, and in terms of our example,

$$MRS = \Delta H / \Delta C \qquad (3\text{-}1)$$

where ΔH is the decrease in hamburger consumption necessary to maintain utility at the same level given a one-unit increase in coke consumption, ΔC. (The Greek letter Δ, uppercase delta, is the conventional symbol for denoting a change in a variable.)

Since convexity of an indifference curve means that the slope will decrease progressively as we move from left to right down an indifference curve, it also means that the MRS will diminish progressively as we give up one good in favor of another. In terms of Figure 3-1, the MRS between points B and A on indifference curve I_1 is the ratio $BE/EA = 2$. The MRS for the next (third) coke per week is equal to the ratio $AG/GF = 1$. Observing Figure 3-1, you can see that the MRS for the fourth coke is approximately 0.5 and that the MRS continues to diminish as the consumer exchanges more hamburgers for cokes along indifference curve I_1.

- NOTE: The MRS declines because it is equal to the ratio of the marginal utility of the product on the horizontal axis divided by the marginal utility of the product on the vertical axis. That is,

$$MRS = MU_c/MU_h \qquad\qquad (3\text{-}2)$$

To appreciate this, note that the movement from point B to point A along indifference curve I_1 in Figure 3-1 left the consumer at the same level of utility after substituting one coke for two hamburgers. The marginal utility attached to the extra coke received must have been equal to the marginal utility given up by sacrificing two hamburgers. Thus the ratio of the marginal utility of cokes to the marginal utility of hamburgers is equal to two. Similarly, from point A to point F, total utility stays constant as the consumer gives up one more hamburger for one more coke. Thus the marginal utilities attached to the two products must be equal, and their ratio is equal to one. Since the MRS is equal to the ratio of the MU of the product being acquired (cokes) to the MU of the product given up (hamburgers), and since we have assumed diminishing marginal utility for all products, it is clear that MRS must diminish, since MRS is the ratio of a numerator (MU_c) that is falling and a denominator (MU_h) that is rising, as we move down along any given indifference curve. Thus the assumption of diminishing marginal utilities causes indifference curves to be convex to the origin.

The Consumer's Budget Constraint

To maximize utility, the consumer must choose a combination on the highest indifference curve possible. The limits of possibility are defined by the consumer's ability to afford the combinations desired. Were it not for a constraint on current income (and/or accumulated wealth), the consumer might proceed upward and to the right to a state of infinite euphoria. The budget constraint, however, keeps our consumer's feet on the ground, since certain combinations of goods are simply not affordable. (I'm sure you'll find *that* easy to understand!)

- DEFINITION: The *budget constraint* is defined as the total income or wealth the consumer is able to spend on goods and services per period. In the simple two-commodity situation we can write the budget constraint as

$$B = P_h H + P_c C \qquad\qquad (3\text{-}3)$$

where B is the total dollar budget available to the consumer; P_h and P_c are the prices per physical unit of hamburgers and cokes respectively; and H and C are the number of hamburgers and cokes purchased.

In this equation three symbols represent *parameters* that are constant (at least temporarily) and known to the consumer, namely, the budget available (B), the price of hamburgers (P_h), and the price of cokes (P_c). The remaining symbols (H and C) are variables that will take on the values necessary to maximize the consumer's utility. Equation (3-3) is actually a linear equation in those two variables. This will be more obvious if we rearrange terms and express the equation in terms of one of the variables. Subtracting B and $P_h H$ from both sides, and dividing both sides by $-P_h$ gives us

$$H = B/P_h - (P_c/P_h)C \qquad (3\text{-}4)$$

In this form we show H as a linear function of C and the three parameters, where B/P_h is the intercept term, and the coefficient to C (namely, $-P_c/P_h$) is the slope term.

- EXAMPLE: Suppose the parameters take the values $B = \$10.00$, $P_h = \$2.00$, and $P_c = \$1.00$. To solve for the intercept value we set $C = 0$, and find $B/P_h = 5$. Thus, if the consumer spends his entire budget on hamburgers, he will be able to purchase 5 units weekly. Alternatively, if he spends his total available income on cokes, he can purchase 10 units weekly. In Figure 3-2 we show equation (3-4) plotted in product space. Note that it intercepts the vertical axis at 5 units and the horizontal axis at 10 units. Starting from the vertical intercept, if coke consumption is increased from zero to 1, we note from equation (3-4) that the value of H is drawn down in the ratio $-P_c/P_h$. This ratio of prices is, of course, the slope of the line and is constant throughout the length of the line since prices are constant.

All combinations of hamburgers and cokes that occur on that line cost exactly $10, as may be verified from Figure 3-2. All combinations that lie above and to the right of the income constraint line are unattainable combinations, since they cost more than $10, and all combinations lying below the line cost less than $10.

Utility Maximization

Let us now superimpose the indifference curves of Figure 3-1 on the budget constraint line of Figure 3-2. This combined graph is shown in Figure 3-3. Suppose the consumer is at point E, spending all his available income on three hamburgers and four cokes and enjoying a utility level denoted by indifference curve I_2. It can be seen that point F is superior to point E and, moreover, that it would allow Steve to reach the highest attainable indifference curve. Any higher indifference curve would lie completely above the budget line and therefore is not affordable. The combination of hamburgers and cokes that appears to maximize our consumer's utility is thus approximately two and one third hamburgers and five and one third cokes.[2] By a quick calculation we can confirm that this combination does not break the consumer's income constraint. The two and one third hamburgers will cost approximately $4.67, and the five and one third cokes will cost approximately $5.33, making a total expenditure of $10.00.

- RULE: Utility maximization requires that the consumer choose the combination on the budget constraint line where this line is tangent to an indifference curve. Tangency between the budget line and an indifference curve means that their slopes must be equal. Since the slope of an indifference curve is the marginal rate of substitution and the slope

---

[2]Don't worry about these fractional units. By extending the time period, the numbers will come out as whole numbers. In this case, over three weeks, Steve would buy seven hamburgers and sixteen cokes, to maximize his utility.

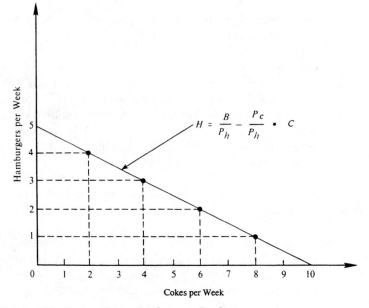

$$H = \frac{B}{P_h} - \frac{P_c}{P_h} \cdot C$$

FIGURE 3-2.   The Budget Constraint between Products

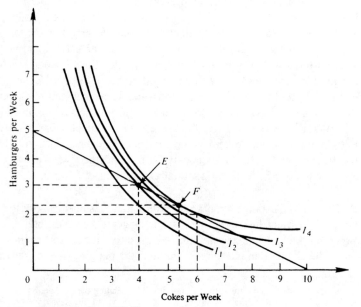

FIGURE 3-3.   Maximization of Utility from Products

of the budget line is the price ratio, we can express the condition for utility maximization as

$$\text{MRS} = -P_c/P_h \tag{3-5}$$

given that all available income is spent. We have previously seen in equation (3-2) that

$$\text{MRS} = \text{MU}_c/\text{MU}_h$$

Thus, we may alternatively express the maximizing condition as

$$\text{MU}_c/\text{MU}_h = -P_c/P_h \tag{3-6}$$

Rearranging terms, we have

$$\text{MU}_c/-P_c = \text{MU}_h/P_h \tag{3-7}$$

Thus the condition for maximizing utility is to spend the available income such that the ratio of marginal utility to price is the same for all products purchased.[3] In the hamburger/coke example it is clear that the consumer must expect to derive twice as much utility from the marginal hamburger, as compared with the marginal coke, since the price of a hamburger is twice that of a coke.

The Price Effect and the Law of Demand

The preceding analysis is concerned with the consumer's decision to buy goods that will maximize his or her utility, given a set of available products, their prices, and the consumer's income. We now consider the consumer's utility-maximizing response to changes in the price of one of the products.

• DEFINITION: The *price effect* is defined as the change in the quantity demanded of a particular product that is due to a change in the price of that product, *ceteris paribus*.[4]

• EXAMPLE: In the upper part of Figure 3-4 we show the indifference curves of an individual consumer between self-service and full-service gasoline.[5] Suppose the initial

---

[3]Note that both sides of equation (3-7) are negative, since MU_h will have a negative value (because it is the marginal utility lost by giving up the last hamburger).

[4]We know that *ceteris paribus* means "all other things remaining the same," which means in this case that the consumer's monetary income and the price of all other available products must remain the same. The price effect requires a constant *monetary* income, while the substitution effect, explained on page 80, requires a constant *real* income.

[5]We can legitimately regard these as separate products since they are composed of different attributes. Full-service gas comes complete with smiling attendant eager to check your oil, fan belt, filters, radiator water and hoses, tire pressure, and to wash your windows, headlights, and taillights. (This is clearly a *textbook*

prices of self-service gas (SSG) and full-service gas (FSG) and the consumer's income level are such that the appropriate budget line is N_1M_1. Thus the consumer maximizes utility at point A, at which he purchases X_3 units of FSG and the indicated amount of SSG. Let us suppose that the price of FSG is now reduced. This price change causes the budget line to swing around to that shown as N_1M_2, since its vertical intercept is unchanged while the slope coefficient falls. The consumer responds by moving to point B with a higher level of utility. Notice that after the price reduction for FSG, the consumer's consumption of this product was raised from X_3 to X_4. Now suppose that the price of FSG is raised, such that the appropriate budget line is N_1M_3. The consumer will now maximize utility by attaining the point C, where consumption of FSG has fallen to X_2 units. If the price of this product were raised still further, such that the appropriate budget line was N_1M_4, the consumer would select point D on that budget line and would maximize utility by consuming X_1 units of FSG and the indicated amount of SSG.

If we join the points A, B, C, and D, we obtain what is known as the *price consumption* curve (PCC), which is the locus of the points of tangency between the appropriate budget constraint line and the highest attainable indifference curve at various price levels of the product on the horizontal axis. It shows how the consumption of one product (and implicitly of the other as well) changes as the price of that product varies. It is apparent that the relationship between the price of a product and the quantity demanded of that product is an inverse one, when all other things stay the same. Indeed, we have just uncovered the theoretical support for the law of demand.

- DEFINITION: The *law of demand* states that as the price is raised the consumer demands progressively less of the product, and, conversely, as the price is reduced the consumer demands progressively more of the product, *ceteris paribus*. The law of demand is an empirical law, meaning that it is commonly observed in practice. It is expressed graphically as a negatively sloping line relating price to units of quantity demanded; this line is the *demand curve*. The consumer's demand curve for full-serve gasoline is shown in the lower part of Figure 3-4.

Notice that the actual data that underlie the demand curve depend on the individual's reaction to changes in the price. This consumer's demand curve is not likely to be exactly the same as the demand curves of other consumers, who have their own taste and preference patterns and hence their own reactions to changes in the price of the product. These differences in reaction may be traced back to different marginal rates of substitution in their taste and preference patterns, as reflected in indifference curves having greater or lesser degrees of curvature. Repeating the preceding analysis for other consumers with differing taste and preference patterns would demonstrate that although other consumers may not react to the same *degree* as our present example, they will react in the same *direction* in response to a change in price if they are attempting to maximize their

---

example.) Self-service gas comes without the above but with a significant saving per tankful and no anxiety about lost gas caps. Many consumers will demand both types of gas since they desire the attributes of each at different times.

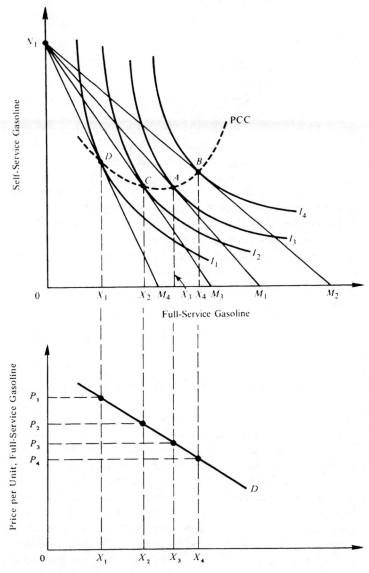

FIGURE 3-4.   *The Price Consumption Curve and the Demand Curve*

utility from a limited income source. Since consumers typically attempt to get the most out of their money, we expect the law of demand to hold for consumers in general, although some consumers may react to price increases or decreases to a greater or lesser degree than others.[6]

The Income and Substitution Effects of a Price Change.   The price effect can be thought of as comprising two separate effects, known as the income effect and the substitution effect. When a product's price falls (and all other things remain unchanged), the consumer experiences an increase in his or her real income. *Real income* is the purchasing power of money income. When the price of a particular good falls, the consumer can buy the same combination as before and have some money left over. This additional real income can then be spent, both on the product whose price has fallen and on other products. Normally, the income effect of a price reduction causes the consumer to buy a little more of the product in question, but if the product in question is an inferior substitute for some other product, the consumer may reduce purchases of the inferior product (whose price fell) in favor of increased purchases of the superior substitute.

The second part of the price effect is the substitution effect. When the price of any product falls, consumers will tend to substitute in favor of that product because it is now cheaper relative to other substitute products that serve the same need. Thus, when the price of a product falls, *ceteris paribus*, the consumer would normally buy more of that product, first because his or her real income has increased, and second because he or she substitutes toward that product and away from other substitutes that are now relatively more expensive. (A detailed treatment of the income and substitution effects of a price change is presented in the appendix to this chapter.)

The Impact of Changes in Consumer Income

When the consumer's money income, also known as *nominal income*, rises (and all other things, but particularly prices, remain the same), there is necessarily a rise in the consumer's real income to the same extent. The preceding discussion concerning the income effect thus applies. Normally, increases in money income, *ceteris paribus*, will lead to increased demand for the products available to the consumer. We show such a situation in Figure 3-5, where the consumer's income has increased and that consumer subsequently purchases more of both products available. Note that at the initial prices and income level, and given the consumer's taste and preference pattern (indicated by the indifference curves), the consumer maximizes utility at point *A*. An increase in money income causes the budget constraint line to shift outward, *parallel* to its earlier position (since the intercept term in-

---

[6]It is important to remember that demand curves presuppose a constant value of the monetary unit as part of the *ceteris paribus* requirement. When there is inflation, such that the value of the dollar declines as time passes, one should correct for the change—for example, by dividing the nominal prices by an index of the price level, such as the Consumer Price Index—before using observations of price and quantity demanded that are collected in different time periods. Such time-series data are always suspect in economics, since a variety of other things are likely to have changed during the period of the data collection, and these changes must be controlled for. We consider this problem further in Chapter 5.

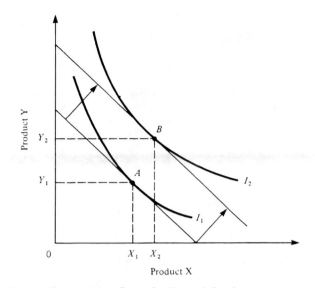

FIGURE 3-5. *Income Consumption Curve for Normal Goods*

creases while the slope term remains constant). In this case the quantity demanded of both products increases as a result of the increase in the consumer's income. Since income and quantity demanded moved in the same direction, we say that the income effect was positive for both goods. We call such products "superior" or "normal" goods.

For some products the income effect is negative, meaning that if income increases, the quantity demanded of those products actually declines. This may happen to a product that is an inferior substitute for some superior product. As people become richer, they tend to switch away from inferior goods to superior substitutes. Conversely, as incomes fall (in a recession, for example), people tend to switch back to the inferior substitutes as they find themselves unable to afford the superior substitutes.

In Figure 3-6 we show the income effect for an inferior good. The product on the horizontal axis, travel by train, is an inferior good, and travel by air is a superior substitute, *for this particular consumer*. Note that when the consumer's income increases and the budget line moves outward, the quantity demanded of travel by train actually decreases while travel by air increases. This consumer, now able to afford more air travel, substitutes away from the inferior good and in favor of the superior good. Looking at this from the opposite perspective, if the consumer's income were to fall from the higher level to the lower level, the consumer would reduce consumption of the superior good and increase consumption of the inferior good.

For any particular product at any particular point in time, some consumers may regard that product as a superior good while others may regard it as an inferior good. This difference in attitude toward a particular product stems from a difference in income levels and/or a different pattern of tastes and preferences. Just as the price effect varies between and among consumers, the income effect should also be expected to vary be-

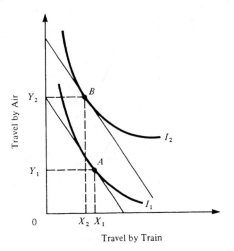

FIGURE 3-6.   *Income Consumption Curve Where X Is an Inferior Good*

tween and among consumers, being high and positive for some, perhaps, while being low, or even negative, for others.

Changes in Consumer Tastes and Preferences

In the preceding analysis, consumer tastes and preferences were assumed to remain constant while changes took place in price and income levels. We now consider changes in the consumer's tastes and preferences. This may happen in response to the latest fashions or trends or as the result of the advertising and promotion expenditures of business firms. However induced, changes in consumer tastes and preferences should be expected to have an impact on the quantity demanded of particular products.

- EXAMPLE: Suppose the sellers of product X begin an advertising campaign to promote their product. In the absence of simultaneous new campaigns from the sellers of other products, we would expect this campaign to influence at least some buyers in the direction of product X. Referring to Figure 3-7, suppose the initial situation is represented by the tangency at point A on the dotted indifference curve I_1. An advertising campaign that causes product X to be regarded more favorably than previously would cause that particular *level* of utility represented by indifference curve I_1 to be attained by the consumption of fewer units of product X, since X is now regarded more highly. Suppose that, whereas consumers previously required X_1 units of product X to attain the utility level depicted by indifference curve I_1, it now takes only X'_1 units of product X to attain the *same level* of utility, in conjunction with Y_1 units of product Y. In effect, then, indifference curve I_1 has swung downward and to the left, since the same level of utility can be obtained with lesser combinations of X and Y due to the new appreciation the consumer has for product

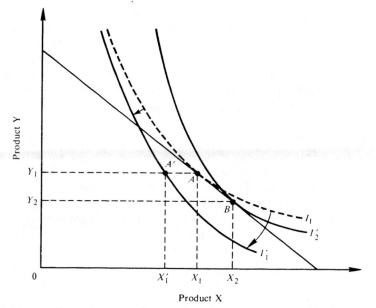

FIGURE 3-7. *A Change in Tastes and Preferences in Favor of Product X*

X. Under the new taste and preference conditions, indifference curve I_1 is now irrelevant, since it refers to the previous pattern of tastes and preferences.

Note that the consumer could remain at the same level of utility by shifting back from point A to point A'. But a utility-maximizing consumer will wish to reallocate his or her budget such that utility is maximized under the new circumstances. Indifference curve I'_2 is the highest attainable indifference curve given the budget constraint, and hence the consumer reallocates his or her income between products X and Y such that he or she is located at point B. Notice that the change of tastes and preferences in favor of product X has led to an increase in the consumption of product X from X_1 to X_2. Note also that in this simple two-product model the gain of product X necessarily came at the expense of product Y, whereas in a multiproduct system the shift of tastes and preferences in favor of product X would be at the expense of some, but not necessarily all, of the other products.

3.2 THE ATTRIBUTE APPROACH TO CONSUMER CHOICE

The traditional model of consumer choice among products suffers from several shortcomings that have prevented its widespread use as a predictive model. For practical purposes, such as the marketing of a firm's products, it would be desirable if we could apply the model to explain, for example, why some consumers in the market for a particular product, such as a car, prefer brand A, whereas others prefer brand B. Alternatively, we might wish to predict the increase in market share following an improvement of our product or to foresee the vulnerability of our sales to the emergence of a new product.

Kelvin Lancaster introduced the *attribute analysis* of consumer behavior in 1966 and expanded it substantially in 1971. This new theory of demand, while continuing to use utility and indifference-curve analysis, departed from the traditional approach by asserting that consumers derive utility not from the products themselves but from the characteristics or attributes provided by the products.[7]

- EXAMPLE: An automobile is desired not for its "automobileness"—its physical composition of nuts, bolts, steel, and plastic—but for the services it provides—transportation, comfort, convenience, prestige, security, and privacy. Consumer demand for an automobile (or any other product) is thus a *derived* demand, in the sense that it is derived from the demand for various services or attributes; the automobile simply provides those attributes. Similarly, a meal in a quality restaurant is not purchased simply to fill one's stomach but rather to enjoy the attributes of pleasant surroundings, courteous service, exotic food, good company, and no mess to clean up. Likewise, skydiving is undertaken not because one wants to jump out of an airplane, but because it provides exhilaration, solitude, exclusiveness, an outlet for one's courage, and a conversation opener.

If it is the attributes that are desired, rather than the products in which they are found, it is instructive to examine the consumer's demand for the attributes directly, rather than indirectly as in the products approach. This is especially useful when a particular attribute—excitement, for example—is available in a wide variety of products, such as bungee jumping, skydiving, and roller coasters. Naturally, the consumer may derive an excitement quota from some but not necessarily from all of the available sources of supply. Unlike the product approach, which takes the consumer's preferences between and among products as an imponderable fact, the attribute approach allows us to explain the choices among different products on the basis of their efficiency in supplying the desired attributes. Thus, the attribute approach greatly facilitates the explanation of consumer choice within groups of substitutes. Moreover, it readily allows us to incorporate new products into the analysis.

Depicting Products in Attribute Space

We now assume that the consumer derives utility from the consumption of attributes but must buy products to obtain the desired attributes. For the purposes of our graphical analysis here, we shall consider only two attributes and assume that each product supplies both attributes in a particular ratio.

- EXAMPLE: To demonstrate how a consumer might choose among products to maximize utility derived from the attributes, consider the case of Mr. Magnus Corpus, who dines

---

[7]See K. Lancaster, "A New Approach to Consumer Theory," *Journal of Political Economy*, 74 (April 1966), pp. 132–57; and *Consumer Demand: A New Approach* (New York: Columbia University Press, 1971).

out frequently and has a choice of six local restaurants. Magnus chooses among six products (the meal and its associated attributes at each restaurant), so his utility is maximized. He seeks only two attributes—exotic atmosphere and haute cuisine—and the restaurants provide these attributes in differing ratios and at different prices. Let us suppose that after visiting all six restaurants Magnus rates each one on a scale of 100 for both exotic atmosphere and haute cuisine, as shown in Table 3-1.

TABLE 3-1. *Attributes and Prices of Meals at Six Restaurants*

Restaurant	*Price of Meal ($)*	*ATTRIBUTE RATING*		*Ratio of Atmosphere to Cuisine*	*Meals per $100*
		Atmosphere	*Cuisine*		
A	22.22	89	22	4.05	4.50
B	25.00	94	50	1.88	4.00
C	27.30	76	86	0.88	3.66
D	26.47	57	90	0.63	3.78
E	18.95	18	72	0.25	5.28
F	19.74	10	77	0.13	5.07

In Figure 3-8 the six products are depicted in attribute space as rays from the origin. The slope of each ray is determined by the ratio of exotic atmosphere to haute cuisine, as listed in Table 3-1. If Magnus has a meal at restaurant A, he "travels out" along the steepest ray, absorbing the two attributes in the ratio 4.05:1—that is, 4.05 units of exotic atmosphere to each unit of haute cuisine. The other restaurants (products) are indicated by the lower rays because these offer the two attributes at lower ratios. Notice that a product for which one of the attributes was completely absent, such as home cooking, would be represented by one of the axes. (You decide which axis!)

The Budget Constraint and the Efficiency Frontier

How far along each ray could the gourmet go? That is, how much of each product is it possible to purchase? The limit, of course, is his budget constraint. Suppose Magnus allocates $100 monthly to eating in restaurants. The prices at these restaurants for a given meal are not identical, as shown in Table 3-1. If he spends the entire $100 in restaurant A, he could have 4.5 meals at the price of $22.22 per meal (including taxes and tip) before exhausting his budget. Note that 4.5 meals at restaurant A produce 4.5 × 89 = 400.5 units of the attribute exotic atmosphere and 4.5 × 22 = 99 units of the attribute haute cuisine. This point in attribute space is marked as point A in Figure 3-9. It shows the maximum intake of the two attributes that can be obtained by consuming product A, given the budget constraint of $100. Repeating this procedure for each of the other five restaurants, we find the points B, C, D, E, and F on each product ray, which represent the entire budget (hypothetically) spent at each of the restaurants. Joining the points *ABCDEF* we have what is known as the efficiency frontier in attribute space.

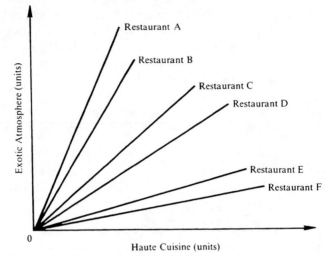

FIGURE 3-8.   Depicting Products in the Attribute Approach

• DEFINITION: The *efficiency frontier* is the outer boundary of the attainable combinations of the desired attributes, given the budget constraint. We shall presently see that any point on the frontier is attainable by consuming combinations of the two adjacent

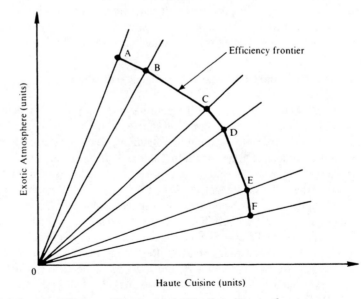

FIGURE 3-9.   The Efficiency Frontier in the Attribute Approach

products; it is called "efficient" because only combinations on this frontier allow the consumer to maximize utility.

Maximizing Utility from Attributes

Just as consumers can express preference or indifference between combinations of products, they can express preference or indifference between combinations of attributes. At any particular combination of exotic atmosphere and haute cuisine, our gourmet will be able to express a marginal rate of substitution between the two attributes: At any point, an extra unit of haute cuisine will be worth giving up some amount of exotic atmosphere. Thus Magnus will have an indifference map in attribute space expressing his tastes and preferences between the two attributes at all levels of those attributes. As before, higher curves are preferred to lower curves, the curves have negative slopes throughout, they neither meet nor intersect, and they are convex to the origin.

Since both the indifference map and the efficiency frontier are in attribute space, we can superimpose one on the other to find the combination of attributes that allows the consumer to reach the highest attainable indifference curve. In Figure 3-10 we show indifference curve I^* as tangent to the efficiency frontier at point M. Thus the combination of attributes Y_2 of exotic atmosphere and X_2 of haute cuisine allows Magnus to maximize his utility.

The Mixability of Products. Notice that combination M lies *between* the rays representing restaurant D and restaurant E. There is no restaurant available that provides the attributes in exactly the ratio represented by point M. Magnus can attain combination M, however, by mixing product D and product E. That is, by visiting restaurant D and restaurant E a number of times each, he can absorb—by aggregating the attributes absorbed at each restaurant over his total number of visits during the month—exactly the combination of attributes represented by point M. If Mr. Corpus visits restaurant D until he reaches point N on that ray, he will accumulate Y_1 units of exotic atmosphere and X_1 units of haute cuisine. At point N he should then switch to restaurant E to accumulate the attributes in the ratio necessary to achieve point M. The line NM in Figure 3-10 has the same slope as the ray representing restaurant E. By spending the remainder of the $100 in restaurant E, the gourmet derives an extra $Y_2 - Y_1$ units of exotic atmosphere and $X_2 - X_1$ units of haute cuisine, bringing his total to Y_2 units of the former and X_2 units of the latter, thereby maximizing his utility.

Alternatively, the gourmet could attain point M by visiting restaurant E until he had in effect reached point P on the ray representing restaurant E, and he could then switch to restaurant D to accumulate the remaining units of the two attributes in the ratio necessary to reach point M. The two paths to maximum utility are thus ONM or OPM in Figure 3-10. Since $ONMP$ is a parallelogram, however, the path OPM is equivalent to ONM, because $ON = PM$ and $OP = NM$. Magnus may visit either restaurant first, and in whatever sequence suits his whims, as long as the attributes accumulate to the combination M without exceeding the \$100 budget constraint.[8]

- NOTE: You may think it strange that the consumer patronizes only two of the six restaurants. This result is a function of our two-attribute model. The more attributes the consumer desires, the more products one would expect to be necessary to supply the optimum combination of those attributes. In the two-attribute case, the optimum combination of attributes could have been supplied by just one of the available products if the highest attainable indifference curve had touched one of the corners (points A, B, C, D, E, and F) of the efficiency frontier. Where the highest attainable indifference curve is tangent to a flat section of the efficiency frontier, a combination of two goods is necessary, as in the preceding case. In general, if the consumer desires n attributes, as many as n products (restaurants) might be required to provide the optimal combination of attributes.[9]

Indivisibility of Products.   Where the price of a product is large in relation to the consumer's income, or products are available only in discrete units, the consumer may have to settle for a suboptimal combination of attributes. With a very large and indivisible purchase, such as an automobile, the consumer must choose one product or another and is therefore constrained to one of the corners on the efficiency frontier. Consider Figure 3-11, in which we show three automobiles in economy-comfort attribute space. Brand A automobile offers a relatively high ratio of economy to comfort, followed by brands B and C. If these products were mixable, the efficiency frontier would be the kinked line ABC, and the consumer would maximize utility by mixing brands A and B at point W to attain indifference curve I^*.

However, if the consumer cannot mix brands A and B (by renting both cars or by agreeing with another person to buy the other car and then share), the consumer must be content to attain either point A, point B, or point C. Of these options, point A allows the attainment of the highest indifference curve, shown as I_0. The indivisibility of the products thus prevents the consumer from reaching indifference curve I^*, and the consumer must be satisfied with the suboptimal point A on indifference curve I_0. Given the constraint imposed by the indivisibility of the product, the consumer chooses the best available option.

---

[8]The consumer could arrive at point M by combining nonadjacent products, for example, D and E. This is inefficient, however, since it would cost more than \$100. One hundred dollars spent on some combination of D and F brings the consumer to a point on a straight line joining points D and F, since it is a linear combination of those points. The straight line joining D and F must necessarily lie below the section of the frontier DEF, and therefore does not include point M. To reach point M by combining nonadjacent products, therefore, will cost more than \$100. See Lancaster, ''A New Approach to Consumer Theory.''

[9]The assumption that products are mixable has drawn criticism from Reuven Hendler, ''Lancaster's New Approach to Consumer Demand and Its Limitations,'' *American Economic Review*, 65 (March 1975), pp. 194–99. It is clear that in some cases a consumer is not indifferent to combinations of goods that give identical combinations of attributes at the same price. Among other examples Hendler cites two medium-sweet apples versus one extremely sweet apple and one completely unsweet apple. Both combinations offer the same sweetness, but the consumer is not likely to be indifferent to them.

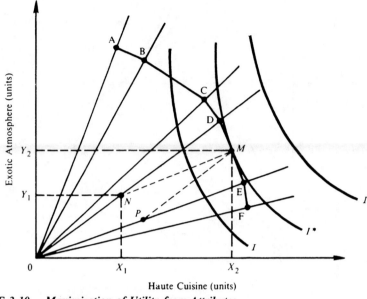

FIGURE 3-10.   Maximization of Utility from Attributes

Thus the efficiency frontier will be a series of facets joining the affordable-limit points on each product ray, given the mixability and divisibility of products. Note that the location of the frontier depends on three things, namely the prices of the products, the consumer's income, and the consumer's perception of the attribute content of each product. To appreciate this fact more fully, we shall examine the impact of changes in these parameters. As might be expected, a change in any one of these things causes a shift of the efficiency frontier.

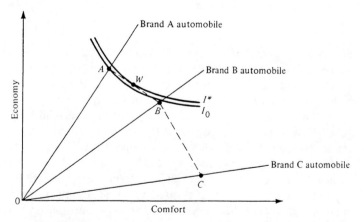

FIGURE 3-11.   Indivisibility of Products Necessitating a Suboptimal Combination of Attributes

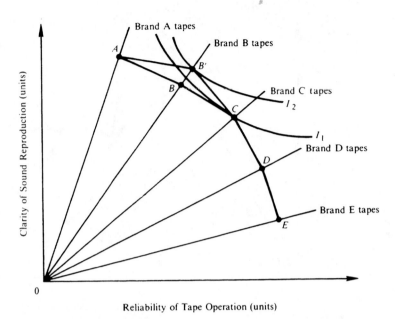

FIGURE 3-12.   The Price Effect Shown by the Attribute Approach: Singer

Changes in Price and the Law of Demand

The affordable-limit point on each ray is given by the ratio of income to the product's price multiplied by the attribute content of each unit of the product. Given constant consumer perceptions and income, a change in the product's price will therefore shift the affordable-limit point, and, consequently, the efficiency frontier. If the product's price were reduced, the frontier would shift outward along the product ray, and, conversely, the frontier would shift inward along the product ray if the price were increased.

- EXAMPLE: Consider a singer who frequently purchases new tapes. She desires two major attributes in these tapes, namely clarity of sound reproduction and reliability of tape operation. There are five brands available, and we show the efficiency frontier and two of the singer's indifference curves in Figure 3-12.

   Initially, the prices of the five brands are such that the efficiency frontier is $ABCDE$, and the consumer is able to maximize utility at point C, where indifference curve I_1 just touches the frontier. Now suppose that the price of brand B is reduced, such that the efficiency frontier moves out along the brand-B ray to point B' and is now represented by $AB'CDE$. The singer can now attain a higher indifference curve (I_2) by switching to brand B tapes. Product B offers the attributes in a different ratio to the previously preferred product C, but the consumer exhibits a marginal rate of substitution between the attributes and is willing to trade off some reliability for more clarity at the lower price to increase her total utility derived.

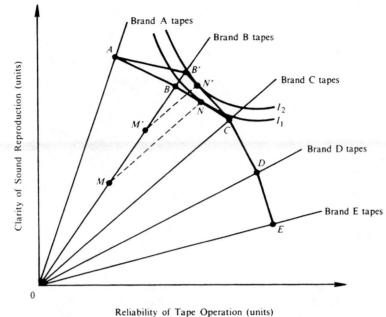

FIGURE 3-13. **The Price Effect Shown by the Attribute Approach: Musician**

In Figure 3-13 we show a different case in which a different consumer, a musician, is initially mixing two products to obtain the desired combination of attributes. This musician has a different taste and preference pattern between the two attributes, as compared with the singer depicted in Figure 3-12. The musician's indifference map is such that his highest-attainable indifference curve, given the initial efficiency frontier *ABCDE*, is tangent to the frontier at point *N*. This consumer prefers to purchase both brand B and brand C tapes, presumably using the brand B tapes for applications where clarity is relatively more important. Let us suppose his path to the frontier is *OMN*.

Again we reduce the price of brand B tapes, and the new efficiency frontier becomes *AB'CDE*. Our musician is able to increase utility by moving to point *N'* on indifference curve I_2. He still purchases both brand B and brand C tapes, but he now will purchase more brand B tapes and fewer brand C tapes. Whereas his previous path to the frontier was *OMN*, it was now *OM'N'*. The segment *OM'* exceeds *OM*, indicating the consumer's greater absorption of the attributes from product B and hence greater purchases of product B. The segment *M'N'* is shorter than *MN*, indicating the musician's reduced purchases of product C. Thus the law of demand is demonstrated by the behavior of both tape buyers: Each one responded to the reduced price of brand B tapes by buying more of that brand and less of a substitute brand.

Pricing a Product Out of the Market. Given a consumer's perception of the attributes embodied in a particular product, there is a maximum price that he or she will pay for

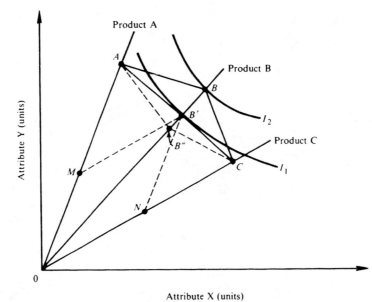

FIGURE 3-14.   Pricing a Product Out of the Market

that product even if it exactly mirrors his or her taste and preference pattern. In Figure 3-14 we show a simple case when three products offer the two desired attributes X and Y. The initial price situation generates the efficiency frontier ABC, and the consumer maximizes utility on indifference curve I_2 by purchasing only product B. Suppose the price of product B is now increased such that the efficiency frontier becomes $AB'C$. The consumer is now unable to reach indifference curve I_2 and must be content with the lower curve I_1 at point B', still purchasing only product B but necessarily purchasing fewer units of product B because of its higher price and the consumer's unchanged budget.

   If the price of product B is raised still further, such that the consumer's entire budget spent on product B would purchase only the combination of attributes shown by point B'', for example, this consumer will no longer buy any units of product B. The efficiency frontier remains at $AB'C$, and product B has fallen inside the frontier. Purchase of product B would now be an inefficient use of the consumer's budget, since the other products provide the desired attributes more inexpensively. The consumer is still able to attain point B' on the efficiency frontier and on indifference curve I_1, but will now travel via the path OMB' or ONB' rather than along the ray representing product B. That is, the consumer will now prefer to combine products A and C to maximize utility from a given budget rather than purchase any of product B. Thus, product B has been priced out of reach for this consumer, even though it provides the attributes in exactly the preferred ratio. (I feel the same way about Ferraris.)

   Thus we see that the price effect, or the law of demand, still applies to products even though they are purchased as a means of acquiring desired attributes. As price falls, consumers already purchasing the product in question will purchase more units, and other

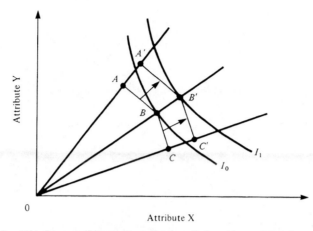

FIGURE 3-15. *The Income Effect where Product B Is a Normal Good*

consumers will begin to buy their first units of that product. Alternatively, as price is increased, consumers will buy fewer units or will drop out of the market for that product completely. Substitute products will tend to sell more units when the price of a product on an adjacent ray increases and will tend to sell fewer units when the price of that product is reduced.

Changes in Income for Superior and Inferior Goods

Given the consumer's perception of attribute content in each product and the prices of the products, an increase in the consumer's income or budget constraint will shift the efficiency frontier outward: A reduction in income will shift the frontier inward. The new frontier shifts in a parallel fashion, since the affordable combinations of attributes change in the same proportion for each product.

We noted earlier that the income effect may be either positive (for superior or normal goods) or negative (for inferior goods). That is, the change in quantity demanded of a product may be in the same direction as the change in income, indicating a superior good, or in the opposite direction, indicating an inferior good. In Figure 3-15 we show an increase in the consumer's income, *ceteris paribus*, that leads to an increase in the quantity demanded of product B. The initial frontier is *ABC*, the highest attainable indifference curve is I_0, and the consumer purchases only product B. Then an increase in the consumer's income shifts the frontier out to $A'B'C'$, allowing the attainment of indifference curve I_1. The consumer's utility-maximizing response to the increase in income is to purchase a larger quantity of product B.

Now suppose that a different consumer regards product B as an inferior good. What does this mean in the attribute context? It must reflect the presence of an attribute that this consumer regards as inferior, and this attribute must occur more frequently in product B than in at least one other (superior) product. Suppose that attribute X is sweetness, attribute Y is nutrition, and the products shown in Figure 3-16 are candy bars A, B, and C. As before, the

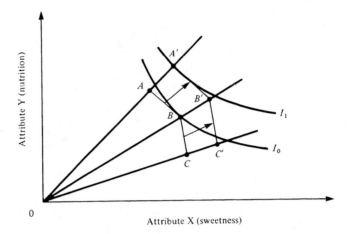

FIGURE 3-16.   The Income Effect where Product B Is an Inferior Good

increase in income shifts the frontier out from *ABC* to *A'B'C'*. In this case, however, the consumer switches from product B at the lower income to product A at the higher income. This consumer is apparently nearing his or her saturation point for sweetness and maximizes utility by reducing sweetness intake slightly in favor of a substantial increase in nutrition. Since candy bar A has a higher ratio of nutrition to sweetness, it is regarded as a superior product, and candy bars B and C are viewed as inferior products, when rising income brings the consumer nearer to his or her saturation level for sweetness.

Approaching the saturation point for an attribute is just another way of saying that the consumer's marginal utility is very close to zero for that attribute. Thus the income effect for a product may be positive or negative, depending on the consumer's relative marginal utilities derived from the attributes contained in the product. As the marginal utility of an attribute approaches zero (and the marginal utility of other attributes remains relatively high), that attribute becomes inferior and products containing a relatively high ratio of that attribute become inferior as a consequence.[10]

Changes in Consumer Perceptions

The attribute content of a product depends critically on the consumer's perception of those attributes. In the production process, a product may be endowed with great strength and durability, but if a consumer thinks it looks flimsy, then this strength and durability are not perceived. Advertising and promotional activity by sellers of particular products, as well as information from other sources (word of mouth or published reports by con-

---

[10]Note that the indifference curves are drawn to indicate this consumer's decreasing fondness for attribute X relative to attribute Y, as he or she is able to afford more of both. The higher indifference curve is markedly flatter than the lower curve as we move out along any ray from the origin. This change in shape indicates that the consumer's marginal rate of substitution of attribute Y for attribute X is falling as the quantity of both is increased, in turn because of the more rapidly falling values of the marginal utility of attribute X relative to attribute Y.

sumer testing agencies), may change the consumer's perception of the quantity of particular attributes embodied in each unit of a particular product. We now examine the impact that such changes might have on the demand for the product.

- NOTE: The first thing we must do is to make the distinction between changes in perceptions and changes in tastes. A consumer's perceptions relate to the amount of each attribute perceived to exist in each unit of the product. A consumer's tastes refer to the amount of utility expected from each unit of the product. Attribute analysis allows us to separate these quite neatly: A change in perceptions shifts one or more of the product rays and may shift the efficiency frontier, whereas a change in tastes shifts the indifference curves (through changes in marginal utilities that are involved in the marginal rate of substitution and hence the slope of indifference curves).

Suppose that in a particular market there are several products supplying two main attributes, and the sellers of one of these products begins a promotional campaign. The advertisements are aimed at convincing the consumer that product B, for example, has more units of attribute X and attribute Y than do products A and C. As a result of these advertisements, the consumer's perceptions of product B may change. If the consumer perceives the attributes to have increased in the same proportion, then the product ray keeps the same slope, and the affordable-limit point simply moves outward along the ray, pushing out the efficiency frontier at that point. More likely the advertisements will stress one attribute more than another, and the consumer's perception of the product's attribute contents will change in different proportions.

If the new information received causes the consumer to believe that the attribute content of a product has changed in different proportions, the product ray changes its slope in attribute space. Refer to Figure 3-17, in which we depict three economy cars in the comfort-economy attribute space. Suppose that initially the efficiency frontier is *ABC* and the consumer chooses product C, attaining indifference curve I_0. Now suppose that car maker B begins to advertise its model, which happens to have a diesel engine, using the theme that *economy* means more than just fuel economy. In the campaign they stress that *operating economy* includes the savings on electrical parts and tune-ups one expects with a diesel engine. They argue that since diesel engines have no carburetor, no spark plugs, no points, no condenser, no distributor (and no power, too!) the absence of these parts saves money, since they do not have to be recalibrated and replaced periodically.

Let us assume the consumer is convinced by this reasoning and now perceives the diesel model to contain the same amount of comfort as before, but more economy. In terms of Figure 3-17 the consumer perceives an extra $X_1 - X_0$ units of economy in the diesel model. This causes the product ray to shift from *OB* to *OB'*, and the efficiency frontier to move from *ABC* to *AB'C*. The consumer can now attain a higher indifference curve by switching to the diesel product from product C.[11]

---

[11]If a product is an inefficient supplier of the desired attributes, changed perceptions of this product do not change the efficiency frontier, unless these changes are sufficient to cause the product to be viewed as an efficient supplier of the attributes. Conversely, of course, new information or experience with a product may

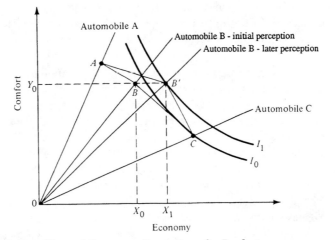

FIGURE 3-17.   *Changed Consumer Perception of a Product*

Note that an advertising campaign could cause both a changed perception of a product's attribute content and a change in the consumer's taste and preference patterns. As an example, suppose the advertising campaign also causes the consumer to want to be more socially responsible by using less fuel. This desire is reflected by a steepening of the consumer's indifference curves in comfort-economy space. The consumer's marginal rate of substitution (MRS) between comfort and economy would increase as a result of this change in taste for the attributes. A change in the indifference map is likely to cause a new point of tangency, of course, and the consumer may rearrange his or her purchases as a result.

- NOTE: It is important to see that this change in tastes is independent of any change in perceptions of the attribute content of the products. A change in perceptions typically changes the shape and location of the efficiency frontier, while a change in tastes changes the slope and location of the indifference curves. The attribute approach allows us to make this distinction, whereas the product approach simply says consumers (for whatever reasons) have changed their tastes between or among products, without being able to distinguish whether this was caused by changes in perceptions of the products, changes in tastes for the attributes, or some combination of the two.

New Products

The advent of new products presents no difficulty for the attribute approach: A new product can be represented on any existing graph as a new ray. If the ratio of attributes offered by the new product is the same as for an existing product, it will occupy the same

---

cause a consumer to view a product as inefficient for the first time. A distasteful or boring advertising campaign could change a consumer's perceptions of attribute content downward.

ray as that existing product. If, however, the new product offers more of this combination of attributes per dollar, as compared with the existing product, the new product will push the efficiency frontier outward and will eclipse the existing product in the eyes of rational consumers. Since the new product offers more utility per dollar than the old, no rational consumer would buy the older product. In the case of market entry by a new product that is not identical in its offering of product attributes when compared with existing products, there will be a new ray in the figure. If the highest affordable point on that ray occurs outside the existing frontier, the new product will serve to push the frontier outward at a point where it was previously flat. In both these cases, where the new product extends the frontier, some consumers will change their consumption in favor of the new product, since the new frontier will now poke through their previously attained indifference curves and allow them to reach a higher curve.

- EXAMPLE: In Figure 3-18 we show an initial situation of only three products—A, B, and C. The initial efficiency frontier perceived by the consumer is thus *ABC*, and he or she attains indifference curve I_1 by purchasing product B. We now suppose a new product is launched that competes with products A, B, and C by also offering attributes X and Y. The new product offers these attributes in a different ratio, however, intermediate between products B and C. We also suppose that the new product is priced so the efficiency frontier is extended to *ABNC*. The consumer is now able to reach indifference curve I_2 by switching to the new product. Notice that the new product steals sales from both B and C but does not affect A unless there are more than two attributes desired by consumers. In the real world, of course, consumers do demand more than two attributes simultaneously, and we should expect the advent of a new product (or new model of an existing product) to affect the sales of a range of other products.

Market Segments

- DEFINITION: *Market segments* are groups of consumers who have similar taste and preference patterns and who therefore tend to buy similar products. Groups of consumers with similar marginal rates of substitution, at a particular combination of attributes, will tend to find their highest-attainable indifference curve tangent to the efficiency frontier at similar points. Consumers with relatively *low* MRS between the attributes will tend to buy products with relatively *high* attribute ratio rays, and vice versa.

- EXAMPLE: In the case of the audiotapes discussed earlier, we may characterize the music clarity segment as consisting of those who will have low marginal rates of substitution (relatively flat indifference curves) between clarity and reliability and who therefore tend to purchase brands A and B. On the other hand, consumers with relatively high marginal rates of substitution (relatively steep indifference curves) will tend to buy brands D and E and may be characterized as the reliability segment. Similarly, consumers with a low MRS between exotic atmosphere and haute cuisine tend to eat at restaurants A, B, and C and might be characterized as the exotic segment of the market, whereas the patrons of restaurants D, E, and F might be called the gourmet segment.

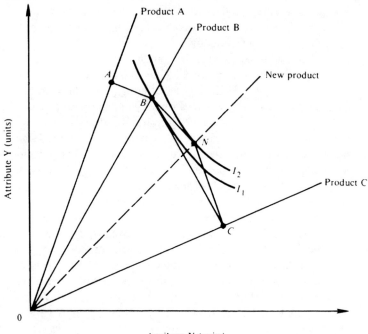

FIGURE 3-18.   *Addition of a New Product to an Existing Group of Products*

Knowledge of the tastes of consumers for the various attributes allows firms to design their products to incorporate the attributes in the ratios desired by a particular group of consumers. This group of consumers becomes the firm's *target market*. Similarly, consumers in a particular market segment seek out firms that supply products providing the attributes in the desired ratios.

Problems of Identifying and Measuring Attributes

Some attributes are readily identifiable and measurable, such as the power and economy associated with an automobile. Objective measurement of power might proceed on the basis of engine horsepower, horsepower divided by vehicle weight, or some similar measure. Economy, likewise, can be measured by a standard unit of measure, such as miles per gallon or liters per hundred kilometers. Problems arise, however, with attributes that are measurable only subjectively, such as modern styling, prestige, status, comfort, and security. The consumer will typically have an intuitive evaluation of these attributes and will be able to make what appears to that consumer as an optimal decision in light of the information held.

The identification and measurability problems arise when we attempt to explain or predict consumer behavior in real-world situations. The implications of attribute analysis for the pricing, promotion, product, and distribution strategies of the business firm are profound. If the firm is able to identify which attributes consumers base their choices on and on *what basis* they evaluate the attributes, it is in a better position to increase sales and profits by adjusting one or more of its marketing strategies.[12] We return to this issue in the contexts of pricing policy in Chapter 10 and product design in Chapter 14.

3.3 SUMMARY

In this chapter we have demonstrated how the rational consumer is expected to adjust to changes in economic variables. The price effect gives rise to the individual's demand curve for individual products. In general, these demand curves show an inverse relationship between the price of the product and the quantity demanded by a particular consumer. This price effect can be divided into two component parts: the income effect and the substitution effect. The income effect may be either positive or negative, depending on the taste and preference pattern of the consumer in question and the level of income of each consumer. The substitution effect is always negative; that is, the relationship between price and quantity demanded, with real income constant, is an inverse one. The net effect of a price change, given *ceteris paribus*, is that quantity demanded will increase when price is reduced and decrease when price is raised. This relationship is known as the law of demand. In the real world the law of demand may sometimes be obscured by the effects of inflation or by the simultaneous movement of another variable that influences demand.

Changes in the consumer's income will change the quantity demanded at a given price level. The quantity demanded of superior (or normal) goods will move in the same direction as income, whereas the quantity demanded of inferior goods will move in the opposite direction to income. Similarly, changes in the consumer's taste and preference pattern will cause changes in the quantity demanded of goods, given the prevailing price and income levels. If tastes change in favor of a product, for example, its quantity demanded will increase at the expense of substitute products.

The attribute approach to consumer behavior gives several valuable insights into consumer choice, which are not so readily apparent using the product approach. The attribute approach allows the entire range of substitutes available to the consumer to be depicted on the same graph. It is thus able to explain clearly why a consumer buys one brand of a product in preference to the other brands available: The preferred brand offers the consumer the greatest amount of the preferred attribute mix per dollar. Moreover, the analysis easily explains why a consumer will purchase combinations of substitute products: Doing so allows the consumer to obtain the desired attribute ratio even when there

---

[12]In marketing research the technique of *conjoint analysis* is being used to establish consumers' perceptions and trade-offs between attributes embodied in competing products. See, for example, Paul E. Green and V. Srinivasan, "Conjoint Analysis in Consumer Research: Issues and Outlook," *The Journal of Consumer Research*, 5 (September 1978), pp. 103–23. Also Albert Madansky, "On Conjoint Analysis and Quantal Choice Models," *Journal of Business*, 53 (July 1980), pp. S37–S44.

is no product that offers the attributes in this ratio. New products are easily handled by the attribute approach, since they are simply added to the existing analysis. The implications for marketing policy are more obvious under the attribute approach: The price level determines the degree to which the product extends the efficiency frontier, and the firm's promotion, product quality, and distribution policies determine the combination of attributes and hence the product's placement on the frontier.

Studying individual consumer behavior is important, for it explains why consumer response to changes in economic variables are basically predictable, in *direction* if not always in *magnitude*. When price changes are regarded in the real, or purchasing power, sense and when the impact of other variables can be accounted for, we must expect a negative price effect to prevail. The ramifications of this expectation for revenues, profits, and general business decision making are explored in subsequent chapters.

DISCUSSION QUESTIONS

3-1. Explain the diminishing marginal rate of substitution between two products in terms of the marginal utilities of those products.

3-2. Explain how the MRS, at a particular combination of the two products, would differ between two consumers—one who likes hamburgers and loves cokes and another who loves hamburgers and merely likes cokes.

3-3. Demonstrate that an increase in a consumer's income could lead to either an increase or a decrease in the consumption of a particular product, using first the product approach and then the attribute approach.

3-4. Show how a change in the consumer's tastes and preference pattern will cause a change in the quantity demanded of any two products, using first the product approach and then the attribute approach.

3-5. In the self-service versus full-service gasoline example used in the text, how would the indifference map of a person who is knowledgeable about preventive maintenance, economy minded, and not lazy compare with that of another person who is the opposite in these respects?

3-6. How would the indifference map between X and Y look different for a consumer who regards X as a normal good (or attribute) as compared with another who regards X as an inferior product (or attribute)?

3-7. What attributes do you think are being sought by a consumer who chooses to fly somewhere for a holiday as compared with another consumer who would drive the same distance for the same holiday?

3-8. Why would a consumer not be acting rationally in purchasing a product that fell short of the efficiency frontier in attribute space?

3-9. Distinguish between a change in consumer perceptions and a change in consumer tastes.

3-10. How would new-product policy benefit from an analysis of the attributes demanded by consumers in the overall market for several substitute products?

PROBLEMS AND SHORT CASES

3-1. Show graphically the effect of a price *increase* on the quantity demanded of a product by a particular consumer. Verbally explain the income and substitution effects of this price change.

3-2. Explain why the *ceteris paribus* assumption is so important in the economic analysis of consumer behavior. Then, using graphs, show the effects of the following series of events: a price reduction for product X, followed by an increase in the consumer's income, followed by a change in the consumer's tastes away from product X.

3-3. Company A sells product X, which has several close substitutes. At its present price, however, it is not making a sufficient contribution to the firm's profitability. A price rise is contemplated. The marketing manager is adamant that an advertising campaign must be undertaken before the price is raised. The finance department says that this expenditure is unnecessary. Explain the marketing manager's reasoning in terms of the attribute approach to consumer behavior.

3-4. Imagine two consumers—Mr. A, who simply appreciates classical music, and Ms. B, who is wildly enthusiastic about it. Suppose that in a simple two-product situation both buy classical music records in conjunction with some other product Y.
   (a) Using the indifference maps you think are appropriate for each consumer, derive each of their demand curves from their price consumption curves. (Assume that they have the same income and face the same prices.)
   (b) Aggregate their individual demands to find their total demand for the records at each price.

3-5. In the automobile market, various segments of the market are catered to by the manufacturers. Show graphically why three different consumers might choose three different automobiles in the simple case where they desire only two attributes, power and economy. Verbally explain the *n*-attribute case, where *n* is a large number.

3-6. In a western region two brands of beer are sold which between them share almost all the market. Through careful research it has been found that their main differences are perceived to be in the attributes lightness and thirst-quenching. Brand A is perceived to contain 10 units of thirst-quench and 5 units of lightness and costs $0.80 per bottle. Brand B is perceived to contain 5 units of thirst-quench and 10 units of lightness and costs $0.67 per bottle. Research has also indicated that a significant share of the market would become available if a third beer were introduced, as long as its price was not too high. The Norbert Brewing Company has a new premium beer that incorporates 10 units of each attribute in each bottle. For a consumer who has $10 monthly to spend on beer and who perceives the attributes in the ratios implied above,
   (a) What is the maximum price that may be charged for Norbert's beer such that $10 will buy a combination of the attributes that lies on the efficiency frontier? (An approximate answer derived from your graph will suffice.)
   (b) Supposing that Norbert prices the new beer at $0.72 per bottle, will the aforementioned consumer necessarily switch to Norbert's beer or stay with one or the other of the initial brands? Why?

3-7. The MacFarlane Chocolate Company has a product called Snackers in the health-food segment of the candy bar market. Each Snackers bar contains 150 grams of protein and 150 calories. The two rival products are Healthnut bars, containing 200 grams of protein and only 100 calories, and Hi-energy bars, containing 50 grams of protein and 200 calories. Each of these bars weighs 4 ounces. Snackers bars sell for $1.75, compared to $2 for Healthnut bars and $1.50 for Hi-energy bars. Recently the cost of peanuts and chocolate has been increasing while the cost of sugar has been falling substantially. As a consequence, MacFarlane's management is considering changing the composition of Snackers to include less protein and more calories. In effect they are considering repositioning their product in the market. The proposal being considered is to make Snackers contain only 100 grams of protein but raise the caloric content to 200. The price would stay the same, but promotional efforts would stress the extra energy packed into the Snackers bar. Market research indicates that the typical customer spends $10 weekly on these so-called health-food bars. With the current Snackers bar, MacFarlane has about 30% of the market. Healthnut has 25%, and Hi-energy has the remaining 45%. The protagonists of the new bar argue that the new Snackers bar will steal sales from Hi-energy bars. The antagonists argue that it will lose more sales to the Healthnut bar than it will gain from the Hi-energy bar.

(a) Using attribute analysis, show how the Snackers bar would be repositioned in nutrient-calorie space and how this would change the efficiency frontier for the typical consumer.

(b) Given the current market share information, advise management whether or not to reposition the Snackers bar. Do you have any other suggestions?

(c) State all assumptions and reservations underlying your conclusion.

3-8. One of the domestic auto manufacturers (which we shall call company D) is considering some strategic changes to its luxury-subcompact model. Its research indicates that consumers consider two main attributes when purchasing a subcompact car, namely fuel economy and comfort. It recognizes that in the design of a subcompact car there is a trade-off between fuel economy and comfort, since features that increase fuel economy (such as smaller size, better aerodynamics, and lighter weight) have the opposite impact on comfort. Similarly, features that improve comfort, like a longer wheelbase, more soundproofing, and larger seats, come at the expense of reduced fuel economy. Fuel economy is measured by the EPA's fuel economy rating (average for city and highway driving), and comfort is measured by an index that industry insiders have developed to incorporate interior dimensions, the weight of sound-deadening materials, and so on. Based on these two scales, the current competitors in the luxury subcompact segment of the market are rated as follows:

> Competitor A: fuel economy, 55; comfort 40
>
> Competitor B: fuel economy, 45; comfort 90
>
> Competitor C: fuel economy, 30; comfort 120

Company D's luxury subcompact is rated at 40 miles per gallon and has a comfort index of 100. Each of these cars is priced within a few dollars of $10,000 in basic trim (as rated here). The current market shares of the firms in this segment are as follows: A has 40%, B has 25%, C has 15%, and D has 20%.

Two competitive strategies are being considered for the next model year. Plan 1 is to keep fuel economy the same through improvements in engine efficiency while increasing the comfort index to 110 by additional sound deadening. Plan 2 is to lighten the car dramatically and incorporate an electronic fuel management system, such that the car will be rated at 50 miles per gallon with a comfort index of 80. In either case the price would be left at its current level, because of consumers' high degree of price sensitivity in this market.

(a) Show graphically how plan 1 and plan 2 differ from the status quo.

(b) Speculate, on the basis of the market share data given, which would be the better strategy assuming that the new model would cost the same as the current model once it got into production, that the initial costs of the two plans would be roughly the same, and that these costs would equal the usual costs of the annual model change.

(c) State all assumptions and reservations that underlie your analysis.

3-9. Richard Poirier has recently graduated from college, and upon receipt of his first paycheck he began planning to buy a sports car. He is considering four major attributes: prestige, performance, reliability, and resistance to rust. The value he attaches to these attributes varies depending on whether he will drive the car all year round or in the summer only. The latter decision depends on whether he is to be transferred 1,500 miles north by his employer. If he moves north he will use the car in the summer only. If he is to drive the car only in the summer, Richard considers performance to be twice as important as reliability, prestige to be three times as important as reliability, and rust resistance to be only half as important as reliability. For year-round driving, he considers rust resistance to be three times as important as reliability, performance half as important as reliability, and prestige twice as important as reliability. Richard has found three sports cars for sale: Each one is secondhand and costs $5,000. All are in good condition, and he decides to buy one of the three. After considering the problem and talking with some experts, he has rated each car on a scale of 10 for each of the four attributes, as follows:

	Car A	Car B	Car C
Prestige	8	9	6
Performance	8	8	9
Reliability	7	6	9
Rust resistance	8	7	6

(a) Please advise Richard about which sports car he should buy to maximize his expected utility if he is in fact transferred 1,500 miles north.

(b) Which car should he buy if he is sure that he will not be transferred?

(c) Which car should he buy if the probability of his being transferred north can be reliably estimated at 0.7? (Explain your reasoning in each case.)

3-10. The demand for telephone installation peaks around the first day of each month, since many subscribers request service on that day because they are moving to a new house or apartment. The Tanguay Telephone Company (T.T.C.) is examining a means to reduce this monthly demand peak, which accounts for 40% of all installations. The problem has been aggravated in recent years by the increasing hourly cost of labor, the reluctance of unionized employees to work overtime, the increased no-access problems caused by the greater number of working households, and the decline of profitable auxiliary sales to the subscriber (colored telephones, extension phones, etc.) due to access being given by a third party (landlord, neighbor, etc.).

T.T.C. is considering opening several "Phoneshops" in its area, so customers may obtain their telephones and install them in their own homes. The company would prewire all homes in its territory, installing one or two phone jacks in each room; the installation by the customer could simply involve plugging in the sets where desired. The company would continue to offer home installation for those unable or unwilling to visit the Phoneshops. Two types of Phoneshops are being considered: more conveniently located stores which would offer a moderate saving as compared with the traditional home installation, and less conveniently located stores which would offer a more substantial saving due to the lower overhead costs in the less convenient locations.

A market survey has found that telephone subscribers want two major attributes in their purchase of a new installation—convenience and economy. A typical customer has been found who rates the three options on a 100-point scale of convenience as follows: home installation, 100; more convenient store, 75; and less convenient store, 25. The economy of the second and third options will be measured by the savings from the $20 it will continue to cost to have home installation. Thus economy will be determined by prices that T.T.C. decides to charge for the latter two options.

(a) Supposing initially that T.T.C. prices the more convenient (MC) Phoneshop service at $16 and the less convenient (LC) Phoneshop service at $12, show the consumer's options in attribute space, with convenience on the vertical axis and dollars saved on the horizontal axis. (Since the consumer wants *one* unit only of *one* of the three services, these options will be represented by points in attribute space, not rays.)

(b) For a consumer who has an MRS $=$ 10 at the point represented by the MC Phoneshop (i.e., who is prepared to give up 10 units of convenience for $1 saved), which of the three options should be selected?

(c) For a person who has an MRS $=$ 15 at the point represented by the MC Phoneshop, which of the three options should be selected?

SUGGESTED REFERENCES AND FURTHER READING

AULD, DOUGLAS. "Imperfect Knowledge and the New Theory of Demand," *Journal of Political Economy*, 80 (November, December 1972), pp. 1287–94.

BAUMOL, W. J. *Economic Theory and Operations Analysis* (4th ed.) chap. 9, Englewood Cliffs, N.J.: Prentice-Hall, Inc., 1977.

CORNELL, B. "Relative vs. Absolute Price Changes: An Empirical Study," *Economic Inquiry*, 19 (July 1981), pp. 506–14.

GREEN, P. E., and V. SRINIVASAN, "Conjoint Analysis in Consumer Research: Issues and Outlook," *The Journal of Consumer Research*, 5 (September 1978), pp. 103–23.

HENDLER, R. "Lancaster's New Approach to Consumer Demand and Its Limitations," *American Economic Review*, 65 (March 1975), pp. 194–99.

HIRSHLEIFER, J. *Price Theory and Applications* (4th ed.) chaps. 3 and 4. Englewood Cliffs, N.J.: Prentice-Hall, Inc., 1988.

HYMAN, DAVID N. *Modern Microeconomics: Analysis and Applications*, esp. chaps. 3 and 4. St. Louis: Times Mirror/Mosby College Publishing, 1986.

LANCASTER, K. "A New Approach to Consumer Theory," *Journal of Political Economy*, 84 (April 1966), pp. 132–57.

———. *Consumer Demand: A New Approach*. New York: Columbia University Press, 1971.

LEIBENSTEIN, H. "Bandwagon, Snob and Veblen Effects in the Theory of Consumer Demand," *Quarterly Journal of Economics*, (May 1950), pp. 183–207.

MANSFIELD, E. *Microeconomics: Theory/Applications*, esp. chaps. 3 and 4. New York: W. W. Norton & Company, 1985.

RATCHFORD, BRIAN T. "The New Economic Theory of Consumer Behavior: An Interpretive Essay," *Journal of Consumer Research*, 2 (September 1975), pp. 65–75.

———. "Operationalizing Economic Models of Demand for Product Characteristics," *Journal of Consumer Research*, 6 (June 1979), pp. 76–84.

ROSEN, SHERWIN, "Hedonic Prices and Implicit Markets: Product Differentiation in Pure Competition," *Journal of Political Economy*, 82 (January, February 1974), pp. 34–45.

ROTH, TIMOTHY P. "On the Predictive Power of the New Approach to Consumer Theory," *Atlantic Economic Journal*, 7 (July 1979), pp. 16–25.

SCHOEMAKER, P. J. H. "The Expected Utility Model: Its Variants, Purposes, Evidence and Limitations," *Journal of Economic Literature*, 20 (June 1982), pp. 529–63.

Appendix 3A

INDIFFERENCE-CURVE ANALYSIS OF THE INCOME AND SUBSTITUTION EFFECTS OF A PRICE CHANGE

EXECUTIVE SUMMARY

The quantity demanded of any product should be expected to decline as its price is raised, holding all other determinants of demand constant. This is known as the price effect and gives rise to the negative slope of the demand curve. **The price effect has two distinct components, known as the income effect and the substitution effect**.

The income effect is the change in the quantity demanded that is due to the change in the consumer's *real* income, which in turn is due to the change in the price level. **We expect the income effect to be positive for superior (or normal) goods and negative for inferior goods**. That is, real income and quantity demanded will move in the same direction for superior goods and in opposite directions for inferior goods. The substitution effect is the change in the quantity demanded that is due solely to the change in relative prices, given a constant real income. **We expect the substitution effect to always be negative**: that is, the quantity demanded due to the substitution effect will always move in the opposite direction to the price change.

In this appendix indifference curves are utilized to separate these two effects in a clear and concise way. This demonstrates that the substitution effect is either supported by the income effect (for superior goods) or is offset to some degree by the income effect (for inferior goods). In the extreme case of a Giffen good the negative income effect would outweigh the substitution effect.

Nominal versus Real Income

It is important to make the distinction between a consumer's monetary, or *nominal*, income and his or her *real* income. Nominal income is the amount of money the consumer has to spend. Given a set of product prices, the consumer can buy certain amounts of various products. Suppose the price of one product is now reduced. The consumer is thus able to buy the same combination of goods and services as before but now spends a *smaller* amount of nominal income. The consumer thus has some money left over to purchase more of the commodity whose price has decreased or any other product. This increase in purchasing power, which follows the reduction of any product price, represents an increase in the consumer's *real* income. Real income, or the purchasing power of nominal income, may be expressed as the ratio of nominal income to a price index that represents the prices of all commodities. Hence, if the price index is reduced because of the lowering of any particular price, the consumer's real income is increased. Conversely, if the price of any product is raised, the consumer's real income is reduced.

Since the substitution effect requires constant real income, we need to adjust the consumer's nominal income to compensate for the change in real income that follows a price change. In Figure 3A-l we illustrate the isolation of the substitution effect. Suppose that the consumer's initial point of equilibrium is point A on the indifference curve I_1 and budget line MN. At this point the consumer chooses to purchase X_1 units of product X. Suppose now that the price of X is reduced, such that the income constraint line swings around to the new line MN', allowing the consumer to attain point B on indifference curve I_2. The consumer now chooses to purchase X_2 units of product X, and the total effect of the price change is to increase his or her consumption of product X by the distance $X_2 - X_1$. It can be seen that this total effect of the price change is what we have called the price effect, since a line joining points A and B would be part of the consumer's price consumption curve. We are now aware, however, that some part of this price effect is caused by an increase in the consumer's real income, which we have called the income effect. Thus the price effect is comprised of the income effect and the substitution effect.

How to Separate the Income and the Substitution Effects

If we can account for and eliminate the income effect, we will be able to identify the remainder of the price effect as the substitution effect. We can account for the income effect by adjusting the consumer's monetary income until it allows the same level of real income as it did before the price change. To eliminate the increase in the real income, we must reduce the consumer to his or her previous level of real income. A method of comparing levels of real income is to compare the utility that may be derived from particular levels of nominal income. Hence, if we were to reduce this consumer to the initial level of utility by a reduction in his or her nominal income, we would, in effect, have reduced the consumer to the initial level of real income. Thus we wish to move the consumer from the level of utility at point B in Figure 3A-l down to a level of utility which is equivalent to point A and therefore lies on the indifference curve I_1.

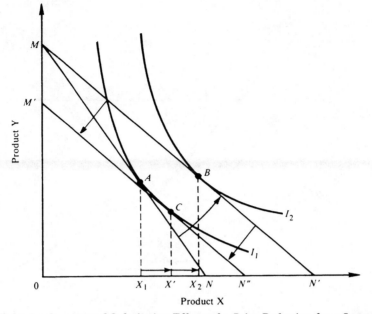

FIGURE 3A-1. *Income and Substitution Effects of a Price Reduction for a Superior Good*

By hypothetically reducing the consumer's nominal income, we begin to move the MN' budget constraint line downward and to the left, such that it remains parallel to MN'. When this hypothetical budget line is tangent to indifference curve I_1, the consumer's level of utility is reduced to a level of real income equivalent to that previously derived from point A. This occurs with budget line $M'N''$ at the tangency point C. At the hypothetical point C the consumer would choose to purchase X' units of product X. The movement from point C to point B, or from X' units to X_2 units, is the income effect, since a line joining points C and B would, in fact, be part of this consumer's income consumption curve. The remaining part of the total effect of the price change from X_1 to X' is the substitution effect. The change in consumption of X from X_1 to X' is simply the result of the differing price ratio, exhibited by the slope of budget line $M'N''$ as compared to the initial line MN, since all other factors, including consumer's real income, remain unchanged.

To reinforce your understanding of the process of separating the income and substitution effects of a price change, let us repeat the process, this time for a price increase.

A Price Increase for a Superior Good

In Figure 3A-2 we show a price increase for product X. This causes the budget line to swing inward from MN to MN'. Accordingly, the consumer adjusts purchases from the combination represented by point A to the smaller combination represented by point B. The price effect is the reduction in quantity demanded of product X from X_1 to X_2. To ascertain how much of this is due to the substitution effect, we must hypothetically in-

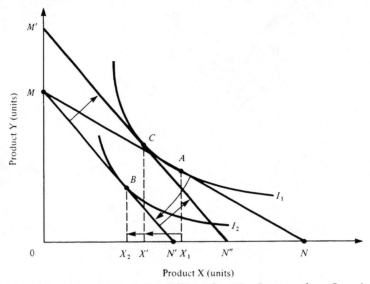

FIGURE 3A-2. Income and Substitution Effects of a Price Increase for a Superior Good

crease the consumer's income to compensate for the reduction in real income caused by the price increase. The new budget line MN' is shifted upward until it just touches the initial indifference curve I_1, at point C. Since points A and C are on the same indifference curve, they represent equal purchasing power in terms of total utility derived. Thus the movement along indifference curve I_1 from A to C, or from X_1 to X' in terms of the quantity demanded of product X, is the substitution effect, since real income is held constant and the only difference is the price ratio. The remaining part of the price effect, from C to B, or from X' to X_2 in terms of the quantity demanded of product X, is the income effect of the price change. Note that the income effect and the substitution effect both work in the same direction to reduce consumption of X when its price increases, and in Figure 3A-1 both worked to increase consumption of X when its price fell.

Inferior Goods

In Figure 3A-3 we show the income and substitution effects of a price change for an inferior good.[1] Again the initial point is a tangency between budget line MN and indifference curve I_1 at point A. The price of product X is reduced such that the budget line

---

[1] The indifference-curve map must reflect the inferiority of product X for our graphs to work out correctly. When product X is regarded as inferior, the indifference curves will not be parallel but will be closer together at the top end than they are at the bottom end, as shown in Figure 3A-3. While indifference curves are everywhere dense (meaning that one passes through every point on the graph), they are also infinitely narrow, so the multitude of indifference curves that exist between the lower parts of curves I_1 and I_2 have no problem squeezing through the more narrow space at the top end of those curves.

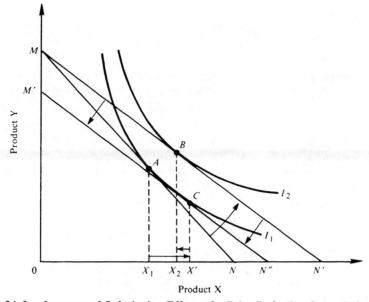

FIGURE 3A-3. *Income and Substitution Effects of a Price Reduction for an Inferior Good*

swings around to *MN'*, allowing the consumer a new higher level of utility at point *B* on indifference curve I_2. The total effect of the price change, or the price effect, is the movement from *A* to *B*, which in terms of product X is a change in consumption from X_1 to X_2. To isolate the income effect, we hypothetically reduce the consumer's income until a budget line with the same slope (that is, with the same price ratio) as budget line *MN'* is just tangent to the original indifference curve. This occurs at point *C*. The income effect is thus the movement from *C* to *B*, or in terms of product X from *X'* to X_2.

In this case the income effect is negative, since the increase in real income caused by the price reduction was accompanied by a decrease in the quantity demanded of product X. A line drawn between the points *C* and *B*, which is part of the consumer's income consumption curve, would have a negative slope, confirming that product X is regarded by this consumer as an inferior good. The substitution effect is once again the movement along the initial indifference curve from point *A* to point *C*. The substitution effect of a price reduction for product X is thus an increase in the quantity demanded of product X from level X_1 to *X'*. This is partly offset by a negative income effect from *X'* to X_2, such that the total effect (or the price effect) is from X_1 to X_2.

- NOTE: Notice that in both the normal goods case and the inferior goods case the substitution effect was negative. Given the general validity of the assumptions that underlie the construction of a consumer's indifference curve, the substitution effect is always negative; that is, for price reductions corrected for the income effect the consumer will always purchase more of the product, while for price increases corrected for the income effect the consumer will always purchase less of the product. The income effect, however, may be either positive or negative, and, if negative, it offsets part of the substitution effect.

Giffen Goods.   It is theoretically possible that a large negative income effect could more than offset the substitution effect, in which case a price reduction would be followed by a decline in the quantity demanded, or a price increase would be followed by an increase in the quantity demanded. A product that behaved in this way would exhibit a positive price effect and would therefore run counter to the empirical law of demand. Such a product is known as a *Giffen good.*[2] A modern-day example of a Giffen good is difficult to find, keeping in mind that we require *ceteris paribus* to hold when the price of the product in question is changed. A situation that may seem to indicate a Giffen good is one in which a product sells for a while at one price and later sells more units at a higher price. If and only if *ceteris paribus* prevailed over the entire period of the observations would the product be a Giffen good. More likely, however, one or more of the underlying factors has changed during the period (such as consumer tastes, incomes, and the prices and availability of other products). If so, the two observations are not on the same demand curve but are on separate demand curves, because of a shift of the demand curve caused in turn by a change in an underlying determinant.

• EXAMPLE: Suppose a merchant offers hand towels for sale at $0.59 each and demand for these towels is somewhat less than enthusiastic. If the merchant now raises the price to $0.99 and customers eagerly purchase the towels, does this mean that those hand towels are a Giffen good? The answer is probably no. Consumers tend to make price-quality associations when they are unable to judge quality on any other basis. At the lower price the hand towels were perceived as low-quality hand towels, whereas at the higher price they were perceived as better-quality hand towels. The consumers' taste and preference patterns between low-quality and high-quality hand towels are probably the same as they were when they were first confronted by the hand towels. The error in calling hand towels a Giffen good rests on failing to distinguish that consumers regard the higher-priced hand towels as a different product from the lower-priced hand towels. Our analysis of the income and substitution effects of a price change for a particular good depends on successive units of that product being identical with the preceding and following units.

---

[2]The existence of such perverse price effects was noted in the case of potatoes during the Irish famine of 1846 to 1849. Although the price of potatoes had increased as a result of a blight affecting the crops and reducing supplies, many families were consuming more potatoes than they were at earlier prices. The Irish peasant was typically so poor that potatoes formed the major part of the family diet, supplemented by meat and other foodstuffs. When the price of potatoes was increased, the demand for potatoes actually increased, since the money left over for meat and other foodstuffs (after buying the same quantity of potatoes) was insufficient to buy enough of these less bulky items to satisfy the family appetite. Thus demand for the more filling potato was increased despite its higher price. See G. J. Stigler, "Notes on the History of the Giffen Paradox," *Journal of Political Economy,* 55 (April 1947), pp. 152–56.

In the preceding example the two observations are most likely part of two separate negatively sloping demand curves, rather than of a single positively sloping demand curve. Shifts versus movements along demand curves are discussed in detail in Chapter 4, and the identification problem, which causes confusion between shifts and movements along demand curves in practice, is discussed in Chapter 5.

Summary

The price effect is composed of an income effect and a substitution effect. The income effect is the change in quantity demanded because of the change in real income which accompanies a price change, given *ceteris paribus*. The substitution effect is the change in quantity demanded because of a change in the relative prices of two products, given *ceteris paribus*. To isolate the income effect, we move the new budget line into tangency with the initial indifference curve to return the consumer to the initial level of real income. The change in quantity demanded that this would cause is the income effect, and the remainder of the price effect is the substitution effect.

DISCUSSION QUESTIONS

3A-1. What is the income effect of a price change? Does the change in the price of one product have income effects on other products as well?

3A-2. What is the substitution effect of a price change? How is its definition different from the definition of the price effect?

3A-3. Why is the same level of total utility (at points *A* and *C*, for example) taken as a proxy for the same level of real income?

3A-4. Why is the (hypothetical) compensating change in income always shown as a parallel shift of the budget line?

3A-5. What do we mean when we say that the substitution effect is always negative, regardless of whether the price increases or decreases?

PROBLEMS AND SHORT CASES

3A-1. The Consumer Price Index is derived by comparing the cost of a given combination of the many products that are usually included in the household's budget. For example, if the price of any one of those goods decreases and other things remain unchanged, the CPI decreases. Explain how the income and substitution effects would work in a multiproduct case like this, with reference to a change in the CPI.

3A-2. Using graphs, show the separation of the income and substitution effects of a price *increase* for an *inferior* good, and explain why the consumer reacts in the way shown.

3A-3. See if you can devise a set of indifference curves that show product X to be a Giffen good. Using these curves, show the separation of the income and substitution effects of a price reduction for that Giffen good. (Hint: Giffen goods are extremely inferior goods, and the indifference curves must reflect this fact.)

SUGGESTED REFERENCES AND FURTHER READING

DWYER, G. P. JR. and C. M. LINDSAY. "Robert Giffen and the Irish Potato," *American Economic Review*, (March 1984), pp. 188–92.

GILLEY, O. W. and G. V. KARELS. "In Search of Giffen Behavior," *Economic Inquiry*, 29 (January 1991), pp. 182–89.

HIRSHLEIFER, JACK. *Price Theory and Applications*, 4th ed. esp. chaps. 3 and 4. Englewood Cliffs, NJ.: Prentice-Hall, Inc., 1988.

HYMAN, DAVID N. *Modern Microeconomics: Analysis and Applications*, esp. chaps. 3 and 4. St. Louis: Times Mirror/Mosby College Publishing, 1986.

MANSFIELD, E. *Microeconomics: Theory/Applications*, esp. chaps. 3 and 4. New York: W. W. Norton & Company, 1985.

STIGLER, GEORGE J. "Notes on the History of the Giffen Paradox," *Journal of Political Economy*, 55 (April 1947), pp. 152–56.

Chapter 4

MARKET DEMAND ANALYSIS FOR DECISION MAKING

EXECUTIVE SUMMARY

The **collective actions of consumers constitute the market demand** for the product markets, and consequently consumers are responsible, in conjunction with the actions of producers on the supply side of each market, for the determination of the price and output levels in each market. In Chapter 3 we examined the behavior of individual consumers who make utility-maximizing decisions to purchase goods and services. They make these decisions on the basis of their incomes, their preferences, the prices, and the availability of various products. When discussing consumer behavior, we do not expect the actions and reactions of any individual consumer to change the environment or subsequent behavior by that consumer. But **consumers in aggregate can and do influence the prices and availability of goods and services.**

The total demand in any particular product market is an important force in the economic system because it enters the product markets supported by the income that consumers expect to spend to maximize their utility. These consumer expenditures become sales revenue from the firm's point of view. In this chapter **we consider the major factors likely to influence the total demand and sales revenue for a product** as well as the probable direction of the influence in each case. We then examine the relationships among the important revenue concepts, namely **total revenue, marginal revenue, and average revenue** (or price per unit). A means of measuring and summarizing the direction and magnitude of the influence that each variable has on the total demand for a particular product is provided by the concept of **elasticity of demand**, and we consider several different elasticity measures and their application to decision-making problems.

4.1   THE DEMAND FUNCTION AND THE DEMAND CURVE[1]

Let us immediately make the following distinction. The demand *function* refers to the relationship that exists between the quantity demanded of a particular product and *all determinants* of demand. The demand *curve* refers to the relationship that exists between the quantity demanded of a particular product and the *price* of that product, with all other influencing factors held constant. The demand curve is thus a subset of the demand function where *ceteris paribus* applies to all of the independent variables except price.

The Independent Variables in the Demand Function

The quantity demanded of X, or Q_x, is known as the dependent variable in the demand function, since its value depends on the values of the influencing variables, which are known as independent variables. What are the independent variables that influence Q_x? Let us discuss them one by one.

Price.   We have seen in the preceding chapter that quantity demanded varies inversely with the price of the product, given *ceteris paribus*. For increases in the price of X we expect the quantity demanded to rise, and vice versa.

Prices of Related Products.   Consumers choose a particular product from within a group of *substitute* products because of its superior value to them. In their view the chosen product offers the best combination of attributes (quality) for the price. Now if the price of one of the substitute products were to increase, we expect the demand for product X to increase, since some consumers will switch away from that substitute product and toward other substitutes, including product X, because they now feel that a different product offers them better value. Conversely, a reduction in the price of a substitute product will cause some consumers to stop buying product X.

    Complementary goods, on the other hand, are products that are typically consumed in conjunction with product X. For example, coffee and cream, gasoline and tires, and beer and peanuts are pairs of complementary goods for many people. If the prices of complementary goods rise, we expect the quantity demanded of product X to decrease, since the consumption of product X and its complementary product is now more expensive. Conversely, if the prices of complements decrease, the quantity demanded of X should increase, since the package price for X and its complements is now reduced.

Advertising and Promotional Efforts.   Advertising and other promotional efforts by the sellers of product X can be expected to influence the quantity demanded of that product, since these efforts are designed to influence the taste and preference patterns of consumers. Advertising related to product X is expected to be followed by an increase in the

---

[1]Chapter 3 is not a prerequisite to this chapter, although it does allow a more thorough understanding of individual consumer behavior. In this chapter the consumers' reactions to change in their economic environment are restated briefly, and this will allow a sufficient understanding of market demand analysis.

quantity demanded of product X. On the other hand, advertising of substitute products is expected to have a negative influence on the quantity demanded of X, since it should be expected to induce consumers to switch their consumption from product X toward one of the substitute products. Conversely, advertising of a complementary good is expected to have a positive influence on the quantity demanded of product X, since consumers tend to buy product X and that complementary good in some proportionate way.

Product Quality and Design. Consumers typically appreciate quality and good design and are expected to purchase more of a product when they perceive it to be of higher quality or of a more functional design, given similar prices. Conversely, if the quality is judged inferior to other products or represents a reduction in quality, as compared to the firm's earlier production, consumers are expected to reduce their demand for the product. Quality can be designed into the firm's product itself, or it can be attached as a peripheral attribute like courteous service, a comprehensive guarantee, or a convenient and well-trained service network. In addition, consumer perceptions of quality and design may be influenced by the firm's advertising and promotional efforts.

Distribution Outlets and Place of Sale. Total demand for the firm's product is directly influenced by the number of sales or distribution outlets and by the location of these outlets. Having a larger number of outlets allows the firm to reach consumers who may not otherwise be exposed to the product, to make it more convenient for consumers to purchase the product, and to offer ancillary services (such as technical advice, repairs, and warranty service) which help to augment total sales. The location of sales outlets is also an important consideration. A retail store in a busy shopping center may have triple the sales volume of a similar store on a low-traffic side street. Thus firms choose the locations of their wholesale and retail outlets with an eye to the potential sales volume (and hence sales revenue) that is expected to result from each location.[2]

Consumer Incomes. The relationship between consumer incomes and quantity demanded of product X can be expected to be either positive or negative, depending on the product in question and the level of consumer income. We saw in Chapter 3 that for some consumers at some levels a particular commodity could have a negative income effect, whereas for other consumers at other income levels the income effect might be positive. We are interested here in the *aggregate* income effect. Thus, if to most purchasers the product is an inferior good, its demand will decrease when income levels rise or increase when income levels fall. On the other hand, if it is a normal or superior product for most purchasers, quantity demanded and income levels move in the same direction.

---

[2]Distribution strategy is covered in detail in marketing courses. See Philip Kotler, *Marketing Management: Analysis, Planning, Implementation, and Control*, 7th ed. (Englewood Cliffs, N.J.: Prentice Hall, 1991), chapters 19 and 20. Marketers speak of the four Ps—price, promotion, product design, and place of sale—as the firm's controllable variables among those that influence consumer demand. Other influencing variables, such as actions by competitors, consumer incomes, and population, are uncontrollable, and others, such as tastes and preferences and expectations, may be regarded as partially controllable by the firm through its product design and promotional strategies.

Consumer Tastes and Preferences.   The tastes and preferences of consumers may be expected to be in a continual state of flux, with some people shifting their purchases toward a particular product and others shifting away, as consumers learn more about other products that are available and as they change their minds about what attributes are more important to them. In explaining market demand, we are interested in the general trend of tastes and preferences toward or away from the product in question. An index of consumer preferences for a particular product may be constructed and periodically updated by surveys of consumer attitudes toward that product. If these surveys indicate that the product is, for example, becoming more widely appreciated, or that the strength of consumers' desire for the product is increasing, this shift would be captured by an increase in the value of the index.

Consumer Expectations.   Consumer expectations about the future price, availability, and substitutability of product X influence their present demand for product X. For example, if you expect gasoline to be significantly more expensive or less readily available in the near future, you may be motivated to increase your current demand for gasoline by keeping your tank full most of the time or even by filling extra containers with gasoline. Similarly, if you expect a new model of product X to be released in the near future and if you expect this new model to be a significant improvement, you may reduce your purchases of X now and wait for the new model. Thus consumer expectations have a positive impact on current demand for product X if the expectations are pessimistic with respect to future prices, availability, or quality of product X. Conversely, consumer expectations have a negative impact on current demand if the expectations are optimistic.

Other Factors.   Every demand function will have its own particular set of determinants, reflecting the reasons people purchase the product. For example, the demand for umbrellas in a particular market depends on the amount of rainfall in that area. The demand for many other products, including clothing, sporting equipment, and types of transportation demanded, is also dependent on the weather. Government policy affects the demand for many products. The government may pursue an industrial strategy that encourages production of high-technology goods, for example. Or the government may increase tariff protection for the firm's product, or act to reduce the external value of the dollar, with subsequent impacts on demand for the firm's product. Reduced or increased surveillance of the firm's pricing and advertising policies by the Federal Trade Commission may impact on the effectiveness of the firm's policies. Finally, we should note that the demand for most products is positively related to the number of people in the market, or the size of the population.

The determinants of demand are summarized in Table 4-1. Note that we can categorize them into four main groups. The firm's strategic variables are those it can adjust to influence demand directly. We also call these the controllable variables. The remaining three groups of determinants are not controllable by the firm, although the firm may be able to influence some of them, including consumer tastes and preferences, the actions of competitors and producers of complementary products, and government policy.

TABLE 4-1. The Determinants of Demand for a Product

$$Q_x = f \quad (P_x, A_x, D_x, O_x, \quad I_c, T_c, E_c, \quad P_y, A_y, D_y, O_y, \quad G, N, W, \ldots)$$

| Strategic variables | Consumer variables | Competitor variables | Other variables |

Controllable variables   Uncontrollable variables

where

Q_x is the quantity demanded of product X, per period
P_x is the price of product X
A_x is advertising/promotion for product X
D_x is design/style/quality of product X
O_x is outlets for distribution of product X
I_c is incomes of consumers/customers/clientele
T_c is tastes and preference patterns of consumers
E_c is expectations of consumers regarding future prices, etc.
P_y is prices of related goods (substitutes, complements)
A_y is advertising/promotion for related goods
D_y is design/style/quality of related goods
O_y is competitor distribution outlets
G is government policy, industrial strategy
N is number of people in the economy
W is weather conditions

The Form of the Demand Function

The specific form of the demand function for a particular product is an empirical question. That is, collection and analysis of data may reveal Q_X to be a linear function of its determinants or, alternatively, a multiplicative function of several independent variables. The linear form of the demand function is exemplified by the following:

$$Q_x = \alpha + \beta_1 P_x + \beta_2 P_y + \beta_3 A_x + \beta_4 A_y + \beta_5 I_c + \beta_6 T_c + \beta_7 E_c + \beta_8 N \qquad (4\text{-}1)$$

where α (the Greek letter alpha) is that part of quantity demanded determined exogenously or by other variables not explicitly mentioned in the demand function, and $\beta_1, \beta_2, \beta_3, \ldots, \beta_n$ (β is the Greek letter beta) are the coefficients of the demand function indicating the marginal impact of each independent variable on the quantity demanded. Equation (4-1) represents a specific demand situation and the independent variables that were significant determinants of Q_x in that situation. The symbols representing the independent variables are explained in Table 4-1, which shows a more general specification of independent variables that might prove to be determinants of quantity demanded in particular instances.

In some cases, two or more variables may have a multiplicative impact on Q_x, as follows:

$$Q_x = \alpha P_x^{\beta 1} N^{\beta 2} O_x^{\beta 3}$$

(4-2)

In this case, the quantity demanded for product X depends on the price of X, total market population, and number of outlets for product X.

The coefficients in the demand function (namely α, β_1, β_2, and so on) may be estimated using regression analysis and other techniques, as we shall see in Chapter 5. Equations (4-1) and (4-2) are, in effect, symbolic models of the demand function of product X. Each one is an explanatory model used to explain the demand for X in terms of the levels of each of the independent variables. Such models explain changes in the value of Q_x as the result of a change in one or more of the independent variables. A model of the demand function can also be used for predictive purposes, given estimates of all the β coefficients and the residual term α.

- EXAMPLE: Suppose the demand function for product X has been estimated (using regression analysis) to be

$$Q_x = 5,030 - 3,806.2P_x + 1,458.5P_y + 256.6A_x - 32.3A_y + 0.18I_c$$

(4-3)

where the symbols for the independent variables are the same as introduced in Table 4-1, and the α and β parameters are replaced by their numerical equivalents. Note that the positive or negative sign preceding the coefficient to each independent variable indicates the direction of the influence that variable has on Q_x. Given this specification of the demand function, we can predict the sales level for product X, given the values of the independent variables. Suppose $P_x = \$8$; $P_y = \$6$; $A_x = \$168$ (in thousands); $A_y = \$182$ (in thousands); and $I_c = \$12,875$. Substituting for these variables in equation (4-3), we find

$$Q_x = 5,030 - 30,449.6 + 8,751.0 + 43,108.8 - 5,878.6 + 2,317.5 = 22,879.1$$

Thus we predict that at the current values of the independent variables, quantity demanded of product X should be 22,879.1 units, given *ceteris paribus*.

The Demand Curve Derived from the Demand Function

The demand curve is a special subcase of the demand function in which *ceteris paribus* applies to all independent variables except the price of the product in question. Since none of the other independent variables or the residual term α vary when *ceteris paribus* is in force, we can aggregate them all into a single term, A, and express the demand function as follows:

$$Q_x = A + \beta_1 P_x$$

(4-4)

where $A = \alpha + \beta_2 P_y + \beta_3 A_x + \beta_4 A_y + \beta_5 Y_c + \beta_6 T_c + \beta_7 E_c + \beta_8 N$ (using equation 4-1 as an example) and includes the influence of all other determinants of Q_x *except for the product's own price, P_x.*

* NOTE: Since a demand curve expresses the relationship between Q_x and P_x with all other things remaining the same, equation (4-4) *is* a demand curve. But economists, following the convention set by the great classical economist Alfred Marshall, traditionally place the independent variable (price) on the vertical axis for their graphical analysis, and speak in terms of an inverse demand curve where P_x is expressed as a function of Q_x, as follows[3]

$$P_x = a + b_1 Q_x \qquad (4\text{-}5)$$

Given this convention, it is important for efficient communication that we also observe this practice, keeping in mind that Q_x is really the dependent variable and P_x is the independent variable.[4] Equation (4-5) is easily obtained from equation (4-4) by a couple of manipulations and substitutions. Working on equation (4-4), subtract A from both sides and divide both sides by β_1 to find

$$P_x = -A/\beta_1 + 1/\beta_1 Q_x \qquad (4\text{-}6)$$

Letting $-A/\beta_1 = a$, and $1/\beta_1 = b$, we have $P_x = a + bQ_x$. Note that the numerical value of β_1 is expected to have a negative sign because of the law of demand. Thus the parameter a will be a positive number and b will be a negative number.

* EXAMPLE: From the numerical example introduced earlier, we can add together the α term (5,030) and the influence of all other independent variables except P_x to find that $A = 53,328.7$. Thus

$$Q_x = 53,328.7 - 3,806.2 P_x \qquad (4\text{-}7)$$

It is usually more convenient when dealing with large numbers to express them in larger units, such as thousands or millions, in order to simplify calculations. To express Q_x in thousands of units, we simply shift the decimal point three places to the left, to obtain

$$Q_x = 53.3287 - 3.8062 P_x \qquad (4\text{-}8)$$

---

[3] See Alfred N. Page. "Marshall's Graphs and Walras' Equations: A Textbook Anomaly," *Economic Inquiry*, 18 (January 1980), pp. 138–43.

[4] In perfectly competitive markets (see Chapter 9) when short run quantity supplied is fixed (as in agricultural markets for, example) price *does* depend on quantity demanded. But in most markets price is set by the firm or other organization and buyers make their purchase decision given that price.

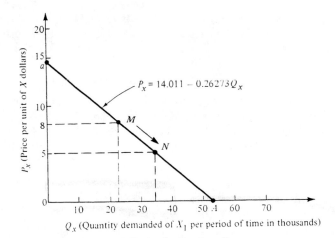

FIGURE 4-1.   The Market Demand Curve for Product X

Now to invert this expression to the form $P_x = a + bQ_x$ we subtract 53.3287 from both sides and divide both sides by 3.8062 to find

$$P_x = 14.011 - 0.26273Q_x \qquad (4\text{-}9)$$

Note that price is now expressed as a linear function of quantity demanded, where a (= 14.011) is the intercept value on the vertical (price) axis and b (= −0.26273) is the slope term. In Figure 4-1 we show that this demand curve intercepts the price axis at the value a and slopes downward at the rate $b = 1/\beta_1$. The intercept on the horizontal axis is, of course, the value A, since this is the value of Q_x when P_x is zero. Note that the price-quantity combination shown as point M on the demand curve in Figure 4-1 occurs when P_x = $8 and Q_x = 22,879.1, as calculated earlier.[5]

Movements Along versus Shifts of the Demand Curve

A *movement along* the demand curve will occur when there is a change in price (and consequently quantity demanded) while all other determinants of demand remain constant. In Figure 4-1 we show a price change from $8 per unit to $5 per unit, which causes quantity demanded to increase from 22,879.1 units to 34,297 units. (The latter figure is calculated by substituting the value 5 for P_x in equation 4-8 or 4-9.) In effect, there has

---

[5]We should be cautious about extending the analysis to extreme values of P_x and Q_x. It is sufficient to say that the intercept terms a (on the vertical axis) and A (on the horizontal axis) simply *locate* the demand curve at its appropriate height. We expect the demand curve to depict the relationship between P_x and Q_x adequately only within the relevant range of observations which is in the vicinity of the current price and demand levels. For the same reason is a sufficient approximation to show the demand curve as linear through the relevant range, although for extreme values of P_x and Q_x the demand curve is likely to become curvilinear.

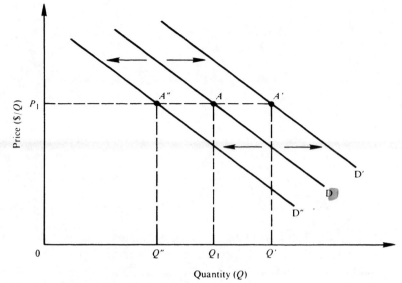

FIGURE 4-2. *Shifts of the Demand Curve for Product X*

been a movement along the demand curve from point M to point N as a result of the price change, given *ceteris paribus.*

A *shift* of the demand curve will occur when *ceteris paribus* does not hold, and thus the value of the intercept term changes. In Figure 4-2 we show shifts of the demand curve which are the result of changes in one or more of the other factors while price is held constant. Suppose that the initial demand curve is that shown as D, such that at price P_1 quantity demand is Q_1. If, for example, consumer incomes increased (or there was an increase in some other variable that has a positive coefficient in equation 4-3 or a decrease in a variable that has a negative coefficient), the demand curve would shift to the right, as shown by the movement to demand curve D'. For the same price level P_1 the quantity demanded is now Q'; the additional quantity demanded is caused by a change in one or more of the other variables. On the other hand, if there was a reduction in consumer incomes (or a shift in consumer tastes away from product X or any of a number of other changes in the determining factors), the demand curve would shift to the left, to a position such as that shown by demand curve D''.

Thus changes in price will, *ceteris paribus*, lead to a *movement along* an existing demand curve, whereas changes in any of the other variables will cause a *shift* of the demand curve. Given the new set of the other variables, there will be a new demand curve that is appropriate, and the initial demand curve will now be inappropriate. When analyzing the effect on quantity demanded of a change in the price level, it is extremely important to ascertain whether or not any of the other factors have changed before concluding that there has been a movement along the demand curve.

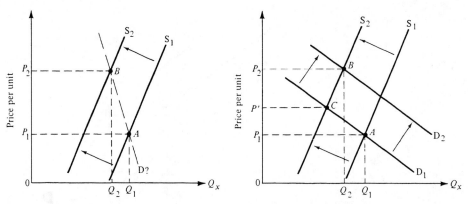

FIGURE 4-3.   Shifts Distinguished from Movements along Demand Curves

- EXAMPLE: To illustrate the combined impact of movements along demand curves and shifts of demand curves, consider the price of coffee, which always jumps up to reflect increases in the cost of imported coffee beans. The left-hand part of Figure 4-3 shows the price and quantity demanded of coffee in supermarkets before and after the increase in coffee bean prices (P_1, Q_1 and P_2, Q_2, respectively). A superficial analysis of this situation might lead to the conclusion that the supply curve for coffee had shifted from S_1 to S_2, causing a movement along the market demand curve from point A to point B. This interpretation would indicate that consumers' demand for coffee was not very sensitive to price increases, and may lead coffee manufacturers to consider further price increases.

  But more careful analysis reveals that the substantial change in the price level was the result of both a movement along *and* a shift of the demand curve. The right-hand part of Figure 4-3 shows the supply curve having shifted from S_1 to S_2 as a result of the increase in coffee bean prices. This change alone would cause supply and demand to be equal at price P', considerably below the actual price that eventuated, P_2. The actual price was higher because there is also a *shift* of the demand curve: Fearing that coffee might not be available in the near future, many consumers will buy more than they normally would to build personal stockpiles. This reaction manifests itself as a shift of the demand curve from D_1 to D_2, and is due to a change in consumers' expectations concerning future prices and availability of the product. Thus the price change was the result of two separate influences: from P_1 to P' as the result of a movement along the initial demand curve, and from P' to P_2 as a result of the shift of the demand curve from D_1 to D_2.

  This example points out the danger of assuming that the change in quantity demanded is entirely due to the variable the manager has adjusted (in the case of a controllable determinant of demand) or has seen move (in the case of an uncontrollable determinant of demand). A naive view of what happens in the coffee market (the interpretation in the left-hand side of Figure 4-3) would lead the manager to conclude that the demand for coffee is really quite unresponsive to changes in price. The quantity demanded seems to fall only slightly whenever the price rises substantially. This manager might be inclined to raise the price further, expecting quantity demanded to fall only slightly. A more informed view, recognizing that *ceteris* were not *paribus*, would lead to the conclusion that quantity demanded would fall very substantially for an additional price increase. But a further price increase would cause a movement along the new demand curve D_2, and the new quantity demanded would come as a great surprise to the naive manager who mistakenly believes the demand curve to be much steeper than it is.

Relationships among Price, Total Revenue, and Marginal Revenue

We are interested in the relationship between price and quantity demanded because of its impact on total sales revenue when price is changed. In Table 4-2 we demonstrate the variation in total revenue for the demand curve specified by $P_x = 11 - 0.001Q_x$.

- EXAMPLE: Suppose this expression represents the demand curve for a carton of twelve cans of dog food at a discount supermarket during a particular month. For this simple demand curve the intercept on the price axis is $11, and the slope is -0.001. Thus, for every $1.00 price reduction, quantity demanded will increase by 1,000 cartons. Substituting different values of price into this equation, we are able to determine the quantity that will be demanded at all prices, as shown in the second column of Table 4-2. Total revenue at each price is derived by multiplying the price by the quantity demanded at that price, to find the total revenue associated with each price (or quantity) level. It can be seen that total revenue increases progressively as price is lowered from $10 to $6, that the price reduction to $5 leaves the total revenue unchanged, and that further price reductions cause total revenue to decline.

    Note that high prices are not necessarily the best prices. By lowering the price we were able to increase total revenue up to a point. But similarly, neither is a very low price necessarily a good strategy; although it does expand the quantity demanded, it causes a smaller total revenue as compared with that which may be earned at a higher price level. The fourth column in Table 4-2 shows the marginal revenue associated with each price level.

- DEFINITION: *Marginal revenue* is defined as the change in total revenue that results from a one-unit increase in quantity demand. Since quantity demanded increases by blocks of 1,000 units in Table 4-2, marginal revenue is calculated here as the row-to-row difference in the total revenue column divided by the change in quantity demanded. It can be seen that marginal revenue falls progressively to zero and becomes negative as price is reduced.

    In Figure 4-4 we plot the values for the demand curve (given by the price/quantity combinations) and the total revenue and marginal revenue curves to illustrate the relationships that exist between and among these curves. These relationships hold for any demand curve that is negatively sloped. Total revenue increases at first as prices are lowered, reaches its maximum, and thereafter declines as prices are reduced further. Marginal revenue will always be less than price at each output level and will fall to zero

TABLE 4-2. Revenue Implications of the Law of Demand

Price ($/unit)	Quantity Demanded (units)	Total Revenue ($)	Marginal Revenue ($/unit)
10	1,000	10,000	—
9	2,000	18,000	8
8	3,000	24,000	6
7	4,000	28,000	4
6	5,000	30,000	2
5	6,000	30,000	0
4	7,000	28,000	−2
3	8,000	24,000	−4
2	9,000	18,000	−6
1	10,000	10,000	−8

at the point where total revenue reaches its maximum. It will take negative values if price is reduced any further, since this causes an absolute reduction in total revenue.[6]

Price and Marginal Revenue.   The relationship between the demand curve and the marginal revenue curve bears further observation. Since both may be derived from the total revenue curve, it is clear that there must be a relationship between them. To find this relationship we begin by expressing the total revenue as the product of price and quantity:

$$TR_x = P_x \cdot Q_x \qquad (4\text{-}10)$$

Substituting $a + bQ_x$ for P_x from equation (4-5), we obtain

$$TR_x = aQ_x + bQ_x^2 \qquad (4\text{-}11)$$

Since *marginal revenue* is defined as the change in total revenue for a one-unit change in quantity demanded, it can be expressed as the first derivative of equation (4-11) with respect to Q_x Thus,[7]

$$MR_x = a + 2bQ_x \qquad (4\text{-}12)$$

---

[6]The price reductions shown in Table 4-2 were made by discrete $1.00 units, and hence the changes in quantity-demanded observations were in blocks of 1,000 units. Marginal revenue calculated from these data is strictly the *average* change in total revenue per one-unit change in quantity demanded for each of the 1,000-unit blocks. If we had shown smaller price reductions, we would have found that the price generating the highest revenue would be $5.50. At this price level, 5,500 units would be demanded and total revenue would be $30,250. Strictly, then, marginal revenue is zero at these price and quantity levels, as shown in Figure 4-4, rather than the more crude approximation shown in Table 4-2.

[7]The derivative of equation (4-11) was obtained using the *power rule*, which is explained in Appendix A at the end of this text.

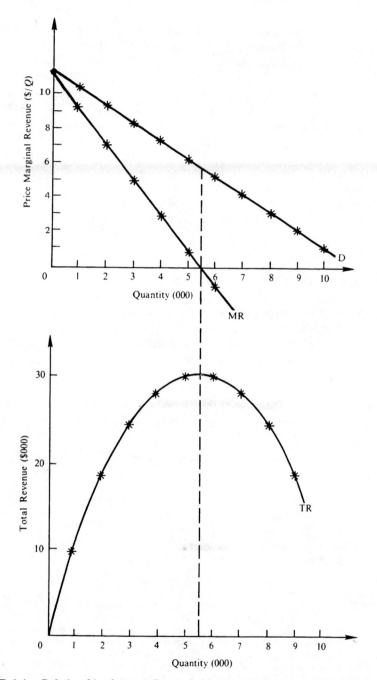

FIGURE 4-4. *Relationships between Demand, Marginal Revenue, and Total Revenue*

Now compare the expression for the demand curve, equation (4-5), with the expression for the marginal revenue curve, equation (4-12). The intercept term of each is a, indicating that both curves must emanate from the same point on the vertical axis of the graph, and the slope term in the marginal revenue expression, $2b$, is exactly twice the slope term in the price or demand curve expression. Thus the marginal revenue curve does have a fixed relationship with the demand curve from which it is derived. It begins at the same point on the price axis and slopes downward at twice the rate of the demand curve.[8]

- EXAMPLE: From the estimated demand function provided earlier, we had derived the following expression for the demand curve: $P_x = 14.011 - 0.26273Q_x$. The marginal revenue curve relating to this demand curve will have the same intercept term, and twice the slope, and can therefore be expressed as $MR_x = 14.011 - 0.52546Q_x$.

4.2   PRICE ELASTICITY OF DEMAND

The relationships between price, marginal revenue, and total revenue can be summarized in a single number known as the price elasticity of demand. The concept of *elasticity* is used widely in economics and expresses the responsiveness of a dependent variable to a change in an independent (determining) variable.

- DEFINITION: *Price elasticity of demand* is defined as the percentage change in quantity demanded divided by a small percentage change in price (which caused the change in quantity demanded). That is,

$$\epsilon = \frac{\% \text{ change in } Q_x}{\% \text{ change in } P_x} \tag{4-13}$$

where ϵ (the Greek letter epsilon) is the conventional symbol for price elasticity of demand. Expanding equation (4-13) we have

---

[8]We have confined our discussion to *linear* demand curves. A linear specification of the demand curve is typically a sufficient approximation over the relevant range of prices and outputs. It is nevertheless also true that the marginal revenue curve for a *curvilinear* demand curve will have the same intercept and twice the slope of the demand curve at any given output level. That is, a tangent to the (curvilinear) marginal revenue curve will have twice the slope of a tangent to the curvilinear demand curve at any given output level. This assumes that the demand curve is *convex* to the origin, which is in keeping with the economic theory of consumer behavior. Horizontal demand curves, such as in pure competition, are coextensive with the marginal revenue curve and thus have the same intercept and the same slope. But since the slope of a horizontal line is zero and since twice zero is still zero, the general rule (that MR has the same intercept and twice the slope of the demand curve) is not violated.

$$\epsilon = \cfrac{\dfrac{\Delta Q_x}{Q_x} \cdot \dfrac{100}{1}}{\dfrac{\Delta P_x}{P_x} \cdot \dfrac{100}{1}}$$

$$(4\text{-}14)$$

where Δ (the Greek letter delta) connotes a small change in the variable following. Canceling the 100/1 terms and rearranging, we have

$$\epsilon = \frac{\Delta Q_x}{\Delta P_x} \cdot \frac{P_x}{Q_x}$$

$$(4\text{-}15)$$

Note that $\Delta Q_x/\Delta P_x$ is equal to β_1, or the reciprocal of b, the slope term in the demand curve. Hence price elasticity is equal to the reciprocal of that slope weighted by the ratio of price to quantity demanded, $P_x Q_x$. Along a linear demand curve the slope term is constant, and therefore the term $\Delta Q_x/\Delta P_x$ is constant in equation (4-15). But because the P_x/Q_x term varies throughout the length of the demand curve, price elasticity also varies as we move along the demand curve. At points high on the demand curve the ratio of P_x to Q_x is relatively large, whereas for points low on the demand curve the ratio P_x/Q_x is relatively low. In fact, this ratio approaches infinity as we move toward the intercept on the price axis, and it approaches zero as we move toward the intercept on the quantity axis. It is thus apparent that the price elasticity must vary from infinity to zero as we move from the price intercept down a linear demand curve toward the quantity intercept.

- NOTE: The value of price elasticity varies from *minus* infinity to approach zero from the negative side, because $\Delta Q_x/\Delta P_x$ has a negative sign. (Either ΔQ_x or ΔP_x is negative, depending on whether we move up or down the demand curve.) By convention, however, we speak of price elasticity in *absolute* terms, saying, for example, that $\epsilon = -5$ is *greater* than $\epsilon = -3$.

It is important to understand that price elasticity is equal to -1 at the midpoint of the demand curve. To see this, consider a demand curve specified by $P_x = 5 - 0.625 Q_x$. You can visualize this demand curve as having a vertical intercept of $5, since $P_x = 5$ when $Q_x = 0$, and a horizontal intercept of 8 units, since $Q_x = 8$ when $P_x = 0$. This demand curve is shown in Figure 4-5. The slope of the demand curve is $\Delta P_x/\Delta Q_x = -0.625$, which is, of course, equal to $-5/8$, the negative of the ratio of the vertical intercept value over the horizontal intercept value. The reciprocal of the slope, $\Delta Q_x/\Delta P_x$, which enters the elasticity calculation, is therefore $-8/5$, or -1.6.

For the value of price elasticity to be equal to -1, and given $\Delta Q_x/\Delta P_x = -8/5$, the other half of the elasticity formula, the price-quantity ratio, must equal $5/8$. The *only* pair of price-quantity observations on this demand curve having the ratio $5/8$ is the mid-

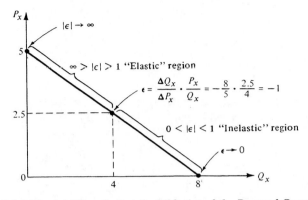

FIGURE 4-5.   *Price Elasticity Equals 1 at the Midpoint of the Demand Curve*

point combination $P_x = 2.50$ and $Q_x = 4$. Thus elasticity is equal to -1 at the midpoint of the demand curve.[9]

- NOTE: Thus price elasticity ranges from -1 to minus infinity above the midpoint and from -1 to zero below the midpoint. By convention, we say demand is *elastic* when ϵ is greater than 1 and it is *inelastic* when ϵ is less than 1 (in absolute terms). At the midpoint there is *unitary* elasticity. The knowledge that the midpoint divides the demand curve into these two ranges of elasticity is quite useful since we can, by inspection of any point on a demand curve, immediately conclude whether its elasticity exceeds, is equal to, or is less than 1. This, in turn, conveys useful information to us about the behavior of total and marginal revenues.

Price Elasticity, Marginal Revenue, and Total Revenue

We first examine the relationship between price elasticity and marginal revenue. Since the MR curve begins at the same intercept on the price axis as the demand curve but has twice the slope of the demand curve, it must intersect the quantity axis in half the horizontal distance as compared to the demand curve. Thus, in terms of Figure 4-5, the marginal revenue curve must pass through the point where $Q_x = 4$. It is therefore apparent that the marginal revenue is negative when elasticity is less than unity.

Now consider the relationship between price elasticity of demand and total revenue. Note that, as shown in Figure 4-4, when marginal revenue is positive (that is, when elasticity exceeds unity), total revenue increases for successive increases in quantity; and when marginal revenue is negative (that is, when elasticity is less than unity), total revenue decreases for successive increases in quantities. In Table 4-3 we summarize what

---

[9] That the coordinates $P_x = 2.50$ and $Q_x = 4$ are the midpoint of the demand curve can be proven using congruent triangles. Since the demand curve is a straight line and the axes form a right angle, the midpoint values of price and quantity will be precisely half of the price and quantity intercept values.

TABLE 4-3. Relationship between Price Elasticity and Total Revenue

Elasticity Value	Price Increases	Price Decreases
$\infty > |\epsilon| > 1$	TR falls	TR rises
$\infty > |\epsilon| = 1$	TR constant	TR constant
$0 < |\epsilon| < 1$	TR rises	TR falls

happens to total revenue for price changes when elasticity is greater than 1, equal to 1, and less than 1.

The relationship between price changes, price elasticity, and the change in total revenue should be intuitively obvious when one recalls our initial definition of price elasticity. We defined it as the percentage change in quantity demanded divided by the percentage change in the price. Thus, elasticity exceeds unity when the percentage change in quantity exceeds the percentage change in price. Hence it should be obvious that if, for example, a price is raised by 10% and the quantity demanded falls by 15%, total revenue must fall since the reduction in quantity demanded is proportionately greater than the increase in the price level. The extra revenue per unit from the quantity actually sold is outweighed by the loss of the revenue from the units that were previously being sold but that are not now being sold.

Point versus Arc Elasticity

We distinguish between *point* elasticity of demand and *arc* elasticity of demand on the basis of the size of the change in price and quantity represented by Δ in the preceding elaboration of the elasticity concept. We use point elasticity when the changes in price and quantity are infinitesimally small, since such a small price change represents a virtual point on the demand curve. For more substantial price changes we speak of arc elasticity, since we are considering a discrete movement along, or an arc of, the demand curve.

For point price elasticity, the formula is modified to read

$$\epsilon = \frac{dQ_x}{dP_x} \cdot \frac{P_x}{Q_x} \tag{4-16}$$

where the letter d is substituted for Δ to reflect the infinitesimally small changes in the variables P_x and Q_x.

Point price elasticity is the appropriate concept for finding the elasticity value at a particular price level if the demand curve is *known*. That is, if you already know the slope of the demand curve, you simply weight the reciprocal of that slope by the appropriate price-quantity ratio to find the elasticity.

In the example introduced earlier, we found that when $P_x = \$8.00$, $Q_x = 22,879.1$. So what is the price elasticity at this point on the demand curve? Using the formula for point price elasticity, equation (4-16), we insert the known values for P_x and

Q_x and recall that dQ_x/dP_x is the reciprocal of b, the slope of the demand curve. From equation (4-9) we know $b = -0.26273$. Thus,

$$\epsilon = \frac{1}{-0.26273} \cdot \frac{8}{22,879.1} = -1.33$$

Thus demand is elastic at the price of $8, meaning total revenue would increase if price were reduced or would decrease if price were raised. (Alternatively, we could have multiplied the dQ_x/dP_x term, which was given in the initial estimate of the demand function as $\beta_1 = -3,806.2$, by the price-quantity ratio to arrive at the same value for point price elasticity.)

In real market situations a firm will know its present price-quantity coordinate but may not know how its demand curve slopes through that point. To find out, the firm must change the price and see what happens to the quantity demanded. But infinitesimally small price changes are not likely to attract the attention of consumers in the marketplace: *Discrete* price changes, or significant and noticeable movements of the price level, are necessary to overcome consumer thresholds of price awareness. Thus the $\Delta Q_x/\Delta P_x$ data that we can obtain will have Δs that are relatively large, as compared with the infinitesimally small changes in price and quantity that are required for the point elasticity formula.

- DEFINITION: *Arc price elasticity* is defined as the relative responsiveness of quantity demanded to a *discrete* change in price, whereas point price elasticity is defined as the relative responsiveness of quantity demanded to an *infinitesimal* change in price.

- EXAMPLE: Suppose a small store has been selling hanging flowerpots over the last few months at a price of $8 per unit and sales have stabilized at about 32 units per week. The store manager now reduces the price of those flowerpots to $7 per unit and after a couple of weeks finds that sales have stabilized at a new level of 44 units per week. If all other factors entering the demand function have remained constant, we expect that the two price-quantity combinations above are points on the demand curve for those flowerpots.

The store manager can estimate the $\Delta Q_x/\Delta P_x$ term required for the elasticity calculation as follows:

$$\frac{\Delta Q_x}{\Delta P_x} = \frac{Q_1 - Q_2}{P_1 - P_2} \tag{4-17}$$

where the subscripts refer to the sequence of the observations. Substituting for the two price and quantity observations, we have

$$\frac{\Delta Q_x}{\Delta P_x} = \frac{32 - 44}{8 - 7} = \frac{-12}{1}$$

Given this estimate of the $\Delta Q_x / \Delta P_x$ value, we can conclude that point price elasticity at $P_x = \$8.00$ and $Q_x = 32$ is $(-12/1 \times 8/32 =) -3.00$, while at $P_x = \$7.00$ and $Q_x = 44$ point price elasticity is $(-12/1 \times 7/44 =) -1.9091$. As we should expect, the point price elasticity is lower for the lower price, because it represents a point further down the demand curve. Thus, the point elasticity formula has provided us with two different figures for the responsiveness of quantity demanded to the same change in the price level, depending on which price-quantity combination we use as the reference point.

Arc elasticity, on the other hand, is designed to provide a *summary measure* of price elasticity over the range of prices between $7.00 and $8.00 per unity. For the arc elasticity calculation, we weight the $\Delta Q_x / \Delta P_x$ term by the average price and average quantity demanded. That is,[10]

$$\epsilon_{arc} = \frac{\Delta Q_x}{\Delta P_x} \cdot \frac{(P_1 + P_2)/2}{(Q_1 + Q_2)/2}$$

Substituting for ΔQ_x and ΔP_x from equation (4-17) and allowing the 2s to cancel out, we have

$$\epsilon_{arc} = \frac{Q_1 - Q_2}{P_1 - P_2} \cdot \frac{P_1 + P_2}{Q_1 + Q_2} \tag{4-18}$$

Inserting the values for P_1, P_2, Q_1, and Q_2 into equation (4-18), we find

$$\epsilon_{arc} = \frac{32 - 44}{8 - 7} \cdot \frac{8 + 7}{32 - 44} = \frac{-12}{1} \cdot \frac{15}{76} = -2.368$$

Note that the arc elasticity value lies *between* the two point elasticities calculated earlier. We should expect this, since the arc elasticity is, in fact, the point elasticity at the midpoint of the arc. As such, it is a better *summary measure* of the elasticity over the arc than is either point elasticity, which represents the extreme values on that arc. The arc elasticity value becomes progressively less accurate as we move toward the end of the arc, but the degree of inaccuracy is much less than the value given by the point elasticity at the *other* end of the arc.

---

[10]We choose the average price and quantities as the weights to calculate arc elasticity because these represent the midpoint of the arc. The midpoint values of price and quantity minimize the variance from all other price and quantity points on the arc, as compared to any other point on the arc. Other formulas have been suggested for elasticity, such as using the new price and the old quantity or the old price and the new quantity. These formulations are inferior, since they base the elasticity calculation on a combination of P and Q which does not lie on the demand curve.

Implications for Optimal Prices

Having obtained an estimate of the slope of this demand curve, what can the manager do with this information? He or she can derive an expression for the demand curve for flowerpots and check whether or not the present price level is profit maximizing.

We know that the firm's demand curve is of the form $P_x = a + bQ_x$, that P_x is currently \$7.00, Q_x is currently 44 units, and that $b = -12/1$. Only a, the intercept value, remains to be found. Substituting the known values into the demand curve expression, we have

$$7 = a - 0.08333(44)$$

Solving for a, we find $a = 10.6667$. The expression for the firm's demand curve is therefore

$$P_x = 10.6667 - 0.08333Q_x$$

The marginal revenue expression (with the same intercept and twice the slope) is therefore

$$MR = 10.6667 - 0.16667Q_x$$

Profit maximization requires MC = MR. Let us assume that marginal costs are constant at \$5.00 per unit regardless of output levels. Setting MC = MR = \$5.00 and solving for Q_x, we find:

$$5 = 10.6667 - 0.16667Q_x$$

and hence

$$Q_x = 34$$

This is the profit-maximizing output level where MC = MR. To find the profit-maximizing price, we substitute the profit-maximizing output of 34 for Q_x in the demand curve expression:

$$\begin{aligned} P_x &= 10.6667 - 0.08333(34) \\ &= 10.6667 - 2.8333 \\ &= 7.8333 \end{aligned}$$

Thus the profit-maximizing price is \$7.83 per unit, rather than the current \$7.00.

Now suppose instead that the manager wants to maximize total revenue from the sale of the flowerpots. What price level would serve this objective? To maximize total revenue, we know that marginal revenue must fall to zero. (See Figure 4-4.) Setting the expression for MR (obtained above) equal to zero and solving for Q_x, we find

$$0 = 10.6667 - 0.16667Q_x$$

hence

$$Q_x = \frac{10.6667}{0.16667}$$
$$= 64.00$$

Substituting for $Q_x = 64$ in the demand curve expression, we find

$$P_x = 10.6667 - 0.08333(64)$$
$$= 5.333$$

Thus the revenue-maximizing price is $5.33, at which 64 units of the flowerpot are expected to be sold. We can verify this by observing that this price-quantity combination represents the midpoint of the demand curve. The price, $5.33, is halfway to the intercept on the price axis, and the quantity, 64 units, is halfway to the intercept on the horizontal axis ($Q_x = 128.00$ when $P_x = 0$).

The *A Priori* Guesstimation of Price Elasticity

The theory of consumer behavior points to the following two factors as the major determinants of the value of price elasticity:

1. The substitutability of the product.
2. The relative expense of the product.

We saw in the Chapter 3 that the substitution effect of a price change is always negative; that is, a price change in one direction will lead to a quantity-demanded response in the opposite direction. This substitution effect is the result of consumers' seeking alternative means of satisfying a particular desire by switching to an available substitute product. Thus, the greater the number of substitute products and the more closely substitutable those products are, the more we would expect consumers to switch away from a particular product when its price rose (or toward that product when its price fell.) Thus the more substitutes there are, and the more closely these substitutes resemble the product in question, the greater we expect the price elasticity of demand to be.[11]

---

[11]A feature of products that is related to this substitutability is their versatility, or the number of uses to which they may be put. A product is more versatile if it can serve two or more purposes rather than only one purpose. A *more versatile* product is likely to be *less substitutable*, since it may require two or more other

We must distinguish between substitutability of products from within the same group of products and substitutability with goods from other groups of products. For example, coffee is a group of products in the larger family of beverages; but within the product group there are many different brands and types of coffee. If we are concerned with the price elasticity of a particular brand of coffee, such as Maxwell House, and the prices of all other coffees and other beverages remain unchanged, we should expect the price elasticity for Maxwell House coffee to be relatively high. On the other hand, if all coffee prices were likely to rise in unison (due to an increase in the cost of imported coffee beans, for example), there would be little or no substitutability between or among coffee brands, but there would be some substitution away from coffee toward other beverages. Therefore, in the case where all close substitutes are expected to follow a similar price strategy, we expect the price elasticity to be somewhat lower, since the substitutability will be toward only the more distant substitutes.

The relative expense of the product as a determinant of price elasticity is related to the income effect of a price change. We argued in Chapter 3 that when the price of a product is increased, for example, the consumer suffers a loss in real income. The consumer is then able to buy less of all products, including the product for which the price has risen. The larger the fraction of the consumer's budget that the product's price represents, the larger will be the impact on the consumer's real income level of a change in that product's price. For example, a 10% change in the price of an automobile would cause the consumer's real income to be changed considerably, whereas a 10% change in the price of bread would have a minimal impact.

Now let's try some elasticity guesstimation. Consider kitchen salt. In view of these factors influencing price elasticity, would you expect its price elasticity to be high or low? Salt has few close substitutes for its kitchen uses, and the proportion of the consumer's income spent on salt is always very low. Thus both the substitutability and the relative expense factors militate in favor of salt having a relatively low price elasticity of demand. On the other hand, consider the demand for a particular automobile, such as the Saturn. There are numerous substitute automobiles, many of them quite close substitutes while others are more distant substitutes. The proportion of the consumer's income that is involved in the purchase of an automobile is typically high. Hence, both determinants militate in favor of the price elasticity for a particular automobile being quite high. If the price of all automobiles rises simultaneously, such as might follow a new wage agreement with the automobile workers, the elasticity of demand faced by the Saturn will be somewhat lower, since the substitutability toward other products is limited to the more distant substitutes such as secondhand cars, mass transit, bicycles, and walking.

In some cases the substitutability of a product will indicate high price elasticity, while the relative expense will indicate low price elasticity, or vice versa. Guesstimation of the value of price elasticity must then proceed on the basis of judgment about which factor will be stronger, if a decision must be made immediately. If the decision can be delayed, research into the nature of the demand function and its elasticities should be

products to serve the purposes of the more versatile product. Hence, the more versatile the product is, the less sensitive to price changes its demand is likely to be, and vice versa.

undertaken. This is the subject of the following chapter. We now turn to some other important elasticity measures.

4.3 INCOME ELASTICITY OF DEMAND

• DEFINITION: The *income elasticity* of demand may be defined as the percentage change in quantity demanded divided by the percentage change in consumer income, *ceteris paribus*. That is,

$$\Theta = \%\Delta Q_x / \%\Delta I \tag{4-19}$$

where Θ (the Greek letter theta) is the conventional symbol for income elasticity and I is the consumer's income, or budget constraint.

Expressing this in terms of proportionate changes, as in the earlier discussion of price elasticity, we have

$$\Theta = \frac{dQ_x}{dI} \cdot \frac{I}{Q_x} \tag{4-20}$$

Notice that the size of dQ_x/dI is undefined as yet. If we knew the relationship between income and quantity demanded of product X (from regression analysis of the demand function), we could calculate *point* income elasticity by substituting (for dQ_x/dI) the coefficient to consumer incomes in the demand function. If, on the other hand, we need to observe a discrete income change to ascertain the effect on Q_x, we would find the *arc* income elasticity as follows:

$$\Theta = \frac{Q_1 - Q_2}{I_1 - I_2} \cdot \frac{I_1 + I_2}{Q_1 - Q_2} \tag{4-21}$$

where the subscripts reflect the sequence of the observations of the two quantity and income levels.

Earlier in the chapter, in equation (4-3), we had estimated a demand function as

$$Q_x = 5,030 - 3,806.2P_x + 1,458.5P_y + 256.6A_x - 32.3A_y + 0.18I_c$$

where the variable I_c represented the average disposable income of consumers or some other measure of spending power, such as gross national product (GNP) per capita. Note that the coefficient to the income term in the demand function, 0.18, represents the dQ_x/dI term we need to calculate the income elasticity. Given our knowledge of the current value of I_c, which we said was \$12,875, and the current value of Q_x, which we calculated to be 22,879.1, the point income elasticity using equation (4-20) is

$$\Theta = 0.18(12,875)/(22,879.1) = 0.101$$

As an example of *arc* elasticity, suppose that in a different situation per capita disposable income is \$15,650 and that the quantity demanded of stereo amplifiers is 36,000 per month. Now suppose that (real) per capita disposable income rises to \$17,215 because of cuts in personal income taxes. As a result (with *ceteris paribus*), we observe an increase in the quantity demanded of stereo amplifiers to 40,320 units per month. Using equation (4-21) for the arc income elasticity calculation, we find

$$\Theta = \frac{36,000 - 40,320}{15,675 + 17,215} \cdot \frac{15,675 + 17,215}{36,000 - 40,320} = 1.189$$

What do these numbers mean? The income elasticity of demand allows us to classify products as either luxuries, necessities, or inferior goods and gives insights into the direction and magnitude of the shift of the demand curve that will follow changes in consumer incomes.

Luxuries, Necessities, and Inferior Goods

- DEFINITION: *Luxuries* are products for which the proportionate change in quantity demanded is greater than the proportionate change in consumer income levels; income elasticity for luxuries is, therefore, positive and greater than unity.

The arc elasticity calculation in the preceding section indicates that stereo amplifiers are luxury goods, since $\Theta = 1.189$. Other examples of luxury goods are items such as fur coats, travel by air, and the use of hotel accommodations. Note that *luxury good* is now a definitional term, a piece of our jargon with a special meaning. In common usage you might refer to something as a luxury, but here the connotation is that it is a product whose quantity demanded responds more than proportionately to changes in consumer incomes.

Graphically, the impact of a change in consumer incomes is reflected by a *shift* of the demand curve for product X. Recall that the quantity demanded of product X that is caused by the income variable becomes part of the intercept term of the demand curve. If consumer incomes change, the intercept term of the demand curve changes, and we must have a shift of the demand curve. In Figure 4-6 we show that the demand curve for the luxury good has shifted from D to D' as a result of an assumed increase in consumer incomes.

- DEFINITION: *Necessities* are products which have an income elasticity of demand which is positive but less than 1. This means that the quantity demanded increases as income increases but that the change in Q_x is less than proportionate to the change in income. The first example calculated above is, therefore, classified as a necessity good, since its income elasticity is 0.101. In this example, if income changed by 10%, we

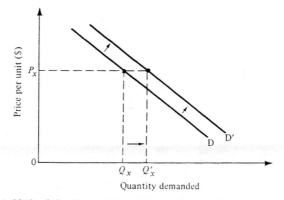

FIGURE 4-6. **A Shift of the Demand Curve for a Luxury Good, Given an Increase in Income**

would expect Q_x to change by only 1.01%. Examples of necessities are some foodstuffs and items of clothing.

Graphically, the impact of an increase in income on the demand for a necessity good, given *ceteris paribus*, can also be shown as a shift outward of the demand curve. The extent of the outward shift will be less than for a luxury good, of course, since the demand for necessities is less responsive to changes in income than it is for luxury goods. Note that both luxuries and necessities exhibit a positive income effect, and in Chapter 3 we called them superior (or normal) goods. In fact, we have now divided superior goods into two subclasses, luxuries and necessities, depending on whether the demand for these items responds more or less than proportionally to changes in income.

• DEFINITION: *Inferior goods* are products which exhibit a negative income effect and, consequently, have negative income elasticity. The quantity demanded of these products declines as real income levels rise. Conversely, if real income levels decline, the quantity demanded of an inferior good will increase. Examples of inferior goods may be items such as potatoes, baked beans, ground beef, bologna, low-quality clothing, and travel by train. As incomes rise, people tend to switch away from these items to more desirable substitutes. As incomes fall, people reluctantly switch away from the more desirable but typically more expensive substitutes and back to these cheaper but less desirable substitutes.

The shift of the demand curve for an inferior good will be in the opposite direction to the change in incomes. In Figure 4-7 we show the demand curve shifting back to the left, following an increase in consumer incomes. Consumers now buy *less* of this product than they did before, as a result of the increase in their incomes. The extent of the shift depends, of course, on the value of income elasticity: Small negative values mean small shifts to the left while relatively large negative income elasticities mean relatively large shifts to the left, in response to an increase in real incomes.

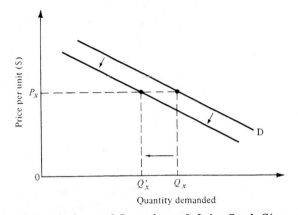

FIGURE 4-7. A Shift of the Demand Curve for an Inferior Good, Given an Increase in Income

Table 4-4 summarizes the relationships that are indicated by income elasticities that are greater than 1, between zero and 1, and less than zero.

Business Implications of Income Elasticity

The implications of income elasticity of demand to the business decision maker are considerable. If the income elasticity for your product exceeds unity, the demand for your product will grow more rapidly than does total consumer income, *and* it will fall more rapidly than does total consumer income when income levels are generally falling. Hence, while income elasticity greater than 1 in a growing economy indicates a growth industry, it also indicates a greater vulnerability to downturns in the level of aggregate economic activity. On the other hand, if the income elasticity of demand for your product is positive but less than 1, the demand for your product will grow more slowly than the gross national product or consumer income, but it will be relatively recession proof in the sense that the demand will not react in the volatile fashion of luxury goods. Third, if your product is regarded as an inferior good by the market as a whole, you must expect the quantity demanded of your product to decline as the gross national product rises, yet

TABLE 4-4. *Income Elasticity and Luxuries, Necessities, and Inferior Goods*

Income Elasticity	Product Class	Increased Income	Decreased Income
$\infty > \theta > 1$	Luxuries	Q_x increases by greater percentage	Q_x decreases by greater percentage
$1 > \theta > 0$	Necessities	Q_x increases by lesser percentage	Q_x decreases by lesser percentage
$0 > \theta > -\infty$	Inferior goods	Q_x decreases	Q_x increases

increase during economic downturns. Good corporate and product planning would there-fore indicate the desirability of having all three types of products in your product mix.

4.4 CROSS ELASTICITIES AND OTHER ELASTICITIES

We now consider the responsiveness of quantity demanded of product X to changes in the prices of related products. *Related* products are either substitutes or complements. The cross elasticity of demand provides a measure of the degree of substitutability, or complementarity, between product X and some other product.[12]

Substitutes and Complements

* DEFINITION: *Cross elasticity of demand* is defined as the percentage change in quantity demanded of product X, divided by the percentage change in the price of some product Y. That is,

$$\eta = \%\Delta Q_x / \%\Delta P_y \tag{4-22}$$

where η (the Greek letter eta) is the conventional symbol for cross elasticity.

Following our earlier analysis, we can restate this as a *point* cross elasticity mea-sure, as follows:

$$\eta = \frac{dQ_x}{dP_y} \cdot \frac{P_y}{Q_x} \tag{4-23}$$

In practice it may be necessary to have a significant change in P_y before an impact is noticed on Q_x. In this case, we would use the *arc* cross elasticity formula, as follows:

$$\eta = \frac{Q_1 - Q_2}{P_1 - P_2} \cdot \frac{P_1 + P_2}{Q_1 - Q_2} \tag{4-24}$$

Note that the Q symbols refer to Q_x, the P symbols refer to P_y, and the subscripts reflect the sequence of the data collection.

From the estimated demand function introduced earlier (equation 4-3), we can cal-culate the point cross elasticity of demand between products X and Y, because the term dQ_x/dP_y has already been estimated. It is, of course, the coefffcient to the term P_y in the

---

[12]Cross-elasticity is the abbreviated name for cross-price elasticity, since we are concerned with the impact of a change in P_y on Q_x. Given that product Y is a substitute, we should also expect a cross-*advertising* elasticity, for example, indicating the impact of a change in Y's advertising efforts on Q_x. By convention, cross elasticity means cross-price elasticity unless specifically noted otherwise.

demand function for Q_x and was 1,458.5. Using equation (4-23) and substituting for variables P_y and Q_x, we have

$$\eta = 1,485.5(6)/(22,879.1) = 0.382$$

What does this number tell us? It says that for a 1% change in the price of product Y, the quantity demanded of product X will change by 0.382%. Note that the changes will be in the same direction since the sign of the cross elasticity is positive. The positive sign indicates that there is a movement of consumers from product Y as its price rises across to product X, given *ceteris paribus*, and that, hence, products X and Y must be substitutes for each other.

- DEFINITION: *Substitutes* are pairs of products between which the cross elasticity of demand is positive. Suppose that the price of product Y is reduced from $10 to $9 and that this reduction induces a change in the quantity demanded of product X from 100 units to 85 units, as shown in Figure 4-8. Since these are discrete price changes, the arc cross elasticity formula is appropriate. Inserting these values into equation (4-24), we see that the cross elasticity between product X and product Y is

$$\eta = \frac{100 - 85}{10 - 9} \cdot \frac{10 + 9}{100 + 85} = 1.54$$

In terms of Figure 4-8, it is clear that products X and Y must be substitutes for each other, since when the price of product Y was reduced the quantity demanded of product X was reduced from 100 units back to 85 units. Given *ceteris paribus*, the gain of quantity demanded for product Y must have been at the expense of the demand for product X. Recall that the price of product Y enters the demand function for product X as a shift parameter; a reduction in the price of product Y would cause the demand curve for product X to shift to the left, such that at price P_x the quantity demanded for product X would be somewhat less. Examples of a pair of substitute products include the product groups of tea and coffee, or pairs of product within either of these groups, such as Maxwell House coffee and Yuban coffee.

- DEFINITION: *Complements* are pairs of products between which the cross elasticity of demand is negative. Suppose that a 10% price reduction for product Y leads to a 20% increase in demand for product X. For example, P_y falls from $1.00 to $0.90 and Q_x increases from 100 units to 120 units. The cross elasticity is

$$\eta = \frac{100 - 120}{1.00 - 0.90} \cdot \frac{1.00 + 0.90}{100 + 120} = -1.73$$

This situation is illustrated in Figure 4-9. In this case the fall in P_y, while accompanied by an increase in the quantity demanded for product Y, also coincided with an

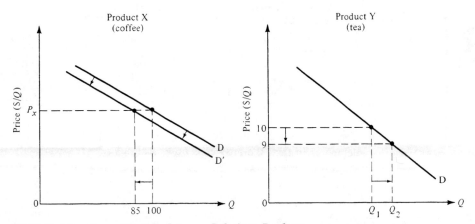

FIGURE 4-8. *Cross Elasticity between Substitute Products*

increase in the demand for product X. Given *ceteris paribus*, it is clear that the increase in consumption of product Y called forth an increase in the consumption of product X. Hence, products X and Y are apparently used jointly in consumption, perhaps in some predetermined ratio. Examples of products with negative cross elasticity are coffee and cream, beer and pretzels, and gasoline and tires.

Of course, a change in the price of one product may have zero or minimal impact on the demand for another product. In this case we conclude that these products are unrelated in consumption. That is, products X and Y are neither substitutes nor complements if their cross elasticity is zero or close to zero. Table 4-5 summarizes the cross-elasticity relationships that may exist between the two products under examination.

What level of cross elasticity indicates a pair of strong substitutes, as compared with weak substitutes? Alternatively, how large and negative must the cross-elasticity

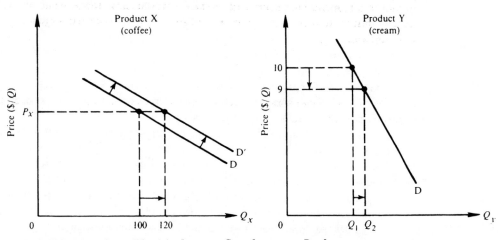

FIGURE 4-9. *Cross Elasticity between Complementary Products*

TABLE 4-5. Substitutes, Complements, and Cross Elasticities of Demand

Cross Elasticity	Relationship	Increase in P_y	Decrease in P_y
$\infty > \eta > 0$	Substitutes	Q_x rises	Q_x falls
$\eta \approx 0$	Unrelated	Q_x unchanged	Q_x unchanged
$0 > \eta > -\infty$	Complements	Q_x falls	Q_x rises

value be before we decide that the products are strong complements rather than simply weak complements? In fact, the answer is quite arbitrary. A cross-elasticity value of 1 will mean that a competitor's price adjustment will have a significant impact on your quantity demanded, but whether we would call this a strong or a weak relationship is essentially a matter of taste. Certainly if another product shared a cross elasticity of 5 with your product, for example, we would be able to say that the latter product is a *stronger* substitute for your product than is the former product.

Advertising and Cross-Advertising Elasticities

We know from the demand function that the quantity demanded of product X will typically show a positive response to the advertising in support of product X, a negative response to the advertising of substitutes, and a positive response to the advertising of complements.

The advertising elasticity of demand for product X measures the responsiveness of the change in quantity demanded to a change in the advertising budget for product X. We expect a positive relationship between advertising and quantity demanded, but we also expect that the responsiveness of sales to advertising will decline as advertising expenditure continues to increase. If advertising expenditure is not to be carried beyond the optimal level, there will be a lower limit on the value of the advertising elasticity. We defer this issue until Chapter 13, where we will see that the critical value of advertising expenditure (and hence advertising elasticity) depends on the profit contribution expected from each additional unit sold as a result of the advertising.

Cross-advertising elasticity of demand measures the responsiveness of quantity demanded of product X to a change in the advertising efforts directed at another product, Y. As indicated earlier, we expect cross-advertising elasticity to be negative between substitute products and positive between complementary products. For example, increased advertising efforts for a particular movie would be expected to reduce the quantity demanded of admission tickets to other movies and attractions but to increase the sales at the refreshment kiosk in the lobby of that particular movie theater. In effect, the increased advertising would have shifted the demand curves to the left for all substitute attractions, while shifting the demand curve to the right for the refreshment kiosk.

It is clear that we might calculate the elasticity of demand with respect to any of the independent variables in the demand function. Using the general concept of elasticities, we can construct the appropriate formula and measure and elasticity that may be useful for decision-making purposes.

The Value of Elasticities

Some would argue that the various elasticities of demand simply summarize information that is already known to the decision maker and that if one has the information necessary to calculate the elasticities of demand, the elasticity value is redundant. (In the case of price elasticity, for example, if one knows the two price and quantity coordinates, one can simply calculate the change in total revenue that results when moving from one coordinate to the other.) So the question arises, Why calculate elasticities?

Essentially the value of elasticities is twofold. First, they are useful summary measures which impart information about the impact of changes in variables on the firm's quantity demanded. The magnitude, and in some cases the sign, of the various elasticity measures says in the briefest way possible what there is to know about the relationship between the two variables. Second, by categorizing this relationship in terms of a single number, we are able to reduce a variety of relationships between products to a common denominator, such that we may rank the values of elasticity for comparison purposes. Hence, if product X is related to a number of other products, we might rank those other products in order of their cross elasticity with product X. Those with the highest value of cross elasticity would be the strongest substitutes, and those with the largest negative values would be the strongest complements.

Moreover, we shall see in Chapter 10 that the calculation of price elasticity facilitates selection of the optimal markup to be applied to unit costs to determine the profit-maximizing prices of various products. In fact, price elasticity provides the link between the pricing theory of economics and the pricing practice of the marketplace.

4.5 SUMMARY

In this chapter we examined the *demand function*, which expresses the dependence of the quantity demanded (or sales) of a particular product on a variety of independent variables. We considered the direction and magnitude of the impact these independent variables might have on the quantity demanded of a particular product. The *demand curve* was defined as a special case of the demand function when only price is variable, holding all other determinants of demand constant. When all other determinants remain constant and price changes, there is a movement *along* a particular demand curve. If any of the other factors (covered by the *ceteris paribus* assumption) do not remain constant, we must expect a *shift* of the demand curve, which will cause a different quantity to be demanded at the prevailing price level.

The relationship between price, quantity demanded, total revenue, and marginal revenue was examined, and it was determined that for any negatively sloping demand curve, total revenue would initially increase as a price is reduced but would later decline. Consequently, marginal revenue would initially be positive and later negative. Moreover, the marginal revenue curve would have the same intercept and twice the slope of the demand curve.

Several measures of the elasticity of quantity demanded were discussed. Price elasticity of demand is particularly useful for indicating the direction of change in total revenue when there is a change in price. Moreover, when a firm has several products, the relative price elasticities of these products will indicate which of these products can best sustain a price increase versus those for which a price increase would be a poor strategy. Income elasticity of demand is important for growth and stability considerations in the firm, since the demand for luxury products will tend to be relatively responsive to changes both up and down in the aggregate level of activity. Similarly, we argued that necessity goods are relatively recession proof and that inferior goods are expected to exhibit countercyclical demand patterns.

Cross elasticities of demand allow the summary and classification of the relationships existing between a particular product and all other products. The decision maker should be interested in knowing which of the other products on the market represent the most serious competition for his or her products. Similarly, negative values of cross elasticity indicate product complementarity and the relative strength of this complementarity.

The concepts and principles outlined in this chapter will be called on in subsequent chapters. Pricing the firm's product requires a strong knowledge of the demand conditions existing in a particular market, and an understanding of the responsiveness of demand to the various factors that influence that demand is therefore of considerable importance.

DISCUSSION QUESTIONS

4-1. Which factors do you think should be held constant in a discussion about the demand curve for season tickets to the home games of a National Football League team?

4-2. What is the relationship between the coefficient of price in the demand function and the slope term in the demand curve? Explain.

4-3. Set up a matrix with $\epsilon > 1$, $\epsilon = 1$, $\epsilon < 1$ down the left-hand side and "TR increases" and "TR decreases" across the top. Fill in the six parts of the matrix to indicate whether there is an increase or a decrease in the price level.

4-4. Summarize the methodological error and the resultant overestimate or underestimate that is involved when the point elasticity formula is used to calculate elasticity from observations of discrete price and quantity changes.

4-5. Explain how you could calculate the price elasticity at any particular price if you know the parameter values in the mathematical expression for a particular demand curve.

4-6. Classify the probable price elasticity value of the following products as either relatively high or relatively low:
(a) soft drinks
(b) Coca-Cola
(c) Diet Pepsi
(d) compact automobiles
(e) Levi's jeans

4-7. Explain how you would derive the demand curve for a particular product X, given the information that $P_x = \$4.50$; $Q_x = 25$; and price elasticity of demand is -1.5.

4-8. Explain why you would expect the demand for luxury goods such as fur coats and jewelry to be more volatile in periods of fluctuating incomes as compared with items such as groceries and meat.

4-9. How would you explain a situation in which two products have both a positive cross-price elasticity of demand and a positive cross-advertising elasticity of demand?

4-10. Define the rainfall elasticity of demand for umbrellas, using your knowledge of the elasticity concept. What possible usefulness could such an elasticity have?

PROBLEMS AND SHORT CASES

4-1. The Silverstein Coffee Company faces the following demand schedule in the relevant price range for one of its products.

Price (lb)	Quantity Demanded (lb/wk)
$5.00	970
4.95	1,000
4.90	1,026
4.85	1,049
4.80	1,071
4.75	1,085
4.70	1,095
4.65	1,105
4.60	1,114
4.55	1,122

(a) Plot the associated demand curve, marginal revenue curve, and total revenue curve on a graph.
(b) Calculate the price elasticity for each price change.
(c) Over what range is demand (1) elastic, (2) inelastic, (3) unitary elastic?

4-2. Billabong Boomerangs, Inc., and Swahili Spears are direct competitors in the fast-growing segment of the hunters' equipment market. Because of recent intense competition, both companies have redeveloped their main product, requiring the users' skills to be less developed than before and thus avoiding extensive field trips by company representatives for on-the-job training. This also reduced the need for costly instruction manuals. Stephen Pesner, president of Billabong Boomerangs, has decided to hire a local market research company to assist his company in planning its strategy. After extensive research using modern methods of data collection and statistical analysis, the researchers came up with Billabong's demand function:

$$Q_b = -1,700P_b + 750Y_h + 350A_b - 250A_s + 1,585P_s + 1.05H + 7.25W$$

where Q_b is the quantity demanded of boomerangs; P_b is the price of boomerangs; Y_h is the average income of hunters (in thousands); A_b is the advertising budget for Billabong Boomerangs (in thousands); A_s is the advertising budget for Swahili Spears (in thousands); P_s is the price of spears; H is the total number of hunters (in millions); and W is the estimated population of wildlife (in hundreds). The current values of the independent variables are P_b = 29.95; Y_h = 12.5; A_b = 680; A_s = 525; P_s = 32.25; H = 24.68; and W = 8.75.

(a) What is the current level of demand for Billabong boomerangs?

(b) Calculate the values of price elasticity, cross-price elasticity, and advertising elasticity.

(c) Is the price of boomerangs too high or too low in view of Mr. Pesner's desire to maximize profits? Explain.

4-3. The demand function for Fritz Reinhart premium beer has been estimated as

$$Q_x = 37,986.5 - 4,476.9P_y + 2,994.2P_y + 668.2A_x - 849.7A_y$$

where Q_x is the demand for the Reinhart beer (in sixpacks); P_x is the price of the Reinhart beer (in dollars); P_y is the price of the main rival beer (in dollars); A_x is the advertising expenditure for Reinhart ($000); and A_y is the expenditure for the rival beer ($000). The current values of the independent variables are P_x = 9.95; P_y = 8.95; A_x = 36; and A_y = 22.

(a) Calculate the price elasticity of demand for Reinhart beer.

(b) Calculate the cross-price elasticity of demand for Reinhart beer.

(c) If the marginal cost of producing Reinhart beer is constant at $4.00 per sixpack, should the firm change its price to maximize profits? Explain.

(d) Suppose instead that the Reinhart company wishes to maximize sales revenue from this beer. What price should it set?

4-4. The demand function for Crispie Chips has been estimated as follows:

$$Q_x = - 27.6887 + 0.2315A_x + 44.1177P_s - 37.73585P_x$$

where Q_x represents thousands of packets of chips; A_x is thousands of advertising dollars; P_s is the average price of substitute-brand chips; and P_x is the price of Crispie Chips (all prices in dollars per packet). The current values of the independent variables are A_x = 216.0; P_s = 0.85; and P_x = 0.79.

(a) What is the price elasticity of demand at the current price level? Explain what this value implies.

(b) Derive an expression for the demand curve from an estimated demand function.

(c) Supposing that marginal costs are constant at $0.19 per unit, what is the profit-maximizing price for Crispie Chips?

(d) What is the sales-revenue-maximizing price for Crispie Chips?

(e) Explain in detail the assumptions and qualifications which underlie your price and output predictions.

4-5. The Belcher Brewing Company has undertaken market research for the purpose of ascertaining the responsiveness of consumers to changes in the price level for their premium beer. Analysis of results has led to the following estimate of the demand relation:

$$Q = 15.996 - 1.47297P$$

where Q represents thousands of cases of one dozen bottles and P represents the price per case in dollars. Belcher's present price is $5.95 per case at the retail level, and the marginal cost of production is $3.00 per case regardless of volume (within the foreseeable range of possible volumes).

(a) What is the price elasticity of demand at the current price level? Comment on this figure.

(b) Express the demand relation in terms of a conventional demand curve.

(c) Is the current price profit maximizing? If not, what is the profit-maximizing price?

(d) What is the total revenue-maximizing price?

(e) State explicitly all assumptions and qualifications which underlie your answers.

4-6. The Gutowski Grocery Company markets a brand of a particular food item for which there are a number of reasonably similar substitutes. The company has been subject to a series of cost increases recently but feels that the present level of costs is expected to continue in the near future. These recent cost increases have caused the monthly profit to fall below the target of $15,000, and management feels that this target could be attained if the price were reduced to $3.99 per unit, presuming that rivals are unlikely to retaliate. Average variable costs are constant up to the maximum output level of 120,000 units. The following data refer to this month's operations:

Variable costs per unit	$2.74
Fixed costs per unit	1.57
Price per unit	4.45
Total profit for month	$11,431.28

(a) What is the price elasticity of demand for the product in the vicinity of the present and contemplated price levels?

(b) Find the profit-maximizing price and the maximum profit level. (Show all calculations and defend your methodology.)

(c) What qualifications and assumptions underlie your analysis?

4-7. The Thompson Textile Company has asked you for advice about the optimality of its pricing policy with respect to one of its products, product X. The following data are supplied:

Sales (units)	282,500
Price per unit	$2.00
Marginal cost per unit is constant at	$1.00
Price elasticity of demand	-3.25

(a) Is the present price level optimal if the firm wishes to maximize profits? If not, can you say what price it should charge?

(b) What is the sales-revenue-maximizing price for product X?

(c) Explain to the management of Thompson Textile Company the assumptions underlying your analysis and the sensitivity of your price recommendations to these assumptions.

4-8. The Bustraen Company is one of five firms that manufacture washing machines. The five firms are all about the same size, have approximately equal market shares, and produce very similar products. Bustraen sells approximately 200,000 washing machines per annum. The company has engaged a market research consultant to provide estimates of the price elasticity and cross elasticity of demand for its product. These estimates have just been received and are as follows: price elasticity of demand for Bustraen's washing machines, -1.85; cross elasticity of demand for Bustraen's washing machine, 0.45 vis-à-vis any one of the other firm's machines; and price elasticity of demand for all washing machines (if all prices changed together), -0.55.

(a) Explain what Bustraen should expect to happen to its sales if it were to raise prices by 10% and no other firm changed its price.

(b) Explain what Bustraen should expect to happen to its sales if one of its rivals were to raise its price by 10%, *ceteris paribus*.

(c) Explain what would happen if Bustraen raised its price 10% and all other firms did the same.

(d) What assumptions and qualifications underlie your analysis?

4-9. Paul McLaughlin recently purchased the MFF Company, a large company that specializes in the manufacture of minifreezers. Mr. McLaughlin has a reputation for revitalizing companies and reselling them, and he has purchased this company with the intention of holding onto it for a period of two years, after which he would sell the entire operation. The management of the MFF Company gave Mr. McLaughlin the following demand function for their product, which they said was based on a number of years of experience:

$$Q = 3,000 - 800P + 0.05A + 2Y$$

where Q represents the quantity demanded each quarter; P is the price; A represents advertising expenditures (dollars per quarter); and Y is personal disposable income per capita (dollars per annum). As Mr. McLaughlin's special consultant, you are faced with the following problems:

(a) Mr. McLaughlin wishes to maximize sales revenue. He informs you that he is allocating $23.5 million each quarter for advertising expenditures and that the estimated personal disposable income per capita is $11,000. To maximize his sales revenue, what price should be charged for his product, and how many minifreezers can he expect to sell at this price level? Illustrate this both mathematically and graphically.

(b) Alternatively, let us assume that Mr. McLaughlin had originally priced his product at $450 and had set his sales goal at 2 million minifreezers for the four quarters of the first year. Price ($450) and personal disposable income ($11,000) have remained constant throughout the first three quarters and are not expected to change during the fourth quarter. His advertising expenditures were as follows:

First quarter	$18,000,000
Second quarter	$15,000,000
Third quarter	$23,000,000

Given these figures, what should his advertising expenditures be for the fourth quarter so he will be able to reach his goal of 2 million products sold?

4-10. The Alpha Beta Company produces and sells toaster ovens. Mr. Learmonth has just been appointed marketing vice-president and is determined to be the first VP to guide the company past the million-dollar sales mark. To do so, ABC must average $84,000 per month for the last nine months of the year. Mr. Learmonth has been given a free hand to run the marketing side of ABC, subject to the following constraints:

1. Perceived social responsibilities dictate that ABC, as the town's largest employer, produce a minimum of 5,800 units per month to avoid layoffs. With overtime the plant can turn out a maximum of 8,100 units per month.

2. Budgetary considerations have limited increases in advertising to 15% above current monthly levels ($5,000). ABC has already contracted for a minimum of $5,000 per month with local media.

Mr. Learmonth's first move as VP was to have Econsult, a local marketing research firm, do some analytical work, and this company has developed the following normative model based on statistics supplied by Mr. Learmonth:

$$Q = 3,000 + 0.3A + 0.4Y - 300P$$

where Q represents the number of ovens demanded; A represents the monthly advertising expenditure; Y represents the per capita income; and P represents the selling price of the ovens. Current selling price is \$14, and current values of A and Y are \$5,000 and \$14,000, respectively. You have been asked to recommend a strategy for the remainder of the year. (Make any assumption required for the solution of the problem, indicating why they were made. Show all calculations.)

(a) What price level do you recommend?

(b) What do you recommend with regard to advertising?

(c) Calculate the income elasticity. What does this indicate about the nature of the product?

SUGGESTED REFERENCES AND FURTHER READING

FERGUSON, C. E., and S. C. MAURICE. *Economic Analysis; Theory and Application* (3rd ed.), chap. 2. Homewood, Ill.: Richard D. Irwin, Inc., 1978.

HIRSHLEIFER, J. *Price Theory and Applications* (4th ed.), chap. 5. Englewood Cliffs, N.J.: Prentice-Hall, Inc., 1988.

JOHNSON, A. C., JR., and P. HELMBURGER. "Price Elasticity of Demand as an Element of Market Structure," *American Economic Review,* December 1967, pp. 1218–21.

LEFTWICH, R. H. *The Price System and Resource Allocation* (7th ed.), chaps. 3, 5. Hinsdale, Ill.: The Dryden Press, 1979.

MANSFIELD, E. *Microeconomics* (5th ed.), chap. 5. New York: W.W. Norton & Co., Inc., 1985.

MARTIN, R. L. "Price Elasticity and a Shifting Demand Curve," *Economic Inquiry,* 17 (January 1979), pp. 153–54.

MILLER, R. L. *Intermediate Microeconomics*, chap. 5. New York: McGraw-Hill Book Company, 1978.

NICHOLSON, W. *Intermediate Microeconomics and Its Application* (2nd ed.), chaps. 4, 5. Hinsdale, Ill.: The Dryden Press, 1979.

OGAKI, MASAO, "The Indirect and Direct Substitution Effects," *American Economic Review,* 80 (December 1990), pp. 1271–75.

SIMON, H. "Dynamics of Price Elasticity and Brand Life Cycles: An Empirical Study," *Journal of Marketing Research*, 16 (November 1979), pp. 439–52.

THOMPSON, A. A., JR. *Economics of the Firm* (3rd ed.), chap. 5. Englewood Cliffs, N.J.: Prentice-Hall, Inc., 1981.

WAN, F. C. "Elasticities and Effects of Price Change on Revenue," *Atlantic Economic Journal,* 11 (September 1983), p. 115.

Empirical Case 2

DEMAND CURVES FOR THE SUZUKI SAMURAI

Suzuki Motor Co. enjoyed impressive sales growth of its Samurai model during its first three years in the U.S. However, during June of 1988, Consumers Union condemned the Samurai as ''not acceptable'' because of its alleged tendency to roll over during sudden turns.[1] As a result of this negative advertising and subsequent unfavorable reports both in the press and on television,[2] unit sales of the Samurai for the month of June plunged to 2,199, a 70.6% decline from May 1988 levels.

To counter the negative publicity, Suzuki mounted its own advertising campaign.[3] The company provided taped evidence suggesting that Consumers Union's results were suspect. Moreover, it was argued that safety was no more an issue for the Samurai than for other similar vehicles. As a consequence of this effective advertising, Samurai unit sales increased to 6,327 in the month of July.

Company officials believed that monthly unit sales could be further improved but that any such improvements would have to come through strategic price changes. During the latter part of July, Suzuki Samurai introduced $2,000 in dealer incentives, which allowed dealers to slash 25% from the Samurai's $7,995 base price. The result was dramatic, with unit sales totaling 12,208 for the month of August. According to Douglas Mazza, general manager of the automotive division of American Suzuki Motor Corp., ''Consumer confidence is back in the Samurai''.

1. List the sequence of events and the corresponding price-quantity relationship for the Samurai from May to August 1988.

2. From the information you obtained in question 1, graph the demand curve(s) faced by Suzuki for the period from May to August 1988.

3. Calculate and interpret an estimate of the price elasticity of demand for the Suzuki Samurai. Does this estimate make sense? Explain.

4. What assumptions, if any, did you make in arriving at your elasticity estimate?

5. From an economic perspective, do the nonprice and price strategies employed by Suzuki make sense? Explain.

---

[1]The test results were published in the July 1988 issue of *Consumer Reports*.

[2]Do you remember Ted Koppel's ''Nightline'' program showing the safety test results?

[3]An article entitled ''Suzuki Lashes Out at Samurai's Critics, Calling Testing of Vehicle Distorted'' appeared in the June 10, 1988 issue of the *Wall Street Journal*.

Chapter 5

ESTIMATION OF THE DEMAND FUNCTION

EXECUTIVE SUMMARY

This chapter examines **methods that are used to obtain demand data** for the solution of business decision problems. Given the prior expectation that the value of the information will exceed the search costs of obtaining that information, the decision maker can generate demand data using a variety of techniques from market research and statistical analysis.

Demand estimation means the process of finding *current* values for the coefficients in the demand function for a particular product, while **demand forecasting** means the process of finding values for demand in *future* time periods. Current values are necessary to evaluate the optimality of current pricing and promotional policies and to make day-to-day decisions in these strategy areas. Future values are necessary for planning production, inventories, new-product development, investment, and other situations where the decision to be made has impacts over a prolonged period of time. This chapter is confined to the issue of demand estimation. Demand forecasting, which often proceeds on the basis of demand estimation, is treated in the appendix to this chapter.

We consider direct methods of demand estimation, such as **interviews, surveys, and market experiments,** in which the potential buyer is asked questions about his or her reactions to hypothetical changes in price and other variables, or, alternatively, is observed reacting to changes in such variables. Indirect methods of demand estimation involve the statistical analysis of data to ascertain the impact of changes in determining variables on the quantity demanded. We introduce and discuss the use of **regression analysis** as a tool to quantify the dependence of quantity demanded on each of the determining variables in the demand function. Special attention is given to the interpretation of the regression results and the avoidance of the six major pitfalls of regression analysis.

5.1 INTRODUCTION TO DEMAND ESTIMATION

In Chapter 4 (equation 4-1) we considered the demand function in the form

$$Q_x = \alpha + \beta_1 P_x + \beta_2 P_y + \beta_3 A_x + \beta_4 A_y + \beta_5 I_c + \beta_6 T_c + \beta_7 E_c + \beta_8 N$$

where the demand for a product is expressed as a function of that product's own price, prices of related goods, advertising, consumer incomes, consumer tastes and expectations, and whatever other variables are thought to be important in determining the demand for a particular product.

The β coefficients represent the amount by which sales will be increased (or decreased) following a one-unit change in the value of each of the variables. The present level of each of the variables is known or can be found with some investigation. It is the coefficient to each of these variables that is the subject of the demand estimation exercise and that is important to us for decision making. That is, we wish to know what will happen to the sales level if we change a particular independent variable by a certain amount, holding all other variables constant. Stated from a more practical viewpoint, we wish to know whether or not a change in the value of any of these variables from their present levels would have a beneficial impact on the firm's profits, or net worth.

Of course, not all of these independent variables are *controllable*, in the sense that we have the ability to adjust their level. The controllable variables are price, promotional efforts, product design, and the place of sale, which may be known to you as the four Ps of marketing. The *uncontrollable* variables in the demand function are those that change independently of the firm's efforts, and they include such variables as consumer incomes, tastes and expectations, the actions of competitors, population, weather, and political, sporting, and social events or happenings. But even if the firm is unable to influence these variables, knowledge of the probable value of the coefficients is useful, since it reduces the uncertainty of the impact of changes in those variables. Given an expectation of the effect of increased consumer incomes, for example, the firm is able to plan more effectively its production, inventories, and new-product development, in view of expected changes in the affluence of consumers.

Direct versus Indirect Methods of Demand Estimation

Methods of estimating the values of these beta coefficients may be classified as either direct or indirect. *Direct* methods directly involve the consumer and include interviews and surveys, simulated market situations, and controlled market experiments. Consumers are either asked what their reactions would be to a particular change in a determining variable, or they are observed when actually reacting to a particular change. *Indirect* demand estimation uses data that have been collected and attempts to find statistical correlations between the dependent and the independent variables. You may have already encountered these statistical approaches in a quantitative methods or statistics course, and you may find that the direct methods of demand estimation are covered in more detail in a marketing research course. Here we confine ourselves to applying these methods to the problem of estimating the parameters of the demand function, and we refer the reader to the sources cited at the end of this chapter for more detailed treatments and other applications.

5.2 INTERVIEWS, SURVEYS, AND EXPERIMENTS

Interviews and Surveys

The most direct method of demand estimation is simply to ask buyers or potential buyers about their potential reactions to changes in the price or other determinants of their decision to buy the product. One might ask how much more or less they would purchase of a particular product if its price (or advertising, or one of the other independent variables) were varied by a certain amount. Focus groups may be assembled for such discussions, or questionnaires may be administered to a representative sample of buyers. Although seemingly simple, this approach is fraught with difficulties.

The first problem concerns the *randomness* of the sample. The individuals interviewed or surveyed must represent the market as a whole so the results will not be biased. Thus a sufficiently large sample, generated by random procedures, must be interviewed to form a reasonable and unbiased estimate of the market's reaction to a proposed change.

A second problem is *interviewer bias*, defined as the distortion of the interviewee's response caused by the presence of the interviewer. Where the true answer would make the respondent feel a little stupid, imply gluttony or drug dependence, expose the person as a tax cheat, or involve any other potential embarrassment, the respondent may give an incorrect answer to avoid the embarrassing moment. Interviewer bias will occur in personal interviews, telephone interviews, and even mailed-in questionnaires (because someone reads them). Telephone and mailed questionnaires avoid eye contact and lessen the potential embarrassment to a large extent, but at the same time the respondents may be less well chosen and their responses less well considered, as compared to personal interviews. Anonymity of respondents may reduce interviewer bias, but the lack of accountability may cause less thought to be given to the responses.

Third there is the *best of intentions* problem. The consumer may have truly intended to buy the product at the time of interview, but by the time the marketing strategy is implemented something may have intervened to change the consumer's mind. Other things may not stay equal long enough for the action to have the anticipated result.

Finally, the responses may be unreliable if any question is *confusing, misinterpreted,* or *unknowable* (if it involves things beyond the realm of the respondent's knowledge or imagination). New products, for example, when described briefly for the first time, cannot easily be pictured as part of the consumer's lifestyle. For example, early estimates of personal computer sales underestimated the dramatic growth of business demand for them in the early 1980s.

To combat these problems, a great deal of research has gone into the problems of questionnaire formulation to derive reliable results from interviews, surveys, and focus groups. Rather than asking questions directly, researchers may derive the answers to a specific question from the respondent's answer to a number of other questions. Reliability of responses to specific questions may be checked by asking the same questions in a different form at a later point during the interview or further down the questionnaire. The form of the question can influence the nature of the results: Open-ended questions allow the consumer to express in his or her own words what the response may be, while structured questions, such as multiple-choice questions where the respondent must use one of four or five specific responses, may suggest an answer to the consumer and may bias the results toward something the researcher expected to find. The choice of words is an important consideration, since nuances may be involved and some words have different meanings to different people. The questions must be sequenced in a way that creates and holds the subject's interest, provokes accurate responses, and does not create an emotional reaction that may influence subsequent answers or cause the respondent to refuse to continue.[1]

In summary, considerable care and thought must be invested in the construction of the questionnaire, and reasoned analysis must be involved in interpreting the results of the survey. Let us consider the results of a particular market survey.

- EXAMPLE: The Sylvain Leather Products Company intends to introduce a new wallet and wishes to estimate the demand curve for the new wallet. They have conducted a questionnaire survey of 1,000 people interviewed while shopping for goods of a similar nature. The interviewees were each asked whether they would actually purchase the new wallet at each of five price levels. For each price level, they were asked to choose one of the following six responses: a = definitely no; b = not likely; c = perhaps, maybe; d = quite likely; e = very likely; and f = definitely yes. The number of people responding in each category at each price level is shown in Table 5-1. The analysts have determined that the probabilities of actually buying the product for each of the six responses are 0.0 for response a; 0.2 for response b; 0.4 for response c; 0.6 for response d; 0.8 for response e; and 1.0 for response f.

TABLE 5-1. Sylvain Leather Products Company: Summary of Questionnaire Responses

Price ($)	NUMBER OF PEOPLE RESPONDING AS						Expected Quantity
	(a)	(b)	(c)	(d)	(e)	(f)	
9	500	300	125	50	25	0	160
8	300	225	175	150	100	50	335
7	100	150	250	250	150	100	500
6	50	100	100	300	250	200	640
5	0	25	50	225	300	400	800

---

[1]See, for example, P. E. Green and D. S. Tull, *Research for Marketing Decisions*, 3rd ed. (Englewood Cliffs, N.J.: Prentice-Hall, 1975), esp. chaps. 4 and 5; and D. J. Luck, H. G. Wales, and D. A. Taylor, *Marketing Research*, 4th ed. (Englewood Cliffs, N.J.: Prentice-Hall, 1974), esp. chaps. 9 and 10.

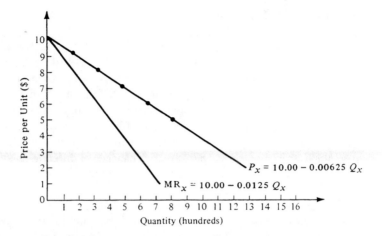

FIGURE 5-1. *Sylvain Leather Products Estimated Demand and Marginal Revenue Curves*

From these data, we can find the expected value of quantity demanded at each price level. At a price of $9, for example, the expected value of quantity demanded is the sum of the expected value of sales to each group of respondents. That is,

$$E(Q) = 500(0.0) + 300(0.2) + 125(0.4) + 50(0.6) + 25(0.8) + 0(1.0)$$
$$= 160 \text{ units}$$

Proceeding similarly, we can calculate the expected quantity demanded at prices of $8, $7, $6, and $5, as shown in Table 5-1. Plotting these price-quantity coordinates on a graph, as in Figure 5-1, we see that they trace out a demand curve which intercepts the price axis at approximately $10.00 and which has a slope of approximately $-5/800$, or -0.00625. This quick estimate of the slope is obtained by noting that as price falls from $10 to $5 (rise $= -5$), quantity demanded increases from zero to 800 units (run $= 800$). Thus the estimate of the demand curve is $P_x = 10.00 - 0.00625Q_x$. From this the firm can easily find $MR_x = 10.00 - 0.0125 Q_x$, since the marginal revenue curve has the same intercept and twice the slope as the demand curve.

- NOTE: This estimate of the demand curve relates to the *sample*, which is some small fraction of the total market for the product (the *population* of potential buyers). Thus, if only 1% of the population were sampled, the expected quantity demanded will be 100 times greater than for the sample. In effect, the demand curve shown in Figure 5-1 would become 100 times flatter, as the quantity demanded at any price level would be 100 times larger. A more simple means of modifying the graph, of course, is to multiply the horizontal scale by 100.

    To convert the estimated sample demand curve into an estimated population demand curve, we simply multiply the slope term by the sampling proportion. In this case, the slope term (-0.00625) would be multiplied by 1/100 (or simply divided by 100) to find the estimated population demand curve $P_x = 10.00 - 0.0000625Q_x$.

Simulated Market Situations

Another means of finding out what consumers would do in response to changes in price or promotion efforts is to construct an artificial market situation and observe the behavior of selected participants. These so-called *consumer clinics* often involve giving the participants a sum of "play" money and asking them to spend this money in an artificial store environment. Different groups of participants may be faced with different price structures among competing products and differing promotional displays. If the participants are randomly selected to be representative of the market for these products, we may, after observing their reactions to price changes of different magnitudes and to variations in promotional efforts, conclude that the entire market would respond in the same way.

Results of such simulated-market test situations must be viewed carefully, however. Participants may spend someone else's money differently from the way they would spend their own money, a phenomenon amply demonstrated by executives' use of expense accounts. Alternatively, participants may overreact and feel that they must choose a particular product (when they notice its price is reduced) to demonstrate that they are thrifty and responsible shoppers (the interview bias problem). Consumer clinics are likely to be an expensive method of obtaining data, however, since there is a considerable setup cost, participants must be provided with the products they select, and the process is relatively time consuming. Given these costs, there will be budgetary pressures to keep the samples small, and hence the results may not be representative of the entire market's reaction to the pricing and promotional changes. Nevertheless, such experiments frequently do provide useful insights into the awareness of buyers regarding price levels and their general reactions to changes in specific promotional variables.

- EXAMPLE: The Brazilian Gold Coffee Company wanted information on the responsiveness of consumer demand to changes in the price of its coffee. Six hundred shoppers were organized for a simulated market experiment and divided into six groups. The membership of the groups was chosen such that the socioeconomic characteristics of the groups were roughly equal and similar to the market in total. On the same day, each group was allowed thirty minutes to shop in a simulated supermarket. Each participant

TABLE 5-2.   Simulated Market Experiment for Brazilian Gold Coffee

Group	Price per Packet ($)	Sample Demand (Packets)	Population Demand (Estimated Packets)
1	3.39	112	11,200
2	3.29	123	12,300
3	3.49	94	9,400
4	3.19	154	15,400
5	3.69	37	3,700
6	3.59	71	7,100

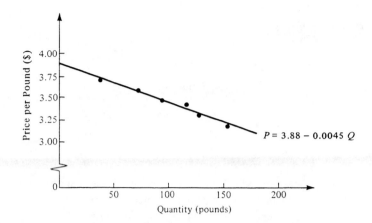

FIGURE 5-2. *Estimated Demand Curve for Brazilian Gold Coffee (Sample)*

was given $30 in play money to purchase any items on display. Brazilian Gold coffee was displayed prominently alongside the best-selling brand of coffee. For each of the six groups, Brazilian Gold was priced at different levels, while the prices of all other products were held constant. The price levels and the quantities demanded by each of the six samples are shown in Table 5-2.

In Figure 5-2 we plot the price-quantity coordinates for Brazilian Gold coffee and sketch in the sample demand curve which seems to be indicated by these data points. Note that we have not simply joined the observations with a jagged line but have, instead, superimposed a line of best fit. In the next section we shall see how to calculate the exact line of best fit using regression analysis. In the present example, we have simply "eye-balled" the line of best fit across the data points. That is, we have sketched in the demand curve that seems visually appropriate to the points shown. We show it as a straight line for simplicity and because the data do not clearly indicate a nonlinear relationship between price and quantity demanded. The intercept of this line with the price axis occurs at approximately \$3.88, and the slope of the line is approximately -0.0045, which is calculated by taking a particular vertical change (e.g., \$3.88 to \$3.38, or $\$-0.50$) and dividing this by the horizontal change indicated by the line of best fit (in this case, from zero to about 110 units). Thus, $-0.50/110 = -0.0045$.

Thus the simulated market experiment has generated data that allow the *sample* demand curve for Brazilian Gold coffee to be estimated as $P_x = 3.88 - 0.0045Q_x$, *ceteris paribus*. Assuming a 1% sample of the population, the *population* demand curve is estimated to be $P_x = 3.88 - 0.000045Q_x$. The firm can then determine the expression for its marginal revenue curve or calculate the price elasticity of demand at any price level. Note that for the price elasticity calculation one would use the reciprocal of the slope term, namely $1/-0.000045$, or $-22,222.22$, as the term dQ_x/dP_x and calculate the coordinates P_x and Q_x from the estimated population demand curve. For example, at price \$3.59, population quantity demanded would be calculated as

$$3.59 = 3.88 - 0.000045Q_x.$$

Hence

$$Q_x = 6444.44$$

Price elasticity at price \$3.59 would be

$$\epsilon = -22{,}222.22 \cdot \frac{3.59}{6{,}444.44}$$

$$= -12.38$$

Note that we have used the *estimated* quantity demanded of 6,444.44 units for the population (or 64.44 units for the sample), calculated from the estimated demand curve (the line of best fit) rather than from the observed sample purchases of 71 units. We do this because we recognize that all the observations probably contain random errors and we expect (from consumer behavior theory) that the demand curve will be a smooth line between price-quantity combinations. The next time we set price at \$3.59 the random disturbances may cause demand to be, for example, only 58 units. Our best estimate of demand at price \$3.59 is given by the line of best fit, and therefore our best estimate of price elasticity at that price should be based on the estimated demand curve rather than on the actual data observed.[2]

Direct Market Experiments

Direct market experiments involve real people in real market situations spending their own money on the goods and services they want. The firm will select one or more cities, regional markets, or states and conduct an experiment in these test markets that is designed to gauge consumer acceptance of the product and to identify the impact of a change in one or more of the controllable variables on the quantity demanded. In a regional market, for example, the firm might reduce the price of its product by 10% and compare the reaction of sales in the market over a particular period with previous sales in that market or with current sales in a similar but separate regional market. Alternatively, the firm may increase its advertising or introduce a promotional gimmick or campaign in a particular market to judge the impact of that change before committing itself to the greater expense and risk of instituting this change on a nationwide basis.

• EXAMPLE: Many firms in the United States launch new products and conduct experimental promotional campaigns in regional test markets. San Diego, California, was used by the Miller Brewing Company as a test market for its new ''Special Reserve'' beer

---

[2]If we had only two pairs of price-quantity observations, such as those for the prices \$3.69 and \$3.59, we would calculate *arc* elasticity of demand and we would have to use the observed price-quantity points in that calculation. Given more observations, however, we are able to see that the slope of the line joining the two coordinates is not our best estimate of the slope of the demand curve. Given more than two data points, we are able to estimate the line of best fit (demand curve) and use the information provided by this curve (rather than the raw data containing probably random disturbances) for our elasticity calculations.

during 1981, prior to the nationwide availability of that beer. Similarly, light (low calorie) wines were test marketed first in the San Diego area by Taylor California Cellars to evaluate market acceptance of the product and to judge consumer reaction to the price level and promotional campaign. San Diego is used as a test market because it is said to be demographically representative of southern California. Similarly, Denver, Baltimore, Phoenix, and Providence were chosen as test markets by Miller for the new beer since they are representative of other areas of the United States in terms of demographics, income levels, lifestyles, and so forth.[3]

Direct Marketing. Once known by the now obsolete term "mail-order marketing," direct marketing is a channel of communication between buyers and sellers that is ideally suited to market experiments. The consumer responds to an advertisement placed by the seller in any of several media, including newspapers, magazines, radio, television, and direct mailings to consumers. The mail and telephone orders that follow a firm's advertisement or direct mailing represent cash up front and are much more reliable indicators of market demand than are simple statements of consumer intentions. By placing different advertisements and price offers in different samples within the same region (using direct mailings to randomly selected samples of the target market), the impact of different prices and promotional strategies on the entire target market can be reliably estimated. As a bonus, the feedback is usually fairly quick. Responses to television advertisements requiring mail or telephone orders are concentrated within the next few days following the advertisement, while magazine advertisements and direct mailings generate the great majority of the total responses within six or eight weeks. Note, however, that direct marketing represents a different channel between the producer and the consumer and may appeal to a different type of consumer, with the result that the findings from experiments using direct marketing may not be generally applicable to other marketing channels, such as retailing through suburban and city stores.[4]

- NOTE: With any change in price or other marketing strategy, there is likely to be an initial or impact effect followed by a gradual settling of the market into the new longer-term relationship between price (or other controllable variable) and the sales level. Consumers will eagerly try a new product or respond to a price reduction or a promotional campaign, but having tried the product, many will go back to the rival product they were previously purchasing. Consumers may respond to a price reduction by purchasing several cartons of the product to build up their personal inventory of the product in the belief that the lower price is only temporary. The initial surge in consumer demand for a new product or for an established product at a lower price (or following a promotional campaign) may substantially overstate the sales gain the firm can expect in several weeks or

---

[3]Lanie Jones, "San Diego's Role as Test Market Toasted as Cap Comes off New Beer," *Los Angeles Times,* August 17, 1981, pt. 2, pp. 1, 10; also Dan Berger, "Miller Introduces New Beer Here," *San Diego Union,* August 13, 1981.

[4]See Bob Stone, *Successful Direct Marketing Methods,* 2nd ed. (Chicago: Crain Books, 1979).

months after consumers have finished making their adjustments in response to the change in prices, product availability, promotion, or some other variable.

To observe more than the impact effects of a change, market experiments must be conducted over a reasonably prolonged period of time. During this period, however, one or more of the uncontrollable variables are likely to have changed, and thus the observed change in sales over the period will not be due simply to the change in the controllable variable. To separate the effects of changes in other variables, the firm should also observe a control market, which should be chosen to exhibit a similar socioeconomic and cultural profile and be subject to the same climatic, political, and other uncontrollable events as is the test market. The change in sales in the control market over the period of the experiment will be solely the result of the uncontrollable factors. Assuming that the same change would have occurred in the test market, this magnitude is deducted from (if positive) or added to (if negative) the change in sales in the test market to find the change in sales caused by the manipulation of the controllable variable(s).

If an uncontrollable variable changes in the test market but remains constant or changes to a different degree in the control market, the results of the market experiment will be less reliable. Even when the control market is nearby, the climatic influence may vary, local politics may intervene, or some other event may cause an impact on the sales level. Competitors may react to the change in the test market by lowering prices or increasing promotional efforts, for example, while maintaining the status quo in the undisturbed control market. Under such circumstances the market experiment could prove to be worthless.

Thus direct market experiments must be implemented with caution; some luck must be forthcoming so that uncontrollable variables do not distort the results, which must be interpreted with care. If the pitfalls are largely anticipated and subsequently avoided, such experiments may provide information whose value (in terms of the present value of the additional future sales revenue) far exceeds its cost. We now turn to a means of estimating the demand coefficients from secondary data, in contrast to the previous reliance on primary data.

5.3 REGRESSION ANALYSIS OF CONSUMER DEMAND

- DEFINITION: *Regression analysis* is a statistical technique used to discover the apparent dependence of one variable on one or more other variables. It is thus applicable to the problem of determining the coefficients of the demand function, since these express the influence of the determining variables on the demand for a product. For regression analysis we require a number of sets of observations, each consisting of the value of the dependent variable Y plus the corresponding values of the independent X variables. Regression analysis allows conclusions to be drawn from the pattern that emerges in the relationships between these pairs or sets of observations, and it can be applied to either time-series or cross-section data.

Time-Series versus Cross-Section Analysis

- DEFINITION: *Time-series analysis* uses observations that have been recorded over time in a particular situation. For example, monthly price and sales levels of a product in a particular firm may have been collected for the past twelve months.

    A problem with time-series analysis is that some of the uncontrollable factors that influence sales tend to change over time, and hence some of the differences in the sales observations will be the result of these influences rather than the result of any changes in the price level. If the changes in the uncontrollable variables are observable and measurable, we may include these variables as explanatory variables in the regression analysis. Actions of competitors and changing consumer income levels, for example, should be quantified (either directly or by use of a suitable proxy variable) and incorporated into the analysis.

    Changing taste and preference patterns, on the other hand, are difficult to observe and measure, but they are likely to change over time. Using time as an explanatory variable in the regression analysis will pick up the influence of tastes and any other factors (not otherwise included in the analysis) that tend to change over the period in a consistent direction.

- DEFINITION: *Cross-section analysis* uses observations taken from different firms or situations at the same point or period of time. Hence cross-section analysis largely eliminates the problem of uncontrollable variables that change over time, but it introduces other factors that may differ between and among firms at a particular point of time. The effectiveness of sales personnel, cash flow positions, levels of promotional activity, and objectives of management may well differ among firms and should be expected to have differing impacts on the sales level. Again, if these factors can be quantified and data obtained, they may be entered into the regression analysis to determine their impact on the dependent variables.

The Linearity of the Regression Equation

Having hypothesized that Y is a function of X or of several X variables and having collected data on the variables, we must then specify the form of the dependence of Y on the X variables. Regression analysis requires that the dependence be expressed in the *linear* form

$$Y = \alpha + \beta_1 X_1 + \beta_2 X_2 + \ldots + \beta_n X_n + e \qquad (5\text{-}1)$$

where the e term is added to represent the error or residual value that will arise as the difference between the actual value of each Y that has been observed in association with each set of X values, and the estimated value of each Y that the regression equation would predict for the X values given. For individual observations we should expect either a positive or a negative residual term, because of random variations in the value of Y.[5]

Nonlinear relationships between the Y and X values (such as quadratic, cubic, exponential, hyperbolic, and power functions) should be used if these best fit the data. Fortunately, these nonlinear forms may be converted to linear form by a simple mathematical transformation, so that linear regression may be used to estimate the relationships among the variables. The most commonly used nonlinear form is the power function, such as

$$Y = \alpha \, X_1^{\beta_1} \, X_2^{\beta_2} e \tag{5-2}$$

where the independent variables, X_1 and X_2 in this case, have a multiplicative (rather than additive) influence on the dependent variable Y. This curvilinear relationship can be expressed as a rectilinear relationship by logarithmic transformation. Taking logarithms of the values for Y, X_1, and X_2, we can express equation (5-2) as

$$\log Y = \log \alpha + \beta_1 \log X_1 + \beta_2 \log X_2 + \log e \tag{5-3}$$

In this form, the equation is linear, and the coefficients β_1 and β_2 can be found directly using regression analysis. The coefficient α can be found by reversing the transformation (that is, taking the antilog) of the log α value provided by the regression analysis. We shall work through an example of this procedure in Chapter 8, in the context of cost forecasting.

Alternatively, you may feel that the appropriate functional form between the dependent variable and the independent variables is quadratic, like the form for the total revenue curve. A quadratic function can be expressed linearly as in equation (5-4). Note that the last variable in this expression is the same independent variable (X) squared.

$$Y = \alpha + \beta_1 X + \beta_2 X^2 + e \tag{5-4}$$

Finally, if the appropriate functional form is thought to be a cubic function, as in the case of a production function or total cost function (to be discussed in Chapter 6), we can postulate the relationship to be

$$Y = \alpha + \beta_1 X + \beta_2 X^2 + \beta_3 X^3 + e \tag{5-5}$$

and use regression analysis to determine the values of the parameters.

---

[5]For the accurate calculation of the coefficients in the regression equation, we require that the errors, or residual terms, fulfill four conditions. They must occur randomly, be nomally distributed, have constant variance, and have an expected value of zero. When the pattern of the residuals does not conform to these restrictions, several problems arise, as we shall discuss later in the section "Problems in Regression Analysis: Six Major Pitfalls."

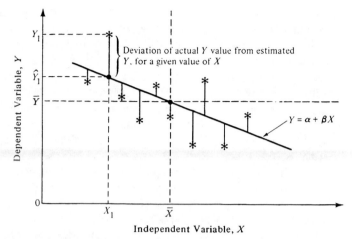

FIGURE 5-3. *The Line of Best Fit*

Estimating the Regression Parameters

The method of least squares is used to find the α and β parameters such that the regression equation best represents or summarizes the apparent relationship between the X_i values and the dependent variable Y. To illustrate this method, we use a simple example of only one independent variable. (This is usually referred to as simple regression or correlation analysis, rather than multiple regression analysis, which is used when we have two or more independent variables.)

- EXAMPLE: Suppose that we have collected ten pairs of observations on the variables Y and X: that is, the Y value and its associated X value on each of ten different occasions in a single situation (time-series data) or from ten different situations during the same period of time (cross-section data). These data points are shown as the asterisks in Figure 5-3. Observing these data points, we hypothesize a relationship of the form $Y = \alpha + bX$ to best fit (or represent most accurately) the apparent relationship between the variables Y and X.

    The method of least squares, often called ordinary least squares (OLS), is a mathematical process which chooses the intercept and slope of the line of best fit such that the sum of the squares of the deviations (or errors) is minimized. These deviations are shown in Figure 5-3 as the vertical distance between the line of best fit and the actual value of Y observed for a particular value of X. For example, given X_1 in Figure 5-3, the estimated value of Y is $\hat{Y}_1$ (known as Y_1 "hat" where the "hat," a circumflex, over the Y_1 indicates the estimated, or expected, value of Y_1 given X_1). The vertical difference between the observed Y_1 and the estimated $\hat{Y}_1$ is known as the deviation, residual, or error term, and was connoted as e in equation (5-2).

    Thus the regression equation specifies the line of best fit. It is selected by a mathematical procedure that positions the line such that the sum of the squared errors is minimized. We square the errors to avoid the positive deviations (points above the line of best fit) cancelling out against negative deviations (points below the line of best fit), and to weight more heavily the larger deviations. Note that the line of best fit passes through the point representing the mean values ($\overline{Y}$ and $\overline{X}$) of the variables. The regression equation explains part of the variation of each Y observation from the $\overline{Y}$ value, in terms of the difference between the associated X observation and the $\overline{X}$ value. In Figure 5-3, when $X = X_1$, the regression equation predicts $\hat{Y}_1$, explaining the variation from $\overline{Y}$ (that is, $\overline{Y} - \hat{Y}_1$), in terms of the variation in X (that is, $\overline{X} - X_1$). The unexplained residual, or error term, is the difference between the actual observation of Y and the predicted value of Y (that is, $Y_1 - \hat{Y}_1$).

Since computer software programs (even in hand calculators) for obtaining correlation and regression equations are becoming readily available, and since the theory underlying regression analysis is typically covered in other courses, we shall not go too deeply into the theory or calculation of regression equations. It is instructive, however, to work through a simple two-variable case to demonstrate some of the issues and problems involved. Without proof, we state the following expressions for α and β.[6]

$$\alpha = \overline{Y} - \beta\overline{X} \qquad (5\text{-}7)$$

and

$$\beta = \frac{n\Sigma XY - \Sigma X \Sigma Y}{n\Sigma X^2 - (\Sigma X)^2} \qquad (5\text{-}8)$$

where $\overline{Y}$ is the arithmetic mean of the Y values; $\overline{X}$ is the arithmetic mean of the X values; Σ (sigma) connotes the sum of the term indicated (for example, ΣXY is the sum of the products of X and Y for all pairs of X and Y); and n is the number of observations or data points.

Given a set of X and Y observations, we can use these equations to solve for the line of best fit for the relationship that appears to exist between those two variables. Let us introduce a hypothetical example.

- EXAMPLE: Suppose a chain of department stores sells its own brand of frozen broccoli in each of its six stores. The Pricing Manager is interested in knowing the price elasticity of demand for this product. Its six stores are in similar middle-income suburban neighborhoods and all are currently selling the item at $0.79 per package. Monthly sales at the six stores average 4,625 units per store, with no store's sales being more than 150 units away from this level. Suppose the manager decides to conduct an experiment: Prices will be set at different levels in each of the six stores to observe the reactions of sales to the

---

[6]See J. Johnston, *Econometric Methods* (New York: McGraw-Hill Book Company, 1963), pp 9–19. Note that your calculator, if it has a regression-equation program, may be programmed for a simplified formula, and you may, as a consequence, arrive at a slightly different answer. The degree of inaccuracy is usually very small, however.

different price levels. As a control, price will be held at $0.79 in the first store. The prices and the sales levels (in thousands) at each of the six stores over the one-month period of the experiment are shown in Table 5-3.

TABLE 5-3.   Price/Sales Observations for Broccoli at Six Stores, and the Calculations for Regression Analysis

Store No.	Price X ($)	Sales Y (000)	XY	X^2	Y^2
1	0.79	4.650	3.6735	0.6241	21.6225
2	0.99	3.020	2.9898	0.9801	9.1204
3	1.25	2.150	2.6875	1.5625	4.6225
4	0.89	4.400	3.9160	0.7921	19.3600
5	0.59	6.380	3.7642	0.3481	40.7044
6	0.45	5.500	2.4750	0.2025	30.2500
	4.96 (ΣX)	26.100 (ΣY)	19.5060 (ΣXY)	4.5094 (ΣX^2)	125.6798 (ΣY^2)

$$\bar{Y} = \frac{\Sigma Y}{n} = \frac{26.1}{6} = 4.35$$

$$\bar{X} = \frac{\Sigma X}{n} = \frac{4.96}{6} = 0.8267$$

Table 5-3 includes the calculations necessary for the solution of the α and β parameters. Using equation (5-8), we have

$$\beta = \frac{6(19.506) - 4.96(26.1)}{6(4.5094) - (4.96)^2} = \frac{-12.42}{2.4548} = -5.0595$$

and from equation (5-7), we have

$$\alpha = 4.35 - (-5.059)(0.8267) = 8.5327$$

Thus, $Y = 8.5327 - 5.0595X$ is the line of best fit to the data, when quantity demanded is measured in thousands of units. As shown in Figure 5-4, the intercept of this line is 8,532.7 units on the Y axis, and the slope is $-5,059.5$ units of sales per dollar increase in price.[7]

---

[7]The intercept value should not be interpreted as the sales level that would be expected at the price of zero, since the range of price observations is from $0.45 to $1.25, and the values of α and β are estimated only for that range. Outside this range a different relationship may hold between X and Y. The intercept parameter serves only to locate the line of best fit such that it passes through the observations at the appropriate height. To interpret the intercept as the sales value when price is zero would be an example of the dangerous practice of extrapolation.

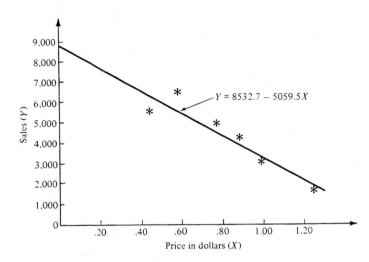

FIGURE 5-4. Graphical Plot of Price/Sales Observations

This regression equation shows the dependence of quantity demanded the price per unit. We can easily invert this into the form $P = a + bQ$ traditionally used to represent the demand curve. Substituting for Q and P in the regression equation, we have

$$Q = 8.5327 - 5.0595P \qquad (5\text{-}9)$$

Subtracting Q from both sides, adding $5.0595P$ to both sides, and dividing both sides by 5.0595, we have

$$5.0595P = 8.5327 - Q$$
$$P = 1.6865 - 0.19765Q \qquad (5\text{-}10)$$

The marginal revenue curve is obtained from this estimate of the demand curve, based on our knowledge that it must have the same vertical intercept value and twice the slope value. Thus,

$$\text{MR} = 1.6865 - 0.3953Q \qquad (5\text{-}11)$$

Price elasticity of demand at any price level may be estimated using $dQ/dP = -5.0595$ from the regression equation (5-9) and the estimated quantity demanded at that price level. For example, given $P = 0.85$, we would find Q by substituting for P in equation (5-9) as follows:

$$Q = 8.5327 - 5.0595(0.85) = 4.2321$$

Inserting these values into the point price elasticity expression,

$$\epsilon = \frac{dQ}{dP} \cdot \frac{P}{Q} \tag{4-16}$$

we find

$$\epsilon = \frac{-5.0595}{1} \cdot \frac{0.85}{4.2321} = -1.0162$$

The price elasticity of demand at the price level of $0.85 is thus slightly above unity, indicating that total revenue would be virtually constant for (very small) price increases or price reductions around the price of $0.85. In effect, this price and quantity combination is very close to the highest point on the *TR* curve, and *TR* would decline for any substantial price change, either up or down.

The Coefficient of Determination

- DEFINITION: The *coefficient of determination*, conventionally expressed as R^2, is a statistic that indicates the proportion of the variation in the dependent variable which is explained by the variation in the independent variable(s).

In effect, the R^2 value tells us how well the regression equation fits the data. An R^2 value of 0.98, for example, indicates that changes in the value(s) of the independent variable(s) account for 98% of the changes in the dependent variable. An R^2 value of 1.0 would indicate that *all* the sample variation in Y is explained by the sample variation in the X variable(s), and consequently, all data points would actually lie on the line of best fit. Conversely, a lower R^2 value of, say, 0.30, would indicate a broadly scattered set of data points with relatively large deviations from the line of best fit, indicating a relatively weak relationship between the dependent and independent variables.

The coefficient of determination can be calculated using the following formula:[8]

---

[8] See Johnston, *Econometric Methods*, pp. 30–32. This formula facilitates hand calculation of the coefficient of determination, but it does little to explain why this statistic indicates the proportion of variation in Y explained by X. Note that the OLS method minimizes the sum of the squared residuals, or the total variation of the Y observations from the mean value of Y, namely $\Sigma(Y_i - \bar{Y})^2$, where Y_i, represents the ith observation of the variable Y (where $i = 1,2,3, \ldots , n$). In turn,

$$\Sigma(Y_i - \bar{Y})^2 = \Sigma(\hat{Y}_i - \bar{Y})^2 + \Sigma(Y_i - \hat{Y}_i)^2$$

That is, the total variation is equal to the variation in Y (the difference from the mean) that is explained by the regression equation, plus the residual variation (the difference of the actual observation from the value predicted by the regression equation). Now, dividing through by the total variation, we have

$$\frac{\Sigma(Y_i - \bar{Y})^2}{\Sigma(Y_i - \bar{Y})^2} = \frac{\Sigma(\hat{Y}_i - \bar{Y})^2}{\Sigma(Y_i - \bar{Y})^2} + \frac{\Sigma(Y_i - \hat{Y}_i)^2}{\Sigma(Y_i - \bar{Y})^2}$$

The coefficient of determination is the term following the equal sign, since it is the ratio of the variation explained to the total variation. Since the term on the left is equal to 1,

$$R^2 = \left(\frac{n\Sigma XY - \Sigma X\Sigma Y}{\sqrt{[n\Sigma X^2 - (\Sigma X)^2][n\Sigma Y^2 - (\Sigma Y)^2]}} \right)^2$$ (5-12)

• EXAMPLE: Inserting the values calculated for the broccoli example in Table 5-1, we have

$$R^2 = \left(\frac{6(19.506) - 4.96(26.1)}{\sqrt{[6(4.5094) - (4.96)^2][6(125.6798) - (26.1)^2]}} \right)^2$$

$$= 0.8624$$

Thus we are able to say that more than 86% of the sample variation in the sales observations was due to the influence of the sample variation in the price level. The remaining unexplained variation is therefore due to other influences on sales and might be due to differences in promotional activity, consumer incomes, consumer tastes, or other factors that may differ between and among the six stores.

The Standard Error of Estimate

Most computer regression programs include as standard output several other statistics that allow the decision maker to evaluate the confidence that may be placed in certain predictions. The first of these is the standard error of estimate. ·

• DEFINITION: The *standard error of estimate* is a measure of the dispersion of the data points from the line of best fit. Given the standard error of estimate (S_e), we can calculate the confidence interval (around the estimated value for the dependent variable) for different levels of confidence. The confidence interval is the range of values within which we expect the actual observation to fall a given percentage of time. For example, we can be confident at the 95% level that the actual value of Y for a given X will fall within a certain range of outcomes above and below the estimated value (that is, $\hat{Y}_i$) if we know that 95% of the time it *should* fall within this interval.

Assuming that the error terms (the deviations or residuals) are normally distributed about the line of best fit, we can use the properties of a normal distribution to say that there is a 68% probability that actual observations of the dependent variable will lie within the range given by the estimated value plus or minus one standard error of the estimate. Furthermore, there is a 95% probability that the future observations will lie

---

$$R^2 = 1 - \frac{\Sigma(Y_i - \hat{Y}_i)^2}{\Sigma(Y_i - \bar{Y})^2}$$

Thus R^2 is equal to 1 minus the proportion of the total variation not explained by the regression equation. When $\Sigma(Y_i - \hat{Y}_i)^2$ is zero (meaning all observations lie on the line of best fit), R^2 is equal to 1, signifying a perfect fit of the line to the data. When $\Sigma(Y_i - \hat{Y}_i)^2$ is relatively large, R^2 is relatively small, signifying a poor fit to the data and showing that X is a relatively unimportant determinant of Y.

within plus or minus *two* standard errors of its predicted value. Finally, we can assert that there is a 99.7% probability that the observed value will lie within plus or minus *three* standard errors of the estimated value.

By adding and subtracting the standard error of the estimate to and from the estimated value of $\hat{Y}_i$ for each value of X_i, we establish a band within which we can expect the value of Y to fall for a particular value of X. A broader band is established when we add or subtract two standard errors of the estimate, and as noted previously the probability is raised to 95% that the actual observation will lie within this band. The 95% band is perhaps the most widely used in decision making, and it establishes what are known as the upper and lower 95% confidence limits. That is, we can be 95% confident that the actual observation will lie in the band and that the best and worst outcomes associated with the particular value of the independent variable will be not further than the limits of the band.

We calculate the standard error of estimate using the following expression:[9]

$$S_e = \sqrt{\frac{\Sigma Y^2 - \alpha \Sigma Y - \beta \Sigma XY}{n - 2}} \tag{5-13}$$

- EXAMPLE: For the broccoli example we can insert the values that were calculated in Table 5-3 and the α and β values subsequently derived to find the standard error of estimate associated with the line of best fit:

$$S_e = \sqrt{\frac{125.6798 - (8.5327)(26.1) - (-5.5095)(19.506)}{6 - 2}}$$
$$= \sqrt{0.41673}$$
$$= 0.64555$$

---

[9]See R. Levin, *Statistics for Management*, 2nd ed. (Englewood Cliffs, N.J.: Prentice-Hall, 1981), pp. 471–77. Again this formula facilitates computation. Equivalently,

$$S_e = \sqrt{\frac{\Sigma(Y_i - \hat{Y}_i)^2}{n - k}}$$

where k is the number of parameters estimated (the intercept and the slope). In this form you can see that the standard error of estimate is effectively the average absolute value of the deviations (corrected for degrees of freedom). Again, when $\Sigma(Y_i - \hat{Y}_i)^2$ is zero, then $S_e = 0$, signifying a perfect fit to the data. When S_e is relatively large, it signifies a poor fit to the data. Note that the value of S_e calculated using equation (5-13) is only accurate at the mean values of X and Y and that it understates the confidence intervals by progressively more as we move away from $\bar{X}$ and $\bar{Y}$. The *exact* value of the standard error for each value of X_i, can be calculated using

$$S_p = \sqrt{S_e^2 \left(1 + \frac{1}{n} + \frac{(\bar{X} - X_i)^2}{\Sigma X^2 - n\bar{X}^2}\right)}$$

From this expression, you can see that S_p diverges from S_e as n becomes smaller and X_i is more distant from $\bar{X}$. Thus the confidence intervals given by the rule of thumb (for example, plus or minus $2S_e$ around $\hat{Y}$ indicates the 95% confidence interval) are accurate at $\bar{X}$ and for reasonably large values of n, but *understate* the confidence intervals for X_i more distant from $\bar{X}$ and when n is relatively small. For greater accuracy when using small samples, the S_e should be multiplied by the appropriate t statistic (rather than simply 2) to find the 95% confidence interval. See Levin, pp. 476–77.

Thus the standard error of estimate is 0.64555 (or 645.55 units, since the sales data were in thousands). To find the 95% confidence interval, we would simply add twice this figure to $\hat{Y}$ to find the upper confidence limit and subtract twice this figure to find the lower confidence limit. Selecting a price near $\overline{X}$, such as $0.85, we estimate sales to be

$$\hat{Y} = 8.5327 - 5.0595(0.85) = 4.2321$$

Thus, when the price is $0.85, our best estimate of sales is 4,232.1 units. However, we don't really expect the actual sales to fall at exactly that number because the estimate is derived from data that exhibited deviations from the line of best fit. The standard error of estimate uses the observed deviations to establish confidence intervals on the presumption that later observations will similarly contain random disturbances and tend to scatter around the line of best fit. The upper bound of the 95% confidence interval is equal to

$$\hat{Y} + 2S_e = 4.2321 + 2(0.64555) = 5.5233$$

and the lower bound of the 95% confidence interval is equal to

$$\hat{Y} - 2S_e = 4.2321 - 2(0.64555) = 2.9409$$

Thus we can be confident at the 95% level that when price is set at $0.85, sales will fall within the range 2,940.9 units to 5,523.3 units. Clearly, we would prefer to discover a smaller standard error of estimate, since the confidence interval would then be smaller, and we could be more confident of experiencing an actual outcome close to the expected outcome Y.

The Predictive Power of the Regression Equation.   If the confidence interval is relatively narrow because of a relatively small value of the standard error of estimate, we say that the regression equation has greater predictive power than it would if the value of S_e were relatively large and the confidence interval relatively broad. How do we judge whether the S_e value is relatively large or small? Relative to what? A convenient rule of thumb is to relate it to the mean value of the Y observations. If the ratio of $S_e/\overline{Y}$ is less than 0.05, then the average deviation from the predicted value of Y should be less than 5% of the predicted value of Y. Note that the S_e value increases as the predicted value of $\hat{Y}$ diverges from the mean value $\overline{Y}$ (see footnote 9), so this rule of thumb becomes progressively less accurate as the value of Y diverges from $\overline{Y}$. If the ratio of $S_e/\overline{Y}$ is less than 0.05, then we have a reasonably accurate predictive equation with relatively tight confidence limits (or a relatively narrow confidence interval) at the desired level of confidence. Note that if we want to be even more secure in our predictions, we could set the $S_e/\overline{Y}$ test at 0.02, for example, and only use predictive equations that have an $S_e/\overline{Y}$ ratio less than 0.02.

For the broccoli case we note that $S_e/\overline{Y} = 0.64555/4.35 = 0.148$. Thus the standard error of estimate is nearly 15% of the typical value of sales. This result, in conjunction with the relatively broad confidence interval calculated, indicates that the predictive accuracy of our regression equation is not especially good.[10]

The Standard Error of the Coefficient

- DEFINITION: The *standard error of the coefficient*, S_β, is a measure of the accuracy of the calculated value of β, the coefficient estimating the marginal relationship between the variables Y and X. The standard error of the coefficient, if relatively small, allows us to express confidence that the calculated value of $\hat{\beta}$ is very close to the true value of β. The true value of β could be verified if we had the entire population of observations linking the variables Y and X, rather than just a sample. In short, $S_{\hat{\beta}}$ is the standard deviation of the sampling distribution of $\hat{\beta}$.

Assuming that the deviations are normally distributed, we can again use the features of a normal distribution to say that there is a 68% probability that the true coefficient will lie in the interval of the estimated coefficient plus or minus one standard error of the coefficient; a 95% probability that the true coefficient will lie in the interval given by the estimated coefficient plus or minus two standard errors of the coefficient; and a 99.7% probability that the actual relationship will be within plus or minus three standard errors of the coefficient of the estimated marginal relationship. Clearly, the smaller the standard error of the coefficient, the greater the confidence we can have in the regression coefficients generated by the data as reliable indicators of the true marginal relationships between the X_i values and the Y value.

The standard error of the coefficient can be calculated using the formula[11]

$$S_\beta = \frac{S_e}{\sqrt{\Sigma X^2 - n\bar{X}^2}} \qquad (5\text{-}14)$$

- EXAMPLE: For the broccoli example, the estimated coefficient $\hat{\beta}$ was -5.0595. What are the 95% confidence limits associated with this estimate? Inserting the data calculated earlier into equation (5-14), we find

$$S_\beta = \frac{0.6456}{\sqrt{4.5094 - 6(0.8267)^2}} = \frac{0.6456}{\sqrt{0.4088}} = 1.5792$$

---

[10]Other, very similar, measures of predictive power are the mean absolute deviation (MAD) and the mean square error (MSE). MAD $= \Sigma|Y_i - \hat{Y}_i|/n$ and MSE $= \Sigma(Y_i - \hat{Y}_i)^2/n$. Note that the MAD is a simple average absolute measure of the deviations without correction for degrees of freedom, but the MSE squares the deviations to give greater weight to the larger deviations. The square root of the MSE, known as the root mean square of errors (RMS), is then very similar to the standard error of estimate formula shown in footnote 9, except that the RMS is not corrected for degrees of freedom. Thus, for relatively small sample sizes, the MAD and the RMS would both underestimate the standard error of estimate.

[11]See Levin, *Statistics for Management*, pp. 491–93.

Thus the 95% confidence limits for the estimated coefficient are $-5.0595 + 2(1.5792) = -1.9009$ for the upper limit, and $-5.0595 - 2(1.5792) = -8.2181$ for the lower limit.

A simple rule of thumb to test for confidence in the regression coefficient is to take twice the value of the standard error of the coefficient and compare it with the estimated regression coefficient. If the regression coefficient exceeds twice its standard error, we can be 95% confident that the estimated coefficient is significantly different from zero and that there is a statistically significant relationship between the variables. In the present example, $\beta = -5.0595$ and is substantially more than twice the size of S_β so we can be confident at the 95% level that the price level *is* a statistically significant determinant of the quantity demanded of the broccoli.[12]

The foregoing discussion in the context of simple regression, or correlation analysis applies, *mutatis mutandis*, to multivariate regression analysis. The formulas for calculating the regression parameters for multivariable situations are given below.[13] The calculations become increasingly more complex and time consuming as the number of variables is increased, and are thus ideally suited to computer solution. The wide availability of computer programs for regression analysis means that essentially we need to know only how to enter the data and to interpret the results rather than to know the mechanistic processes of obtaining the results.

Problems in Regression Analysis: Six Major Pitfalls

There are six major problem areas likely to be encountered in regression analysis. If one or more of these problems do arise, the regression analysis will provide unreliable parameter estimates and statistics, and potentially give misleading explanations and poor predictions. (The computer presumes that researchers know what they are doing.) We shall address the major problems in turn.

---

[12]Alternatively, if the regression program generates t statistics for each independent variable, we would require that the t value exceed 2, since the t statistic is calculated as the correlation (or regression) coefficient divided by its standard error adjusted for the degrees of freedom. See Levin, *Statistics for Management*, pp. 491–93.

[13]For the multivariate regression equation $Y = \alpha + \beta_1 X_1 + \beta_2 X_2$, we can find α, β_1, and β_2 by simultaneous solution of the equations:

$$Y = n\alpha + \beta_1 \Sigma X_1 + \beta_2 \Sigma X_2 \tag{5-1}$$
$$\Sigma X_1 Y = \alpha \Sigma X_1 + \beta_1 \Sigma X_1^2 + \beta_2 \Sigma X_1 X_2 \tag{5-2}$$
$$\Sigma X_2 Y = \alpha \Sigma X_2 + \beta_1 \Sigma X_1 X_2 + \beta_2 \Sigma X_2^2 \tag{5-3}$$

See Levin, *Statistics for Management*, pp. 511–16. For more than two independent variables the equations are commensurately more complex. Using computer programs, such as the STATPAK Multiple Regression Program, complex regression equations can be solved much more quickly and accurately. The *Computer Courseware Package and Manual* that is ancillary to this text includes a multiple-regression program, named MULTREG, available on disk for IBM and compatible personal computers. Your instructor can get a copy of the disk from Prentice Hall, and you may copy it. Details of the Courseware package are included in both the *Study Guide/Workbook* and the *Instructor's Manual*.

Specification Errors.   The first place to create unreliability in the results is in the specification of the relationship that is hypothesized to exist between the dependent variable and the independent variable(s). Two main types of problems occur under this heading. First, there is the use of the *wrong functional form* of the relationship. We noted previously that the regression equation must be calculated in linear form, but that this could be achieved for nonlinear relationships by logarithmic transformation of the function to linear form. The first specification error is to specify the relationship as linear when in fact it is nonlinear of some form, or vice versa. How do we know which functional form is the true relationship? We find which functional form best fits the data by comparing the coefficient of determination (R^2) for various functional forms. By running the data in both the linear form, equation (5-2), and, for example, the power form, equation (5-3), the R^2 statistics can be compared to determine which functional form best explains the variance in the dependent variable. For bivariate correlation analysis, of course, a simple plot of the Y values against the X values should allow a visual assurance that the relationship is either linear or nonlinear.

The second specification error involves the *omission of an important explanatory variable*. This leads to probable unreliability in the regression coefficients and the likely violation of the restrictions that we place on the error terms. Essentially, since one or more of the explanatory variables are not included in the regression equation, the influence of these variables is attributed to the variables that are included, or it shows up as an unexplained residual.

- EXAMPLE: To illustrate this problem, recall the broccoli example discussed earlier. Suppose we now learn that *ceteris paribus* did not hold for the period of the experiment: The promotional activity of the six stores differed during the period because of differences in the availability of advertising space in the suburban weekly newspapers and differences in the circulation of these newspapers. Multiplying pages of advertising by circulation in each area, we obtain a proxy measure of advertising exposure of each store as shown in Table 5-4 with the original price and sales data.

TABLE 5-4.   *Price, Sales, and Advertising Exposure for Six Stores during the Experiment*

Store No.	Sales Y (000)	Price X_1 ($)	Advertising X_2 (proxy units)
1	4.650	0.79	23,000
2	3.020	0.99	18,500
3	2.150	1.25	24,600
4	4.400	0.89	26,200
5	6.380	0.59	25,100
6	5.500	0.45	16,800

We now hypothesize that $Y = a + \beta_1 X_1 + \beta_2 X_2$, and we use a computer to estimate the α and β parameters. The regression equation that best fits the data in Table 5-4 is

$$Y = 5.71802 - 5.80262X_1 + 0.000153X_2$$

and we are provided with the following statistics:

Standard error of estimate:	S_e	= 0.23838
Standard error of the X_1 coefficient:	S_{β_1}	= 0.39975
Standard error of the X_2 coefficient:	S_{β_2}	= 0.00298
Coefficient of determination:	R^2	= 0.986

Note that the relative magnitudes of these standard errors indicate that the independent variables are reliable for predictive purposes, according to the rules of thumb mentioned earlier. The coefficient of determination indicates that the two variables, price and advertising exposure, jointly explain 98.6% of the variance of Y. Note also that the coefficient to X_1 has changed by the addition of the second explanatory variable, and that the R^2 value has increased, when compared with our earlier correlation analysis. Thus the omission of a significant determining factor in the earlier analysis led to a misleading coefficient for the price variable and to a subsequently misleading estimate of the price elasticity of demand.

Measurement Errors.   The next pitfall to be avoided is the improper measurement of the variables. In the broccoli problem, for example, does the proxy measure of advertising exposure accurately depict the determining variable we wish to measure? To the extent that some suburban weeklies may have a superior advertising format, or to the extent that the newspaper tends to lie neglected on the porches (or under the Porsches!) of some suburbs, the simple measure of advertising exposure may not accurately depict the influence of advertising efforts on sales.

The price variable is notorious for its problems of measurement. The most readily available measure of price is usually the list price or manufacturer's suggested price, but in many instances this may not accurately depict the actual price paid. Whenever bargaining, discounts, or trade-ins are involved, the actual money changing hands may be somewhat less than the list price. For all variables, if the data used do not accurately measure the level of the variables, the programmers' adage "garbage in, garbage out" is likely to be appropriate.

Simultaneous Equation Relationships.   Regression analysis proceeds on the assumption that a single equation explains the entire relationship. One problem with demand estimation arises because the price level is the result of the solution of the simultaneous equations for both demand and supply.

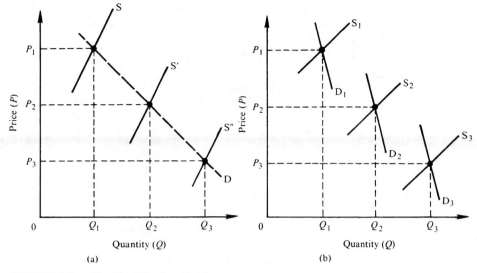

FIGURE 5-5. The Identification Problem

- EXAMPLE: Suppose we have three price/quantity observations that have been collected over a period of time and are as shown in Figure 5-5. They seem to indicate a negative relationship between price and quantity and hence may be thought to trace out the demand curve shown in part (a) and be the result of a shifting supply curve that has moved to the right over time, causing progressively lower intersection points on the demand curve. Alternatively, the three observations may be a result of the scenario depicted in part (b) of the figure. The first price/quantity observation may be the result of the intersection of supply and demand curve S_1 and D_1, while the subsequent price/quantity observations are the result of shifting demand and supply curves as indicated. Regression analysis, however, would conclude that part (a) is the appropriate interpretation of the data, which, if erroneous, would give a misleading view of the slope and placement of the demand function.

The problem arises because there are insufficient data in the regression analysis to identify the shifts of the demand curves, and hence this is often called the identification problem. This problem arises particularly with time-series data in demand estimation, since we cannot expect the demand function to remain stable for any extended period of time because of changing influences such as consumer incomes and preference patterns. In this case the problem may be avoided by inclusion of the determining variables which cause the demand curve to shift.

Multicollinearity. The problem of multicollinearity arises when the independent variables are not independent (of each other) at all. If two or more of the explanatory variables vary together because of their dependence on each other or on another variable, the $\hat{\beta}$ coefficient assigned to each of the variables by the regression solution may have no relationship to the true marginal influence of these variables on the dependent variable.

The regression analysis is unable to detect the true relationships and will assign an arbitrary value to the coefficients. Besides reducing the explanatory and predictive power of the regression equation, the presence of multicollinearity is likely to cause the standard error of the coefficient (or a *t* test) to be an unreliable indicator of the statistical significance of the coefficients.

The presence of multicollinearity may be uncovered by checking the correlation coefficients between pairs of independent variables. Most computer regression programs will generate a correlation matrix. If any two independent variables are found to be highly correlated with each other, one of the two should be excluded from the regression equation, and a new, more reliable estimate of the intercept and slope parameters may then be obtained.[14]

- NOTE: Multicollinearity can be tolerated in the regression equation if the purpose of that equation is simply predictive. Recall that in Chapter 1 we acknowledged three purposes of models: namely, pedagogical, explanatory, and predictive. The demand function estimated by regression analysis may be used as either an explanatory model or as a predictive model. As an explanatory model, it is important that there be no multicollinearity in the data, since we ascribe importance and significance to the individual coefficients in the regression equation. For example, the β coefficient for price is used to calculate price elasticity and to find the slope of the demand curve. Consequently, it is important that this β coefficient be an accurate estimate of the marginal relationship between Q_x and P_x and that it not be distorted by the presence of multicollinearity. However, when the estimate of the demand function is used to predict, or forecast, Q_x in a subsequent period, given estimates of the values of all the independent variables, we look at the impact of the independent variables on Q_x as a group rather than individually. Thus it does not matter if individual coefficients are inaccurate because of multicollinearity, since it is the total effect on Q_x which interests us. Recall from Chapter 1 that predictive models do not have to be realistic or based on accurate assumptions—the test of a predictive model is how well it predicts. Thus, if the presence of multicollinearity increases the R^2 and makes the regression equation a better predictor, it can be tolerated as long as the equation is used only for predictive purposes, with the independent variables viewed as a group rather than individually.

Heteroscedasticity.   The regression analysis presumes homoscedasticity of the error terms; that is, it assumes that the residuals or deviations from the line of best fit occur randomly with respect to the magnitude of the independent variables. When the error terms do not occur randomly but exhibit a systematic relationship with the magnitude of one or more of the independent variables, we have the condition of heteroscedasticity. The presence of heteroscedasticity is likely to cause the standard error of the coefficient to give misleading indications and cause the coefficient of determination to overstate the explanatory power of the regression equation.

---

[14]See Levin, *Statistics for Management*, pp. 201–6; or see A. S. Goldberger, *Topics in Regression Analysis* (London: Macmillan, Inc., 1968), pp. 79–83.

A simple means to discover the presence of heteroscedasticity is to plot the values of the residuals against the values of the independent variable(s). Many regression programs will produce these graphs for visual inspection: Any systematic relationship that appears will indicate the presence of heteroscedasticity. For example, the residuals associated with each of the X observations may become progressively larger (or smaller) as the value of X is larger. This problem may be removed by respecifying the independent variables, by changing the functional form of the relationship, by a transformation of the data, or by using a weighted least-squares regression technique.[15]

Autocorrelation.   Autocorrelation is another problem that arises when the error terms do not conform to the restrictions required for regression analysis. Autocorrelation (also known as *serial correlation*) can only occur in time-series data and is indicated by a sequential pattern in the error terms. That is, if the size of the error term becomes progressively larger or smaller, or exhibits a cyclical or any other pattern as the X observations are arrayed in chronological order, this pattern indicates that some other variable is changing systematically and influencing the dependent variable. Autocorrelation may be removed by adding to the regression equation the variable thought to explain the systematic pattern. For example, if the residuals appear to follow a cyclical pattern over time, dummy variables might be required to account for seasonal variation. If the cycles are longer and appear to be related to the state of the economy, a variable to reflect national income, such as GNP, might be added in an attempt to eliminate the autocorrelation. A continuing upward or downward trend in the residuals could be eliminated by adding time (e.g., number of weeks) as an explanatory variable.

Most regression programs will produce either a sequence plot of the residuals or the Durbin-Watson statistic, which is calculated to indicate the presence or absence of autocorrelation. A Durbin-Watson statistic around the value of 2 indicates the absence of autocorrelation, while values significantly greater than or less than 2 indicate that the residuals do not occur randomly and, therefore, that the results are likely to be unreliable.[16]

In summary, regression analysis is an extremely useful tool for estimating the coefficients of the demand function. But precautions must be taken with the use of this tool. Most regression programs will produce the various statistics mentioned above and will plot the residuals such that the experienced researcher can readily discover the presence of one or more of the major problems that may occur. Clearly, the greatest care must be taken in the initial steps of specifying the assumed relationship and collecting the data. Once the regression analysis has been conducted, the researcher must carefully interpret the results before concluding that these results are a sufficient basis for decision-making purposes.

---

[15]This takes us into the big league. These rectifications are discussed in advanced statistics texts, such as in N. R. Draper and H. Smith, *Applied Regression Analysis* (New York: John Wiley & Sons, Inc., 1966), pp. 77–81.

[16]See Johnston, *Econometric Methods*, Chapter 7.

5.4   SUMMARY

Demand estimation is concerned with finding the values of the parameters in the demand function that are currently appropriate. This information is important for current decision making and in evaluating whether decisions are optimal in terms of the current demand situation.

Buyers' reactions to changes in the independent variables in the demand function may be gauged by interviews and surveys, simulated market situations, or direct market experiments. Care must be taken to ensure the selection of a sufficiently large and random sample that properly reflects the target market, to allow confidence in the findings. Questionnaire design is critical to the accuracy of the predictions from interviews and surveys. Consumer intentions do not always accurately translate into actions at a later point. Interviewer bias and lack of consumer interest or information may also distort the estimates derived.

Simulated market situations and direct market experiments allow the observation of the consumer during the consumption-decision process, and conclusions may be drawn from the actual behavior of consumers. Care must be taken to isolate impact effects from longer-term effects and to ascertain whether the behavior of people in consumer clinics accurately reflects their usual behavior patterns. Direct marketing techniques provide an ideal opportunity to test the impact of different levels of price or other strategic variables, and regional test markets have proved useful for ascertaining the impact of different strategies at the retail level.

Regression analysis of data collected allows the calculation of the coefficients in the demand function, as well as the calculation of several statistics which indicate the confidence that can be attached to the estimates derived. Regression analysis is a powerful tool, when used correctly, for estimating the parameters of the demand function on the basis of the statistical association that appears between and among variables in either time-series or cross-section data observations. The pitfalls that may invalidate this technique include specification error, measurement error, the identification problem, multicollinearity, heteroscedasticity, and autocorrelation. These potential problems were outlined in some detail so the researcher can better set up the problem for analysis and better interpret the results of that analysis.

DISCUSSION QUESTIONS

5-1. Why is it useful to the decision maker to have an estimate of the impact (on the quantity demanded) of variables that are not controllable by the decision maker?

5-2. List the problem areas that one must be cautious about when using interviews and surveys to derive estimates of the market demand function for a particular product.

5-3. List ten questions you would ask a sample of people to estimate their demand function for a specific brand of toothpaste.

5-4. Suppose you were to interview a large number of people, asking each person whether he or she would buy a particular product at a series of prices starting from a relatively low price and then raising the price until each person would not buy the product. How would you translate this information into an estimated demand curve?

5-5. Design a simulated market situation intended to ascertain customers' responses to changes in prices, packaging, and point-of-purchase promotion for a particular product.

5-6. What factors must be monitored while conducting a direct market experiment to allow confidence that the results obtained give reliable information about the demand function?

5-7. Suppose you had data on the annual quantity demanded of newsprint and the price per ton of newsprint over the past twenty years and that you had found the regression equation relating quantity demanded to price. Why would this be an unreliable estimate of the demand curve?

5-8. Explain the importance of the assumptions concerning the residuals, or error terms, to the accuracy of the estimate of the demand function derived using regression analysis.

5-9. Explain how you would satisfy yourself that your analysis did not contain any specification errors.

5-10. Summarize the issues you would need to check before concluding that the results of a regression analysis were a reliable basis for estimating the demand function.

PROBLEMS AND SHORT CASES

5-1. Jose Hermanos Liquors has conducted a simulated market experiment aimed at finding the price that would maximize total revenue from the sale of one item in its product line, namely Hermanos Gold Tequila. Six samples of 100 persons each were assembled at intervals one hour apart and allowed to select bottles of liquor up to a total value of $50 from a simulated liquor store display. The Hermanos tequila was displayed prominently between two major brands of tequila and its price was different for each sample of shoppers. All other prices and promotional variables remained the same over the six tests.

After the six groups of shoppers had finished the experiment, the following results were tabulated:

Group	Price ($)	Quantity demanded
1	9.55	17
2	7.85	24
3	8.25	21
4	10.75	10
5	6.45	32
6	6.95	28

(a) Sketch the line of best fit representing the demand curve for Hermanos Tequila for this sample of 100 consumers. Estimate the intercept and slope terms of this demand curve.

(b) Generalize this demand curve to the total market in the region, estimated to be 1 million people.

(c) What price promises to maximize total revenue for Hermanos Tequila?

(d) What is the value of the price elasticity of demand at that price? Explain what this value indicates.

5-2. The Direct Deal Marketing Company operates a mail and telephone order business, selling products directly to consumers who order DDMC's products after seeing advertisements in magazines or after receiving informational materials and samples through the mail. At the present time, DDMC is considering a mailing to 500,000 subscribers of *Road and Track* magazine, offering custom-fitted sheepskin seat covers to fit most automobiles sold in North America. Before incurring the major expense associated with this large mailing, however, DDMC has conducted a market experiment to ascertain consumer responsiveness to price. It has rented four separate lists of names of *Road and Track* subscribers, each list randomly generated by computer from the total subscription list and each containing 2,500 names and addresses. In its mailing to these four subsamples, all other promotional and information material was the same, but each sample was offered a different price. After two months DDMC has received orders from each of the subsamples, as shown below, and considers that all orders are in after waiting this long:

Subsample	Price	Pairs Ordered
A	$179.95	51
B	$199.95	38
C	$219.95	26
D	$239.95	14

(a) Estimate the intercept and slope term for DDMC's demand curve for the seat covers, given that the proposed mailing will reach 500,000 subscribers.
(b) What is the price elasticity of demand at each of the four price levels indicated?
(c) Suppose that the marginal cost to fulfill each order is $150 per pair, including postage and handling costs. What price should DDMC establish for the proposed mailing to maximize its profits from this particular product?
(d) State all assumptions which underlie your analysis and predictions.

5-3. Acton Auto Accessories has manufactured a new product, a center-high-mounted brakelight for aftermarket installation on cars not originally fitted with one of these devices. AAA has test marketed its new product for one month by advertising on independent local television stations in ten regional markets. These markets range from Portland, Maine to Portland, Oregon. In each market the pitch was the same, but the asking price was different. Viewers were given an 800 number to call and were urged to order directly by telephone. The sales volumes for each regional market have been multiplied by an appropriate factor (equal to the inverse of the ratio of that region's population to the national population) to give the number of units that would have been sold if the product had been advertised across the entire country at that price. The prices asked, and the adjusted monthly sales volume at each price, are shown below:

Region	Price	Volume
1	$16.95	2,208
2	12.50	2,682
3	19.99	2,061
4	13.99	2,526
5	18.88	2,158
6	22.95	1,732
7	11.99	2,877
8	15.50	2,312
9	12.75	2,606
10	14.99	2,488

The purpose of this test was to ascertain the demand curve for the product in order that the price for the national campaign could be set at the profit-maximizing level. Acton's marginal cost of production is $10, regardless of production volume. If the product is to be marketed nationally, it will be offered through a national chain of auto supply stores, and supported by a national advertising campaign in *Autoweek* and other automotive periodicals. This campaign will cost an estimated $200,000, all spent within the first month.

(a) Derive an expression for the monthly demand curve facing Acton's new product. Express this in the conventional way.

(b) What are the profit-maximizing price and monthly output levels?

(c) What is the price elasticity of demand at the profit-maximizing price? What does this indicate?

(d) What is the 95% confidence interval for sales volume at the profit-maximizing price? Comment on this.

(e) Regarding the market test results, express any misgivings you might have with the data generated. Would you like additional data on any other variables? What other assumptions and qualifications underlie your recommended price and expected sales levels?

5-4. Simpson Footwear has estimated the demand function for its "El Condor" men's shoe, using regression analysis, to be:

$$Q_x = 250.684 + \underset{(65.583)}{240.928P_y} + \underset{(70.431)}{180.328P_z} - \underset{(150.108)}{410.308P_x} + \underset{(1.473)}{1.235Y}$$

where Q_x represents quantity (pairs) demanded per month; P_y is the price of a competitor's shoe; P_z is the price of another competitor's shoe; P_x is the price of the El Condor shoe; Y is GNP per capita, representing consumers' incomes; and the figures in parentheses are the standard errors of the coefficients.

The regression analysis also provided the coefficient of determination, which was 0.9325, and standard error of estimate, which was 1,265.613. The current values of the independent variables are: $P_y = 74.99$; $P_z = 82.50$; $P_x = 79.99$; and $Y = 15,250$.

(a) Calculate the cross-elasticities of demand between your product and the other two, and the price and income elasticities of demand for your product. What do these values indicate?

(b) Suppose that the marginal cost of El Condor shoes is constant at $50. What is the profit-maximizing price?

(c) At the profit-maximizing price, what range of sales volumes can be expected at the 95% confidence limits?

(d) Outline all the assumptions and qualifications which underlie your sales prediction at the new price level.

5-5. The Lifestyle Leisure company produces and sells hot tubs for the southern California market. It has recently been varying the price of its best-selling unit and observing the quantity sold at each price level. Based on these data, the following regression equation has been calculated:

$$Q_x = 38,658.235 - 8.667P_x$$

where Q_x is quantity sold and P_x is price per unit. The regression analysis also produced the following statistics: coefficient of determination, 0.723; standard error of estimate, 3,251.625; and standard error of the coefficient, 5.213.

Lifestyle Leisure's marginal cost of producing these hot tubs is constant at $1,500 per unit for all foreseeable output levels.

(a) What is the profit-maximizing price for the hot tubs?

(b) What is the sales-revenue-maximizing price?

(c) Calculate the price elasticity of demand at the profit-maximizing price and comment on the value obtained.

(d) At the profit-maximizing price, what is the 95% confidence interval for sales?

(e) What other qualifications and assumptions underlie your prediction?

5-6. Ambivalent Autronics has commissioned a study to quantify the determinants of the demand for its cruise-control device. This device is installed in an automobile to allow the vehicle to maintain a constant cruising speed, with subsequent fuel economy advantages.

Based on the data available to it from sources, the Demand Data Research Company has calculated the following regression equation:

$$Q_x = 125{,}062.85 - 1{,}862.52P_x + 1{,}226.94P_s + 524.18A_x + 28{,}672.74Y + 0.035S$$

where Q_x is quantity demanded of the cruise-control unit per month; P_x is the price per unit set by Ambivalent Autronics (in dollars); P_s is the average price (in dollars) of the three other cruise control units that are considered the closest substitutes for AA's unit; A_x is AA's advertising budget per month (in thousands of dollars); Y is the level of per capita disposable income per month (in thousands of dollars); and S is the level of sales of new automobiles per month. The regression analysis also provided the following statistics:

Coefficient of determination (R^2): 0.8675

Standard error of estimate: 6,432.75

Standard errors of the coefficients: for P_x, 725.6; for P_s, 482.8; for A_x, 106.2; for Y, 188.1; for S, 0.015

AA's cost of production of the cruise-control units has stabilized, and it can produce for all foreseeable demand situations at a constant marginal cost of $132.50 per unit. The current values of the independent variables are $P_x = 189.95$; $P_s = 195.00$; $A_x = 12.65$; $Y = 1.53$; and $S = 895{,}645$.

(a) Calculate the price elasticity, the cross elasticity, and the income elasticity of demand for the product and comment on the values obtained.

(b) Derive expressions for the firm's demand and marginal revenue curves for the product.

(c) Calculate the profit-maximizing price for the cruise-control unit.

(d) At that price, in what range of figures do you expect quantity demanded to fall at the 95% confidence level?

(e) What other qualifications underlie your analysis?

5-7. The demand function for product X has been established, using regression analysis as follows:

$$Q_x = -5{,}154.605 - 35.83P_x + 82.97P_y + 78.67P_z - 64.03P_w$$

where P_x, P_y, P_z, and P_w are the prices of products each identified by the subscript. The current price levels are as follows: $P_x = \$188.50$; $P_y = \$103.75$; $P_z = \$119.25$, and $P_w = \$32.50$.

The regression program also generated the following statistics: $R^2 = 0.92$; $S_e = 80.01$; standard errors of the coefficients: for P_x, 8.62; for P_y, 33.91; for P_z, 60.82; and for P_w, 35.82.

(a) What price would maximize sales revenue from the sale of product X?

(b) Suppose the marginal cost of producing X is constant at $100 per unit. What price would maximize profits from the sale of product X?

(c) Suppose the price of product Y is raised to $114.95. Does this increase have any impact on the profit-maximizing price for X? Explain.

(d) What qualifications and/or assumptions underlie your analysis?

5-8. The Jumping Jack Flash Company has developed a new lightweight camera with an automatically triggered flash which (naturally) pops up and flashes just as you press the shutter-release button. This product was introduced last year and a follow-up survey has just been completed, giving rise to the following regression equation:

$$Q_x = -190.1366 - 1.0457P_x + 3.9824A_x + 3.6145Y + 1.8794P_s$$
$$(32.11) \qquad (0.18) \qquad (1.25) \qquad (1.92) \qquad (0.63)$$

where Q_x is the quantity demanded in thousands; P_x is the price per unit in dollars; A_x is the advertising budget per month in thousands; Y is per capita disposable income in thousands; and P_s is the price per unit (average) of competing cameras. The figures in parentheses represent the standard errors of the coefficients. The coefficient of determination was 0.922, and the standard error of estimate was 0.3871.

Jumping Jack's cost of production for these cameras has stabilized at $25 per unit, and the current price is $48.88. The current values of the other variables are $A_x = 36$, $Y = 5.865$, and $P_s = 46.86$.

(a) Calculate the price elasticity, the income elasticity, and the cross elasticity of demand for JJF's camera, and comment on the values obtained.

(b) Derive expressions for the firm's demand and marginal revenue curves.

(c) Suppose JJF wishes to maximize total revenue—what price should be set for these cameras? At that price, what is the expected sales volume?

(d) What qualifications and assumptions underlie your analysis?

5-9. The demand function for compact Hertz rental cars at Boston's Logan Airport has been estimated, using regression analysis, to be

$$Q_x = 26.0071 + 2.4490P_{cc} + 1.8233P_{sc} - 3.6075P_x$$
$$(8.624) \qquad (0.816) \qquad (0.631) \qquad (1,508)$$

where Q_x represents the number of compact cars rented per day by Hertz; P_{cc} is the average rental price of competitor's compacts; P_{sc} is the rental price of Hertz's subcompacts; P_x is the rental price of Hertz's compacts; and the figures in parentheses are the standard errors of the coefficients. The regression analysis also provided the coefficient of determination, which is 0.8325, and the standard error of estimate, which is 2.5613. The current values of the independent variables are $P_{cc} = 24.50$; $P_{sc} = 21.95$; and $P_x = 24.95$.

(a) What are the cross elasticities of demand between Hertz's compact cars and other cars, and what do these figures indicate?

(b) Derive an expression for the demand curve for Hertz's compact cars.

(c) What is the sales-revenue-maximizing price (daily rate) for Hertz compact cars?

(d) At that price, what range of sales volumes can be expected at the 95% confidence limits?

(e) Outline all the assumptions and qualifications which underlie your sales predictions.

5-10. The demand function for Blitz brand economy beer at a major suburban supermarket has been estimated, using regression analysis, to be

$$Q_x = -109.093 - 2.8985P_x + 10.044P_y + 5.126P_z + 41.665A_x - 25.631A_y + 0.0581M$$
$$(8.62) \qquad (0.86) \qquad (1.03) \qquad (1.58) \qquad (15.33) \qquad (10.88) \qquad (0.12)$$

where Q_x represents the number of cases of Blitz sold per week; P_x is the price per case of Blitz economy beer; P_y is the price per case of Sudds economy beer; P_z is the price per case of the store's generic (no brand) beer; A_x is the advertising expenditure per week (in thousands of dollars) for those weeks when Blitz beer was featured as a special; A_y is the advertising expenditure per week (in thousands of dollars) for those weeks when Sudds beer was featured as a special; and M is the mean weekly take-home income per household for the store's customers (in dollars). The figures in parentheses are the standard errors of the coefficients. The coefficient of determination is 0.85, and the standard error of estimate is 0.75. The data were collected weekly over a six-month period within the store. Mean income of customers was estimated by the average response to the income question on the questionnaire required from those wishing to enter the store's weekly lottery. (The winner is given a refund for the money spent in the store in the preceding week.) The store prepares a weekly advertising supplement to accompany the Sunday newspaper and always features either Blitz or Sudds beer. The generic beer is never advertised.

The current values of the independent variables are $P_x = 7.99$; $P_y = 8.49$; $P_z = 6.49$; $A_x = 1.25$; $A_y = 1.5$; and $M = 350.96$.

(a) Calculate the elasticities of demand for Blitz beer, with respect to its own price, the prices of the other beers, and consumers' incomes. What do these figures indicate?

(b) Derive an expression for the demand curve for Blitz beer, and express this in the conventional way.

(c) What is the sales-revenue-maximizing price for Blitz beer?

(d) Supposing the store's marginal cost is $2 per case, what is the profit-maximizing price for Blitz beer?

(e) At that price, what range of sales volumes can be expected at the 95% confidence limits?

(f) Outline all the assmuptions and qualifications which underlie your sales predictions.

SUGGESTED REFERENCES AND FURTHER READING

BAUMOL, W. J. *Economic Theory and Operations Analysis* (4th ed.), chap. 10. Englewood Cliffs, N.J.: Prentice-Hall, Inc., 1977.

BENNETT, S. and J. B. WILKINSON, "Price-Quantity Relationships and Price Elasticity under In-Store Experimentation," *Journal of Business Research*, 2 (January 1974), pp. 27–38.

DRAPER, N. R., and H. SMITH, *Applied Regression Analysis*. New York: John Wiley & Sons, Inc. 1966.

GOLDBERGER, A. S. *Topics in Regression Analysis*. London: Macmillan, Inc., 1968.

GREEN, P. E. and D. S. TULL, *Research for Marketing Decisions* (3rd ed.), esp. chaps. 3-5. Englewood Cliffs, N.J.: Prentice-Hall, Inc., 1975.

JOHNSTON, J. *Econometic Methods*, chaps. 1, 2, 4, 7, and 8. New York: McGraw-Hill Book Company, 1963.

KOTLER, P. *Marketing Management* (3rd ed.), chap. 19, Englewood Cliffs, N.J.: Prentice-Hall, Inc. 1976.

LEVIN, R. L. *Statistics for Management* (2nd ed.), chaps. 11 and 12. Englewood Cliffs, N.J.: Prentice-Hall, Inc., 1981.

LUCK, D. J., H. G. WALES, and D. A. TAYLOR, *Marketing Research* (4th ed.), esp. chaps. 9, 10, 12, and 14. Englewood Cliffs, N.J.: Prentice-Hall, Inc., 1974.

PESSEMIER, E. A. "An Experimental Method for Estimating Demand," *Journal of Business*, 33(October 1960), pp. 373–83.

STONE, B. *Successful Direct Marketing Methods* (2nd ed.), esp. chap. 15. Chicago: Crain Books, 1979.

Empirical Case 3

ESTIMATING THE DEMAND FOR GASOLINE

In 1987, the United States experienced a budget deficit of approximately $150 billion. For some time, the government has considered raising the gasoline tax as a partial solution to the deficit problem. A preliminary estimate of the government's annual revenue gain is approximately $1 billion for every additional penny levied on gasoline consumption.[1] If, for example, the gasoline tax was increased by 20 cents per gallon, tax revenues would increase by approximately $20 billion per year.

From an international perspective, the current U.S. tax on gasoline of approximately 9 cents per gallon tax pales in comparison to that levied by other free-market economies. For example, this same tax ranges from $1.50 per gallon in the United Kingdom and Germany to more than $2.00 per gallon in France, Italy, and the Netherlands.[2]

In addition to its direct revenue benefits, the higher gasoline tax is expected to generate several positive externalties. For example, the resulting higher effective price of gasoline should encourage more efficient driving, which in turn would reduce environmental pollution, congestion on urban roads and highways, and traffic fatalities. Moreover, the expected decline in gasoline consumption resulting from the increased tax will, in turn, lower U.S. reliance on the OPEC community,[3] reducing U.S. vulnerability to another OPEC crisis. A recent estimate of U.S. dependence on OPEC production shows that approximately 40% of U.S. oil consumed is purchased from the OPEC cartel.

To examine these issues more carefully, consider the following: The consulting firm you work for has been hired by the U.S. government to provide an independent analysis of the demand-side effects of a gasoline tax. Your division manager has asked you to conduct an economic study of short-run consumer demand for gasoline.

In consultation with your staff, you have decided to include several quantifiable economic factors in your investigation. Given that the focus of the analysis is the impact of the gasoline tax on the quantity of gasoline consumed, you have asked your staff to decompose the price of gasoline into the service station price (P_S) exclusive of tax and the retail price (P_R) inclusive of tax. Obviously, the difference between these two ($P_R - P_S$) is the combined state and federal tax. You remind your staff that they must deflate the retail price of gasoline by the Consumer Price Index (CPI), since the quantity demanded of a commodity depends on its real rather than its nominal price.

To complete the modeling of the short-run demand function, you hypothesize that the annual quantity of gasoline consumed (Q^D) is a function of constant dollar disposable

---

[1]Mike Evans, "It's Time for a Gas Tax", *Industry Week*, November 20, 1989, p. 68.

[2]John Greenwald, "Fueling Up a Brawl", *Time*, January 23, 1989, pp. 42–43.

[3]Martin and Kathleen Feldstein, "Raise the Gasoline Tax", *Boston Globe*, May 9, 1989.

income (RY_D), the constant dollar price of public transportation (RP_T), the total number of registered vehicles (N), and the miles per gallon of an average vehicle (MPG).

TABLE 1

Year	Q^D	P_S	P_R	CPI	RP_T	N	MPG	RY_D
1962	43771	20.36	30.64	90.6	87.4	66638	14.37	6271
1963	45246	20.11	30.42	91.7	88.5	69842	14.26	6378
1964	47567	19.98	30.35	92.9	90.1	72969	14.25	6727
1965	50275	20.70	31.15	94.5	91.9	76634	14.15	7027
1966	53312	21.57	32.08	97.2	95.2	80106	14.1	7280
1967	55110	22.55	33.16	100.0	100.0	82367	14.05	7513
1968	58524	22.93	33.71	104.2	104.6	85793	13.91	7728
1969	62448	23.85	34.84	109.8	112.7	89156	13.75	7891
1970	65784	24.55	35.69	116.3	128.5	92095	13.7	8134
1971	69514	25.20	36.43	121.3	137.7	96144	13.73	8322
1972	73463	24.46	36.13	125.3	143.4	100658	13.67	8562
1973	78011	26.88	38.82	133.1	144.8	106119	13.29	9042
1974	74217	40.41	52.41	147.7	148.0	109823	13.65	8867
1975	76457	45.44	57.22	161.2	158.6	111679	13.74	8944
1976	78847	47.44	59.47	170.5	174.2	115170	13.93	9175
1977	80677	50.70	63.07	181.5	182.4	118711	14.15	9381
1978	83233	53.09	65.71	195.4	187.8	121717	14.26	9735
1979	80233	74.33	87.79	217.4	200.3	125750	14.49	9829
1980	73375	104.73	119.1	246.8	251.6	127448	15.32	9722
1981	71718	112.75	131.1	272.4	312.0	129123	15.68	9769
1982	72848	102.65	122.2	289.1	346.0	129500	16.36	9725
1983	73156	95.36	115.7	298.4	362.6	131723	16.81	9930
1984	71180	91.46	112.9	311.1	385.2	133751	17.8	10419
1985	69450	89.64	111.5	322.2	402.8	137308	18.28	10622
1986	71404	63.63	85.7	328.4	426.4	140693	18.35	10947
1987	70984	66.33	89.7	340.4	441.4	142209	19.26	10976

Q^D = Gasoline consumption for passenger cars, millions of gallons.

P_S = Service station price, excluding taxes, cents per gallon.

P_R = Retail price of gasoline (includes state and federal taxes), cents per gallon.

CPI = Consumer Price Index (Base year 1967), total.

RP_T = Consumer Price Index (Base year 1967), public transportation.

N = Number of registered passenger cars, thousands.

MPG = Average miles traveled per gallon.

RY_D = Real per capita disposable income, 1982 dollars.

Sources: Q^D, P_S, P_R, N, and MPG come from the *Basic Petroleum Data Book*, published by the American Petroleum Institute, 1989.

CPI, RP_T, and RY_D come from the *Economic Report of the President*, 1988.

A multiple regression analysis is to be conducted using annual time-series data on each of these variables for the period from 1962 to 1987. The empirical model is as follows:

$$Q^D = a_0 + a_1 RP_R + a_2 RP_T + a_3 N + a_4 MPG + a_5 RY_D + e$$

where a_0, a_1, a_2, a_3, a_4, and a_5 represent the parameters to be estimated using a statistical regression software package, RP_R is the deflated retail price of gasoline, and e is the error term in the model, assumed to possess all of the conventional statistical properties. Table 1 presents the data to be used in the estimation.

QUESTIONS

1. Using economic theory, what are the hypothesized signs of the parameters (a_0, a_1, a_2, a_3, a_4, a_5) in the model? Explain.

2. Using the results from your regression analysis, are your estimated parameters statistically significant? Compare your hypothesized signs (Question 1) with your estimated signs. If there are any discrepancies, provide an appropriate explanation.

3. Using 1987 data, what are your estimated elasticities with respect to each independent variable? Interpret each elasticity.

4. Recall that the government made the claim that for every one cent of tax on gasoline there would be $1 billion increase in tax revenue. Use your estimated model to support or refute the government's claim.

5. Can you think of any direct or indirect negative effects associated with the gasoline tax? Can these explain why the government has been reluctant to raise the tax? Explain.

Empirical Case 4

ESTIMATING THE DEMAND
FOR DOMESTIC AUTOMOBILES

Empirical estimation of demand conditions in the domestic automobile market has become an increasingly important subject of economic analysis. Over the past two decades individual manufacturers have been struggling with a series of much-publicized problems ranging from poor productivity performance to intense foreign price competition. In addition to these firm-specific problems, the industry itself has had to adjust to other pressures associated with a changing macroeconomic environment. Automobiles are a cyclical consumer durable good sold in a marketplace that is dramatically affected by such factors as disposable income and consumer interest rates. Consequently, cyclical changes in these macroeconomic variables can detrimentally affect aggregate industry demand, which, in turn affects demand at the firm level.

To investigate these important issues, economists use regression analysis to estimate demand conditions at both the industry and firm level. Analytically, the link between industry demand and the demand faced by the firm follows from microeconomic theory. Recall that industry demand is modeled as the horizontal summation of individual demand curves. Thus, if one assumes constant market shares across firms, it is theoretically possible to translate industry demand changes to firm-specific demand changes. Specifically, predicted quantity demanded at the industry level can be multiplied by firm market share to derive an estimate of predicted quantity demanded at the firm level.

Even if this hypothesized link between industry and firm demand can be quantified, there is still the problem of actually estimating industry demand. The empirical demand specification must be selected from among many possible functional forms. In addition, the appropriate set of explanatory variables must be selected in accordance with economic theory. For example, in the automobile industry, it is critical to include a price variable, a consumer income variable, and an interest rate measure.

To illustrate the entire estimation process in the context of the automobile market regression analysis is proposed using annual time-series data on each of these variables for the period from 1970 to 1987. The demand specification is a nonlinear model represented as follows:

$$Q^D = a_0 RPN^{a_1} RYD^{a_2} i^{a_3}$$

where a_0, a_1, a_2, and a_3 represent parameters to be estimated, RPN is a real price index of new cars, RYD is real disposable income, and i is the prime rate of interest. Table 1 presents the data to be used in this analysis.

As explained in the text, one of the benefits of this particular specification is the intuitive interpretation of the parameter estimates. Taking logarithms of the variables transforms the nonlinear equation into a linear equation. The resulting parameter estimates measure the percentage change in the dependent variable given a percentage change in each independent variable.

TABLE 1

Year	Q^D	RPN	RYD	i
1970	7115274.603	107.6	1668.1	7.91
1971	8676408.090	112.0	1728.4	5.72
1972	9321305.126	111.0	1797.4	5.25
1973	9618508.232	111.1	1916.3	8.03
1974	7448339.497	117.5	1896.6	10.81
1975	7049843.199	127.6	1931.7	7.86
1976	8606856.110	135.7	2001.0	6.84
1977	9104932.233	142.9	2066.6	6.83
1978	9304247.497	153.8	2167.4	9.06
1979	8316018.868	166.0	2212.6	12.67
1980	6578359.219	179.3	2214.3	15.27
1981	6206688.802	190.2	2248.6	18.87
1982	5756614.512	197.6	2261.5	14.86
1983	6795226.090	202.6	2331.9	10.79
1984	7951786.23	208.5	2469.8	12.04
1985	8204694.894	215.2	2542.2	9.93
1986	8222475.891	224.4	2645.1	8.33
1987	7080889.531	232.5	2676.1	8.22

Q^D = Annual domestic auto sales, number of units. From *Automotive News, Market Data Book*, various issues.

RPN = Real price index of new cars. From *Economic Report of the President*, 1988.

RYD = Real disposable income. From *Economic Report of the President*, 1988.

i = Prime rate of Interest from *Economic Report of the President*, 1988.

QUESTIONS

1. Using economic theory, what are the hypothesized signs of the parameters (a_0, a_1, a_2, and a_3,) in your model? Explain.

2. Examine the results from your regression analysis. Are your estimated parameters statistically significant? Explain.

3. What are the estimated elasticities with respect to each explanatory variable? Interpret each elasticity.

4. Using your regression results, what does your model predict regarding quantity demanded of domestic automobiles for 1987? How confident are you with this estimate?

5. Given that GM's 1987 domestic market share was 48.7%, determine an estimate of their sales for 1987.

6. Can you think of any additional variables that should be included in the analysis? If so, what are they, and how might they affect your estimates of industry demand?

Appendix 5A

DEMAND FORECASTING

EXECUTIVE SUMMARY

Forecasting the future level of demand is an issue of concern for business firms as well as governments, banks, and other institutions. Consequently, there is a considerable amount of forecasting activity at the aggregate, sectoral, and industry levels. Decision makers in firms and institutions have access to the results of much of this forecasting activity and should utilize this material in forming their own forecasts. If the demand for their particular products is closely correlated with GNP or some other measure of aggregate activity, published forecasts are available, such as those in the *Business Conditions Digest* issued by the U.S. Department of Commerce. Such **publications will serve as in inexpensive source of data** on future demand levels. On the other hand, the firm's demand may move against the general trend, or it may exhibit lags or leads, and the decision maker may need to construct a forecast to suit the specific circumstances of the individual firm.

We start by **extending regression analysis to forecast future values** of quantity demanded, given estimates of future values of the determinants of the firm's demand. This is a causal forecasting model, since we attempt to model the causes (determinants) of future demand based on our prior observations and explanatory models of demand. Next, we consider time-series analysis and the **decomposition of a time series into its trend, seasonal, cyclical, and random components.** Future values can then be predicted by projection of the trend and adjustment for the expected seasonal and cyclical effects. **Exponential smoothing** is another technique to improve predictions of future demand. Finally, we examine **several methods of predicting the state of the economy,** and, from this prediction (and prior knowledge of a relatively stable relationship between the firm's demand and some aggregate variable), we derive a forecast for the firm's demand.

Regression Analysis as a Forecasting Tool

Regression analysis was utilized in Chapter 5 both as an explanatory model of the determinants of demand and as a predictive model of the quantity demanded, given estimates of the coefficients and known values of the variables that determine quantity demanded. Estimation of the firm's demand function in the present period allowed the regression equation to be used as a predictive model to predict the impact of changes in the firm's price (or any other determining variable) on the quantity demanded of the firm's product. The predictive power of the regression equation is easily applied to future periods as well. If we can generate predicted values for the determining variables in a future period and can be confident that the coefficients estimated in the present period remain reliable in the future period, we can derive a forecast of demand in the future period.

The future-period values of the determining variables may be estimated by a variety of means, each involving information-search activity. The most simple procedure would be to project any trend displayed by each variable into the future period and insert the projected value of each variable in the regression equation. A simple trend projection for each variable may be established by regressing the variable against time and using the line of best fit to provide an estimate of the variable's value in the future period. The regression equation for the variable as a function of time should be checked for its predictive power (the R^2, standard errors, and S_e/Y ratio) before using the projected value in the regression equation to forecast demand.

A second method is to establish a probability distribution for the uncertain future value of each variable in the regression equation. For such variables as competitors' prices and advertising budgets, which might have been constant throughout the period of the time-series data, the decision maker might estimate the probability distribution relating to possible levels of that variable in the next period. For example, you might estimate that the firm's main competitor may raise its price by 10% with probability 0.40, may maintain its price at the same level with probability 0.50, or may reduce its price by 5% with probability 0.10; you would then use the expected value of the competitor's future price in the regression equation representing the demand function.

Third, one might use published sources to establish a consensus forecast—that is, one might average the values forecast by several well-known forecasting firms or individuals—for those variables that are widely discussed and predicted, such as the consumer price index (CPI), interest rate, gross national product (GNP), imports and exports, and industrial production. If these variables are significant determinants of your firm's demand, you might use the consensus, or average, prediction of the various experts who routinely follow and forecast these variables. Alternatively, their forecasts of these variables may assist in determining your estimate of the variables in your demand function. The forecast value of CPI may be the most likely indicator of movements in competitors' prices in the next period, or forecast values for GNP may be the best information you have about the likely movement in consumer incomes.

Finally, for other variables that are specific to your demand function, marketing research and professional forecasting firms employ high-powered people and techniques to generate their forecasts of these variables, and it may well be cost-effective to utilize their services rather than attempt to duplicate their efforts.

In addition to an explanatory model of the demand function for current-period decision-making purposes, the firm may be able to develop a separate predictive model that has greater predictive power when used to forecast future values of quantity demanded. For predictive purposes only, a regression model may safely fall into some of the pitfalls of regression analysis. Multicollinearity, spurious and illogical dependence, and autocorrelation may be permitted to exist if the regression equation is to be used only to forecast future quantity demanded. Essentially, any variable (with any lag applied) may be included in the regression equation as long as it increases the value of the R^2 and consequently reduces the standard error of estimate. This is not to say that the firm's forecasting model should be totally unrealistic; such a situation would carry with it the danger that if the true causes of quantity demanded are not incorporated to a large extent, their values might change and cause the forecast to be substantially wide of the mark.

The multiproduct firm may be more interested in its total sales revenue in a future period than the quantity demanded (and hence sales) of a particular product or product line. A regression model can be constructed to predict the firm's total sales in a future period, using independent variables suggested by consumer behavior theory. For example, the next period's sales should be expected to depend on the next period's general price level and consumer incomes. The CPI is a measure of general prices that is applicable here, and GNP is a broad measure of total consumer incomes. (A better measure is disposable income, DI, which is aggregate personal income after taxes, estimates of which are also readily available.) If the firm's products are often bought on credit, then the cost of borrowing money, or the interest rate r, is a likely determinant of future sales. Estimates of future interest rates are published regularly in the financial pages. Thus an explanatory (or casual) model to forecast the firm's total sales revenue (TR), might be

$$TR = \alpha + \beta_1 CPI + \beta_2 DI + \beta_3 r \qquad (5A-1)$$

The constant term α and the β coefficients may be estimated using past data. For example, using data collected for each year since 1975, actual sales revenues might be regressed on these independent variables to establish a regression equation that best fits the data. The R^2 and standard errors also generated will indicate the predictive power of the model. If this is not high enough, then other probable determinants of sales should be entered into the regression equation until an acceptable predictive equation is obtained. Then, using current estimates of the next period's CPI, DI, and r, a predicted value of the next period's total sales may be calculated from the regression equation.

Time-Series Forecasting Models

Time-series forecasting models generate a forecast of future values based entirely on past values of the variable to be predicted. They therefore exclude any changes in the current period or those expected in the next period which the manager may be aware of, since these changes will not yet be reflected in the past data. In this sense, these models are naive. In terms of complexity they run all the way from simple projections through moving averages, exponential smoothing, and time-series decomposition.

Simple Projections.   The simple trend projection method takes the present period's value of the time-series variable and multiplies it by the trend that has become evident in the past to obtain a forecast of the next period's quantity demanded, or sales, level. That is,

$$\hat{Y}_{t+1} = (1 + b)Y_t \tag{5A-2}$$

where the subscripts indicate the period (t is the present period, $t + 1$ is the next period, $t - 1$ would be the preceding period, and so on). The coefficient b is the slope term derived from the regression of past Y values against time. Of course it is unlikely that the value of Y_{t+1} will fall exactly on the trend line, since a multitude of influences may operate to cause the observed value to fall above or below the trend line. Cyclical, seasonal, and random variations about the trend will be discussed below. For longer-term projections, simple extrapolation of trend may be useful, but it is unlikely to be very reliable for short- to medium-term forecasts. For *very* short-term forecasts, such as for next month's sales, it may be relatively useful since the cyclical and seasonal factors may not be expected to change much in the very short term.

Moving Averages.   If the time series is subject to unexpected fluctuations, a moving average may generate an acceptable prediction of future period values of the variable. Suppose that sales have fluctuated over the past six periods as shown in Table 5A-1. Taking a four-period moving average of sales in column 4 (equal to the value in column 3 divided by 4), we see that the moving average rises and then falls. We take the moving average for periods t to $t - 3$ (namely, $7,068,000) as our forecast of sales in period $t + 1$, the next period. Adding this figure into the four-period total (and dropping the $t - 3$ sales figure), we find a new four-period total and a new moving average of $7,070,000, which becomes our forecast of sales in period $t + 2$. The use of a forecast value of a variable to generate the forecast of the following value of the variable is called recursive forecasting.

   If a trend exists within the data, the moving average would tend to move up or down over time. Note, however, that the moving-average method weights equally each of the past periods that are included in the moving average. Thus the moving average would systematically underestimate the future values if there is an upward trend, or overstate future values if the trend is downward. A *weighted* moving average, weighing the more recent periods more heavily, would show the trend effect and more accurately predict future values of the variable. One could experiment with the weights assigned to the past periods until one found the combination that minimizes the sum of the squared deviations of the forecast values from the actual values in past periods, and then use these weights to forecast the value of the variable in future periods. However, one would probably be better off using an exponential smoothing model, as we shall see below.

TABLE 5A-1. Forecasting Using Moving Averages

Period [1]	Sales ($000) [2]	Four-Period Total ($000) [3]	Four-Period Moving Average ($000) [4]
$t - 6$	7,000		
$t - 5$	7,200		
$t - 4$	6,820		
$t - 3$	7,060	28,080	7,020
$t - 2$	7,120	28,200	7,050
$t - 1$	6,872	27,872	6,968
t	7,220	28,272	7,068 (forecast for $t + 1$)
$t + 1$	7,068*	28,280	7,070 (forecast for $t + 2$)
$t + 2$	7,070*		

*Forecast values based on four-period moving average.

Exponential Smoothing Models.   These models attach exponentially declining weights to the past observations, starting with the largest weight being assigned to the most recent period. A major advantage of these models over weighted-moving-average models is that exponential smoothing models adjust each prior forecast to reflect its forecast error. Thus these models adjust more quickly to changing conditions than do moving-average models. The forecast value of $\hat{Y}_{t+1}$ can be written as

$$\hat{Y}_{t+1} = \hat{Y}_t + a(Y_t - \hat{Y}_t) \tag{5A-3}$$

This equation says that the forecast for period $t + 1$ is equal to the forecast for period t plus a times the difference between the actual Y_t and the previously forecast $\hat{Y}_t$. Thus the new forecast is adjusted by some proportion a of the error involved in the prior forecast. If a is chosen to be close to 1, a relatively large weight is placed on the most recent observation. Conversely, if a is close to 0, more weight is placed on the previous forecast than on the previous outcome, reflecting the belief that the most recent outcome probably contains a significant random fluctuation. This is seen more easily if we rewrite the preceding equation as follows:

$$\hat{Y}_{t+1} = aY_t + (1-a)\hat{Y}_t \tag{5A-4}$$

Thus the forecast value of $\hat{Y}_{t+1}$ is the sum of the actual outcome in period t (that is, Y_t) weighted by a and the forecast value of $\hat{Y}_t$ (made in period $t-1$) weighted by the complement of a. The value of a is chosen, after experimentation with past data, to minimize the sum of the squared deviations of the predicted Y values from the actual values. Note that the estimate of $\hat{Y}_t$ must have been

$$\hat{Y}_t = aY_{t-1} + (1 - a)\hat{Y}_{t-1} \tag{5A-5}$$

and the estimate of $\hat{Y}_{t-1}$ in turn must have been

$$\hat{Y}_{t-1} = aY_{t-2} + (1 - a)\hat{Y}_{t-2} \qquad (5A\text{-}6)$$

Thus the forecast value of $\hat{Y}_{t+1}$ can be rewritten, after substituting for $\hat{Y}_t$, $\hat{Y}_{t-1}$, and $\hat{Y}_{t-2}$, as

$$\hat{Y}_{t+1} = aY_t + (1 - a)Y_{t-1} + a(1-a)^2Y_{t-2} + a(1 - a)^3Y_{t-3} + \ldots \qquad (5A\text{-}7)$$

Thus $\hat{Y}_{t+1}$ is a weighted average of the prior levels of Y, where the weights decline exponentially as the prior period goes further back into the past. Since the previous values of Y are all involved in the $\hat{Y}_{t+1}$ forecast, we may simply use equation (5A-3) or, equivalently, (5A-4) to calculate the new forecast for $\hat{Y}_{t+1}$. A major practical advantage of the exponential smoothing model is that one does not need to keep, or retrieve, data going back a large number of years. One simply modifies last year's forecast by a proportion of its error.

If we were going to start using an exponential smoothing model, we would need to collect the actual Y value data for several years back to generate the optimal value for the weight a. Alternatively, we might simply begin with any forecast of $\hat{Y}_t$, start with $a = 0.5$, and refine the model over the next several periods. Note that the weights decline exponentially, which means quite rapidly. If $a = 0.5$, for example, the weights in equation (5A-7), shown as a, $a(1 - a)$, $a(1 - a)^2$, and so on, are $0.5, 0.25, 0.125, 0.0625,$ $0.015625,$ and so on. Placing a greater weight on the most recent outcome means that the influence of past outcomes diminishes even faster.

There are many more complex time-series forecasting models, such as double exponential (and several other) smoothing models, and the Box-Jenkins model, but we have probably gone far enough for our purposes here. Hopefully your appetite is whetted for a course in business and economic forecasting, which would complement this course very nicely. If you cannot wait for that, I refer you to a good forecasting text.[1]

Time-Series Decomposition.   A time series may be decomposed into four potential elements, namely the trend, cyclical, seasonal, and irregular components of the series. The trend is the general rate of increase or decrease of the variable's value as time passes, and it is captured by the line of best fit to the observations when plotted chronologically. The cyclical component is the oscillation around the trend that results from alternating expansions and recessions in general business activity. Seasonal variation in the data, represented by a cycle within each year, is caused by the influence of weather and by events that take place on an annual basis, such as pre-Christmas sales and Thanksgiving weekend. The irregular component is the residual, which is not explained by the other three components. We expect the irregular component to be positive or negative and to depend on random events. Since these components interact with each other to determine the

---

[1]See, for example, Dale G. Bails and Larry C. Peppers, *Business Fluctuations: Forecasting Techniques and Applications* (Englewood Cliffs, N.J.: Prentice-Hall, 1982).

value of the time-series variable, we can specify the model in multiplicative form as follows:

$$Y_t = T_t \cdot C_t \cdot S_t \cdot I_t \tag{5A-8}$$

where Y_t is the value of the time-series variable in time period t (such as quantity demanded in the fourth quarter of 1992). Essentially, the future value of $\hat{Y}_{t+1}$ is equal to the projected trend value T (calculated using the line of best fit), multiplied by three index numbers representing the cyclical, seasonal, and random variation expected. The cyclical index will be greater than 1 if the variable is above the trend line, less than 1 if below the trend. The seasonal index will be greater than 1 if the current observation is above the quarterly (or monthly) average, and less than 1 if below the quarterly (or monthly) average. The irregular component will have an expected index value of 1 if indeed the residual component component is due to random events.

To isolate the components we would first deseasonalize the data. Deseasonalizating requires calculation of a moving average, over four quarters if the observations are quarterly, or over twelve months if the observations are monthly, for example. The ratio of the actual observation in a particular period to the moving average centered on that period is the seasonal index number S for that period. Dividing each Y observation ($Y = T \cdot C \cdot S \cdot I$) by the seasonal index number leaves us with the deseasonalized data ($Y/S = T \cdot C \cdot I$). The next step is to calculate the trend line of the deseasonalized data by regressing $T \cdot C \cdot I$ against the period number in which each data point was observed (1 for the first quarter, 2 for the second quarter, and so on). From the resulting regression equation a series of predicted $T \cdot C \cdot I$ values will be generated. The ratio of the observed $T \cdot C \cdot I$ value to the predicted value for each observation is the cyclical index number C. Dividing each observed $T \cdot C \cdot I$ value by its cyclical index number we have $T \cdot I$, or the trend component multiplied by the irregular index number. Since we are unable to predict the irregular component's direction or magnitude, we expect $I = 1$, and hence we are left with the trend component that is subject to unexpected variations caused by random events. This method of decomposing a time series is shown in more detail in elementary statistics and business forecasting textbooks.[2]

• EXAMPLE: Suppose we have the following regression equation for the firm's (deseasonalized) quantity demanded:

$$Q_t = 12{,}586.83 + 452.39_t$$

where t is the number of the periods over which the observations were collected. Suppose further that this equation was estimated over twenty periods and we wish to forecast $\hat{Q}_{21}$ the value in the twenty-first period, which is, say, the first quarter of the sixth year. Inserting 21 for t in the equation, we find $\hat{Q}_{21} = 22{,}087.02$, which is the trend value

---

[2]See Robert R. Johnson and Bernard R. Siskin, *Elementary Statistics for Business*, 2nd ed. (Boston: Duxbury Press, 1985), chapter 18. See also Bails and Peppers, *Business Fluctuations*, esp. chapter 4.

(subject to irregular variation) expected for quantity demanded in the future period. In other words, this is the $T \cdot I$ value of Q.

Now suppose that the cyclical index C has been rising over the past several quarters and a reasonable projection of it for the future period is the value 1.035, indicating that demand will be 3.5% above trend because of the expansion of the economy during this period. Multiplying the $T \cdot I$ value of Q by the cyclical index number, we find the $T \cdot C \cdot I$ value of $\hat{Q}_{21} = 22,860.07$. Finally, assume that the seasonal index number S for the first quarter is given as 0.925 (that is, quantity demanded is typically only 92.5% of the four-quarter moving average during the first quarter of the year). Multiplying the $T \cdot C \cdot I$ value of Q by $S = 0.925$, we have $\hat{Q}_{21} = 21,145.56$. Thus the firm's forecast quantity demanded ($T \cdot C \cdot S \cdot I$) for the future period is 21,145.56 units. The standard error of estimate associated with the regression equation would be used to establish the confidence interval (caused by the irregular component) in which the actual observation is expected to fall with a particular level of confidence.

Macroeconomic Forecasting

We turn now to the forecasting of macroeconomic aggregates, such as gross national product (GNP) and other measures of national income, the general price level, and the level of interest rates. Our interest in these variables is a derived interest: They may provide information that allows the firm to make better forecasts of the demand for its products. National income, or more appropriately, disposable income (national income less net taxes) measures aggregate consumer income, and it may be the best indicator of changes in the income of the firm's clientele.

Indices of the price level, such as the consumer price index (CPI) and the wholesale price index (or producer price index), indicate the general trend of prices of products purchased by consumer and producers, respectively. These price indices, along with the measure of disposable income, may prove useful to the firm considering whether or not to raise its own prices.

Forecasts of the interest rate, actually a structure of interest rates based on the Treasury bill rate (with more risky securities and longer-term loans typically carrying higher-risk premiums), may be important determinants of sales for firms in interest-rate-sensitive markets. Demand for much of construction, housing, automobiles, and other consumer durables, including furniture and appliances, depends on the prevailing and forecast borrowing rate, since much of this demand is supported by credit.

Readers of the *Wall Street Journal, Business Week, Fortune*, and other business periodicals will already be familiar with the ongoing discussion of the trends in the aforementioned macroeconomic variables. For the forecaster, and for managers in general, I believe these periodicals should be mandatory reading. They report on virtually everything of interest to the business decision maker, including the presentation of periodic forecasts of disposable income, prices, and interest rates.

The following discussion is confined to two related issues. First we examine the intention surveys conducted monthly, quarterly, or semiannually by a variety of government and private sources. Second we examine the use of barometric indicator forecasting to track and forecast the general level of economic activity.

Intention Surveys. Two main intention surveys are conducted periodically: the survey of consumer intentions and the survey of investor intentions.[3] Both are used to judge the level of confidence the consumer or investor feels concerning the desirability of spending for consumption or investment in the future. If consumers are hesitant about continuing their purchases of consumer durables or semidurables in the near or not-too-distant future because of pessimistic expectations about the state of the economy (and, indirectly, the likelihood of their income remaining at high levels), we might forecast an attenuation of the demand for these products in future periods. For many purchases, especially nondurables such as food, the consumer's purchases may be expected to continue at a relatively constant level almost regardless of the level of aggregate economic activity. For durables and semidurables, however, the consumer may postpone such purchases if the immediate outlook is less promising. If consumer expectations take a general turn toward the pessimistic, we would expect demand for such products to fall in the ensuing period.

Investors' intentions are important not only as an indicator of the future level of aggregate economic activity but also for the implications these intentions have for the demand for a variety of products, such as construction materials, office supplies, and plant and equipment. Decision makers interested in the demand for these products must therefore remain aware of such intentions for the implications that they will have on the demand for their own products.

Investors' intentions are similarly highly dependent on investors' expectations about the future levels of aggregate activity. Investors will feel more confident about investing if they expect aggregate activity to remain high or to increase from its present level, since this expectation has implications for the degree of idle capacity in future periods. If investors' expectations are relatively pessimistic, we might expect investment projects to be postponed or canceled, with subsequent impacts on the level of aggregate economic activity. The ironic feature about both consumers' and investors' expectations is that these expectations tend to become self-fulfilling prophecies. To counter this phenomenon, governments, banks, and business leaders often express great confidence in the future levels of aggregate economic activity at times when all other indications imply the opposite.

The problems with intention surveys as a forecasting device are similar to those that occur when surveys are used to estimate present levels of the demand parameters. However, some of these problems are increased by our asking consumers or investors to predict their actions far into the future instead of our simply observing the current actions

---

[3]Consumer intentions to purchase homes, automobiles, and a variety of consumer durable goods are surveyed by the Census Bureau and also by the Survey Research Center at the University of Michigan. Investors' intentions are surveyed quarterly in the *Survey of Current Business* by the U.S. Department of Commerce, as well as by the Securities and Exchange Commission and the National Industrial Conference Board. Purchasing plans of business executives are surveyed monthly by the National Association of Purchasing Agents. Business periodicals report on these surveyes on an ongoing basis.

of the people who make the demand decisions. Any change in expected future demand levels should become immediately apparent. Thus decision makers have an advance warning of likely changes and can plan their production, inventories, and other matters more effectively.

Barometric Indicators: Leading Indicators and Diffusion Indices.   A barometer is a device that predicts changes in one variable (weather) by measuring the change in another variable (air pressure). Since falling air pressure foretells the arrival of relatively inclement weather and rising air pressure indicates that the weather will begin to improve, the barometer is able to predict tomorrow's weather on the basis of today's air pressure. Barometric indicators in forecasting are named for the same ability: Movements in the barometric indicator typically lead movements in the variable that we wish to predict. Thus by observing the level of the barometric time series and its changes, we are able to predict changes in the variable of interest based on the previous association between these two time series.

Leading Series Indicators.   The first type of barometric indicator consists of a single leading series. In this case the firm will attempt to find a particular time series that tends to consistently lead the performance of the demand for its products.[4] By "lead the performance" we mean that the barometric indicator will experience turning points (the changes in direction from growth to contraction or from contraction to growth) in advance of the turning points of demand for a firm's products. In addition, a pattern may emerge between the rate of growth or decline of the barometric series and the rate of change of the demand. Examination of time-series data for various industries and sectors should unearth a time series that tends to act as a leading indicator for the sales of a company's products. We may find, for example, that the shipments of coal and the production of steel vary as indicated in Table 5A-2.

In Table 5A-2 it can be seen that reductions in steel production (the negative percentage changes) tend to precede the reductions in coal shipments by two quarters, just as the increases in steel production tend to precede the increases in coal shipments by two quarters. We can rationalize this as the time period it takes for the steel producers to become aware of the reduction in demand for their product and to organize a reduction in their orders for coal. Producers of coal thus have a six-month warning for turning points in demand for their product, which should aid their production and inventory planning considerably. In this case, then, steel production acts as a barometric indicator of changes in the level of demand for coal.

Single-series leading indicators are unlikely to consistently lead the series they are intended to, and moreover they are unlikely to lead by a consistent lead period. A multitude of other factors influence the demand for steel in the preceding example or the barometric indicator in the general case. It is difficult in practice to find a leading indicator that leads even 90% of the time, since random factors intervene to cause the baromet-

---

[4]For an extensive listing of leading, lagging, and coincident indicators, see the *Business Conditions Digest*, a monthly publication of the U.S. Department of Commerce.

TABLE 5A-2. Steel Production as a Leading Indicator for Coal Shipments (Hypothetical)

Year	Quarter	Steel Production % Changes (qtr. to qtr.)	Coal Shipments % Changes (qtr. to qtr.)
1990	1	2.5	1.6
	2	3.1	3.2
	3	1.8	2.4
	4	−0.2	1.8
1991	1	−1.4	1.2
	2	−1.8	−0.4
	3	0.6	−3.8
	4	2.4	−4.1
1992	1	3.0	1.6
	2	−1.2	3.2
	3	−2.1	3.6
	4	0.8	−2.5

ric indicator to indicate continued growth when in fact the dependent time series is already falling, or vice versa.

Composite Leading Indices. To avoid the problem of the unreliability of a single indicator, composite barometric indices have been established. Several leading indicators are aggregated to form an index, with the result that the random movements in any one series tend to be offset by opposite movements in one or more of the other series. The result is that the composite index provides a more reliable indication of actual turning points in the series we are attempting to predict. Table 5A-3 shows the major leading, coincident, and lagging indicators, as identified by the National Bureau of Economic Research and by other sources. The value of the latter two categories for forecasting is their ability to indicate when the peak or trough has in fact passed. Since the coincident indicators are expected to turn at about the same time as GNP or aggregate economic activity and since lagging indicators are expected to turn after the GNP has turned, we may be confident when we observe these series turning that GNP has in fact turned as indicated by the leading indicators, without having to wait for actual measurement of GNP to confirm that there has been a turning point.

The Diffusion Index. A third category of barometric indicators involves the diffusion index, which shows the proportion of the total number of series in a chosen collection that are rising at any point of time. For prediction of GNP, for example, when the diffusion index exceeds 50% we expect that GNP will be rising, and when it is less than 50% we expect that GNP will be falling. We can construct a diffusion index to predict the sales of any product by using past data to choose the series to be included in the index so it will best predict turning points of sales for that product. In Figure 5A-1 we show the relationship between the diffusion index and the variable that we are hoping to predict by use of the diffusion index. In the ideal situation where the series in the diffusion index are

TABLE 5A-3.   Selected Leading, Coincident, and Lagging Indicators

Leading Indicators
  1. Average work week, production workers, manufacturing
  2. Nonagricultural placements
  3. Index of net business formation
  4. New orders, durable goods industries
  5. Contracts and orders, plant and equipment
  6. New-building permits, private-housing units
  7. Change in book value, manufacturing and trade inventories
  8. Industrial materials prices
  9. Stock prices, 500 common stocks
 10. Corporate profits after taxes
 11. Ratio, price to unit labor cost, manufacturing
 12. Change in consumer debt

Roughly Coincident Indicators
  1. Employees in nonagricultural establishments
  2. Unemployment rate, total (inverted)
  3. GNP in constant dollars, expenditure estimate
  4. Industrial production
  5. Personal income
  6. Manufacturing and trade sales
  7. Sales of retail stores

Lagging Indicators
  1. Unemployment rate (unemployment > 15 weeks, inverted)
  2. Business expenditure, new plant and equipment
  3. Book value, manufacturing and trade inventories
  4. Labor cost per unit of output, manufacturing
  5. Commercial and industrial loans outstanding

From Table 2 in J. Shiskin and L. H. Lempert, "Indicator Forecasting," in W. F. Butler, R. A. Kavesh, and R. B. Platt, *Methods and Techniques of Business Forecasting* (Englewood Cliffs, N.J.: Prentice-Hall, 1974), pp. 48–49.

weighted by the exactly appropriate amounts, as the diffusion index rises to 50% and above, the variable to be predicted reaches its lower turning point and continues to rise. When the diffusion index reaches a maximum, the variable to be predicted should exhibit an inflection point, and as the diffusion index drops below 50% the variable to be predicted will attain a maximum and thereafter fall. There are likely to be random shocks to the diffusion index such that it will not appear smooth, as in Fig. 5A-1. To better judge the direction of change of the diffusion index, we may need to use a moving average of the past few weeks or months.

The major limitation of barometric indicators generally is that they predict turning points only and not the magnitudes of the change, so we must use some other method to find the likely magnitude of the change in the variable to be predicted. Thus barometric indicators, like surveys, are more suited to short-run forecasting, since they require little lead time and indicate turning points rather than the general longer-term direction of sales. Projection techniques, on the other hand, require substantial preparation time in

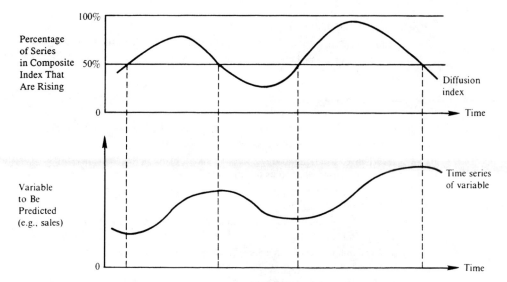

FIGURE 5A-1.   *Relationship between a Diffusion Index and a Time Series*

some cases, and in all cases they generate the general trend of the data and may incorrectly predict the immediate direction and magnitude of the change in the variable.

Summary

Demand forecasting is concerned with the future values of the parameters and independent variables of the demand function, and it is clearly vital for decision problems where expected sales in future periods must be forecast.

   Regression analysis is an important forecasting tool. A regression equation may be a causal (or explanatory) model of the relationship between the demand for a product and its major determinants. Alternatively, the regression equation may be simply a predictive model that best explains the variation in the firm's demand or sales, without necessarily being completely logical and without necessarily avoiding all the pitfalls that may apply to explanatory regression models.

   Time-series forecasting models naively project future values of the time-series data based solely on the past values of the data. Moving-average forecasts allow the average of the most recent observations to be used as the forecast value of the next period. Weighted moving averages must be used if a trend is apparent in the data, to weight the most recent observations more heavily. Exponential smoothing models weight the more recent observations more heavily and also adjust the forecast for errors in previous forecasts. The time-series decomposition technique decomposes the time series into its trend, cyclical, seasonal, and irregular components. The projected trend value is then adjusted up or down by the use of cyclical and seasonal indices (calculated on the basis of past observations) to arrive at the forecast value for the next period.

   Forecasts of macroeconomic variables and surveys of consumer and producer intentions are also useful in helping the firm forecast its future demand situation. The technique of barometric indicator forecasting was examined in some detail. Such forecasts and survey results are published periodically and should be incorporated into, or at least checked for consistency with, the firm's own forecast of its future demand.

DISCUSSION QUESTIONS

5A-1. Distinguish between causal forecasting models and time-series forecasting models. How can a complex model be naive?

5A-2. When is a moving-average forecast likely to be better than the simple projection of the current-period value plus a trend factor?

5A-3. What are the advantages of exponential smoothing models over weighted-average forecasting models?

5A-4. Explain how the forecaster would arrive at the weight to be used in an exponential smoothing model.

5A-5. Explain how a time series may be decomposed into its four components and how a forecast value for the next period may be arrived at.

5A-6. What are leading indicators? Name several, and speculate as to why they are leading indicators.

5A-7. Why is the use of a composite leading index usually preferable to a single leading index? What is the advantage of a diffusion index?

5A-8. Outline how you might generate a demand forecast for a particular product group, such as for automobiles.

PROBLEMS AND SHORT CASES

5A-1. The Lieberman Plastics Company wishes to predict sales for its plastic pails for the 1992 year. It has recorded data for its past ten years' demand and has obtained data on the number of households within its market area. This information is listed in the following table.

Lieberman Plastics Company

Year	Sales of Pails (units)	Number of Households (000)
1982	7,000	350
1983	6,750	462
1984	7,150	548
1985	8,300	610
1986	8,000	694
1987	9,200	830
1988	9,050	985
1989	10,100	1,080
1990	10,300	1,210
1991	10,600	1,330

(a) Plot the annual sales data against the number of households in the market area and draw in the line of best fit that seems to be visually appropriate.

(b) Measuring the intercept and slope of the line of best fit, state the approximate functional relationship between the two variables.

(c) Suppose the number of households is projected as increasing by 165,000 in 1992. Use the functional relationship to forecast the demand for plastic pails during 1992.

(d) Comment on the probable accuracy of your forecast.

5A-2. The Johnston Raymond Corporation has established a composite index of demand which has been relatively accurate in predicting the annual quantity demanded of its cement products. A number of variables are included in the index, such as GNP in current dollars, the index of industrial production, personal disposable income, manufacturing and trade sales, and industrial materials prices. Also included is the average price of JRC's cement products and the prices of substitute products. By trial and error, JRC has adjusted the weights to each of these variables such that the composite index has performed very well in predicting sales in the recent past. Historical data for the past twelve years are shown in the following table:

Johnston Raymond Corporation:
Historical Data

Year	Sales (units) (Y)	Demand Index (X)
1980	1,950	500
1981	2,570	658
1982	3,140	801
1983	3,280	843
1984	3,360	853
1985	3,570	917
1986	3,750	953
1987	3,980	995
1988	5,800	1,485
1989	6,170	1,567
1990	6,650	1,729
1991	7,130	1,845

(a) Calculate the regression equation showing the relationship between the quantity demanded and the value of the composite index.

(b) How reliable is the composite index as an explanatory variable?

(c) Form a projection of the value of the composite index over the next five years.

(d) Use this projection in the regression equation to forecast the quantity demanded in each of the next five years.

5A-3. Avon Cosmetics Company markets its products directly to customers in eighteen separate campaigns annually. Sales brochures are prepared and printed for each campaign and are sold to the sales representatives, who are paid by commission only. To allow time for printing and distribution and to give the sales representatives sufficient time to utilize the brochures while making their normal rounds to clientele, it is necessary to forecast sales of the brochures three campaigns in advance. The quantity of brochures sold to representatives in a particular territory for each campaign during 1989, 1990, and the first six campaigns of 1991 are shown in the accompanying table, along with the scheduled print runs for campaigns 7, 8, and 9.

Actual Brochure Sales

Campaign	1989 (000)	1990 (000)	1991 (000)
1	1,013	865	997
2	923	811	965
3	779	712	877
4	897	712	877
5	819	774	965
6	874	831	1,051
7	879	845	1,091*
8	885	878	1,122*
9	906	840	1,100*
10	869	824	
11	844	800	
12	823	803	
13	834	786	
14	789	847	
15	833	878	
16	986	1,011	
17	1,027	1,090	
18	1,024	1,141	

*Scheduled print runs.

(a) Have you any comments on the levels of the printing runs for the seventh, eighth, and ninth campaigns of 1991?

(b) Forecast the sales of brochures for the tenth, eleventh, and twelfth campaigns of 1991, using trend projection.

5A-4. Halley Appliances has determined that quarterly sales of its household appliances depend on changes in consumers' incomes, the general price level, and the rate of interest. (Halley always sets its prices roughly equal to its major competitors, so these prices do not show up as significant determinants of quantity demanded.) Halley has generated the following regression equation:

$$S = 34,586.29 + 108.97INC - 28.73CPI - 15.43INT$$
$$(681.22) \qquad (23.86) \qquad (9.71) \qquad (11.84)$$

where S is sales revenue per quarter, INC is the number of percentage points by which aggregate disposable income has changed in the prior quarter, CPI is the (percentage points) change in the Consumer Price Index in the prior quarter, and INT is the (percentage points) change in the three-month Treasury bill rate in the prior quarter.

The coefficient of determination is 0.858, and the standard error of estimate is 1,238.77. The standard errors of the coefficients are shown in parentheses underneath the coefficients in the equation.

Estimates of this quarter's INC, CPI, and INT have just come to hand and are 1.85, 0.65, and 1.25, respectively.

(a) Using this equation, forecast sales for the next period.

(b) What is the 95% confidence interval for that forecast?

(c) What comments do you have on the predictive power of this regression equation?

(d) What suggestions do you have that might improve the predictive power of the regression forecasting technique used by Halley?

5A-5. The demand for stereo and video equipment repair depends on breakdowns occurring, and thus the demand for Ace Electronic Service (AES) varies unexpectedly from month to month. This variability creates extra costs for AES's owner, since his two repair technicians always seem to be either too busy or not busy enough. Each technician can handle about 1.5 jobs per seven-hour working day (there are, on average, twenty working days per month). With an extra three hours of overtime per day, which costs AES $10 per hour instead of the regular $7, each technician can do two complete jobs per day. Over the past year, AES has employed two technicians on a full-time basis and has used overtime when necessary. The owner of AES would like you to set up a forecast of the number of repair jobs that he might expect in November, based on the past twelve months' data supplied:

Month	Service Calls	Revenue Generated*
November	42	$2,060
December	80	3,840
January	58	3,016
February	24	1,392
March	66	2,904
April	44	2,376
May	72	4,032
June	64	3,200
July	38	2,390
August	53	2,862
September	76	3,572
October	28	1,624

*Revenue generated is net of the actual cost of parts installed, which are charged to the customer at actual cost plus a markup, which varies depending on the type of part. This revenue thus contributes toward labor and overhead costs. Overheads, comprising only rent, utilities, and depreciation, average $500 per month.

(a) Construct a three-period moving average of the number of repairs in November. Comment on this forecast.
(b) Based on the past year's demand, should AES employ any more or fewer full-time repair technicians? Explain and defend your answer.
(c) The productivity of the technicians could be improved if they did not have to answer the phone and receive customers. They say they could do three jobs each, in the normal seven-hour workday, if a receptionist were employed. Overtime productivity would also be doubled. A receptionist would raise overhead by $750 per month. Should AES hire one?
(d) Alternatively, new diagnostic equipment would cost $4,000 but would raise the technicians' productivity to 2.5 jobs per day each, or 3.25 including overtime. This equipment will last at least a year. Should AES buy it? (Assume that monthly demand will fluctuate around the average of the past twelve months.)
(e) Consider as an alternative a proposed incentive scheme that would pay each technician $10 for each job completed in addition to wages. This is expected to have the same impact on productivity as the new diagnostic equipment. Should AES implement this plan instead?

5A-6. Hubert Hockey Equipment faces cyclical, seasonal, and irregular variations in the trend for its hockey sticks. It has generated the following regression equation of past quantity demanded (deseasonalized) against time:

$$Q = 12,564.89 + 128.47t$$

where t is the month of the observation. The coefficient of determination for this equation is 0.933, and the standard error of estimate is 886.94. HHE has seventy-two months of data collected and wishes to forecast next month's ($t = 73$) quantity demanded. The cyclical index for next month, calculated on the basis of published forecasts of disposable income, is 0.956. The seasonal index, on the other hand, is 1.122, since this is one of the main months of the hockey season.

(a) Derive a forecast of the quantity of hockey sticks likely to be demanded next month, based on this information.

(b) Using the standard error, establish the 95% confidence interval around the trend value for quantity demanded next period.

(c) Suppose that 90% of the standard error is due to cyclical variation and the remainder to random deviations. Now establish a confidence interval around your forecast value of Q.

(d) What assumptions and qualifications underlie your forecast?

5A-7. The Four Squares Company has used exponential smoothing as a forecasting technique for several years and has established the optimal weight to be 0.85. The company's forecast value for sales last quarter was $1.265 million, and actual sales were $1.385 million.

(a) Derive a forecast of the current quarter's sales using the company's exponential smoothing model.

(b) Does the size of the optimal weight tell you anything about the pattern of their sales? Can you deduce why the company would get better forecasts by using a relatively heavy weight like this, rather than weighting the most recent observation less heavily?

(c) For what type of data pattern would a time-series decomposition model give better forecasts than an exponential smoothing model?

(d) What kind of data pattern would cause a simple moving-average model to give better forecasts than an exponential smoothing model?

SUGGESTED REFERENCES AND FURTHER READING

BAILS, D. G., and L. C. PEPPERS. *Business Fluctuations: Forecasting Techniques and Applications*. Englewood Cliffs, N.J.: Prentice-Hall, Inc., 1982.

BUTLER, W. F., R. A. KAVESH, and R. B. PLATT. *Methods and Techniques of Business Forecasting*, esp. pts. 1,2, and 4. Englewood Cliffs, N.J.: Prentice-Hall, Inc., 1974.

CHISHOLM, R. K., and G. R. WHITAKER, JR. *Forecasting Methods*. Homewood, Ill.: Richard D. Irwin. Inc., 1971.

GRANGER, C. W. J. *Forecasting in Business and Economics*. New York: Academic Press, 1980.

HANKE, J. E., and A. G. REITSCH. *Business Forecasting*. Boston: Allyn and Bacon, 1981.

JOHNSON, R. R., and B. R. SISKIN. *Elementary Statistics for Business*, 2nd ed. Boston: Duxbury Press, 1985.

NELSON, C. R. *Applied Time Series Analysis for Managerial Forecasting*. Oakland, Calif.: Holen-Day, 1973.

U.S. DEPARTMENT OF COMMERCE. *Survey of Current Business and Business Conditions Digest*. Springfield, VA.: National Technical Information Service, current issue.

Empirical Case #5

FORECASTING THE DEMAND FOR DOMESTIC AIR TRAVEL

Imagine that it is June 30, 1988, and you have just been hired as an airline industry analyst for Drexel, Burnham, Lambert. That's the good news. The bad news is, you have been informed by the director of your section that he needs a six-month forecast of domestic air travel by the end of the day.

Ideally, you would approach this problem by relying on your extensive economic background and develop an appropriate econometric model of domestic airline travel. However, given the immediate deadline, you decide to estimate a trend line and adjust for seasonal variations. Your statistical model is as follows:

$$\text{Trend line: } Y_t = a_0 + a_1 \text{ Time} + u_t$$

Where Y_t is a proxy for air travel quantity demanded; Time equals 1 for the first month's observation, 2 for the next month, etc.; a_0 and a_1 represent the intercept and slope parameters of your trend line and will be estimated by least-squares analysis; and u_t represents a well-behaved random error component.

TABLE 1.

Year	Month	RPM	Year	Month	RPM	Year	Month	RPM
1986	1	18,244	1987	1	20,926	1988	1	21,773
	2	17,486		2	21,392		2	22,021
	3	21,817		3	26,688		3	26,641
	4	20,318		4	24,757		4	24,768
	5	20,980		5	25,385		5	25,123
	6	22,027		6	25,330		6	26,225
	7	23,679		7	27,290			
	8	25,349		8	28,204			
	9	19,671		9	21,585			
	10	21,049		10	23,129			
	11	19,916		11	21,717			
	12	22,174		12	22,993			

RPM = Monthly revenue passenger miles (000). From *Aerospace and Air Transport, Industry Surveys, Standard and Poor's,* various issues.

Preliminary investigation of the industry indicates that the conventional measure of quantity demanded is revenue passenger miles (RPM), which captures the quantity of paying customers. You collect monthly data for the period from January 1986 to June 1988, which is given in Table 1. Use this data to estimate the trend line for domestic air travel. Then use your results to answer the following questions.

QUESTIONS

1. Plot the data to see if there is any apparent trend. Does the trend appear to be upward or downward sloping?
2. Does your regression analysis support your casual observation? Graph your estimated trend line on your plot. Why are there discrepancies between the actual observations and your trend line?
3. Using your estimated trend line, what are your forecasts for the period from July 1988 to December 1988? How confident are you with these forecasts?
4. Does there appear to be any seasonal variation in airline travel? What are some of the methods that can be used to adjust for these seasonal differences? Choose one such method and present an adjusted forecast.
5. Which forecast, trend or seasonally adjusted, are you going to present to your director? Explain.

Chapter 6

PRODUCTION FUNCTIONS AND COST CURVES

EXECUTIVE SUMMARY

In this chapter we consider **the firm's production process** and the implications of this for the cost of producing the firm's output. A thorough understanding of the **interrelationships between the cost of the inputs and the cost of the output** is essential for good management decisions.

Production is the process whereby resources are transformed into products. Production turns inputs into outputs. In this chapter we introduce several new terms and concepts to better understand the relationships involved in the production process. We are concerned with **the economic efficiency of production:** that is, we wish to minimize the cost of producing any particular output level during a given period of time.

The efficiency of the production process depends on the ratios in which the various inputs are employed, the absolute level of each input, and the productivity of each input at each input level and ratio. Since inputs are generally not free but have a cost attached, **the degree of efficiency in production translates into a level of costs per unit of output.**

Production and costs are thus intimately related. In this chapter the theory of production and costs is presented in a way that demonstrates the impact of changing efficiency in production on the shape and placement of the **cost curves.**

We examine the theory of production and costs to lay a sufficient **conceptual foundation for the discussion of practical cost concepts** and techniques of cost estimation in the two subsequent chapters.

6.1   THE SHORT-RUN VERSUS LONG-RUN DISTINCTION

In production and cost theory, the distinction is made between the *short run,* in which the quantities of some inputs are variable while others are in fixed supply, and the *long run,* in which all factors may be varied. Consequently, it is useful to classify the inputs on the basis of whether or not they are variable in the short run. Since *labor* has traditionally been variable and *capital* is typically fixed in the short run, these headings are commonly used to denote, respectively, all variable and all fixed resources. When using the terms *labor* and *capital* in this sense, we should think of one unit of labor as including, say, one hour of a worker's time plus a "package" of all the necessary raw materials, fuel, and other variable inputs, and we should think of capital as including all the plant, equipment, land, buildings, managers' salaries, and other expenses that do not vary with the level of output.[1]

It is important to understand that *the long run* does not refer to a long period of time. It is a peculiarity of the economists' jargon that the term has no direct connection with time at all, and that the firm is likely to be in a long-run situation for relatively short periods of time. When intending to change its scale of production, the firm must continue to operate in a short-run situation until its most-fixed factor becomes variable. At this point the firm is in a long-run situation, since it can vary the input levels of all factors. As soon as the firm has installed its new levels of plant, buildings, and other fixed facilities, it will begin to operate in a *new* short-run situation, since the input of these factors is now fixed at their new levels. Notice that the firm might be constrained to the short run for as little as a few days for some very simple types of firms (such as a street vendor selling flowers from a wheelbarrow) or as much as five years for large manufacturing concerns (such as steel mills or automobile producers). Thus the phrase *in the long run* should be taken to mean "when factors that are currently in fixed supply can be increased or decreased." Since the long run may be either a short or a long time coming, we will use *the long term* to refer to an extended period of time and reserve *the long run* for its specific meaning in the jargon of economics.

In most production processes there is a significant gestation period, or a time lag, between the conception of the idea to change plant size and the birth of the new plant. This time lag means that the firm must make its long-run decision (choice between available plant sizes) during a short-run period and continue in that short-run situation until the new plant is fabricated and installed, at which time it shifts into the new short-run situation. Also, firms with multiple outputs tend to be continually changing plant size for one or another of their multiple production process.

---

[1]The human resources utilized by the firm may be effectively fixed in many production functions, particularly if strong labor unions mean that people cannot be fired or retrenched at management's discretion. Even without strong unions, in many cases only unskilled labor can be regarded as a variable input, as the firm is usually reluctant to retrench or fire skilled labor due to the subsequent recruiting and retraining costs when these resources are needed again.

• EXAMPLE: Consider the assembly process for an automobile. Which inputs are fixed and which are variable? Remember that the criterion is whether or not the inputs must vary to cause changes in the output level. Certainly the land and building are fixed inputs and are not varied from day to day to cause changes in the output level. So too are the assembly lines, the computerized plant and equipment, and the various tools and machines used to assemble the cars. What about the assembly-line workers? To the extent that management can increase or decrease the input of human resources as production needs dictate, these workers are a variable input. Increases in human resource input can usually be effected by paying overtime rates to workers who continue into the next shift or by hiring new workers. Other inputs, such as component parts, fuel, and power, are certainly variable inputs to the production process.

6.2 PRODUCTION IN THE SHORT RUN

The Production Function

• DEFINITION: A production function is a technical specification of the relationship that exists between the inputs and the outputs in the production process. In general form, it says simply that the quantity of output depends on the quantity of the inputs used, as follows:

$$Q = f(K, L) \qquad (6\text{-}1)$$

where Q is the quantity of output; f represents the functional relationship existing between the inputs and the output; and K and L are the conventional symbols representing the input levels of capital and labor, respectively.[2]

In specific form the functional relationship is stated explicitly as a precise mathematical relationship. Output may be expressed, for example, as a linear function of the inputs, or alternatively as a multiplicative power function of the inputs. The exact mathematical specification of the production function depends on the productivity of the input factors at various levels of all inputs, and is an empirical issue.

The State of Technology. The productivity of a factor of production refers to the amount of output that can be produced by that input, holding constant the input of all other factors of production. Obviously, an input, such as human resources, can be more productive if it works with modern mechanical and computer-assisted equipment and high-quality raw materials. Similarly, the plant or equipment can be more productive if it is being operated by highly skilled and well-trained workers. We use the phrase *the state of technology* when we refer to the quality of the resources involved in the production

---

[2]In this chapter we confine our attention to production processes with a single output. Linear programming analysis allows us to deal with the multiple-output case and is treated in Appendix 6B, following this chapter.

process: Higher states of technology are associated with more productive inputs. Thus the state of technology refers to the inherent ability of factors of production to produce output, given the simultaneous efforts of all other inputs to the production process. For example, three units of labor and two units of capital may combine to produce fourteen units of output. If technology improves (that is, if either or both labor and capital become more productive), the same combination of labor and capital may then be able to produce, say, eighteen units of output. Thus the state of technology is incorporated into the specification of the production function and is reflected by the precise mathematical form taken by any particular production function.[3]

Given the specific form of the production function, we can insert values for labor and capital and find for every combination of labor and capital the output that would result. A tabular array of the output levels associated with various input levels of all factors for the hypothetical case of automobile assembly by a small company that produces sports cars is shown in Table 6-1. The numbers in the body of the table show how many vehicles can be assembled by each combination of capital and labor. For example, when capital is set equal to 2 units (2,000 machine hours) and 5 units of labor (500 labor hours) are added to this capital, the number of assembled vehicles produced will be 23.

Note that there is another combination of capital and labor that will also produce twenty-three assembled vehicles, namely, $K = 4$ and $L = 2$. This combination is clearly a more capital-intensive production process, apparently involving more automated techniques (such as robot welders and other mechanical and computer-assisted processes) and fewer units of labor per unit of output. This example demonstrates the substitutability of capital and labor in the production process. The same output level can usually be attained by several different combinations of capital and labor. This substitutability is also evident for the production of eight assembled vehicles: These may be produced either by setting $K = 3$ with $L = 1$ or by setting $K = 2$ with $L = 2$. In fact there are other combinations of capital and labor that will also produce eight vehicles. Note that $K = 1$ with a labor input somewhere between 3 and 4 (say, $L = 3.4$) could also produce eight vehicles. So too could $L = 3$ with capital input somewhere between 1 and 2 units (say, $K = 1.15$). The same could be found for any other output level.

There is typically a variety of input combinations, ranging from those that are relatively labor intensive to those that are highly capital intensive, which can be utilized to produce any given output level. In Appendix 6A, following this chapter, we introduce isoquant-isocost analysis to demonstrate that the input combination chosen by the firm depends on the relative cost of the capital and labor inputs. Suffice it to say here that when the cost of labor is cheaper, relative to the cost of capital, firms

---

[3]A linear production function can be expressed as $Q = \alpha + \beta_1 K + \beta_2 L$, where the $\alpha + \beta$ parameters are estimated from observed input and output data using regression analysis. A power function, such as $Q = AK^\alpha L^\beta$, enables us to compute the multiplicative effect of capital and labor, if it exists. Regression analysis using logarithmic transformation (see Chapter 8) can be used to estimate the parameters A, α, and β. This power function is often referred to as the Cobb-Douglas production function, named for C. W. Cobb and P. H. Douglas. See their "A Theory of Production," *American Economic Review*, 16 (1928), pp. 139–65, and P. H. Douglas, "Are There Laws of Production?" *American Economic Review*, 38 (March 1948), pp. 1–41.

TABLE 6-1. Motor Vehicle Assembly Production Function

| | | Labor Units (L) (hundreds of person hours) | | | | | | | |
		1	2	3	4	5	6	7	8
Capital	1	1	3	7	10	12	13	13.5	13
Units (K)	2	3	8	14	19	23	26	28	29
(000s of	3	8	18	29	41	52	62	71	79
machine	4	11	23	36	50	65	78	90	101
hours)	5	12	26	42	60	80	98	112	124

will choose more labor-intensive production methods. Conversely, when the cost of labor is high relative to the cost of capital, firms will choose more capital-intensive production methods.

- NOTE: Table 6-1 depicts both the short run and the long run. In the short run the level of capital input would be fixed at a particular level, and output is constrained to that shown in the *row* opposite that level of capital. In the long run, that is, when all input quantities are variable, any point in the table may be achieved. Thus if only 3,000 machine hours were available, output levels would vary as shown along the third row of Table 6-1 as we added or subtracted labor. Given the opportunity to change its plant size, the firm could move to any other row of the table, to which it would be constrained for the duration of the following short-run period.

The Law of Diminishing Returns

- DEFINITION: The *law of diminishing returns* states that as additional units of the variable factor are added to the fixed factors in the short run, after some point the increment to total product will decline progressively.

    The law of diminishing returns is concerned with the relative productivity of the marginal units of the variable factors as we progressively add them to the fixed inputs. Prior to the point where diminishing returns set in, there may be increasing returns to the variable factors followed by constant returns to the variable factors. The law of diminishing returns can be stated more broadly as the law of variable proportions, which states that as more and more of the variable factors are added to a given quantity of the fixed factors, the increment to output attributable to each of the additional units of the variable factor will increase at first, will later decrease, and will eventually become negative.

    Notice that this phenomenon relates to the short run, since fixed inputs are involved, and it can be witnessed in any row of Table 6-1, where the differences between the adjacent numbers increase at first and later decrease as more labor is added to a particular level of capital. In Table 6-2 we show the increments to output as we move along the third row of the production function exhibited in Table 6-1. Notice

TABLE 6-2. *The Law of Variable Proportions Exhibited by the Marginal Product of the Variable Factors*

Units of the Variable Factor (L)	Units of Output (for K = 3) (total product)	Increment to Output over Preceding Row (marginal product)	Returns to the Variable Factor (for K = 3)
0	0	—	—
1	8	8	Increasing
2	18	10	Increasing
3	29	11	Increasing
4	41	12	Increasing
5	52	11	Diminishing
6	62	10	Diminishing
7	71	9	Diminishing
8	79	8	Diminishing

that increasing returns prevail up to and including the fourth unit of labor when applied to three units of capital, after which point diminishing returns to the variable factor prevail.

Total Product and Marginal Product Curves

The total output from a production process is also known as the *total product* of the inputs to that production process. Thus the second column in Table 6-2 shows the total product for several levels of labor input (given capital input fixed at 3 units). In Figure 6-1 we plot the total product data on the vertical axis against the number of units of labor input on the horizontal axis. Note that for higher input levels (beyond that shown in Table 6-2) total product reaches a maximum and actually falls as still more labor input is added to the fixed capital inputs. This indicates that the ratio of variable to fixed inputs is too high, causing congestion of the work place, which results in total output falling despite the additional units of the variable inputs.

Note that the law of variable proportions is evident from the shape of the *TP* curve shown in Figure 6-1. It is convex from below at first, showing output increasing at an increasing rate as labor units are added. After the point of inflection the curve is concave from below, reflecting diminishing returns to the variable factors. The change in total product, as the result of a one-unit change in the variable input, or the rate of change of total production in relation to that of labor, is defined as the marginal product of labor. In Figure 6-1 we also show the marginal product curve, which can be derived from the total product curve.

DEFINITION: *Marginal product* is defined as the rate of change of total product as labor is increased, and it is equal in mathematical terms to the first derivative of the total product function with respect to labor. This is the same as saying that marginal product is

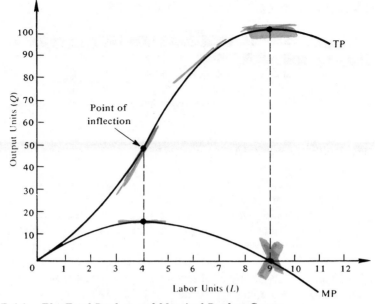

FIGURE 6-1. *The Total Product and Marginal Product Curves*

given by the slope of the total product curve at each level of labor input. Note that at the point of inflection, where the total product curve changes from being concave upward to concave downward, the total product curve is at its steepest, and marginal product attains its maximum value. Similarly, at the input level where total product reaches its maximum and later falls, marginal product falls to zero and becomes negative. The law of variable proportions can thus be expressed in terms of the behavior of the marginal product of the variable factor: There are increasing returns to the marginal unit of the variable factor while marginal product is rising, and there are decreasing returns thereafter as the marginal product falls.

The law of variable proportions is an empirical law, which is to say it has frequently been observed in actual production situations. Unlike a judicial law, however, there is no compulsion for every production function to behave like this. The range of increasing returns to the variable factors may be quite brief or indeed absent in many production processes. The point of inflection may be extended to exhibit a prolonged range of constant returns to the variable factor. But decreasing returns to the variable factor are a necessary feature of all short-run production situations, however. Sooner or later, as units of the variable factor are added to the fixed supply of capital resources, the marginal product of the variable factor must begin to decrease, because of simple overcrowding if for no other reason. Hence, this law is more commonly referred to as the law of diminishing returns. But note that the law of diminishing returns refers only to the section of the total product curve that is concave from below, after the point of inflection, or to the negatively sloped portion of the marginal product curve.

6.3   SHORT-RUN AND LONG-RUN COST CURVES

The total product curve shows the number of units of output associated with each level of the variable factors of production. At the same time, it implicitly shows the number of units of the variable factor required for each level of output. Since each unit of the variable factor costs money, it is a simple step to find the total cost of the variable inputs for each level of output, which is otherwise known as the total variable cost of each output level.

The Total Variable Cost Curve

The Total Variable Cost (TVC) curve can be derived from the TP curve simply by multiplying the level of variable inputs by the cost per unit of those inputs and by plotting these cost data against the output level. Suppose that the variable factor units cost $10 each. Using the data from the total product curve, shown on the right-hand side of Figure 6-2, and multiplying each unit of the variable factor by $10, we can plot the cost of the variable input against the output, in the left-hand side of Figure 6-2.

For simplicity we have chosen the scale on the left-hand side of the horizontal axis to be ten times that on the right-hand side, so the TVC curve is a mirror image of the TP curve. Note that three units of the variable factors, or $30 spent on the variable factors (which amounts to the same thing), will produce Q_1 units of output. Similarly, five units, or $50 spent on the variable factors, will produce Q_2 units of output. Thus the shape of the total variable cost curve derives directly from the form of the production function and the number of units of capital employed, since these factors underlie the shape of the total product curve.

Average Variable and Marginal Costs

- DEFINITION: *Average variable cost* (AVC) is equal to TVC divided by output Q at every level of Q. That is,

$$AVC = \frac{TVC}{Q}$$

(6-2)

In Figure 6-3 we show the TVC curve tipped on its side (rotated 90 degrees to the right) with the associated average variable and marginal cost curves. The AVC for each output level is equal to the ratio of the vertical distance from the quantity axis to the TVC curve. Average variable cost at point A on the TVC curve is equal to the ratio AR/OR, or the value of the slope of the line OA, and is shown as point A' on the AVC curve vertically below.

It can be verified that the slopes of rays from the origin joining points on the TVC curve become progressively flatter as we begin to move up the TVC curve away from the origin. Thus the AVC, which is equal to the value of these slopes, must fall over this range. A point is reached, however, where the ray from the origin can become no flatter

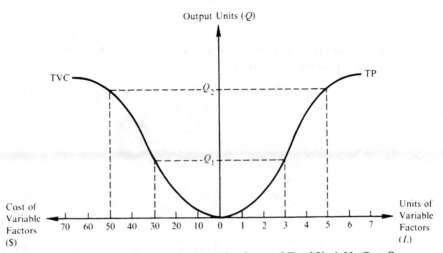

FIGURE 6-2. Relationship between the Total Product and Total Variable Cost Curves

and still touch the TVC curve. Point C, where the ray is just tangent to the TVC curve in Figure 6-3, signifies the lowest value for AVC. Since the rays become steeper for points on the TVC to the right of the tangency point, AVC must rise after this output level, as shown in the figure.

• DEFINITION: *Marginal cost* (MC) is the change in total costs caused by a one-unit change in output:

$$MC = \frac{\Delta TC}{\Delta Q} \qquad (6\text{-}3)$$

where $\Delta Q = 1$. Since output changes cause only variable costs to change, we can equivalently define marginal costs as the change in total variable costs for a one-unit change in output. Hence,

$$MC = \frac{\Delta TVC}{\Delta Q} \qquad (6\text{-}4)$$

where $\Delta Q = 1$. In this form you see that marginal cost is defined as the (vertical) movement up the TVC curve divided by the (horizontal) change in output. MC is thus equal to the slope of the TVC curve at each output level.

If we were to put tangents against the TVC curve at every output level, we would see that the slopes of these tangents would fall at first, up to the point of inflection on the TVC curve, and would then rise. In Figure 6-3 the point of inflection occurs at point B, where the TVC curve changes from convexity to concavity (when viewed from above). The slope of the TVC becomes progressively flatter until point B, and it becomes pro-

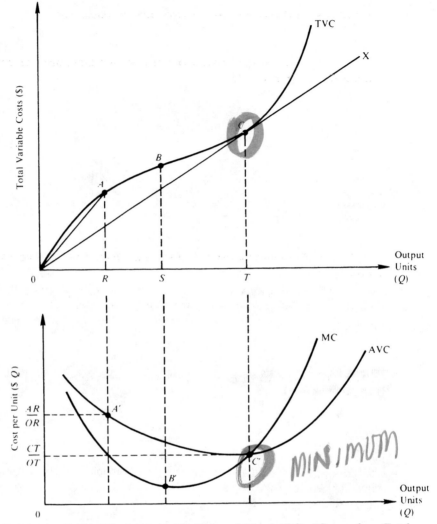

FIGURE 6-3.   *Derivation of Average Variable and Marginal Cost Curves from Total Variable Cost Curve*

gressively steeper after point *B* as output is increased. This indicates that the marginal cost curve is U-shaped, falling to a minimum at the output level where the TVC exhibits its inflection point and rising thereafter.

• NOTE: When the marginal cost curve lies below the average variable cost curve, the latter is falling. In effect, the lower marginal cost is pulling down the average. Conversely, when the MC curve lies above the AVC curve, the latter must be rising, being pulled up by the marginal costs. It follows that when the MC crosses the AVC, the AVC must be at its minimum value. This can be verified in Figure 6-3 at point *C* on the TVC curve.

Marginal costs and average variable costs must be equal, since both are given by the slope of the tangent to the TVC curve at that point.

Note that marginal costs are inversely related to the marginal product of the variable factors. When marginal productivity of labor is falling, marginal cost of output is rising, and vice versa. But if the efficiency of the marginal units of the variable factor is constant, output can be produced at a constant level of marginal cost. These relationships can be confirmed by another look at Figure 6-2. Notice that when the TP curve is concave from above, exhibiting increasing marginal productivity of the variable factor(s), the TVC curve is indicating decreasing marginal costs per unit of output. Alternatively, when diminishing returns set in for the variable factor(s) after the inflection point, the TVC curve begins to increase at an increasing rate, and marginal costs are increasing over this range.

Short-Run Average Costs

- DEFINITION: *Short-run average costs* (SAC) are defined as total costs (TC) per unit of output.

$$SAC = \frac{TC}{Q} \tag{6-5}$$

Total costs are the sum of TVC and total fixed costs (TFC). To complete the short-run cost picture, therefore, we need to add the costs of the fixed factors. TFC is a horizontal line when plotted against output, as shown in Figure 6-4, since these costs are constant whatever the level of output. To find the total of fixed and variable costs, we add vertically the TFC and TVC curves on the graph. This procedure, in effect, causes the TVC curve to be moved upward a constant distance equal to the total fixed costs. Thus the total cost (TC) curve and the TVC curve have the same shape, as is evident in Figure 6-4. As noted previously, the marginal cost curve can thus be derived from the TC curve instead of the TVC curve.

Average total costs, or short-run average costs (SAC), may be derived from the TC curve by the same technique as was used to derive the AVC curve. The slope of a ray from the origin to a point on the TC curve gives the value of SAC for each output level. Thus at point *B* in the upper part of Figure 6-4, SAC is equal to the ratio *BF/OF*, or the slope of the line *OB*. At the same output level, AVC = *CF/OF*, or the slope of *OC*. In the lower part of the figure these values are shown as points *B'* and *C'* respectively. Given the shape of the TC curve, SAC must fall at first, reach a minimum, and then rise. Note that at the minimum point, found where the ray from the origin is just tangent to the TC curve, the slope of the ray is equal to that of the TC curve, and hence SAC and MC are equal at that output level.[4]

---

[4]Alternatively, one can derive the SAC curve by adding the average fixed cost (AFC) to the AVC. The AFC will be a rectangular hyperbola, sloping downward to the right as output is increased, because total fixed

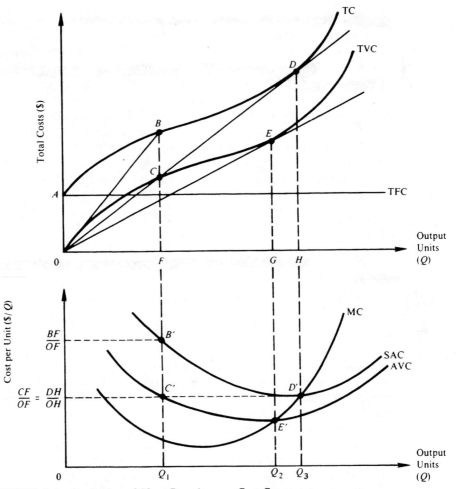

FIGURE 6-4. *Derivation of Short-Run Average Cost Curve*

Different Production Functions Cause Different Cost Curves

The specific form of the TP curve is an empirical question: For some plants it may indeed be a cubic function, as indicated by the S-shaped curves in Figures 6-1 and 6-2. But for other production situations it might be a quadratic or a power function, and it may even be sufficiently approximated by a linear function (over the relevant range) in other plants. Estimation procedures (considered in Chapter 8) will ascertain the shape of the TP curve in any particular production process. The cubic function we have been using is the most

cost (a constant) is spread over an increasingly larger output base. Note that AVC and SAC must converge on each other as output increases, since they differ by a decreasing margin, namely the decreasing value of AFC.

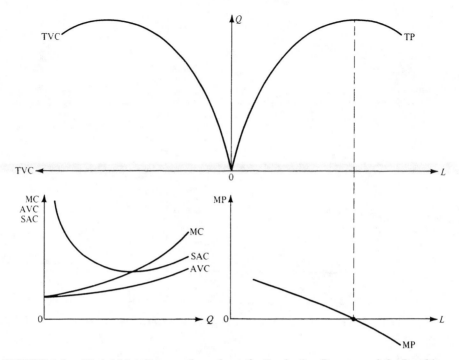

FIGURE 6-5. **Diminishing Returns throughout the Production Process and the Resulting Cost Curves**

general case, since it allows for the entire range of returns to the variable factors: It shows increasing returns at first, then constant returns (momentarily, at the point of inflection), and finally diminishing returns, after the point of inflection.

In some production processes we may expect diminishing returns to set in immediately; that is, for marginal product to decline from the outset. This may be true of very small plants which allow the variable inputs to be most efficient at low output levels. In Figure 6-5 we demonstrate that diminishing returns from the outset imply a quadratic TP curve (or other curve which increases at a decreasing rate, such as a power function). The TVC will take its shape from the TP curve, and resulting AVC and MC curves must be upward sloping throughout. Note that the SAC curve falls at first because of the influence of falling average fixed costs, but rises later as the rising AVC outweighs the falling average fixed costs.

Finally, there are cases in which it can be argued that constant returns to the variable factors prevail throughout, or at least over an extended range of output levels. This may occur in a production process in which variable inputs interact primarily with each other and there is minimal impact with the fixed inputs. For example, the marginal product of the variable inputs in a basket-weaving production process may be constant over a wide range of outputs, since the variable inputs (labor and the straw) interact with each other virtually independently of the fixed factors (which provide shelter, marketing sup-

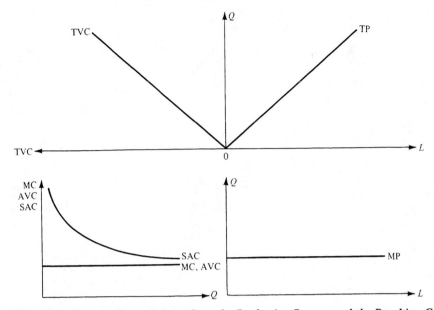

FIGURE 6-6.   Constant Returns throughout the Production Process and the Resulting Cost Curves

port, and so on). In Figure 6-6 we show a linear TP and MP curve and the resulting linear TVC curve. The cost-per-unit curves which are associated with the linear TVC curve are shown in the lower left-hand part of Figure 6-6. Note that MC is constant from the outset and is, therefore, coextensive with the AVC curve. Note also that SAC converges on AVC because of falling average fixed costs.

Linear TVC Curves Resulting from Plant Divisibility

In many production processes the fixed factors are indivisible, in the sense that the firm must utilize all of the fixed factors or none at all. In a steel mill, for example, the blast furnace is either on or off, and it tends to be relatively inefficient at low volumes. Similarly, the assembly line in an automobile plant is either moving or not moving. The TVC curve associated with such plants might reasonably be expected to be a cubic function of the variable inputs, reflecting falling marginal costs at first and rising marginal costs later. In other production processes, however, the plant, or some parts of it at least, are divisible in the sense that the variable inputs are not obliged to work with the entire plant but may instead work with a more efficient subset of the plant. In these cases the firm may be able to avoid situations in which too few units of the variable factors are working with too much capital and may instead be able to maintain the capital-labor ratio at the most efficient level over a considerable range of output levels.

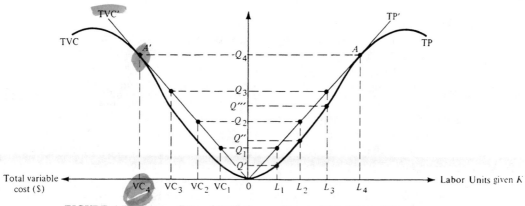

FIGURE 6-7. Linear TP and TVC Curves Due to Divisibility of Plant

- EXAMPLE: Consider a firm that manufactures stuffed toys. Its variable inputs are labor (operators for the cutting machines and sewing machines), cloth material, filler, cotton thread, and electrical energy to power the machines. Its fixed inputs, or plant, include four cutting machines, eight sewing machines, the building, fixtures, all related overhead costs, and the inputs of the managers, administrators, secretaries, clerks, and so on. Some part of the plant is divisible—namely the cutting and sewing machines. At low levels of output, with low levels of the variable inputs, some cutting and sewing machines would not be used at all but would be temporarily "mothballed." If demand for the product were to grow, the firm would then hire more labor, order more materials, and expand output by starting up these idle machines.

In terms of Figure 6-7, suppose that L_1, L_2, L_3, and L_4 represent the first four units of the variable factors. For example, L_1 might represent one cutting-machine operator, two sewing-machine operators, 30 yards of cloth, 50 pounds of filler, 100 yards of cotton thread, and the electrical energy to run one cutting machine and two sewing machines. These variable inputs, if applied to all four cutting machines and eight sewing machines, might produce only Q' units of output on the curvilinear total product curve shown as TP. Doubling the inputs of the variable factors to L_2 would increase output Q''; tripling inputs to L_3 would produce Q'''; and quadrupling inputs to L_4 is the level of variable inputs that maximizes the average product of the variable inputs (Q_4/L_4). The average product of the variable inputs is given by the slope of the ray from the origin to a point on the total product curve and is maximized at the point where this ray is tangent to the curvilinear TP curve. From the total variable cost (TVC) curve on the left-hand side of the figure, we see that average variable cost (AVC) is also minimized at the output level Q_4 and the underlying input level L_4.

Note that at input level L_4 there are four cutting-machine operators operating four cutting machines and eight sewing-machine operators operating eight sewing machines (because we are assuming that the most efficient ratio of operators to machines is 1 to 1 for both the cutting and sewing machines). Now suppose output had to be reduced because of a drop in demand. The firm would reduce its variable inputs back to L_3 units, but instead of asking the remaining workers to operate *all* the machines, it would close down one cutting machine and two sewing machines, maintaining the most efficient ratio of operators to machines. Thus output would fall only to Q_3 rather than Q'''. Thus AVC stays at the minimum level. Similarly, if variable inputs were reduced to L_2 units, the firm could maintain AVC at its minimum level by shutting down another cutting machine and two more sewing machines.

Thus, if the firm can divide its fixed factors into units which may or may not be operated depending on the demand for its product, it may be able to maintain the most efficient ratio of its variable factors to those divisible fixed factors, such that it can regard the straight lines TP' and TVC' as its total product and total variable cost curves, respectively. In this case the firm's marginal and average variable costs will not be U-shaped but will be linear, for output levels up to Q_4, as shown in Figure 6-6.[5]

Other Ways to Stabilize Unit Costs

Stable marginal and average variable costs are highly desirable, since they facilitate the firm's pricing decisions and its profit planning. We have just seen that the firm may keep AVC equal to MC at the minimum AVC level, if it is able to maintain the optimal ratio of variable to fixed inputs as a result of the divisibility of strategic fixed inputs (namely, the fixed inputs with which the variable inputs interact directly in the production process).

Inventories. By initially building up a desired level of inventories (or stocks) of finished goods, the firm has another way to stabilize unit costs in the face of fluctuating demand. The firm would maintain its output rate at a constant rate per period and run down its inventories when there is an unexpected increase in demand, rather than be forced to produce at higher levels of marginal cost. Later reductions in demand will give the firm the opportunity to rebuild its inventories to the desired levels. Thus, when demand is uncertain, a firm may choose to produce the expected value of quantity demanded in each period, adding to inventories when demand falls short of expectations and selling from inventories when demand exceeds expectations. Its desired inventories should be such that the marginal cost of holding an item in inventory does not exceed the additional production cost avoided by not producing the item on demand.[6]

Contracting Out. Another way to avoid rates of output that involve higher marginal and average variable costs is to have the firm contract out for additional production rather

---

[5]Output can be increased beyond Q_4 either by adding more units of L (labor, materials, and energy) to the existing plant (in which case the MC and AVC curves would begin to rise) or by adding both L and K in the optimal ratio (in which case MV and AVC would remain constant while AFC and SAC would shift upward). The latter implies a long-run adjustment, of course.

[6]Inventory control theory is beyond the scope of this text. Suffice it to say that it is only worth holding an item in inventory if the cost of holding that item does not exceed the difference between the MC of producing the item at the time it is demanded and the MC of producing it in advance.

than produce this output itself. If producing the output would cause the firm's MC values to rise steeply, the firm may be able to purchase the items at lower cost from another firm that has excess capacity and can produce the same product at a similar quality level. Initial setup costs may be involved, if the subcontractor has to imprint the firm's logo or follow the firm's special design, for example. But if the sum of these costs, plus the subcontractor's price per unit times the number of units, is less than the additional cost to the firm of producing those units itself, the firm should contract out rather than produce the additional units. We consider this make-or-buy decision in more detail in Chapter 7.

Backlists. Finally, unit costs can be kept constant by maintaining output rates (when demand exceeds the firm's capacity to supply) and putting customers on a backlist, or in a queue or waiting line for delivery as soon as possible. That is, customers are asked to wait for delivery until the firm can catch up with orders once the rate of new orders decreases. This approach may only be feasible if the firm's products are unique or customized, or if the delay causes the customer minimal problems, or if all rival suppliers are similarly operating with a backlist or waiting line. It may pay the firm to offer a discount for delayed delivery rather than incur the additional cost of producing the item on demand. This discount would encourage advance orders, which would help the firm in its production planning. If customers will wait for varying lengths of time, queuing theory may be utilized to calculate the optimal length of time spent in the queue. Queuing theory balances the sales lost because some customers will not wait at all (or not wait any longer than a certain time) against the cost of additional production facilities that would allow the queue to be shortened.[7]

The Short-Run Supply Decision

In the short run the firm must incur its fixed costs, since it cannot, by definition, change the input of these factors of production. The firm's variable costs, on the other hand, are discretionary, in the sense that the firm may decide whether or not to incur these costs, since the input of variable factors can be varied all the way back to zero. What induces a firm to incur costs? We argued briefly in Chapter 1 that the firm is profit oriented and will incur costs when it expects to more than cover those costs with revenues. Thus a firm will set up a plant and incur fixed and variable costs to produce a particular product because it expects to make a profit.

Once committed to its present size of plant, however, the fixed costs of that plant are *obligatory* in the short run. That is, the firm must incur them because it cannot vary them in the short run, by definition. But variable costs are *discretionary* and should be incurred only if the firm expects revenues at least to cover these variable costs. Suppose that in a particular situation price exceeds average variable cost but is less than the average total cost, meaning that the firm is making a loss. If the firm continues production when P is greater than AVC but less than SAC, there is, for each unit sold, some excess

---

[7]Queuing theory is also beyond the scope of this text. It may be encountered in production management or optimal control theory texts.

of revenue over variable costs that contributes toward the fixed costs. Therefore, the firm reduces its losses by continuing to produce when SAC > P > AVC, rather than by ceasing production. If it were to cease production, its loss would equal the entire fixed costs, rather than just part of fixed costs.

• RULE: Thus the firm should incur variable costs, and hence supply the product to the market, whenever price exceeds the firm's average variable cost level. If price also exceeds the SAC level, the firm makes a profit. If price falls below SAC, the firm suffers a loss, but it can minimize its loss by staying in production as long as P > AVC. If price slips below AVC, the firm would minimize losses by ceasing production and waiting until either the price rises above AVC again or until it can liquidate its fixed factors and terminate the associated fixed costs. The latter option implies a long-run situation, of course.

In most business situations, where the firm has multiple products, the rule governing the decision to supply or not to supply is more clearly stated in terms of total revenues and total variable costs, rather than in terms of (per unit) prices and average variable costs. That is, if TR > TVC, the firm should supply its product(s), whereas if TR < TVC, it should not incur the variable costs and, consequently, not supply the product(s). In the business world, quantity demanded tends to vary day by day and month by month because of seasonal factors, chance circumstances, weather conditions, and competing attractions. In effect, the demand curve shifts back and forth in response to these shift factors. Most firms cannot change their prices daily to reflect the differing states of demand that eventuate. Rather, they set prices on the basis of some notion of the average, or normal, demand situation and hold these prices steady as sales fluctuate daily, monthly, or seasonally around this conceptually normal volume. Hence price is constant while AVC varies substantially from day to day depending on the volume produced. In such situations the firm may find it easier to decide whether or not to supply its product in the short run on the basis of whether or not it expects TR to exceed TVC.

• EXAMPLE: During a severe snowstorm or hurricane, many stores may close early (or not even open at all) because the manager predicts that sales would be so small that it would not be worth keeping the store open and incurring the associated variable costs. Similarly, a coffee shop might stay open until 3 A.M. on Saturday night but close at midnight or earlier on week nights, based on the manager's expectation that sales revenues would or would not cover the total variable costs involved after the designated closing times. In these cases, fixed costs are being incurred and would be incurred regardless of whether the firm is open for business. The supply decision depends on whether or not the total sales revenue is expected to exceed the discretionary total variable costs relevant to the time period under consideration.

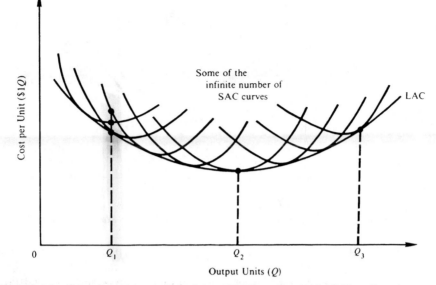

FIGURE 6-8. *Long-Run Average Cost Curve: Envelope Curve of All Short-Run Average Cost Curves*

The Long-Run Average Cost Curve

• DEFINITION: The *long-run average cost* (LAC) curve shows the least cost of production for each level when all inputs may be varied. It is the locus of points from various SAC curves which allow each output level to be produced at lowest cost, given the ability to change plant size (that is, to vary continuously the input of capital).

To derive the long-run average cost curve we can proceed by finding a series of SAC curves, one for every level of fixed inputs. Each level of capital (fixed factor) input will give rise to a TP curve, from which we can derive a TVC curve and ultimately obtain the appropriate SAC curve, as we did earlier. This procedure would give us a series of SAC curves, each with a slightly larger capital input level as we move from left to right. As shown in Figure 6-8, the long-run average cost (LAC) curve is the "envelope curve" of all these short-run curves. A corollary of this is that for any point on the LAC curve there is an SAC curve lying tangent at that point.

The LAC curve may not be a smooth line for many firms in the real world, since the smoothness depends on the availability of a large number of different plant sizes, with the sizes of these plants varying by relatively small increments from the smallest available to the largest available. In many industries there are only a few alternative sizes of plant, each one significantly different in size from the next largest and the next smallest.

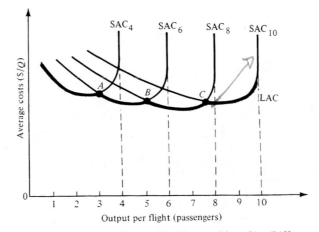

FIGURE 6-9. Long-Run Average Costs with Discrete Plant Size Differences

- EXAMPLE: Consider a small airline company that plans to initiate a feeder service from a remote town to a major city. In choosing the aircraft for this route, the firm must, in effect, choose its size of plant, since light aircraft are available in four-, six-, eight-, and ten-seat models. In this case, plant sizes are available only in discretely increasing, rather than continuously increasing, sizes, and the LAC curve will exhibit a series of kinks, or scallops, rather than being a smooth line. In Figure 6-9 we show the LAC curve as the heavy line encompassing only those sections of each SAC curve which allow output to be produced at lowest cost.

    The four SAC curves represent the available plant sizes, with the subscripts indicating the maximum number of seats in each plant size. Note that each SAC becomes vertical at the point where it reaches its maximum output (passenger) level. The LAC curve is the envelope curve of these four SAC curves: It contains kinks at points A, B, and C, where it becomes less costly (per passenger) to choose the next largest plant size. Note that if there were an aircraft available that seated five passengers (including the pilot), the SAC curve of that plant size would have nestled between SAC_4 and SAC_6, and it would have caused the kink in the LAC curve at point A to disappear and be replaced by two smaller kinks. Similarly, if planes were also available with seven and nine seats, the other kinks might be removed and be replaced by smaller kinks. It follows that if plant size were continuously variable, the kinks would disappear and the LAC curve would be a smooth line. In the real world, however, the LAC curve is most likely to exhibit kinks because plant size is not continuously variable.

Choice of Plant Size in the Long Run.   In the short run the firm is confined to its current plant size, but in the long run it will be able either to enlarge or reduce its plant to the size that best serves its objectives. Thus, if a firm finds itself with a plant that is either too large or too small in relation to its current quantity demanded, it may undertake the steps necessary to reduce or increase plant size. If it wants to reduce plant size, it has to find buyers for plant and buildings, wait until employment and other contracts expire, and so on. If the firm wishes to increase its plant size, it must order the fabrication and construction of new plant and buildings, search for new managers, hire and train more workers, and so on. All these things are possible; they simply take time to accomplish.

Given the freedom to choose any size of plant in the long run, which one should the firm choose? It should choose the plant size that minimizes the average cost of producing the firm's desired output level. Refer back to Figure 6-8 and suppose that the firm wishes to produce output level Q_1 (because Q_1 is the net-worth-maximizing output level, for example). Three different plant sizes that can produce output level Q_1 are shown in Figure 6-8, but the plant size chosen will be the one that produces this output level at the lowest average cost. Note that the plant size chosen will be the one with its SAC curve just tangent to the LAC curve at the desired output level. For "kinky" LAC curves, as shown in Figure 6-9, the plant size chosen will be the one with its SAC curve coextensive with the LAC at the desired output level. For example, when quantity demanded is expected to be eight passengers (including the pilot), the optimal plant size is the 10-seat aircraft.

In many cases the costs are known, but demand is uncertain. How then does the firm select its plant size? We can apply expected-value analysis to find the plant size that minimizes the expected value of average costs. Since the uncertain demand may be represented by a probability distribution of potential demand outcomes, we can transfer those probabilities to the output levels necessary to satisfy each of those demand levels, and note that each output level has a known average cost level in any particular plant. This process is demonstrated in Table 6-3. The probability distribution of quantity demanded is shown in the first two columns. The average cost at each of those output levels in a particular plant (plant A) is shown in column 3, and the expected value of average cost in that plant is calculated in column 4, where each value is the product of the value in column 3 multiplied by the probability of its occurring from column 2. The expected value of average cost in an alternate plant (plant B) is calculated in columns 5 and 6.

Note that plant A has lower average costs for smaller output levels but higher average costs for the larger output levels. Further inspection shows that where the weights (the demand probabilities) are highest, plant B has the lower average costs.[8] Thus we see that the weighted average costs, or the expected values of average costs, are lower (at $2.1125 per unit) in plant B. Assuming that these are the best two plant sizes available, the firm should install plant B based on this expected-demand situation.[9]

---

[8]The initial cost of plant B is no doubt higher than for plant A, but this difference is already incorporated into the analysis, since we are dealing with SAC. Included in the AFC part of SAC is a charge for depreciation, which is based on the life of the plant and the difference between its initial and its residual value. (In Chapter 7 we consider whether depreciation is the appropriate measure of the economic cost of the fixed inputs employed in the production process, arguing that it may not accurately reflect the opportunity costs of using the resources in the production process.)

[9]A totally erroneous procedure would be first to calculate the expected value quantity demanded (in this case 1,775 units) and then to base one's decision on the average cost level at that expected value of output in each plant. A quick interpolation between the average cost figure at 1,500 and 2,000 units in Table 6-3 will confirm that this procedure would give an underestimate of average costs in both cases, since larger and smaller outputs tend to have higher costs per unit.

TABLE 6-3.   *The Expected Value of Average Costs: Choice of Plant Size When Costs Are Known but Demand Is Uncertain*

QUANTITY DEMANDED		PLANT A		PLANT B	
Potential Outcome [1]	Prob- ability [2]	Average Cost [3]	Expected Value [4] = [2] × [3]	Average Cost [5]	Expected Value [6] = [2] × [5]
500	0.05	3.00	0.15	5.00	0.25
1,000	0.15	2.50	0.375	3.00	0.45
1,500	0.25	2.00	0.50	1.75	0.4375
2,000	0.35	2.75	0.9625	1.50	0.525
2,500	0.15	3.50	0.525	2.00	0.30
3,000	0.05	4.50	0.225	3.00	0.15
		Expected values	2.7375		2.1125

The Firm's Preference for Excess Capacity.   The firm's choice of its plant size to minimize the average cost (or expected value of the average cost) of production typically leads the firm to build a plant with production capacity greater than the level (or expected value) or quantity demanded. This excess capacity is evident in both the examples referred to previously (in Figures 6-8 and 6-9). In both cases the plant selected has the capacity to produce at a rate substantially higher than the (expected value of) quantity demanded. How do we measure excess capacity? In an absolute sense, the firm can continue to increase output until the SAC curve becomes vertical, but by the time that happens the marginal cost will be approaching infinity. Thus the absolute capacity is not a very useful reference point from which to measure excess capacity.

- DEFINITION: The *full capacity* of a plant is usually referred to as the output level at which MC begins to rise above SAC. Although additional output could be produced by adding more units of the variable factors, MC would typically rise very steeply. Firms usually avoid such "overfull capacity" production wherever possible, preferring instead to produce at a rate somewhat less than full capacity so they have in reserve some excess capacity. Thus *excess capacity* is the difference between the firm's current output level and the output level at which MC rises above SAC, and we recognize that after excess capacity is all used up the firm still has some overfull capacity it may wish to utilize, if it is profitable to do so.

What are the firm's motives for having excess capacity? When the market is growing, excess capacity buys the firm some time to build a larger plant, allowing it to serve an expanding market and maintain or increase its market share without unit costs rising prohibitively. Excess capacity also allows the firm operating under conditions of uncertain demand to defer the expansion decision until it can confirm that the growth in demand is permanent rather than transitory. Moreover, excess capacity allows the firm to produce at a rate higher than its current demand rate, to rebuild depleted inventories, to recover from a labor strike or mechanical breakdown, or to take advantage of a competitor's problem. Thus firms have several good reasons to build plants somewhat larger than they appear to need given their current demand or market share situation.

The Long-Run Marginal Cost Curve

• DEFINITION: *The long-run marginal cost* (LMC) curve shows the marginal cost of producing each additional unit of output when the firm is free to vary the inputs of all factors of production. As you should by now expect, the LMC lies below the LAC when the LAC is falling, and it lies above the LAC when the LAC is rising. In fact, LAC falls precisely because the LMC lies below it, pulling down the average cost. Similarly, LAC rises precisely because the marginal units cost more than the average to produce.

In Figure 6-10 we show the LMC associated with a particular LAC curve and three short-run cost situations. Notice that at output level Q_1, the short-run average cost is equal to the long-run average cost at point A. It follows that short-run marginal cost must equal LMC at this output level, since the two averages have converged on each other precisely because the two marginals were converging on the same value (at point B). Similarly, at output level Q_2 we have $SAC_2 = LAC = LMC = MC_2$. We know that the LMC must pass through the minimum point of the LAC curve and that (short-run) MC must pass through the minimum SAC point. Since SAC = LAC at the minimum points of both, we have four-way equality. Finally, at output level Q_3, average short-run and long-run costs are equal at point D, because marginal short-run and long-run costs are equal at point E.

Returns to Plant Size and Firm Size

• DEFINITION: Economies of plant size, or increasing returns to plant size, are evident when the LAC curve slopes downward to the right, indicating that successively larger plant sizes have corresponding SAC curves lying lower and to the right. These economies arise because larger output levels may allow the firm to utilize more efficient capital-intensive methods (such as computer-controlled assembly lines) and because personnel may specialize in the areas of their greatest expertise. After some point, increasing inefficiencies in other areas, caused perhaps by the increasing bureaucracy of larger establishments, may be expected to offset these cost advantages. The firm experiences diseconomies of plant size when successively larger plant sizes exhibit SAC curves that lie progressively higher and to the right.[10]

---

[10]There is a technical distinction between economies of plant size and economies of scale, although the two terms are used interchangeably by many. Economies of scale occur if unit costs decline when *all inputs are increased in the same proportion* (that is, if the K/L ratio remains constant). Economies of plant size occur if

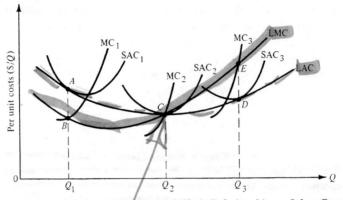

FIGURE 6-10.   Long-Run Marginal Costs and Their Relationship to Other Cost Curves

- NOTE: The LAC curve is *not* the locus of the minimum points of each SAC curve. Since each SAC curve is tangent to the LAC curve, the minimum SAC points would touch the LAC curve only if the LAC curve were horizontal. If economies and diseconomies of plant size exist, the LAC curve will at first be negatively sloping and then positively sloping. Thus tangencies with SAC curves must occur at first on negatively sloping parts of SAC curves and then on positively sloping parts. It follows that SAC curves are tangent to the left of their minimum points when there are economies of plant size, and tangent to the right of their minimum points when there are diseconomies of plant size. Only for the SAC curve that is tangent to the minimum point of the LAC curve, often called the *optimum size of plant,* will the minimum point of an SAC curve be a point on the LAC curve. This is evident in Figure 6-10.

Economies of Firm Size and Multiplant Operation.   Certain other economies arise as a result of the absolute size of the firm. For example, larger firms are usually able to obtain discounts for bulk purchases of raw materials, which gives them a cost advantage over smaller firms. These cost advantages are often referred to as pecuniary economies of plant or firm size, and they are clearly different from the economies of plant size that are dependent on increasing efficiency in production. Many large firms derive further pecuniary economies as the result of operating more than one plant. These cost savings are likely to result from spreading certain underutilized fixed costs, such as managerial talent, computer rental, and advertising expenditures, over more than one plant. The average cost curve for the first plant is, therefore, expected to sink downward to some degree as a result of opening a second and subsequent plants, since some part of the fixed costs

---

unit costs decline as plant size is increased, without any restriction on the K/L ratio. Indeed, in most business situations, the firm would not want to increase all inputs in the same proportion, because unit costs are typically minimized by *increasing* the K/L ratio as plant size is increased. A special case of the production function is the *homogeneous* production function, in which the same K/L ratio is optimal at all output levels. See P. H. Douglas, "Are There Laws of Production?" *American Economic Review*, 38 (March 1948), pp. 1–41, or any upper-level microeconomics textbook.

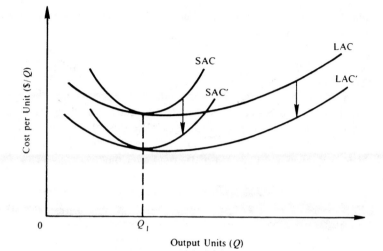

FIGURE 6-11. *Pecuniary Economies Causing Cost Curves to Sink Downward*

previously charged to a single plant are now charged to one of the newer plants. This situation is illustrated in Figure 6-11.

• EXAMPLE: McDonald's fast-food restaurant chain is a good example of a lot of things. Over several decades this chain has burgeoned from a single fast-food restaurant to a worldwide network of almost identical restaurants. Most of the phenomenal growth of McDonald's can be attributed to franchising, whereby local entrepreneurs supply a substantial capital investment in return for part ownership in a new outlet and several container loads of furniture, signboards, equipment, and fixtures that characterize a McDonald's restaurant. This familiar environment attracts customers who have tried McDonald's elsewhere and who know they can expect the same menu, the same quality, and reasonable prices. (This lack of uncertainty about prices and quality is very comforting to the wary consumer, who may have suffered disappointments and surprises at other fast-food restaurants.) In addition, McDonald's attracts new customers and reinforces preference patterns of regular customers by substantial expenditures on advertising and on other promotional efforts.

   On the cost side there seems to be little indication that McDonald's benefits from economies of plant size, since all their restaurants seem to fall within a relatively small size range, although this is largely determined by the size of local markets for each outlet. On the other hand, there is little doubt that McDonald's benefits from economies of multiplant operation. Each additional plant (new outlet) probably allows McDonald's to reduce the per-unit cost of its foodstuffs, since these are prepared in central locations and shipped to each franchised outlet. Advertising and promotion costs per outlet are reduced as the number of outlets sharing these costs is increased. Also, the per-unit cost of chairs, tables, and wall decorations is expected to decrease as the market (number of outlets) for these products increases. Thus we might expect the cost curves of any particular McDonald's outlet to drift downward (in real terms) over time as more and more outlets are opened.

The Learning Curve

It has been observed in particular production processes that the average costs per unit tend to decline over time as the factors of production learn the production process and become more efficient. Kenneth Arrow called this relationship "learning by doing," and empirical studies have shown that costs per unit in many manufacturing processes do exhibit a downward trend (in real terms) over time.[11]

- DEFINITION: The *learning curve*, also known as the experience curve, is a curve relating the cost per unit of output to the cumulative volume of output since that production process first started. Empirical studies indicate that unit costs tend to decline by a relatively stable percentage each time the cumulative output is doubled.

- EXAMPLE: Suppose that after setting up the assembly process for a new calculator, Texas Instruments found that assembly time had fallen to 100 minutes per calculator by the time 1,000 calculators had been assembled. Based on its previous experience that costs decline to 80% of their previous level each time output doubles, the company might predict that the 2,000th calculator would require 80 minutes assembly time; the 4,000th would require 64 minutes (80% of 80); the 8,000th 51.2 minutes (80% of 64); and so on. Given constant wages in real terms, the average cost per unit would be expected to decline along the learning curve depicted in Figure 6-12.

- NOTE: The learning curve plots unit costs against cumulative output. Cumulative output grows over time, and so the learning curve indicates that unit costs will decline over time as cumulative volume grows. The impact of this on the firm's SAC curves, which indicate costs per unit for different rates of output per period of time, will be to cause the SAC curve to sink downward as cumulative volume grows (and time passes). In Figure 6-13 we show the firm's SAC curves sinking downward as cumulative volume (indicated by the subscript to SAC) increases.

In terms of production and cost theory, the learning curve (and its manifestation as a sinking of the short-run cost curves over time) can be explained as a continuing improvement in the productivity of the variable inputs, given constant input prices. From one month to the next, the marginal product curve for the variable inputs shift up, causing the marginal cost curve to shift down, bringing with it the AVC and SAC curves. Note that the learning effect is greatest when a production process first starts, and diminishes as time passes. Mature production processes will find very little learning effect, and subsequently the downward drift of the short-run cost curves from one month to the next

---

[11]K. J. Arrow. "The Economic Implications of Learning by Doing," *Review of Economic Studies*, 29, No. 3 (1962). See also *Perspectives on Experience* (Boston: Boston Consulting Group, 1970).

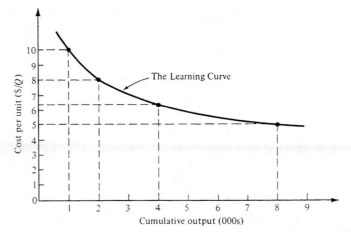

FIGURE 6-12. *The Learning Curve: Declining Average Costs as a Function of Cumulative Output*

will be negligible. Conversely, for new production processes (such as for the production of a new product, or a new way to produce an existing product), we should expect the learning effect to cause a significant downward movement in the short-run cost curves from one month to the next, until cumulative production grows to the level where the learning curve becomes relatively flat.

6.4 SUMMARY

The production process involves the interaction of inputs, or factors of production, to produce output. Inputs are categorized as either fixed or variable, depending on whether or not their input can be varied in the short run. By convention, and for graphical sim-

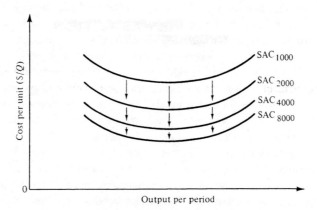

FIGURE 6-13. *Impact of the Learning Curve on the Firm's SAC Curve*

plicity, we call all the variable inputs labor and all the fixed inputs capital. In a particular short-run period, with capital fixed at a given level, output can be varied by varying the input of labor. Output is positively related to input of the variable factors, except at high ratios of the variable inputs to the fixed inputs, when overcrowding of the work place may cause total product to decrease. The total product curve, in its most general form, reflects output as a cubic function of the variable inputs, with marginal product rising at first and then falling. The law of diminishing returns in production, or more generally, the law of variable proportions, is evidenced by the behavior of the marginal product of the variable inputs.

The total variable cost (TVC) curve is derived from the total product (TP) curve by multiplying the variable inputs by their price per unit. Thus the shape of the TVC curve reflects the shape of the TP curve and the underlying increasing, constant, or diminishing returns to the variable factors. If the TP curve is a straight line, or a quadratic function, for example, then so too is the TVC curve. From the TVC curve we can derive the average variable cost (AVC) curve and the marginal cost (MC) curve. Adding total fixed cost (TFC) to TVC, we find total cost (TC), from which we derive the short-run average cost (SAC). If production is a cubic function of the variable inputs, the SAC, AVC, and MC curves will be U-shaped, and the MC curve will pass through the minimum point on both the SAC and the AVC curves.

The AVC and MC curves may be horizontal if there are constant returns to the variable inputs or if the fixed inputs are divisible such that the ratio of variable to fixed inputs can be held at the optimal ratio (where AVC is minimized). Other ways to avoid fluctuations in the value of AVC and MC include keeping the output rate constant and using inventories to accommodate fluctuations in demand, contracting out for production, and having customers wait when demand is unexpectedly or abnormally high.

The long-run average cost (LAC) curve is the envelope curve of all the short-run AC curves. Larger plant sizes are reflected by SAC curves lying further to the right. The LAC curve is the locus of minimum average cost of production when the firm is free to choose any size of plant. If plant size is continually adjustable, the LAC curve will be a smooth line, and the long-run marginal cost (LMC) curve will lie below LAC when it slopes downward to the right (economies of plant size) and lie above it when LAC slopes upward to the right (diseconomies of plant size). If there are several discretely different plant sizes, the LAC curve will comprise elongated sections (rather than simply points) from each of the underlying SAC curves, and it will exhibit kinks where costs would be reduced by changing to new plant size.

The firm's choice of plant size depends on its desired level of output. If demand is predictable with certainty, the plant size chosen is the one that allows the production of the quantity demanded at minimum average cost. If demand is uncertain, the plant size chosen is one that minimizes the expected value of average cost, given the probability distribution formed by the meshing of the demand probabilities and the known cost values at each output level. Choosing plant size on this basis typically means that the firm builds in some excess capacity, which benefits the firm in case of market growth or successful competitive strategies that lead to sales gains at the expense of rivals.

The short-run cost curves of a particular plant, and thus the long-run cost curve as well, will shift downward if the firm benefits from reduced input prices, if it can spread some of its fixed costs over more than one plant through multiplant operation, or if the productivity of its inputs improves because of the learning effect.

DISCUSSION QUESTIONS

6-1. Explain how a tabular representation of a production function represents both the long-run and the short-run situations at the same time.

6-2. Suppose your production process has three inputs—machinery, highly skilled labor, and raw materials. If you wanted a new (larger or smaller) machine, it would take six months to be fabricated, delivered, and installed. Your present workers are all under contract for another eight months. New workers would take three months to acquire, because of the lengthy process of advertising, interviewing, training, and so forth. Raw-material supplies must be ordered four weeks in advance. How long is your short run? When can you make your long-run decision to expand or contract your plant size?

6-3. How does the law of variable proportions differ from the law of diminishing returns?

6-4. Why is the point of inflection on the total product curve the point where diminishing returns begin?

6-5. Explain why the shape of the short-run average variable cost curve depends on the specific form of the production function.

6-6. Discuss three ways that the firm may stabilize its costs per unit in the short run, rather than be forced to produce at varying levels of marginal cost.

6-7. Why would it be erroneous, when demand is uncertain, to choose plant size on the basis of the average cost level at the expected value of demand? What is the correct approach?

6-8. Distinguish between full capacity, absolute full capacity, overfull capacity, and excess capacity.

6-9. Explain the construction of the long-run average cost curve and its relationship with the long-run marginal cost curve and the various short-run average cost curves.

6-10. Distinguish between economies of scale, economies of plant size, and economies of firm size. Under what conditions would a firm's expansion be an example of all three phenomena at once?

PROBLEMS AND SHORT CASES

6-1. Donald K. Brown and Company operates a pearl-diving operation in the North Pacific Ocean. Mr. Brown owns a large trawler and hires local divers from the nearby islands and pays them on the basis of the weight of oysters recovered. He sells the pearls and the oyster meat separately. Over the past month he has been out pearling eight times in the same general area, taking all the divers who showed up for each trip. The particulars are as follows:

Trip Number	Divers Employed	Oysters Recovered (kg)
1	6	38
2	17	76
3	9	56
4	5	32
5	12	74
6	3	15
7	14	80
8	15	78

(a) Over what ranges do there appear to be increasing, constant, and diminishing returns to the variable factor?

(b) What number of divers appears to be the most efficient in terms of output per diver?

(c) What number of divers appears to be mostly efficient in terms of the utilization of the trawler and other equipment?

6-2. Taras Panache is the owner-manager of Panache Shirts Enterprises, which manufactures shirts by using rented space and equipment in a large warehouse. Because of the technical aspects of shirt production and the available equipment, separate production centers are used, each consisting of one cutting machine, two sewing machines, and three operators. Six months ago Mr. Panache had only one such production center, but recently he doubled, then tripled, and finally quadrupled the number of production centers by renting more space and equipment and by hiring more operators. Throughout the expansion Mr. Panache has personally supervised all the operators and has handled all other aspects of the business. He kept a record of the average daily output from the entire plant for each of the four situations, as follows:

One production center:	20.6 shirts/day
Two production centers:	42.4 shirts/day
Three production centers:	60.8 shirts/day
Four production centers:	76.3 shirts/day

Each production center costs $3,000 per month in fixed and variable costs. Mr. Panache pays himself $3,000 per month, and the remaining fixed costs are $1,000 per month. Assume there are twenty working days in a month.

(a) Can the expansion of Panache Shirts be regarded as a case of an increase in the scale of operations or simply an increase in the size of operations? Why?

(b) Are there economies and/or diseconomies of scale/size evident? Explain.

(c) Indulge in some speculation about the probable cause of the economies and diseconomies, if any.

6-3. Greenfield Farms Bakery (GFB) is currently producing below full capacity with a relatively stable demand (of 15,000 loaves per week) from its regular customers in the Boston area. At this output level the business is quite profitable—average cost per loaf is $0.74 while the delivered price is $0.85 per loaf to the stores. Brian Puddington, president of GFB, wants to enter the southern New Hampshire market and has begun negotiations with a major food chain in that area. This would involve a contract for a minimum delivery of 10,000 loaves per week, with additional loaves being supplied as demanded up to a maximum of 30,000 loaves per week. Demand in excess of the minimum delivery would depend on consumer response to GFB bread, and GFB's research staff has compiled the following probability distribution of weekly demand (at $0.85 per loaf) from the New Hampshire market.

Quantity	10,000	15,000	20,000	25,000	30,000
Probability	.4	.3	.15	.10	.05

GFB's present plant could supply up to 30,000 additional loaves per week, but it would prove to be very expensive to run the plant that far beyond full capacity. Alternatively, Mr. Puddington is considering the purchase and installation of a new continuous-process mixing and baking machine which would cost $416,000 (installed and ready to start). This machine could always be resold at its market value, which is expected to decline linearly at 1/6 of the initial cost, and have no scrap value at the end of its 6-year life. Alternatively the funds could be invested at 18% per annum at similar risk. The new plant would not require any other changes in overhead costs, which are currently $3,600 per week and include no depreciation charges since the present plant has been completely depreciated. Variable costs for the present and the proposed plant are estimated as shown below.

Output/Week	Present Plant TVC per Week	Proposed Plant TVC per Week
10,000	6,300	—
15,000	7,500	—
20,000	9,200	—
25,000	12,750	15,000
30,000	18,600	15,300
35,000	26,950	15,400
40,000	40,400	15,600
45,000	76,500	22,950
50,000	—	35,500

(a) Calculate the AVC and SAC values and plot the curves for both the present plant and the proposed plant.
(b) Calculate the expected value of weekly profits under three alternative scenarios: (i) present plant with no additional sales, (ii) present plant with NH contract, and (iii) proposed plant with NH contract.
(c) Supposing that the contract is for an initial two year period and that Mr. Puddington's time horizon is only two years, calculate the expected incremental contribution of the proposed plant alternative.
(d) Advise Mr. Puddington as to what strategy he should follow, stating explicitly all assumptions and qualifications that underlie your recommendation.

6-4. Silver Star Corporation has estimated its production function as follows:

$$Q = 38.6K + 3.2K^2 - 1.8K^3 + 16.3L + 2.8L^2 - 0.85L^3$$

where K represents units of the capital input (in $1,000 units) and L represents units of the labor input (in hundreds of labor hours).
(a) Construct the total product and marginal product curves for the case of $K = 5$.
(b) At what level of labor input do diminishing returns become evident?

(c) If labor were available at no cost (students wishing to gain work experience and willing to work without wages), what input level would you choose? Why?

6-5. Gewurz Fabricators Limited manufactures and assembles small aluminum buildings suitable for garden toolsheds, garages, and children's playhouses. Stephen Gewurz, the owner, is considering opening a new plant to diversify into the production of luxury dog kennels for the expanding large-dogs market. He has carefully considered the labor and capital requirements and the substitutability between these inputs at various output levels and has summarized the production function in the following table.

		Labor Inputs (person years)							
		1	2	3	4	5	6	7	8
Capital	1	30	52	80	110	130	145	155	162
inputs	2	50	80	120	164	200	220	235	248
(machine	3	80	124	175	226	260	274	282	287
years)	4	100	160	218	272	302	320	335	345

(a) Supposing that the cost of each unit of capital is $20,000 and the cost of each unit of labor is $10,000, derive the SAC curve for each of the four plant sizes indicated.
(b) What conclusions can you draw about the returns to increasing plant size in this example?
(c) Which of the four plants should be selected if demand is expected to be (1) 125 units? (2) 250 units? (3) somewhere within the range of 200 to 300 units? (Explain and defend your decision.)

6-6. The newly formed Bangladesh Automobile Corporation plans to produce and export an expensive sports car and has asked your consulting firm for advice on the size of plant to construct. Because of the union contract and technical features of automobile production, labor must be paid the equivalent of $12,000 per person per annum, and each incremental change in plant size involves $900,000 in annual expenses for depreciation, interest, and other fixed costs. The maximum the firm will have available for expenditure on capital and labor is $9 million per annum. BAC has supplied the following details of its production function, meticulously derived by its chief engineer. (The data in the body of the table represent automobiles produced, in units.) Labor can be varied virtually continuously; the table shows units of fifty persons for convenience. All other variable expenses are constant at $2,500 per vehicle produced.

Capital (units of $900,000)	Labor (units of 50 persons)					
	1	2	3	4	5	6
3	40	90	140	170	180	185
4	60	120	180	220	230	236
5	100	170	230	250	260	268
6	170	200	240	270	280	289

BAC's market research indicates that the new vehicle should be sold at around $50,000 per unit and that the expected demand situation is as follows:

Units Demanded (annually)	100	150	200	250
Probability	0.20	0.50	0.20	0.10

(a) Plot the SAC curves suggested by the production function and input cost figures.

(b) Comment on the economies and diseconomies of plant size (if any) which are evident in your graph.

(c) Which plant do you suggest that BAC build, and why?

6-7. The Peachy Cosmetics Company has established the following relationship between the variable inputs and the output level for its production of its face cream products. Each unit of the variable product includes one person working forty hours weekly, the necessary utilities, and a variety of ingredients in the required proportions, including the small glass jars and cardboard boxes in which the cream is packed. These variable inputs cost $600 per unit. Overhead (fixed) costs are $60,000 per week.

(a) Use these data to derive the firm's AVC and SAC schedules for the output levels shown.

(b) Graph the AVC and SAC curves and sketch in your best estimate of the marginal cost curve.

Variable Input (units)	Output (units)
100	6,500
200	14,300
300	20,200
400	24,400
500	27,800
600	30,000

(c) At what output level do you think diminishing returns first start? Explain with reference to the graph and reconcile this result with the input-output data.

(d) What is the full capacity output level? What is average cost at that level? Under what conditions would Peachy produce in the overfull capacity area of its cost curves?

6-8. Suppose that one of the very expensive ingredients in Peachy Cream (see problem 6-7) was suddenly found in abundance, and the cost of the variable units fell to $500 each.

(a) What is the impact of this discovery on the firm's AC, SAC, and MC curves?

(b) Does it change the point where diminishing returns set in?

(c) Now suppose that after the reduction in the price of that ingredient, worker productivity increases as a result of improvements in morale, such that output goes up by 10% at each input level. What is the impact of this improvement on the firm's AVC, SAC, and MC curves?

(d) What is the impact of both changes on the firm's full capacity output level?

6-9. Paxtronix Corporation is considering the installation of plant and equipment to manufacture a nonlethal stun gun for use by law enforcement agencies only. It has a choice of three plant sizes A, B, and C. The average cost schedules for these plants are shown below. Also shown is the estimated probability distribution of demand for each of the first two years.

(a) Plot the average cost curves for plants A, B, and C on the same graph.

(b) Calculate the expected value of average cost for each plant, given the probability distribution of demand.

(c) Which plant size should Paxtronix choose? Support your answer with sensitivity analysis.

(**d**) Given the plant size you have recommended, how much excess capacity will Paxtronix have?

| Output Level | Demand | AVERAGE COST LEVEL ($) | | |
(thousands)	Probability	Plant A	Plant B	Plant C
1	0.10	110	140	180
2	0.20	90	100	110
3	0.35	80	70	80
4	0.20	80	60	50
5	0.10	90	70	40
6	0.05	110	90	50

6-10. Magnocrunch Computer Company is currently producing at full capacity. This firm is fortunate to have fully divisible fixed inputs, such that its average variable cost is constant out to the full capacity level. Demand for the new Magnum computer is increasing, and the firm faces a backlog of 1500 orders. It cannot build inventories and fears that it will lose 20% of the buyers on the backlist if it cannot deliver within another month. The firm is considering two alternative plans. Plan A is to increase the rate of production to an overfull capacity situation, which would raise marginal cost from the present level of $1,500 by $300 for every 100 units beyond the current output rate of 500 computers per month. Alternatively, plan B is to contract out for the manufacture of various components, and then have these assembled into the finished unit by another firm. The firm estimates that these units will end up costing $2,200 per unit, regardless of volume. The present price of the computer is $2,995, and the firm's fixed costs per month are $250,000 per month. The firm's fixed costs are not expected to change, regardless of which plan is selected.

(**a**) Calculate the firm's profit for monthly output levels from 500 to 1500 units, using plan A. What would be the optimal output rate per month?

(**b**) Now consider the profit implications of plan B, holding in-house production at 500 units per month. Of these two alternatives, which is preferable, plan A or plan B? Why?

(**c**) Now consider a combination of plans A and B and make your recommendation to Magnocrunch management.

SUGGESTED REFERENCES AND FURTHER READING

BAUMOL, W. J. *Economic Theory and Operations Analysis* (4th ed.), chap. 11. Englewood Cliffs, N.J.: Prentice-Hall, Inc., 1977.

CHAMBERLIN, E. H. "Proportionality, Divisibility and Economies of Scale," *Quarterly Journal of Economics*, 1948, pp. 229–57.

COLE, C. L. *Microeconomics: A Contemporary Approach*, chaps. 6 and 7. New York: Harcourt Brace Jovanovich, Inc., 1973.

DOUGLAS, P. H. "Are There Laws of Production?" *American Economic Review*, 38 (March 1948), pp. 1–41.

GOLD, B. "Changing Perspectives on Size, Scale, and Returns: An Interpretive Survey," *Journal of Economic Literature*, 19 (March 1981), pp. 5–33.

HYMAN, DAVID N. *Modern Microeconomics: Analysis and Applications*, esp. chaps 6 and 7. St. Louis: Times Mirror/Mosby College Publishing, 1986.

LEFTWICH, R. H. *The Price System and Resource Allocation* (7th ed.), Chaps. 8 and 9. Hinsdale, Ill.: The Dryden Press, 1979.

MANSFIELD, E. *Microeconomics: Theory/Applications* (6th ed.), esp. chaps. 6 and 7. New York: W. W. Norton & Company, 1988.

VARIAN, HAL R. *Intermediate Microeconomics: A Modern Approach* (2nd ed.), chaps. 17-20. New York: W. W. Norton & Company, 1990.

Empirical Case 6

ESTIMATING THE PRODUCTION FUNCTION FOR BUS TRANSPORTATION

Recently you have been hired as production expert by a large metropolitan transportation authority. Your primary task is to examine the structure of the production of area bus transportation services.

You begin your investigation by observing the various combinations of inputs used in the production of transportation services by several large bus lines. You discover that labor, buses, and fuel are the three main inputs employed in the production process. As a result, you intend to concentrate your attention on these three inputs.

The empirical model specified for the production of bus services is a Cobb-Douglas production function:

$$Q = aB^{b_1}F^{b_2}L^{b_3}$$

where

Q = bus transportation output measured in vehicle miles

B = number of buses

L = number of workers

F = fuel measured in gallons

a, b_1, b_2, and b_3 are the parameters to be estimated using a statistical regression package. Table 1 presents the data you have collected for fourteen similar bus lines. Use this data in the specified model to estimate the production structure of bus services. Then use your results to answer the following questions.

QUESTIONS

1. Confirm that the Cobb-Douglas production function is an appropriate model for this industry. Do this by testing whether the coefficients on buses, fuel, and labor are statistically significant. Do these estimates conform to economic theory? Explain.

2. Determine the estimated bus, fuel, and labor production elasticities and give an economic interpretation of each estimate. Why are these elasticities important to a bus line?

3. Determine whether this production function exhibits increasing, decreasing, or constant returns to scale. Explain. Why would this concept be of interest to the transportation authority?

TABLE 1

Bus Line	Q	B	F	L
1	102,940	2,940	31,384.14	8,272
2	16,746	526	4,784.57	1,814
3	51,522	1,764	15,379.70	4,410
4	28,945	1,023	8,744.71	2,022
5	77,046	2,295	26,845.29	7,345
6	23,193	1,000	6,761.81	2,393
7	24,107	450	7,131.95	2,013
8	38,093	1,240	9,894.29	2,535
9	27,826	1,044	7,116.62	2,110
10	74,369	2,345	14,005.46	7,800
11	22,613	1,100	5,813.11	1,631
12	36,862	1,455	12,934.03	2,500
13	33,268	1,026	9,241.11	2,381
14	29,135	1,195	7,451.41	2,320

Q = vehicle miles, measured in thousands

B = number of buses

F = gallons of fuel, measured in thousands

L = number of workers

Source: All data from the 1983 edition of *National Mass Transportation Statistics*, published by the U.S. Department of Transportation.

Appendix 6A

ISOQUANT-ISOCOST ANALYSIS OF PRODUCTION AND COSTS

EXECUTIVE SUMMARY

The firm's production problem is to choose the optimal levels of all inputs that enter the production process, such that output is maximized for a given budget constraint. Alternatively, the production problem may be stated as seeking to minimize the cost of producing a given output level. In this appendix, **isoquant and isocost curves** are introduced to enable a somewhat more rigorous treatment of the firm's production problem. An isoquant curve is a locus of alternate input combinations that can produce the same output level, while an isocost curve is a locus of alternative input combinations that require the same total expenditure. Using these concepts, it is a simple matter to demonstrate the principles involved in output maximization and cost minimization.

We distinguish between **technical efficiency**, whereby there is no wasted resources, and **economic efficiency**, whereby there is no waste of expenditure. That is, economic efficiency means that the cost of producing a given output level is minimized. With plant size fixed, the **least-cost input combinations** give rise to the firm's short-run cost curves. Under long-run conditions, the firm's **expansion path** shows the least-cost combinations of inputs that would be utilized if the firm were to increase its output progressively, given the freedom to adjust its plant size by the optimal amount each time.

Changing prices and changing productivities of inputs must be adjusted for if the firm is to minimize the cost of producing a given output level or to maximize the output from a given expenditure budget. The profit-maximizing firm will adjust to such changes by a **substitution away from an input when its relative price rises and/or when its relative productivity falls**. Given that relative input prices and productivities vary across countries, and even within countries, this explains why we observe relatively labor-intensive production in some areas while production in other areas is relatively capital intensive.

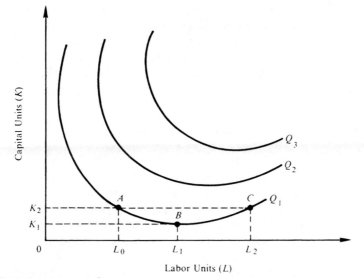

FIGURE 6A-1. Isoquant Curves

Isoquant-Isocost Analysis

- DEFINITION: An *isoquant* is a line joining combinations of inputs which generate the same level of output. The word *isoquant* comes from the Greek word *iso* meaning equal and the Latin word *quantus* meaning quantity. As with indifference curves, there will be a family of isoquant curves, with higher curves preferred to lower curves. Similarly, the curves do not cross, and they are convex to the origin. Unlike indifference curves, however, isoquant curves are not negatively sloped throughout their length. Isoquants may bend back, as shown in Figure 6A-I, at both relatively high and relatively low ratios of capital to labor. The reason for this difference is that in consumer theory we assumed that marginal utility would never be negative, whereas in producer theory we make no such restrictive assumption concerning marginal products.

We saw in Chapter 6 that the marginal product of the variable inputs will take on negative values when its input is "too large" relative to the fixed inputs. Conversely, the marginal product of the fixed inputs (in the long-run context) may become negative if the ratio of capital to labor becomes "too high." Just as the slope of an indifference curve is equal to the negative of the ratio of the marginal utilities, the slope of an isoquant is equal to the negative of the ratio of the marginal products. Specifically, with capital on the vertical axis, the slope of an isoquant is equal to the negative of the marginal product of labor over the marginal product of capital.[1] When the marginal product of labor goes

---

[1]The slope of the isoquant curve can be represented by $\Delta K/\Delta L$, the vertical change over the horizontal change. Note that a negative ΔK, with L held constant, causes a reduction in output, ΔQ (a move to a lower

negative, at low capital-labor ratios, the slope term must be positive. Hence the isoquant bends upward at the right-hand end. Conversely, where the marginal product of capital goes negative, at relatively high capital-labor ratios, the slope of the isoquant must again take a positive value, and thus the curve bends back at the left-hand, or uppermost, end as well. In between, where both marginal products are positive, the slope must be negative.

Technical and Economic Efficiency

A combination of capital and labor is *technically efficient* if none of either factor can be subtracted without reducing the output level, given *ceteris paribus*. All combinations on negatively sloped sections of the isoquant curves are technically efficient, since if one factor input is reduced while the other factor input is held constant, output will decline and the new input combination will lie on a lower isoquant curve. On the other hand, all combinations on positively sloped sections of isoquant curves are *technically inefficient*, since some of both factors may be subtracted without output being reduced. In terms of Figure 6A-1, output level Q_1 can be produced by different combinations of capital and labor at points A, B, and C. Combination C is technically inefficient, however, since the same output level could be produced at combination A by subtracting $L_2 - L_0$ units of labor or at combination B by subtracting both $L_2 - L_1$ units of labor and $K_2 - K_1$ units of capital. By the same process of reasoning, *all* points on positively sloped sections of the isoquants are technically inefficient combinations of the inputs.

The slope of an isoquant at any point can also be expressed as the ratio of the amount of capital that can be subtracted from the production process to the amount of labor that is added to the production process, such that output level remains constant. For a one-unit increment in the labor input, this ratio is known as the *marginal rate of technical substitution* of capital for labor.

- DEFINITION: *The marginal rate of technical substitution* (MRTS), is the rate at which labor can be substituted for capital in the production process, *such that output remains unchanged*. Note that it is equal to the amount of capital that can be subtracted from the production process for a one-unit increase in labor added to the production process. Thus,

$$\text{MRTS} = \frac{\Delta K}{\Delta L} \tag{6A-1}$$

---

isoquant curve). This $\Delta Q = \Delta K \times \text{MP}_K$, or the number of units of capital multiplied by the marginal product of those units. Now, to get back on the same isoquant curve, we need a positive ΔL, with K held constant, that causes the same absolute magnitude ΔQ (but in the other direction). This $\Delta Q = \Delta L \times \text{MP}_L$. Since the first ΔQ equals the negative of the second ΔQ, we know $\Delta K \times \text{MP}_K = -\Delta L \times \text{MP}_L$. From this relation we get $\Delta K / \Delta L = -\text{MP}_L / \text{MP}_K$. Thus the slope of an isoquant is equal to the ratio $-\text{MP}_L / \text{MP}_K$.

where ΔK is the decrement to capital that will just allow output to remain unchanged given a one-unit increment ΔL to the labor input. Thus the marginal rate of technical substitution reflects the slope of an isoquant curve, and the MRTS will be negative for all technically efficient combinations of the factors and positive for all technically inefficient combinations. Since the slope is also equal to the negative ratio of the marginal products, we can also say that MRTS $= -\text{MP}_L/\text{MP}_K$.

The combinations of capital and labor on the negatively sloped sections of the isoquants represent the range of possibilities open to the rational firm. The actual combination of capital and labor chosen to produce each output level (in the long-run situation where the firm is free to vary all inputs) will depend on the relative prices of the inputs. Only one of the technically efficient ways of producing each output level will be *economically* efficient; that is, only one will allow the lowest cost of producing that output level. To show this we need to introduce isocost lines which show combinations of capital and labor that cost the same amount.

• DEFINITION: An *isocost* line is a locus of combinations of inputs that require the same total expenditure.

Let us express the firm's expenditure on inputs as

$$E = K \cdot P_K + L \cdot P_L \tag{6A-2}$$

where E is the total dollar expenditure; P_K and P_L are the unit prices of capital and labor, respectively; and K and L are the number of physical units of capital and labor that are to be employed in the production process. This can be rearranged to appear as

$$K = \frac{E}{P_K} - \frac{P_L}{P_K} \cdot L \tag{6A-3}$$

in which form it is perhaps more recognizable as a linear equation explaining K in terms of L and three known values (E, P_L, and P_K) It can therefore be plotted in the same space as the isoquant curves. The intercept of the isocost line on the capital axis occurs when $L = 0$, and this intercept value of K is simply the total expenditure divided by the price of the capital units, resulting in a particular physical quantity of capital units. As we purchase units of labor, it is evident that our purchase of capital units, for the same expenditure (isocost) level, is drawn down in the ratio of the price of labor to the price of capital.

For each output level there will be a minimum-cost combination of the factors necessary to produce that output level. In Figure 6A-2 we show three isoquant curves representing 20, 40, and 60 units of output. The cost of producing 20 units is minimized at point A, since any other capital/labor combination producing 20 units, such as at A', will lie to the right of the isocost line MN and would thus require a larger total expenditure to purchase. Recall that the intercept on the capital axis is equal to E/P_K, where P_K is presumed to remain unchanged. Hence, larger total expenditures are represented by

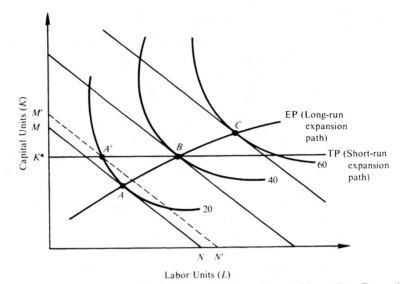

FIGURE 6A-2. *Isoquant-Isocost Analysis Showing Short-Run and Long-Run Expansion Paths*

higher intercept points and higher isocost lines. Similarly, the output level of 40 units is produced at the least-cost by the input combination represented by point *B*, and 60 units are produced at the least-cost by the input combination at point *C*.

- RULE: Output is maximized for a given input expenditure level where the isocost line representing that expenditure level is just tangent to the highest attainable isoquant curve. Equivalently, input cost is minimized for a given output level, where the isoquant curve representing that output level is just tangent to the lowest attainable isocost line. Note that at the point of tangency between the isoquant and the isocost curves the slopes of these curves are the same. The slope of the isoquant curve is the MRTS, and the slope of the isocost curve is equal to the negative of the input price ratio, $-P_L/P_K$. Thus MRTS $= -P_L/P_K$ at the point of tangency. Since MRTS $= -MP_L/MP_K$, we also have $-MP_L/MP_K = -P_L/P_K$. Rearranging terms we have $MP_L/P_L = MP_K/P_K$ as an alternative statement of the output-maximizing, or cost-minimizing, rule. Thus the firm should utilize all inputs such that the ratios of the marginal products to prices of all inputs are equal. This rule generalizes to the *n* input case, where n is any number of different inputs. That is, $MP_1/P_1 = MP_2/P_2 = \ldots = MP_n/P_n$.

The Expansion Path: Long Run and Short Run

- DEFINITION: A locus of the tangency points between various isoquants and various isocosts is called the *expansion path*, since it shows the least-cost combinations of labor and capital a firm would choose as it expanded its output level, if it were free to vary both labor and capital and if it were given constant factor prices and a constant state of technology. This expansion path is shown as the line EP in Figure 6A-2. Note that this must be the *long-run* expansion path, since all factors must be variable to allow the adjustment in both capital and labor involved in the movement along the line EP.

Suppose the firm wishes to produce 40 units of output and thus selects the combination of factors represented by point *B* on the long-run expansion path. The firm's capital input will now be fixed at K^* units, and the firm is in a short-run situation. If the firm wishes to vary its output level in the short run, it must simply add or subtract labor to or from the fixed capital input K^*. The *short-run expansion path* is therefore a horizontal line at the capital input level K^*, and we have shown it as the line TP in Figure 6A-2. This short-run expansion path is in fact the total product curve, viewed from a different perspective.

Notice that for every output level except the one where TP crosses EP, it costs more to produce the output in the short run than it does in the long run. Any isocost line that *intersects* an isoquant curve on the TP line must lie farther to the right when compared with the isocost line that is *tangent* to each isoquant curve. This statement is demonstrated in Figure 6A-2 for the output level of 20 units. In the long-run situation the optimal input combination is at point *A*, and the lowest attainable isocost line is shown as *MN*. In the short-run situation with capital input of K^*, 20 units must be produced by the input combination represented by point *A'*, since the firm is constrained to the "short-run expansion path," TP. The minimum cost of producing 20 units with combination *A'* is shown by the isocost line *M'N'*, which lies to the right of the line *MN*. The short-run situation costs more than the long-run situation for all except one output level, because the firm is unable in the short run to change the input of capital and is thus forced to have an inappropriate factor combination for all except one output level. In the case shown, only at the output of 40 units does the level of capital (K^*) allow the tangency situation of economic efficiency to be attained.[2]

Factor Substitution Resulting from Changed Factor Prices

Economic efficiency depends on the relative factor prices. If the price of one factor changes, with *ceteris paribus*, the profit-maximizing firm will attempt to substitute away from the factor that has become relatively more expensive and in favor of the factor that has become relatively less expensive. Suppose the initial situation in Figure 6A-3 is at

---

[2]We saw in Chapter 6 that each short-run average cost (SAC) curve is tangent to the long-run average cost (LAC) curve at a single point when plant size is continuously variable. Note that the long-run expansion path (EP) contains all the data necessary to derive the LAC curve, namely, the minimum total cost required to produce each output level, given the variability of both capital and labor. Similarly, the minimum total cost of producing each output level under short-run conditions can be derived from the values of the isoquants and isocosts crossing the short-run expansion path (TP). Thus the firm's SAC and LAC curve would be tangent at 40 units of output, and the SAC would lie above the LAC for all other output levels. Similarly, the TP curve for any other level of capital input would cross the EP line at a particular output level, and this would be the output level at which that plant's SAC curve was just tangent to the LAC curve.

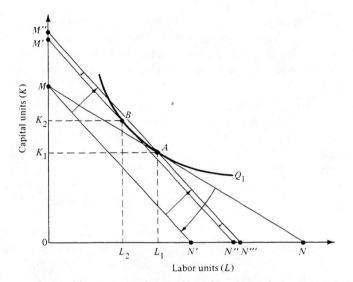

FIGURE 6A-3.   Factor Substitution Resulting from Changed Relative Factor Prices

point A. Output level Q_1 is being produced economically efficiently by the factor combination K_1 units of capital and L_1 units of labor, and factor prices are such that the lowest attainable isocost line is MN.

Suppose now that labor prices rise, for example, because of a new agreement with a labor union or because of legislation requiring the firm's contribution to an employee health scheme or to similar benefits. Imagine that the increase in the cost of labor is such that the isocost line swings down from MN to MN'. If the firm wishes to maintain its output level at Q_1, to hold its market share, for example, it will need to spend more money on the inputs to produce Q_1.

In the short run, the firm is constrained to the plant size indicated by K_1, and must produce Q_1 units of output at point A. This constraint necessitates the total expenditure indicated by the isocost line $M''N'''$. Given a long-run situation, the firm can adjust both capital and labor inputs and will increase its plant size to K_2 units of capital and reduce labor input to L_2 units to produce Q_1 units of output with economic efficiency at point B, given the new factor-price ratio. Thus the firm substitutes away from labor and in favor of capital when the price of labor increases relative to that of capital, given time to adjust the input of all factors. History has given us the opportunity to observe this phenomenon, of course: As the price of labor has increased relative to that of capital, we have observed that production processes have become relatively more capital intensive with the introduction of labor-saving equipment such as mobile assembly lines by Henry Ford and the more recent use of computerized production technology.

• EXAMPLE: There are hundreds of thousands of robots working in American industry. These computer-controlled machines, which in some cases have visual and tactile skills, have replaced human labor for two main reasons. First, they are cheaper. General Motors reports that where robots are used in automobile assembly, they cost only about $6 an hour, compared with the average $20 an hour paid to assembly labor. Second, robots are more productive than the humans they replace. Hour after hour they methodically and precisely repeat their tasks, never stopping for coffee breaks, chats, washroom visits, and the like. Similarly, absenteeism and sick leave are human foibles. Should the robots break down, they are quickly repaired, since they can indicate which part needs replacing. General Electric (GE) found that robots were 10% to 35% more productive than humans in coating dish racks with polyvinyl. Although their initial cost averages $50,000 each, GE found that their first robot paid for itself in ten months as a result of its greater productivity.[3]

Different Factor Price Ratios in Different Economies

If the relative costs of capital and labor differ between different countries or even between regions within the same country, we should expect to see differing capital-labor ratios being utilized in these different situations.

- EXAMPLE: The cotton textile and apparel industry is remarkable in that it is found around the world with significantly differing degrees of capital and labor intensiveness. In the United States and Canada, for example, this industry is relatively *capital intensive*, using computer-controlled equipment and relatively few people per unit of output. In many less developed countries, on the other hand, production processes are relatively *labor intensive*, with dozens of people using much more rudimentary equipment to produce a given output level. Does this statement mean that the industry is inefficient in these less developed countries? Quite the contrary, as we shall see.

   In terms of isoquant-isocost analysis, firms in both situations are trying to attain tangency between their isocost line and the appropriate isoquant line. Suppose a firm in each group wishes to produce a particular output level, shown as Q^* in Figure 6A-4. In the less developed economy, labor is relatively cheap, whereas capital is relatively expensive, giving rise to an isocost line like M_2N_2. The economically efficient input combination for the firm in this situation is thus K_2, L_2, where the isocost curve is tangent to the isoquant at point B. In the more highly developed country, labor is relatively expensive, and capital is relatively cheap, giving rise to an isocost line like M_1N_1, which is tangent to the isoquant line at point A, indicating that K_1 and L_1 constitute the economically efficient input combination for the firm in the more developed economy.

   Thus both situations are probably both technically and economically efficient given the factor productivities and factor prices facing the firm in each situation. The crunch comes for Americans when their economically efficient input combination for any given output level costs *more* than the economically efficient input combination in less devel-

[3]See Joann S. Lublin, ''Steel-Collar Jobs: As Robot Age Arrives, Labor Seeks Protection Against Loss of Work,'' *Wall Street Journal*, October 26, 1981, pp. 1, 17.

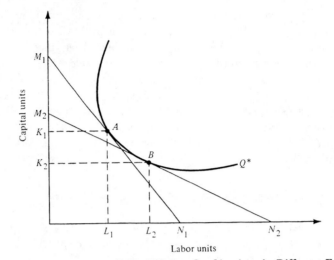

FIGURE 6A-4.   *Different Economically Efficient Combinations in Different Economic Situations*

oped economies. Hence the U.S. textile industry finds itself subject to the competition of imported textiles that are sold at a lower price in its market.

A similar example is found in the automobile industry. In the early 1980s, automobile assembly workers in Japan were paid only about $12 per hour in wages and benefits, compared with $20 per hour in the United States.[4] The cost of capital in these countries (and for large automobile companies) is more nearly equal, however, given the greater international mobility of capital and the international capital markets. Thus we should expect the Japanese automobile industry to be somewhat more labor intensive than the U.S. automobile industry. Given their labor cost and other cost advantages, said to amount to $1,500 per car, the Japanese are able to compete very effectively in the American market and have enjoyed significant growth in their market share in recent years.

Isoquant-Isocost Analysis of Short-Run Production Problems

Isoquant-isocost analysis can be used to solve short-run production problems as well. Variable inputs are often substitutable for each other, and the firm faces a short-run decision concerning the combination of variable factors (in conjunction with fixed factors) which would minimize cost for a particular output level. A firm may have the choice of hiring either generalist labor (who can accomplish a sequence of tasks) or, alternatively, hiring specialist labor who can each do only one of the required tasks. Thus these two different types of labor are substitutable in the short run, presuming each can be hired or fired at management's discretion.

---

[4]See Robert L. Simison, "Ford Asks for 50% Pay-Benefit Cut in Bid to Align Labor Costs with Japanese," *Wall Street Journal*, October 22, 1981.

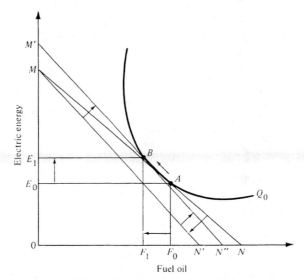

FIGURE 6A-5. Response of Cost-Minimizing Firm to a Change in Fuel Oil Costs

Similarly, labor may be substitutable for raw materials in some production processes. For example, three workers and 10 yards of cloth may combine (along with the fixed factors) to produce five shirts per hour. Alternatively, five workers and 8 yards of cloth may combine to produce five shirts per hour. The extra labor allows more careful cutting of the cloth so there is less waste of the material. A further example is the substitutability among different sources of energy. A firm can install electric heating to supplement or replace its oil heating system if the cost of oil rises relative to that of electricity.

• EXAMPLE: The energy crises of 1974 and 1979 spurred the movement away from petroleum-derived energy and toward alternative energy sources. Oil prices shot up dramatically during 1979, following the turmoil in Iran, and after a short decline, continued their upward thrust when war broke out between Iran and Iraq in September 1980. Heating oil consumption in the winter of 1980–1981 was substantially below projections, however, indicating the shift from petroleum as an energy source to competing energy sources.[5]

In terms of Figure 6A-5, where we show fuel oil on the horizontal axis and electrical energy on the vertical axis, suppose that the initial price ratio was such that the isocost line in early 1979 was MN. To produce output level Q_0, the firm would choose the combination of fuel oil and electrical energy represented by point A, or F_0 units of fuel oil and E_0 units of electrical energy. The rise in oil prices is indicated by the shift of the isocost curve to MN'. To maintain its output at level Q_0, the firm (and households which had the ability to do so) would prefer to substitute away from fuel oil and toward electric energy to point B on isoquant Q_0. Thus, after the adjustment process, the firm

---

[5]See Mary Greenebaum, "The Sudden Popularity of Heating Oil Contracts," *Fortune*, February 23, 1981, pp. 127, 130.

would purchase E_1 units of electrical energy and F_1 units of fuel oil. In fact, we observed a shift away from petroleum-derived energy and toward a variety of other energy sources, including solar and nuclear energy.

Summary

In this appendix we have used isoquant-isocost analysis to examine the firm's production problem. The firm should always operate on the negatively sloped section of an isoquant, to avoid technical inefficiency, which means the waste of inputs. While there are many technically efficient input combinations for every level of output, only one input combination will be economically efficient, given the cost of capital and labor.

The firm's choice of plant size in the long-run context is indicated by the tangency of the isoquant for the desired output level and the lowest attainable isocost line. The level of capital input indicated is the optimal plant size for that output level. Short-run fluctuations in the quantity demanded will cause the firm to move along a horizontal line which is effectively the total product (TP) curve. Except for the output level where the TP curve crosses the expansion path (EP), a given output level will cost more in the short run than in the long run, because the firm is unable to adjust its fixed inputs to the optimal level in the short run.

Isoquant-isocost analysis can also be used for short-run production problems—namely, the optimal combination of variable inputs when these are substitutable in production. Given the underlying fixed factors, a given output level will be attainable from a variety of combinations of the variable inputs, and the firm should choose the least-cost combination by reference to a tangency between the isoquant and isocost curves.

DISCUSSION QUESTIONS

6A-1. Distinguish between technical and economic efficiency in the production process.

6A-2. The smooth curve of an isoquant curve implies the ability to substitute small amounts of capital for small amounts of labor. Given that a person is not physically divisible, how can the firm use a fraction of a person's time? Similarly, how can it increase capital by very small increments?

6A-3. Why do isoquant curves bend back at relatively high and relatively low capital-labor ratios?

6A-4. What is the rule for the optimal input combination? State this rule verbally, and then symbolically. Generalize it to the n input case.

6A-5. Why would you expect the production of any particular product to be typically more capital intensive in more highly developed countries, as compared to less developed countries?

PROBLEMS AND SHORT CASES

6A-1. The Himam Foods Corporation is a relatively small firm producing grocery items. Recently its research department developed a new salad dressing. Production of this new dressing would involve the use of the firm's mixing machine, which combines, shakes, rotates, and warms the ingredients to a specified temperature before pouring the mixture into bottles, which are then capped and labeled. Some of the above procedures can be done manually, however, and Himam wants to choose the optimal proportions of machine time and labor time. The production function has been estimated as follows:

Himam Foods—Production Function
(output in thousands of units)

Machine hours per year (000)	LABOR HOURS PER YEAR (000)					
	1	2	3	4	5	6
1	25	80	110	120	125	115
2	70	102	120	135	145	150
3	86	117	140	160	175	182
4	96	125	150	170	185	195
5	95	130	155	175	192	205
6	90	127	158	178	196	210

Machine hours cost $25 per hour, and labor costs are $10 per hour. (Raw-material costs are constant per bottle and are covered by a separate budget.) Because of the current difficult financial situation, Himam can allocate a budget of only $80,000 for the machine and labor costs of producing the new dressing.

(a) Plot these output levels in input space on a graph and sketch in several isoquant curves that are suggested by the data.

(b) Estimate from your graph the maximum output level which Himam can produce within its budget constraint and the factor combination that is required to achieve this level.

(c) Demonstrate what would happen if the cost of labor hours were to increase to $15 per hour. Estimate the new optimal factor combination and output level.

6A-2. The long-run production function for the Burnstein Apparel Company is represented by the following input-output table. Capital units cost $100,000 each, and labor units cost $50,000 each. The firm has an annual budget of $0.5 million.

Capital Units	LABOR UNITS					
	1	2	3	4	5	6
1	20	40	70	90	100	108
2	30	50	100	130	140	147
3	40	90	140	170	180	185
4	60	120	180	220	230	236
5	100	170	230	250	260	268
6	170	200	240	270	280	289

(a) Plot these output levels in input space, and sketch in the isoquant curves representing 50, 100, 150, 200, and 250 units of output.

(b) Superimpose the isocost line, and estimate the maximum output level that Burnstein can expect to achieve, given its budget constraint.

(c) Assuming capital is divisible, how much do you recommend that they spend on fixed factors of production annually?

(d) Given that they implement your recommended plant size, what change do you expect in their total variable costs if they expand output in that plant by 25% to meet an increase in their quantity demanded?

6A-3. The Vermont Maple Syrup Company has estimated the relationship between its fixed and variable inputs and the resultant output level over the range shown in the following table. The units of fixed inputs cost $50,000 each, and the units of the variable inputs cost $10,000 each. The company believes it can sell 150 units of the product next year. (Each unit is 1,000 pints of grade A maple syrup.)

Fixed Inputs	VARIABLE INPUTS						
	1	2	3	4	5	6	7
1	30	52	80	110	130	145	155
2	50	80	120	164	200	220	235
3	80	124	175	226	260	274	286
4	100	160	218	272	302	320	335

(a) Plot these outputs in input space and sketch in your best estimate of the isoquants representing 50, 100, 150, and 200 units of output.

(b) Draw in the isocost line that represents the minimum cost level for the production of 150 units of output.

(c) What is your best estimate of the minimum total cost of producing 150,000 pints of maple syrup, based on this data?

(d) What will happen to total costs if the cost of the variable inputs goes up by 10% and the firm still wishes to produce 150,000 pints of syrup?

SUGGESTED REFERENCES AND FURTHER READING

HYMAN, DAVID N. *Modern Microeconomics: Analysis and Applications*, esp. chap. 6. St. Louis: Times Mirror/Mosby College Publishing, 1986.

LEFTWICH, R. H. *The Price System and Resource Allocation*, 7th ed., esp. chap. 8. Hinsdale, Ill.: The Dryden Press, 1979.

MANSFIELD, E. *Microeconomics: Theory/Applications*, 5th ed., esp. chap. 6. New York: W. W. Norton & Company, 1985.

Appendix 6B

LINEAR PROGRAMMING ANALYSIS

EXECUTIVE SUMMARY

Linear programming is a solution technique that has a wide variety of business applications. Given linear objectives and constraints, the manager can find the least-cost input combination, the shortest sales route that visits each of several cities, the most nutritious, or least calorie, combination of foods, and so on. For the objectives and constraints to be linear, we simply require that input and output prices are constant over the range of inputs and outputs involved.

In this appendix we confine our attention to the firm's production problem but introduce a new aspect of that problem. We consider the **multiproduct firm** in which the manager must decide how much of each of several different products to produce, given their differing demands on limited inputs and available productive capacity, and the differing profitabilities associated with each product.

We consider the **graphical solution of the linear programming problem** first and then approach more complex problems **algebraically**. This leads us to the solution of the so-called dual problem, which generates "shadow prices" of the constrained resources. These **shadow prices** indicate the marginal value of the fixed inputs and indicate whether or not it is worth expanding the capacity of those inputs.

Software packages are available quite cheaply which allow the simple solution of linear programming problems on the personal computer. It is nonetheless valuable to understand the importance of the linearity condition, the solution process, and the meaning of the shadow prices, in particular. Without such understanding, this effective tool of the manager may be applied inappropriately, with adverse impact on the firm's profitability.

The Linearity Assumptions

To apply linear programming to a particular problem, both the decision maker's objective function and the constraints that confine the decision must be linear (or sufficiently approximated by linearity) over the range of outputs to which the decision applies. Supposing that the firm's objective function is the maximization of profits, this implies that the profit per unit of output must be constant for profit to be a linear function of output. This in turn requires that both price and average variable costs be constant over the range of outputs affected by the decision.

Under what circumstances would prices be constant over a range of output levels? This situation applies in markets in which the individual firm supplies such a small proportion of total industry output that it may presume that its output decision will not influence the market price. Clearly, as we consider progressively larger firms this assumption becomes more tenuous unless the range of outputs being considered is correspondingly reduced. Thus a relatively large firm may consider that for small variations in its output level it will not cause a change in the price level.

Constant average variable costs imply constant returns to the variable inputs. The statistical studies referred to in Chapter 8 indicate that constant AVC may be observed within many firms over limited ranges of output.

The second linearity requirement is that each of the possible outputs use each of the constraints as a linear function of the output of each product. If, for example, the first unit of product X uses twenty minutes of machine time,[1] so must all subsequent units of product X. Thus the efficiency of the fixed resources is constant and does not depend on the output level of each particular product to be produced. In any particular machine or plant facility, therefore, there will be a constant trade-off between product X and product Y, or more generally between any two products that may be produced by that machine.

In the following sections the emphasis will be on understanding the technique of linear programming so it can be correctly applied to decision problems. Simple linear-programming problems may be solved either graphically or algebraically, but more complex problems demand the assistance of computer programs designed to search for the optimal solution.

Graphical Solution of a Linear-Programming Problem

Suppose a small firm is in the business of making chromed shelf display units for city stores and boutiques. It has the necessary plant and equipment plus a small work force whose members regard their labor input as being fixed at certain weekly maximum levels. The firm has tapped a market for two particular shelf units and has found that demand exceeds its capacity to produce either product. It could specialize in either product X or product Y or produce some combination of the two products.

---

[1]This should be interpreted as the first unit in the relevant range of outputs, rather than the very first unit produced. All we require is that, over the range of output levels likely to contain the optimal output level, the relationship between input usage and output rate is constant.

Suppose that product X involves a more complex design and has a constant per-unit cost of $300 and that any feasible output of the firm can be sold at the current market price of $600 per unit. Product Y is a more simple design, has constant variable per-unit costs of $200, and can be sold within the range of feasible outputs at a market price of $400. Thus product X contributes $300 per unit toward fixed costs and profits, whereas product Y contributes only $200 per unit. (We call the excess of price over AVC the per-unit contribution of the product in question. Similarly, the excess of TR over TVC is the total contribution of the product in question.)

The firm has three processes which have limited capacity to produce both product X and product Y. The first process consists of cutting the material to the appropriate size and configuration on the firm's power hacksaw. The power hacksaw is available for only thirty-two hours weekly, since the operator of this machine is available for this period only. The second process consists of welding the materials to construct the shelf units, and the availability of the welding equipment and its operator is limited to thirty hours per week. The third process involves immersing the units in the chrome bath, and this facility and its operator are available for forty hours a week only.

Representation of the Constraints. Product X requires eight hours per unit in the first process, six hours per unit in the welding process, and five hours per unit in the chrome bath. Product Y requires four hours of the hacksaw time per unit, five hours of the welding time, and eight hours of the chrome bath time per unit. It can be seen that while product Y contributes less per unit, its demands on two of the processes are less than the demands of product X. Alternatively, product X demands more time per unit for two of the three processes yet has a significantly higher contribution than does product Y. Thus it is not obvious that the firm should specialize in either product X or product Y, and in fact we shall see that a combination of the two products will allow a maximum contribution to overheads and profits. The linear-programming problem is to find the output mix that will achieve the maximum contribution to overheads and profits, given the constraints imposed on the production of these two products.

Let us state the linear-programming problem in symbolic form. Supposing the firm wishes to maximize the total contribution of its operations, it thus wishes to maximize an objective function of the form

$$\pi = AX + BY \qquad (6B\text{-}1)$$

where π represents the total contribution to overheads and profits, X and Y are the number of units of each product to be produced, and the coefficients A and B represent the per-unit contribution expected from each of the two products. Using the price per unit and average variable cost data outlined above, we can deduce that the contribution per unit of product X is $300, and for product Y it is $200. Thus we can express the objective function as

$$\pi = 300X + 200Y \qquad (6B\text{-}2)$$

The constraints on the maximization of contribution can be expressed as follows:

$$\textit{Process 1: } 8X + 4Y \leq 32 \tag{6B-3}$$

$$\textit{Process 2: } 6X + 5Y \leq 30 \tag{6B-4}$$

$$\textit{Process 3: } 5X + 8Y \leq 40 \tag{6B-5}$$

Equation (6B-3) says in effect that the sum of the time utilized by the production of both product X and product Y must not exceed the time available in the first process. Since each unit of product X demands eight hours of the power hacksaw's time and each unit of product Y demands four hours, the number of units of products X and Y produced are constrained to that which can be produced within thirty-two hours' utilization of the power hacksaw and its operator. Similarly for the welding process, where each unit of product X requires six hours and each unit of product Y requires five hours, the sum must not exceed thirty hours in total. Finally, for the chrome bath process, each unit of product X requires five hours and each unit of product Y requires eight hours, and the total utilization of this process must be less than or equal to forty hours weekly.

Since linear programming is a mathematical procedure, it is likely to assign both positive and negative values to the variables X and Y unless we instruct it otherwise. Since negative values of output for product X and product Y make economic nonsense, we must add the condition that

$$X \geq 0, Y \geq 0$$

These are known as the nonnegativity requirements of linear-programming analysis.

The problem to be solved is thus to maximize profit contribution as shown by equation (6B-2) subject to the constraints indicated by equations (6B-3) through (6B-5) and the nonnegativity requirements on the variables X and Y. Thus we wish to choose values of X and Y such that none of the constraints are broken and π is maximized. We can solve this problem graphically by expressing the constraints and the objective function on a specific graph and finding the output level for which profits are maximized. To find the feasible combinations of X and Y, that is, those that it is possible to produce without violating one or more of the constraints, we must delineate between those combinations that are possible on each process and those that are impossible to produce given the total time available in each process. Beginning with the first process, it is clear that the limits of possible combinations will be achieved where all of the available thirty-two hours weekly are used in the production of X and Y. Thus we can remove the inequality from equation (6B-3) and state that

$$8X + 4Y = 32$$

or in terms of Y:

$$4Y = 32 - 8X$$
$$Y = 8 - 2X \tag{6B-6}$$

We now have an expression that shows Y as a linear function of X. In a graph with product Y on the vertical axis and product X on the horizontal axis, the first term is the intercept on the Y axis, and the coefficient to the X term represents the slope of the line relating products Y and X. In Figure 6B-1 we show the first constraint graphed against products Y and X. Those combinations of Y and X that lie outside the line are clearly unobtainable, since they would demand more than thirty-two hours of the time available in process 1.

To find the feasible output combinations under the other two processes, we proceed similarly. Thus for the second constraint

$$6X + 5Y = 30$$
$$5Y = 30 - 6X$$
$$Y = 6 - 1.2X \tag{6B-7}$$

and for the third process

$$5X + 8Y = 40$$
$$8Y = 40 - 5X$$
$$Y = 5 - 0.625X \tag{6B-8}$$

As shown in Figure 6B-1, the second constraint has an intercept value of 6 and a slope of -1.2, and the third constraint has an intercept value of 5 and a slope of -0.625.

The irregular area encompassing all combinations of X and Y that lie below all the constraint lines is known as the *feasible region* of the production problem and is shown as the shaded area $OABCD$ in Figure 6B-1. The feasible region has several linear facets at its outer boundary, each corresponding to a particular constraint that is binding on the feasible combinations of X and Y.

Isoprofit Lines. To find which of the feasible combinations allows the highest profit contribution, we introduce the concept of isoprofit lines, which are analogous to the isocost lines discussed in Appendix 6A. An isoprofit line is a locus of the combinations of products X and Y that allow the same total profit to be derived. Expressing the profit function, equation (6B-2), in terms of product Y, we have

$$Y = \frac{\pi}{200} - \frac{300}{200} X$$

or

$$Y = \frac{\pi}{200} - 1.5X \tag{6B-9}$$

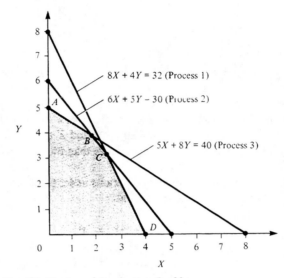

FIGURE 6B-1.   Feasible Region of Production Problem

Thus we have represented the isoprofit function in terms of Y and X. On any given isoprofit line the value of π will be known, and hence we may find the combinations of X and Y that preserve the equality shown in equation (6B-9). Suppose we wish to find the combinations of X and Y that allow a profit level of $1,000. Substituting in equation (6B-9), we have

$$Y = \frac{1,000}{200} - 1.5X$$
$$Y = 5 - 1.5X \qquad\qquad\qquad (6B\text{-}10)$$

Hence equation (6B-10) represents the equation for the isoprofit line along which profits are $1,000. We note that the intercept of this line on the Y axis must be at five units, and the slope of this line is -1.5 as the production of X is increased in one-unit increments. This isoprofit line is shown in Figure 6B-2 along with two other arbitrarily chosen profit levels. Notice that higher levels of profits are represented by higher isoprofit lines and that all isoprofit lines are parallel, since the slope of the isoprofit function is unchanged by variations in the value of π.

By superimposing the relevant isoprofit map on the relevant feasible region, we are able to ascertain which of the combinations of X and Y allows the attainment of the highest possible isoprofit line. In Figure 6B-3 we reproduce the feasible region of the production problem from Figure 6B-1 and show that the highest isoprofit line that can be obtained is the line representing $1,350, which just touches point C on the feasible region. Any other point on the feasible region must lie on a lower isoprofit line, and any higher isoprofit lines will not touch the feasible region. Thus the optimal combination of

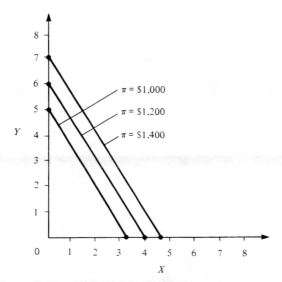

FIGURE 6B-2. *Isoprofit Map for Production Problem*

Y and *X* is three units of *Y* and two and one half units of *X* per week. (The fractional value of *X* does not worry us: Every two weeks five complete units of product X will be produced.)

Note that the solution occurs at one of the corners of the feasible region. Since the isoprofit lines are linear, and the constraints are linear, this must always be the case. In the event that the isoprofit line has the same slope as one of the constraint lines, the highest attainable isoprofit line would coincide with the facet of the feasible region that represents that particular constraint. In Figure 6B-4 we show such a situation. In this case the highest attainable isoprofit line coincides with the section *CD* of the feasible region. Note that any output combination of *X* and *Y* along the facet *CD* allows the same level of profits to be attained. Thus the earlier statement that the solution will always occur at a corner of the feasible region is vindicated, since the corners represented by the points *C* and *D* represent equivalent levels of profit contribution when compared with any point on the facet of the feasible region, and thus either one will be an optimal solution.

A second interesting point depicted in Figure 6B-4 is the horizontal facet of the feasible region, labeled *AB*. This indicates a constraint that operates only on the production of product Y. It is thus a process that is not needed for the output of product X, and which when utilized fully by product Y allows 0*A* units of *Y* to be produced. Similarly, a process that is utilized only by product X would give rise to a vertical section on the feasible region (if it is a binding constraint).

Confirming the Solution Algebraically. The preceding discussion indicates that the slope of the constraint equations, in comparison with the slope of the isoprofit line, can be used to find the solution values for *X* and *Y*. Referring back to Figure 6B-3, notice that the slope of the isoprofit curve is greater than the slope of the third constraint (shown by

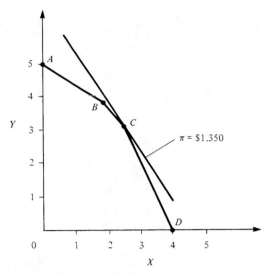

FIGURE 6B-3.   Solution to Production Problem

the section *AB* of the feasible region) and is greater than the slope of the second constraint (shown by the segment *BC*), but it is less than the slope of the first constraint (shown by the segment *CD*). Thus we might have simply compared the slopes of the profit function with the slopes of the constraint lines to find, in comparison with the profit function, the next-steepest constraint line and the next-flattest constraint line. The intersection of these two constraint lines will thus define the point at which profit contribution is maximized, unless one of these constraints lies outside the feasible region. The

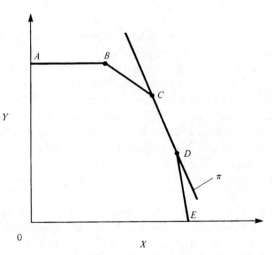

FIGURE 6B-4.   Isoprofit Line Coinciding with a Facet of the Feasible Region

comparison of the slopes of the objective function and the constraint functions that bound the feasible region thus acts as a check on our graphical procedures.

Since the solution line lies at the intersection of the first and second constraint lines, we are able to confirm the graphical results by simultaneous solution of those two equations for the values of X and Y, as follows:

$$8X + 4Y = 32 \tag{6B-11}$$

$$6X + 5Y = 30 \tag{6B-12}$$

We proceed to eliminate Y by multiplying equation (6B-11) by 5 and equation (6B-12) by 4:

$$40X + 20Y = 160 \tag{6B-13}$$

$$24X + 20Y = 120 \tag{6B-14}$$

and subtracting equation (6B-14) from equation (6B-13), we have

$$16X = 40$$

or

$$X = 2.5$$

Substituting for X in equation (6B-11) to find Y:

$$8(2.5) + 4Y = 32$$
$$4Y = 12$$
$$Y = 3$$

To find the profit level, we substitute for X and Y in the isoprofit function, equation (6B-2):

$$\pi = 300(2.5) + 200(3)$$
$$= 750 + 600$$
$$= 1,350$$

It is clear that process 1 and process 2 are fully utilized by the production of the three units of Y and the two and a half units of X per week. Process 3, however, is not fully utilized, since this output combination requires less than forty hours of the third process. To confirm this, let us substitute the optimal values for X and Y into the constraint inequality given by equation (6B-5).

$$5X + 8Y \leq 40$$
$$5(2.5) + 8(3) \leq 40$$
$$12.5 + 24 \leq 40$$
$$36.5 \leq 40$$

Thus there are 3.5 units (hours) of the third process remaining unutilized at the optimal output combinations.

Algebraic Solution of the Linear-Programming Problem

Given the knowledge that the solution to linear-programming programs will occur at one of the corners, we could solve for the values of X and Y at each of the corners, substitute these values into the objective function, and choose that pair of values that generates the greatest value in the objective function. To solve the problem algebraically, however, all constraints must be expressed as equations rather than inequalities.

To cause all constraints to be expressed as equalities, we insert what are known as "slack variables" in each of the constraint expressions. The slack variables take up the slack if the constraint is not binding and are thus valued at the amount of idle capacity remaining in a particular process. Obviously, if a constraint is binding, the value of the slack variable is zero.

Algebraic solution of the linear-programming problem offers two main advantages over the graphical solution. First, it allows us to handle problems in which there are three or more variables; and second, the values of the slack variables provide information that is extremely useful for decision-making purposes. To demonstrate the algebraic solution of a linear-programming problem, suppose that the small firm making the shelf display units discovers that a market exists for a third product, product Z, which is essentially a smaller version of product X. Suppose that its price is expected to remain constant at $250 per unit and that its costs will be $150 per unit, such that the contribution will be $100 per unit. It will require two hours of hacksaw time, four hours of welding time, and three hours of the chrome bath time to produce each unit of product Z. Modifying the earlier objective function and constraints by the addition of the information relevant to product Z, and inserting slack variables, we may state the linear-programming problem algebraically as follows:

Maximize

$$\pi = 300X + 200Y + 100Z \tag{6B-15}$$

subject to

$$8X + 4Y + 2Z + S_1 = 32 \tag{6B-16}$$
$$6X + 5Y + 4Z + S_2 = 30 \tag{6B-17}$$
$$5X + 8Y + 3Z + S_3 = 40 \tag{6B-18}$$

with the nonnegativity requirements

$$X \geq 0, \; Y \geq 0, \; Z \geq 0, \; S_1 \geq 0, \; S_2 \geq 0, \; S_3 \geq 0$$

We wish to find the values of X, Y, and Z at each of the corners or peaks of a three-dimensional feasible region. The constraint equations (6B-16) to (6B-18) provide a system of three equations in six unknowns, and the system is therefore underdetermined. We know, however, that at each of the corners or peaks of the feasible region the values of some of the variables will be zero. In the three-dimensional case, three variables will be zero at each corner.[2]

To identify each corner, we take the six variables (three output variables and three slack variables) and consider every combination in which three of these variables are zero and the other three have positive values. We then evaluate the profit function at each of these combinations. In Table 6B-1 we show the value of each of the variables at each corner of the feasible region. At corner 0, the origin, output of the three products is zero, and the slack variables must take the maximum values. At corner A, the values of X and Z are zero and the third constraint is binding, such that the slack variable S_3 is also zero. At this corner the value of Y is 5, and we find the values of S_1 and S_2 by substitution of $Y = 5$ in equations (6B-16) and (6B-17). Since X and Z are zero in each of these expressions, and Y is known, it is a simple matter to find $S_1 = 12$, and $S_2 = 5$. At corner B, $Z = 0$, $S_2 = 0$, and $S_3 = 0$. This procedure collapses equations (6B-17) and (6B-18) into the following system of two equations in two unknowns:

$$6X + 5Y = 30 \tag{6B-19}$$

$$5X + 8Y = 40 \tag{6B-20}$$

By simultaneous solution of equations (6B-19) and (6B-20) we find $X = 1.74$ and $Y = 3.91$. Substituting these values into equation (6B-16), we find the missing value of slack variable S_1, which is 0.44. Substituting the calculated values for X and Y into the objective function (6B-15), we find the total profit contribution at this corner to be \$1,304. The values of the variables and the objective function at the other corners are calculated in similar fashion. The values of the objective function at the corners of the feasible region are calculated by substitution of the values of X, Y, and Z in the objective function equation (6B-15) and are shown in the next to the last column of Table 6B-1. It can be seen that contribution is maximized at corner C, as it was in the earlier two-dimensional case. Thus, the addition of product Z does not change the optimality of the earlier solution, since the contribution of product Z relative to its use of the constrained processes is lower than for the original two products. Thus the firm would maximize total product

---

[2]Imagine a three-dimensional surface, like a peaked roof. Where three planes intersect, as at the end of the roof, there will be a point. In a three-variable linear-programming problem this point corresponds to the intersection of three constraint planes. If the isoprofit surface sits on this point, then three of the processes will be fully utilized.

TABLE 6B-1.   Algebraic Solution of a Linear-Programming Problem

Corner Name	VALUE OF VARIABLES						VALUE OF OBJECTIVE FUNCTION	
	X	Y	Z	S_1	S_2	S_3	Initial	Later
0	0	0	0	32	30	40	$ 0	0
A	0	5	0	12	5	0	1,000	500
B	1.74	3.91	0	0.44	0	0	1,304	870
C	2.5	3	0	0	0	3.5	1,350*	988
D	4	0	0	0	6	20	1,200	1,100
E	3.4	0	2.4	0	0	15.8	1,260	1,115*
F	0	4.12	2.35	10.8	0	0	1,059	588
G	0	0	7.5	17.0	0	17.5	750	563

* Maximum

contribution by producing 2.5 units of X, 3.0 units of Y, and ignoring the market opportunity for product Z.

Response to a Change in the Parameters of the Problem.   The above optimal combination of the three products depends on their relative contributions to overheads and profits and their relative use of the three production processes. If either of these factors changed or if we were able to relax one of the constraints, we should expect a new combination of the three products to be optimal. To illustrate, let us suppose that market conditions change and the relative contributions of the three products change. Suppose a new firm begins making these units in direct competition with product Y, but causes the prices of products X and Z to be reduced also, such that the new objective function becomes

$$\pi = 275X + 100Y + 75Z \qquad (6B\text{-}21)$$

Note that there has been no change in the availability of any of the production processes or in the usage rates of these processes by any of the products. Thus the corner solutions found earlier are still applicable. Inserting these values for the variables into the new objective function, we find the value of the objective function at each corner as shown in the last column in Table 6B-1. Note that profit contribution is now greatest at corner E rather than at corner C: Under the new market conditions it is now more profitable to drop product Y and increase the production of both products X and Z. This result comes about because the isoprofit plane has shifted because of the change in the relative contributions of the three products, and the highest attainable isoprofit plane now touches the feasible region at the corner E, whereas previously the highest attainable isoprofit plane rested on point C.

   If the capacity of a particular process could be increased, that is, if the constraint could be relaxed, would we expect a change in the optimal combination of outputs and

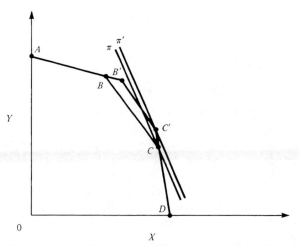

FIGURE 6B-5. *Relaxation of a Constraint and Its Impact on Profit Contribution*

the total profit contribution? The answer to this question is yes to both issues if the constraint is binding, but it is no if slack exists in the particular constraint. For additional availability of a constraint process to cause the solution to change, availability of additional capacity must cause the frontier of the feasible region to move outward and poke through the previously highest attainable isoprofit line or surface, such that a new higher isoprofit line or surface can be attained. This statement is demonstrated in the two-variable case in Figure 6B-5. Here the constraint represented by the facet *BC* has been relaxed by a certain amount to cause the feasible region to expand to the area bounded by 0*AB'C'D*. Whereas the previously highest attainable isoprofit curve was that shown by π, tangent at point *C*, the new feasible region allows the higher isoprofit line π' to be attained at point *C'*.

Shadow Prices of the Constraints. The *shadow price* of a constraint is defined as the increment to the value of the objective function that results from that constraint being relaxed by one unit. From the preceding discussion it is clear that only those constraints that are binding will have positive shadow prices, since those constraints with slack remaining will add nothing to profit contribution if increased further.

Graphically we could find the shadow price of each constraint by expanding the frontier for each constraint, finding the new highest attainable isoprofit line, and calculating the value of this level of profit from the intercept value of this isoprofit line. Algebraically, the procedure is similar. We would expand one constraint by one unit—for example, $8X + 4Y + 2Z + S_1 = 33$—and solve for the optimal combinations of X, Y, and Z in conjunction with the other two constraint equations in their original form. We would then substitute the solution values for X, Y, and Z in the objective function to find the new profit-contribution level. A simple subtraction of the earlier maximum profit contribution from the new maximum profit contribution would generate the shadow price of the constraint that was augmented.

An alternative algebraic method of obtaining the shadow prices is to solve the ''dual'' of the linear-programming problem.

The Dual Problem

In the preceding discussion we have worked with what is by convention called the primal problem. A primal problem may be to maximize some variable subject to various constraints, as in the above example, or it may be to minimize a variable subject to several constraints in a different problem. Every primal linear-programming problem has a dual problem associated with it. For every maximization problem there is an associated (dual) minimization problem, and for every minimization problem there is an associated (dual) maximization problem. This relationship derives from the mathematical nature of the linear-programming technique. Although it may not be intuitively obvious, for every problem in which a particular variable is to be maximized (or minimized) subject to certain constraints, there is another variable that, if minimized (or maximized) subject to another set of constraints, will derive the same values for the crucial variables. In the case discussed above, we maximized profit contribution subject to the limited availability of three production processes, by choosing the optimal output mix of products X, Y, and Z. The dual to this problem is to minimize the value of these three production processes subject to the constraints that the value of the production processes used in the production of each unit of output do not exceed the contribution generated by each unit of each output. When this minimization problem is solved, the output mix of products X, Y, and Z will be the same as it would have been in the primal maximization problem. The virtue of solving the dual problem is that the solution imputes a value to the marginal units of each of the constraints, which of course are the shadow prices we seek.

Let us now return to the simple two-variable problem discussed previously, which was to maximize

$$\pi = 300X + 200Y$$

subject to

$$8X + 4Y + S_1 = 32$$
$$6X + 5Y + S_2 = 30$$
$$5X + 8Y + S_3 = 40$$

with the nonnegativity requirements that X, Y, S_1, S_2, and S_3 are all ≥ 0.

To establish the dual problem, we must define a number of new variables as follows:

$V =$ the total value of the three production processes,
$W_1 =$ the shadow price of the first process,
$W_2 =$ the shadow price of the second process,

W_3 = the shadow price of the third process,

R_1 = slack variable in the constraint that the value of the resources used in production of a unit of X should not exceed the contribution from a unit of X, and

R_2 = the slack variable in the constraint pertaining to product Y.

We can now state the dual problem:

Minimize

$$V = 32W_1 + 30W_2 + 40W_3 \qquad \text{(6B-22)}$$

subject to

$$8W_1 + 6W_2 + 5W_3 + R_1 = 300 \qquad \text{(6B-23)}$$
$$4W_1 + 5W_2 + 8W_3 + R_2 = 200 \qquad \text{(6B-24)}$$

with the nonnegativity requirements that W_1, W_2, W_3, R_1, and R_2 are all ≥ 0.

Solving the Dual Problem. The objective function of the dual problem is thus to minimize the total value of the firm's fixed resources, measured in terms of the shadow prices of each resource times the availability of that resource in units. The constraints are that the total cost of the firm's resources involved in the production of each product should be less than or equal to the contribution from each of the products. We insert the slack variables to allow the constraints to be represented as equalities.

Equations (6B-23) and (6B-24) are a system of two equations in five unknowns, and this system is thus underdetermined. However, our knowledge of the nature of the solution to the linear-programming problem allows us to predict that at each corner of the feasible region three of the variables will take zero values, and hence we may iteratively assign zero values to combinations of three variables and find the combination that provides the minimum value of the objective function. We could array the values of the variables and the objective function in a table, as we did for the primal problem in Table 6B-1, where each line would represent the values of the variables and the objective function at one of the corners. That corner that meets all the nonnegativity requirements and shows the minimum value for V will represent the optimal solution. At that corner the values of the variables W_1, W_2, and W_3 will represent the shadow price of each of the constraints.

Rather than follow the above procedure, however, we shall use the knowledge gained from the solution of the primal problem to assign zero values to three of the variables in the system of equations (6B-23) and (6B-24) such that we may solve for the values of the shadow prices at the optimal solution. We know that in the primal problem the first and second constraints were binding. Thus W_1 and W_2 in the dual problem will have positive values, while W_3, R_1, and R_2 must take zero values. Eliminating the latter three variables from equations (6B-23) and (6B-24), we have

$$8W_1 + 6W_2 = 300 \qquad\qquad (6B\text{-}25)$$
$$4W_1 + 5W_2 = 200 \qquad\qquad (6B\text{-}26)$$

which is a system of two equations in two unknowns and can thus be solved by simultaneous solution. Multiplying equation (6B-26) by 2, we have

$$8W_1 + 10W_2 = 400 \qquad\qquad (6B\text{-}27)$$

Subtracting equation (6B-25) from (6B-27) to eliminate W_1, we have

$$4W_2 = 100$$

or

$$W_2 = 25$$

Substituting into equation (6B-25) to find W_1:

$$8W_1 + 6(25) = 300$$
$$8W_1 = 150$$
$$W_1 = 18.75$$

Thus the shadow prices of the two constraints that are binding are $25 for the hacksaw process and $18.75 for the welding process. That is, an extra hour of utilization of either process would add those amounts to the total contribution to overheads and profits. If an additional hour of the hacksaw operator's time plus associated expenses could be employed for less than $25, the decision maker should do so. Similarly, if an additional hour of the welding equipment's utilization could be employed for less than $18.75, the decision maker would be advised to do so, since there would result a net increase in the contribution to overheads and profits.

    An alternate method that finds both the optimal values of the variables and the shadow prices of the constraints is the simplex method.[3] Essentially, the simplex method uses the knowledge that the solution must occur at a corner of the feasible region, and that at each corner the number of nonzero variables is exactly equal to the number of constraints in the problem, to search for the solution. The simplex method starts at the

---

[3]The simplex method is attributed to the mathematician George M. Dantzig. See Dantzig, *A Procedure for Maximizing a Linear Function Subject to Linear Inequalities* (Washington, D.C.: Headquarters U.S. Air Force, Comptroller, 1948). Although the word *simplex* might imply simplicity, a simplex is the *n*-dimensional analogue of a triangle. The simplex technique is named for its procedure of systematically evaluating the objective function at the simplexes of the feasible region.

origin of the feasible region and proceeds to compare the profitability of that corner point with an adjacent corner point. If the adjacent corner yields a greater profit, the next corner point is evaluated and compared. When the adjacent corner yields a lower profit, the procedure ceases, and the previous highest profit point is taken to be the optimal solution.

We shall not go into any detail concerning the simplex method, since it is a tedious method prone to error when calculated by hand. Computer programs are now readily available that use the simplex method to compute the optimal values of the variables and the shadow prices of the constraints quickly and accurately. It is important for the decision maker to understand the underlying principles of linear programming, and then use the most cost-effective means of utilizing the linear programming technique.

Other Applications of Linear Programming

In this appendix we have confined our attention to the solution of a product-mix problem. Linear-programming analysis is applicable to a wide variety of decision problems that arise in the business firm or institutional environment. Linear programming is commonly used to solve transportation problems in which the shortest route must be found between a number of delivery points, subject to the constraints imposed by the highway or railroad system.[4] The classic diet problem involves minimizing the cost of supplying patients in a hospital with the minimum required amounts of certain vitamins and other nutrients which are contained in differing quantities in various foodstuffs, which in turn cost differing amounts.[5] This problem is analogous to a firm wishing to minimize the cost of meeting all specifications on a particular project when there is more than one way to meet each specification. In marketing, linear programming may be used to find the minimum costs of obtaining a certain level of advertising exposure given the different costs and availabilities of the various media. These examples serve to indicate the range of applications of linear-programming analysis. As long as the objective function and the constraints can be expressed linearly in terms of the variables, linear programming will serve as a valid solution procedure.

Summary

In this appendix we have outlined the application of linear programming to the product-mix problem. Linear programming allows the optimal combinations to be found, given the presence of certain absolute constraints. Simple two-variable cases can be solved graphically by graphing the constraints in the two-variable space and finding the corner solution that supports the highest attainable isoprofit line. At this corner solution, two of the constraints will be equalities and thus can be solved for the values of the two vari-

[4]See, for example, W. J. Fabrycky and G. J. Thuesen, *Economic Decision Analysis* (Englewood Cliffs, N.J.: Prentice-Hall, 1974), pp. 324–32.

[5]See R. Dorfman, P. A. Samuelson, and R. M. Solow, *Linear Programming and Economic Analysis* (New York: McGraw-Hill, 1958), chap. 2.

ables at the optimal combination point, and the optimal level of profits will be found by substituting the solution values of the variables in the objective function equation.

More complex cases can be solved algebraically on the basis of the knowledge that the nature of the solution is such that the number of nonzero variables will equal the number of constraints at the solution point. Thus, if we have n constraints and m variables, we could set $m - n$ variables equal to zero and solve for the remaining n variables in the n equations provided by the constraints. We would do this for all combinations of the variables. For each of the $m - n$ zero-valued variables and n positively valued variables that would result, we would evaluate the objective function and choose as a solution the combination that gave the optimal value to the objective function. The solution of the dual problem may be easier than solving the primal problem, but in any case it provides values for the shadow prices of each constraint, which provide valuable information for the decision maker.

The mechanistic nature of the linear-programming solution lends itself to computer programming, such that this technique is able to handle extremely complex decision problems. It has wide applicability in business situations, but the decision maker must be assured that the problem to be solved can be fairly represented by linear constraints and a linear objective function.

DISCUSSION QUESTIONS

6B-1. Outline the features necessary to make a problem suitable for solution by linear-programming analysis.

6B-2. When would a constraint line be horizontal or vertical in the graphical approach to linear programming analysis?

6B-3. Why is linear programming a technique suitable for short-run production problems rather than for long-run production problems?

6B-4. If a firm produces two products, both of which make exactly the same demands on resources and contribute the same to profits, how is the optimal product mix determined?

6B-5. What is the logic behind changing the inequality to an equality to depict each constraint graphically?

6B-6. For algebraic solution of the linear-programming problem, we insert slack variables to express the constraints as equalities. Why?

6B-7. Outline the process involved in the algebraic solution of the linear-programming problem. Why are we able to confine our attention to the corner solutions?

6B-8. What happens to the shape of the feasible region if a production process suddenly becomes more efficient in terms of the output of one product?

6B-9. What should the decision maker do after having ascertained the shadow prices of each constraint?

6B-10. Outline the relationship between the primal problem and its dual problem in linear-programming analysis.

PROBLEMS AND SHORT CASES

6B-1. Frank's Fish Packing Company produces two items, fish cakes (for human consumption) and fish meal (for animal consumption). The light-meat parts of the fish are separated from the rest of the fish for the fish cakes, and the rest of the fish is used for the fish meal. The ratio of fish cakes output to fish meal output can vary as more or less of the lighter meat is separated from the rest of the fish. As the fresh fish comes into the plant, it goes through four processes: separating, shredding, packing, and canning. Each of these processes has a maximum input available because of the labor available with the required training for each process, and these workers' prior agreements with management as to the length of their work week. The total time available in each process, and the time required in each process per 1,000 pounds of output for each of the products, is as follows:

Process	Total Time Available (hours weekly)	HOURS REQUIRED (PER 1,000 LB) Fish Cakes	Fish Meal
Separating	205	22.78	13.67
Shredding	106	10.60	8.83
Packing	188	14.46	17.09
Canning	65	5.00	5.00

Frank's sells the fish cakes for $0.80 per pound and the fish meal for $0.70 per pound. All costs, including the fresh fish, are joint costs, and hence these revenue figures can be treated as the per-unit contribution to joint (overhead) costs and profits.

Solve this product-mix problem using graphical analysis. Confirm your answers algebraically.

(a) What is the contribution-maximizing product mix?

(b) What is the maximum contribution attainable?

(c) Which processes are at full capacity?

6B-2. The Munchies Cake Company wishes to minimize the materials cost for its Jumbo fruit-and-nut cakes. The company has found that market acceptance of these cakes is maximized when they contain at least 250 grams of currants, 375 grams of sultanas, 150 grams of citrus peel, and 225 grams of nuts, and it consequently wishes to maintain at least these levels of these components in each cake. Neither of the two commercially available fruit-and-nut mixes comes in exactly these proportions, however, and Munchies combines these two mixes to achieve a mix that meets the above constraints on the minimum weight of each component. Brand A fruit-and-nut mix costs $2.15 per kilogram, and brand B fruit-and-nut mix costs $2.35 per kilogram. Each kilogram of these two mixes contains the following percentage breakdown of the four components:

	Currants	Sultanas	Peel	Nuts
Brand A	30%	40%	10%	20%
Brand B	15%	35%	25%	25%

(a) Using graphical analysis, find the combination of brand A and brand B fruit-and-nut mix that minimizes cost subject to the minimum weights being achieved for each of the four components. Confirm your answers algebraically.

(b) What is the minimum fruit-and-nut mix cost per Jumbo cake?

(c) Which constraints are binding? What would you suggest Munchies do? Why?

6B-3. The Grimes Gravel Company produces three mixtures of sand, pebbles, and rocks for eventual sale in 20-kg bags to the home handyperson for use in cement work. The sandy mixture is composed of 10 kg sand, 7 kg pebbles, and 3 kg rocks. The pebbly mixture is composed of 6 kg sand, 10 kg pebbles, and 4 kg rocks. The rocky mixture is composed of 2 kg sand, 8 kg pebbles, and 10 kg rocks. The market prices prevailing are $2.75 for the sandy mixture, $2.50 for the pebbly mixture, and $2.25 for the rocky mixture. Grimes Gravel feels that the market prices will hold regardless of the volume of each product it supplies.

Grimes Gravel wishes to maximize sales revenue from its present plant and equipment. The constraints on output are the limited size of the storage bins for the sand, pebbles, and rocks. These bins hold 2,000, 3,000, and 2,000 kilograms, respectively, and replenishment of supplies can only be made once weekly.

(a) Use the algebraic approach to find the optimal output of each of the three products.

(b) What is the maximum weekly revenue that Grimes Gravel can obtain?

(c) Which constraints are binding?

6B-4. Corpulent Foods, Inc., wishes to minimize the ingredient cost of its Krunchy-Karamel chocolate bar. This chocolate bar has become its major seller over the past year, but increasing costs have reduced the contribution margin below acceptable levels. The Krunchy-Karamel bar is now comprised of 45% chocolate, 35% caramel, and 20% nuts. It weighs 100 grams, and Corpulent Foods wholesales the bar at 10 cents apiece (in bulk) and expects to continue paying $1.25 per kilogram for chocolate, $0.85 per kilogram for caramel, and $0.50 per kilogram for nuts.

Corpulent Foods' marketing research department has been conducting tests with experimental compositions of the Krunchy-Karamel bar. Using bars with various combinations of chocolate, caramel, and nuts, it has ascertained that as long as the bars contain at least 30 grams of chocolate, 15 grams of caramel, and 10 grams of nuts, and score at least 150 on the crunch index and 300 on the flavor index, all consumers who initially preferred the (regular) Krunchy-Karamel bar over the rival bars will still prefer the (modified) Krunchy-Karamel bar. The score on the crunch and flavor indices reflects the average subjective evaluation given by the consumer-participants to each experimental bar, on a scale of zero to 500. Regressing these average crunch and flavor scores against the contents of the various experimental bars, it was found that chocolate gives 2 units of crunch and 3.3 units of flavor per gram, caramel gives 1 unit of crunch and 5 units of flavor per gram, and nuts give 7 units of crunch and 2 units of flavor per gram.

(a) Formalize the above problem by expressing its objective function and six constraints algebraically.

(b) Solve for that minimum cost combination of ingredients that satisfies all constraints by systematically assigning zero values to some variables and evaluating the objective function at each of the feasible corner solutions.

(c) Should Corpulent Foods change the present composition of its Krunchy-Karamel bar? Why?

6B-5. The P.M.D. Light Company produces and sells three standing lamps. The contribution to overhead and profit for these lamps is constant at the following levels regardless of output level: model A, $8.75; model B, $13.25, and model C, $16.80. All three models go through the basic assembly process; then models A and B go through the fabric installation process while model C goes through the antique-bronzing process. The requirements of each model in each process and the weekly availability of these processes are as follows:

Process	Hours Available	HOURS REQUIRED PER UNIT		
		A	B	C
Assembly	800	0.2	0.3	0.35
Fabric	480	0.1	0.12	—
Bronzing	160	—	—	0.8

Using the simplex method, solve for the contribution-maximizing output mix, the maximum contribution available, and the shadow prices of the constraints.

(a) Should P.M.D. Light continue to produce all three models? Why?

(b) Suppose overtime labor was available in each process at a cost of $12 per hour compared with the regular $8 per hour. Would you advise P.M.D. Light to employ this overtime labor? Explain.

SUGGESTED REFERENCES AND FURTHER READING

BAUMOL, W. J. *Economic Theory and Operations Analysis* (4th ed.), chaps. 5 and 6. Englewood Cliffs, N.J.: Prentice-Hall, Inc., 1977.

BRIGHAM, E. F., and J. L. PAPPAS. *Managerial Economics* (2nd ed.), chap. 7. Hinsdale, Ill.: The Dryden Press, 1976.

CHARNES, A., and W. W. COOPER. *Management Models and Industrial Applications of Linear Programming*, vols. 1 and 2. New York: John Wiley & Sons, 1961.

DANO, S. *Linear Programming in Industry: Theory and Applications*. Vienna, Austria: Springer-Verlag, 1960.

DANTZIG, G. M. *Linear Programming and Extensions*, esp. chaps. 1-5. Princeton, N.J.: Princeton University Press, 1963.

DORFMAN, R. "Mathematical, or Linear, Programming: A Nonmathematical Exposition," *American Economic Review*, 63 (December 1953), pp. 797–825.

DORFMAN, R., P. A. SAMUELSON, and R. M. SOLOW. *Linear Programming and Economic Analysis*, chaps. 1–7. New York: McGraw-Hill Book Company, 1958.

FABRYCKY, W. J., and G. J. THUESEN. *Economic Decision Analysis*, chap. 15. Englewood Cliffs, N.J.: Prentice-Hall, Inc., 1974.

HEINEKE, J. M. *Microeconomics for Business Decisions: Theory and Applications*, chaps. 4 and 5. Englewood Cliffs, N.J.: Prentice-Hall, Inc., 1976.

NAYLOR, T. H., and J. M. VERNON. *Microeconomics and Decision Models of the Firm*, chaps. 6–8. New York: Harcourt, Brace & World, 1969.

Chapter 7

COST CONCEPTS FOR DECISION MAKING

EXECUTIVE SUMMARY

In this chapter we introduce **cost concepts relevant for day-to-day decision making by the business executive**. In some cases these are crude when compared with the theoretical nicety of the concepts discussed in the preceding chapter. But real-world business situations seldom provide the data necessary for direct application of the theoretical concepts. Nevertheless, an understanding of the theoretical concepts is important to ensure the proper application of the concepts that will be discussed in this chapter. Decision makers sometimes apply convenient rules of thumb to problems that confront them without first examining the applicability of those rules to the particular problem at hand. The danger of incorrectly applying these shortcuts is perhaps nowhere greater than in the area of costs, since poor decisions here operate directly to erode profitability.

In this chapter we shall first examine the differences between **economic and accounting concepts of costs** and profits. We shall see that some accounting costs, such as the depreciation of an asset purchased in an earlier period or the cost of an item taken from inventory that was purchased at an earlier, lower price, must be evaluated in terms of the current or future cost for economic decision-making purposes. This leads to a discussion of the **relevant costs** for decision making: Some costs are relevant and others are irrelevant to the decision problem at hand. The relevant costs are all **incremental costs**. The three main types of incremental costs are introduced and discussed. **Contribution analysis** is based on the incremental costs of a decision, and the last section of this chapter uses contribution analysis in the context of several types of decision problems. The appendix to this chapter considers breakeven analysis, with an examination of its applications and its limitations in the decision-making process.

7.1   ECONOMIC VERSUS ACCOUNTING CONCEPTS OF COSTS AND PROFITS

The data for decision making with respect to costs typically come not from economists but from accountants. In most cases these data are adequate and appropriate, but in some cases, since they were derived for different purposes, they are less suitable for direct insertion into economic decision-making procedures. We shall examine several different economic and accounting cost concepts and the relationships between them.

Direct and Indirect Costs

In the business firm some costs are incurred that can be directly attributed to the production of a particular unit of a given product. The use of raw materials, labor inputs, and machine time involved in the production of each unit can usually be determined. On the other hand, the cost of fuel for heating, electricity, office and administrative expenses, depreciation of plant and buildings, and other items cannot easily and accurately be separated and attributed to individual units of production (except on an arbitrary basis). Accountants speak of the *direct*, or *prime*, costs per unit when referring to the separable costs of the first category and of *indirect*, or *overhead*, costs when referring to the joint costs of the second category.[1]

Direct and indirect costs are not likely to coincide exactly with the economist's variable cost and fixed cost categories. The criterion used by the economist to divide cost into either fixed or variable is whether or not the cost varies with the level of output, but the criterion used by the accountant is whether or not the cost is separable with respect to the production of individual output units. To bring the accounting costs into line with the economic concepts, we must find that part of the indirect or overhead costs that varies with the output level. Accounting statements often divide overhead expense into variable overhead and fixed overhead categories, in which case we would add the variable overhead expense per unit to the direct cost per unit to find what economists call *average variable cost*.

- EXAMPLE: Suppose that a company reports that during the past month it manufactured 1,480 units of output, and the accountant provides you with figures for the total expenditures on direct labor, direct materials, variable overhead, and fixed overhead, as shown in the left-hand side of Table 7-1. The sum of the first three expenditures constitutes the total variable cost (TVC), and adding to it the fixed overhead, which we call total fixed cost (TFC), we arrive at total costs (TC). Per-unit costs, shown on the right-hand side of the table, are found by dividing the total cost figures by the output level.[2]

---

[1]See, for example, C. T. Horngren, *Introduction to Management Accounting*, 5th ed. (Englewood Cliffs, N.J.: Prentice-Hall, 1981), chap. 3.

[2]Simply adding variable overhead to direct labor and materials to find total variable cost, and hence AVC, may still involve error if the assignment of costs to the variable or fixed overhead categories was made on any basis other than the variability of the cost with respect to changes in the output level. In Chapter 8 we examine the gradient method and other cost estimation techniques which allow a more precise estimate of average variable and marginal costs. At that time we will stress the importance of examining changes in all cost

TABLE 7-1.   The Interpretation of Accounting Reports in Economic Terms

Costs of Production	Total Costs	Average Cost
Direct labor	$ 77,700	$ 52.50
Direct materials	36,260	24.50
Variable overhead	4,930	3.33
	TVC = $118,890	AVC = $ 80.33
Fixed overhead	TFC = $ 36,800	AFC = $ 24.86
Total costs	TC = $155,690	AC = $105.19

Explicit and Implicit Costs

The accounting process is predominantly concerned with explicit costs. These are costs that actually involve a transfer of funds from the firm to another party that had previously supplied some materials or services. These are out-of-pocket expenses in the current time period, since they are an actual cash outflow in payment for resources. Other cost items, however, are implicit costs, in the sense that they do not involve an actual cash outflow in the current time period.

- EXAMPLE: One such cost in the accounting framework is *depreciation*, which is a charge against each year's revenue of some portion of the cost of acquiring the capital equipment necessary to generate that revenue. The accounting procedures involve taking the initial cost of the asset, subtracting from this the asset's estimated scrap or salvage value at the end of its useful life, and apportioning this net cost against revenues over the life of the asset. Straight-line depreciation procedures allocate the net cost evenly over the life of the asset, while other methods, such as the sum-of-the-digits methods and double-declining-balance methods, allocate proportionately more of the net cost against revenues early in the asset's life.[3] Thus the accountant charges an implicit cost against revenues each year to spread the explicit cost of the asset over the period during which the asset is being used in the production process.

Opportunity Costs and Historic Costs

Accountants are constrained by the tax laws and by the laws governing financial reporting to shareholders to express many costs in terms of the actual or historic costs paid for the resources used in the production process. For decision-making purposes, however, both accountants and economists agree that the appropriate cost concept is not the past

---

categories to see that the changes were output related and not simply due to changes in factor input prices or some other reason.

[3]See Horngren, *Introduction to Management Accounting*, pp. 344–46.

cost at which the resource was purchased, but the current or future cost at the time in which it is involved in the decision to be made.

- DEFINITION: *Opportunity costs*, or alternative costs as they are often called, refer to the value of a resource in its best alternative employment. For resources that are purchased outright or hired, such as raw materials and labor inputs, there is usually little difference between historic costs and opportunity costs. The market price at which they are purchased or hired should reflect their opportunity cost, since producers must bid for these goods in their respective markets. If not willing to pay at least what the resources are worth in their best alternative usage, the firm will not be able to purchase the services of these resources.

  A difference will almost certainly arise between historic cost and opportunity cost if the resources are purchased and held in inventory for some time before they are used in the production process. If the market value of those resources changes, the opportunity cost diverges from the historic cost. Given the continuing problem of inflation, input prices tend to move upward on a more or less continuous basis, although in some cases rapid technological advances can cause the market value of resources held in inventory to decline. For decision-making purposes, the current market value of the resource is its implicit cost to the firm, and this cost should be incorporated into any decision process rather than the (either higher or lower) historic cost.. Note that if the firm wanted to replenish its inventories it must pay the current market price for the resource, or alternatively, if it wanted to sell the resource to another firm, it could do so at the current market value rather than at the historic cost of the resource.

  Now let us reconsider depreciation, which is intended to represent the implicit cost of assets such as land, buildings, and equipment purchased in the past. The accountant depreciates the cost of these assets by allocating a portion of the net cost of the asset against the current period's revenues. The economist determines the opportunity cost of these services on the basis of what the land and buildings might have earned in alternative employment or on the basis of the interest which the funds tied up in those assets could have earned in alternative investment, whichever is greater. The opportunity costs of the capital tied up in land, buildings, and equipment may be quite different from the depreciation charge made against revenues, since the latter is determined on an entirely different basis. For decision making-purposes, depreciation of assets involved in the production process must be treated as the opportunity cost of those assets.

- EXAMPLE: The owner of a small farm might forego $10,000 per annum in camping fees by continuing to use the land for farming rather than to take in campers. This is the opportunity cost of the land, unless the market value of the land is so high that the interest earned on the proceeds of the farm's sale would earn more. Suppose the farm could be sold for $100,000, which the farmer (supposing he owns the farm free and clear) could deposit for 15% interest. Thus the opportunity cost of continuing to farm the land is $15,000, this being the *best* alternative use of the resource.

The farmer's own labor must similarly be valued at its opportunity cost. If he could alternatively work for another farmer or take a job demonstrating and selling farm machinery, at say $20,000 per annum, this figure is his opportunity cost and should be included in the analysis for decision-making purposes.

Costs and Profits

The economist's concept of profit differs from that of the accountant. Both consider profit as the excess of revenues over costs, but they regard costs differently. The accountant subtracts from revenues only the costs that are actually incurred plus an allowance for depreciation of some of the previously incurred one-time expenditures, such as the cost of plant and machinery. Profits thus represent the net income to the owners of the firm; profits are their reward for having invested time and capital in the venture. The economist, on the other hand, is concerned with the wider notion of efficient allocation of resources and is thus concerned that all resources are employed where they will earn the maximum for their owners. A means of ensuring this is to consider the opportunity cost of each resource.

• EXAMPLE: Let us illustrate with an example of a small-store owner who has $50,000 invested as equity in a store and inventory. As shown in Table 7-2, the annual sales revenues were $160,000, from which must be deducted the cost of goods sold, salaries of hired labor, and depreciation of equipment and buildings. The accounting profit to the store is thus $15,000.

In Table 7-3 we show the economic statement of profit of the same store. Note that the sales revenues, cost of goods sold, salaries, and depreciation are the same as in the preceding table. (We suppose that we have checked and found that the market values of the equipment and buildings have in fact declined by $5,000 over the current year and that the depreciation charge, therefore, fairly reflects the opportunity costs of these resources.)

The economist, however, would add two other items relating to the implicit cost of resources that are owned by the manager. Suppose that the owner-manager could earn $15,000 as a departmental manager in a large store and that this is his best opportunity for salary. Then we would add a cost to the business of $15,000, the imputed salary of

TABLE 7-2. Accounting Income Statement for the Small-Store Owner

Sales		$160,000
Cost of goods sold	$120,000	
Salaries	20,000	
Depreciation expense	5,000	145,000
Accounting profit		$ 15,000

TABLE 7-3. *Economic Statement of Profit to Small-Store Owner*

Sales		$160,000
Cost of goods sold	$120,000	
Salaries	20,000	
Depreciation expense	5,000	
Imputed salary to owner-manager	15,000	
Imputed interest cost on equity	4,000	164,000
Economic profit		$ − 4,000

the owner-manager.[4] Similarly, the owner-manager has $50,000 equity in the store and inventory, a sum of money that could easily be employed elsewhere for financial gain. Suppose it could be banked or invested elsewhere at comparable risk and would receive 8% interest on the principal, or $4,000 per annum. By choosing to invest the $50,000 in the store rather than elsewhere, the owner-manager is therefore foregoing an income of $4,000 per annum, and the economist adds this as an implicit cost on the income statement. Thus the total economic costs, or the opportunity costs of all resources used in the production process, are $164,000, and in economic terms the store owner has incurred a loss of $4,000. That is, the store owner could have earned $4,000 more with the resources at his disposal if he had sold the building and inventory, invested the money at 8% per annum, and worked in a similar job elsewhere for a salary of $15,000 per annum.[5]

Normal and Pure Profits

- DEFINITION: *Normal profits* are earned when total revenues equal total costs, if total costs are calculated to reflect the opportunity costs of *all* services provided. If revenues just equal these costs, then all factors are earning the same in that particular employment as they could earn elsewhere. If revenues exceed these costs, we say that the firm is earning a *pure*, or economic, profit. Remembering that the owners of the firm are the effective suppliers of the services of the land and buildings mentioned, you will see that an economic profit means that the owners of the firm are earning more profit than they could by investing their capital elsewhere. The accounting profit must be adjusted for the opportunity cost of the owned resources—that is, for what the firm would pay for the services of those resources if they were purchased or hired—before the alternative invest-

---

[4]If the owner-manager were to make drawings from the business of cash or goods, these must be accounted for. Suppose he had drawn $10,000 from the business in cash and goods over the year. This plus another $5,000 should be charged against sales revenues, so his opportunity cost is properly valued at $15,000.

[5]Psychic income, or the utility derived from being one's own boss in this case, should always be considered. This storekeeper should continue in his own store if the monetary value of being his own boss exceeds $4,000 per annum. Similarly, many business school professors continue to teach in business schools, rather than accept positions with substantially higher salaries in business and government, because of the psychic income associated with the academic life. (Occasional consulting work represents a nice compromise.)

ment possibilities can be assessed. Accounting profit will exceed economic profit if some implicit opportunity costs are not subtracted from revenues.

This is not to say that either the accountant's or economist's view of profit is incorrect; each is designed for a different purpose. The accountant's purpose is to find, once the capital has been invested in a particular pursuit, the return to the owners of that capital. The economist's purpose is to ensure that all resources are employed in their most efficient uses. The existence of economic profit confirms this.

- NOTE: A normal profit (when TR = TC) does not mean *no* profit. Since total costs in the economic sense include the opportunity cost of all resources used, the return on capital invested is included as a cost, rather than counted as a residual in the accounting sense. Normal profit means a *sufficient return* on the owner's investment in the firm, sufficient to prevent him or her from liquidating this investment and investing it in the next best alternative investment, since the return on the next best alternative investment opportunity is included as an economic cost of production. Normal profit, therefore, means as much profit as the owners could get elsewhere.

Normal Profits and Risk Considerations

Considering that investments are not equally risky, we need to qualify our concept of normal profits to take into account the different degrees of risk in investment opportunities. Investing money in government bonds is relatively risk free, for example, since there is virtually no risk of default in mature economies. Dividends are paid on schedule, and bonds are redeemed on the due date as long as the government exists. Investing money in the development of a new product, on the other hand, is relatively risky. Investors may not receive dividends on their investments, and in many cases they may lose all the capital they put in. Accordingly, government bonds pay a relatively low rate of interest (5% to 10%), whereas companies prospecting for oil and minerals, introducing new products, and engaging in other high-risk businesses must offer relatively high rates of interest (15% to 20%) to attract the required investment funds. Although investors are generally averse to risk, they are willing to take risks, but only if there is a promise of sufficiently higher returns to compensate for the risks they are taking. The extra return on high-risk investments necessary to compensate investors is known as the *risk premium*. The higher the risk involved, the larger the risk premium demanded by investors.

Since alternative investment opportunities could earn more or less, depending on the degree of risk, we must confine our considerations to alternative investments of the same or similar degree of risk, for the sake of comparability. In effect, this is the familiar *ceteris paribus* requirement: the comparison of one investment with other investments of *equal* risk. The highest return on these alternative investments of equal risk is the opportunity cost of investing in the chosen area. It follows that the opportunity cost of investing in a low-risk business is lower than the opportunity cost of investing in a relatively high-risk business. In turn, the normal profit of a low-risk business is lower than the normal profit of a high-risk business. In accounting terms, a firm in a low-risk business may be content to earn an 8% return on investment after taxes, whereas a firm in a high-risk industry might require a 15% return on investment after taxes to stay in that particular business.

We turn now to incremental costs, the most important cost concept for decision making.

7.2 INCREMENTAL COST ANALYSIS

- DEFINITION: *Incremental costs* are those costs that will be incurred as the result of a decision. Incremental costs are measured by the change in total costs that results from a particular decision. Incremental costs may therefore be either fixed or variable, since a new decision may require purchase of additional capital facilities plus extra labor and materials. When we compare incremental costs with incremental revenues, that is, with the change in total revenues that occurs as a result of the decision, we can see whether a proposed decision is likely to be profitable or not. Clearly, if incremental revenues exceed incremental costs, the proposed decision will add to total profits (or will reduce losses if the total revenues generated do not cover the total costs incurred).

- NOTE: Incremental costs are not identical with marginal costs. As defined in the preceding chapter, *marginal costs* are the change in total cost for a one-unit change in the output level. Incremental costs, on the other hand, are the aggregate change in costs that results from a decision. This decision may involve a change in the output level of 20 or of 2,000 units, or it may not involve a change in the output level at all. For example, the decision may be whether or not to introduce a new technology of producing the same output level. Knowledge of marginal costs, however, may be very important for the calculation of the incremental costs.

The incremental costs must be accurately identified. Only those costs that actually change as a result of the decision may be included, but all costs that change as a result of the decision must be included. Factors that have been lying idle, with no alternative use, do not have an incremental cost and therefore may be regarded as being costless for the particular decision at hand. Similarly, costs that have been expended in the past for machinery or plant and buildings must be regarded as *sunk* costs and should not enter the decision-making procedure unless their opportunity cost is positive. That is, unless there is a competing and profitable use for an owned resource, the incremental cost of involving that resource in the present decision will be zero.

Relevant Costs and Irrelevant Costs

- DEFINITION: The *relevant costs* for decision-making purposes are those costs that will be incurred as a result of the decision being considered. The relevant costs are, therefore, the incremental costs. Costs that have been incurred already and costs that will be incurred in the future regardless of the present decision are *irrelevant* costs as far as the current decision problem is concerned.

- EXAMPLE: The manager of a gift store thinks that he has found a miracle product that will sell rapidly and give him large profits. It is an "antenna hat" comprised of two brightly colored balls on the end of flexible springs affixed to a headband. When worn by a person, the balls swing around like the antennae of some giant insect. The manager is convinced that these hats will sell and has purchased 5,000 of them. His cost was $1.00 each, payable $0.50 immediately and $0.50 within thirty days. He then spent $2,500 promoting these gimmicks, in newspaper advertisements and by hiring students to wear them around campus and at public events. He set the price at $4.95 and waited for his fortune to come rolling in. Three weeks have passed and he still has 4,975 of these antenna hats. His assistant manager suggested that he cut the price to $1.25 to get rid of what was obviously an ill-considered venture. The manager is adamant that he will never let the price fall that low since "his cost" was $1.50 per unit and he doesn't want to take a loss on this item.

But is $1.50 the relevant cost? The manager is about to make a pricing decision, and, as a result of that decision, costs may or may not be incurred and revenues may or may not be earned. The relevant costs are those that will be incurred as a result of the decision. The initial outlays of $2,500 on the antenna hats and $2,500 on promotion are irrelevant costs since they have already been incurred and cannot be retrieved. These are sunk costs. The second payment of $2,500 for the hats is also an irrelevant cost since it must be paid whether or not the price is changed and whether or not any more of the hats are sold. The relevant costs are those, if any, that will be incurred following the pricing decision. Suppose that storage costs must be incurred if the hats are not sold within another week. These costs will be incremental to a decision to maintain price at $4.95 but not incremental to a decision to cut price to $1.25, presuming that the assistant manager's judgment is correct and all units would sell at the lower price. Note that the marketability of the item is declining; it is a novelty item and must be sold before the public tires of its novelty value. Thus price should be set not with an eye on the irrelevant costs (sunk costs and committed costs) but with an eye on the incremental costs. To include the irrelevant costs in the present decision is to let an earlier bad decision cause another bad decision to be made. In business parlance, the gift-store manager should "cut his losses" and "avoid sending good money after bad."

Incremental Cost Categories

There are three main categories of relevant, or incremental, costs. These are the present-period explicit costs, the opportunity costs implicitly involved in the decision, and the future cost implications that flow from the decision. Let us examine these in turn.

Present-Period Explicit Costs.   Direct labor and materials costs and changes in the variable overhead costs, such as electricity, are fairly easy to anticipate as a consequence of a decision, for example, to increase the output level. If this increase also requires the purchase of additional capital equipment, this capital cost is incremental to the decision and should be included in full rather than apportioned in any way, notwithstanding that the equipment may have a useful life remaining after the present decision has been carried out.[6]

Thus the incremental costs of a decision will include all present-period explicit costs that will be incurred as a consequence of that decision. They will exclude any present-period explicit costs that will be incurred regardless of the present decision.

Opportunity Costs. Items taken from inventory may not have an explicit present-period cost if the firm does not choose to replace them in inventory by current purchases. Nevertheless, the relevant cost is the opportunity cost of that item—it could presumably be sold to another firm for its market value. If an item in inventory is worthless, having no market value (because it is outmoded by a new item, for example), its opportunity cost is zero, regardless of its historic cost. The historic cost of purchasing the item is an irrelevant, sunk, cost for the purposes of the present decision.

The most common application of the opportunity cost doctrine in decision making concerns the situation in which a particular resource has one or more uses at the same point of time. In this case, if the resource is used in the production of a particular output, it precludes the production of one or more other outputs.

• EXAMPLE: Telarah Lite-Fab Industries produces steel gates, fences, balcony and porch railings, and similar items cut and welded from wrought iron. This firm does custom orders but also produces standard gates and railings, which are sold to retail hardware stores. The firm finds it can sell as much as it can produce of the standard gates and railings but prefers to do custom orders since the latter are invariably more profitable. At the present time the firm has no custom orders outstanding, and its labor force is producing standard items at the rate of $10,000 per week sales value. Materials cost is $2,000 per week. Suppose now that a large custom order arrives that would take a week to manufacture and would cost $4,000 in materials. What is the opportunity cost of the firm's resources presently employed in the manufacture of the standard gates and railings? Note that with the standard items the firm is making $8,000 per week over and above materials cost. It must forego this $8,000 contribution to its other costs and profits if it takes the custom order. Thus the firm must make at least $8,000 over and above materials cost on the custom order before it should even consider accepting the order. That is, the materials cost and the opportunity cost of the custom order add up to $12,000, and the firm must set its price at least that high or it would be better off sticking to the standard items.

Future Costs. Many decisions will have implications for future costs, both explicit and implicit. If the firm can form an expectation of a future cost that will be incurred or is likely to be incurred as a consequence of the present decision, that cost must be included in the present analysis. Of course, it will be incorporated in present-value terms if known

---

[6]If future revenues may be expected from an item of equipment or from other capital investment, these will be incorporated into the analysis on the revenue side of contribution analysis, as we shall see in the next section.

for certain or in expected-present-value terms if there is a probability distribution of the future cost's occurring.

- EXAMPLE: A firm decides to produce a special order which it knows will cause severe wear and tear on its equipment, to the point where an overhaul will be required within one year after the job is completed. Otherwise, the equipment would serve out its useful life without a major overhaul. This overhaul is expected to cost $2,000 and will be paid one year from now. Supposing an opportunity discount rate of 15%, the appropriate discount factor is 0.8696, and the present value of that cost is $2,000 × 0.8696 = $1,739.20. This figure should be included as an incremental cost of deciding to produce the special order.

- EXAMPLE: Consider now a future cost which has a probability distribution of outcomes. Suppose a firm is considering copying another firm's design and knows that the other firm may sue for loss of business as a result. The possible legal costs and damages and the probabilities attached to each level of these costs are shown in Table 7-4. Given the congestion in the courts, it will take three years for the case to be resolved. We suppose that the firm's opportunity discount rate is 15%. Thus the discount factor used to find the present value of the expected costs is 0.6575.

    Thus the EPV of the future legal costs is $72,325, a figure that should be included in the incremental costs of the decision to copy the other firm's design. Note that the firm should consider the possibility of such legal claims even when it does not willfully copy another firm's design. It may feel that its design is sufficiently different but that a court may nevertheless rule against it in the event of a lawsuit. In such cases the firm should calculate the EPV of the possible lawsuit and include this in its calculations.

    Other future costs include labor problems, loss of future business, deterioration of supplier relations leading to higher input prices, and cash flow problems necessitating borrowing costs. Any future cost, whether explicit or implicit, which can reasonably be

TABLE 7-4. *Expected Present Value of Future Incremental Costs*

Costs Expected ($)	Present Value	Probability	Expected Value ($)
0	0	0.10	0
50,000	32,875	0.20	6,575.00
100,000	65,750	0.30	19,725.00
150,000	98,625	0.25	24,656.25
200,000	131,500	0.10	13,150.00
250,000	164,375	0.05	8,218.75
	Expected present value		$72,325.00

TABLE 7-5. *Summary of Cost Concepts for Decision Making*

RELEVANT COSTS	IRRELEVANT COSTS	
Incremental Costs[a]	*Committed Costs[a]*	*Sunk Costs[b]*

Present-period explicit costs:
 Variable:
    Direct labor
    Direct materials
    Variable overheads
 Fixed:
    New equipment
    New personnel
	Managers' salaries
	
	 Payments on debt
	
	 Rental and lease costs
	
	 Wage contracts or wages
	 of ongoing workers
		Previously paid-for
		 purchases of assets,
		 including land, buildings,
		 plant and equipment, and
		 depreciation expenses
		 based on these assets
		
		 Prepaid and nonrecoverable
		 expenses

Opportunity costs:
    Contribution foregone on the
    best alternative use of the
    resources involved
	All other payments that
	 must be made regardless of
	 the decision at hand	

Future-period incremental costs:
    EPV of probable costs to
    follow in the future as a
    consequence of the decision		

[a]Future costs
[b]Past costs

expected to follow as a consequence of the current decision should be quantified in EPV terms and included in the incremental costs of the decision.

The cost concepts that were mentioned previously are summarized in Table 7-5. Note that by *relevant* or *irrelevant* we mean with respect to the decision at hand. If a cost is expected to be a consequence of the decision to be made, it is a relevant, or incremental, cost. Some subsequent (future) costs are not consequent (relevant) costs, because the firm is committed to them and they will be incurred anyway. No prior expenditures (sunk costs) are incremental costs.

7.3 CONTRIBUTION ANALYSIS

We proceed now to use the concept of incremental costs in the contribution analysis of decision problems.

• DEFINITION: The *contribution* of a decision is defined as the incremental revenues of that decision less the incremental costs of that decision. It should be interpreted as the contribution made to overhead costs and profits by the decision. Clearly, only those decisions that have a positive contribution should be undertaken; and where decisions are mutually exclusive, the one with the larger expected contribution is to be preferred. We shall illustrate contribution analysis with three common types of decision problems, but first let us clarify the notion of incremental revenues.

Incremental Revenues

- DEFINITION: *Incremental revenues* are defined as the revenues which follow as a consequence of a particular decision. We should expect incremental revenues, like incremental costs, to have an explicit current-period component, a possible opportunity component, and a possible future component.

- EXAMPLE: A firm bidding on a contract to supply electric light fixtures to a government office building tenders a very low bid for $265,000 and expects to avoid layoff costs of $100,000 if it wins the contract. It also expects to win future government contracts if it is the successful bidder on this contract, since this contract provides the firm with the opportunity to prove that it can supply a quality product and meet its production schedule.

  The explicit current-period incremental revenues if the firm wins the contract will be $265,000. But the contract is worth much more than $265,000 to the firm. If it doesn't win the contract, it will have to lay off workers and incur subsequent severance pay and future startup costs associated with recruiting and training totaling $100,000. If the firm does win the contract, this $100,000 is not spent and therefore stays in the bank. Avoidance of a cost as the result of a decision amounts to an opportunity revenue of the same amount.

- DEFINITION: An *opportunity revenue* is a cost avoided as the result of a decision. Although there is no actual inflow of revenues, the outflow of revenues is avoided so money that would otherwise be spent is still sitting in the bank, and the net effect is the same. The *future* revenues associated with this pricing decision will be the expected present value of the contribution to overheads and profits associated with the future business generated as the result of winning the present contract.

- EXAMPLE: Suppose the firm mentioned in the preceding example feels that if it wins the present job, it has a 50% chance of winning a similar contract next year. Suppose further that the next contract would be for $300,000 and would have an incremental cost of $250,000. The contribution from the next contract is, thus, $50,000 (if won). Given an opportunity discount rate of 15%, the present value of this contribution is $50,000 × 0.8696 = $43,480. The expected present value is the present value times the probability of receiving it, or $43,480 × 0.50 = $21,740. Thus the EPV of the future revenue is $21,740, and this figure should be included in the incremental revenue calculation.

  The firm's incremental revenue is the sum of the present-period explicit revenues, the opportunity revenues, and the EPV of future (consequential) revenues. Thus the contract has total incremental revenues of $265,000 + $100,000 + $21,740, or $386,740 in total. This contract would, therefore, offer a positive EPV of contribution as long as incremental costs were less than $386,740.

- NOTE: The EPV of the contribution to be received from future business resulting from the present decision can be regarded as the *goodwill* associated with the present decision. Goodwill is the EPV of contribution from future business, and if a decision involves an increment to goodwill, the amount of that contribution in EPV terms should be included as an incremental revenue. Conversely, the present decision may cause the loss of future business. The EPV of the future contribution lost as the result of the present decision can be regarded as the *ill will* associated with this decision.

- EXAMPLE: Consider a construction firm that is considering bidding for a contract to move city garbage while the garbage workers are on strike. If this contract involves the possibility that the firm will lose future construction contracts because of the buyer's fear of retaliatory disruption by unionized construction workers, the EPV of the contribution expected to be lost on future jobs must be included as an incremental cost of taking the present contract to move the city's garbage.

     Let us now demonstrate the application of contribution analysis in the context of three common types of decision problems.

Project A or Project B?

- EXAMPLE: Suppose a firm is considering adopting either project A or project B but cannot adopt both, since they use the same set of machinery and labor. Project A, as shown in Table 7-6, promises sales of 10,000 units at $2 each, with materials, labor, variable overhead, and allocated overhead costs as shown, such that there is an apparent profit of $2,000. Project B promises sales revenues of $18,000, with materials, direct labor, and variable and allocated overhead as shown. The apparent profit from project B is $4,000, and it would seem that project B is preferable to project A by virtue of its higher profitability.

TABLE 7-6.   **Income Statements for Projects A and B**

Project A			Project B		
Revenues (10,000 @ $2)		$20,000	Revenues (6,000 @ $3)		$18,000
Costs			Costs		
Materials	$2,000		Materials	$5,000	
Direct labor	6,000		Direct labor	3,000	
Variable overhead	4,000		Variable overhead	3,000	
Fixed overhead	6,000	18,000	Fixed overhead	3,000	14,000
Profit		$ 2,000	Profit		$ 4,000

     When contribution analysis is applied to the above decision problem, however, the answer may be surprising. Consider Table 7-7, in which the incremental costs are subtracted from the incremental revenues to find the contribution of each project. Since the fixed overhead was not a cost incurred as a result of this particular decision, it is exclud-

TABLE 7-7. Contribution Analysis for Projects A and B

Project A			Project B		
Incremental revenues		$20,000	Incremental revenues		$18,000
Incremental costs			Incremental costs		
Materials	$2,000		Materials	$5,000	
Direct labor	6,000		Direct labor	3,000	
Variable overhead	4,000	12,000	Variable overhead	3,000	11,000
Contribution		$ 8,000	Contribution		$ 7,000

ed from the contribution analysis, and it can be seen that project A contributes more to overheads and profits than does project B. The danger of including arbitrary allocations of fixed overhead is exemplified here. The fixed overhead was allocated on the basis of a particular criterion, in this case as 100% of direct labor, but if it had been included in the decision process it would have caused an inferior decision to be made. Whatever method of fixed overhead allocation is used, the danger is likely to persist. Hence we use contribution analysis, which allows an incisive look at the actual changes in costs and revenues that follow a particular decision.

Note that in this example we implicitly assumed the absence of all opportunity costs and revenues and that we proceeded as if there were neither future costs nor future revenues associated with either project. In practice, decision makers should not proceed so blithely but instead should assure themselves that *all* incremental costs and incremental revenues are included in the decision analysis. In the above example the difference between projects A and B was only $1,000. Hence, our decision to choose project A was very sensitive to the assumption of zero opportunity and future costs and revenues. Our decision would have been reversed if A had opportunity and future costs (in EPV terms) exceeding $1,000, for example. More generally, if the *net* opportunity and future revenues of project B had exceeded those of A by more than $1,000, the decision would have been reversed.[7]

Make or Buy?

- EXAMPLE: The Wilson Tool Company manufactures high-quality power tools such as drills, jigsaws, and sanders. All these tools require the same roller-bearing unit, which

---

[7]Recall our discussion of sensitivity analysis from Chapter 1. A decision is sensitive to the assumptions on which it is based to the extent that a change in those assumptions would cause a different decision to have been preferable. Thus it is important to consider the dollar amount of cost variability or difference in contribution, which would cause the decision to be inappropriate. It is also useful to express this in terms of the totals, to see the *percentage* cost variability which would change the decision. In the present example, if the incremental costs of project A are understated by more than $1,000 or by more than $1,000/12,000 = 8.33%, and the incremental costs of project B are accurate, the decision would be reversed.

TABLE 7-8. Wilson Tool Company: Bearing Department Costs

	Total	Per Unit
Direct materials	$ 38,640	$ 0.56
Direct labor	126,390	1.81
Allocated overhead	252,780	3.63
	$417,810	$ 6.00
Total bearing units produced:		69,635

the company manufactures in its own bearing department. Pertinent cost data for the past year of operations in that department are shown in Table 7-8.

Demand estimates indicate that the company should expand its production of some of the power tools and that an additional 7,500 bearing units will be required. The company could produce these in its bearing department but is considering having the additional units supplied by a firm that specializes in bearings. Wilson anticipates that it will require an increase of 15% in total direct labor costs and 12% in total materials costs to produce these additional units in house. No additional capital expenditure will be necessary, since some machines currently have idle capacity. A specialist bearing producer who has been approached has studied the specifications and has offered to supply the 7,500 bearing units at a total cost of $30,000, or $4 per unit. Should Wilson make or buy the additional units?

We begin by comparing the incremental costs of the two alternatives facing Wilson. The incremental costs of buying them from the specialist come to $30,000, since this is the dollar amount that Wilson must spend to obtain the additional units. To calculate the incremental costs of making the units in house, we begin by calculating the increases in materials and direct labor costs that would be occasioned by the manufacture of those units. The 12% increase in the total material cost would imply an incremental material cost of $4,637, and a 15% increase in total direct labor costs would imply a $18,959 increase in that cost category. As shown in Table 7-9, the total of these two figures is $23,596, which is less than the incremental cost of buying the units from outside. The decision to make, rather than buy, the additional units would thus appear to save the Wilson Tool Company a total of $6,404.[8]

Variability of Overheads. The preceding analysis, however, does not consider the possibility that some part of overhead expenses may vary with the level of production of the bearing units. It is conceivable that some overhead cost components, such as electricity,

---

[8]Since the incremental revenue is the same whether Wilson makes or buys the parts, we can do the contribution analysis on the basis of the incremental costs alone. Presuming that the incremental revenues exceed the incremental costs, the "make" alternative would seem to contribute more to overheads and profits than does the "buy" alternative.

TABLE 7-9.   Incremental Costs of Making the Bearing Units

	Total	Per Unit
Direct materials	$ 4,637	$0.62
Direct labor	18,959	2.53
Allocated overhead	(?)	(?)
	$23,596	$3.15

office and administration expense, and cafeteria expense, might vary to some degree as a result of producing these units in house. Rather than make arbitrary assumptions about the proportion of overheads that will vary, and since we do not have the information necessary to make a reasoned judgment, let us perform a sensitivity analysis on the decision that has been made. That is, we wish to know by how much the overhead expenses may vary before the decision to make the product would be the wrong decision. The answer is obviously that if overheads vary more than $6,404 as a result of this decision, the best decision would be to buy the product from the outside supplier. A $6,404 variation in overhead represents slightly more than a 2.5% variation in the allocated overhead. It is up to the decision maker to judge whether a variation of this percentage or dollar magnitude is likely to follow the decision to produce the product in house.

Longer-Term Incremental Costs.   A number of other considerations should also enter into this decision. First, there is the issue of long-term supplier relations. Since Wilson may need a specialist producer sometime in the future when it may be unable to produce the bearings in house because of capacity limitations, it can perhaps establish itself as a customer of the supplier by giving this contract out at the present time, so in future situations supply could be assured.

Second, there is the issue of the quality of the bearing units supplied by the outside firm as compared with those produced by Wilson. The decision maker would have to be assured that the units supplied from outside would be at least equal in quality to the standards desired. On the other hand, the specialist producer may be able to produce consistently higher-quality bearing units, with subsequent impact on the quality of Wilson Tools and on long-term buyer goodwill.

Third, the issue of labor relations must be considered. The decision to make the units involves an increase in the labor force, which may lead to crowded working conditions and overtaxed washroom and cafeteria facilities. The data indicate that labor efficiency is decreasing, since the incremental cost per unit to make the additional 7,500 units is $3.15 as compared with the total of $2.37 for direct materials and labor per unit shown in Table 7-8. It is conceivable that the hiring of additional labor units and the resultant increased congestion and reduced efficiency could cause a lowering of employee morale, with subsequent longer-term disadvantages to the profitability of the Wilson Tool Company.

In total, the decision maker must decide whether or not the expected present value of these eventualities, plus the possible variable components in overhead costs, is likely to exceed $6,404. If so, the decision should be to buy the product from outside.

Other Considerations.   There are several additional issues that should be considered. First, the decision maker would need to be assured of the accuracy of the estimations that are involved in this decision. If, for example, demand for the tools does not increase as predicted and Wilson purchased the roller-bearing units from outside, this would be an irreversible commitment involving considerable expense, whereas the decision to make the units in house could soon be suspended. The cost estimates are likewise subject to some doubt. These are presumably extrapolations on the estimated marginal costs of producing the units in house. The decision maker would need to be assured that these extrapolations were based on the most reasonable assumptions concerning the efficiency of direct labor and material usage and that they are, consequently, the best estimates. To the extent that there is a distribution of both demand and cost estimates, a decision based on the most likely point estimate alone may result in an outcome that is quite different from the expected value.

Another question that arises in the problem is whether or not the price quotation received is in fact the lowest-cost source of supply of these bearing units. We might assume that bids were solicited and that the lowest bid was being considered, but if this were not the case the decision maker should consult alternative sources of supply to confirm that the $30,000 price was in fact the best price at which the units may be bought from outside.

With these qualifications in mind, we turn now to the third category of decision problems in which contribution analysis is an appropriate solution procedure.

Take It or Leave It?

- EXAMPLE: The Idaho Instruments Company produces a variety of pocket calculators and sells them through a distributing company. The purchasing agent for a large chain of department stores has recently approached Idaho Instruments with an offer to buy 20,000 units of its model X1 at the unit price of $8. Idaho's present production level of that model is 160,000 units annually, and it could supply the additional 20,000 units by foregoing production (and sale) of 5,000 of its more sophisticated X2 model. Pertinent data relating to these two models are shown in Table 7-10. Because of the highly mechanized production process, the per-unit variable costs of each model are believed to be constant over a wide range of outputs. The sales manager for Idaho Instruments is reluctant to sell the X1 model for $8 when she normally receives $12 from the distributing company, and she has attempted to negotiate with the purchasing agent. The latter, however, insists that $8 is his only offer. Should Idaho Instruments take it or leave it?

Since the average variable cost for both models is expected to be constant over a wide range, we can calculate the incremental cost of this decision on the basis of the average variable cost. The average variable cost is the sum of the first three components

TABLE 7-10.   Idaho Instruments Company: Per-Unit Data on Calculators

	Model X1	Model X2
Materials	$ 1.65	$ 1.87
Direct labor	2.32	3.02
Variable overhead	1.03	1.11
Fixed overhead allocation	5.00	6.00
Profits	2.00	2.40
Price to distributor	$12.00	$14.40

in the table, and hence 20,000 additional units of model X1 (with AVC = $5.00) will add $100,000 to the cost levels. This figure is not the total incremental cost, however, since there is an opportunity cost involved. The production of the additional 20,000 units will come partly from the idle capacity that is to be utilized and partly at the expense of 5,000 units of model X2. The opportunity cost of using the resources that previously produced the X2 is the value of those resources in that alternate use. The net value to Idaho Instruments of employing the resources in the production of 5,000 units of the X2 is the contribution made by those 5,000 units. From Table 7-10 it can be found that the contribution per unit to overheads and profits is $8.40. Hence the opportunity costs are the total foregone contribution, or 5,000 units × $8.40 = $42,000. In Table 7-11 we show the contribution analysis of this problem. The incremental revenues are $160,000, and the incremental costs add up to $142,000. Hence the contribution to overheads and profits that would follow from the decision to take the department store's offer is $18,000. Thus profits would be $18,000 greater than they would be otherwise, or losses would be $18,000 less.

An alternate method of arriving at the same contribution would be to subtract from the incremental revenues the revenues foregone when the 5,000 units of X2 were not sold at $14.40 (that is, $72,000) and subtract from the incremental cost of producing the extra units of the model X1 the decremental costs of not producing 5,000 units of the model X2 (that is, $30,000). The net adjustment as the result of these manipulations is $72,000 − $30,000, or $42,000, which is exactly the opportunity cost figure we have entered in Table 7-11. The opportunity cost method achieves the same results with some economy of effort, but more importantly, perhaps, it draws the decision maker's attention to the possible alternate uses of resources.

The preceding decision is sensitive to some of the underlying assumptions, however. The first issue is that of substitutability between the units sold to the department store and those sold to the distributing company. The analysis has proceeded on the implicit assumption that the sale of 20,000 units to the department store will be *in addition to*, and nonsubstitutable with, the 160,000 units sold through the distributing company. To the extent that some customers now buy this product through the department store rather than through the distributing company, Idaho Instruments will be foregoing an amount of $4 per unit, or the difference in the price charged to the two wholesale buyers. If the department stores will tap a totally new market for the calculators, we can presume

TABLE 7-11. Contribution Analysis of Calculator Decision Problem

Incremental revenues		
20,000 units of X1 @ $8.00		$160,000
Incremental costs		
Variable costs		
20,000 units of X1 @ $5.00	$100,000	
Opportunity costs (contribution foregone)		
5,000 units of X2 @ $8.40	42,000	142,000
Contribution		$ 18,000

that total sales will increase by the entire 20,000 units and that there would indeed be a contribution of $18,000 following this decision. On the other hand, if the sale to the department store reduces normal sales, to what degree could this happen before the decision to take the offer becomes the wrong one? Since the difference in contribution per unit is $4, the number of units that it would take to erode that $18,000 total contribution down to zero is $18,000 ÷ 4 = 4,500. Thus, if in the judgment of the decision maker there are likely to be at least 4,500 units purchased from the department stores that would otherwise have been purchased from the normal distribution channels, the decision should be reversed.

An additional consideration here is that of retailer relations. Doubtless the firms in the normal distributing channels will become aware that the department stores were given a better deal, and these firms may in turn look elsewhere for their supplies. Thus any short-term gain by selling to the department store may be outweighed by longer-term losses from a deterioration of the relationship currently enjoyed with the distributing company and with other firms.[9]

A third area of concern relates to the image of Idaho Instruments' calculators. Presumably the department stores, having purchased at a relatively low cost per unit, will price below the current market price for the model X1. This reduced price may have a detrimental impact on the quality image currently held by that model. Since many consumers judge quality on the basis of price when they have no alternate means of discovering quality or durability, the lowering of the price of the X1 may reduce the consumer's perception of its quality. Alternatively, this contract with the department store may be the beginning of a long and successful relationship with that particular buyer and may add to rather than detract from the image of the calculators and the total sales.

In summary, then, the decision maker must consider all possible future ramifications of the decision and must calculate the expected present value or loss of each eventuality. The net expected present value or loss must be added to or subtracted from the immediate contribution before the final decision is made.

---

[9]In fact, if Idaho Instruments continues to favor the department store with a lower price, it may run afoul of legislation concerning price discrimination. Legal constraints on pricing are discussed in Appendix 10A.

Multiperiod Contribution Analysis

Many decisions involve costs that will be incurred or revenues that will be received in future time periods. As discussed in Chapter 1, these costs and revenues must be converted to present-value terms to make them comparable with cost and revenues incurred or received in the present period. In Chapter 1 we spoke simply of profits in the first and subsequent periods which had to be discounted back to present value. We now know that it is the *contribution* in each future period that is important for decision making, and not profits in either the accounting or the economic sense.

The contribution of a decision in future periods is likely to be subject to uncertainty, and thus expected-present-value (EPV) analysis is involved. Thus multiperiod contribution analysis with uncertain future contributions proceeds in the by now familiar context of decision trees. The only difference is that the *expected present value of contribution* (EPVC) in each period is now the operative concept. Initial costs should now be viewed as the excess of incremental costs over incremental revenues in the current period (that is, a negative contribution). The probability distributions of contribution in future periods must be carefully estimated and placed in the appropriate branches of the decision tree. The EPVC of each decision is then calculated and compared with the EPVC of alternative decisions. The various decision criteria are then applied, using the procedures demonstrated in Chapter 2. Two of the problems at the end of this chapter involve decision trees and multiperiod contribution analysis.

7.4   SUMMARY

The cost concept of prime importance for decision making is that of incremental costs. *Incremental* costs are those that are incurred as a result of the decision under consideration. To calculate incremental costs, however, the decision maker must consider a variety of other cost concepts, such as direct and indirect, explicit and implicit, opportunity and historic, and relevant and sunk costs. Each of these cost concepts was illustrated with reference to a particular business example.

Contribution analysis seeks to ascertain the contribution to overheads and profits, or the excess of incremental revenues over incremental costs, that is expected to follow a particular decision. To calculate the contribution of a decision, the decision maker must consider the present-period explicit costs and revenues arising from the decision, plus the opportunity costs and revenues associated with the decision, plus the expected present value of future costs and revenues that are subsequent to the decision. The expected present value of contribution (EPVC) of each decision alternative is then compared with the EPVC of the other decision alternatives. When uncertainty is involved, as we should expect in multiperiod contribution analysis, the risk attitude of the decision maker must be considered. A risk-neutral decision maker will simply select the decision alternative with the greatest EPVC. A decision maker who is risk averse (or risk preferring) should utilize criteria that adjust for risk, such as the coefficient of variation, certainty equivalent, and maximin.

As before, we should be careful to conduct sensitivity analysis before plunging ahead with a decision based on EPVC calculations. Many of the consequences of a decision may be subject to a high degree of uncertainty, and our best estimates may not be especially reliable. Other issues may be assumed away, on the basis of a presumption that they will not occur. Sensitivity analysis should be undertaken to see whether or not the decision alternative selected would remain the optimal one if our underlying assumptions turn out to be in error. The assumptions most often made that cry out for sensitivity analysis fall under two broad headings, namely data accuracy and *ceteris paribus*. Data-accuracy assumptions include the following: accuracy of the figures used and the lack of any other current-period, future-period, or opportunity incremental costs or revenues. *Ceteris paribus* assumptions include the lack of any impact on labor, customer, and supplier relations (with subsequent current or future cost or revenue implications), as well as the lack of any adverse impact on the firm's product quality, financial stability, public image, and so on.

DISCUSSION QUESTIONS

7-1. How might the accountant's calculation of indirect costs differ from the economist's calculation of fixed costs?

7-2. Explain how the economist would calculate the implicit cost of a fixed factor, such as plant and equipment, which is used in the production process.

7-3. When is the opportunity cost of an input to the production process equal to zero? If an input has several different alternative uses, how is the opportunity cost of that input determined?

7-4. Explain the economist's notions of normal and pure profits. Why wouldn't a firm wish to liquidate its investment and leave the industry if it was simply breaking even with TR = TC?

7-5. Define the *relevant costs* for decision making. When do the relevant costs include some elements of fixed costs?

7-6. Why does contribution analysis ignore the fixed overhead costs that might otherwise be included in the cost analysis of a decision?

7-7. How should future considerations be evaluated and included in contribution analysis?

7-8. In multiperiod contribution analysis, what determines the choice of the appropriate discount factors?

7-9. Explain how you would calculate the incremental cost of a decision that might lead to a future class-action lawsuit by consumers for damages caused by your product.

7-10. Explain and contrast the concepts of opportunity costs and opportunity revenues.

PROBLEMS AND SHORT CASES

7-1. The Muscle-Man Company manufactures forklift tractors, and it supplies some parts to other manufacturers of forklifts. It fabricates most of the component parts but buys the engines, hydraulic systems, wheels, and tires from suppliers. Demand estimates indicate that Muscle-

Man should increase its production level from 60 forklift units monthly to 70 units monthly. Sufficient slack exists in most departments to allow this increase, except that production of 10 extra chassis assemblies could be attained only by reallocating labor and equipment from fork-assembly manufacture to chassis-assembly manufacture. The fork-assembly department currently produces 90 units monthly, and it supplies the 30 surplus units to other manufacturers at $188 each. With the expanded production level, 70 forks would be required, but the labor and equipment responsible for the remaining 20 units is thought to be just sufficient to produce the 10 extra chassis assemblies. Alternatively, the extra chassis assemblies could be purchased from a supplier, and the lowest quote is from Fenton Fabricators, for $305 per unit. The costs of the chassis and fork departments for a representative month were as follows:

		DEPARTMENT	
Costs		Chassis	Fork
Direct materials		$ 4,650	$ 2,070
Direct labor		6,300	4,050
Depreciation		750	500
Allocated burden of fuel, electricity, office, and other overheads		12,600	8,100
(200% of direct labor)			
Total		$24,300	$14,720
Production level		60	90

(a) Should Muscle-Man make or buy the ten extra chassis assemblies?

(b) What qualifications would you add to your decision?

7-2. The Crombie Castings Company produces two products, A and B, for which pertinent data are as follows for the past month:

	A	B
Sales (units)	840,000	220,000
Price per unit ($)	2.50	4.25
Materials cost ($)	386,400	105,600
Direct labor ($)	529,200	277,200
Overheads ($)	567,893	297,467

CCC's plant and labor are operating at full capacity, but the company is unable to meet the demand for product A, which is thought to be 1 million units per month. One way to meet the demand for A would be to reduce the output of product B and to shift resources to the production of A. For each unit reduction in the output of B, the firm could produce two units of A with the labor that is released. Note that average variable costs are constant in both production processes. Alternatively, CCC could contract out to have product A manufactured by another firm in the same industry and sold as if this product were from the CCC plant. Donald, Dodge, and Draper, a firm that holds a minor share of the same markets and has considerable excess capacity, was approached on this issue. DDD is willing to sign a contract to supply the extra 160,000 units of A at a price of $2.25 per unit.

How should CCC resolve this problem? Support your answer with discussion of the various issues involved.

7-3. Commodore Candies produces a 3-pound box of chocolates which it sells at a price of $6.75 to various retail outlets. Commodore's output capacity for this product is 10,000 units per month with a one-shift operation, but it can produce more using overtime labor, which has a premium of 15% over regular labor cost. Variable overhead expenses would be 10% higher per unit of output for overtime production. Average variable costs are constant from 8,000 to 10,000 units and are then constant at the higher level. Costs of production for the current month's output of 8,000 units are as follows:

	Total Costs ($)
Raw materials	9,600
Direct labor	17,600
Variable overhead	9,200
Fixed overhead	14,500

Today Commodore is faced with a decision problem. A large retail chain has offered to purchase a bulk order of 4,000 units at $6 per unit, to be delivered within thirty days. Should Commodore take this order? Support your answer with discussion of the issues involved. Defend any assumptions that you make.

7-4. The XYZ Company produces and sells a product directly to consumers at a price of $6 per unit. Sales have been increasing at 10% per month, and this trend is expected to continue. Average variable costs are expected to remain constant at the current levels. The company's maximum output capacity is 200,000 with the present investment in plant and equipment. Following is a summary record of the firm's January production and cost levels:

	January
Sales (units)	171,661
Materials ($)	211,143
Direct labor ($)	520,133
Indirect factory labor ($)	110,500
Office and administration salaries ($)	64,000
Light and heat ($)	12,116
Other fixed expenses ($)	24,680

A national mail-order company has asked XYZ to consider the following deal: 10,000 units of the product, to be ready at the end of February, at the price of $5 per unit.
(a) Should XYZ accept the order from the mail order company?
(b) What strategy do you suggest?
(c) Support your answer with discussion of the various issues involved.

7-5. A large department store has called for bids for the following contract: A truck plus its driver must be available, given one day's notice, whenever the store's own trucks are fully utilized, to deliver goods to suburban households. The number of days for which a truck will be required is twenty, and the number of miles is expected to be 4,000 for the coming year.

You are the manager of the Clark Rent-a-Truck Company and have a number of trucks that you rent out on a day-to-day basis. One truck is a little older than the others, and it is always the last to be rented out because it does less for public relations than the new trucks. In the absence of a contract with the department store, you expect this older truck to be rented out two thirds of the 300 rental days this coming year. Your normal rental charge is $25.00 per day plus $0.35 per mile.

You estimate the costs of operating the older truck to be as follows, assuming 10,000 miles of rental over the coming year:

Depreciation	$ 800
Interest on investment in truck	360
License fees and taxes	125
Insurance	440
Parking fees (permanently rented space)	300
Gasoline	1,367
Oil, grease, and preventive maintenance	600
Repairs	1,450
Allocated overheads	1,650

You can hire a driver on one day's notice for $50 per day. A one-time cost of $400 will be involved in fitting the truck with a special loading ramp required by the contract. This ramp will not interfere with the normal use of the truck.

On the basis of this information, and making whatever assumptions you feel are necessary and reasonable, calculate your incremental costs of undertaking this contract.

7-6. The Bowen Biscuit Company produces a savory cracker and is currently selling 6,000 units per month at $6.00 per unit. The marketing research director has recently reported that price elasticity is -1.5 at this price level. The production manager now reports the following relationships between observed total variable costs and several different levels of output:

Output (units)	Total Variable Costs ($)
2,000	11,000
4,000	14,400
6,000	18,600
8,000	32,000

Fixed overhead charges are $5,000 per month.

(a) Calculate an expression for the demand and the marginal revenue curves for this particular biscuit, and plot these on a graph.
(b) Calculate the average cost and average variable cost at the various output levels and plot these on the same graph. Sketch in an estimate of the marginal cost curve.
(c) Advise Bowen's management as to the profit-maximizing and sales-maximizing prices.
(d) State explicitly all the assumptions and reservations that underlie your answers.

7-7. The Tico Taco Company has estimated the following total variable cost function from cost and output data pairs observed over the past ten weeks:

$$TVC = 435.85 - 1.835Q^2 + 3.658Q^3$$

where TVC represents thousands of dollars and Q represents thousands of boxes of tacos produced. TTC is currently producing 2,000 boxes weekly and is considering expanding its output to 2,200 boxes weekly. To do so, it will have to hire another taco machine operator ($400 per week) and lease another taco machine ($200 per week).

(a) Estimate the incremental costs of the extra 200 boxes weekly.
(b) State all the assumptions and qualifications which underlie your answer to part (a).

7-8. You are the manager of a ski resort. Based on industry projections of this season's demand, your competitive position, and your estimates of costs, you have set the lift ticket price at $8 per day. Because of the variability of demand between weekdays, weekends, and holidays, you hire labor on the basis of the expected demand for each particular day, based on past years' records and on current snow conditions. Extra labor is readily available on a day-to-day basis from the pool of local "ski bums."

You employ one lift attendant for every 250 tickets sold, in addition to a basic staff of four lift attendants. Ski-patrol persons are required at the rate of one for every 400 tickets sold in addition to the two patrol persons who are required regardless of ticket sales volume. All other labor employees connected with the skiing operation are required regardless of sales volume. Lift attendants are hired at the rate of $25 per day plus a free lift ticket to be used subsequently. Ski-patrol persons receive $30 per day plus a free meal in your restaurant that evening.

Your restaurant serves only one standardized meal for $3 per person. Based on expected demand fluctuations, you have hired various people on a full-time and part-time basis for the season. The $3 price represents the average cost of materials and direct labor plus a 50% markup to contribute to restaurant overheads and profits. Unexpected fluctuations in demand can be handled, since you keep a large inventory of supplies and can hire temporary labor at short notice. There is, however, an additional $10-per-person cost for this temporary labor, since these people are handled through an employment agency and require transportation to the restaurant. To maintain your standard of meals and service, you hire kitchen staff at the rate of one person for every forty-five meals expected to be sold and serving staff at the rate of one person for every eighty meals expected to be sold.

Today you received a phone call from the Students' Association of a nearby university which is asking around various ski resorts for the following deal: Ten busloads of students (500 in total) will come to your resort on Friday of next week if they can get a lift ticket *and* a meal for $4 per person. Your expected sales for that Friday, before this possibility arose, were 1,500 lift tickets and 900 meals.

Should you give the students the deal they are asking for? Explain your decision and state any possible qualifications to that decision.

7-9. The Wyndham Wool Company is considering two alternative strategies to increase its profitability and net worth. Strategy A is to set up a string of retail outlets for exclusive distribution of Wyndham's Scottish kilts, sweaters, jackets, blankets, scarves, and so on. Plan B is to wholesale these items to a limited number of high-quality department stores. The probability distributions of contribution for each strategy are shown in the following table. Wyndham's cost of capital is 15% per annum.

	STRATEGY A		STRATEGY B	
	Contribution ($)	Probability	Contribution ($)	Probability
Current period	− 600,000	1.0	− 100,000	1.0
	200,000	0.3	50,000	0.5
Year 1	400,000	0.5	100,000	0.3
	600,000	0.2	150,000	0.2
	400,000	0.3	100,000	0.4
Year 2	600,000	0.4	200,000	0.5
	800,000	0.3	300,000	0.1

(a) Calculate the expected present value of the contribution from each of the proposed strategies.
(b) Supposing Wyndham to be risk averse, which strategy would you recommend?
(c) State all the assumptions and qualifications that underlie your recommendation. Is your recommendation especially sensitive to any of these?

7-10. The Yankee Jack Company operates a tourist service business in a New England seaside resort area. Wishing to capitalize on the expanding tourist potential of the region, the firm is considering two alternatives. The first is the creation of a wildlife and animal farm, mostly oriented to children and tourists from the big City, and the second is an amusement park, which would cater more to teenagers and young adults. The probability distributions of contribution for both alternatives are shown below. Yankee Jack has accumulated sufficient funds to finance either venture, and the money is currently earning 9% per annum in government Treasury bills.

	WILDLIFE FARM		AMUSEMENT PARK	
	Contribution ($)	Probability	Contribution ($)	Probability
Current period	− 200,000	1.0	− 285,000	1.0
	50,000	0.1	100,000	0.3
Year 1	100,000	0.6	150,000	0.5
	150,000	0.3	200,000	0.2
	100,000	0.2	150,000	0.3
Year 2	200,000	0.5	300,000	0.5
	300,000	0.3	450,000	0.2

(a) Calculate the expected present value of contribution and its standard deviation for each of the two alternatives.

(b) Conduct sensitivity analysis with respect to the opportunity discount rate involved in the calculation above.

(c) Which alternative would you advise Yankee Jack proceed with, and why?

(d) State all assumptions and qualifications that underlie your analysis.

SUGGESTED REFERENCES AND FURTHER READING

DAVIDSON, S., J. S. SCHINDLER, C. P. STICKNEY, and R. L. WEIL. *Managerial Accounting—An Introduction to Concepts, Methods, and Uses*, chaps. 4-6. Hinsdale, Ill.: The Dryden Press, 1978.

GREER, H. C. "Anyone for Widgets?" *Journal of Accountancy*, April 1966. (Despite its title, this paper contains an excellent discussion of relevant and irrelevant costs.)

HARRINGTON, D. H. "Costs and Returns: Economic and Accounting Concepts," *Agricultural Economics Research*, 35 (October 1983), pp. 1-8.

HAYNES, W. W., *and* W. R. HENRY. *Managerial Economics: Analysis and Cases* (3rd ed.), chaps. 2 and 5. Dallas, Tex.: Business Publications, 1974.

HORNGREN, C. T. *Cost Accounting: A Managerial Emphasis* (5th ed.), chaps. 2 and 3. Englewood Cliffs. N.J.: Prentice-Hall, Inc., 1982.

————. *Intoduction to Management Accounting* (5th ed.), chaps. 2-5. Englewood Cliffs, N.J.: Prentice-Hall, Inc., 1981.

PAPPAS J. L., and E. F. BRIGHAM. *Managerial Economics* (3rd ed.), chap. 8. Hinsdale, Ill.: The Dryden Press, 1979.

SIMON, J. L. *Applied Managerial Economics*, chaps. 8 and 9. Englewood Cliffs, N.J.: Prentice-Hall, Inc., 1975.

WEBB. S. C. *Managerial Economics*, chap. 5. Boston: Houghton Mifflin, 1976.

Appendix 7A

BREAKEVEN ANALYSIS: APPLICATIONS AND LIMITATIONS

EXECUTIVE SUMMARY

Breakeven analysis, like the decision tree, is a graphical technique often used as an aid to decision making in practical situations. When applied correctly, it allows the manager considerable insight into the decision problem and is useful for assessing the feasibility of different price, cost, and volume combinations. Indeed, it is often called **price-cost-volume analysis**.

The **breakeven volume** is defined as the sales level for which total revenue equals total cost. Managers are always concerned with the breakeven volume and whether or not sales will actually reach this level, since only if sales volume exceeds the breakeven volume will the manager's decision to go ahead with the product be vindicated by the existence of profits.

Breakeven analysis proceeds on the basis of an assumed price and cost per unit, and, in turn, both the cost per unit and the price per unit presume a particular level of quality, since unit cost will increase with the level of quality desired and higher prices can typically be obtained for a higher-quality product. **Different assumptions about quality, cost, and price per unit** are easily incorporated into breakeven analysis, and the impact on the breakeven volume is readily seen.

The composition of unit costs also has an impact on the breakeven volume. Where average fixed cost is relatively high and average variable cost is relatively low, such **relatively capital-intensive production methods are likely to have higher breakeven volumes than are more labor-intensive production methods**. But once the breakeven volume is attained, the more **capital-intensive method is likely to augment profit more quickly**, since the contribution margin will be higher. Oppositely, although a production method with relatively low fixed inputs will attain breakeven volume sooner, the contribution margin will be smaller beyond the breakeven point. The elasticity of profit with respect to changes in volume is referred to as **operating leverage**.

Breakeven Charts

In Figure 7A-1 we show the breakeven charts under three different cost and revenue situations. In part (a) of the figure you will notice that total revenue and total cost are equal at two separate output levels. At point A total revenue has risen to equality with total costs, and at point B total revenue has fallen to equality with the rising total cost. In the interval between point A and point B the firm is experiencing profits, as shown by the profit curve on the same graph, and to the left of point A and to the right of point B the firm experiences losses. In part (b) of the figure we show a situation where the price level remains constant, while costs are similar to those in part (a). Again there are two breakeven points, and profits are positive in the output range between these two breakeven points. In part (c) of the figure we show the most commonly used form of breakeven analysis, in which both price and average variable cost are constant. Notice that the profit function is therefore a straight line.

The use of linear total costs and total revenue functions, as in part (c) of Figure 7A-1, greatly facilitates breakeven analysis. Typically the decision maker will obtain an estimate of expected volume level and of the cost and price levels at that volume level. Linear extrapolation from those expected cost and price values around the expected volume level obviates the problem of ascertaining the actual variance in average variable costs, and it recognizes that prices are not likely to be variable by small amounts because of the price awareness thresholds of customers.

It is important to recognize, however, that linear revenue and cost functions are generally approximations of the actual form of the cost and revenue functions. The assumption of constant prices and average variable costs is likely to become progressively less accurate as we move away from expected volume levels. Most decision problems, however, will concern output levels within a fairly limited range of expected volume levels, and we call this limited range the *relevant range*. In Figure 7A-2 we show estimated linear revenue and cost functions (TR_E and TC_E) that are tolerably good approximations of the actual curvilinear revenue and cost functions (TR_A and TC_A) over the range of output levels in which the decision maker is interested. Within this relevant range the linear functions are a sufficient approximation of the actual functions for most decision-making purposes.

Applications of Breakeven Analysis

Breakeven analysis can be of considerable value to the decision maker when decisions must be made about the price and quality levels of a proposed product. In Figure 7A-3 a comparison is shown of the breakeven points at two different price and variable cost levels. Suppose that initially the decision maker was considering the price and cost levels represented by the curves TR and TC. The indicated breakeven sales volume is shown as Q_4. Let us suppose that the decision maker feels that it is unlikely that the product will attain that sales volume and hence is likely to incur losses. The decision maker may rectify this situation in one way or in a combination of two ways: First, the price may be raised; second, the average variable cost may be lowered. The latter adjustment has im-

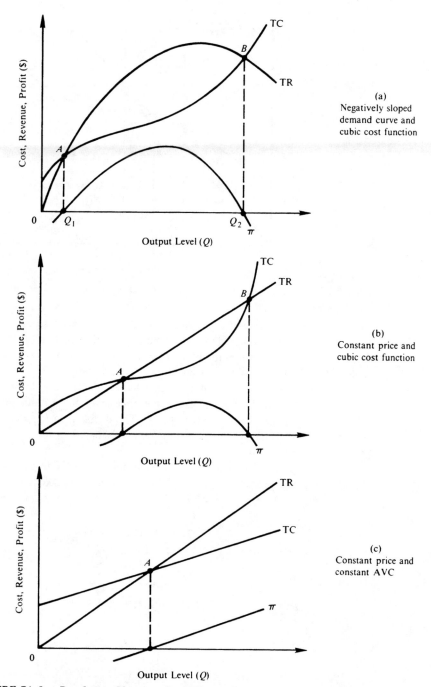

FIGURE 7A-1.   Breakeven Charts under Different Cost and Revenue Conditions

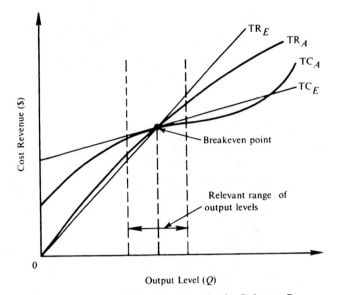

FIGURE 7A-2.   Linear Revenue and Cost Functions in the Relevant Range

plications for the quality of the product, since lowering average variable costs presumably implies the use of lower-quality raw materials or the use of less labor input per unit of output. It can be seen that at the initial price a reduction in the average variable cost level reduces the breakeven volume to that shown as Q_3. Alternatively, an increase in the price level with costs per unit remaining unchanged would reduce the breakeven volume to output level Q_2. Finally, an increase in the price level and a reduction in the cost level would reduce the breakeven volume to Q_1. The decision maker must consider each of these breakeven volume points in conjunction with the estimates of sales volume at those price and quality levels.

Algebraic calculation of the breakeven point is likely to be less time consuming than the graphical procedure. To find the formula for the breakeven volume, recall that it occurs where total revenue equals total costs, which may be expressed as follows:

$$P(Q) = \text{AVC}(Q) + \text{TFC}$$

or

$$Q(P - \text{AVC}) = \text{TFC}$$

or

$$Q = \frac{\text{TFC}}{P - \text{AVC}} \qquad\qquad (7A\text{-}1)$$

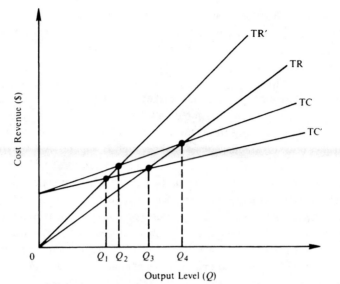

FIGURE 7A-3.   *Comparison of Breakeven Points at Different Price and Variable Cost Levels*

Since $(P - \text{AVC})$ is equal to the contribution margin (CM), we may restate this as

$$Q = \frac{\text{TFC}}{\text{CM}} \qquad \qquad (7A\text{-}2)$$

Thus the breakeven volume may be calculated simply by dividing the total fixed costs by the contribution margin per unit.[1]

In multiproduct firms, where each product must attain a particular profit target to maintain its place in the product mix and to withstand being replaced by another profitable product, breakeven analysis can be used to find the sales volume at which this profit target will be attained. Note that a profit target is a constant dollar value, just as fixed costs are a constant dollar value. Hence the profit target may be added to the fixed cost figure to represent the total dollar amount that must be obtained through contributions from each unit, before fixed costs and the profit target are covered. Algebraically, this relationship may be expressed as follows:

$$Q = \frac{\text{TFC} + \pi}{\text{CM}} \qquad \qquad (7A\text{-}3)$$

---

[1]Note that this form is applicable only for linear TR and TC functions. If either or both of these are not linear, the contribution margin will vary with the level of output.

Having calculated the sales volume necessary to cover the fixed costs and to attain the desired target profit, the decision maker must then consider whether or not that target sales volume is likely to be achieved. If it appears quite unlikely, the decision maker may wish to revise the target profit, change either price or average variable costs, or delete this product from the product mix in favor of a more profitable product.

A third area in which the breakeven analysis may be useful is that where a particular product may be manufactured under two or more technologies of production. Suppose a firm is considering three alternate means of manufacturing a product for which the market price is established at $4.00 per unit. In Figure 7A-4 we show the three technologies under which this product may be manufactured. The total revenue function in each graph is the same, indicating that the firm does not expect to be able to influence market price by its actions. Plant A is characterized by fixed costs of $20,000 and a constant average variable cost of $2.00 per unit of output. Plant B is characterized by fixed costs of $45,000 and a constant average variable cost of $1.00 per unit. Plant C involves the much higher fixed costs of $70,000 but a low and constant average variable cost of $0.50 per unit. Using this information and equation (7A-2), one may verify that the breakeven points are 10,000, 15,000, and 20,000 units, respectively.

Suppose the decision maker's estimate of sales volume is distributed around a mean of 12,000 units. The breakeven charts of Figure 7A-4 indicate that plant A would be the most suitable choice, since its breakeven point is at the low end of this distribution. And barring an eventuality at the extreme left-hand tail of the distribution, plant A would be profitable at the likely sales levels.

In Table 7A-1 we show the profitability levels at various expected sales levels for each of the three technologies. Table 7A-1 summarizes the information given in Figure 7A-4. Plant A remains the most profitable up to the output level of almost 29,000 units, at which point it is overtaken by plant B. Plant C does not become the most profitable technology until it has an output level greater than 50,000 units.

The decision maker must use the breakeven information in conjunction with the probability distribution of expected sales levels before deciding on the size of plant to implement. We would proceed in the way outlined in Chapter 6, namely the calculation of the expected value of average costs in each plant, given the probability distribution of sales/output levels and a predetermined price level. Equivalently, we could assign probabilities to the expected sales levels in Table 7A-1 and calculate the expected value of profits from each plant, selecting the plant with the greatest expected value of profits. The firm should then check to see the relationship between the expected value of output (EVQ) and the breakeven output (BEQ). Clearly the EVQ should be above the BEQ or the plant should not be installed. The firm may wish to adopt a veto rule which incorporates the standard error of estimate S_e (or the standard deviation) pertaining to the probability distribution of sales/output levels. For example, unless the BEQ is less than $(EVQ - 2S_e)$, the firm will not install the plant with the greatest expected value of profit, and will choose instead the next smallest plant size. Such a rule would be interpreted as a risk averter's trade-off between risk and return.

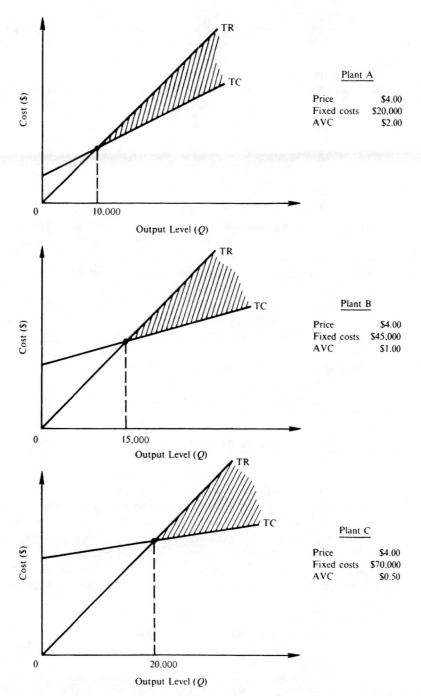

Plant A

Price	$4.00
Fixed costs	$20,000
AVC	$2.00

Plant B

Price	$4.00
Fixed costs	$45,000
AVC	$1.00

Plant C

Price	$4.00
Fixed costs	$70,000
AVC	$0.50

FIGURE 7A-4. Breakeven Charts for Different Production Technologies

TABLE 7A-1.   *Profitability at Various Output Levels with Differing Technologies*

Expected Sales Level	Plant A	Plant B	Plant C
10,000	Breakeven	− 15,000	− 35,000
15,000	10,000	Breakeven	− 22,500
20,000	20,000	15,000	Breakeven
30,000	40,000	45,000	35,000
40,000	60,000	75,000	70,000
50,000	80,000	105,000	105,000
60,000	100,000	135,000	140,000

Operating Leverage.   The differences in the contribution per unit after the breakeven point are due to the extent to which fixed factors are substituted for variable factors in the production process. The greater this substitution, or the more capital intensive the technology, the greater the operating leverage of the production process. *Operating leverage* refers to the extent to which the incremental units sold contribute to overheads and profits. With linear cost and revenue functions, it is constant over the relevant range (equal to the contribution per unit); but with nonlinear total costs or total revenue functions, the operating leverage will vary as the slopes of the functions vary. Operating leverage shows the sensitivity of total contribution to changes in volume. Since the difference between total contribution and total profits is a constant (that is, fixed costs), operating leverage also shows the sensitivity of total profits to changes in volume. When a product is subject to volatile swings in sales in response to fluctuations in general economic conditions, greater leverage involves greater risk of wide variations in profits.[2]

Limitations of Breakeven Analysis

At the beginning of our discussion of breakeven analysis, the cautious note was injected that breakeven analysis is a useful tool *when correctly applied*. It is essential that the form of the total revenue and total cost functions used in breakeven analysis accurately reflect, or at least be a tolerable approximation of, the actual cost and revenue conditions. As indicated, the assumption of linear cost and revenue conditions may be a tolerable approximation within a relatively limited range of outputs but becomes progressively less accurate at higher output levels because of the likelihood of diminishing returns to the variable factors or the necessity of reducing price in order to actually sell those higher output levels.

Second, breakeven analysis must be used in the incremental sense. That is, the total cost function must represent those costs that are incurred as a result of a decision to

---

[2]Operating leverage is in fact an elasticity measure. Since it measures the relative responsiveness of profits to a change in quantity demanded, it can be calculated as the percentage change in profits over the percentage change in quantity demanded. It is the "volume elasticity of profit," if you wish.

produce this particular product, and it must not include costs that would be incurred regardless of this decision. In the case of a firm that produces only one product, the total cost function will represent all costs incurred by the firm. If implicit costs are included at their opportunity cost value, the breakeven point will be the point of zero economic profits. Similarly, within a multiproduct firm where each department produces a single product, the total overhead costs of a particular department may be included in the total cost function in breakeven analysis. Beyond the breakeven point, the profits earned by that department will represent a contribution to the overheads and profits of the entire firm. Otherwise, in multiproduct firms, only the incremental overheads should be included, and then profits are the contribution to the joint overheads and profits of the entire firm. Care must be taken, therefore, that the vertical intercept of the total cost function relates to simply the incremental and separable fixed costs associated with that particular product.

Summary

Breakeven analysis, like the decision tree, is a graphical aid to decision making. It allows the decision maker to consider the sales volumes that would be required to break even, given certain prices and cost structures. By reference to the estimates of the demand curve for a product of a given quality, the decision maker can see whether or not the breakeven volume can be attained. If not, the quality of the product may be upgraded or downgraded if the breakeven volume of the product (at the changed quality and cost level) is attainable.

A simple calculation, namely the division of the fixed costs and profit target by the contribution margin per unit, allows the breakeven volume to be found readily for any combination of price and average variable costs per unit, as long as these are both constant over the relevant range.

Operating leverage measures the responsiveness of profits (or contribution to overheads and profits) to changes in sales volume. In conjunction with the breakeven volume calculation, operating leverage indicates the extent to which profits will increase as sales surpass the breakeven point.

Care must be taken with breakeven analysis to ensure that the cost and revenue functions used are sufficient approximations of the actual incremental costs and revenues.

DISCUSSION QUESTIONS

7A-1. Discuss the applications of breakeven analysis to business decision making.

7A-2. Summarize the limitations involved in the use of breakeven analysis.

7A-3. Derive an expression for the operating leverage of a particular plant, expressed in terms of the percentage changes in the appropriate variables.

7A-4. Under what circumstances is it appropriate to show the TR and TC curves as linear functions of output for breakeven analysis purposes?

7A-5. Derive an algebraic expression for the breakeven volume for the case where TR is a quadratic function of output (and TC is linear).

PROBLEMS AND SHORT CASES

7A-1. For the total revenue curve TR $= 45Q$ and the total cost function TC $= 120 + 12.5Q$, where Q represents thousands of units, perform the following:

(a) Show graphically the breakeven volume. Confirm your answer algebraically.

(b) Suppose now that a demand study estimates the demand curve to be $P = 80 - 10Q$. What do you advise?

7A-2. The Franklin Razor Company is considering the introduction of a new product that will facilitate shaving in the shower. It is considering three alternative quality levels for the product. Produced in plastic without any detailing, the product would cost $0.125 per unit over a wide range of outputs. Produced in a more expensive clear plastic material that allows intricate design work, the product would cost $0.1875 per unit over a wide range of outputs. Produced in an aluminum alloy, the product would cost $0.2225 per unit over a wide range of outputs. Fixed and setup costs would be $120,000, $180,000, and $250,000, respectively, for each of the three alternative quality treatments.

Market research has indicated that consumers would perceive the products to contain good value when priced at $1.25, $1.49, and $1.98, respectively.

(a) Calculate the breakeven volumes for each of the three quality treatments.

(b) What other information would you prefer to have before making your recommendation?

7A-3. Suppose that the data in Table 7A-1 refer to the plant-size decision of Mainstream Motors Company, which intends to build a plant to produce extruded plastic bumper covers for the major automobile builders. Suppose the probability distribution of sales each month at the $4 price has been estimated to be as follows:

Output Level	Probability
10,000	0.01
15,000	0.05
20,000	0.18
30,000	0.45
40,000	0.25
50,000	0.05
60,000	0.01

(a) Calculate the expected value of profit from each of the three plant sizes, given this probability data.

(b) Calculate the standard deviation of profits around the expected value for each plant.

(c) Supposing management is risk averse, advise them which plant size should be selected.

SUGGESTED REFERENCES AND FURTHER READING

DAVIDSON, S., J. S. SCHINDLER, C. P. STICKNEY, and R. L. WEIL. *Managerial Accounting—An Introduction to Concepts, Methods, and Uses*, chap. 6. Hinsdale, Ill.: The Dryden Press, 1978.

HORNGREN, C. T. *Introduction to Management Accounting* (5th ed.), chap. 2. Englewood Cliffs, N.J.: Prentice-Hall, Inc., 1981.

Chapter 8

COST ESTIMATION AND FORECASTING

EXECUTIVE SUMMARY

We make a distinction between cost estimation and cost forecasting. **Cost estimation refers to the present-period cost levels,** whereby we ascertain the likely unit costs or incremental costs of a particular decision to be made in the near future. **Cost forecasting refers to the levels of cost in a future period,** whereby judgments must be made about the probable rate of inflation, the market factors affecting the prices of the different inputs, and changes in input productivities, including the possible effects of the learning curve.

The manager must undertake cost estimation and forecasting **to judge the optimality of present output levels, and to solve problems using incremental cost analysis.** Both fixed and variable cost categories must be scrutinized to ascertain their variability as a consequence of the decision to be made. Although fixed costs do not change with output levels, by definition, they may change for other internal or external reasons (such as a manager's salary being raised, or an increase in the price of a lease arrangement), or because the decision to be made requires a long-run adjustment to the plant's fixed inputs. Management must therefore have an appreciation of the degree of idle capacity remaining in fixed cost categories, since a particular decision may require an increased input of one or more of the fixed factors. When fixed factors are expected to meet their full capacity constraints, such that overtime use or additional facilities or equipment must be purchased, the manager must account for these costs, as well as the variable costs, in estimating the incremental costs of the decision to be made.

This chapter is organized into three main sections, namely: short-run cost estimation, long-run cost estimation, and cost forecasting. In our discussion of cost forecasting we examine the learning curve, whereby unit costs are seen to decline because of the increasing productivity of the inputs as the cumulative volume of output increases.

8.1 SHORT-RUN COST ESTIMATION

In the short run we are concerned principally with the behavior of variable costs, but we must also be aware of other incremental costs, such as those changes in a fixed-cost category that would be necessitated by a particular decision. We shall discuss short-run cost estimation under four headings: simple extrapolation, gradient analysis, regression analysis, and the engineering technique.

Simple Extrapolation

- DEFINITION: *Extrapolation* means to impute values to points outside the range represented by the data base by projecting the relationship which is apparent within the data base.

The most simple method of cost estimation is to extrapolate the present level of marginal or average variable costs backward or forward to other output levels. Firms often express the belief that their marginal and average variable costs are constant over a range of output levels surrounding the current output level. Note that this belief implies constant returns to the variable factors and hence the absence of either increasing or diminishing returns in the short-run production process. If this constant efficiency situation actually exists in the production process, the simple extrapolation method is an adequate method of accurate cost estimation. However, if marginal costs are in fact increasing with additional output units, the simple extrapolation method may cause poor decisions to be made. It is a common error in business situations to assume that marginal costs are constant—in effect, assuming the absence of diminishing returns to the variable factors. It should be intuitively obvious that sooner or later diminishing returns will set in and that the decision maker must be constantly aware of this possibility.

When we have only one cost/output observation (that is, the current level), adjustment for possible diminishing returns must take place on the basis of judgment, experience, or intuition. For example, the decision maker may feel that the most reasonable presumption is that marginal costs are likely to increase by, say, 2% for each additional 1% change in the output level. Clearly, with only one set of cost/output observations, such an assumption is quite risky, since it may easily be significantly inaccurate.

Conversely, the decision maker may feel that marginal costs are more likely to fall if output is increased, or that there is no reason for marginal costs either to rise or fall, and, hence, the best estimate is that marginal costs are constant. Perhaps the best approach, in the absence of any data to the contrary, is to assume constant marginal costs for extrapolation purposes and then to examine the sensitivity of the decision made to the accuracy of that assumption.

- EXAMPLE: The Blissful Underwear Garment Company has an opportunity to sell 500 dozen pairs of panties to a discount store which has made a flat offer of $7.00 per dozen. There has recently been a management shake-up at Blissful Underwear, and the new production manager is appalled that no data have been kept on production or cost levels for these panties and she, therefore, has no idea what the incremental cost would be.

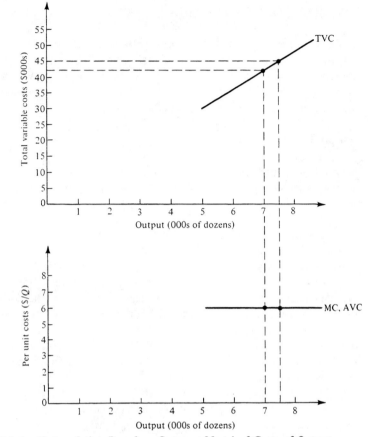

FIGURE 8-1. Extrapolation Based on Constant Marginal Costs of Output

Working quickly, she ascertains that, for the present week, 7,000 dozen pairs were produced at a total variable cost of $42,000. Thus average variable costs (AVC) are $6 per dozen at this output level, she reasons. Planned output for the next several weeks is also 7,000 dozen pairs, so fulfilling the discount store's order would expand the output rate to 7,500 per week, which is well within the plant's capacity.

Without any further information, the production manager has little choice but to extrapolate from the single data point she has observed. In Figure 8-1 we show the TVC, AVC, and MC curves based on an extrapolation of these curves, assuming constant MC, from the output level of 7,000 dozen to 7,500 dozen.

In the absence of any other changes in costs as a result of the decision to fulfill the discount store's order, we estimate that incremental costs will be $3,000 for the additional 500 dozen pairs. The incremental revenue, again in the absence of any other current explicit, opportunity, or future revenues, will be $3,500. Thus the contribution of this decision is expected to be positive, at $500, and the production manager is inclined to fill the order.

How sensitive is this decision to the underlying assumption of constant marginal costs? If TVC is not rising at a constant rate but, in fact, rises at an increasing rate over the next 500 dozen units of output, how much could it rise before the decision should be reversed? The answer is $3,500, at which point there would be no contribution from the decision, so it should not be taken. A $3,500 increase in TVC, bringing it to $45,500, would represent an increase in AVC to $6.0667, or fractionally more than a 1% increase in AVC from the earlier level. Thus the decision is very sensitive to the assumption of constant marginal costs, and we would probably advise Blissful Underwear not to fill the order unless they were very confident that TVC would, in fact, increase at a constant (or decreasing) rate.

Since output levels typically fluctuate to some degree from period to period, we should be able to find two or more cost/output observations, in which case we can conduct gradient analysis.

Gradient Analysis

- DEFINITION: The *gradient* of a total cost curve is defined as the rate of change of those total costs over a particular interval of output levels. Gradient means slope, of course, and the gradient of total costs can be calculated as the change in total costs divided by the change in output levels. That is,

$$\text{Gradient} = \frac{\Delta TC}{\Delta Q} \tag{8-1}$$

- NOTE: The gradient of the total cost, or total variable cost, curve is not exactly the same as *marginal costs,* since the latter is defined as the change in total costs for a one-unit change in outputs. In practice, output typically changes by discrete jumps, and we must, therefore, calculate the gradient over intervals greater than one unit. The gradient does provide us with an estimate of the marginal costs over the range of output levels, as we shall see.

- EXAMPLE: Suppose that Blissful Underwear accepts the order, produces the extra 500 dozen pairs, and notes that the total variable cost of producing 7,500 dozen pairs was $48,750. The gradient of total variable costs can thus be calculated as

$$
\begin{aligned}
\text{Gradient} &= \frac{\Delta TVC}{\Delta Q} \\
&= \frac{48,750 - 42,000}{7,500 - 7,000} \\
&= \frac{6,750}{500} \\
&= 13.50
\end{aligned}
$$

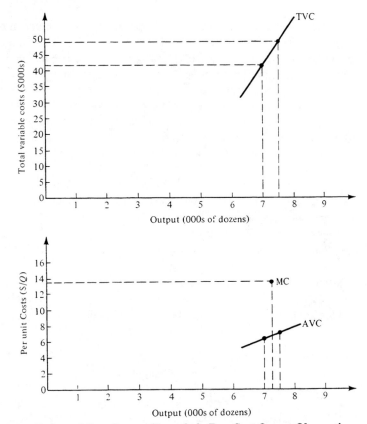

FIGURE 8-2.   Estimated Cost Curves Given Only Two Cost-Output Observations

Thus the rate of change of total variable costs, over the output interval 7,000 to 7,500 dozen, was $13.50 per unit. This is a measure of the marginal cost over that output range. In Figure 8-2 we show our best estimates of the TVC, AVC, and MC curves based on the observation of a second data point.

- NOTE: The single MC point shown in Figure 8-2 is plotted in the *middle* of the output interval over which it is calculated, because the gradient is a single-point estimate of the rate of change of total costs over a discrete range of output levels. It is the *average* rate of change over the output interval, or an estimate of the average MC over that range, and is, therefore, plotted in the center of that range.

Gradient Analysis with Several Observations.   If we have a few more cost-output observations, we can substantially improve the estimates of the TVC, AVC, and MC curves.

- EXAMPLE: The new management of the Blissful Underwear Company, although planning to produce 7,000 dozen pairs per week in the next several weeks, finds that it faces a severe absenteeism problem, with weekly absentee rates ranging between 10% and 25% over the next three weeks, such that its output levels fall below the planned production level in each of these weeks. Total variable costs also fall, however, since absent labor is not paid for time missed, and purchases of raw materials and the use of electrical energy are also positively related to the output level. The TVC and output figures collected over the first five weeks are shown in Table 8-1 and plotted in Figure 8-3. Note that the output levels have been rearranged in ascending order, regardless of the chronology of production, to facilitate the calculation of the gradients over each output interval.

The AVC column in Table 8-1 is simply TVC/Q. The last three columns show the calculation of the gradients (and, hence, the estimated MC at the midpoint of each interval). When these points are plotted in Figure 8-3, we can interpolate between each adjacent pair of points and show our best estimates of the TVC, AVC, and MC curves. Note that the interpolation between the gradient values to find the MC curve indicates that the minimum point on the AVC curve must lie somewhere below 6,000 dozen pairs, since the MC curve must cut the AVC curve at the minimum point of the latter.[1]

TABLE 8-1. *Cost-Output Observations and the Calculation of AVC and MC*

Production Period	Output (doz.)	TVC ($)	AVC ($)	ΔTVC ($)	ΔQ (doz.)	MC ($)
Week 4	4,500	27,000	6.00			
Week 3	6,000	33,600	5.60	6,600	1,500	4.40
Week 5	6,500	37,375	5.75	3,775	500	7.55
Week 1	7,000	42,000	6.00	4,625	500	9.25
Week 2	7,500	48,750	6.50	6,750	500	13.50

Thus the observation of several pairs of cost-output data allows us to form a more complete estimate of the TVC, AVC, and MC curves. Each additional data point allows the shape of TVC to be seen more clearly, so more reliable calculations of AVC and MC may be derived.

Regression Analysis Using Time-Series Data

Given a larger number of cost/output observations, we can apply regression analysis to estimate the dependence of costs on the output level and thus obtain an estimate of the marginal cost.[2] Since we wish to estimate the cost function of a particular firm, we must

---

[1]A smooth interpolation between the gradient values indicates that AVC is minimized at about 5,500 dozen pairs. This is open to debate, of course, since a straighter MC curve would indicate AVC minimized at a lower volume, for example. Our conclusion that AVC is minimized at 5,500 units is, therefore, sensitive to interpolation error.

[2]The principles of regression analysis and the major problems associated with the use and interpretation of the results of this method were discussed in a self-contained section of Chapter 5. The discussion in this chapter presumes your familiarity with the earlier section.

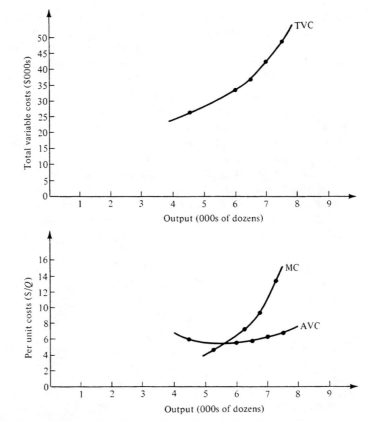

FIGURE 8-3. Estimated Cost Curves Given Several Cost-Output Observations

use time-series data from that firm. This necessity raises some of the standard problems with time-series data: If over the period of the observations some factors have changed, the results of regression analysis will be less reliable. For example, factor prices may change because of inflation or market forces in the factor markets, or factor productivities may change because of changing technology and worker efficiency. To eliminate these problems, the cost data should be deflated by an appropriate price index, and time should be inserted as an independent variable in the regression equation. Any trend in the relative prices or productivities will then be accounted for by the coefficient of the time variable.

Regression analysis of time-series cost data is quite susceptible to the problems of measurement error. The cost data should include all costs that are *caused* by a particular output level, whether or not they are yet paid for. Maintenance expense, for example, should be expected to vary with the rate of output, but it may be delayed until it is more convenient to close down certain sections of the plant or facilities for maintenance purposes. Hence the cost that is caused in an earlier period is not recorded until a later period and is thus likely to understate the earlier cost level and to overstate the later cost level.

Ideally, our cost/output observations should be the result of considerable fluctuations of output over a short period of time with no cost/output matching problems.

• EXAMPLE: Suppose the weekly output and total variable costs of an ice cream plant have been recorded over a three-month period, as shown in Table 8-2. Output of the product varies from week to week because of the rather unpredictable nature of the milk supply from dairies and the impossibility of holding inventories of the fresh milk for more than a few days.

TABLE 8-2. **Record of Output Levels and Total Variable Costs for an Ice Cream Plant**

Week Ending	Output (gallons)	Total Variable Costs ($)
Sept. 7	7,300	5,780
Sept. 14	8,450	7,010
Sept. 21	8,300	6,550
Sept. 28	9,500	7,620
Oct. 5	6,700	5,650
Oct. 12	9,050	7,100
Oct. 19	5,450	5,060
Oct. 26	5,950	5,250
Nov. 2	5,150	4,490
Nov. 9	10,050	7,520
Nov. 16	10,300	8,030
Nov. 23	7,750	6,350

It is apparent from the data supplied that total variable costs tend to vary positively with the output level in this ice cream plant. But what is the *form* of the relationship? The specification of the functional form of the regression equation has resounding implications for the estimate of the marginal cost curve that will be indicated by the regression analysis. If we specify total variable costs as a linear function of output, such as $TVC = a + bQ$, the marginal cost estimation generated by the regression analysis will be the parameter b, since marginal cost is equivalent to the derivative of the total variable cost function with respect to the output level. In Figure 8-4 we show, for a given collection of data observations, the consequent average variable costs and marginal cost curves that would be generated by regression analysis using a linear specification of the relationship. Since average variable costs are total variable cost divided by output level Q, the AVC curve will decline to approach the MC curve asymptotically.

Alternatively, for the same group of data observations, if we specify the functional form as a quadratic such as $TVC = a + bQ + cQ^2$, the marginal cost will not be constant but will rise as a constant function of output. In Figure 8-5 we show the hypoth-

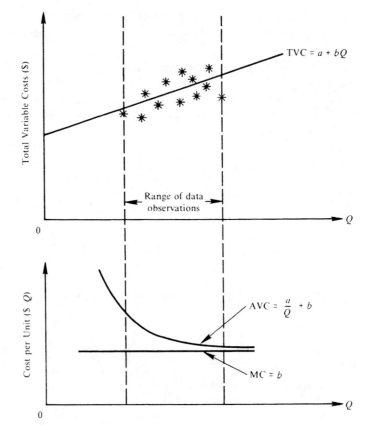

FIGURE 8-4. *Linear Variable Cost Function*

esized quadratic relationship superimposed on the same data observations, with the consequent average variable cost and marginal cost curves illustrated in the lower half of the figure.

Finally, if we hypothesize that the functional relationship is cubic, such as TVC $= a + bQ - cQ^2 + dQ^3$, the marginal cost estimate generated by regression analysis will be curvilinear and will increase with the square of the output level. Figure 8-6 illustrates the cost curves consequent on a cubic expression of the cost/output relationship. Alternatively, a power function or other multiplicative relationship may be appropriate.

Which form of the cost function should we specify? Since the results of the regression analysis will be used for decision-making purposes, we must be assured that the marginal and average cost curves generated are the most accurate representations of the cost/output relationships. By plotting the total variable cost data against output, we may be able to ascertain that one of the above three functional forms best represents the apparent relationship existing between the two variables, and we may thus confidently continue the regression analysis using this particular functional form.

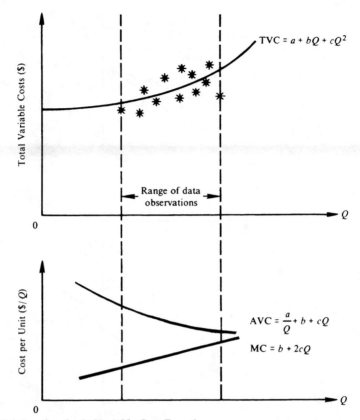

FIGURE 8-5. *Quadratic Variable Cost Function*

If it is not visually apparent that one particular functional form is the best representation of the apparent relationship, it may be necessary to run the regression analysis first with a linear functional form and later with one or more of the other functional forms to find which equation best fits the data base. You will recall from Chapter 5 that the regression equation that generates the highest coefficient of determination (R^2) is the equation that explains the highest proportion of the variability of the dependent variable, and it can thus be taken to be the best indication of the actual functional relationship that exists between the two variables.

• EXAMPLE: Fitting a linear regression equation to the cost-output pairs shown in Table 8-2 resulted in the following computer output:

$$\text{TVC} = 1{,}395.29 + 0.6351Q \tag{8-2}$$

with a standard error of estimate of 182.02 and a standard error of the regression coefficient of 0.0313. The coefficient of determination (R^2) was 0.97614.

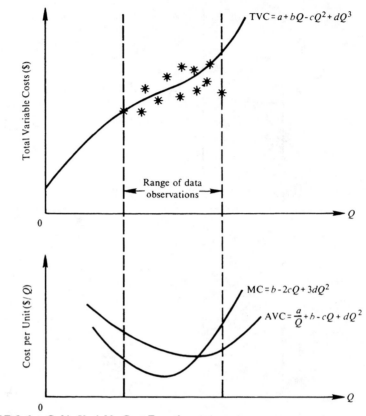

FIGURE 8-6.   Cubic Variable Cost Function

Note that this linear regression equation explains 97.614% of the variation in TVC as resulting from the variation in the output level.[3]

Suppose we now wish to estimate the total variable costs at output levels of 7,000 and 11,000 units. For 7,000 units

$$
\begin{aligned}
TVC &= 1{,}395.29 + 0.6351(7{,}000) \\
&= 1{,}395.29 + 4{,}445.70 \\
&= 5{,}840.99
\end{aligned}
$$

---

[3]Adding extra explanatory variables will inevitably explain more of the variation in the independent variable, even if the extra variables are *not* responsible for variation in the independent variable, since the regression analysis tends to capitalize on chance. In this present case, a cubic function of the form $TVC = a + bQ + cQ^2 + dQ^3$ has $R^2 = 0.97642$ and thus explains fractionally more of the variation in TVC, although the standard errors of the coefficients are so large that one cannot have confidence in the equation's explanatory value. As a predictive equation, we could use the cubic expression, since the individual coefficients are not given any significance. For simplicity, we proceed with the simple linear specification with insignificant loss of accuracy.

Using the standard error of estimate, we can be confident at the 68% level that the actual TVC will fall within the interval of $5,840.99 plus or minus $182.02 ($5,658.97 to $6,023.01), and we can be confident at the 95% level that the actual TVC will fall within the interval of $5,840.99 plus or minus two standard errors of estimate ($5,476.95 to $6,205.03). Thus we can be confident at the 95% level that TVC will be no higher than $6,205.03, given the production of 7,000 gallons of ice cream. These confidence limits allow a best-case/worst-case scenario to be developed. Of course, a highly risk-averse decision maker may wish to extend the confidence limits to plus three standard errors of estimate to find the TVC below which one can be 99% confident that actual TVC will fall.

The estimation of TVC at 11,000 units would proceed in the same way. The result must be viewed with caution, however, because it represents an *extrapolation* from the data base. The regression equation applies over the range of outputs observed and hence can be applied quite confidently for 7,000 units, a case of *interpolation*. Outside the range of the initial observations the relationship between TVC and *Q* may not continue to be linear but may instead be curvilinear, exhibiting diminishing returns to the variable factors, for example. Extrapolation may be undertaken, however, if we have no good reason to expect that the relationship will *not* hold outside the range of observations, as long as we are fully cognizant that the relationship may not hold.[4]

The Engineering Technique of Cost Estimation

- DEFINITION: The *engineering technique* consists of developing the physical production function that exists between the inputs and the output and of attaching cost values to the inputs to obtain a total variable cost figure for each output level. For each output level we must therefore calculate, or test for, the amount of each of the variable factors necessary to produce that output level. Attaching costs to these variable inputs, we can subsequently calculate the total variable cost for each output level and hence the average variable costs and marginal costs at each output level. Let us demonstrate this in the context of a hypothetical example.

- EXAMPLE: Suppose a metal-stamping plant has one large machine that can be operated at five different speeds up to a maximum speed of 100 revolutions per minute (rpm). On each revolution it stamps out one unit of the product, and hence output is proportional to the operating speed of the machine. However, the requirements of materials, labor, electric power, and repairs and maintenance need not be proportional to the operating speed of the machine. In Table 8-3 we show the relationships that have been found between the

---

[4]Throughout the regression analysis we required *ceteris paribus* to hold. Specifically, the prices of the input factors and the productivities of the factors must reasonably be expected to have remained constant over the period of data collection. The same costs and productivities must be expected to prevail over the prediction period as well.

TABLE 8-3. *Physical Requirements of a Metal-Stamping Machine at Various Operating Speeds*

Operating Speed (rpm)	Output per Hour (units)	Materials Used (lb)	Labor (hours)	Power Requirements (kWh)	R&M Requirements (units)
20	1,200	1,320	20	2,585	10
40	2,400	2,880	25	4,523	20
60	3,600	4,680	27	5,262	30
80	4,800	6,720	28	6,708	35
100	6,000	9,000	30	10,954	60

output and the inputs of the variable factors, using this machine at each of its five speeds.[5]

By observing the various input components, you will notice that the ratio of materials used to output per hour increases as the operating speed of the machine is increased, indicating increased wastage or spoilage as the machine is operated at faster speeds. Labor input, however, increases by different amounts as the operating speed is increased. It apparently requires twenty workers to operate the machine at its minimum speed, and the labor requirement increases at an irregular rate as the operating speed is increased, until at maximum speed thirty workers are required per hour of operation. Electric power requirements, measured in kilowatt-hours, increase rapidly at first, then more slowly, and then more rapidly again as maximum operating speed is attained. Repairs and maintenance requirements are indicated by an index of labor and materials necessary to maintain the machine in operating condition, and they evidently increase quite dramatically as the machine attains its maximum operating speed.

Suppose the variable inputs have the following costs per unit: Materials cost is $0.15 per pound; labor cost is $8.00 per hour; power cost is $0.0325 per kilowatt-hour; and repairs and maintenance cost is $10.00 per unit. With this information we can calculate the total variable cost of the output at various levels, as shown in Table 8-4. Dividing total variable cost at each output level by that output level, we derive the average variable cost for each output level, and the marginal cost figures are derived by the gradient method and are in effect the *average* marginal costs over each 1,200-unit interval. Note that both average and marginal costs decline at first and later rise.

In Figure 8-7 we plot these average variable and marginal cost figures against the output level. Interpolating between these observations, we are able to sketch in the average variable and marginal cost curves as indicated by the engineering technique. The production process appears to be most efficient in terms of the variable factors at about 4,600 units, where average variable cost appears to reach a minimum at something like $0.37 per unit. If the speed of the machine were infinitely variable, the firm might wish

---

[5]The figures at any output level should be regarded as the central tendency of the actually observed levels, since we should expect small day-to-day variations in material wastage, labor efficiency, and actual repairs and maintenance requirements.

TABLE 8-4. *Costs Associated with Operating the Metal-Stamping Machine at Various Output Levels*

Output Levels (units)	Materials Cost ($)	Labor Cost ($)	Power Cost ($)	R&M Cost ($)	TVC ($)	AVC ($)	MC ($)
1,200	198	160	84	100	542	0.452	
2,400	432	200	147	200	979	0.408	0.364
3,600	702	216	171	300	1,389	0.386	0.342
4,800	1,008	224	218	350	1,800	0.375	0.343
6,000	1,350	240	356	600	2,546	0.424	0.622

to operate at this output level by running the machine at approximately 77 rpm. If the firm wishes to maximize profits rather than simply minimize costs, it will seek the output level at which marginal revenues from the sale of these output units equal the marginal cost of producing the last unit of output. Note that by multiplying the scale on the horizontal axis in Figure 8-7 by the appropriate factor, the same cost curves will be applicable for output per day, per week, or for a longer period.

Incremental costs associated with any decision to increase or decrease output levels will be determined on the basis of the variable costs as calculated by one or a combination of the above methods, plus an allowance for any opportunity costs that are involved and any incremental fixed costs that may be necessitated. The incremental fixed costs

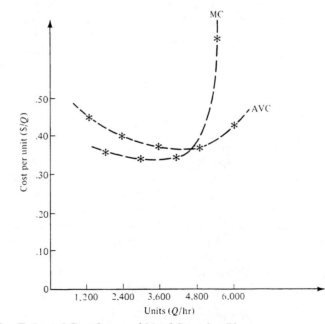

FIGURE 8-7. *Estimated Cost Curves of Metal-Stamping Plant*

must be calculated on the basis of the knowledge of the production capacity of the fixed factors involved. This in turn may require an engineering-type investigation of the output capacities of particular fixed facilities. Similarly, increased costs associated with over-time use of facilities must be estimated on the basis of known overtime labor costs.

Studies of Short-Run Cost Behavior

Numerous studies of the short-run cost functions of particular business firms have been reported. Perhaps the definitive work in this area is the book by Johnston,[6] in which the theoretical and conceptual issues of cost estimation by statistical methods are examined in detail before thirty-one separate studies of statistical cost estimation are summarized by the author. With regard to short-run cost estimation, the preponderant conclusion is that marginal cost tends to be constant in the operating range of the firms studied. Hence average variable cost is constant at the same level (or is asymptotically approaching that level), and average total costs are declining because of the influence of declining average fixed costs. That is, in most cases a linear total variable cost function provided the best fit to the data observations.

In some cases where a curvilinear total variable cost function was hypothesized, the regression analysis generated a high coefficient of determination, but generally the linear equation provided at least as much explanatory power. Thus the general conclusion of the statistical cost studies is that marginal and average variable costs tend to be constant over the output range in which firms tend to operate, or they are sufficiently constant over that range that they may be regarded for decision-making purposes as constant. But constant MC and AVC over the range of recent output levels does not mean that we can expect these unit costs to be constant *outside* this range. For decisions that involve output levels beyond the recent range of output levels, the decision maker must consider the possibility that extrapolation of unit-cost levels is an unreliable procedure because of the possible onset of diminishing returns in the production process. The occurrence of diminishing returns in the incremental units of output should always be suspected, and if these are thought likely to occur the incremental cost figure should be adjusted accordingly.

The observation of constant marginal costs over the range of outputs observed should not be too surprising. We argued in Chapter 6 that the firm would wish to build the plant size that minimizes the expected average cost of production, given the expected output level or the probability distribution of quantity demanded at the chosen price level. This decision will typically lead to the installation of some excess capacity, allowing the firm to operate in a range somewhere below full capacity. Since full capacity is defined as the output level where average costs are minimized, the firm will typically operate somewhere around and to the left of the minimum point of the AVC curve. In Figure 8-7 note that the MC curve is virtually horizontal to the left of the minimum point of the AVC curve. If our observations of the metal-stamping plant have been restricted to

---

[6]J. Johnston, *Statistical Cost Analysis* (New York: McGraw-Hill Book Company, 1960).

output levels in the range from only 2,400 units to 4,800 units, we might well have concluded that marginal costs were approximately linear, yet the full picture shows them rising steeply as the plant approaches full capacity.

8.2 LONG-RUN COST ESTIMATION

In this section we shall outline methods by which the long-run cost curve, or the alternative short-run cost curves available at a particular point in time, may be ascertained. We shall discuss two methods of long-run cost estimation: cross-section regression analysis and the engineering technique applied to plants of various sizes.[7]

Regression Analysis Using Cross-Section Data

Since long-run cost estimation seeks to find the differing sizes of plant available at a particular point in time (while technology and factor prices remain constant), it is clear that we cannot use time-series observations to derive estimates of the long-run cost function. Observations from various plants at a particular point in time (cross-section data) may be analyzed, however, using the technique of regression analysis. Thus we would need to collect pairs of data observations relating the output level to the total cost of obtaining that output level in each plant, at a particular point in time. Care must be taken to avoid errors of measurement relating either to the actual level or rate of output in that period or to the actual level of costs that should be associated with that level of output in each plant observed.

    Specification of the functional form of the equation involves the same problems for long-run cost estimation as it did for short-run cost estimation. We must choose the functional form that best fits a scatter plot of the total cost and output observations. Since we are interested in whether or not there are likely to be economies of plant size, constant returns to plant size, or diseconomies of plant size, we might initially specify the relationship as being cubic, since this relationship is consistent with the presence of increasing, constant, and decreasing returns to plant size. If there are increasing, and later decreasing, returns to plant size, the coefficients to the squared and cubed output terms will show up as significant determinants of the total cost level, with the signs of the coefficients being negative for the squared term and positive for the cubed term. If the cubed term is an insignificant determinant, the sign of the coefficient to the squared term will

---

[7]G. J. Stigler has suggested a third method of estimating the long-run average cost curve based on the principle that the more efficient firms will survive and expand their market share over time. Plant sizes that allow increased market share over time are inferred to have lower average costs, while plant sizes that are associated with reduced market share over time are inferred to have higher average costs. Stigler's study of the U.S. steel industry inferred an LAC curve that was negatively sloping at first, then more or less horizontal for an extended range of outputs, and finally upward sloping at high output rates. This "survivor principle" suffers from several major disadvantages for practical implementation, however. See G. J. Stigler, "The Economies of Scale," *Journal of Law and Economics,* 1 (October 1958), reprinted in his *The Organization of Industry* (Homewood, Ill.: Richard D. Irwin, Inc., 1968); see also A. Koutsoyiannis, *Modern Microeconomics*, 2nd ed. (London: Macmillan, Inc. 1979), pp. 146–48.

indicate increasing returns to plant size, if positive, or decreasing returns to plant size, if negative.

If both the squared and cubed output terms are insignificant determinants of total costs, a linear equation will give a better fit to the data. Attention should then shift to the sign of the constant term in the linear equation. If it is positive, the (long-run) total cost curve has a positive intercept, and long-run average costs (LAC), which are the ratio of (long-run) total cost to output levels, must be falling as output levels increase. Thus the data indicate economies of plant size over the range of observations. Conversely, if the intercept term is negative, LAC must be rising over the range of data observations, and we have discovered diseconomies of plant size. Finally, if the constant term is zero, we would conclude that there are constant returns to plant size over the output range observed. (In each of these three cases a positive slope term is taken for granted.)

If a power function, such as $TC = aQ^b$, best fits the data, then the size of the exponent term b will indicate whether returns to plant size are increasing (if the exponent is less than 1), constant (if equal to 1), or decreasing (if greater than 1).

Two major problems exist with cross-section data for estimation of the long-run average cost curve. The first arises because the observations collected may not be points on the long-run average cost curve at all.

- EXAMPLE: Suppose there are five plants observed, and the current output and total cost levels are as shown in Table 8-5. It seems that economies of plant size exist initially and that diseconomies of plant size prevail for the fourth and fifth largest plants, since the average cost figures decline at first and later rise as we encounter progressively larger plant sizes.

  Suppose that the *actual* short-run cost curves for each of the five plants are as shown by the SAC_1, SAC_2, and so on in Figure 8-8. The observed output/average cost values are shown by the point on each short-run cost curve marked by an asterisk.

Given this insight, we can see that the preceding analysis has overestimated the presence of economies and diseconomies of plant size in this instance because the observation points for each plant were not the points of tangency with the actual LAC curve. This problem is accentuated if smaller plants are operating beyond the point of tangency with the long-run average cost curve and if large plants are operating to the left of the tangency point, but it occurs whichever side of the "actual" tangency point the firms are operating on. Since we cannot expect each firm to be operating at precisely the point of tangency of the short-run average cost curve to the long-run average cost curve, the regression analysis of cross-section data is likely to produce a misleading picture of the actual economies and diseconomies of plant size that may exist. You will note that this is a case of measurement error—the assumption is that the data points are the points of tangency between the short-run average cost curves and the LAC, when in fact the data points are more likely *not* the points of tangency.

The second problem that may arise with cross-section data is that the various plants may not be operating with the benefit of the same factor prices or factor productivities. If the plants operate in differing geographical, political, and socioeconomic environments,

TABLE 8-5. Cross-Section Estimate of the Long-Run Average Cost Curve

Plant	Output (Q)	Total Cost ($)	Average Cost ($/Q)
1	1,500	7,350	4.90
2	3,500	12,600	3.60
3	6,150	18,143	2.95
4	8,750	26,688	3.05
5	11,100	43,290	3.90

we may expect both factor prices and productivities of the factors to differ between and among the plants. If this problem exists, regression analysis may indicate economies or diseconomies of plant size where the cost differences are actually due to differences in factor prices and productivities. Alternatively, the differences in these things may completely obscure the existence of those economies and diseconomies of plant size that would be seen if the influence of differing factor prices and productivities could be removed from the data.

Estimation of the long-run average cost curve presumes that all plant sizes represented are of the same vintage and therefore incorporate the same technology. Moreover, this technology should be the *latest* technology. Part of the differences in labor productivity that will most likely exist in cross-section cost-output data will relate to differing vintages of the plants observed, ranging from almost new plants to older and much less efficient plants. (Any other differences in labor productivity will relate to differences in the workers' education, training, motivation, and so on.) Regression analysis of cross-

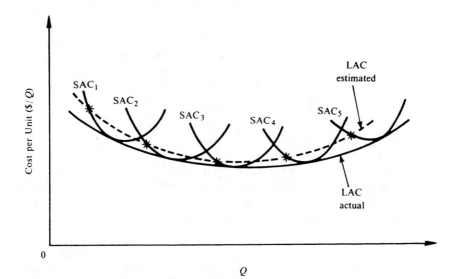

FIGURE 8-8. Estimation of Long-Run Average Cost Curve from Cross-Section Data

section cost-output data from plants of less than current vintage is likely to give unreliable results and should be avoided. A superior approach is to apply the engineering technique to all the different plant sizes that are currently available and that embody the latest technology.

Applying the Engineering Technique to Several Plants

The engineering technique outlined above in the context of short-run cost estimation can be used to find an estimation of the long-run cost function by applying the same analysis to a number of plants of differing sizes at a particular point in time. In the short-run cost estimation section we used the engineering technique to find the cost curves of a particular firm at a particular point in time. If we proceeded in a similar fashion with other plant sizes that are available, we would be able to trace out a series of short-run cost curves that are available to the firm at a particular point in time.

To apply the engineering technique for purposes of long-run cost estimation, we would conduct the analysis as outlined above under short-run cost estimation for each firm. To this we would add the average fixed cost curve for each plant size to arrive at the short-run total cost curve for each of the plant sizes. By the shape and placement of the short-run average cost curves, we could infer the presence or absence of economies and diseconomies of plant size. In Figure 8-9 we show a hypothetical case in which five different sizes of plants have been observed, and the short-run average cost curve of each has been derived by the engineering technique. The envelope curve of these short-run curves is the long-run average cost curve. It can be inferred from the figure that there are economies of plant size initially as one moves from the first plant to the second plant, followed by relatively constant returns to plant size as one progresses to the third and fourth plant, and decreasing returns to plant size with the largest plant available.[8]

Note that the construction of the long-run average cost curve by the engineering technique is predicated on given factor productivity and factor prices. Similarly, the cost curves derived by this analysis are applicable only as long as the factor prices and productivities do not change. If they do, a new set of short-run average cost curves must be derived, and a new long-run average cost curve will be found.

Long-Run Cost Estimation Studies

Various studies of the long-run cost function of firms have been undertaken, and a number of these are summarized by Johnston.[9] The most common finding of these studies was that the long-run average cost curve tended to be not so much U-shaped as L-shaped; that is, there were typically significant economies of plant size at relatively low

---

[8]Typically we should expect discrete differences in the plant sizes that are available to the firm rather than the infinite variability of plant sizes that is implied by a smooth long-run average cost curve.

[9]See Johnston, *Statistical Cost Analysis*, chap. 5.

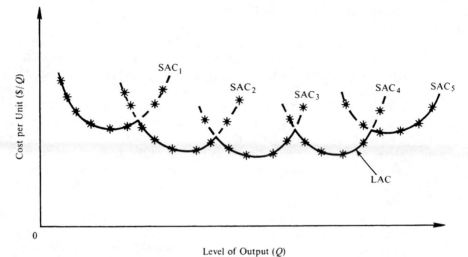

FIGURE 8-9. *Engineering Technique of Cost Estimation Used to Derive the Long-Run Average Cost Curve*

output levels, followed by an extended range of constant returns to plant size with no common tendency for costs per unit to rise at higher output levels. The absence of diseconomies of size in these production processes does not necessarily mean that they would not occur if progressively larger plant sizes were employed. The expectation that costs per unit would increase with a larger plant would presumably cause the firm to operate two smaller plants rather than build one larger plant. Thus the absence of evidence indicating diseconomies of plant size does not mean that they would never occur; it simply means that the data base does not include any plant that is experiencing diseconomies (presumably because of the foresight of the decision makers).

8.3 COST FORECASTING

Cost forecasting is necessary whenever decisions involve cost levels in future periods, such as in bidding for contracts, make-or-buy problems, or any other decision with cost implications beyond the present period. Forecasting the level of costs for various output levels in future periods requires an assessment of the likely changes in the efficiency of the physical production process, plus changes in the prices of the factors involved in the production process. Changes in the efficiency of factors of production will change the shape of the total product curve associated with the production process. If factor prices are expected to change, the relationship between the total product curve and the total variable cost curve that is derived from the total product curve will change. Hence the change in future costs will be the result of two influences, which we shall consider in turn.

Changes in Factor Productivities

When considering the physical efficiency of the production process in future periods, we should expect the productivities of at least some of the factors of production to change as time passes. Machines and equipment, for example, should be expected to become progressively more efficient in terms of output per hour (or by some other criterion) because of the incorporation of technological advances into those machines. The increasing use of computer-controlled plant and equipment has allowed the productivity of capital equipment to increase substantially in recent years. Similarly, labor productivity may be expected to increase as time progresses because of the workers' higher level of education and increased familiarity with mechanical production processes. Conversely, changes in the attitude toward work or other sociological factors may lead us to expect reduced labor productivity in the future.

If trends have become apparent in the productivity of the factors of production, we may apply these trends as an estimate of future changes in the efficiency of the physical production process. This extrapolation of productivity trends should be modified by any changes in the productivity of any factor that may be expected to follow foreseen events of an irregular nature.

Labor productivity is typically measured as units of output per labor unit, and hence it takes the credit for increases in the productivity of capital factors such as machines and equipment. Labor productivity figures are therefore an amalgam of labor and capital productivity, and it may be quite difficult to separate the effects of each. The learning curve, introduced in Chapter 6 and discussed in a subsequent section of this chapter, is concerned with the increasing productivity of labor in conjunction with a particular set of equipment, with the familiar *ceteris paribus* requirement attached to that equipment (when interpreted strictly). Thus the average cost curve for a particular plant drifts downward as cumulative production increases. In practice, improvements are made to the firm's existing plant on an ongoing basis, so our estimates of the learning effect will capture both the increasing productivity of labor and capital.

Changes in Factor Prices

If the costs of all inputs increase over time in the *same proportion*, then the factor combination that is initially optimal for a particular output level will remain optimal, although it will cost more dollars. If all input prices increase at the same rate, the relative prices of the inputs will stay the same, and there will be no profit incentive to substitute away from one input toward another, and thus the optimal input proportions (capital-labor ratio in the simplest case) will remain the same. Costs in a future period will therefore be equal to today's costs plus the expected percentage increase in all costs.

If market forces in the factor markets are expected to be such that the price of one factor will rise *relative* to the prices of other factors, we should expect the firm to want to substitute away from this factor and toward other factors that become relatively cheaper as a result of that price change. Thus, if labor costs are expected to increase faster than capital costs in the future, we should expect the firm to want to substitute capital for labor to minimize the costs of particular output levels. Historically, we have seen this to be the general case, with the increasing automation of production processes. To the extent that this process is expected to continue in future periods, the firm should expect to achieve an increasingly capital-intensive production process in the future.

Forecasting factor price changes—or, more generally, forecasting the rate of inflation—requires techniques similar to those introduced in the appendix to Chapter 5 in the context of demand forecasting. Opinion surveys, trend projections, econometric models, and leading series and other barometric indicators may be used to predict the rate at which costs of production are expected to increase in future periods.[10] Expectations of events likely to influence prices, such as supply shortages or export embargoes, must be incorporated into the cost forecasts. Given a probability distribution associated with future cost levels, we may proceed on the basis of the expected value of cost levels in future periods to obtain a point forecast of future cost levels for pricing or for other decision problems.[11]

In a socioeconomic system where inflation is endemic and relatively low rates of inflation are welcomed for their beneficial impact on business confidence, we should expect a continuing increase in nominal prices of all factors in future periods. To the extent that the firm is able to pass inflationary cost increases along to its customers and maintain the ratio of its prices to costs, the *real* cost of the resources to the firm is unchanged. Thus a current decision involving future production and costs can be made on the basis of today's cost levels modified only for expected changes in factor price ratios and for any inflationary effects that are not expected to be passed along to the purchaser. We shall see in Chapter 10 that the practice of "markup pricing" ensures that the firm will maintain its *real* contribution margin per unit under inflationary conditions. If the price must be set now but costs will be incurred in future periods, as in competitive bidding and price quotations, the price must include the expected inflation factor so the firm's real contribution margin will be preserved.

Estimating the Learning Curve

As discussed in Chapter 6, the learning curve relates the cost per unit to the accumulated volume of production of a particular product. We expect that the productivity of the inputs will increase as those inputs "learn" the production process, such that the cost per unit will decrease as time passes and cumulative volume increases. Evidence indicates that the cost per unit (at a particular output rate per period in a particular plant) tends to decline by a fairly stable percentage each time the cumulative volume is doubled. This rate of learning is typically around 20%. That is, unit costs fall approximately 20% each time the cumulative output level increases by a factor of 2, 4, 8, 16, 32, 64, 128, and so

---

[10]See C. A. Dauten and L. M. Valentine, *Business Cycles and Forecasting*, 4th ed. (Cincinnati, Ohio: South-Western Publishing, 1974), chap. 18.

[11]Costs to be incurred in the future have a present value that is less than their future value, of course. Decisions to be made now, but which involve both costs and revenues incurred or received in future periods, should be evaluated in present-value terms.

TABLE 8-6.   Cost per Unit and Cumulative Volume Observations and Their Logarithms

Date of Observation	Cost per Unit (SAC)	Cumulative Volume (Q)	Log SAC (Y)	Log Q (X)
Sept. 30	9.00	150	0.9542	2.1761
Dec. 15	7.20	275	0.8573	2.4393
March 1	6.50	350	0.8129	2.5441
May 15	5.85	500	0.7672	2.6990

on. Note that for a constant output rate per period, this series of numbers indicates the number of periods before another 20% decline in unit costs is achieved. Thus the change in cost per unit between any two production periods, resulting from the learning effect, is most noticeable when production processes are just new, and it becomes virtually negligible as the production process matures.

The figures for the successive redoubling of output indicate that the learning curve is not a straight line; rather, cost per unit is an exponentially declining function of cumulative output. That is, the learning curve may be expressed as a power (or exponential) function of the form

$$SAC = aQ^b \qquad (8\text{-}3)$$

where Q represents cumulative volume levels, a represents the hypothetical cost of the first unit (or batch of units) produced, and b (typically a negative number) indicates the rate at which SAC will decline as output increases over time.

You will recall from Chapter 5 when we introduced regression analysis that a power function can be made linear by logarithmic transformation. Expressing our observed SAC and cumulative output values in logarithms, we postulate that[12]

$$\log SAC = \log a + b \log Q \qquad (8\text{-}4)$$

and use regression analysis to estimate the parameters a and b.

• EXAMPLE: Suppose that a manufacturing company has observed that the cost per unit of producing a particular product has declined as cumulative output increased, as shown in the first three columns of Table 8-6. The logarithms of SAC and Q are shown in the last two columns. Let us call log SAC the variable Y and log Q the variable X and postulate that $Y = \alpha + \beta X$. The calculations to find the parameters α and β, following the example worked through in Chapter 5, are shown in Table 8-7. Note that $\alpha = 1.7418$

[12]Your calculator may be preprogrammed to find the logarithm (and antilog) of any number. If not, find a set of log tables and think about getting a better calculator. The logs used here are to base 10. Using "natural" logs (to base e) will involve different log values but the same answers.

TABLE 8-7.   *Calculations for Regression Parameters for Learning Curve*

Y	X	XY	X^2
0.9542	2.1761	2.0764	4.7354
0.8573	2.4393	2.0912	5.9502
0.8129	2.5441	2.0681	6.4724
0.7672	2.6990	2.0707	7.2846
3.3916	9.8585	8.3064	24.4426

$$\bar{Y} = \frac{\Sigma Y}{n} = \frac{3.3916}{4} = 0.8479$$

$$\bar{X} = \frac{\Sigma Y}{n} = \frac{9.8585}{4} = 2.4646$$

$$\beta = \frac{n\Sigma XY - \Sigma X\Sigma Y}{n\Sigma X^2 - (\Sigma X)^2} = \frac{4(8.3064) - (9.8585)(3.3916)}{4(24.4426) - (9.8585)^2} = -0.3627$$

$$\alpha = \bar{Y} - \beta\bar{X} = 0.8479 - (-0.3627)2.4646 = 1.7418$$

represents log *a*. To find the parameter *a*, we must take the antilog of 1.7418, which is found to be 55.18. Thus the power function expressing the learning curve is estimated to be

$$SAC = 55.18Q^{-0.3627} \tag{8-5}$$

To forecast cost per unit at, for example, 1,000 units of cumulative volume, we simply substitute for $Q = 1,000$ in equation 8-5 as follows:

$$
\begin{aligned}
SAC &= 55.18(1,000^{-0.3627}) \\
&= 55.18(0.0816) \\
&= 4.50
\end{aligned}
$$

Thus, we expect SAC to decline to $4.50 per unit by the time cumulative volume reaches 1,000 units.[13]

• NOTE: Learning curves are often expressed in terms of the *percentage decline* in average costs for each consecutive doubling of cumulative volume. To find this percentage for

---

[13]To be confident in the prediction, we should calculate the coefficient of determination, the standard error of estimate, and the standard errors of the coefficients. In this example, $R^2 = 0.99$, and thus the standard errors will each be relatively small. The confidence intervals around the estimated SAC will accordingly be quite narrow.

the example here, we simply choose two output levels (one twice the other) and calculate the percentage by which SAC has declined. For example, estimating the SAC at 200 and 400 units of cumulative output from the learning curve, we have for 200 units

$$SAC = 55.18(200^{-0.3627}) = 8.076$$

and for 400 units

$$SAC = 55.18(400^{-0.3627}) = 6.281$$

Thus SAC at 400 units are

$$\frac{6.281}{8.076} \cdot \frac{100}{1} = 77.77\%$$

of what they were at 200 units, and we can see that there has been slightly more than a 22% decline in average costs as cumulative output doubled. We can predict that SAC will continue to decline by approximately 22% for the next and each subsequent doubling of the cumulative output level.

8.4 SUMMARY

Cost estimation is concerned with the levels of cost at various output levels of the firm's plant and with the relative costs of other plant sizes that are currently available to the firm. In the short-run situation we are concerned with the behavior of average variable and marginal costs, plus any other incremental costs that may be required because of the full utilization of some of the existing fixed-factor inputs. Long-run cost estimation involves the cost-per-unit levels of various plant sizes, given the current factor prices and state of technology.

Methods of short-run cost estimation discussed were simple extrapolation, gradient analysis, regression analysis of time-series data, and the engineering technique. Long-run cost possibilities may be estimated by using regression analysis of cross-section data or by applying the engineering technique to plants of various sizes. Empirical studies of cost estimation have frequently shown constant marginal costs in the short run and the absence of diseconomies of scale in the long run.

Cost forecasting requires the estimation of cost levels in future periods, in which factor productivities and prices may be different from today's levels. Trends in factor productivities that have become apparent over recent years may be used to project future changes in cost levels. Factor price changes that are real rather than simply monetary must also be forecast to obtain reliable indications of future cost levels for decision-making purposes.

The *learning curve*, when estimated for a particular production process, allows the cost per unit of future output levels to be predicted, based on the line of best fit to observed average cost data as cumulative volume increases. Production processes tend to become progressively more efficient in the production of an item as the experience in that production process accumulates. Unit costs tend to decline as a decreasing function of the total output, and a firm may use data collected on its past costs per unit to predict, or forecast, future costs per unit.

DISCUSSION QUESTIONS

8-1. Explain the dangers inherent in extrapolation of cost levels beyond the limits of the data base.

8-2. Why are cross-section data likely to be inappropriate for the estimation of short-run cost functions?

8-3. Why is it important to test several specifications of the cost function for their significance and goodness of fit?

8-4. Explain the engineering technique of cost estimation in terms of the production and cost theory of Chapter 6.

8-5. Outline some of the reasons why you might expect raw-material input, labor, and repairs and maintenance not to be simple linear functions of output.

8-6. Discuss the major problems that may arise in regression analysis of cross-section data to estimate the long-run average cost curve.

8-7. Explain why a linear relationship (with positive intercept and slope terms) between total costs (of different plants) and output levels (of different plants) means that the data exhibit economies of plant size.

8-8. Discuss the learning curve and the underlying reasons for its shape. What effect does this have on the firm's SAC curve?

8-9. If the productivities of all factors are expected to improve by the same proportion in the coming years, does this mean that there should be no factor substitution in future periods? Why or why not?

8-10. Summarize the issues involved in the forecasting of cost levels in an inflationary situation.

PROBLEMS AND SHORT CASES

8-1. The Rakita Racquets Company restrings tennis racquets, a business with a highly seasonal demand. The owner-manager, Ian Rakita, has kept a record of the number of racquets restrung and total variable costs for each of the past twelve months, as shown in the following table.

Over the past twelve months Mr. Rakita has experienced a constant price level for all variable factor inputs, and he feels that, because of the regular turnover of employees, employee productivity and materials wastage are neither better nor worse than they have ever been.

Month	Total Variable Cost ($)	Racquets Restrung (units)
June	35,490	9,000
July	42,470	11,150
August	48,980	12,600
September	52,530	13,050
October	37,480	10,650
November	33,510	8,100
December	31,850	5,700
January	27,860	4,900
February	22,160	3,050
March	19,520	1,850
April	25,960	3,850
May	32,980	7,000

(a) Plot the total variable cost levels against output. Draw a freehand line through those observations that appear to represent the line of best fit to the data.

(b) From your freehand TVC cost function, derive the AVC and MC curves for Mr. Rakita's racquet-stringing operation.

(c) Suppose that demand is expected to move from its present level of 7,000 units (May) to 10,000 units next month (June). What is the incremental cost of meeting this additional demand?

(d) Explain how you would set up the data provided to use regression analysis to find the line of best fit. What functional form would you use?

(e) Qualify your answers with any implicit or explicit assumptions that are involved in the above analysis.

8-2. The Minical Electronics Company produces pocket calculators that are sold to various retail outlets at a price of $20. Minical feels it can sell all it is able to produce at this price. The following table indicates the physical input requirements for several weekly output levels, as compiled by the production manager, Paula Wald.

Output (units)	500	650	800	950	1,100
Labor hours	1,000	1,200	1,400	1,600	1,800
Component "packages"	750	1,000	1,275	1,575	1,895
Power (kWh)	225	400	500	650	1,000
Maintenance hours	5	15	23	28	42
Machine hours	20	25	29	32	39

The hourly wage rate paid for assembly labor is $5.50. The cost of a "package" of components is $5.00 each. (These packages each contain all the components necessary to produce one calculator. Because of imperfections in some components and breakage due to rough handling, more than one package per calculator is typically required.) Power costs $0.038 per kilowatt-hour, machine hours are costed at $10 per hour, and maintenance hours cost $25 each.

(a) Using the engineering technique and gradient analysis, construct the AVC and MC curves implied by the physical input/output relationship and the prices of the inputs.

(b) At what output level are the variable inputs (combined) most efficient?

(c) What output level should the firm produce to maximize the contribution from this product?

8-3. The Patches Printing Company has recently expanded its product line to include a set of four-color Christmas and other Seasons Greetings cards. For the past three months it has been building up inventories and keeping records of total costs associated with the output in each month. These are as follows:

> August: 1,500 dozen cards, total cost $8,700
>
> September: 4,650 dozen cards, total cost $24,645
>
> October: 3,300 dozen cards, total cost $14,520

In the meantime PPC's market research group has conducted an investigation into the demand side of the year-end greeting card market and has arrived at the following regression equation and associated statistics:

$$Q = 8.41764 - 0.911P,$$

where Q is quantity demanded in thousands of dozens per month and P is price per dozen at the wholesale level. The coefficient of determination was 0.8652, the standard error of estimate was 0.6385, and the standard error of the coefficient was 0.3861.

(a) Estimate and plot on a graph the demand and marginal revenue curves PPC might expect to face.

(b) Plot on a graph your estimate of the average and marginal cost curves on which PPC is operating.

(c) What is the profit-maximizing price and output level you would recommend for PPC over the year-end sales period?

(d) What qualifications and assumptions underlie your analysis?

8-4. Scruples Footwear Design, Inc. manufactures and sells to distributors a designer "loafer" shoe. The total variable cost function for shoe production has been estimated using regression analysis on weekly observations collected over the past year to be:

$$TVC = \underset{(3.23)}{20Q} + \underset{(0.00343)}{0.00782Q^2},$$

Separately, the demand function for next week has been estimated as:

$$Q = \underset{(382.984)}{1,346.5494} - \underset{(3.29874)}{27.495188P}$$

where Q represents pairs of shoes and the numbers in parentheses represent the standard errors of the coefficients. The coefficients of determination for these two equations were 0.9638 and 0.9422, respectively. The standard error of estimate was 286.22 for the cost function and 30.967 for the demand function.

Scruples plans to adjust its price to the profit-maximizing level on the basis of the above cost and demand functions. Its current price is $32.50, it has been producing well below full capacity, and its inventories are at the desired level of 100 pairs. Scruples currently has several dozen wholesale customers, each selling to retail stores in different regions. Today the purchasing agent of a high-class clothing store chain has asked for a special deal for what would be Scruples' largest order ever—400 pairs of shoes. This represents a big opportunity for Scruples, since this chain would allow its shoes to reach a much wider market, and future sales will grow as a result. The purchasing agent has offered only $28 per pair, however, and says "take it or leave it." This window of opportunity is open for only one week—either the shoes are produced and delivered by the end of the next week or the chain will buy elsewhere, "now and in the future" says the purchasing agent.

(a) From the cost function provided, and the information that fixed costs are $2,000 per week, calculate and plot the per unit cost curves that Scruples faces.

(b) What are the profit-maximizing price and output levels, in the absence of the chainstore deal?

(c) What is the contribution from the chainstore deal, presuming that Scruples adds the 400 pairs on top of its profit-maximizing output?

(d) What do you recommend that Scruples do, with respect to their proposed price change, and concerning the chainstore deal?

(e) What assumptions and qualifications underlie your recommendation?

8-5. A large new stadium is to be built in your city and contracts are being offered to manufacture certain items. Your company produces molded plastic items and is very interested in obtaining contracts to supply the seats for spectators. You have had substantial experience in making these hard plastic seats, ranging from garden furniture to elegant apartment furniture and including two previous contracts for hinged stadium-type seats. The major contractor for the stadium has determined that it will pay $12.50 per seat in batches of 5,000 seats. Several companies are expected to accept one or more of these contracts for 5,000 seats each. Your problem is to decide how many of these contracts your company should undertake.

Your cost estimating department has produced the following physical production requirements for various output levels.

Output Level (units)	Time to Complete (weeks)	Labor Input (hours)	Materials Required (kg)
5,000	2	500	11,000
10,000	3	1,053	23,000
15,000	4	1,724	34,500
20,000	5	2,667	54,000
25,000	6	4,167	77,500

Labor costs $10 per hour, and materials cost $2.50 per kilogram. Variable overheads are reliably estimated to be very close to 50% of labor cost per unit.

Rather than take these contracts, your company could instead devote its attention to making patio chairs for major chain stores and mail-order companies. Your company regularly produces these chairs whenever more lucrative contracts are not forthcoming and adds them to inventory for periodic supply to the chain stores and mail-order firms at a flat rate of $4.50 per chair. In a representative week you can produce 8,000 of these chairs with the following cost structure:

Cost Item	Cost per Week
Labor	$ 5,330
Raw materials	18,000
Variable overheads	2,670
Fixed overhead allocation	7,360

Determine how many contracts (for 5,000 seats each) your company should accept. Explain your answer fully and state explicitly any assumptions or qualifications you feel are necessary.

8-6. The Argus Boat Company manufactures aluminum paddles for use in canoes and small boats. Its demand for this product fluctuates from month to month depending on orders received. ABC manufactures to order only and ships the product immediately, since it has very little space for inventory accumulation. Its regular price is $10.00 per unit. Based on past demand, ABC has compiled a probability distribution of demand for next month, as shown below.

Today ABC's top salesman has asked the sales manager to authorize a special deal to a new customer: 2,000 paddles at $9.00 each. The sales manager in turn has asked the production manager for an estimate of costs per unit and has received the production data shown below. This data was derived by a careful analysis of the input requirements for various output levels and is kept in this form because costs of the inputs frequently change. The production manager advises that input costs are currently $12 per hour for labor; $3.25 per kilogram for materials; and $0.035 per kilowatt-hour for electric energy. He further advises that they are expected to remain at these levels over the next month, during which time the special batch would be scheduled if the order is accepted.

Demand Data

Quantity Demanded per Month	Probability
5,000	0.10
6,000	0.15
7,000	0.20
8,000	0.25
9,000	0.20
10,000	0.10

Production Data

Units of Output	Labor (hours)	Materials (kg)	Energy (kWh)
1,000	477	500	4,885.71
2,000	807	1,000	7,600.00
3,000	1,010	1,500	9,857.14
4,000	1,140	2,000	12,000.00
5,000	1,224	2,520	13,485.71
6,000	1,280	3,050	15,071.43
7,000	1,337	3,600	17,314.29
8,000	1,478	4,180	19,400.00
9,000	1,800	4,690	22,214.29
10,000	2,407	5,320	23,600.00
11,000	3,304	5,970	25,700.00
12,000	4,434	6,660	28,200.00

In addition to the regular production costs, the special batch of 2,000 paddles will require a $3,000 setup cost for the customer's insignia to be imprinted in the metal and another $3,000 for extraordinary packing and shipping costs. Also, the salesman has just submitted his expense account, which contains $1,000 in expenses associated with a special trip to see this potential new client and to bring negotiations to their present stage. ABC's overhead costs are expected to be $24,000 next month.

(a) Derive the marginal and average cost curves from the data given and show these on a graph.

(b) Advise the sales manager about the appropriate decision, giving full supporting reasoning and calculations.

(c) State any qualifications and reservations you have regarding your recommendation.

8-7. The Done Brown Cookie Company produces high-nutrition Brownie biscuits which it sells to retailers for $22.55 per carton of twenty-four packets. Although demand for Brownies is not seasonal, it nonetheless fluctuates during the year. Over the past nine months of operations demand has varied between 6,000 and 10,000 cartons per month, but there is a general growth trend in sales.

The vice-president of corporate planning, Mr. Black, has put forward the proposal that the firm expand its present plant. Having investigated the financial situation of Done Brown, he suggests that the cash that the directors are considering paying out as an extra dividend would be put to better use if invested in plant expansion and renovation. He contends that running a larger plant at half capacity would be more economical than running the present plant.

The vice-president of production, Mr. Green, on the other hand, asserts that the plant is running smoothly and that sales forecasts in no way indicate that a larger plant is necessary at this time. Mr. Black, though, seems to have a convincing argument, having procured the cost figures for a competing brownie manufacturer who has a larger plant than does Done Brown. He suggests that Done Brown should model its plant after that of the competitor.

A task force has been assigned to study the question of expansion. It is to analyze costs for both firms, analyze the sales forecast, as shown below, and submit its findings to the board of directors, along with a recommended plan of action. You are the head of the task force. Is Mr. Black correct? Should Done Brown expand its plant? Support your recommendation with discussion of the issues involved. Defend any assumptions that you feel are necessary.

**Sales Forecast: Average
Sales per Month
over the Next Year**

Volume	Probability
8,000	0.05
9,000	0.20
10,000	0.50
11,000	0.20
12,000	0.05

Done Brown's Production Costs: Past Nine Months

Month	Output Level (cartons)	Materials ($)	Direct Labor ($)	Overhead ($)
April	6,000	88,500	21,000	15,200
May	7,500	107,250	24,000	17,450
June	6,500	94,900	22,100	15,950
July	8,000	113,200	24,800	18,200
August	7,000	101,150	23,100	16,700
September	8,500	118,825	28,475	18,950
October	10,000	148,500	45,000	21,200
November	9,000	126,850	32,400	19,700
December	9,500	136,075	37,525	20,450

Competitor's Production Costs: Past Nine Months

Month	Output Level (cartons)	Materials ($)	Direct Labor ($)	Overhead ($)
April	10,000	140,000	30,500	24,350
May	8,500	127,075	27,025	22,175
June	9,000	133,000	28,550	22,900
July	10,500	144,375	32,025	25,075
August	9,500	136,565	29,875	23,625
September	11,000	151,250	33,550	25,800
October	12,500	173,750	47,875	27,975
November	11,500	158,125	36,675	26,525
December	12,000	165,600	41,600	27,250

8-8. The Victoria Lawrence Frame Company manufactures aluminum picture frames for sale to retail buyers. VLF produces twelve different lengths of frames, and users must buy two packages of the desired lengths in order to have the complete frame. These twelve different products, ranging from 4 inches to 48 inches, each have different material costs but the other variable costs are invariant with respect to frame length. Wholesale prices of these products vary from $2.00 a package to $16.00 a package.

VLF's clientele is composed of several dozen retail stores which sell these frames as well as prints, art supplies and a variety of other products. Their orders arrive monthly and range from 50 units to 1000 units, but average between 200 and 300 units per client. Since these orders typically comprise some units of all twelve frame lengths, VLF has found that its average price per unit is $8.00, and uses this figure in its revenue calculations for simplicity. Similarly its cost figures are looked at in terms of the cost of an average unit, although the smaller frames actually cost less and the larger frames actually cost more than this average.

The monthly production costs of VLF can be derived from the input-output matrix provided in Table 1, and the knowledge that fixed overhead costs are $3,000 per month. The factor costs are $10 per hour for labor; $5 per kilogram of materials; $0.05 per kilowatt hour of energy; and $15 per hour of indirect labor (variable overhead).

TABLE 1   Input-Output Matrix

| Output Units | Input Units | | | |
	Labor (hours)	Materials (kg.)	Energy (kwH)	Var. O/hd (hours)
1,000	400	100	4,000	20
2,000	700	200	9,500	35
3,000	880	300	16,000	60
4,000	990	420	30,000	100
5,000	1,450	560	43,000	170
6,000	2,850	720	63,000	250

The demand for VLF's frames varies from month to month without any marked seasonality. A probability distribution of demand for the next month has been derived on the basis of past experience, and is shown in Table 2.

VLF has recently been approached by Georgian Galleries, a local retailer with whom VLF has done no business to date. Georgian wants the following deal: 2,000 units (of various sizes but involving the average product mix), at a 15% discount below regular prices, to be delivered during the next month.

TABLE 2   Probability Distribution of Demand

Demand	Probabilities
1,000	0.15
2,000	0.25
3,000	0.40
4,000	0.15
5,000	0.05

(a) Calculate and plot the firm's AVC, MC, and SAC curves. At what output level are the variable inputs as a group most efficient? Comment on the diminishing returns which are evident in these data.

(b) What is your best estimate of the contribution to be gained or lost by filling the Georgian order on their terms? Advise VLF whether or not to accept the order from Georgian.

(c) State explicitly the assumptions and qualifications which underlie your recommendation.

8-9. The Whizbang Electronic Games Company has been producing a particular machine for sale to pinball arcades for about a year. At first its costs per unit were relatively high, but these declined as total production grew, as shown below:

Total Production Since Start-up	Average Cost of Production per Unit
300	$1,000
500	870
1,000	700
1,800	540
2,400	520

(a) Estimate the learning curve for this firm, assuming that the relationship is best represented by unit costs as a power function of total production.

(b) What is the percentage of learning implied by the data?

(c) Forecast the average cost per unit when total production reaches 3,000 units.

(d) What qualifications and assumptions underlie your analysis and prediction?

8-10. The Fairway Golf Cart Company entered the American market in 1981 after production began in its Florida plant. Initially, the output rate was low, but it soon picked up as the workers learned their jobs and found ways to save time, materials, and energy in the production process. Suppose that the assembly costs during the first year were as follows and that the variable factors will continue to become more productive as total output continues to increase.

Total Units Produced	Assembly Cost per Unit
1,000	$1,582
2,000	1,215
3,000	1,095
4,000	975
5,000	900

(a) Forecast the assembly cost per unit for each vehicle when total output reaches 10,000 units and 20,000 units.

(b) How well does the learning curve fit the data points? What are the 95% confidence limits to your predictions?

(c) What other qualifications should you attach to your predictions?

SUGGESTED REFERENCES AND FURTHER READING

ABERNATHY, W. J., and K. WAYNE. "Limits of the Learning Curve," *Harvard Business Review*, 52 (September-October 1974), pp. 109–19.

DAUTEN, C. A., and L. M. VALENTINE. *Business Cycles and Forecasting* (4th ed.), chaps. 10 and 18. Cincinnati, Ohio: South-Western Publishing, 1974.

FUDENBERG, D., and J. TIROLE. "Learning by Doing and Market Performance," *Bell Journal of Economics*, 14 (Autumn 1983), pp. 522–30.

HARPAZ, G. "Learning by Dominant Firm," *Managerial and Decision Economics*, 6 (March 1985), pp. 59–63.

JOHNSTON, J. *Statistical Cost Analysis*. New York: McGraw-Hill Book Company, 1960.

MCGUIGAN, J. R., and R. C. MOYER. *Managerial Economics* (2nd ed.), pp. 272–302. St. Paul, Minn.: West Publishing Company, 1979.

MCINTYRE, E. B. "Cost-Volume-Profit Analysis Adjusted for Learning," *Management Science*, 24 (October 1977), pp. 149–160.

NELSON, C. R. *Applied Time Series Analysis for Managerial Forecasting*. Oakland, Calif.: Holden Day, 1973.

PEGELS, C. C. "Start-up or Learning Curves—Some New Approaches," *Decision Sciences*, 7 (October 1976), pp. 705–13.

SIMON, J. L. *Applied Managerial Economics*, chap. 13. Englewood Cliffs, N.J.: Prentice-Hall, Inc., 1975.

SPENCE, A. M. "The Learning Curve and Competition," *Bell Journal of Economics,* 12 (Spring 1981), pp. 49–70.

STIGLER, G. J. "The Economies ot Scale," *Journal of Law and Economics,* 1 (October 1958).

WOMER, N. K., and J. W. PATTERSON. "Estimation and Testing of Learning Curves," *Journal of Business and Economic Statistics,* 1 (October 1983), pp. 265–72.

Empirical Case 7

ESTIMATING THE COST OF SERVICE FOR AN ELECTRIC UTILITY

Regulated industries must pay particular attention to their cost structure. Estimates of their operating costs must be presented to rate-making authorities in support of any request by the regulated firm for a rate increase. As a consequence, these industries rely on rate researchers to empirically estimate the cost of providing their services.

As one would expect, the estimated cost of service has many components. Economic theory states that the short-run cost of providing a good or service consists of both variable and fixed costs. From a practical standpoint, the rate researcher attempts to operationalize these classifications. First, there are explicit variable costs of providing the product. These include all expenses directly related to the production of the good or service, such as labor, energy, and raw-materials expenditures. Second, there are fixed costs, including depreciation expenses, taxes, and capital investment expenditures. The standard formula for cost of service (COS) can be represented by the following:

$$COS = TVC + DEP + TAXES + R \cdot BASE$$

where

$$
\begin{aligned}
TVC &= \text{total variable costs,} \\
DEP &= \text{depreciation expenses,} \\
TAXES &= \text{all appropriate tax expenditures,} \\
R &= \text{allowed rate of return, and} \\
BASE &= \text{capital investment expenditures required to produce the service}
\end{aligned}
$$

The electric utility industry has been the subject of intense investigation regarding its cost of service. Recall from introductory economics that electric utilities are natural monopolies. As such, an unregulated price of electricity would be detrimental to society. The utility would earn economic profits at the expense of consumers, and the presence of extensive economies of scale would prohibit entry by potential competitors. The solution to this problem is for the government to regulate the price such that the natural monopolist earns just a normal rate of return. That is, revenues of providing the service are controlled to be exactly equal to the cost of providing the service.

To illustrate how a rate researcher might estimate the cost of service for a proposed utility in the New England region, you collect the following data on thirteen regional plants for existing utilities. To hold technology constant, you restrict the data to include only fossil-fueled steam-electric plants as opposed to hydro or nuclear plants.

For simplicity, the proposed utility will operate in the same region and will produce the average amount of output, incur the average amount of depreciation expense ($10 million) and taxes ($7 million), and undertake the average amount of capital investment ($250 million). The firm will be allowed to earn a 10% return on its investment.

The only component of the cost-of-service formula not known is the amount of variable cost that will be incurred. To estimate the variable costs of providing the good or service, you specify the average variable cost equation as a quadratic function of output, given as follows:

$$AVC = a0 + a_1Q + a_2Q^2$$

where AVC is the average variable production costs and is the sum of labor and fuel expenditures divided by output.

Estimate the preceding AVC function with the plant-level data given in Table 1 using least-squares regression analysis. Use your results to answer the following questions.

TABLE 1

State	Plant	Output	Labor Expenditures	Fuel Expenditures
Connecticut	Norwalk Harbor	1880.9	6,350	88,590
	Bridgeport Harbor	2635.6	13,431	131,806
	New Haven Harbor	2615.9	6,239	123,242
Maine	Graham Station	25.2	717	1,087
	Walter F. Wyman	2029.5	11,688	107,477
Massachusetts	Mystic	4147.7	23,056	190,474
	New Boston	3512.9	20,744	158,973
	Kendall	191.8	700	14,807
	Cannon Street	117.6	2,696	7,355
	Brayton Point	9203.2	21,922	250,350
	Salem Harbor	3753.5	22,735	141,368
	B. F. Cleary	284.3	3,063	13,455
New Hampshire	Merrimack	3272.7	8,598	65,390

Output = power generation (million kilowatt-hours)

Labor expenditures = total production expense, exclusive of fuel ($000)

Fuel expenditure = fuel production expense ($000)

Source: Historical Plant Costs and Annual Production Expenses for Selected Electric Plants 1984, Energy Information Administration.

QUESTIONS

1. Does your estimated AVC function conform to economic theory? Explain.
2. Use the parameter estimates to obtain estimates of TVC.
3. Given your total variable cost estimation results, determine the estimated cost of service for this proposed utility.
4. Given this cost of service estimate and assuming that the utility sells the average amount of output, what is the price per kilowatt-hour the authorities will allow this firm to charge?

Empirical Case 8

ESTIMATING THE COST FUNCTION FOR FREIGHT TRUCKING

In the United States, the 1980s have been called the decade of deregulation. Transportation industries witnessed a major relaxation of government controls as part of this trend toward a restoration of market forces to the business sector. In particular, regulation of entry conditions and price levels have been removed in both air and land transport industries to let the market determine the number of competitors and the price/quantity allocation of services.

An interesting outcome associated with this process is the altered decision making of high-cost firms formerly protected under regulation from potential entrants. Once entry restrictions were relaxed, these firms had to consider the threat of entry by more cost-efficient firms and the associated decline in market price. Without significant cost reduction, these firms would face short-run losses and eventually exit the market in the long run. Consequently, an accurate assessment of cost conditions is of particular importance in the post deregulatory market.

TABLE 1

Firm	Variable Cost	Output
1	102,813	201,953
2	196,121	377,940
3	296,416	979,267
4	226,356	571,714
5	176,163	340,608
6	450,666	1,413,807
7	607,082	2,071,861
8	624,680	2,195,352
9	636,133	1,670,195
10	222,885	1,466,024
11	378,446	1,367,596
12	579,696	1,701,125

Variable cost = total operating expenses, measured in $000

Output = ton-miles, measured in thousands

Source: All data are given in the 1983 edition of *Trinc's Blue Book of the Trucking Industry,* published by Trinc Transportation Consultants.

You are interested in assessing the short-run relationship between price and quanity supplied for the general freight trucking industry in the deregulated period. To accomplish this, you estimate the industry's short-run cost structure using the following quadratic form:

$$AVC = a0 + a_1Q + a_2Q^2$$

where AVC represents average variable production costs and Q is a measure of output. Table 1 presents the data you have collected for the general freight industry. Use this data to estimate the short-run cost structure. Then use your results to answer the following questions.

QUESTIONS

1. Does the estimated average variable cost function conform to economic theory? Explain.
2. Use the resulting parameter estimates to obtain estimates of AVC and MC.
3. Graph your estimates of the AVC and MC Curves. At what level of Q does AVC reach a minimum? What is the economic interpretation of the output level?
4. What is the market-determined price per ton-mile if a firm supplied the amount of output found in question 3? Explain what this price means.

Empirical Case 9

ESTIMATING THE LEARNING CURVE FOR FAX MACHINES

In recent years the growth of facsimile machines has been substantial. For example, U.S. fax unit sales have grown from 63,900 in 1982 to approximately 785,000 in 1988. Not surprisingly, the average price of a fax machine declined dramatically over this same period. The average price of a fax machine in 1988 was approximately $2,200 compared to $4,400 in 1982.

Industry analysts predict that in the near future fax machines will be available at prices between $200 to $500 per unit. These same analysts suggest that unit production and sales for the U.S. will be approximately 1 million yearly.

In an attempt to explain this market, you propose that a major reason for these price declines is the reduction in short-run production costs associated with the increasing production level of fax machines. In other words, you believe that production of this commodity is subject to a learning phenomenon. This learning effect materializes because of the repetitive nature of the production process. For example, as workers become more familiar with production of the fax and as improved manufacturing methods are introduced and accepted, input productivity rises, causing a decline in per-unit input costs.

You decide to investigate this learning curve effect and begin by collecting the data for the U.S. facsimile market shown in Table 1.

TABLE 1: *Facsimile Machine Data*

Year	Real Per-Unit Cost	Annual Production
1982	$3,666.67	63,900
1983	3,416.66	70,000
1984	3,125.00	100,000
1985	2,583.33	150,000
1986	2,166.67	175,000
1987	1,833.33	400,000
1988	1,787.50	785,000

Source: Based on an article entitled "Fax: Faster than a speeding Fed Ex Truck," Ronald Rosenberg, *Boston Globe,* June 12, 1988.

The model of the learning curve effect that you use is as follows:

$$SAC = aQ^b$$

where SAC represents real per-unit costs, Q is the cumulative production of facsimile machines, and a and b are parameters to be estimated by a statistical software package.

Estimate this model and use your estimates of the learning curve phenomena to answer the following questions.

QUESTIONS:

1. Do your results support the existence of a learning effect in the production of facsimile machines?
2. What is the percentage decline in real per-unit costs when production doubles from 500,000 units to 1 million units?
3. How will future increases in fax sales affect competing companies such as Federal Express? Focus your discussion on sales, prices, and profits.
4. What will be the future impact of increased fax sales on complementary industries such as the telephone company? Focus your discussion on sales, prices, and profits.

Chapter 9

MODELS OF THE FIRM'S PRICING DECISION

EXECUTIVE SUMMARY

Economists have developed a wide variety of models of the firm's pricing decision. These models typically seek to explain the manager's choice of price, and the related output level, on the basis of profit maximization or the pursuit of some other objective. These **pricing models typically bring together the demand curves derived from models of consumer behavior with the cost curves derived from models of the firm's production process.**

The first thing to learn about the theory of the firm is that **there is no single theory of the firm. Rather, there are literally dozens of models of the firm,** each representing a different theory which is reflected in the assumptions that underlie the model under consideration. Each model is designed to explain a firm's pricing decision, or to predict a firm's pricing decision, under a specific set of demand and cost conditions.

Models of the firm's pricing decision can be characterized by their underlying assumptions. **Each model has four structural assumptions and three behavioral assumptions.** The structural assumptions define the demand and cost conditions facing the firm, while the behavioral assumptions define how the firm is expected to behave in its market situation as it pursues its stated objective.

In this chapter we first discuss the seven assumptions underlying any model of the firm's pricing decision, and then proceed to an examination of the traditional microeconomic models of pure or **perfect competition** and the imperfectly competitive markets of **monopoly, monopolistic competition, and oligopoly.** Most business firms operate under imperfect competition, so the greater part of the chapter is concerned with models of oligopoly and monopoly that embody different structural and behavioral scenarios. These include the **kinked demand curve model, conscious parallelism, price leadership, sales maximization, limit pricing, and the satisficing model of the firm's pricing decision.**

9.1 THE FOUR BASIC MARKET FORMS

The Seven Assumptions of a Model of the Firm

Traditional price theory delineates four basic market forms, namely pure competition, monopolistic competition, oligopoly, and monopoly. Pure competition consists of many firms producing identical products in an environment of full information—all firms know where to buy the cheapest inputs, and all consumers know where to buy the cheapest products. Firms operating in pure competition are called *price takers*, because the price of their product is determined by the market forces of demand and supply. Excess demand for the product will drive the market price up, and excess supply will drive the market price down. Since all firms are selling exactly the same product and consumers have full information about all firms' prices, a firm will sell nothing if it raises its price above the market price. Conversely, the firm has no incentive to reduce its price below the market price, since it is small relative to the size of the market and can sell all that it wants to at the market price.

The other three market forms are characterized by product differentiation, and the state of information is not complete. In fact, lack of information may be one of the bases for consumers' differentiating between the products of rival suppliers. Monopolistic competition consists of many firms with slightly differentiated products. Oligopoly consists of a relatively small number of firms whose products are typically substantially differentiated from each others' through some combination of product design, promotional efforts, and place of sale.[1] Monopoly consists of a single seller of a product that has no close substitutes; thus the product is highly differentiated from the products of all other firms.

Firms operating in monopolistic competition, oligopoly, and monopoly are called *price makers*, because they can adjust the price of their product up or down to pursue their objectives. The firm's ability to set prices derives from the differentiation of its product. Each firm can raise its price to some extent without losing all its customers, since the remaining customers believe that the product is worth the extra price being asked.

In Table 9-1 we show the four traditional market forms in terms of the underlying structural and behavioral assumptions. Note that the essential differences between the four market forms arise from assumptions 1 and 4. Thus it is the number of firms and whether or not the firms' products are differentiated that essentially characterize the firms into the four traditional market forms. The three types of price-maker markets are each characterized by differentiated products. Assumption 7 also differs across the market types, but note that this

---

[1]An oligopoly could, in theory, have undifferentiated products. In practice a pure oligopoly is hard to find. Identical products means that all attributes of the product are identical across firms. Thus not only the attributes of the firms' core product, such as steel, but all other (peripheral) attributes of the product, including the convenience of purchasing, the delivery schedules, the product warranty, and the interpersonal relationship between the purchasing agent and the salesperson, must be equal across all firms. Even if the core product is exactly the same, it is unlikely that the buyer will not find one seller a little more convenient or a little more pleasant to buy from. The existence of imperfect information may make the buyer think there is a difference between the sellers even if there is not. If the buyer has any preference for one seller over another when prices are equal, then the products are differentiated as far as the buyer is concerned.

difference is related to assumption 1. When there are many firms in the market, each firm can safely expect no reactions from rivals following the adjustment of its strategic variable, since the effects of this adjustment are spread over many rivals, making an insignificant impact on each one. Conversely, in an oligopoly, where there are relatively few rivals, the firm should expect its strategic actions to have a noticeable impact on the sales of each of its rivals, and therefore expect them to retaliate in some situations. Monopolists expect no reactions because there are no rivals in their markets.

TABLE 9-1.   *Market Forms and the Seven Assumptions Underlying Them*

	PRICE TAKERS	PRICE MAKERS		
	Pure Competition	Monopolistic Competition	Oligopoly	Monopoly
Structural assumptions:				
1. Number of sellers	Many	Many	Few	One
	Underlying the number of sellers is an assumption concerning barriers to entry. The absence of barriers to the entry of new firms means that there will be many firms in the market. Substantial barriers to entry in oligopoly markets limit the rivals to a few. Insurmountable barriers to entry allow the monopolist to remain the only seller of its product.			
2. Cost conditions	For all models we can assume diminishing returns in production in the short run, causing MC to rise. This is not important in oligopoly and monopoly, where constant or declining MC may prevail.			
3. Number of buyers	For all models we assume many buyers, so the dominant force in the pricing decision will not be one, or a few, strong buyers. Variants of the oligopoly and monopoly models, known as oligopsony and monopsony, cover the strong-buyer situation.			
4. Demand conditions	Identical substitutes	Very similar substitutes	Close substitutes	No substitutes
Behavioral assumptions:				
5. Objective function	For all models we initially assume short-run profit maximization. This may be inappropriate for oligopoly, where time horizons typically extend beyond the short run, since high short-run profits may induce the entry of new competitors to cause a more competitive market for the firms later in the planning period.			
6. Strategic variable	In all models we assume the firm can adjust price and quantity supplied, although once the price is in equilibrium, pure competitors will adjust only their quantity supplied. Firms in the other three market types may also adjust their promotional efforts, product design, and distribution channels.			
7. Expectation of rivals' reactions	None, since there are many firms in both these market types. Firms are all small relative to their market, so their actions will go unnoticed by rivals.		Rivals may ignore or match the firm's actions, depending on what serves their objectives.	None, since there are no close substitutes for the monopolist's product.

In managerial economics we are concerned with the firm's pricing problem—namely, to set its price at the level that will best serve its objective. Consequently, we are more concerned with the price-making models than with the price-taker model of pure competition. Nevertheless, the firm may face conditions approaching pure competition in some situations, so a quick review of the pure competition model is appropriate.

9.2 PRICE TAKERS

Price Determination in Pure Competition

In pure competition the equilibrium price is determined by the interaction of the market forces of supply and demand. There are many buyers and many sellers, each too small relative to the market to influence directly the general price level. In aggregate, however, their demand and supply decisions lead to the determination of the equilibrium market price. The market demand curve is negatively sloping, and the market supply curve is positively sloping, as shown in the left-hand part of Figure 9-1. If, at a particular price level, such as P_1, supply exceeds demand, there will be downward pressure on prices because of the desire of firms to reduce inventories to preferred levels. Each firm reduces price to clear its excess inventories and thus avoid costs associated with holding those excess inventories. Since many firms will be independently reducing their prices, the market price falls. One firm alone reducing its price would not cause a reduction in the general price level, since it could sell all it wishes at the lower price without any competing firm suffering a significant loss of sales because of the assumption that firms are small relative to the market. But the combined effect of many firms reducing their prices causes a significant loss of sales to those competitors that have *not* reduced their prices. This in turn causes those firms to suffer excess inventory, and they too will be motivated to reduce price.

Thus excess market supply leads to a reduction in the market price. The lower price causes an increase in the quantity demanded and at the same time causes the firm to be willing to supply a somewhat reduced amount. Prices will continue to fall until finally supply equals demand, as shown in Figure 9-1.

Conversely, if there is excess demand at a particular price level, such as at P_2 in Figure 9-1, there will be upward pressure on prices because of the willingness of some buyers to pay more than the market price rather than go without the product. Firms will find they can raise their price slightly yet still sell all they wish to produce, since although other firms may be maintaining their price at P_2, those firms are unable to supply all the buyers willing to purchase at price P_2, and some of the remaining buyers are willing to pay more than P_2 to obtain the product. The firms setting price P_2 then see that they too can ask for a higher price, and the combined effect is for the market price to move upward. As it does, the quantity demanded is reduced as some buyers drop out of the market, and the quantity that suppliers are willing to put on sale increases until finally supply equals demand and no further incentive exists to raise prices. The price P^* in Figure 9-1 is thus the equilibrium price and is determined not by the actions of any one firm but by the combined effects of individual firms' actions.

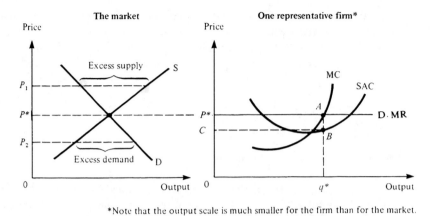

*Note that the output scale is much smaller for the firm than for the market.

FIGURE 9-1.   Price and Output Determination in Pure Competition

Given the market price, the purely competitive firm must decide what output level to produce to maximize its profits. Profits are maximized when the difference between total revenues and total costs is greatest. Since the firm is small relative to its market, it can sell all it wants to at the market price, and its demand curve is therefore a horizontal line at the market price level, as shown in the right-hand part of Figure 9-1. Since the price is constant regardless of the number of units sold, marginal revenue is equal to price, and the demand and marginal revenue curves are coextensive. The short-run average cost (SAC) and marginal cost (MC) curves are added to the firm's graph, and we note that MC = MR at output level q^*. To maximize its profit the firm chooses the output level q^*, where marginal cost rises to equal marginal revenue. Producing one more unit of output would cost more than the revenue it would generate (MC > MR), and producing fewer units of output would save less cost than the revenue foregone (MC < MR). The firm's profit can be visualized as the rectangle P^*ABC, since profit is the product of the price-cost margin ($P^* - C$) times the output level $0q^*$.[2]

• NOTE: Do purely competitive markets exist? There are certainly some markets that have many buyers and many sellers. The most difficult condition to find is that of identical products. All buyers must regard all products from the competing suppliers as identical in all respects. Buyers cannot have personal preferences for particular sellers, nor have differing expectations of quality or after-sales service, nor find it more or less convenient to buy from one seller rather than from another. The package of attributes constituting the product must be viewed as identical in all respects.

---

[2]Note that the purely competitive firm has no incentive either to raise or lower its price away from the market price. If it raised its price above P^* it would sell no units at all, since all its buyers would seek the product from other sellers at the market price. Lowering the price would also lead to reduced profits, since the firm would sell fewer units (because a lower *MR* will cut MC at a smaller output level) at a lower price, without a commensurate reduction in costs per unit. Only when there is excess market demand will the firm have a profit incentive to raise price, and only when there is excess market supply (and there is a cost of holding excess inventories) will the firm wish to reduce its price.

- EXAMPLE: Perhaps the only market in which this condition is fulfilled is the stock exchange, at which hundreds of buyers and sellers meet anonymously (through an agent) to buy and sell a company's stock. Each share in the company has the same rights, benefits, and obligations attached (for each class of shares), and no buyer is likely to care about the identity of the previous owner. In fact, the theory of finance is based on the pure competition model.

Applications of the purely competitive model as an explanatory or predictive device will be inappropriate to the extent that the seven assumptions involved do not accord with the reality of the situation being explained or predicted. The major value of the purely competitive model is probably as a pedagogical model. It allows the theory of the firm to be introduced in a relatively simple context, free of the complications introduced by product differentiation and fewness of buyers or sellers. It thus forms a basis on which we can build an understanding of more complex theories of the pricing behavior of firms.

9.3 PRICE MAKERS—NO REACTIONS EXPECTED

Monopolists and monopolistic competitors can safely ignore the reactions of their rivals, in the former case because there are no close rivals, and in the latter case because the firms are each small relative to the market and are expected to have insignificant impact on each others' sales. Oligopolists may ignore the probable reactions of rivals, but they do so at their own risk. The sales and profits of oligopolists are interdependent, or mutually dependent—the competitive actions of one have a significant impact on the sales of the others and may provoke a competitive reaction. Recognition of mutual dependence (RMD) means that the firms recognize and take into account the probable reactions of rivals before undertaking a competitive strategy. We shall consider oligopoly pricing (with RMD) in the next section. We shall not consider non-RMD oligopoly pricing at all, because of the space constraints of this text and because the topic has limited relevance to managerial economics.[3]

Monopoly Markets

Monopolies exist when there is a single seller of a product in a particular market. They persist over time if the entry of new firms is prevented by *barriers to entry*. Barriers to entry are additional costs that a potential entrant must incur before gaining entry to a market. These costs may arise because the existing firm controls an essential raw material, the best location, necessary information, the right to produce the product (such as a patent or a government mandate), and so on. Consumer loyalty to the existing firm poses

---

[3]These myopic oligopoly pricing models, such as the Cournot and Edgeworth models, do have some pedagogical value, since they demonstrate quite forcefully the implications of myopia in oligopolistic markets. In short, failure to recognize mutual dependence leads to the downward progression of prices to a price floor, as in the Cournot model, or to the fluctuation of prices between a price floor and a price ceiling, as in the Edgeworth model. A particularly thorough treatment of these classical models of duopoly (two sellers) under conditions of unrecognized mutual dependence is found in A. Koutsoyiannis. *Modern Microeconomics*, 2nd ed. (London: Macmillan, Inc., 1979), pp. 216–33.

a barrier to a potential entrant, since the new firm would have to spend substantial amounts on advertising to offset it. In some cases the entry cost is infinite (where it is impossible to acquire the necessary input or permission to produce), and in other cases the cost is simply high enough to prevent a potential entrant from making a profit in the foreseeable future.

Some monopolies are *natural monopolies*, in the sense that the market would inevitably be served by a monopoly even if some other market form were to exist initially. This situation occurs when the monopolist's output capacity is large relative to the market demand. In terms of the long-run average cost (LAC) curve and the monopolist's demand curve, the quantity demanded at the monopolist's price would occur where the LAC curve is still falling. Thus a single firm will benefit from economies of plant size by expanding to supply the entire quantity demanded. If an oligopoly initially existed, the firms would have a profit incentive to merge with (or take over) each other to form a monopoly and subsequently benefit from the economies of plant size.

The profit-maximizing monopolist will wish to expand output until marginal costs rise to equal marginal revenues. Since this firm faces the entire market demand, the firm's demand curve and the market demand curve are one and the same. Thus the *market* marginal revenue curve is the *firm's* marginal revenue curve. We saw in Chapter 4 that the marginal revenue curve associated with a negatively sloping linear demand curve has the same vertical intercept on the graph and *twice* the slope of the demand curve. In Figure 9-2 we show the market demand curve (D) faced by the monopolist and the corresponding marginal revenue (MR) curve. Superimposed on these are the cost curves of the monopolist—the short-run average cost (SAC) and marginal cost (MC) curves. The profit-maximizing monopolist produces up to the point where marginal costs per unit rise to meet the falling marginal revenues. This point occurs at output level Q_m. Notice that every unit to the right of Q_m has a marginal cost greater than its marginal revenue; it therefore *will not* be produced. Conversely, every unit to the left of Q_m costs less than it earns (marginally or incrementally); it therefore *will* be produced and sold. The firm's profits can be visualized as the rectangle $P_m ABC$ in Figure 9-2.

• NOTE: Monopolists in the real world usually do have some peripheral competition from distant and partial substitutes. The post office experiences competition from the telephone company and from such delivery services as United Parcel Service (UPS) for some of the services it provides. The electricity company competes with the gas company in some households. Bootleggers compete with the liquor control board in some areas. In all these cases, however, the extent of substitution of these products for the monopolist's product is quite small. Thus the cross elasticity of demand between the monopolist's product and the distant substitutes, over the market as a whole, is quite low.

Monopolistic Competition

In monopolistic competition markets the firm must choose a price knowing that the consumer has many close substitutes to choose from. If the price is too high, in view of the consumer's perception of the value of the differentiating features of the firm's product, the consumer will purchase a competing firm's product instead. Thus the monopolistic

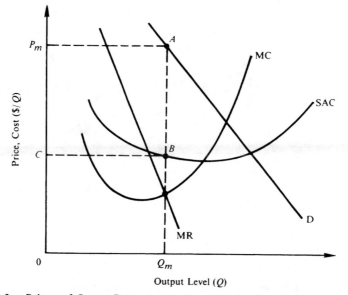

FIGURE 9-2. *Price and Output Determination for a Monopoly*

competitor must expect a relatively elastic demand response to changes in its price level. Yet at the same time, it expects to be able to change price without causing any other firm to retaliate and, consequently, without causing a change in the general price level in the market. This is possible because the firm is one of many firms, and it expects the impact of its actions to be spread imperceptibly over all the other firms, giving no one firm any sufficient reason to react to the initial firm's price change.

Monopolistic competition is so called because it has elements of both monopoly and pure competition. The firm has a significant amount of the monopolist's pricing power by virtue of the differentiation of its product. It can change price up and down without experiencing the extreme response of pure competition. For price increases it will suffer a loss of sales, but this loss is not total, as it would be for the pure competitor. Like a monopoly, the monopolistic competitor can adjust the price upward or downward to the level which maximizes its profits. But like the pure competitor, the monopolistic competitor has many rivals in the short run, compounded by the free entry of new firms in the long run.

- EXAMPLE: Monopolistically competitive markets are found where a large number of vendors gather to sell similar products to a gathering of potential buyers. The weekly fruit and vegetable market in some communities may be characterized as monopolistic competition. Similarly, the gatherings of artisans selling souvenirs and other goods in tourist resorts act like monopolistic competitors.[4]

---

[4]Be wary about characterizing markets as monopolistically competitive unless there are many firms in a relatively compact area and consumers could reasonably be expected to consider purchasing from any one of the firms. Note that seller location (or convenience of purchase) is a relevant attribute in the purchase decision

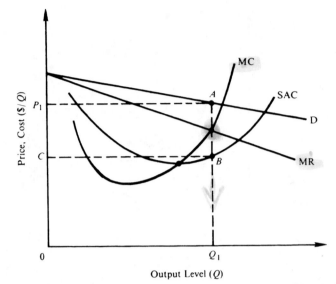

FIGURE 9-3.   Price and Output Determination for a Representative Firm in Monopolistic Competition

The situation of a representative firm in monopolistic competition is depicted in Figure 9-3. Since the demand curve is negatively sloping, the marginal revenue curve must lie below the demand curve, having twice the slope and the same intercept point. The monopolistically competitive firm maximizes its profits at the price and output level where marginal revenue equals marginal costs. Thus price will be set at P_1 and quantity at Q_1; profits are shown as the area P_1ABC.

The prices set by monopolistic competitors need not be at the same level. In real-world situations we should expect to find slight price differentials between and among monopolistic competitors, with some firms being able to command slightly higher prices or larger market shares because of the market's perception of greater value in the product of some firms as compared with others. Firms with more convenient locations, longer operating hours, and quick service, for example, can obtain a premium for what is otherwise the same product (e.g., brand A bread). Quality differences inherent in the product will also form the basis for price differences.[5]

---

for most consumers. Several industries have a large number of producers but are not characterized by monopolistic competition, since the markets for these industries are sparsely dispersed across the nation. There may be thousands of fast-food outlets in North America, but each one seldom competes with more than half a dozen other sellers in its local market. Similarly, there are hundreds of gas stations in and around a large city, but each one is in competition with the three or four gas stations nearest to it, rather than with every other gas station in the entire city. This spatial aspect of some industries means that, rather than being monopolistically competitive, their markets are characterized by intersecting oligopolies, with each firm competing directly with only a few nearby rivals.

[5]Price and market share differences arise in the *asymmetric* monopolistic competition model, where both cost and product differentiation are allowed to differ among firms. This is a considerably more complex model than the *symmetric* case outlined above, in which it is implicit that the representative firm has the same cost structure and product differentiation advantages as all other firms. The asymmetric model will not be consid-

9.4 PRICE MAKING IN OLIGOPOLIES WITH MUTUAL DEPENDENCE RECOGNIZED

- DEFINITION: *Oligopolies* are markets in which there are only a few sellers. (The word *oligopoly* is derived from the Greek word *oligos*, meaning *few*, and the Latin word *polis*, meaning *seller*.) Recall that we use the word *few* to mean a number small enough so the actions of any one firm have a noticeable impact on the demand for each of the other firms.

- EXAMPLE: In the real world the great majority of market situations are oligopolies. Prominent examples are the automobile, steel, aluminum, and chemical industries. These are national and, in some cases, international oligopolies. In your local or regional area, you will notice many more oligopolies. There are probably only half a dozen new car dealerships from which you would consider buying a new automobile. Similarly, there are only a few sellers in a multitude of other lines of business in your area, and these qualify as oligopolies if the actions of any one seller have a significant impact on the sales of any other seller.

Oligopolists are mutually dependent because there are only a few of them sharing a particular market, and any one firm's sales gain, resulting from a price reduction, for example, will be accompanied by sales losses for its rivals. The rival firms must be expected to react to their loss of sales, probably by also reducing price to win back their lost customers. The oligopolist that ignores its mutual dependence will thus receive a rude shock when sales volume and profits do not turn out the way they were expected to. Moreover, such myopic price cutting could precipitate a "price war" which could inflict heavy financial losses on all firms. Conversely, a price increase that is ignored by rivals may lead to a substantial loss of market share and profitability, since at least some of its customers will switch to a rival firm's product.

Thus the oligopolist should attempt to predict the probable reaction of rivals to its strategic actions and decide whether or not an action is likely to be worthwhile in the final analysis before taking that action. The firm's expectation of its rivals' reactions is known as its *conjectural variation*. The firm's conjectural variation may be defined as the expected percentage change in the rivals' strategic variable (such as price) over the contemplated percentage change in the firm's strategic variable. Thus conjectural variation will be zero when the firm expects rivals to do nothing in reaction to its action, unity if the firm expects rivals to exactly match its action, and more than (or less than) unity if rivals are expected to adjust their strategic variables by a greater (or lesser) percentage.

The Kinked Demand Curve Model of Oligopoly

When oligopolists *do* recognize their mutual dependence, there are a variety of different conjectural variations they might make. We shall first examine the *kinked demand curve*

---

ered here except to note that it allows greater realism, at the expense of greater complexity, by explicitly considering differing cost and product differentiation situations between and among firms.

model.[6] This model assumes that the firm's conjectural variation will be twofold: For price increases the firm expects no reaction from rivals, since the other firms will be content to sit back and receive extra customers who switch away from the firm raising its price; and for price reductions the firm expects rivals to exactly match the price reduction to maintain their shares of the market.

Since the firm's conjectural variation for price increases is zero, it envisages a *ceteris paribus* demand curve at all prices above the current level, this curve being more or less elastic depending primarily on the degree of substitutability between its product and rival products. In contemplating price reductions, however, the firm envisages a different kind of demand curve, known as a *mutatis mutandis* demand curve, meaning that it takes into account all reactions induced by or concurrent with the firm's price adjustment. In this case the *mutatis mutandis* section of the demand curve represents a constant share of the total market for the product in question, because if all firms move their prices up or down in unison, their relative prices will remain the same, and we therefore expect each of them to maintain its market share.[7]

In Figure 9-4 we show a firm's current price and output levels as P and Q. For prices above P, the firm envisages the relatively elastic *ceteris paribus* demand curve shown by the line dA. For prices below P, it envisages the relatively inelastic *mutatis mutandis* demand curve shown by the line AD. The demand curve facing the firm is therefore dAD, being *kinked* at the current price level. The marginal revenue curve appropriate to this demand curve will have two separate sections. The upper section, shown as dB in Figure 9-4, relates to the *ceteris paribus* section of the demand curve and therefore shares the same intercept and has twice the slope of the line dA. The lower section, CMR, relates to the *mutatis mutandis* section of the demand curve and is positioned such that it has twice the slope of the line AD, and if extended up to the price axis would share its intercept point with the line AD similarly extended.

You will note that there is a vertical discontinuity in the marginal revenue curve, shown as the gap BC in Figure 9-4. Given the foregoing, it is apparent that the length of this gap depends on the relative slopes of the *ceteris paribus* and *mutatis mutandis* demand curves,[8] which in turn are related to the elasticity of demand under the two conjectural variation situations. If the firm is a profit maximizer, its marginal cost curve will pass through the gap BC. If P and Q are the profit-maximizing price and output levels, this relationship implies that outputs to the left of Q would have marginal revenues exceeding marginal costs, while outputs to the right of Q would have marginal costs exceeding marginal revenues. This observation is true only if the MC curve passes through

---

[6]This model was initially proposed separately by R. L. Hall and C. J. Hitch, "Price Theory and Business Behavior," *Oxford Economic Papers*, May 1939, pp. 12–45; and by P. M. Sweezy, "Demand under Conditions of Oligopoly," *Journal of Political Economy*, August 1939, pp. 568–73.

[7]Note that while the *ceteris paribus* demand curve is appropriate for independent action by a firm not expecting reactions, the *mutatis mutandis* demand curve is appropriate for joint action by firms, taking into account rivals' reactions.

[8]See G. J. Stigler, "The Kinky Oligopoly Demand Curve and Rigid Prices," *Journal of Political Economy*, 55 (October 1947).

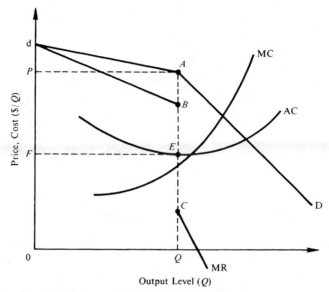

FIGURE 9-4.   The Kinked Demand Curve Model of Oligopoly

either of the points *B* or *C* or through some point in between.[9] The oligopolist's profits are shown by the rectangle *PAEF* in Figure 9-4.

Price Rigidity in the Kinked Demand Curve Model.   The KDC model is not a complete theory of price determination, because it is unable to tell us how the firm arrives at the initial price and output levels. Given this starting point, however, the model is able to tell us several things that are important to our understanding of oligopoly markets. First, it offers an explanation of the observed rigidity of oligopoly prices in the face of changing cost and demand conditions. Recall that in each of the models of firm behavior we have examined so far, the firms set price where marginal costs equal marginal revenue. If either costs or demand conditions change, one of these marginal curves shifts, and a new price level is required if the firm is to maximize profits under the new conditions. In the KDC case, however, the marginal cost and marginal revenue curves may shift to a considerable degree without a new price level becoming appropriate, as we shall see.

In the KDC model the firm does not wish to change price as long as the marginal cost curve passes through the gap in the marginal revenue curve. Thus costs could increase so the MC curve moves upward until it passes through point *B* in Figure 9-5 without the present price becoming inappropriate. Conversely, if variable costs fall, the MC curve could sink downward until it passes through point *C*, and price *P* would remain the profit-maximizing price. As long as marginal revenue exceeds marginal costs

---

[9]See D. S. Smith and W. C. Neale, "The Geometry of Kinky Oligopoly: Marginal Cost, the Gap, and Price Behavior," *Southern Economic Journal*, 37 (January 1971), pp. 276–82.

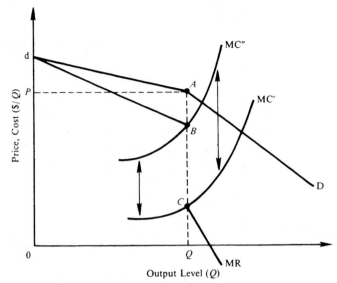

FIGURE 9-5.   *Price Rigidity in Oligopoly Despite Changing Cost Levels*

for higher prices and is less than marginal costs for lower prices, the present price remains the optimal price. Of course, profits are smaller when costs are higher, but profits are *maximized* when the MC curve passes through the MR gap.

Now consider changes in the demand situation. In most real-world market situations, quantity demanded at the prevailing price level fluctuates up and down over time as the result of seasonal, cyclical, or random influences on the factors determining demand. But as we show in Figure 9-6, demand at price P could fluctuate over the range Q to Q' without causing the MC curve to pass outside the relevant MR gap. At quantity Q, the MR curve is shown by dBCMR, and the MC curve passes through point C. This is the extreme leftward point to which the demand curves could shift and yet still allow the MC curve to pass through the gap. The extreme rightward shift of demand, which allows P to remain as the profit-maximizing price, is found when the MC curve passes through point B', as it does at output Q'. Thus demand could fluctuate over the relatively wide range Q to Q' at price P without the firm wishing to change its price. Profits are lower when demand is lower but are maximized at price P as long as the demand shift is not so large as to cause the MC curve to miss the gap in the appropriate MR curve.[10]

---

[10]George Stigler (see footnote 8), and Julius Simon, "A Further Test of the Kinky Oligopoly Demand Curve," *American Economic Review*, December 1969, each presented empirical findings to indicate that prices in oligopolies were adjusted less frequently than were prices in monopoly markets, thus appearing to refute the KDC model's prediction that oligopoly prices would be adjusted less frequently than would monopoly prices. Jack Hirshleifer, in his *Price Theory and Applications*, 4th ed. (Englewood Cliffs, N.J.: Prentice-Hall, 1988), pp. 293–5, points out that there are reasons to expect monopoly prices to be adjusted relatively infrequently, such as fear of attracting regulatory scrutiny and management's pursuit of their own objectives, and these reasons may have been stronger for the monopolists than was the KDC effect for the oligopolists. In addition, it should be recognized that the KDC model is just one model of oligopoly. Other models, such as the price leadership models and the conscious parallelism variant of the KDC model, explain how price adjustments are

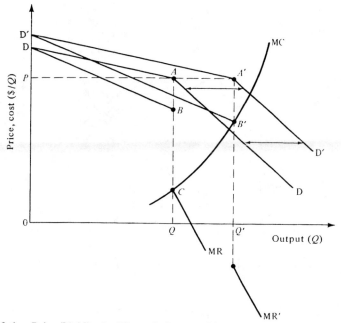

FIGURE 9-6. Price Rigidity in Oligopoly Despite Changing Demand Levels

Price Adjustments in the Kinked Demand Curve Model.   Let us look briefly at a cost change that *will* lead to a change in price. As implied previously, if the change is such that the new MC curve no longer passes through the MR gap, the firm will want to change price. In Figure 9-7, we show a shift of the marginal cost curve from MC to MC′, causing it to intersect the MR curve at point *B′*. The initial price *P* is no longer the profit-maximizing price, since marginal cost exceeds marginal revenue for all the output units between *Q′* and *Q*. The new profit-maximizing price is thus *P′*, where the MC′ curve intersects the MR curve. The firm therefore raises its price to *P′* and experiences a reduction in its quantity demand from *Q* to *Q′*.

Notice that the firm raised its price independently, with the expectation that no other firm would follow its price increase; consequently, it lost part of its market share. Since the firm's price-output coordinate is now point *A′*, it must envisage the new *mutatis mutandis* demand curve, *A′D′*, for any contemplated price reduction. Thus the firm's share-of-the-market demand curve has effectively shifted to the left as a result of its independent price increase. But the firm, being a profit maximizer by assumption, would rather increase profits than worry about market share, and hence it prefers the higher

---

facilitated in oligopoly. Thus we should recognize that the KDC model does not purport to describe the conjectural variations of all oligopolists at all times. But for those firms at those times when the split conjectural variation is appropriate, it is a valuable addition to the decision maker's toolbox.

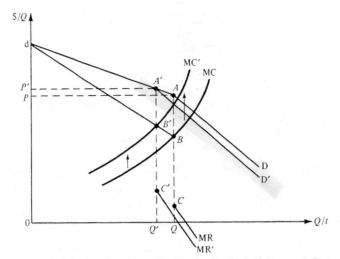

FIGURE 9-7. A Profit-Maximizing Price Change in the Kinked Demand Curve Model

profit situation at price P', given the cost increase that upset the initial equilibrium situation.

Alternatively, we could show the demand curves shifting to the right to such an extent that the firm prefers to raise price (and lose part of its market share) to maximize profits. Conversely, we could show the marginal cost curve failing sufficiently or the demand situation declining sufficiently, causing the MC curve to cut the lower section of the marginal revenue curve. In either of these two cases, the firm would cut its price, notwithstanding its expectation that rivals would immediately follow suit, because cutting price allows profits to be maximized. Since all rivals match the price reduction, all firms maintain their market shares at the lower price level.

Thus the KDC model predicts that firms will hold price steady, despite the fluctuations of variable costs or demand over a significant range of cost or output levels. Outside the limits set by the requirement that the MC curve pass through the gap in the MR curve, the firm *will* be motivated to change price. It will raise or lower price to the new profit-maximizing level, whether or not it expects rivals to do likewise.

Conscious Parallelism

Under some conditions the firm's conjecture that other firms will ignore its price increase may give way to the expectation that other firms will *follow* a price increase rather than ignore it. Such a situation may arise when a cost increase applies to all firms, such as an increase in the basic wage rate or an increase in the cost of an important raw material. In the case of cost increases that apply to all firms, the individual firm may reasonably expect that all firms would like to maintain profit margins by passing the cost on to consumers. Especially if there is a history of this practice in the industry, the firm's conjectural variation for a price increase, up to the extent necessary to pass on the cost increase, may be unity.

- DEFINITION: The simultaneous adjustment of prices with the expectation that rivals will do likewise has been called *conscious parallelism*.[11] The firms consciously act in a parallel manner, given their expectation that all other firms are motivated to act in the same way.

    The relevant demand curve for a consciously parallel price increase is the *mutatis mutandis* demand curve. As indicated in Figure 9-8, the kink in the demand curve moves up the *mutatis mutandis* section to the new price level chosen. It will kink at the level that passes on the cost increase, because the firm expects that any further price increase will not be matched by rivals and therefore expects to experience a more elastic demand response above that price level. The firm's conjectural variation is unity up to the price level that is expected to be agreeable to all firms, and it is zero for price levels above that.[12]

    In terms of Figure 9-8, the firm has experienced a shift in its marginal cost curve from MC to MC'. Based on its expectation that rival firms have suffered a similar cost increase and will be raising their prices, the firm raises its price from P to P' to pass on the cost increase to consumers. The firm expects its price-quantity coordinate to move from point A to A', along the *mutatis mutandis*, or share-of-the-market, demand curve. If its expectation (that rivals will similarly raise prices) is borne out, it will in fact move to A', its new kinked demand curve will be $d'A'D$, and its new marginal revenue curve will be $d'B'C'MR$.

    Since all firms are expected to act jointly, each firm expects to maintain its share of the market at the higher price level, and, by passing on the cost increase to consumers, each firm expects to maintain its profit margin per unit (the difference between price and average costs). In the next chapter we see that the prevalent practice of *markup pricing* allows firms to practice conscious parallelism in the real world, even when they don't know how their demand curves slope away from the present price level.

Price Leadership Models

A number of oligopoly models rely on the notion of *price leadership* to explain the upward adjustment of prices in oligopoly markets. The major difference between conscious parallelism and price leadership is that in the former situation all firms take the initiative in adjusting prices, confident that their rivals will do likewise, whereas in the latter situation one firm will lead the way and will be followed within a relatively short

---

[11]See W. Hamburger, "Conscious Parallelism and the Kinked Oligopoly Demand Curve," *American Economic Review*, 57 (May 1967), pp. 266–68.

[12]The extent to which price is raised depends on the extent to which the firm expects other firms to raise prices simultaneously; it may be more than, less than, or equal to the cost increase. It would be (joint) profit maximizing to raise price all the way to the point where the MC curve cuts the *mutatis mutandis* MR curve (extended upward). But if some firms are not expected to raise price that far, the demand curve will kink and that MR is thus inappropriate.

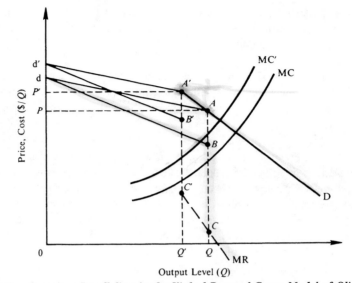

FIGURE 9-8.   *Conscious Parallelism in the Kinked Demand Curve Model of Oligopoly*

period by all or most of the other firms adjusting their prices to a similar degree. The price leader is the firm willing to take the risk of being the first to adjust price, but, as we shall see, this firm usually has good reason to expect that the other firms will follow suit. The risk involved here relates especially to price increases, since if the firm raises price and is not followed by other firms, it will experience an elastic demand response and a significant loss of profits before it can readjust its price to the original level.

- NOTE: Conjectural variation for the price leader is unity, since this firm expects all rivals to adjust prices up or down to the same degree that it does. For the price followers, conjectural variation is zero for self-initiated price increases, since price followers do not expect to have all firms follow their price increases. For price decreases, the price follower may expect all firms to follow suit to protect their market shares, and so the conjectural variation is unity for price reductions. It should be immediately apparent to the reader that the price follower faces a kinked demand curve.

   There are three major types of price leaders: the barometric price leader, the low-cost price leader, and the dominant firm price leader.

The Barometric Price Leader.   As the name implies, the barometric price leader possesses an ability to accurately predict when the climate is right for a price change. Following a generalized increase in labor or materials costs or a period of increased demand, the barometric firm judges that all firms are ready for a price change and takes the risk of sales losses by being the first to adjust its price. If the other firms trust that firm's judgment of market conditions, they too will adjust prices to the extent indicated. If they feel the increase is too much, they may adjust prices to a lesser degree and the price leader may bring its price back to the level seemingly endorsed by the other firms. If the other firms fail to ratify the price change, the price leadership role could shift from firm to firm over time and will rest with the firm that has sound knowledge of market supply and demand conditions, the ability to perceive a consensus among the firms, and the willingness to take the risk of sales losses if its judgment on these issues is faulty.[13]

The Low-Cost Price Leader. The low-cost price leader is a firm that has a significant cost advantage over its rivals and inherits the role of price leader largely because of the other firms' reluctance to incur the wrath of the lower-cost firm. In the event of a price war the other firms would suffer greater losses and be more prone to the risk of bankruptcy than would the lower-cost firm. Out of respect for this potential power of the lower-cost firm, the other firms tacitly agree to follow that firm's price adjustments.[14]

In Figure 9-9 we show the demand curve D as the curve faced by either firm when each firm sets price at the same level. This curve is thus a *mutatis mutandis* demand curve, predicated on the simultaneous adjustment of the other firm's price to the same level. In price leadership situations, price adjustments are more or less concurrent, and the demand curve D in this case represents a constant (half) share of the total market at each price level.[15] The marginal cost curves of the two firms are shown as MC_A for firm A, the lower-cost firm, and MC_B for firm B, the higher-cost firm. The lower-cost firm maximizes its profit from its share of the market by setting price P and output level Q, and firm B follows the lead and also sets price P.

Given that it sets price P, what output level should the higher-cost firm produce? Being a profit-maximizing firm, by assumption, it will simply choose the output level that maximizes profits, subject to the (self-imposed) constraint that its price will be the same as the price leader's. The demand curve facing firm B is the kinked line dAD. If the high-cost firm raises its price, it expects to do so alone, along the *ceteris paribus* section dA. If it sets its price below P, the other firm will match this price reduction to avoid having its sales fall dramatically. The marginal revenue curve associated with the kinked demand curve dAD is the disjointed line dBCMR. Firm B should therefore choose output level Q, since below this output level marginal revenue exceeds marginal costs, and above this level marginal costs exceed marginal revenue. The firms thus share the market equally at the price level chosen by the lower-cost firm.

Price Leadership with Price Differentials. When product differentiation is asymmetric, we should expect a range of prices among the rival firms, reflecting the different cost and demand situations facing each firm. Price leadership in this situation requires one

---

[13]Barometric price leadership was first proposed by J. W. Markham, "The Nature and Significance of Price Leadership," *American Economic Review*, December 1951, pp. 891–905. For a thorough discussion of barometric price leadership, see F. M. Scherer, *Industrial Market Structure and Economic Performance*, 2nd ed. (Chicago: Rand McNally & Company, 1980), chap. 6.

[14]This agreement is likely to be ruled illegal price fixing if the firms *explicitly* agree on price levels. Price fixing is discussed in Appendix 10A.

[15]If product differentiation is *symmetric*, the share of the firms will be equal when prices are equal, and each firm would lose sales at the same rate following an independent price increase. This is a simplifying assumption, since in practice we should expect to find *asymmetric* product differentiation, whereby market shares are unequal when prices are equal, and the slopes of the firms' *ceteris paribus* demand curves are not necessarily equal.

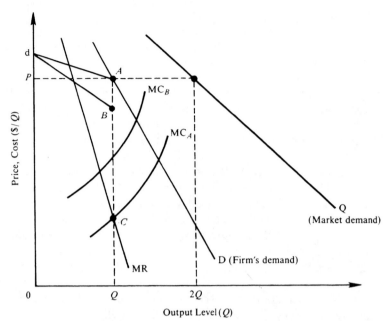

FIGURE 9-9. Low-Cost Firm Price Leadership: Simple Two-Firm, Identical Products Case

slight modification to the preceding analysis. The price leader may adjust its price by a certain amount, and the price followers will adjust their prices by the *same percentage* as is represented by the price leader's price adjustment. Thus the relative price differentials that prevailed prior to the price changes are unchanged, and no firm expects to gain or lose sales from or to a rival. The price leader simply initiates an upward (or downward) adjustment in the entire price structure of that particular market.

In Figure 9-10 we show a situation in which three firms produce asymmetrically differentiated products. Firm A is the acknowledged price leader and sets price P_A, selling Q_A units. Firms B and C are price followers, not wishing to initiate price adjustments in case this might precipitate a price war in which the lower-cost firm A would have a definite advantage. Firm B's price is above the price leader's price, and firm C's price is below the other two prices. Firm B's product may be a higher-quality item desired by a relatively small segment of the market. This firm's higher cost level may well be the result of higher-quality inputs and more hand finishing of the product, for example. Firm C's product is both lower priced and more expensive to produce, as compared with the price leader's. The lower price may be due to the market's perception of inferior after-sales service, an inferior location, or absence of other attributes, while the higher costs may be the result of more expensive sources of the inputs, inefficiencies in production, or a plant size too small in view of the present output level.

The price followers face the kinked demand curves shown because they expect no reaction from rivals for price increases but expect the price leader and the other price follower to match any price reductions. The price leader's demand curve is simply the

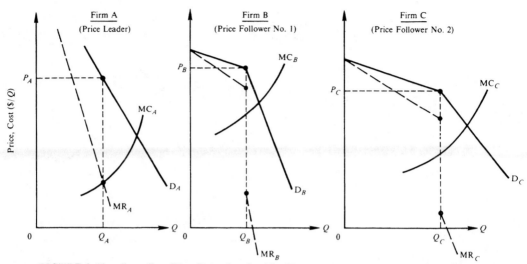

FIGURE 9-10. **Low-Cost Firm Price Leadership: Two or More Firms, Asymmetric Product Differentiation and Cost Conditions**

mutatis mutandis demand curve: The price leader expects the other firms to follow both price increases and price reductions. If, for example, the price leader's costs increase, it will adjust price upward along the D_A curve. The price followers, who have probably incurred a similar cost increase, will follow the lead and adjust prices upward. But for this particular price increase they do not expect *ceteris paribus*; they expect that the other firms will be simultaneously adjusting their prices upward (or have seen them do so). Thus the kinks in the price followers' demand curves will move upward, extending the *mutatis mutandis* section of their demand curves, as in the conscious parallelism case shown in Figure 9-8.

We shall see in Chapter 10 that the common business practice of *markup pricing* allows firms to adjust prices to cost increases by a similar proportion. We turn now to the third type of price leader.

The Dominant-Firm Price Leader.   As the name implies, the dominant firm is large relative to its rivals and its market. The smaller firms accept this firm's price leadership perhaps simply because they are unwilling to risk being the first to change prices, or perhaps because they are afraid that the dominant firm could drive them out of business, for example, by forcing raw-material suppliers to boycott a particular small firm on pain of losing the order of the larger firm. In such a situation the smaller firms accept the dominant firm's choice of the price level, and they simply adjust output to maximize their profits. In this respect they are price takers, similar to pure competitors who can sell as much as they want to at the market price. Like pure competitors, they will want to sell up to the point where their marginal cost equals the price (equals marginal revenue). The dominant firm recognizes that the smaller firms will behave in this manner and that it

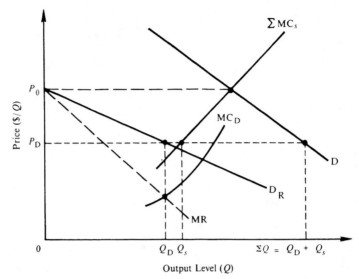

FIGURE 9-11.   Price Determination by the Dominant-Firm Price Leader

must therefore choose price to maximize its profits with the knowledge that the smaller firms will sell as much as they want to at that price.

The first task of the dominant-firm price leader is, therefore, to ascertain how much the smaller firms will want to supply at each price level. Since each of the smaller firms will want to supply up to the point where MC = MR, and since MR = P in a situation where the individual firm is so small that it does not influence market price, each of the smaller firms will regard its MC curve as its supply curve. Note that a supply curve shows the quantity that will be supplied at each price level. At each price level the firms supply the amount for which marginal cost equals price. The MC curve therefore indicates how much the firm will supply at each price level. It follows that a horizontal aggregation of these curves will indicate the total amount that the smaller firms will supply at each price level. In Figure 9-11 we depict this aggregation of the smaller firms' marginal cost curves as the line ΣMC_s.

Knowing how much the smaller firms will supply at each price level, the dominant firm can subtract this quantity from the market demand to find how much demand is left over at each price level. This residual demand can be measured as the horizontal distance between the ΣMC_s and the market demand curve D at each price level, and is shown as the demand curve D_R in Figure 9-11. Only at prices below P_0 is there any demand left for the dominant firm after the smaller firms have supplied their desired amounts. This residual demand curve is the amount that the dominant firm can be assured of selling at each price level, since the smaller firms will have sold as much as they wanted to and yet there remain buyers willing to purchase at those price levels.

The dominant firm will choose the price level to maximize its own profits from this residual demand. The marginal revenue curve associated with the residual demand curve is shown as the curve *MR* in Figure 9-11. The dominant firm's marginal cost curve is depicted by MC_D. The dominant firm therefore selects price P_D and output Q_D to maximize its profits. Faced with the price P_D, each of the smaller firms produces up to the point where its marginal costs equal that price, and hence the smaller firms in aggregate produce the output level Q_s. Since the residual demand curve was constructed to reflect the horizontal distance between the ΣMC_s and the D curves, the total amount supplied to the market, ΣQ, is equal to the market demand, and an equilibrium situation exists. The dominant firm thus chooses price to maximize its profits under the constraint that the smaller firms will supply the amount at that price level which will maximize their profits.

- NOTE: An interesting long-run implication of the dominant-firm price leadership model is that if the chosen price allows the smaller firms to earn economic profits, the dominance of the large firm will be eroded over time. The reason for this erosion is that in the long run the small firms will expand their plant sizes in search of even greater profitability, and new firms will enter the industry—if the barriers to entry can be overcome—in search of this profitability. Unless the market grows faster than the small firms, the residual demand remaining for the dominant firm must be reduced, and the price leader will be forced to set a lower price and accept a reduced market share. Eventually, of course, the dominant firm will no longer be dominant, and the aforementioned system of market price determination will give way to some other form of price leadership, conscious parallelism, or independent price setting.

- EXAMPLE: Alcoa is said to be an example of a firm that was initially a monopoly, later a dominant-firm price leader, and more recently simply one of several large oligopolists in the aluminum industry.[16] Alcoa was effectively a monopoly at first because it held most of the known reserves of bauxite, from which aluminum is derived. As more bauxite was discovered, other firms entered the industry but were small in relation to Alcoa. As time passed and Alcoa's chosen price level allowed the other firms to prosper and grow, Alcoa's dominance in the industry waned to the point where it is no longer the price leader at all. Rather, Alcan has emerged as the low-cost price leader because of its cheaper source of electric power.

9.5 PRICING FOR LONGER-TERM OBJECTIVES

The behavioral assumption of short-run profit maximization, which we have used in all the models of pricing discussed previously, may be criticized for its lack of realism in oligopolistic markets where high short-run profits may induce new firms to overcome the barriers to entry and obtain a share of the market and thus dilute future profits of the existing firms. We should expect that the time horizon envisaged by oligopolists will extend beyond the short-run period and that these firms will be likely to forego immediate profits in order not to attract the entry of new firms. This observation suggests, of

---

[16]See J. V. Koch. *Industrial Organization and Prices*, 2nd ed. (Englewood Cliffs, N.J.: Prentice-Hall, 1980), pp. 282 and 289.

course, that a more appropriate objective function for the oligopolist is the maximization of long-term profits.

By maximization of long-term profits we must mean the maximization of the expected present value of present and future profits, since the firm will face uncertainty in the future and must employ present-value analysis to make the future profits comparable to present-period profits. We argued in Chapter 1 that this objective is the equivalent of net worth maximization (in EPV terms). Thus the firm should choose the price level that maximizes the EPV of profits. A quick look at what this choice involves will convince you that the search costs of implementing this decision rule will most likely be prohibitive. Estimates must be made of the probabilities of entry in future periods, relating to each of the possible current-period price levels. Then the impact of new firms on the price level must be forecast. The growth (or decline) of the overall market, as well as the firm's share of the market in each future period, must be forecast. The firm's costs must be forecast in each of the future periods, in conjunction with the demand forecasts, before a profit forecast can be formulated. In some cases the search cost of this procedure will be considered worthwhile, but more often we should expect the search costs to be prohibitive.

It is more likely that firms wishing to maximize their long-term profits will adopt a "proxy" objective function. That is, they will pursue a policy that gives approximately the same results but is much more simple and inexpensive to administer. In the following sections we shall examine a number of such proxy policies which, it can be argued, are a short-term means of achieving the long-term objective of profit maximization.

Sales Maximization with a Minimum Profit Target

W. J. Baumol has suggested that the appropriate objective function for many firms is the maximization of sales in the short term, subject to the attainment of a certain minimum profit level.[17] First let us consider the minimum profit requirement, which is necessary for two main reasons: (1) A sufficient minimum profit must be forthcoming to prevent shareholders from becoming disgruntled and voting for a new board of directors; and (2) the value of the firm's shares on the stock exchange depends, in part, on the current profitability of the firm, since the expectation of dividend payments has a positive influence on the market value of the shares. If, as a result of low current profits, the shares become undervalued in view of the firm's longer-term prospects, the firm may be subject to a takeover bid by another firm, which again involves the risk that managers may lose their jobs. Therefore, managers will be motivated to keep profits at a level sufficient to stave off these two possibilities while at the same time making sure that profits are not so large as to attract the entry of new firms.

---

[17]W. J. Baumol, *Business Behavior, Value, and Growth* (New York: Harcourt Brace Jovanovich, Inc., 1967). Note that we mean sales *volume*, not sales *revenue*. Maximizing sales revenue simply means finding the point where MR = 0 and requires no reference to the firm's cost situation. This may be desirable if the firm faces an immediate cash flow problem, but completely neglects the profit implications since it ignores the cost side. Maximization of sales volume (subject to a profit target) amounts to maximizing the firm's market share and seems empirically more supportable.

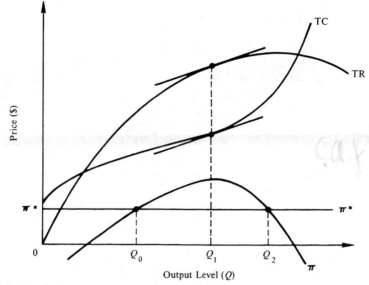

FIGURE 9-12.   Sales Maximization Subject to a Minimum Profit Constraint

Having determined the minimum acceptable, or target, level of profits, the firm will wish to maximize its sales subject to this profit constraint. We can show the sales-maximization decision on the same graph as the one for short-run profit maximization. Figure 9-12 shows the familiar total revenue and total cost curves, with the profit curve indicating the excess of total revenue over total costs at each output level. Suppose the minimum profit constraint is the vertical distance indicated by $0\pi^*$. The profit constraint is satisfied anywhere between output levels Q_0 and Q_2, but sales are maximized, subject to this constraint, at output level Q_2. It is clear that this output level is larger than the short-run profit-maximizing output level Q_1 and must be offered at a lower price than the short-run profit-maximizing price, since the firm faces a negatively sloped demand curve.

But why is the maximization of sales volume in the short run a proxy for the maximization of longer-term profits? The lower price level, as compared with the short-run profit-maximizing price, has three major implications for future profits. First, it will tend to inhibit the entry of new firms whose costs may exceed that price level because of the extra expenses associated with overcoming the barriers to entry. Second, it will introduce more customers to the product now and will thus operate to gain more repeat sales in future periods, because of the goodwill and brand loyalty that will develop over time as customers use the product. This cultivation of consumer loyalty and goodwill acts to raise one of the barriers to entry, since a potential entrant firm would need to spend even more on advertising and promotion of its own product to induce customers to try that product. Third, the larger market share in the short term provides a larger base for complementary sales in the longer term. This is especially important in the market for some durable consumption goods, such as automo-

biles and cameras, where apparently quite lucrative markets exist for specialized replacement parts and accessories.

- EXAMPLE: The Kodak 110 camera appears to have been priced with a view to maximizing its sales volume in the short run. When it was first introduced, it seemed to offer
excellent value and became very popular as a Christmas and birthday gift, particularly for
children. As every parent found out, of course, the cost of the camera was simply the
start of a series of expenditures benefiting Kodak. Sales of special film cartridges, flash
bulbs, developing, printing, and enlarging services all served to keep the sales revenue
flowing to Kodak. Kodak's strategy appears to have been to get the widest possible
penetration of the market with their camera, at a modest profit margin, and to rely on
subsequent sales of accessory items to generate continued revenues and profitability. Gil-
lette, who pioneered several advances in shaving equipment during the 1970s, appears to
have followed a similar strategy. For both their twin-blade and swivel-head (Atra) blade,
they priced the handle at a price that must barely have covered their variable cost per unit
and were content to take their profits on the later sales of razor blades.

A policy of sales maximization in the short run thus operates to inhibit the entry of
new firms and to generate future sales of the firm's product(s). The resultant profit
stream probably comes reasonably close to that which could be attained by the present-
value calculation for long-term profit maximization, since there are likely to be considerable search costs associated with obtaining the information necessary to make that calculation. Sales maximization is a relatively simple and inexpensive rule-of-thumb procedure that can be applied in each period, and it thus obviates the cost, effort, and
uncertainty associated with the continual recalculation of the price that maximizes the
expected present value of the firm's profit stream.

Limit Pricing to Deter Entry

- DEFINITION: The *limit price* is the price that is not quite high enough to induce the
entry of new firms. For the potential entrant whose objective is short-run profit maximization, the limit price is the highest price that can be set without allowing the potential
entrant to make normal profits. If the potential entrant takes the longer view and would
be prepared to take losses initially if it could foresee profits later, the limit price is the
highest price that can be set without allowing the potential entrant's expected present
value of profits to be positive.
    Limit pricing may also be regarded as a proxy for long-term profit maximiza-
tion. Preventing the entry of new firms serves to avoid having to share the market
with new firms in the future. Thus the firm expects its future sales and the EPV of
profits from the present to its time horizon to be greater if it successfully prevents the
entry of new firms.

Deterring Entry of a High-Cost Firm.   In many cases the entrant firm is expected to
have higher costs than the existing firms, as a result of its probable smaller scale of
operation and the additional product differentiation expense it must incur to offset con-

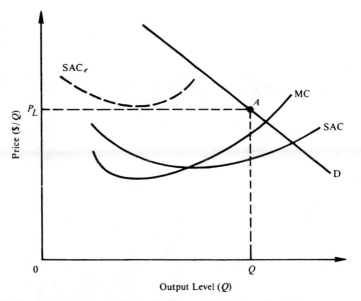

FIGURE 9-13. Limit Pricing to Deter the Entry of a Higher-Cost Firm

sumer loyalty to the existing products. Thus the established firms, at the suggestion of a price leader perhaps, choose a price that does not allow the potential entrant to earn even a normal profit at any output level. In Figure 9-13 this price is shown as P_L, which is lower than any point on the potential entrant's short-run average cost curve, SAC_e.

The demand curve D should be interpreted as the *mutatis mutandis*, or share-of-the-market, demand curve of one of the existing firms. Given that the existing firm will not wish to set a price above P_L, it faces, in effect, the kinked demand curve $P_L AD$. Its profit-maximizing output, subject to the self-imposed constraint, is thus Q, where marginal cost and marginal revenue come nearest to being equal.[18]

Since the price set by the existing firms is less than the expected minimum cost per unit of potential entrant firms, new firms will not enter, and thus the existing firms' future market shares and profitability are protected from incursions from this quarter at least. Pursuit of a limit-pricing policy is, therefore, like sales maximization, a relatively simple short-run means of approximating a long-term objective. This is not to say that entry will not occur, since there may well be entry of a new firm if the existing firms incorrectly estimate the costs of the potential entrant, if the new firm employs the latest technology while existing firms continue to use older, less efficient plants, or if the entrant firm is prepared to take a loss for a protracted period while gaining a foothold in an expanding market.

---

[18]The marginal revenue curve is not shown in Figure 9-13, but you should be able to figure out where it goes. It will be coextensive with the dotted line $P_L A$ out to output level Q, then have a vertical discontinuity at output level Q, and then fall below the axis with twice the slope of the demand curve for output levels greater than Q. Thus the MC curve passes through the vertical discontinuity of the MR curve and the limit price is the profit-maximizing price subject to this self-imposed constraint.

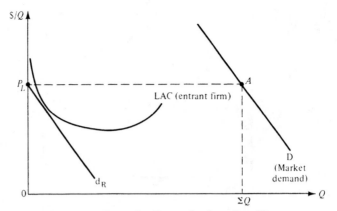

FIGURE 9-14. *Limit Pricing to Deter the Entry of a Low-Cost Firm*

Deterring Entry of a Low-Cost Firm.   Let us now consider the case in which the potential entrant has access to the same technology and factor markets and hence has the same or lower cost structure as compared to the existing firms. In this case there is no point in pricing below the new entrant's costs, since all firms would incur losses. Instead, the firms choose price such that the extra quantity supplied by the entry of another firm would cause the market clearing price to be depressed below the level of cost for all firms. The prospect of losses thus prevents the potential entrant from actually entering unless it expects market demand to expand over time or the existing firms to reduce output level such that price is not depressed below cost.[19]

In Figure 9-14 we demonstrate the limit price that deters entry of a potential entrant that has costs equal to or lower than existing firms. The market demand curve is shown as D, and the potential entrant firm's long-run average cost curve is shown. To simplify the figure, the existing firms' *mutatis mutandis* and *ceteris paribus* demand curves are not shown. Suppose that the existing firms follow a price leader and establish the market price shown as P_L. At this price they collectively supply ΣQ units to the market. Note that this means that all buyers willing to pay at least price P_L for the product (that is, those above point A on the demand curve) have been able to obtain the product.

The strategy for deterring entry requires the existing firms to make known the threat that, if a new firm enters, the existing firms will maintain their output levels at the current levels, or ΣQ in aggregate. Thus the new firm's output would be additional to ΣQ and could only be sold at a lower price. In effect, the new firm would be looking at the market demand curve *below* point A. This is the residual demand left for the new firm after the existing firms have supplied ΣQ units to the market. Shifting this residual section (AD) of the market demand curve over to the vertical axis, we have the demand curve d_R that is faced by the potential entrant firm. Now we see why P_L is the limit price: There is no part of the residual demand curve d_R that lies above the potential entrant

---

[19]F. M. Scherer, *Industrial Market Structure and Economic Performance*, 2nd ed. (Chicago: Rand McNally & Company, 1980). chap. 8.

firm's LAC curve. Thus the entrant could not make a profit at any output level, in any plant size.

- NOTE: The limit price to deter the entry of a low-cost (or lower-cost) firm is, therefore, the price that causes the residual demand curve to lie everywhere below the potential entrant firm's LAC curve. There is then no plant size the entrant can select that would allow normal profits. Notice, however, that the deterrent to entry is simply the threat that existing firms will maintain their output levels, thereby allowing the new firm's output to cause the market price to fall to a lower level until demand equals supply. But at this lower price level, existing firms do not make profits either, since they have no cost advantage over the entrant. It is clear that if the new firm actually does enter the market, the established firms would be better off to reduce their output levels (and market shares) and have the price leader choose a price that would allow all firms to make at least normal profits.

  Thus, if a potential entrant firm "calls the bluff" of the existing firms and does enter the market, the firms would be better off to reduce their output levels, despite their earlier threats, and to follow their price leader to a new price level that is acceptable to all. The potential entrant that foresees this and that expects to incur losses, initially in any case, may not be deterred at all.

Contestable Markets. A recent advance in the theory of markets has been made by Baumol, Panzer, and Willig.[20] Building on earlier work demonstrating that barriers to entry are critical elements influencing the pricing behavior of firms, they define a contestable market as one that may be entered by a new firm without significant cost. This potential for entry prevents the existing firms in that market from pricing to make any more than a normal profit, since doing so would attract new firms into the market that will compete with the existing firms and drive prices below cost. Pure competition and monopolistic competition markets are therefore contestable markets, but so too are some monopoly and oligopoly markets. If there are no significant barriers to entry but the size of plant chosen by the firms is large relative to the market, then there is only room for one firm (a natural monopoly) or a few firms in the market (a natural oligopoly). However, these monopoly and oligopoly markets are also contestable. That is, the prospect of losing their market shares because of entry by a new firm will force the existing firms to keep prices close to their average costs to avoid attracting the entry of new firms.

- EXAMPLE: The passenger airline industry serves literally thousands of different markets, where each market is defined as a "city pair." In larger markets, such as the New York–Los Angeles route, there are six or more different airlines offering services (an oligopoly). Most routes will be oligopolies, offering the passenger a choice between at least two or three carriers. Between other city pairs, where demand for flights is much smaller, there is a single airline offering service (a monopoly). Because the airline industry has been deregulated, any carrier may offer a service between any city pair. Entry to a

---

[20]See W. J. Baumol, J. C. Panzer, and R. D. Willig, *Contestable Markets and the Theory of Industry Structure* (San Diego: Harcourt Brace Jovanovich, 1982).

particular market involves very little initial (setup) cost relative to the firm's operating costs. Note that the entrant will have operating costs that are similar to the other airlines serving the market—that is, the same landing fees, ticket sales and baggage-handling expenses, aircraft fuel and maintenance cost, and so on. The minimum efficient size for most city-pair markets involves a multiengine jetliner capable of carrying at least 100 people, which is relatively large compared to the market (at a particular time each day, for example).

Thus there are more airlines contesting larger markets and fewer airlines contesting smaller markets. Although we might expect these oligopolies and monopolies to set prices considerably in excess of average costs, following the traditional theory of market forms, we observe rather competitive prices being set in contestable markets to avoid attracting the entry of a new competitor into that market. Thus the firms are effectively practicing limit pricing to deter entry.

Satisficing: Achieving Targets as a Managerial Objective

Following Baumol's sales-maximization hypothesis, which represented a break with the traditional short-run profit-maximizing theory of the firm, several managerial and behavioral theories of the firm were developed. It has been suggested that firms wish to maximize the rate of growth of the firm, or, alternatively, that managers wish to maximize managerial utility.[21] The satisficing model of firm behavior says that firms do not try to maximize anything—they simply set targets and are satisfied if they can reach those targets.[22] The targets typically relate to profits, sales or market share, worker productivity, or inventory/sales ratios, and can be seen to be either revenue- or cost-related.

The satisficing theory of the firm[23] is based on the proposition that firms face considerable uncertainty about costs and demands even in the short run and that they adjust prices, promotional expenditures, and other variables whenever it appears that one of their targets is not going to be attained. Once the profit target is met, for example, managers apply their efforts to satisfying the next constraint that has not yet been met, on the basis of their imperfect information systems and their imperfect expectations of the impact of the adjustments they make. In effect, satisficing managers appear to act according to short-run criteria designed to ensure the continued existence and maintained market standing of the firm they control.

The satisficing model of firm behavior is, in effect, an extension of Baumol's sales-maximization model, if we accept that a minimum profit target is the firm's first objective. After attaining this minimum profit level, the firm may pursue a target market

---

[21]See E. Penrose, *The Theory of the Growth of the Firm* (Oxford: Oxford University Press, 1959); and R. Marris, "A Model of the Managerial Enterprise," *Quarterly Journal of Economics*, 77 (May 1963), pp. 185–209.

[22]H. A. Simon, "Theories of Decision Making in Economics and Behavioral Science," *American Economic Review*, 57 (March 1967), pp. 1–33. The principal-agent problem, mentioned in Chapter 1, is an outgrowth of the managerial-utility-maximization model.

[23]See R. M. Cyert and J. E. March, *A Behavioral Theory of the Firm* (Englewood Cliffs, N.J.: Prentice-Hall, 1963), and H. A. Simon, "Theories of Decision Making in Economics," *American Economic Review*, 49 (June 1959), pp. 253–83.

share. Having attained this target, it may pursue a target inventory-to-sales ratio, and so on. In fact, all these targets are simultaneously monitored, and attention is directed primarily to whichever of these targets seems to be in jeopardy at any particular time. The targets themselves, or aspiration levels, are set by management consensus and usually reflect past achievements plus an additional margin to act as an incentive for improved performance. Thus the targets, or aspiration levels, may be consistently revised upward, as the firm becomes more and more efficient in its operation. R. H. Day has argued quite plausibly that this continued revision of aspiration levels can mean that a satisficing strategy eventually converges on the long-term, profit-maximizing strategy.[24]

• NOTE: The above short-run proxy policies (for the maximization of the expected present value of present and future profits) may not lead to exactly the price and output levels in each period that would allow maximum EPV of profits over the firm's planning period. But these proxies would still be optimal if the amount of revenue lost (by not having the "correct" prices and output levels) is less than the search costs avoided. In such cases the firm would be better off using a relatively simplistic short-run objective function than it would by incurring the search costs and having the "correct" price and output level at all times. Thus the firm, anticipating high search costs, may actually make more profits by proceeding simplistically than by incurring the search costs and proceeding elegantly. But the firm should always attempt to evaluate the search costs necessary to obtain the required information, and it should proceed without more information only if it is persuaded that the costs outweigh the benefits that could be derived. We shall pursue this subject further in Chapter 10.

9.6 SUMMARY

In this chapter we introduced the notion that models of the firm's pricing behavior can be characterized under seven assumptions. The four structural assumptions relate to number of sellers, cost conditions, number of buyers, and degree of product differentiation. The three behavioral assumptions refer to the firm's objective function, its strategic variables, and its conjectural variation. The models of pricing behavior differ from each other only to the extent that one or more of the seven basic assumptions is different. The difference in one or more of the underlying assumptions, however, leads to a different pattern of behavior of the firm. Thus the price and output levels chosen by a firm depend on the structural and behavioral conditions under which the firm operates.

The four basic market forms were analyzed for the pricing and output behavior of the firm in each of those market situations. Under conditions of pure competition, monopolistic competition, and monopoly, the pricing and output decision was based on a *ceteris paribus* demand curve because of the expectation that a firm's price or output adjustment would not induce any changes in any other variables. Under oligopoly we introduced the *mutatis mutundis*, or "joint action," demand curve. In the kinked demand

---

[24]See R. H. Day, "Profits, Learning, and the Convergence of Satisficing to Marginalism," *Quarterly Journal of Economics*, May 1967.

curve model of oligopoly the firm envisages no reaction for price increases but expects rivals to match any price reductions. Given these expectations, the oligopolist faces a kinked demand curve, since the *ceteris paribus* section for price increases will be more elastic than the *mutatis mutandis* section for price reductions. The kinked demand curve offers an explanation for price rigidity despite changes in the cost and demand conditions, within limits. Outside these limits of cost and demand movements the firm will change price or output levels.

Conscious parallelism is the process by which firms separately but collectively raise prices in response to common cost or demand changes. This process allows price adjustments to be coordinated, so no firm expects to suffer loss of market share because each firm is anticipating the price changes of its rivals. Price leadership may be provided by a firm that has a keen awareness of industry cost and market demand conditions, as well as a willingness to risk loss of market share by being the first to adjust price. The price followers accept the leader's judgment and raise prices to the same level (or by a similar proportion). The price followers thus avoid the risk of market share loss, as well as the search costs which might otherwise be spent to ascertain the price change required. Barometric, low-cost, and dominant-firm price leadership situations were discussed, and the pricing implications were examined.

When the firm's time horizon falls beyond the present period, a change in the objective function is indicated. The appropriate objective function for the firm facing uncertainty in future periods is the maximization of the expected present value of future profits. Given the search costs involved, however, we expect firms to pursue short-run objective functions which are, in effect, proxies for long-term profit maximization. Sales maximization subject to the attainment of a profit target, limit pricing, and satisficing were each argued to be short-run policies which could approximate the maximization of the firm's EPV of future profits over its planning period. Given the search costs avoided, of course, these policies do not need to indicate the actual prices and outputs which would maximize the EPV of future profits; they merely need to get sufficiently close to the optimal price and output levels, so at least as much profit is earned.

With this grand tour of the theory of the firm behind us, we are now in a position to move to pricing and output decisions in actual business situations. The solution of actual business pricing and output problems is generally facilitated by, and optimized with the aid of, a sound understanding of the models of firm behavior covered in this chapter.

DISCUSSION QUESTIONS

9-1. In what single dimension does monopolistic competition differ from pure competition? In what dimension(s) does oligopoly differ from both of these?

9-2. Characterize according to the simple spectrum of market forms the markets in which the following groups of firms operate:
(a) Automobile dealerships in a large city.
(b) Colleges and universities marketing their degrees to potential students.
(c) An art dealer who wants to sell a unique painting, such as the Mona Lisa.
(d) A grain farmer selling wheat to one of forty or fifty flour-milling companies.

9-3. Given that an oligopolist envisages a kinked demand curve, explain why it is sometimes profit maximizing to raise prices and incur a loss of market share.

9-4. Why would you expect the price rigidity implications of the kinked demand curve model more likely to be observed in practice if the cost changes or demand shifts are firm specific, rather than common to all firms?

9-5. Discuss conscious parallelism in the context of price leadership and followership. Which firms are leaders and which, if any, are followers? Should the firm expect conscious parallelism if a cost change is confined to just that firm?

9-6. Why do firms follow the price leadership of another firm? Is it simply fear of the consequences if they do not? Explain.

9-7. What is the connection between the kinked demand curve model and the low-cost firm price leadership model?

9-8. Explain why the objective sales maximization subject to a minimum profit requirement may be said to be an operational means of pursuing long-term profit maximization.

9-9. For oligopolists to practice limit pricing, what behavioral assumptions must be applicable?

9-10. What has the magnitude of search costs got to do with the short-run policy of satisficing and with the adequacy of any one of the proxy policies for long-term profit maximization?

PROBLEMS AND SHORT CASES

9-1. Show graphically the situation in which a purely competitive market suffers a temporary reduction in consumer demand. Summarize what happens to
(a) The price level.
(b) A representative firm's output level.

9-2. Suppose the automobile producers are confronted with an increase of 10% in the negotiated wage for assembly labor, yet prices of their products remain constant.
(a) Explain with the aid of graphs why the firms might not wish to increase their prices.
(b) Why might you expect these firms to raise prices at the start of the next model year, rather than during the present model year?

9-3. The Prangle Company manufactures and sells several styles of jeans which are branded as the Sizzlers. Several years ago the company introduced the stylized jean look, and Prangle sales increased dramatically. Over the past two years, however, sales have been declining steadily for their stylized jean because of the incursion of several look-alike competing products, even though the total market for stylized jeans is still expanding.

As a result of the increased supply of stylized jeans, the other companies have been selling their competitive jeans at a price below that of Prangle. Prangle's price has not changed from the original price set by the company at the introduction of the jean on the market. Prangle's price at retail was $24, with the retailer paying $18. Other firm's products are retailing for around the same price, with the retailer paying $16.

As a result of the increased supply in the market and Prangle's declining sales volume, Gail Morin, the sales manager, decided to review the cost structure to determine if the margin offered to the retailer could be widened to recoup some of the sales share. If she could significantly reduce the price to retailers, Prangle could recapture some of its lost market.

At the present time, variable production costs (including raw materials and labor) are constant at $8 per pair. The sales volume now is 400,000 pairs of jeans. Ms. Morin is wondering what effect a reduction in price would have on sales and on the profitability of the line. The accounting department and the market research department have estimated cost and demand figures applicable for a reduction in Prangle's price to the retailer. If the price were lowered to that of the competition ($16), demand would increase by 150,000 pairs; if the company lowered the retailer's price even further (to $14), demand is estimated to increase to 625,000 pairs. With such an increase in production the firm could more efficiently use its resources and production facilities. The advantages acquired in bulk buying of raw materials and the more efficient use of labor both help to chisel down the variable costs per pair to $7.50 per unit under the latter demand condition.

Ms. Morin has considered all of the information the market research and accounting departments have provided and is about to make a pricing decision. You are asked to advise on the following issues:

(a) Explain why the Prangle Company suffered declining sales in a market that was actually expanding.

(b) Explain the proposed price reductions in terms of the demand curve the Prangle Company is apparently facing, assuming the data are accurate.

(c) Advise Ms. Morin about the contribution-maximizing price level.

9-4. To demonstrate your understanding of the issues involved, draw the graph for and explain the price and output determination in the three-firm, symmetrically differentiated products case of low-cost firm price leadership. Now expand this model to include conscious parallelism when common cost increases are involved, with price leadership remaining in effect when market demand changes. Explain the conjectural variation of the price followers.

9-5. There are two firms in the prefabricated homes industry producing metal-frame houses. The cost structure of Struktatuff, Inc., is considerably lower than that of its rival, Steeldeal, Inc., although both firms are about the same size in terms of output capacity. The cost functions have been estimated as $TC = 160,000 + 4,850Q$ for Struktatuff, and $TC = 120,000 + 5,250Q$ for Steeldeal. These firms face the market demand curve specified by $P = 36,384 - 1.25Q$.

In past years it has become evident that Struktatuff is the effective price leader. Steeldeal twice tried to set a lower price, but each time Struktatuff undercut this price and forced a return to the price that maximized its own contribution. Product differentiation is such that when prices are equal, Struktatuff always has two thirds of the market while Steeldeal has the remaining one third.

(a) On separate but adjacent graphs, show the *mutatis mutandis* demand curves for both Struktatuff and Steeldeal.

(b) Show the price level that Struktatuff will prefer.

(c) Calculate the output level that will be produced by each firm.

9-6. In a dominant-firm oligopoly, the market demand curve has been estimated by the dominant firm to be $P = 100 - 1.25Q$, where Q represents thousands of units. There are twenty very small firms who each have a cost structure estimated by $TC = 10 + 15Q + 11.25Q^2$.

(a) Show graphically the derivation of the dominant firm's residual demand curve.

(b) Suppose the dominant firm's cost structure is represented by $TC = 500 + 10Q + 0.25Q^2$. Show on your graph the profit-maximizing price the dominant firm will choose.

(c) Calculate the profits earned by the dominant firm and by each of the small firms.

(d) Comment on what you expect may happen in the long run.

9-7. In the market for introductory economics textbooks there are several competitive textbooks, whose prices range from $31.95 to $44.95. One of the established texts is the major seller and is considered to be the price leader in this field. A new text has recently become available, and its publishing company has priced it at $43.95 and expects to sell 60,000 copies. At this price the company expects to maximize contribution to its overheads and profits. The author of this text receives royalties which are a fixed percentage of total sales receipts. He feels that if the price were reduced to around $32 each, the market would demand 140,000 copies. The publisher feels that the author's perception of the market situation is unrealistic and that a lower price would *reduce* both the contribution and the royalties, as compared with the company's selected price.

(a) Explain the author's side of the argument. What is his objective function and why does he wish to select a lower price than does the publishing company?

(b) Explain the publisher's side of the argument. What is its perception of the market situation? Why does it expect both sales revenue and contribution to fall at lower prices?

9-8. The cement industry in a particular region is characterized by five firms producing what are highly similar products. Over the years these firms have found that active price competition is to be avoided, since this strategy has led to prolonged periods of low profitability. At the same time, each firm jealously guards its market share and will quickly match any price reduction by a competitor. Whenever costs increase for all firms, the firms act, as if by consensus, to raise prices concurrently to preserve their profit positions.

It has become obvious recently that a cement producer in another region is considering entering the market by building a sixth plant in the vicinity of the plants of the existing five firms. This firm would have higher costs per unit, however, because the existing five firms control all nearby sources of the basic raw material, limestone.

The existing firms have similar cost structures and find that their marginal costs per ton are virtually constant at $20 per ton. At current output levels of about 200,000 tons each per annum, the firms must cover $5 per ton in overhead costs. and they now price their cement at $32 per ton. The potential entrant's average variable costs are expected to be 20% higher and its total fixed costs per annum are expected to be 15% lower than those of the five existing firms. If entry takes place next year, the new firm is expected to gain about 10% of the market in the first year (pricing at $32 per ton), gradually improving its position to an equal share as a result of the very slight product differentiation involved with this product. The overall market demand for the product is expected to be constant over the next few years, and the market price elasticity of demand is quite low, at -0.2.

(a) Should the existing firms practice limit pricing to forestall the entry of the sixth firm? What price would be necessary to prevent entry?

(b) If the sixth firm does enter the industry, what price level would maximize contribution for each firm after the entrant firm achieves an equal share of the market?

9-9. Fiori Pasta Company produces high-quality pasta products. It has estimated its demand curve for its spaghetti to be $P = 39.898 - 0.03757Q$, where Q represents thousands of cartons (each containing five dozen packets of spaghetti) demanded per year by its wholesale customers. Its cost of producing this spaghetti has been estimated as $TC = 2,500,000 + 12Q + 0.01538Q^2$. Fiori is having a management meeting to reconsider its pricing strategy. Its current price for the spaghetti is $27.50 per carton. The president, Don Fiori, wants to maximize sales volume subject to earning a target profit of $500,000 per year. The vice-president of sales, Tony Fiori, wants to maximize sales revenue, since his bonus relates only to sales revenue. The vice-president of production, Gina Fiori, wants to maximize profits so they can afford to install the latest high-technology manufacturing equipment. You have been hired to give an impartial analysis of the problem facing Fiori Pasta.

(a) Calculate the profit-maximizing price and output level, and the profits at that price level.

(b) Calculate the price, output, and profit levels that would be preferred by Tony Fiori.

(c) Plot the TC, TR, and profit curves on a graph, and estimate from the graph the output level that would satisfy Don Fiori. What is the associated price level?

(d) Prepare your report for presentation at the Fiori management meeting.

9-10. Two bakeries serve a small, isolated rural community. Golden Bread Company is the low-cost price leader, and Farmer's Family Bakery is the price follower. Golden's cost function has been estimated as $TC = 8,000 + 6.5Q + 0.00047Q^2$, where TC is the firm's total cost per month and Q represents dozens of loaves of bread. The market demand curve has been estimated as $P = 24 - 0.00125Q$. The market views the products of the two bakeries as essentially similar, and so they share the market equally when their prices are equal.

Popular Bakery is a major city bakery that is considering entering the rural market. Its production facilities are large, and its average variable cost per unit is constant at a level about 20% less than Golden's minimum average cost. However, the additional transportation cost that Popular would have to incur would mean that its delivered cost would be about

50% more than its average variable cost. Popular is expected to enter the rural market if the price is at least 20% over its delivered cost per dozen.

(a) Show graphically (and confirm algebraically) the profit-maximizing price that Golden will set if it ignores the potential entry of the Popular Bakery Company. Calculate the firm's profits at that price.

(b) What is the limit price that will keep the Popular Bakery Company out of the rural market? What will be Golden's output and profit levels at that price?

(c) Suppose that you are the manager of Golden. What price strategy would you choose, and why?

SUGGESTED REFERENCES AND FURTHER READING

ALCHIAN, A. A. "Uncertainty, Evolution, and Economic Theory," *Journal of Political Economy*, 58 (June 1950), pp. 211–21.

BAIN, J. S. *Barriers to New Competition*. Cambridge, Mass.: Harvard University Press, 1956.

BAUMOL, W. J. *Business Behavior, Value, and Growth* (2nd ed.), esp. chap. 6. New York: Harcourt Brace Jovanovich, 1967.

BAUMOL, W. J. "Contestable Markets: An Uprising in the Theory of Markets," *American Economic Review,* 72 (March 1982), pp. 1–15.

BAUMOL, W. J., J. C. PANZER, and R. D. WILLIG. *Contestable Markets and the Theory of Industry Structure*. San Diego: Harcourt Brace Jovanovich, 1982.

BHAGWATI, J. "Oligopoly Theory, Entry Prevention, and Growth," *Oxford Economic Papers*, 22 (1970), pp. 297–310.

CHAMBERLIN, E. H. *The Theory of Monopolistic Competition*. Cambridge, Mass.: Harvard University Press, 1969.

COHEN, K. J., and R. M. CYERT. *Theory of the Firm*, esp. chaps. 15–17. Englewood Cliffs, N.J.: Prentice-Hall, Inc., 1965.

CYERT, R. M., and J. E. MARCH. *A Behavioral Theory of the Firm*. Englewood Cliffs, N.J.: Prentice-Hall, Inc., 1963.

DEMSETZ, H. "Barriers to Entry," *American Economic Review*, 72 (March 1982), pp. 47–57.

EATON, B. C., and R. G. LIPSEY. "Exit Barriers Are Entry Barriers: The Durability of Capital as a Barrier to Entry," *Bell Journal of Economics* 11 (Autumn 1980), pp. 721–29.

FLAHERTY, M. T. "Dynamic Limit Pricing, Barriers to Entry, and Rational Firms," *Journal of Economic Theory,* 23 (October 1980), pp. 160–82.

FRANCIS, A. "Company Objectives, Managerial Motivations, and the Behavior of Large Firms: An Empirical Test of the Theory of 'Managerial' Capitalism," *Cambridge Journal of Economics*, 4 (December 1980), pp. 349–61.

GASKINS, D. W., JR. "Dynamic Limit Pricing: Optimal Pricing under Threat of Entry," *Journal of Economic Theory*, 3 (September 1971), pp. 306–22.

HALL, R. L., and C. J. HITCH. "Price Theory and Business Behavior," *Oxford Economic Papers*, May 1939, pp. 12–45.

HAMBURGER, W. "Conscious Parallelism and the Kinked Oligopoly Demand Curve," *American Economic Review*, 57 (May 1967), pp. 266–68.

HOLTHAUSEN, D. M. "Kinky Demand, Risk Aversion. and Price Leadership," *International Economic Review*, 20 (June 1979), pp. 341–48.

KLING, A. "Imperfect Information and Price Rigidity." *Economic Inquiry*, 20 (January 1982). pp. 145–54.

LOOMES, G. "Why Oligopoly Prices Don't Stick," *Journal of Economic Studies*, 8. No. 1 (1981), pp. 37–46.

MARKHAM, J. W. "The Nature and Significance of Price Leadership," *American Economic Review*, 41 (December 1951), pp. 891–905.

MCDONALD, IAN M., "The Setting of Retail Prices in a Customer Market," *Economic Record*, 66 (December 1990), pp. 322–8.

OSBORNE, D. K. "The Role of Entry in Oligopoly Theory," *Journal of Political Economy*, 72 (August 1964), pp. 396–402.

ROBINSON, J. *The Economics of Imperfect Competition*. London: Macmillan, Inc., 1933.

SCHERER, F. M. *Industrial Market Structure and Economic Performance* (2nd ed.), chaps. 5-8. Chicago: Rand McNally & Company, 1980.

SMITH, D. S., and W. C. NEALE. "The Geometry of Kinky Oligopoly: Marginal Cost, the Gap, and Price Behavior," *Southern Economic Journal*, 37 (January 1971), pp. 276–82.

STIGLER, G. J. "The Kinky Oligopoly Demand Curve and Rigid Prices," *Journal of Political Economy*, 55 (October 1947), pp. 432–49.

SWEEZY, P. M. "Demand under Conditions of Oligopoly," *Journal of Political Economy*, 47 (August 1939), pp. 568–73.

WELCH, P. J. "On the Compatibility of Profit Maximization and the Other Goals of the Firm," *Review of Social Economics*, 38 (April 1980), pp. 65–74.

WILLIAMSON, J. "Profit, Growth and Sales Maximization," *Economica*, 33, No. 129 (1966), pp. 1–16.

Appendix 9A

FURTHER MODELS
OF PRICING BEHAVIOR

EXECUTIVE SUMMARY

In this appendix we examine five somewhat more complicated, but at the same time more realistic and useful, models of the firm's pricing decision.

First, we consider the pricing and output decision of **the multiplant firm**. This firm must decide how much to produce in total and what price is profit maximizing, and then it must apportion its total output between or among its two or more separate plants.

Second, we examine **cartels**, which are groups of firms acting in unison to set price and apportion output among their various plants.

Third, we examine **price discrimination** by a firm that can subdivide its customers into separate groups or markets. We show that a firm can increase its profit by charging a higher price to the buyers whose demand is less elastic and by asking a lower price from those buyers whose demand is more elastic, provided certain preconditions are met.

Fourth, we discuss **transfer pricing**. Transfer prices are the prices set for transactions that take place between divisions or profit centers within the same firm or organization. Since such transactions are an internal matter, they may not be subject to market forces, and the temptation exists to set them in an arbitrary fashion. The optimal transfer price is the one which induces each division to act in the best interests of the firm as a whole.

Finally, we consider the pricing decision where buyers are spread out in geographical space and the costs of transportation or delivery must be incorporated into the selling price. This is called spatial competition, and prices are quoted as **delivered prices**.

The Multiplant Firm

Many firms operate more than one plant. They may have built two or more smaller plants to avoid diseconomies of plant size that would occur if they tried to serve their market from a single, much larger, plant. A second reason for multiplant operation is relatively high transportation costs for the finished goods. If the market is spread over a wide geographical area, the firm will find it more economical to operate two or more plants in two or more locations if the savings in transportation costs more than outweigh the economies of plant size foregone. Third, the firm may operate two or more plants as a result of a merger or takeover, and the costs of scrapping both plants and building another larger one more than offset the economies of plant size foregone.

The multiplant firm must determine its profit-maximizing price and total output level, and at the same time it must determine the cost-minimizing allocation of the total output among its two or more plants.

The standard profit-maximizing rule, that marginal costs should equal marginal revenue, remains applicable, but our interpretation of the marginal cost curve must reflect the fact that marginal costs now derive from two or more production sources. The relevant marginal cost curve must show the marginal cost for each incremental unit produced when the firm is free to choose the plant in which that incremental unit should be produced. Clearly, the firm will always nominate the plant that can produce the incremental unit at the lowest additional (or marginal) cost. A simple means of ensuring this result is demonstrated in Figure 9A-1.

For simplicity, we assume just two plants being operated by a particular firm. To make the exercise nontrivial, we have assumed differing cost structures for the two plants: Plant A has a higher cost structure than plant B, perhaps because of its location in a high-land-value area or another factor cost disadvantage or because of the inability of this plant to achieve the same degree of production efficiency as plant B.

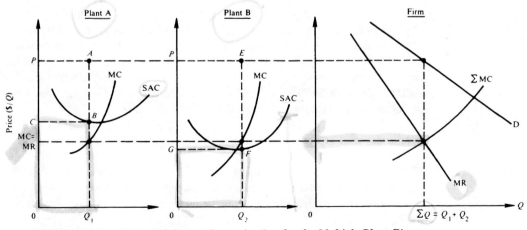

FIGURE 9A-1. Price and Output Determination for the Multiple-Plant Firm

The marginal cost curves of plants A and B are summed horizontally to find the curve ΣMC shown in the "firm" part of the figure. This curve shows the combined marginal costs of the firm—that is, for a particular output level, some part of the output will have been produced in plant A and the remainder will have come from plant B, taking care always to select the incremental unit from the plant that can produce it at lowest marginal cost. It follows that at any total output level, the marginal cost from each plant should be approximately equal, since if this were not true the last unit might be taken away from the plant with the higher marginal cost and might be produced instead by the plant with the lower marginal cost, and thus reduce the marginal cost, to the firm as a whole, of the last unit produced. The ΣMC curve thus shows the marginal cost to the firm of each successive output unit, given the ability of the firm to have that unit produced in whichever of its plants can produce it most efficiently.

The firm's profits will be maximized at the output level when the combined marginal cost just equals the marginal revenue. This is shown as output level ΣQ in Figure 9A-1, and the demand curve indicates that the firm should set price P. The intersection of the ΣMC and MR curves indicates the *level* at which marginal costs are equal to marginal revenue. If we extend a line at this level across to the cost curves of plants A and B, it will indicate how the total output ΣQ should be divided between the two plants. Marginal costs in plant A come up to this critical level at output Q_1, and in plant B marginal costs meet this level at output Q_2. Outputs Q_1 and Q_2 together add up to ΣQ by virtue of the method of construction of the curve ΣMC. Thus, when the output ΣQ is divided among the plants in this way, the marginal cost of plant A equals the marginal cost of plant B, and both of these equal the marginal revenue of the final unit sold. The firm's profit is shown as the sum of the two rectangles *PABC* (from plant A) and *PEFG* (from plant B), which show the per-unit profit margin times the number of units produced, in each of the two plants.

The above analysis of the multiplant firm applies to any market situation where a firm envisages a negatively sloping *ceteris paribus* demand curve. It is thus appropriate for monopoly, monopolistic competition, or oligopoly situations. For oligopolistic markets where mutual dependence is recognized, price may be determined by a price leader or by "conscious parallelism," rather than independently, as suggested in the preceding discussion, and the demand curve depicted in Figure 9A-1 would represent the firm's *mutatis mutandis*, or share-of-the-market, demand curve. But the rule for allocation of output between or among multiple plants remains the same. The firm should ensure that the marginal cost of the last unit produced in each plant is approximately the same and is equal to the marginal revenue obtained for those last units.

Cartel Price and Output Determination

• DEFINITION: A *cartel* is a group of firms acting as one, determining their price and output levels from within a central administering body. Cartels are illegal in most Western countries, but a couple of major international cartels continue to exist, immune from national legislation.

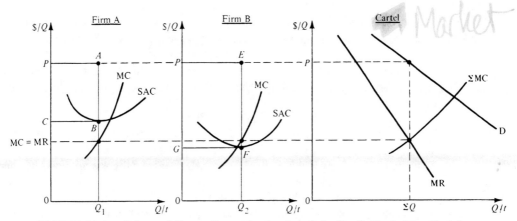

FIGURE 9A-2. *Price and Output Determination by a Joint-Profit-Maximizing Cartel*

- EXAMPLE: The International Air Transport Association (IATA) determines air fares and many elements of nonprice competition for its members, such as types of meals, beverage prices, and in-flight movie prices. During the 1970s, higher levels of excess capacity resulting from the advent of jumbo jets, as well as the vigorous competition of third world airlines, reduced IATA's market control to a significant degree. The Organization of Petroleum Exporting Countries (OPEC), undoubtedly the most powerful cartel in the late 1970s, was able to elevate the prices of petroleum products dramatically as its members jointly raised prices to the levels agreed on. The influence of OPEC waned considerably as the "oil glut" of the 1980s induced members to offer discounts below the cartel price. As implied by these two examples, the life of cartels tends to be short and stormy. We shall see that cartels are inherently unstable because of the incentives facing each firm to cheat on the cartel agreement.

A cartel may be either profit maximizing or market sharing. The profit-maximizing cartel attempts to maximize the *joint* profits of the firms. The firms then take a share of the total profits as determined by prior agreement or as actually earned. The market-sharing cartel establishes rules that allow each firm to maintain its predetermined or historical share of the market. We examine here each type in turn.

The Profit-Maximizing Cartel. The profit-maximizing cartel has exactly the same price and output decisions to make as does the multiplant firm. The cartel is like the multiplant firm except that it does not own each of the plants; it simply controls their pricing and output decisions.

For simplicity we assume there are two members in the cartel and that the firms have differing cost structures: Firm A has a higher cost structure than firm B, as shown in Figure 9A-2.

The marginal cost curves of A and B are summed horizontally to find curve ΣMC shown in the part of the figure labeled *cartel*. This curve shows the combined marginal costs of the cartel; that is, for a particular output level, some part of the output is produced in firm A and the remainder in firm B, taking care always to select the incremental unit from the firm that can produce it at the lower marginal cost. From this it follows that at any particular total output level the marginal cost from each firm should be approximately equal. The ΣMC curve thus shows the marginal cost to the cartel of each successive output unit, given the ability of the cartel to have that unit produced by the firm that can produce it most efficiently.

The cartel's profits are maximized at the output level where the combined marginal cost just equals the marginal revenue. This is shown as output level ΣQ in Figure 9A-2. The demand curve indicates that the cartel should set price P. The intersection of the ΣMC and MR curves indicates the level at which marginal costs are equal to marginal revenue. If we extend a line at this level across to the cost curves of firms A and B, we see how total output ΣQ should be divided between the two firms. In firm A marginal costs come up to this critical level at output Q_1, and in firm B they come up to this level at output Q_2. Outputs Q_1 and Q_2 together add up to ΣQ, by virtue of the method of construction of the curve ΣMC. Thus, when the output ΣQ is divided among the firms in this way, the marginal cost of firm A equals the marginal cost of firm B. Both of these equal the marginal revenue of the final unit sold. The cartel's profit is shown as the sum of the two rectangles *PABC* (from firm A) and *PEFG* (from firm B). These rectangles show the per-unit profit margin times the number of units produced, in each of the two firms.

Side Payments and the Incentive to Undercut the Cartel Price.   The two member firms may agree to keep the profits they have each earned. Alternatively, there may be a prior agreement that the more profitable firm B must give some of its profits to the less profitable firm A. This *side payment* may be thought necessary to help firm A resist the temptation to undercut the cartel price and temporarily, at least, to enjoy an elastic demand response for its product. In fact, both firms face the temptation of large sales gains and higher profits if they can secretly undercut the cartel price. If either firm can set a price below the cartel price, while the other firm continues to set the cartel price, the price-cutting firm will face a relatively elastic *ceteris paribus* demand curve, on which there will be a lower, more profitable price. Let us illustrate, using firm A as the price cutter in Figure 9A-3.

Initially, firm A is setting the cartel price P and producing Q_1 units of output. When contemplating independent price adjustments, the firm envisages the *ceteris paribus* demand curve shown as d. Associated with that curve is the marginal revenue curve, mr, which intersects the firm's marginal cost curve, MC_A, at output level Q'. Profits at the lower price P' are equal to the area $P'A'B'C'$ and are considerably larger than the profits *PABC* available to the firm as a member of the cartel. Thus there is considerable profit incentive to leave the cartel and price independently. Firm A might require a side payment equal to the difference in these two profit rectangles to keep it in the cartel.

But notice that the firm would earn these extra profits only as long as *ceteris paribus* prevailed. As soon as the other firm noticed its loss of sales and ascertained that firm A was "chiseling" the cartel price, it would probably match A's price reduction to maintain its share of the market. Alternatively, it might undercut A's price to teach it a

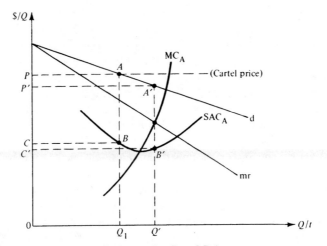

FIGURE 9A-3.   The Incentive to Undercut the Cartel Price

lesson, and a price war might ensue. The extra profits are available to firm A only as long as the price reduction remains unknown to firm B. If A is able to give customers secret discounts, and if sales normally fluctuate considerably in any case, firm B might not discover the duplicity for several weeks or months, during which time A can earn extra profits, which may be worth the risk of setting off a price war or of facing other disciplinary action by the cartel.

The more firms there are in a cartel, the more difficult it is, *ceteris paribus*, for the cartel to control prices or outputs of individual firms. The more firms, the more difficult it is for cartel members to find out that they are being undercut, since the "chiseler's" sales gain is comprised of proportionately smaller sales losses for each firm. There is thus a greater inclination for individual firms to undercut the cartel price. In actual business practice the life of cartels has usually been short and stormy, ending with a rapid decline in prices after the discovery that one or more firms were undercutting the cartel price.

The Market-Sharing Cartel.   In some instances oligopolists may wish to come to an agreement regarding their share of the market as a primary objective, rather than allow the market share to be the outcome of the price-fixing agreement, as in the preceding discussion. Firms that are geographically dispersed, for example, may feel that they have a right to sales in their own territory and will want to preclude encroachment by rivals into that territory. In this case the total market would be shared on the basis of the firms' locations and the density of population (and consequent demand) in each territory. Alternatively, firms with large output capacities may feel that they deserve a larger share of the market than would be allocated to them under a joint profit-maximizing cartel agreement. The other firms may be willing to allow these firms to take more than their (joint profit-maximizing) share, rather than risk a breakdown of the cartel's price agreement.

The agreement on market share may be quite an explicit arrangement (firm A gets 15% of industry sales) or an implicit, general understanding among the firms concerning each one's annual output levels (firm A has a quota of about 200,000 units annually). We immediately see that problems arise in business situations, since these agreements involve an estimate of annual market demand. Different conceptions of the market, different projections about the coming year's demand, and different perceptions of the same phenomena are likely to lead to disagreements about what constitutes a 15% share, for example. Compromises on these issues may leave some firms feeling less happy than others and perhaps more likely to violate the agreement at a later time. Similarly, agreements on the boundaries of each firm's geographical territory may be hard to arrive at and may be quite fragile when finally made.

When business is booming, firms have little time or reason to think about how the market-sharing agreement puts them at a disadvantage. When demand slackens in periods of recession or depression, however, firms may be considerably more inclined to undercut the cartel price or to encroach on another firm's territory and compete for sales. Such price cutting, probably in the form of secret discounts, generous trade-in allowances, or additional goods and services for the same price, soon comes to the attention of other firms. The cartel agreement would be expected to break down as other firms begin to take defensive measures to avoid losing any more of their market shares.

Cartel price and market-sharing agreements might be expected to work a lot better if the participant firms have similar cost structures and either identical or symmetrically differentiated products. In such cases a single market price and equal market shares are likely to be relatively palatable solutions to the uncertainty faced by oligopolists.

Price Discrimination

- DEFINITION: *Price discrimination* is the practice of charging different prices to different buyers or groups of buyers for essentially the same product, where these price differences do not simply reflect the cost differences associated with serving different buyers or markets. The monopolist may find it both possible and more profitable to discriminate among buyers on some basis—to charge a higher price to some buyers and a lower price to others, rather than set the same price for all buyers. Price discrimination in the economic sense must be distinguished from price discrimination in the legal sense. In Appendix 10A we briefly examine the illegal methods of price discrimination. In perhaps most instances, economic price discrimination is not illegal.

- NOTE: Three major conditions must exist before it is possible and profitable to practice price discrimination. First, the buyers or groups of buyers (markets) must be *separable*. That is, it must be possible to identify and keep separate the two or more buyers or markets, to prevent arbitrage selling from the lower-price to the higher-price buyer or market. Second, the two or more buyers (or markets) must exhibit *differing price elasticities of demand* at any particular price level, to make price discrimination profitable, as we shall see below. Third, the markets must be characterized by a *lack of price competition* from rival firms, to prevent price levels' being eroded from the profit-maximizing levels in each market. Clearly, price discrimination is most likely to work well in a monopoly situation, where there are no rivals to worry about, but it is also feasible in oligopoly markets, where the firms coordinate their pricing strategies using conscious parallelism, price leadership, or cartel pricing.

Price discrimination has been categorized into three distinct types. *First-degree price discrimination* occurs when each buyer is forced to pay the maximum that he or she would have been willing to pay for the product. In situations where there is no price discrimination, all but one of the buyers pay *less* than they would have been willing to pay, since there is only one price at which the product is offered, and the last buyer is the one who is only just willing to pay the price asked. All other buyers (those higher on the demand curve) would have been willing to pay more but were not asked to.[1] First-degree price discrimination involves asking each buyer to pay the maximum he or she would be willing to pay or else go without the product. In practice, of course, this is a difficult pricing decision, since one cannot know the preference structures of all the potential buyers.

- EXAMPLE: One means of accomplishing first-degree price discrimination in practice is the so-called Dutch auction in which the price starts at a very high level and the auctioneer calls out prices at slowly reducing price levels. The first person to accept the called price as the purchase price gets the product. This person will have paid the maximum he or she would have been willing to pay, since this buyer did not know what the second-most-eager buyer would have paid and therefore must bid as soon as the price falls to the maximum level he or she would have paid. The more conventional auction, in which price is bid upward, ensures that the successful bidder pays only slightly more than the second-most-eager buyer was willing to pay, rather than the maximum he or she was willing to pay.

Second-degree price discrimination involves discriminating among groups of buyers on a time or urgency basis. Those most eager to purchase the product will pay a higher price than those prepared to wait a little longer, and so on.

- EXAMPLE: An amazing example of second-degree price discrimination was the early sale of ballpoint pens, which reportedly sold for around thirty dollars each because of their novelty and utility value. Later, as technology advanced and costs fell, and as the market became progressively more saturated, the price fell to the level we know today. Products that have undergone a similar reduction in prices in more recent years are electronic calculators and quartz-crystal wristwatches. One further example is the pricing of tickets for new-movie releases. First runs in city theaters are priced substantially above second runs in suburban theaters, and so on down the line until finally the movie appears on television for virtually no charge at all.

Third-degree price discrimination is a situation whereby the firm can charge different prices in two or more different markets at the same point in time.

---

[1]Consumer surplus is the name given to the amount of money the consumer would have been willing to pay over and above the price actually paid. In regular markets all buyers except the last one receive some amount of consumer surplus. With first-degree price discrimination all consumer surplus is expropriated by the seller from every buyer, and it is added to the producer's surplus, which is profit. For more on consumer surplus, see R. A. Bilas, *Microeconomic Theory*, 2nd ed. (New York: McGraw-Hill Book Company, 1971), pp. 97–107.

- EXAMPLE: Examples of third-degree price discrimination are telephone and electricity price differentials between households and business establishments and a firm that charges a higher price for a particular product in a downtown store than in a suburban store. Telephone companies also practice third-degree price discrimination by separating their markets on the basis of the time of day and the day of the week. Long-distance telephone calls during business hours cost more than during early morning hours or on weekends. Business establishments are willing and able to pay the higher prices during the day, since business must be conducted when other businesses are also operating. If the prices were the same twenty-four hours a day, many home users would write letters instead. Recognizing the more elastic nature of home demand, the telephone company offers cheaper calls at less convenient hours to increase the use of long-distance telephone calls in two ways: First, it attracts buyers who would not otherwise purchase the service; and second, it shifts some of the demand into the offpeak hours, which saves the company from building a larger plant just to handle peak traffic.

To practice third-degree price discrimination the firm must decide what its total output should be, how it should distribute this output between or among the separate markets, and what price it should set in each market, so profits are maximized. The methodology for solving this problem is similar to that for the multiplant firm's allocation problem. The firm should distribute each successive output unit to the market in which the unit contributes most to total revenues and should continue up to the point where the marginal revenue derived from the sale of the last unit is just equal to the marginal cost of producing that last unit. Figure 9A-4 shows two market situations, A and B. Market A has the more inelastic demand situation, perhaps because of fewer competitors or higher incomes of the buyers, or simply because of different taste patterns of the buyers in that market. If the firm were to begin with its first output unit, it would certainly sell this unit in market A, at a price near P_0, since the marginal revenue of the first unit is higher there than in market B. As the firm lowers its price to sell successive units, these units too will be best sold in market A, at least initially. But when price P_1 is reached in market A, a price of P_2 in market B would generate the same marginal revenue ($= P_2$). Thus buyers in market B begin to enter the market, and the firm should now allocate successive output units back and forth between markets A and B, taking care to allocate each incremental unit to the market in which it derives the greatest marginal revenue. The curve ΣMR in the "firm" part of the figure indicates the marginal revenue to the firm when it is free to allocate each successive unit to the market in which marginal revenue is highest. It is found by the horizontal summation of the marginal revenue curves in markets A and B. Clearly, it must begin at price level P_0 and kink at price level P_2, since below this level it is the horizontal sum of both MR curves rather than just the one.

In Figure 9A-5 we superimpose the firm's short-run cost curves upon the ΣMR curve. The output level that maximizes the firm's profits is shown as ΣQ, where its marginal costs rise to equality with its declining marginal revenues. The intersection of the MC and ΣMR curves defines the *level* at which marginal revenues in each market should be equated to the firm's marginal costs. Extending a line at this level across to the graphs for markets A and B, we see that the firm should allocate Q_A units to market A

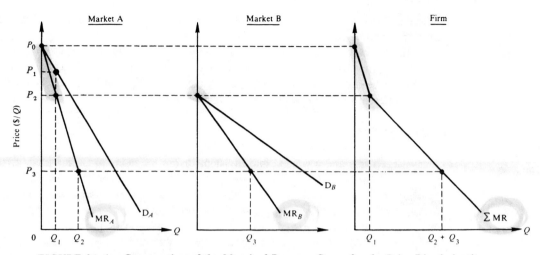

FIGURE 9A-4.   Construction of the Marginal Revenue Curve for the Price-Discriminating Firm

and Q_B units to market B, since marginal revenues in each of these markets at these output levels have fallen to the level to which marginal costs have risen. In market A, quantity Q_A should be priced at price P_A, and quantity Q_B will be sold at price P_B in market B. Note that the more inelastic market is charged the higher price. The firm's total profits may be calculated as the sum of the price-cost margin in each market times the quantity sold in each market. That is, profits in market A will be the shaded area $P_A C \times 0Q_A$, and in market B profits will be the shaded area $P_B C \times 0Q_B$.

   The output level ΣQ, and the allocation of this output between the markets as shown, is optimal, because if another unit was produced its marginal cost would exceed the marginal revenue in either market, and if the last unit was taken from either market and sold in the other, its marginal revenue would be less than its marginal cost. Thus any

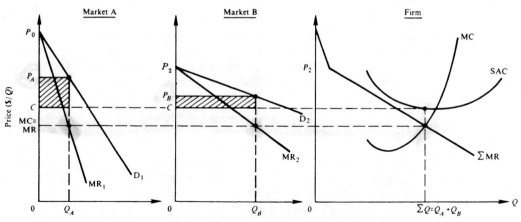

FIGURE 9A-5.   Prices and Output Determination by the Price-Discriminating Firm

different output level or allocation of output between the markets would cause the firm's total profits to be reduced.

In summary, price discrimination involves charging different prices to different buyers or groups of buyers when their demand situations differ. If markets or individual buyers can be identified and kept separate, the monopolist can increase its profits by setting different prices for each one.

Transfer Pricing

Many large firms are organized into divisions or profit centers to facilitate the efficient operation of the firm. The decentralization of decision making in this way is considered to have a beneficial impact on the firm's overall efficiency and profitability, since each division manager is judged by the profit performance of his or her division or profit center. A problem can arise, however, when one division or profit center supplies a component product (or intermediate product) to another division or profit center that uses this intermediate product as the basis for the firm's finished product, which is sold to consumers. This transaction is essentially internal to the firm and does not take place in the market for that intermediate product, if indeed there is a market for it. If the transfer price is set at a relatively high level, the supplying division will make more profits and the buying division less, presuming there is competition of some sort in the market for the finished product. If the transfer price is set at a relatively low level, the opposite will prevail. The firm as a whole will wish to set the transfer price at a level which serves to maximize the profit of the firm as a whole, rather than at some arbitrary or negotiated level that may not best serve the firm's objective.

We shall analyze the transfer pricing problem under three scenarios, first considering the case where there is no external market for the intermediate product, then considering the existence of a purely competitive external market for the intermediate product, and finally considering the existence of an imperfectly competitive market for the intermediate product.

Transfer Pricing with No External Market.   The marginalist rule, that marginal cost equals marginal revenue, determines the profit-maximizing output and price level for the firm as a whole. But if the firm has two divisions, for example, its overall marginal cost at any output level will be the sum of the marginal costs in its two divisions. Suppose a firm has two divisions, A and B. The intermediate product is produced in division A, and then packaged and marketed by division B. We suppose that each division has an upward-sloping marginal cost curve, as shown in Figure 9A-6. The vertical sum of these two MC curves is shown as the MC_F curve, and the firm maximizes profit at the price P^* and output level Q^*.

What transfer price should be established to induce division A to produce exactly the profit-maximizing output of the intermediate product? Similarly, what transfer price will induce division B to set the market price at the level P^* such that the firm's profits are maximized? In Figure 9A-6 we show the optimal transfer price as P_T chosen to equal division A's marginal cost at output level Q^*. As a result, division A faces a horizontal demand curve at the transfer price—it can sell as much as it wants to at that price.

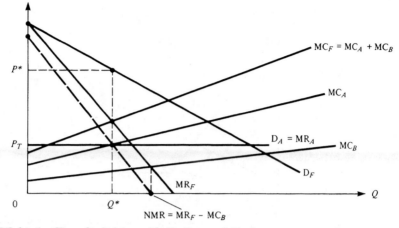

FIGURE 9A-6.   *Transfer Pricing with No External Market*

However, it will only want to produce Q^* units, since its marginal cost (MC_A) equals its marginal revenue (MR_A) at that output level. Thus setting the transfer price at the level P_T induces division A to produce and supply exactly the optimal amount.

From the viewpoint of division B, the net marginal revenue (NMR) from the sale of the intermediate product is equal to $MR_F - MC_B$ or the market marginal revenue minus division B's marginal cost. At output/sales level Q^*, note that $NMR = MC_A$ (because $MR_F = MC_F$ at output Q^*, hence $MR_F - MC_B = MC_F - MC_B = MC_A$). That is, the marketing division's net marginal revenue equals the marginal cost of the intermediate product that it buys from division A, which is in turn is equal to the transfer price. Thus division B maximizes its profits by setting market price P^* and output/sales level Q^*. At any other price and output combination in the market for the finished product, division B's NMR would either exceed or fall short of the transfer price (its effective marginal cost of the intermediate product), and its divisional profit would not be maximized.

Thus establishing the transfer price at the level P_T provides the appropriate incentives for both divisions to produce and sell at the firm's profit-maximizing output level Q^*. Each division maximizes its profits by producing Q^* units, and the overall firm's profits are also maximized. Any other transfer price may have higher profits for either division A or B, but would have lower profit for the firm as a whole, not to mention a shortage or surplus of the intermediate product.

Transfer Pricing with a Purely Competitive External Market.   Now suppose that the intermediate product is available from other suppliers as well as division A. Moreover, division A's product is identical to that of other suppliers. There will be a market price for the intermediate product determined by the forces of supply and demand in that external market. In this case the transfer price must be set equal to the market price for the intermediate product. If it is set higher, division B will prefer to buy from the external market rather than from division A. If the transfer price is set below the external market price, division A will prefer to sell to the external market rather than to division B. If, at

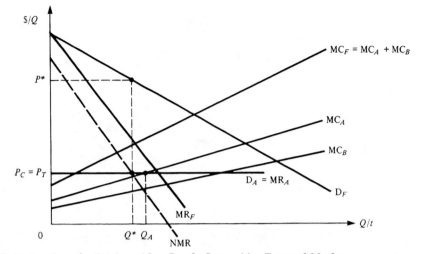

FIGURE 9A-7.   Transfer Pricing with a Purely Competitive External Market

the transfer price (equal to the market price), division A wants to produce more than division B wishes to purchase, it can sell the balance in the external market. Conversely, if division B wants to purchase more than division A wishes to produce, it can buy the remainder in the external market.

In Figure 9A-7 we show the transfer price set at the external market price P_C. Note that division A will wish to produce Q_A units, such that $MC_A = MR_A$. Division B will demand only Q^* units, since $NMR = MR_F - MC_B = P_T$ at that output level. Thus division A will sell the remainder, shown by the distance $Q_A - Q^*$, in the external market for the intermediate product. Had the competitive external market price been lower, such that $Q_A < Q^*$, division B would have purchased some from division A and the remainder from the external market.

Transfer Pricing with an Imperfectly Competitive External Market.   Now we suppose that the intermediate products are not identical across firms, and thus each supplier to the external market faces a downward-sloping demand curve in that market. In Figure 9A-8 we show the demand and marginal revenue curves for the external market in the middle panel of the figure. In the left-hand panel we show the net marginal revenue (NMR) curve for (the marketing) division B of the firm, which is responsible for setting the market price and output level in the market for the finished product. Division A again has two markets for its output—it can sell to either division B or it can sell to the external market. However, since the elasticities of demand are different in these two markets in this case, division A will find it profitable to practice price discrimination between the two markets.

The analysis proceeds as in the third-degree price discrimination case. The firm will sum horizontally the marginal revenue from its markets, and equate the ΣMR with its marginal cost of production MC_A. But note that from the firm's point of view it must consider only the net marginal revenue from the internal market (sales to division B), since otherwise it would be ignoring division B's marginal cost. The intersection of the ΣMR and MC_A curves determines division A's total output level Q_A, which must then be allocated between the internal and external markets. By extending a horizontal line back across the panels representing the external and internal markets, we see that Q^* should be allocated to the internal market and Q_E should be allocated to the external market, such that the marginal revenue in each market equals the firm's marginal cost of production.

The optimal transfer price is shown as P_T in the left-hand panel of Figure 9A-8. Division B treats this price as a constant marginal cost of the intermediate product and demands Q^* units, which it will sell at the price indicated by the demand curve for the finished product (not shown). In the external market the buyers are willing to pay a higher price, P_E, for the quantity Q_E, and thus division A discriminates against the external buyers and charges them a higher price for the intermediate product. In this way the overall profit of the firm is maximized.

Transfer pricing gets much more complicated than this example. If the demand or cost functions of the divisions are not independent, as assumed above, the issue becomes decidedly more complex. Within General Motors, for example, the demand curves of Chevrolet, Buick, and a third division producing electrical components are interdependent because their products are either substitutes or complements for each other. On the cost side, if they compete in the same input markets, their cost functions may be interdependent as well. Multinational firms, with divisions or profit centers in different countries, must also consider the tax rates, import and export duties, and a variety of other issues that are involved. The interested reader is referred to the literature on transfer pricing for these extensions.[2]

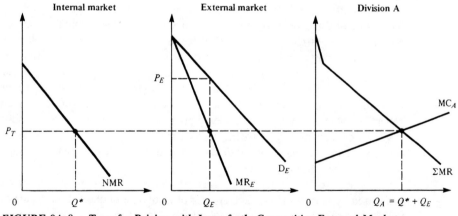

FIGURE 9A-8. *Transfer Pricing with Imperfectly Competitive External Market*

[2]See Joel Dean, "Decentralization and Intracompany Pricing," *Harvard Business Review*, July–August 1955, pp. 65–74; Jack Hirshleifer, "On the Economics of Transfer Pricing," *Journal of Business*, 29 (July 1956), pp. 172–84, and "Economics of the Divisionalized Firm," *Journal of Business*, 30 (April 1957), pp. 96–108; Charles T. Horngren, *Cost Accounting: A Managerial Emphasis*, 5th ed. (Englewood Cliffs, N.J.: Prentice-Hall, 1982), esp. chap. 19; and Stefan Robock, Kenneth Simmonds, and Jack Zwick, *International Business and Multinational Enterprises*, 3rd ed. (Homewood, Ill.: Richard D. Irwin, 1983), pp. 532–36.

Delivered Prices and Spatial Competition

When rival producers and consumers are dispersed geographically from each other, transportation costs become a significant element in the pricing decision. Either the consumer must pay the producer's price at the place of production and then incur the cost of transporting the product to the place of consumption, or the seller will incur the transportation cost and deliver the product to the consumer, charging a "delivered price." The former solution is called f.o.b. pricing, where f.o.b. stands for "free on board," meaning that the seller may help load the item into your car or truck, if it is heavy, but then you are on your own. Clearly, this is the kind of pricing that most consumers experience. In general, where the transportation cost is trivial, or is not incremental to the consumer, or is more cheaply provided by the buyer, the buyer will assume that cost rather than pay the seller to provide it. Delivered prices are more common in industrial purchasing and for heavy consumer items.

The dispersion of sellers and buyers over geographical space gives rise to what is known as spatial competition. A particular consumer may be quoted different prices by different suppliers, because of some combination of different "factory door" prices, different transportation costs per mile, and different transportation distances arising from the suppliers' differing locations. To secure a sale to a particular customer, the lucky seller must have the lowest delivered price, other things being equal.

In Figure 9A-9 we show buyers spread evenly along the horizontal axis, which measures distance, while sellers are located at the points *A, B, C,* and *D*. The vertical axis measures delivered prices. For simplicity, the base price of each firm at the factory door is the same, and the firms face the same transportation costs. The curved lines show the price to the buyer located at each point along the horizontal axis. Each buyer pays the base price plus the price of transportation services, which comprises an initial loading cost plus a freight rate per mile. Note that as the distance from the seller increases, the transportation costs, and hence delivered prices, increase at a decreasing rate. That is, the transport cost per mile diminishes as the loading cost is spread over an increasing distance traveled. The limit to each firm's sales is found where its price lines intersect with those for neighboring sellers. The buyers at each intersection point have a choice of two sellers, each quoting the same delivered price. All other buyers have one seller offering a price lower than its rivals, owing to its transport cost advantage. Note that delivered prices are a form of price discrimination, as buyers are discriminated among on the basis of their distance from the supplier.

"Basing-point" pricing is a form of delivered pricing. In this variant, the base price used by all firms is the factory door price of a particular firm at a particular location (the basing point). The agreement of all firms to set the same base price amounts to an agreement to share the market based on geographic proximity of the buyers to the sellers, which we have earlier characterized as a market-sharing cartel. It is particularly effective where product differentiation is minimal or nonexistent, as in the markets for steel, grain, lumber products, and petroleum. In the past, these industries have been subject to scrutiny by the Federal Trade Commission for collusive basing-point pricing agreements.

Basing-point pricing may well be the pricing convention chosen by colluding oligopolists, but the existence of delivered pricing with similar base prices does not imply

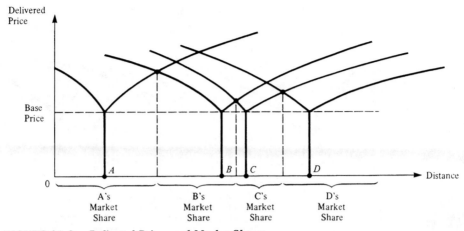

FIGURE 9A-9. *Delivered Prices and Market Shares*

collusion, as Haddock has argued.[3] Suppliers in a purely competitive market, who will all have similar production costs and face similar transportation costs, must use a delivered pricing scheme to compete for sales in a spatial market. Their base prices will tend to be equal to their marginal and average cost of production, because of the unrestricted entry of new competitors if pure profits are earned. Noncollusive oligopolists, such as price leaders and followers, will set the base price initiated by the price leader and quote different prices on the basis of transportation cost.

In fact, an analysis of delivered pricing highlights the ways in which oligopolists may compete effectively with each other in a spatial market. Efficiency in production, leading to a lower base price than that set by rivals, will expand the firm's market, since it increases the distance from its plant that a firm can set a lower delivered price than its competitors. In Figure 9A-10 we show the impact of a reduction in firm B's base price. The dotted price lines indicate the old pricing schedule based on the higher base price. The new, lower, base price allows firm B to expand sales both to the right and the left, at the expense of firms A and C. Note, however, that it also allows firm B to be the lowest-priced supplier to the right of firm C, where it consequently steals sales from both firm C and firm D.

Similarly, increased efficiency in transportation will cause a firm's delivered price lines to be flatter, and thus lower, at any particular location, allowing it to be the lowest-priced supplier further from its plant than it was before, and thus to gain sales at the expense of rivals. Finally, in the long run, the firm may relocate to a less crowded part of the market or build a second plant in another location to gain market share.

In Figure 9A-10, firm B's sales in what was formerly C's and D's markets will lead to what is called "cross hauling"—firm B's trucks heading to this area will pass firm C's trucks heading in the opposite direction to service the buyers located to the left-hand side

[3]David D. Haddock, "Basing-Point Pricing: Competitive vs. Collusive Theories," *American Economic Review*, 72 (June 1982), pp. 289–306. See also George J. Stigler, "A Theory of Delivered Price Systems," *American Economic Review*, 39 (December 1949), pp. 1143–59.

Delivered
Prices

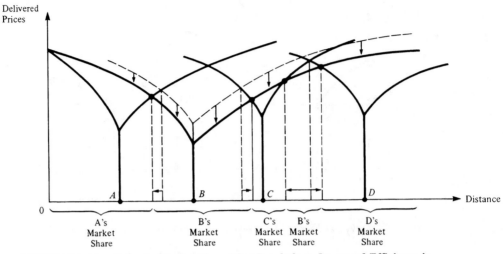

FIGURE 9A-10.   Gains in Market Share That Result from Increased Efficiency in
Production

of its plant. Cross hauling is often interpreted by the courts as evidence of collusive behavior, since it might occur in market-sharing cartels (where the agreement is based on firms having no competition for their "traditional" customers).[4] It is clear that the cross hauling evident in Figure 9A-10 is due to competitive behavior. Haddock, cited above, points out some other noncollusive reasons for cross hauling. First some buyers will prefer to buy from more than one supplier as an insurance policy against one's inability to supply at a critical time. The extra transportation cost is merely the premium paid for that insurance policy. Second, the cost of information leads to cross hauling. The buyer must incur search costs to identify the lowest-priced supplier, and where prices change frequently such that information held may not be correct, cross hauling will occur because of ignorance. Further, although it would be more profitable for firms to switch customers rather than cross haul, some cross hauling will go undetected because the managerial cost of detecting it will exceed the excess transportation costs incurred. Finally, the existence of product differentiation in a spatial market will cause cross hauling, because some buyers will pay more for what they perceive to be the superior product.

Summary

In this appendix we considered several models of the firm's pricing behavior in addition to those in Chapter 9, each one relating to a particular pricing problem that may face the firm. The multiplant firm must select the profit-maximizing price and output level, while at the same time allocating the output level between or among its two or more plants such that total costs are minimized. The technique for solving this problem involves the hori-

---

[4]See John S. Magee, "Cross Hauling—A Symptom of Incomplete Collusion under Basing Point Systems," *Southern Economic Journal*, 20 (April 1954), pp. 369–79.

zontal summation of the marginal cost curves from each of the plants to obtain a hypothetical ΣMC curve. Total output is determined where this curve cuts the firm's MR curve, and market price is read from the demand curve at this total output level. To allocate the profit-maximizing total output between the plants such that total cost is minimized, the level of ΣMC at which it equals MR is observed, and production in each plant is taken to the point where the MC in that plant rises up to the level at which $\Sigma MC = MR$.

The profit-maximizing cartel's price and output decision proceeds along the same lines. The incentive to cheat on the cartel exists for every member of the cartel, although it will be stronger for some than for others. A secret price reduction will allow any one firm to set a lower price along a relatively elastic *ceteris paribus* curve and increase its profits until the other firms discover the cheating and retaliate. The firm must weigh these additional profits against the benefits of price and output stability that are provided by the cartel. Side payments may be necessary to bribe an unhappy cartel member to remain in the cartel. Market-sharing cartels prescribe territorial limits to sales, allocate particular buyers to particular sellers, or simply prescribe output limits, and allow the prices to be determined by the individual firms. Cartels tend to be relatively short-lived, and they are more likely to break down when the members have substantial excess capacity available.

Price discrimination allows the firm that is able to separate its buyers into markets on some basis to increase its profit. First-degree price discrimination discriminates against those with higher incomes or wealth, second-degree price discrimination discriminates against those unable or unwilling to wait, and third-degree price discrimination discriminates against those with less elastic demand for the product.

Transfer pricing is involved whenever a firm is divisionalized, or organized into separate profit centers each with responsibility for its own profits. To ensure that the firm's overall profits are maximized, a centralized decision must be imposed concerning the transfer price for sales from one division to another. In general, the transfer price should equal the supplying division's marginal cost of production or the competitive market price for the intermediate product if such a market exists. If the external market for the intermediate product is imperfectly competitive, the supplying division will contribute to the maximization of the firm's profits by practicing price discrimination between the internal and external market for its output.

Delivered pricing systems occur where producers and consumers are located at different places and the consumer is charged the cost of production plus the transportation costs involved in transporting the product from the place of manufacture to the place of consumption. Given identical products, the buyer will buy from the seller with the lowest delivered price, which is not necessarily the nearest seller. Cross hauling will also occur because of lack of full information, because of product differentiation, and as a result of risk aversion.

DISCUSSION QUESTIONS

9A-1. State what the ΣMC curve represents for the multiplant firm.

9A-2. Discuss the operation of cartels and the incentive to undercut the cartel price. Does it make a difference when the products are differentiated and the "cartel price" is in reality a structure of prices around a particular level?

9A-3. Outline the principle of profit maximization as applied to a firm that operates three plants within the same market.

9A-4. In principle, explain how a firm may increase its profits by discriminating between two distinct markets for its products.

9A-5. Do you think that OPEC is still an effective cartel? Or is it a price leader instead? Why?

9A-6. Outline the three degrees of price discrimination. What is the basis of discrimination in each case? What conditions must be fulfilled to allow the firm to practice price discrimination?

9A-7. What is the transfer pricing problem? What might happen if the marketing division of the firm was required to accept whatever the manufacturing division of the firm produced at a transfer price equal to the latter's average cost of production plus a margin for profit?

9A-8. In spatial competition, why does the delivered price increase at a decreasing rate as the distance from the buyer and seller increases?

9A-9. In what ways can a firm increase its sales in a spatial market?

9A-10. What is cross hauling? List several reasons why you would expect to see cross hauling in spatial markets.

PROBLEMS AND SHORT CASES

9A-1. Analyze graphically the case of a two-plant firm that practices price discrimination in two separate markets. Assume two sets of cost conditions and two demand situations, and show the following:
(a) How the firm determines total output.
(b) Allocation of production to each plant.
(c) Allocation of output to each market.
(d) Prices in each of the two markets.

9A-2. The Thomas Tent Company has two separate markets for its midsize tent. The domestic market is characterized by the demand curve $P = 100 - 15Q$, and the foreign market is characterized by the demand curve $P = 60 - 2.5Q$, where P represents the price in dollars and Q represents thousands of units demanded. The firm's one plant has a total cost function approximated by $TC = 10,800 + 20Q + 0.1Q^2$ in the relevant range of outputs.
(a) What is the profit-maximizing output level of midsize tents?
(b) How should Thomas divide this output between the two markets?
(c) What price should be set in the domestic market?
(d) What price should be set in the foreign market?

9A-3. The Bartram Bitumen Company has two plants producing bituminous tar for its market, in which it has a virtual monopoly because of the remote location of other firms producing bituminous tar. The marketing manager has estimated the firm's demand curve as $P = 68.5 - 0.005Q$; and the production manager has estimated the monthly cost functions as $TC = 5,850 + 1.5Q + 0.005Q^2$ for plant A, and $TC = 6,250 + 1.2Q + 0.003Q^2$ for plant B, where Q represents pounds of tar in all cases.
(a) Please advise Bartram about the profit-maximizing output level from both plants in total.
(b) How much of this output should come from plant A?
(c) What price should Bartram set?

(d) Demonstrate that total contribution would decline if the last 100 units to be produced in plant A could not be produced there because of a breakdown and had to be produced in plant B instead.

9A-4. Holiday Pleasure Tours is a small company that provides a one-week holiday package on a Caribbean island. It is a member of the Association of Island Tour Operators. which is effectively a cartel that sets the prices for tourist packages in the Caribbean Islands. Holiday's tour package involves air fare from New York, transfers, hotel accommodation, a rental car, and daily use of sailboats, snorkeling equipment, and so on. The cartel price for this tour is $1,600 per person, and Holiday's current quantity demanded is 400 per month. Holiday is considering a secret discount, to be advertised in the *New York Times* travel section. A market research firm has estimated that Holiday faces a *ceteris paribus* demand curve specified by $P = 2,000 - Q$, following its conjecture that quantity demanded would increase by one unit for every dollar the price is reduced. Holiday's cost function for this tour package is estimated to be $TVC = 50,000 + 400Q + 0.25Q^2$.
(a) Calculate Holiday's monthly contribution at the current price and output levels.
(b) If Holiday were to set a lower price, what is the profit-maximizing price level, with *ceteris paribus*?
(c) What is Holiday's expected contribution at the new price level?
(d) What issues would you consider before advising Holiday to go ahead with the price reduction?

9A-5. General Statics Corporation is organized into a manufacturing division and a marketing division. Each division manager is responsible for his or her division's profits. The manufacturing division makes an electronic ignition system which the marketing division packages and distributes to automobile manufacturers. The firm's demand curve for this product is estimated to be $P = 1,000 - 0.625Q$, where Q represents thousands of units. The manufacturing division's marginal cost is estimated to be $MC = 200 + 0.375Q$, and the marketing department's marginal cost is estimated to be $MC = 100 + 0.5Q$.
(a) Assuming there is no external market for the ignition systems, calculate the profit-maximizing transfer price.
(b) Assuming there is a purely competitive external market for these ignition systems in which the price is currently $350 per unit, how many units should be produced? How many of these should be sold internally and how many should be sold externally?
(c) Finally, assuming that the external market demand curve is described by $P = 1,200 - 0.8Q$, what is the profit-maximizing transfer price and the optimal allocation between the internal and external markets? What price should be charged in the external market? (An answer derived from a careful graphing of the problem will suffice.)

9A-6. The IXL Company, which manufactures tomato sauce, has recently acquired Robinson Farms, Inc. its tomato supplier. As a result of this takeover, IXL will be organized into two main divisions, the agricultural division and the manufacturing division. Now, instead of IXL buying the tomatoes from Robinson at a negotiated price, the manufacturing division will buy tomatoes from the agricultural division at a transfer price that will be chosen to maximize the firm's overall profits.

The firm's demand function for tomato sauce has been estimated to be $Q = 15.0376 - 0.75188P$, where Q represents thousands of cases and P is the price per case. The total variable cost schedules for the agricultural division and the manufacturing divisions are estimated to be $TVC = 3Q + 0.5Q^2$ and $TVC = Q + 0.25Q^2$ respectively. Note that a case of tomatoes (40 kgs) holds exactly enough tomatoes to make a case of tomato sauce (24 cans).
(a) Supposing there to be no external market for tomatoes within a reasonable distance, calculate (i) the optimal transfer price, (ii) the optimal output, and (iii) the optimal price level.
(b) Now supposing that there is a nearby market for fresh tomatoes, and that the competitive price for tomatoes is $6 per case, what is (i) the optimal transfer price, (ii) the

amount transferred, (iii) the amount bought and sold in the market, and (iv) the optimal output and price for IXL's tomato sauce.

(c) Now suppose, instead, that there is an imperfectly competitive market for the agricultural division's tomatoes, since people in the local town think Robinson's fresh sunripened tomatoes are different from other tomatoes. The external demand curve for the tomatoes is estimated to be $P = 16 - 0.75Q$. What is the (i) optimal transfer price, (ii) the price to the external market, (iii) the total amount of tomatoes produced and the split of this between the internal and external markets, and (iv) the profit-maximizing price of IXL's tomato sauce?

(d) Explain why the transfer price changes up or down in each circumstance—that is, what are the economic reasons for the different transfer prices under the three scenarios?

(e) Outline the assumptions and qualifications that underlie your analysis.

9A-7. Greener Grass Pty Ltd (GG) competes with one other firm, Better Lawns and Gardens (BLG) in the supply and installation of in-ground lawn sprinkler systems, in the wealthy western suburbs of a major east coast city. Last year, GG's price for the typical lawn was $1,995, compared with BLG's $2,100. GG installed 9,130 systems, or about 55% of the systems professionally installed last year, and BLG installed the rest. (No doubt many additional systems were installed by "do-it-yourselfers" since the parts are available at hardware stores.)

GG has substantial excess capacity: it could easily install 25,000 systems annually, as it has the equipment and funds and finds it easy to hire and train installers. Accordingly, GG is considering expansion into the eastern suburbs, where the houses are much older and the people less wealthy. In past years, both GG and BLG have installed several hundred systems in the eastern suburbs, but their sales efforts are usually met with the response that the systems are too expensive.

GG has hired Douglas Research Associates to investigate the market demand in each of the markets, and to recommend a pricing strategy for the coming season. You are one of the associates assigned to this task. You and your colleagues have so far estimated two distinct demand curves. For the western suburbs:

$$Q_w = 1,035.548 - 6.07164\ P_w + 2.83\ P_b + 2,100\ A_g - 1,500\ A_b + 0.2348\ Y_w$$

where

Q_w is the number of systems demanded in the western suburbs;
P_w is the price charged by GG in the Western suburbs;
P_b is the price charged by BLG;
A_g is the advertising budget ($millions) of GG;
A_b is the advertising budget ($millions) of BLG; and
Y_w is the average household income in the western suburbs.

GG expects to spend $1.5m on advertising, and predicts that BLG will spend $1.2m on advertising, this year. Average household income is expected to be $55,000.

For the eastern suburbs:

$$Q_e = 49,714.29 - 30.7692\ P_e + 6.984\ P_b + 1,180\ A_g - 950\ A_b + 0.0825\ Y_e$$

where the variables represent the same as above, except that the subscript e refers to the eastern suburbs market. The average household income in the eastern suburbs is $25,000. The advertising expenditures also apply to both markets, since the media are common to both. GG does not expect BLG to change from last season's price, since it has already printed and distributed its glossy brochures (with the $2,100 price shown) in both the western and eastern suburbs, and production of its TV commercial is already completed.

GG's cost structure has been estimated as TVC $= 755.363 + 0.005\ Q^2$ where Q represents single units of the irrigation system.

(a) Derive the demand curves for GG's product in each of the two markets.

(b) Plot graphically the demand and MR curves for each market, and also show GG's combined MR curve and its MC curve. Show graphically the quantities that should be produced and sold, and the price that should be charged, in each market.

(c) Confirm your quantity and price results algebraically.

(d) Calculate the price elasticities in each market at the prices chosen, and relate these to the prices charged in each market.

(e) Defend your pricing recommendations, including your estimate of the increase in their revenues and profits that are to be obtained by following a price discrimination strategy.

(f) Add a short note to your boss outlining the reservations and qualifications underlying your recommendation.

SUGGESTED REFERENCES AND FURTHER READING

COYNE, T. J. *Managerial Economics: Analysis and Cases* (5th ed.), chap. 10. Plano, Tex.: Business Publications, Inc., 1984.

DOUGLAS, E. J. *Intermediate Microeconomics: Theory and Applications*, esp. chaps. 8, 10, and 12. Englewood Cliffs, N.J.: Prentice-Hall, Inc., 1982.

HOLMES, THOMAS J., "The Effects of Third-Degree Price Discrimination in Oligopoly," *American Economic Review*, 79 (March 1989).

ISMAIL, B. E. "Transfer Pricing under Demand Uncertainty." *Review of Business and Economic Research*, 18 (Fall 1982), pp. 1–14.

LEFTWICH, R. H. *The Price System and Resource Allocation* (7th ed.), chap. 11. Hinsdale, Ill.: The Dryden Press, 1979.

LOTT, J. R., JR. and R. D. ROBERTS, "A Guide to the Pitfalls of Identifying Price Discrimination," *Economic Inquiry*, 29 (January 1991), pp. 14–23.

MANSFIELD, E. *Microeconomics: Theory and Applications* (5th ed.), esp. chaps. 9, 10, and 11. New York: W. W. Norton Company, 1985.

McGUIGAN, J. R., and R. C. MOYER. *Managerial Economics* (3rd ed.), chap. 15. St. Paul, Minn.: West Publishing Company, 1983.

PAPPAS, J. L., E. F. BRIGHAM, and M. HIRSCHEY. *Managerial Economics* (4th ed.), chap. 11, appendix 11A. Chicago: The Dryden Press, 1983.

SEO, K. K. *Managerial Economics: Text, Problems, and Short Cases* (6th ed.), esp. chap. 16, appendix 16A. Homewood, Ill.: Richard D. Irwin, Inc., 1984.

WEISMETH, H. "Price Discrimination Based on Imperfect Information: Necessary and Sufficient Conditions," *Review of Economic Studies*, 49 (July 1982), pp. 391–402.

Chapter 10

PRICING DECISIONS IN PRACTICE

EXECUTIVE SUMMARY

The pricing models of Chapter 9 were discussed in the context of certainty. That is, the shape and location of the firm's demand and cost curves were assumed known, and the decision maker proceeded to select the price and output levels that were profit maximizing or that otherwise best served the firm's objective. In this chapter we deal with **pricing under uncertainty,** where full information on the demand and cost situation is not available or is deemed too expensive to acquire.

We deal first with **marginalist pricing** under uncertainty, where estimated demand and cost curves are used to predict the optimal price and output levels. Subsequent observations of the actual sales and profit levels will serve to support or refute the accuracy of the estimated demand and cost curves.

Markup pricing is then discussed in considerable detail. It is reconciled with the marginalist approach, where it is seen that the profit-maximizing markup is dependent on the price elasticity of demand: More elastic demand dictates a lower markup for profit maximization. It is demonstrated that markup pricing, by avoiding search costs, can remain optimal despite shifts in the demand and cost curves. Markup pricing also serves as a coordinating device for oligopolists concerned with the simultaneous actions of rivals.

Pricing in established markets is treated in this chapter, while the pricing of new products is treated separately in the next chapter. In this chapter we discuss **price positioning, product-line pricing, pricing to infer quality, and the pricing of product bundles, including quantity discounts.** The notion of search, experience, and credence goods is introduced in the context of **promotional pricing,** or the practice of placing a product temporarily "on sale." It is noted that search goods are better candidates for promotional pricing (and price wars) than are experience and credence goods.

10.1 PRICING WITH INCOMPLETE INFORMATION

Marginalist Pricing under Uncertainty

There are three main ways of practicing marginalist pricing under uncertainty, each of which has been outlined in preceding chapters. We shall now summarize the three methods in turn.

Given Estimated Demand and Marginal Cost Curves. Suppose we have estimated the demand curve or have derived the demand curve from an estimate of the demand function, as outlined in Chapter 5. We know that the marginal revenue curve has the same intercept value and twice the slope value as compared with the demand curve, and thus we can quickly derive an estimate of marginal revenue. Suppose also that we find marginal cost to be constant over the relevant range of output, or explained by a linear or other function of output, as outlined in Chapter 8. Setting the expression for marginal revenue equal to that for marginal cost, we can solve for the quantity level that preserves the equality. Inserting the result back into the demand curve gives us the price that, to the best of our knowledge, will maximize contribution and hence profits.

Given Estimated Price Elasticity and Marginal Costs. If we are supplied with an estimate of price elasticity for a product in the vicinity of the current price, we can use the elasticity formula ($\epsilon = dQ/dP \times P/Q$) to deduce the slope of the demand curve ($b = dP/dQ$), since we already know the values ϵ, P, and Q. We then deduce the value of the intercept term a in the demand curve expression ($P = a + bQ$), since we would then know the value of P, b, and Q. We then proceed as in the above situation to find the MR expression, and the optimal price and quantity. This method was shown in detail in Chapter 4 in the section entitled "Implications for Optimal Prices." (See page 132.)

Given Estimates of Incremental Costs and Revenues. The incremental or contribution approach is a marginalist approach, since it is concerned with changes in both total revenues and total costs. Unlike the marginal revenue/marginal cost approach, however, the incremental approach does not require the ability to adjust output by one unit at a time. Thus demand indivisibilities and discontinuities can be handled using the incremental approach. Suppose that the following demand situation exists: As price is progressively reduced the quantity demanded will increase by discrete blocks, as a result of gaining particular orders at the lower prices. For example, at a price of $3.80 per unit we may expect to sell 12,000 units, but at $3.79 we expect to sell 14,500 as a result of gaining a particular order at the slightly lower price.

 Where demand contains indivisibilities or discontinuities, we cannot construct the marginal revenue function since the total revenue curve is not continuous and therefore is not differentiable. Instead, we must compare the incremental costs and incremental revenues at each price level and choose the price that allows the maximum contribution to be made.

These methods of price determination are only as sound as the underlying information. To put our faith in the price that is indicated, we should be highly confident that both the demand and the cost estimates do in fact represent the actual situations and that the underlying *ceteris paribus* assumption can reasonably be expected to hold true. If, for example, our calculations indicate a price substantially below the prices of close rivals, we should expect those firms to react in some way and thus violate the *ceteris paribus* assumption. Because the demand and cost data are simply estimates, the actual outcomes may differ substantially from the expected outcomes. This is the nature of decision making under uncertainty, however: We must make decisions on the basis of the best information available, and if new information comes to light at a later point in time, this information forms the basis for a subsequent decision (which may involve the reversal of the initial decision).

Search Costs and Rule-of-Thumb Pricing Practices

In many cases the decision maker may expect that the cost of obtaining the estimates of the MC and MR relationships will exceed the extra revenue that might have been obtained using these estimates. Before attempting to obtain the additional information, the decision maker must expect that the additional revenues to be earned as a result of making the optimal decision (as compared with the revenues expected from the decision to be made on the basis of existing information) will exceed the cost of obtaining that information. Clearly, in many business situations the decision maker would have no such expectations. Thus it is not surprising that business decision makers, notwithstanding the elegant models of the economists, tend to adopt simple *rule-of-thumb procedures* when setting or changing prices.

Rule-of-thumb pricing procedures should be viewed as shortcut decision-making methods that economize on search costs and on the decision maker's time. These procedures usually result in a suboptimal decision being taken when that decision is compared with one that might be taken if full information were available. In terms of profits gained by the firm, however, the rule-of-thumb decision-making procedure may be optimal. Although it may never lead to the optimal decision in any specific instance, consistent decision making by a rule-of-thumb procedure may approximate the same net profit levels over the longer term. The inefficiency of rule-of-thumb decision procedures arises from the fact that some amount of profitability is lost because the optimal decision in specific instances is not taken. But to know what the optimal decision is requires additional information which in turn has search costs attached, and hence all rule-of-thumb pricing procedures need to do is *lose less* than the information would cost.

The most common rule-of-thumb pricing procedure is known as *markup pricing*, and we examine this in the next section. We will see that under a broad range of conditions it may be more profitable for the firm to practice markup pricing than to incur the search costs necessary to implement marginalist pricing. Nevertheless, the principles involved in marginalist pricing are indispensable to the optimal use of markup pricing, and the firm should periodically seek cost and demand data to confirm that its prices are at levels which best serve the firm's objectives.

Following the discussion of markup pricing, we consider a variety of pricing issues and strategies used in practice, including price positioning, product-line pricing, pricing to infer quality, temporary price "deals," pricing product "bundles," and price "breaks" (quantity discounts).

10.2   MARKUP PRICING

- DEFINITION: *Markup pricing,* also known as *cost-plus* pricing, is the practice of determining price by adding a percentage markup to the direct cost (or average variable cost) of the product.[1] Thus,

$$P = \text{AVC} + X\%(\text{AVC}) \tag{10-1}$$

where X is the markup percentage chosen. This markup, in dollar terms, is the per-unit contribution to overheads and profits, and hence choosing the size of the markup amounts to choosing the contribution margin. Thus equation (10-1) may be expressed as follows:

$$P = \text{AVC} + \text{CM} \tag{10-2}$$

Hopefully, the markup will be large enough so that, at the actual level of sales volume, the total contributions to overheads and profits actually cover the overheads and allow a profit to be made. The size of the markup is constrained, however, by the willingness of consumers to pay the higher prices associated with a higher markup. Even a firm that has a monopoly over a certain product must acknowledge that at higher prices consumers in aggregate will buy fewer units. Oligopolists must take into account the relative prices of competitors. An individual firm will lose sales to rivals if its price is significantly above the prices of its rivals and if consumers do not think the item is worth the extra money.

Markup pricing is often thought to be simply cost based, but it is evident that the amount by which price can be marked up is highly dependent on the demand conditions facing the firm. When asked what factors determine the size of the markup percentage, businesspeople often respond that they choose the markup with an eye to "what the market will bear" or "in order to meet the competition."[2] These statements carry an

---

[1]Full-cost pricing is a variant of markup pricing in which the *average cost* is marked up by some percentage rate to determine the price per unit. Note that this practice necessarily involves an estimate of sales volume, to determine the value for average fixed cost to be added to the average variable cost. Since sales volume depends on price, however, the markup rate, the full-cost price, and the quantity demanded at that price must be determined simultaneously. Most firms using full-cost pricing have a notional standard volume around which they expect to produce with minor variations that result from fluctuations of demand. They use as their full cost the average cost at this standard volume, and the markup rate is the rate that will bring their price into line with rivals' prices in the market, with minor adjustments to reflect differences in product quality and service.

[2]See A. Silberston, "Price Behavior of Firms," *Economic Journal,* 80 (September 1970).

implicit message about the price elasticity of demand facing the firm, and hence the size of the markup is both cost and demand based, contrary to the naive view that markup pricing depends on cost alone.

Since firms tend to use markup pricing in practice, does this mean that they are ignoring the marginalist principles of pricing? No, it does not. We shall see that markup pricing is not necessarily inconsistent with the marginalist principles. In fact, if the mark-up rate is chosen correctly, it will give exactly the profit-maximizing price.

Reconciliation of Markup and Marginalist Pricing

For every price level which is determined by the marginalist procedure of setting $MC = MR$, there is an *implied* markup percentage. For example, if the profit-maximizing price is $6.00 and the AVC is $4.00, the implied markup is 50%, since $6.00 is 150% of $4.00. In Figure 10-1 we show this situation. In part (a), we show the marginalist deter-mination of price: $MR = MC$ at output level Q_0 and the profit-maximizing price is found to be P.[3] In part (b), we show the markup approach—without benefit of data on the demand and marginal revenue curves, the firm simply applies a 50% markup to AVC and arrives at the *same* price P. At price P, the quantity demanded will be Q_0, and the firm will be setting the profit-maximizing price, even though it did not know where its de-mand curve was. (It now knows one point on its demand curve, namely point A, since consumers demanded Q_0 units at price P.)

In this case we suppose the firm using markup pricing under uncertainty was just lucky—it *happened* to apply the profit-maximizing markup implied by the marginalist approach and, thus, set the profit-maximizing price without having to spend money on search activity to estimate the shape or placement of its demand curve. How will the firm

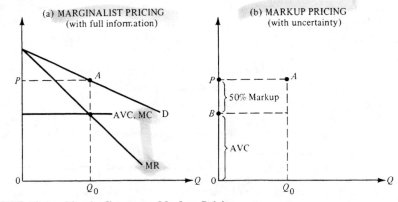

FIGURE 10-1. *Marginalist versus Markup Pricing*

---

[3]Note that we show a horizontal MC curve, with $AVC = MC$ in keeping with the empirical studies noted in Chapter 8. Constant MC over the relevant range greatly facilitates the analysis of markup pricing. The decision maker should be content that MC is constant in the situation under review before applying the simple markup-pricing rules without the modifications necessary if MC is in fact not constant over the relevant range.

know whether its markup is profit maximizing or not? By reconciling the two approaches, we can derive a simple rule which will indicate whether or not the markup rate is profit maximizing. To reconcile the markup and the marginalist approach to price determination, we must incorporate the marginalist rule, MR = MC, into the markup pricing equation (10-1). We start by finding an expression for marginal revenue that incorporates the price elasticity. Recall from Chapter 4 that total revenue is the product of price and quantity:

$$TR = P \cdot Q$$

Marginal revenue is the first derivative of total revenue with respect to output. Using the chain rule,[4] since P also depends on Q, we have

$$MR = P + Q\frac{dP}{dQ} \tag{10-3}$$

We now perform a manipulation on equation (10-3) which will allow a substitution. Multiply and divide the last term by P such that we obtain

$$MR = P + \frac{QP}{P} \cdot \frac{dP}{dQ} \tag{10-4}$$

Factoring out P we obtain

$$MR = P\left(1 + \frac{Q}{P} \cdot \frac{dP}{dQ}\right) \tag{10-5}$$

Note that the compound term in the brackets is simply the reciprocal of the expression for price elasticity. (See equation 4-16 in Chapter 4 if this is not clear.) Substituting for elasticity ϵ into equation (10-5) we obtain

$$MR = P\left(1 + \frac{1}{\epsilon}\right) \tag{10-6}$$

Given this expression for the relationship between marginal revenue, price, and elasticity we are now ready to perform the reconciliation. Marginalist pricing requires MC = MR. Setting MC equal to the above expression for MR we have

$$MC = P\left(1 + \frac{1}{\epsilon}\right) \tag{10-7}$$

---

[4]The chain rule of derivation is explained in Appendix A at the end of this book, in case you are not familiar with it.

Expressed in terms of price, this may be restated as[5]

$$P = MC\left(\frac{\epsilon}{\epsilon + 1}\right) \tag{10-8}$$

In business situations average variable costs are often constant (or viewed as constant) over the relevant range of outputs. Under such circumstances, marginal cost is equal to average variable cost. Hence we may restate equation (10-8) as

$$P = AVC\left(\frac{\epsilon}{\epsilon + 1}\right) \tag{10-9}$$

which can be rewritten as[6]

$$P = AVC +\left(\frac{-1}{\epsilon + 1}\right)AVC \tag{10-10}$$

Thus the markup rate X in equation (10-1) is equal to the negative reciprocal of one plus the price elasticity.[7]

Let us now substitute into equation (10-10) an arbitrary value for elasticity, say $\epsilon = -5$. In this case,

$$P = AVC + \left(\frac{-1}{-5 + 1}\right)AVC$$

$$P = AVC + \left(\frac{1}{4}\right)AVC$$

$$P = AVC + 25\%(AVC)$$

Thus a 25% markup on average variable cost is the profit-maximizing markup percentage if the elasticity value is equal to -5.

---

[5]Note that since MC $= P(1 + 1/\epsilon)$, $P = MC[1/(1 + 1/\epsilon)]$. In the latter expression the term in parentheses can be rewritten as $[1/(1/1 + 1/\epsilon)]$, or the reciprocal of a pair of fractions. To add fractions we use their common denominator, which is the product of the denominators. In this case the common denominator of $1/1$ and $1/\epsilon$ is ϵ. The sum of these fractions is thus $(\epsilon + 1)/\epsilon$. Thus we have $P = MC\{1/[(\epsilon + 1)/\epsilon]\}$ or $P = MC[\epsilon/(\epsilon + 1)]$.

[6]To follow this, note that $\epsilon/(\epsilon + 1) + 1/(\epsilon + 1) = [\epsilon/(\epsilon + 1)]/[\epsilon/(\epsilon + 1)] = 1$. Thus $\epsilon/(\epsilon + 1) = 1 - 1/(\epsilon + 1)$. Thus $P = AVC[1 - 1/(\epsilon + 1)]$, or $P = AVC + [-1/(\epsilon + 1)]AVC$.

[7]Note that equation (10-10) is not a formula to find the profit-maximizing price given an estimate of price elasticity at some other price, since P and ϵ vary together. Rather, equation (10-10) is the optimality condition: If the price level and its associated elasticity value are such that the equality of equation (10-10) is preserved, then the markup rate is profit maximizing. If there is an inequality, the optimal markup rate must be found by constructing the firm's demand and marginal cost curves (from the elasticity estimate) and deducing the profit-maximizing markup rate, as in Figure 10-1.

In Table 10-1 we show the profit-maximizing markup rates for a variety of other elasticity values. Note that the optimal markup rate varies inversely with the absolute value of price elasticity.[8]

TABLE 10-1. The Profit-Maximizing Markup Rate Given Price Elasticity

Elasticity Value	Markup Rate (%)
−1	∞
−2	100
−3	50
−4	33.3
−5	25
−6	20
−7	16.7
−8	14.3
−9	12.5
−10	11.1

Thus products with higher price elasticities of demand should be expected to have relatively lower percentage markups to make the maximum total contribution to overheads and profits. You will recall from Chapter 4 that we expect price elasticity to be higher the greater the number of substitutes and the greater the proportion of income that is spent on that particular product. In practice we know that markups on individual items of groceries, for example, tend to be low and that on gift items they tend to be high, in keeping with the above analysis.

Do firms choose their markup with an eye to the value of price elasticity? Certainly most do not. Rather, they find their best markup by trial and error or by adopting the same markup that is applied by other firms or choosing the markup that brings their price into line with the price set by the price leader in their market. This is not to say, however, that marginal analysis is of limited usefulness to the decision maker. Although firms may not use marginalist analysis in choosing the price levels, they may act as if they do. Marginalist analysis may thus predict the pricing actions of firms, even if in practice they use a markup-pricing procedure. To the extent that they choose the size of the markup with reference to market conditions and to the extent that they wish to maximize the contribution to overheads and profits, the markup price level may closely approximate the price that would be indicated by marginalist procedures.

---

[8]Note that the formula only works for $\epsilon < -1$. But for $\epsilon > -1$, MR < 0 and hence we cannot have MC $=$ MR, since MC must be nonnegative. The profit-maximizing markup rate is infinite for $\epsilon = -1$, because profit maximization requires MC $=$ MR, and since MR $= 0$ when $\epsilon = -1$, MC $=$ AVC must also be zero. Thus the profit-maximizing price is an infinite multiple of AVC, and it is equal to the revenue-maximizing price, when AVC $=$ MC $= 0$.

The Range of Acceptable Markup Levels[9]

Since the markup-pricing procedure avoids the search costs associated with estimating the demand curve, the markup level can vary within certain limits and still be acceptable, in the sense that the firm makes at least as much profit as it would if it first incurred the search costs and then set the MC = MR price.

Consider Figure 10-2, in which we show the total revenue (TR) curve associated with the actual demand curve faced by the firm. The total cost (TC) curve is shown as a straight line, reflecting constant marginal and average variable costs on top of a base comprising the total fixed costs (TFC). Profits, the vertical distance between TR and TC at each output level, are represented by the curve π. Now consider search costs. If the

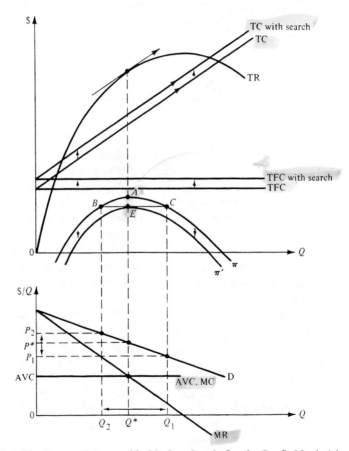

FIGURE 10-2.   *The Range of Acceptable Markup Levels for the Profit-Maximizing Firm*

---

[9]More detail on this topic may be found in my "Pricing for Economic Objectives Given Search and Price Adjustment Costs," *Journal of Cost Analysis*, 1 (Spring 1984), pp. 59–74.

firm decides to spend funds to estimate the demand curve, this expenditure will shift total fixed costs and, hence, total costs upward by the amount spent on search activity. (Search costs must be regarded as a fixed cost, since they are not related to the output level.) Thus the profit curve must shift down by the same vertical distance, to that shown as π' in Figure 10-2.

The profit-maximizing price, shown as P^* in the lower part of the figure, is found where MC = MR or where TC and TR have the same slope in the upper part of the figure. Note that this price is still the profit-maximizing price, whether or not search costs are incurred. That is, point A is the highest point on profit curve π, and point E is the highest point on profit curve π'. However, once the firm incurs the search costs, point E is the *best* it can do. If it does not incur the search costs, it might be lucky enough to set price P^* and maximize profits at point A. But note that any point on the profit curve π between B and C involves *more profit* than does point E. In terms of the demand curve in the lower part of the figure, any price between P_1 and P_2 promises more profit (without search costs) than does price P^* (after search costs have been spent). Sales can vary between Q_2 and Q_1 for prices between P_1 and P_2 and the firm will be at least as well off as (*at* prices P_1 or P_2) or better off than (*between* prices P_1 and P_2) it would be with full information and the "correct" price (where MC = MR).

In terms of the level of the markup, the rate applied to average variable costs could be anywhere between the low rate $(P_1 - \text{AVC})/\text{AVC}$ and the high rate $(P_2 - \text{AVC})/\text{AVC}$, and the firm would make more profits by *not* undertaking search activity to ascertain its demand curve. From Figure 10-2 you will note that in this example any markup between about 50% and 100% would appear to offer more profits, as compared to the alternative of incurring search costs and setting the "correct" price.[10]

Periodic Tests to Ensure Acceptability of the Markup.   The firm may wish to assure itself from time to time that its markup is in fact within the range of markup levels that allow greater profits as compared with the "correct" price after search costs have been incurred.

A simple test that should involve minimal search costs is the use of the markup rate to infer the value of price elasticity that would be required for the markup level to be profit maximizing.

• EXAMPLE: Earlier, in Table 10-1, we saw that a markup rate of 50% over AVC is profit maximizing if the price elasticity is equal to -3. Thus a firm using a 50% markup and wishing to maximize profits must ponder the question of whether or not its price elasticity of demand is equal to or close to the value -3. (That is, it should ask "would quantity demanded change by 30% if price were changed by 10%?") If the implied price elasticity

---

[10]The range of acceptable markups will be wider or narrower depending on the magnitude of search costs and the shape of the firm's profit curve. The greater the search costs and the flatter the profit curve, the wider will be the range of acceptable markups. The less elastic is demand in the vicinity of the profit-maximizing price or the lower is the firm's marginal and average variable cost, the flatter will be the profit curve. (You can easily verify this relationship graphically.) Thus firms with relatively elastic demand (many substitutes or a price that is high relative to incomes) will have a narrower range of acceptable markups, *ceteris paribus.*

seems *too high*, given management's knowledge of the market conditions, the markup percentage is probably *too low*, given the inverse relationship between the price elasticity and the profit-maximizing markup percentage. Thus the firm might try a higher markup and observe its impact on profit (or the contribution to profit generated by this particular product).

- NOTE: A simple formula to find what price elasticity *should* be for the current markup rate to be profit maximizing can be derived as follows. We know from equation (10-10) that the profit-maximizing markup rate is $-1/(\epsilon + 1)$. The markup rate is also measured by the difference between price and average variable cost over the average variable cost. Thus,

$$\frac{P - AVC}{AVC} = \frac{-1}{\epsilon + 1} \tag{10-11}$$

Solving for ϵ we find

$$\epsilon = \frac{-AVC}{P - AVC} - 1 \tag{10-12}$$

- EXAMPLE: Bonne Nuit sleeping pills are sold to retailers for $1.15 per packet, approximately 30% over the wholesaler's average variable cost, which is constant at $0.88 per packet. What must price elasticity be if this contribution margin represents the profit-maximizing markup? Substituting in equation (10-12), we find

$$\epsilon = \frac{-0.88}{1.15 - 0.88} - 1$$
$$= \frac{-0.88}{0.27} - 1$$
$$= -3.26 - 1$$
$$= -4.26$$

Thus, price elasticity must be something close to -4.26 if the 30% markup is profit maximizing. The manufacturer must now consider whether or not, for example, a 10% price decrease *would* expand sales by 42.6%. If even the most optimistic estimate is that sales would increase by only 20%, the markup is too low and the firm might cautiously adjust its price upward to determine the impact on profits.

- NOTE: If the firm does adjust its price up or down as a result of its view that the markup and the price elasticity are out of alignment, it will be able to generate information on the slope of its demand curve, as long as *ceteris paribus* holds. Given this estimated slope term, it can quickly solve for the intercept term in the expression for its demand curve and subsequently derive an expression for its marginal revenue curve. Given its knowledge of average variable costs (or marginal costs if AVC is not constant), it can solve for the profit-maximizing price, the sales-maximizing price, or the limit price and adjust its markup percentage to reflect the ratio $(P - AVC)/AVC$ given by the optimal price. It can then use that markup percentage in subsequent periods. As we shall see, the optimal markup percentage will remain optimal despite shifts in the demand curve and under conditions of inflation, given certain conditions. In any case, as we saw previously, the markup has only to stay within the range of *acceptable* markup rates in future periods.

Rather than change price experimentally, the firm might commission a study to estimate the price elasticity of demand around its present price. Such a study will generate information that will allow the firm to ascertain the profit-maximizing price, or the sales-maximizing price, or the limit price, as in the preceding discussion. The firm should undertake search expenditures whenever management expects the value of the information (in terms of the additional contribution generated) to more than cover the search costs of generating the information. It would seem prudent, given human fallibility, to incur these search costs *periodically,* in any case, to ensure that the firm's price does in fact best serve the firm's objective function.[11]

Markup Pricing and Iso-elastic Demand Shifts

We can show that if the firm has selected a markup rate which is profit maximizing, it may simply maintain that markup rate despite considerable shifts in its demand curve, and the price will continue to best serve the firm's objective. Consider Figure 10-3, in which we show an initial demand situation represented by the demand curve D and marginal revenue curve MR. Given $MC = AVC$, the profit-maximizing price is P, implying a markup rate of about 70% over AVC, and the profit-maximizing output level is Q_0 units. Suppose that the quantity demanded increases by the *same percentage* at every price level—in Figure 10-3 a 40% increase in quantity demanded at each price level is indicated by the shift of the demand curve to D'. This is called an *iso-elastic shift* of the demand curve since it maintains the price elasticity of demand at each price level at the same value as it was before the shift. For example, the price elasticity at points A and B is the same; $\epsilon = -2.4$ at each point.

Thus the profit-maximizing price P remains the profit-maximizing price despite the shift of the demand curve from D to D'. Thus, the 70% markup can be applied to AVC

---

[11]Surprisingly, perhaps, a firm wishing to maximize sales subject to the attainment of a minimum profit target should *not* periodically incur search costs. To see this, note that search costs would reduce profit below the minimum level and thus place the managers' jobs in jeopardy. Managers would then have to raise the price level to restore profit to the target level. This price increase would reduce sales and thus be directly contrary to the firm's objective. Such a firm is better off lowering price to increase sales until the profit objective is just attained, and need not know any more about its demand curve. Note also that the sales maximizer's price will be lower than the profit maximizer's price, presuming that the target profit is less than the maximum attainable profit. For the same cost structure this statement implies that the sales maximizer will always use a lower percentage markup. This procedure is consistent with the sales maximizer's underlying objective (to maximize long-term profits, or the EPV of net worth) because demand elasticities are invariably higher in the long term than in the short run, since buyers have more time to adjust their purchases and their habits.

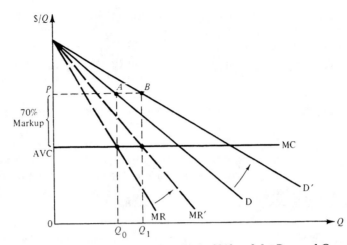

FIGURE 10-3.   *Constant Markup Given Iso-elastic Shifts of the Demand Curve*

despite shifts in the demand curve, as long as these shifts are iso-elastic and MC remains constant. Iso-elastic shifts in the demand curve are an intuitively appealing notion and may well approximate the actual shifts that firms experience. In any case, we have seen that if the firm starts from, or periodically adjusts price to, the "correct" price (in terms of its objective function and given full information), it can afford to slip away from the "correct" price to a degree before it would be better to undertake search and reestablish the correct price. Thus, even, if demand shifts are *not* iso-elastic, the markup can be expected to remain within the optimal range over some range of demand variations at the existing price level.

Markup Pricing under Inflationary Conditions

A markup-pricing policy applied to increasing levels of variable costs per unit will lead to a commensurate increase in the price level. In Table 10-2 we show a situation where average variable costs have increased over a one-year period by 10%. The 40% markup, when applied to that cost base at the beginning of the year, resulted in a price of $8.40. The 40% markup applied to the higher average variable cost figure at the year's end results in a 10% increase also in the size of the markup, or the contribution margin. Since both components of price have increased by 10%, it is not surprising that price itself has also increased by 10%.

Thus markup pricing under conditions of inflation tends to pass the cost increase along to the consumer of the product. You will notice, however, that the increase in average variable costs was $0.60, while the increase in the price amounted to $0.84. The difference arises, of course, because the absolute amount of the contribution has risen by $0.24. Since this contribution has risen by 10% and the cost level has also increased by 10%, the contribution at the end of the period of inflation has the same purchasing power as the contribution had at the beginning of the period of inflation: It will now take $2.64

TABLE 10-2. Markup Pricing with Inflation

	Jan. 1 ($)	Dec. 31 ($)	Change (%)
Average variable costs	6.00	6.60	10
40% markup	2.40	2.64	10
Price	8.40	9.24	10

to purchase what was previously purchasable for $2.40. Thus markup pricing, as well as passing the cost increase along to the consumer of the product, also serves to maintain the purchasing power (or real value) of the firm's contribution to overheads and profits.

• NOTE: If during this regime of inflation buyers' incomes have also gone up by 10%, this product will still require the same proportion of their incomes as it did before the inflation. Thus the 10% change in the price level is not a *real* price change in the sense that it does not cause consumers' purchasing power to be reduced, but it is a simple monetary price change resulting from the depreciation of the monetary unit. Such a price increase should not be regarded by purchasers as causing the product to become more expensive in terms of their incomes, and hence their quantity demanded should remain constant following the monetary price increase.

This situation is illustrated in Figure 10-4. Note that the demand curve has shifted vertically by a constant percentage, 10% in this case. This shift reflects each consumer's willingness to pay 10% more for the *same* quantity demanded as before, given that con-

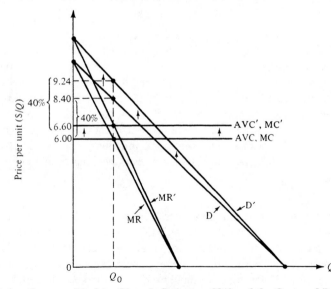

FIGURE 10-4. Constant Markup Given Inflationary Shifts of the Cost and Demand Curves

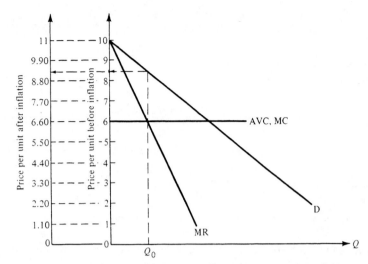

FIGURE 10-5.   Constant Purchasing Power Analysis of Price and Cost Changes under Inflationary Conditions

sumer incomes have gone up by 10%. Thus the vertical intercept of the demand curve shifts up by 10%, while the horizontal intercept remains unchanged, so at each quantity level price is, therefore, 10% higher than before. Note that the new marginal revenue curve MR' cuts the new marginal cost curve at the *same* output level Q_0. At the new price level, \$9.24, consumers buy the same quantity as before, since both their incomes and the price have risen by the same proportion.

- NOTE: The above analysis was conducted entirely in *nominal-dollar* terms. In *real-dollar* terms, or constant purchasing-power terms, neither the cost curve nor the demand curve has shifted. In Figure 10-5 we show two vertical scales on the graph—the inner scale is in constant-dollar terms, showing the initial price at \$8.40 when AVC = \$6.00. The outer scale is in nominal, or monetary, terms, reflecting the nominal cost and price levels after the inflationary period. In effect, the purchasing power of the dollar, for both the firm and its customers, has shrunk by 10%; it now takes 10% more in nominal dollars to purchase what one could before the inflationary period. Deflating the nominal price and costs by 10%, we find that in real terms there has been no change in price or quantity demanded.

    To the extent that consumers' incomes rise *less rapidly* than the firm's average variable costs in nominal-dollar terms, use of a constant-markup rate will cause the price to rise above the profit-maximizing level. Being cognizant of this danger, the firm should consider whether or not its consumers' incomes have risen by the same proportion as the firm's costs. If not, the firm should *reduce* its markup rate commensurately. Conversely, if by some chance its consumers' incomes have risen by a higher proportion than its costs, the firm may *raise* its markup rate commensurately.

Markup Pricing as a Coordinating Device

We know that a crucial element in the oligopolist's decision-making process is the decision maker's conjecture whether or not rival firms are likely to adjust prices at the same time and by similar magnitudes. To the extent that price changes are coordinated among firms, the market shares are likely to remain stable. On the other hand, if one firm raises price and rival firms do not, we expect that firm to suffer an elastic demand response and subsequently lose some part of its market share. Similarly, if all firms were to raise prices, yet one firm raised price by a significantly larger amount, that firm would be expected to lose part of its market share.

The existence of an established markup-pricing policy in a particular industry acts as a coordinating device when price changes become necessary. All firms are likely to be faced by similar changes in their cost structure, since they purchase labor and raw materials in the same or in similar markets, and if they each apply the same markup percentage to these average variable costs, their prices will rise by a similar percentage. Hence the *relative* prices of the firms will remain undisturbed at the new general level of prices. Markup-pricing policy and a common markup percentage allow a common and predictable strategy for price increases. Under conditions of conscious parallelism, each firm will expect that other firms will raise their prices to the extent of the familiar markup proportion on the change in unit costs. Thus, when a cost component changes, the firm may confidently adjust its price upward in the expectation that all rival firms will be doing likewise. An established markup-pricing procedure within an industry thus allows the decision maker to predict with a high degree of certainty the responses of rival firms to change in cost conditions.

- NOTE: The size of the markup that will maximize profits, maximize sales subject to a profit constraint, or limit the entry of new firms will be chosen by the price leader or by the collective consensus of firms operating under conditions of conscious parallelism. Once a level of the markup is found that seems to achieve these objectives, this markup percentage will become institutionalized in the industry and be the standard percentage applied by the firms, as long as the objective functions and general market conditions do not change significantly.

This is not to imply that competing firms must necessarily mark up their average variable costs by exactly the same percentage figure. We shall see in the following section that the industry standard markup acts as a point of reference which allows the firm to bring its price into the correct "ball park," but in many cases a further price adjustment, or deviation from the standard industry markup percentage, may be desirable. Let us now turn to an examination of pricing in the context of established market situations.

10.3 PRICING IN ESTABLISHED MARKETS

In established product markets the general price level may be regarded as historically determined, in the sense that it has gravitated to the current level over a prolonged period of time and to the general satisfaction or acquiescence of the firms involved. We might therefore claim, by backward induction, that the general price level prevailing in established markets is the level that serves the objective of the price leaders or of the firms in general. In established markets we would expect the general price level to be revised upward or downward whenever deemed desirable by the price leader or by the firms in general, and this price revision may be achieved by each firm individually applying its usual markup to the new level of direct cost.

The essence of the pricing decision in established markets is therefore not so much to choose the general level of price as it is to choose the specific level of price relative to the prices of one's competitors. The price ball park is established; the firm must choose its price positioning within that ball park.

Price Positioning

The price of a product relative to the prices of its competing products should presumably be set higher or lower depending on the presence or absence of desirable attributes perceived in that product by consumers in general.

- EXAMPLE: In the market for personal computers there are a variety of computers, and variations of each computer, available at a variety of prices. Those with more memory, with hard and floppy disk drives, and a better reputation for quality and service command above-average prices, or a price premium over the average price. Conversely, those with less memory and the absence of other desirable features command below-average prices, or a discount from the average price level. The price premium, or price discount, that a particular firm may add to or subtract from the general, or average, price level will depend on the market's appreciation of the value of the total package of attributes involved in that firm's product relative to the offerings and prices of all competitive products.

How might we determine the value of specific product attributes or the value of a total package of attributes embodied in that product? Market research techniques must be applied to find the value placed on the presence of certain attributes or groups of attributes in a particular product. If a large sample of consumers were canvassed, their consensus regarding the extra amount they would be prepared to pay for certain features could be used as a guide for pricing variants or new models of an established product.

The maximum amount that a buyer will pay for a product is known as that buyer's reservation price. Similarly a buyer will have reservation prices for attributes perceived to be supplied by the product. The buyer will buy the product only if the reservation price is greater than the seller's asking price. If an attribute may or may not be included in the product, such as a "luxury package" in an automobile, the buyer will only buy that attribute along with the basic product if his or her reservation price for that attribute exceeds the seller's asking price for that attribute. Buyers will be reluctant to divulge their reservation prices, since sellers would use this information to set the price just at or below the buyer's reservation price, and thus leave the consumer with little or no consumer surplus. (Consumer surplus is the difference between what the consumer had to pay for a product—the seller's asking price—and the maximum he or she would have been willing to pay rather than go without—the buyer's reservation price.)

Carefully conducted market research could supply the firm with the reservation prices (of a sample of buyers surveyed) for a particular product and for each attribute that may or may not be included in the product. Putting these in descending order essentially graphs out the sample's demand curve for that product or the attribute in question. Generalizing this information to the market as a whole, a market demand curve and associated marginal revenue curve could be derived. A profit-maximizing firm would then have a simple pricing decision—namely, price the product or the attribute such that the marginal revenue equals the marginal cost of production. An oligopolist must consider the probable reactions of its rivals if the price indicated by this analysis was significantly above or below the prices of the rivals' versions of this product or the attribute in question.

- EXAMPLE: One version of a particular brand of personal computer might contain 256K bytes of memory, and another might contain twice that amount. If the computers are otherwise the same, what is the appropriate price premium for the computer with the larger memory? The firm could establish the short-run profit-maximizing price or the long-term profit-maximizing price (proxied by the sales-maximizing price, for example), given information regarding the buyers' demand curve for the extra 256K bytes of memory and given its own cost data. Alternatively, rather than incur the search costs, the firm might prefer to simply mark up its average variable cost of purchasing and installing the extra 256K memory chip to arrive at the price premium for the 512K model. Should the markup rate be relatively high or low? Ask yourself whether price elasticity is likely to be relatively high or low. In the case where a prospective buyer is considering either the 256K model or the 512K model, we would probably expect relatively elastic demand for the extra 256K, and thus a relatively low markup. But if the buyer already owns a 256K computer and wants an extra 256K-byte chip installed, we would expect relatively inelastic demand and thus a relatively high markup rate for retrofitting the extra 256K. In both cases an oligopolistic seller will wish to be sure that its price premium for the computer with extra 256K, and its price for retrofitting the extra 256K, is not too far different from the prices of its rivals, other things being equal.

In general, the firm will attempt to price its product such that its position in the price range is reflective of its position in the quality range, where the word *quality* is used broadly to mean the presence of desirable attributes. Thus a product with more desirable attributes will command a higher price than one that is lacking some of the attributes desired by some buyers. Buyers will buy the product that gives them the most consumer surplus for the collection of attributes that they want, namely the product with the lowest asking price, other things being equal. Since buyers have different preferences, we should expect to see the simultaneous offering of a wide range of quality at a similarly wide range of prices. In fact we observe this structure in most oligopoly markets.

- EXAMPLE: In the market for videocassette recorders (VCRs) one can find several basic models (two video heads, twelve or fourteen preset channels, and one or two preselected programs) selling for about $150 at the time of this writing. As additional features are added, the competitive price for the product increases. A wireless remote control commands a premium over the wired type. The next step up is additional channels, and four programs over a two-week period, for which additional premiums are charged. Two more video heads with special-effects capabilities, stereo capability, and a quartz tuner each add another premium, and so on. At each quality level there are typically a dozen or more competing brands, and the prices tend to be similar. Each firm must consider the prices of rivals for the similar package of attributes, because buyers are aware of the availability of competing brands.

A more complicated price positioning decision must be made when the firm offers several different models of their product in a market where the quality demands of buyers differ. In the markets for automobiles, computers, VCRs, and so on, we find the firms each offering a product line—a series of related products. Some of these products are substitutes for each other, being located at different points along the quality spectrum, such as small cars and large cars. Other products in the product line are complementary to each other, such as a particular car and spare parts for that car. We turn now to product-line pricing.

Product-Line Price Strategy

In perhaps the majority of cases the decision maker is not simply concerned with the price of one product, but with the prices of a line of related substitute and complementary products produced or sold by that firm. Price differentials between and among these products should reflect their place in the overall product line, and the spacing of price levels should be adjusted so the firm's objective function is maximized.[12]
The reconciliation of the markup-pricing and marginalist-pricing procedures indicates that products with a lower price elasticity should be expected to contribute a greater relative amount to overheads and profits than those with a higher price elasticity. Keeping in mind that higher price elasticities result from a product's having a variety of substitutes or being relatively expensive, we would thus expect the decision maker to consider each product in the light of its absolute cost to consumers and the availability of substitutes both within and outside that decision maker's particular price line before deciding on the appropriate markup over average variable costs.[13]
This relatively simple approach—choosing the markup rate with respect to the estimated price elasticity of demand—implicitly assumes that the demand for each of the items in the product line is *independent* of the demand for any of the other items in the

---

[12]See Michael Mussa and Sherwin Rosen, "Monopoly and Product Quality," *Journal of Economic Theory,* 18 (1978), pp. 301–17; and S. Oren, S. Smith, and R. Wilson, "Pricing a Product Line," *Journal of Business,* 57 (January 1984), pp. S73–S99.

[13]If the search costs involved in determining the value of price elasticities are relatively high, it may in fact be contribution maximizing to apply a common markup percentage to all products in a product line, as long as the revenue foregone is less than the search cost not expended. More likely, the manager will have some idea of the relative elasticities and vary the markups on that basis.

product line. But items that are substitutes or complements have *dependent* demand functions. Recall from Chapter 4 that an increase in the price of one product will cause a shift outward of the demand curves for its substitutes and a simultaneous shift inward of the demand curves for its complements. In the product-line case, the firm must take account of these demand interdependencies. Raising the price of one product, for example, will increase the sales of the next-higher-quality substitute, and also of the next-lower-quality substitute, but reduce the sales of the product itself and of its complements in the product line. Alternatively, improving the consumer's perception, or image, of one product in the line, as well as increasing the sales of that product, may also have positive spillover effects for sales of all other products carrying the firm's brand name.

The total contribution to overheads and profits will be maximized when the contribution from each item in the product line is chosen with respect to both its place and function in that product line and the extent of competition it faces on the market. Where products in the line are complementary goods, such as cameras, attachments, films, and projecting equipment, it may be desirable to price the basic item (cameras) with a relatively low markup to achieve broad penetration of the market. If the complementary products must be purchased from the same manufacturer (for example, special film cartridges), sales of these items in the future will be enhanced by greater sales of the basic item now. In some cases, total contribution from the product line may be maximized by using the basic item as a "loss leader," or promotional item, pricing it at a level below that which would be indicated by the short-term price elasticity considerations.[14]

Where two or more products in the line are substitutes, the price of the bottom-of-the-line product must be chosen quite carefully. Potential customers may be attracted to the store by price information and once in the store may be convinced of the virtues of more expensive products in the line. Consequently, it may enhance total contribution to price the bottom-of-the-line product somewhat lower than would be suggested by price elasticity considerations. Automobile manufacturers might be expected to price their vehicles on this basis, since potential customers are likely to be attracted by relatively low advertised prices on items that are expensive in absolute terms. Once in the showroom the customer may be convinced by a salesperson to purchase a more luxurious version or a larger model (with higher contribution margins) or to "dress up" the basic vehicle with a number of higher-markup options and accessories. For obvious reasons, this type of pricing and personal selling strategy has been called "trading up."

In a line of substitutes the bottom-of-the-line, or entry-level, product is priced first, with an eye to the prices of rivals' similar products. If its quality is marginally better, or inferior, when compared to rivals' products at that area in quality space, it may be priced a little higher, or a little lower, than those products. This simple price positioning would then be modified to some extent if the firm takes into account the demand interdependencies. Suppose the firm wishes to promote an image of offering better value to consumers

---

[14]"Loss leader" is generally used to mean pricing one item below full costs to attract customers into the store, where they will (or the store hopes they will) also buy other items at the regular prices. It is being used here in the sense of attracting a customer to the product line with (it is hoped) subsequent sales of related items at the regular prices.

than do rival firms. It might therefore set the price below rivals' prices for the similar item, expecting this "better-value" image to be associated with its brand name and therefore shift outward the demand curves for all other products in the line, leading to increased sales for these products as well.

Another demand interdependency occurs when repeat purchases are a factor. Consumer loyalty, the propensity of a buyer to be a repeat purchaser, is developed following the buyer's satisfactory experience with the seller's products on earlier occasions. A first-time buyer is valued, not just for the present purchase, but also for the expected value of future contributions following repeat purchases that will follow (with some probability) if the buyer in fact makes the first purchase. In cases where the seller expects the buyer to move up the product line to higher-quality (more expensive) products in the future, there is an incentive to price the entry-level product using a lower markup than would be applied to products higher in the product line. Automobile dealers tend to follow this pattern, expecting favorable experience with their smaller (lower markup) cars to induce consumers to buy their larger (higher markup) cars in the future.

After the lowest-quality product in the line is priced, the next product in the line is then priced with a view to the value of the additional attributes that it contains when compared to the entry-level product, again with an eye to the prices of rivals' products at approximately the same quality level. This process continues as we move up the product line. We might expect higher markup percentages as we move up the product line, since the buyers of these items will typically have higher incomes and may also derive more utility from quality, and thus their reservation prices will be higher as compared with the buyers of the lower quality products. Throughout the product line, the firm will reduce the price of a particular item if it expects this to have a positive net effect on profit because of the demand interdependencies perceived to exist.

At the top of the line of substitutes we have the firm's "flagship" item, and it might be priced with yet another consideration in mind as well. Demand for this product is probably quite limited, because of its relatively high price, and thus exclusivity enters as a relevant attribute in the buyer's decision. Some buyers will pay heavily for exclusivity, or for "scarcity value," other things being equal. Antiques exemplify this phenomenon, of course, but so do limited production runs of collectors' items, and exotic automobiles like the Rolls Royce Camargue.

In pricing a line of substitutes, the firm can shift demand uphill (to the next-higher-quality substitute) or downhill (to the next-lower-quality substitute) by varying the price of any product. It can do this by raising or lowering the price of that product. Some buyers will then consider the next-higher-quality substitute to be the better deal and others will consider the next-lower-quality to be the better deal. (Buyers will select the substitute that gives them the higher consumer surplus, or the greatest difference between their reservation price and the seller's asking price.) In the short run the seller might find that quantity demanded for a particular item exceeds the supply available, or the firm's full capacity output rate, while for the adjacent levels of quality the firm has excess supply or production capacity. In this case it will increase profit to shift demand away from the more heavily demanded product toward the substitutes for which demand is lower, relative to supply or production capacity.[15]

Demand shifting up or down the product line may also be practiced to meet externally imposed constraints. For example, the automobile manufacturers must comply with the CAFE (corporate average fuel economy) requirement set by the EPA (Environmental Protection Agency). Larger and more powerful cars tend to consume more gas per mile than do smaller and less powerful cars in the firms' product lines. To meet the CAFE requirements, the firm may have to reduce the prices of its more economical models or increase the prices of its less economical models.

- EXAMPLE: In January 1985, Chrysler Corporation and Ford Motor Company announced increased prices for selected cars and light truck models, following the lead of General Motors, which had earlier announced its price increases. Chrysler's price hikes applied to its midsize and larger cars, as well as its "hot-selling" minivans and its light trucks. The boom in light truck sales, and the continued strong demand for larger automobiles, was also behind the price increases for these by Ford and General Motors. But prices were not increased for compact trucks, such as Ford's Ranger and GM's S-10 truck. A Ford spokesman said that stiff competition (mainly from imports) was the reason for holding the line on compact truck prices. Small-car prices were expected to hold steady because of the expected relaxation of the quota on imported Japanese cars. The Ford spokesman said options for larger engines and heavier transmissions had higher than average increases, to encourage the purchase of more fuel-efficient equipment.[16]

This example indicates several things. First, General Motors is the acknowledged price leader in this market, largely because of its lower cost structure. Second, the increased demand for larger cars, minivans, and light trucks allowed the firms to jointly raise prices on these items in their product lines, while the competition from imports militated against price increases on smaller cars and compact trucks. Third, the price changes for each item in their product lines were made with an eye to rivals' prices of their similar items. Finally, an important consideration underlying the adjustments to the firms' prices was the CAFE requirement. Raising prices on less economical cars would induce some buyers, at the margin, to substitute in favor of a more economical automobile, and subsequently enable the firms to meet the CAFE requirement.

---

[15]A similar demand-shifting strategy is known as *peak-load pricing*, whereby higher prices are set for a product during periods when the demand is strongest, and prices are reduced at off-peak times. Peak-load pricing is practiced by the airlines, the telephone companies, and electricity companies in some areas. In these cases the firm's product at one point in time is a substitute for itself at another point in time. Consumers who are able to defer consumption until the off-peak prices come into effect may receive more consumer surplus by doing so. Thus the firm utilizes its limited production capacity during the peak periods by supplying only those who cannot wait, or prefer not to wait, for the product or service. In effect the firm discriminates against those buyers for whom the demand is more urgent. We called this process second-degree price discrimination in Appendix 9A.

[16]See Doron P. Levin, "Chrysler, Ford Increase Prices on Some Lines," *Wall Street Journal,* January 7, 1985, p. 5; and Amal Nag, "Auto Makers are Quietly Raising Prices Higher Than First Promised," *Wall Street Journal,* January 8, 1985, p. 39.

Pricing to Infer Quality

It is often claimed that pricing a product higher will make the consumer perceive it as a higher-quality item and cause sales and profits to be greater than if the product were priced at a lower level.[17] Given our knowledge of consumer behavior theory, we can think of two arguments to support this assertion.

First, if the consumer has no other means of judging quality of the product, price will be the consumer's best indicator of quality, *a priori*. Purchase of the product and subsequent experience with the product should provide other indications of quality which the consumer can use in subsequent purchase decisions. But the absence of *all* other means of estimating quality implies a situation in which the consumer cannot tell by looking, feeling, or shaking the product, or it implies a situation in which there are no consumer reports, comparative tests, word-of-mouth recommendations (or warnings), or any other information available to the consumer. Certainly, there are products for which it is difficult to judge the quality without actually using them.

- EXAMPLE: If your car breaks down, you could buy replacement parts made by a different manufacturer rather than by the original equipment manufacturer (OEM). The OEM parts are usually more expensive and the inference is that they are of higher quality. Objective comparison tests may show that there is no difference or even that the OEM parts are inferior to some of the cheaper alternatives. Other examples include electronic air purifiers, burglar alarms, stereo systems, brand-name aspirin, and so on.

Most of these examples beg the question, "Why doesn't the consumer do some investigating and find out more information about the quality of the product?" The consumer could shop around, read *Consumer Reports*, ask people who own or use the product, and so on. This brings us to the second argument for using price as an indicator of quality.

Second, if the search costs necessary to ascertain the quality of the product are expected to exceed the consumer's notional value of the information derived, the consumer would rationally use price as an indicator of quality rather than incur those search costs. Note that search costs include time and money; it may take you several hours to find the information, plus the cost of buying magazines, such as *Consumer Reports, Road and Track, Stereo Review*, or whichever magazine has published a comparison test on the item. Rather than spend the equivalent of $20 searching, the consumer may simply pay the extra few dollars for the more expensive item and hope to get the quality he or she seeks. Notice that it is the price difference between the higher-priced item and the lower-priced item (which are under consideration) that determines the amount of search activity the consumer should conduct. Obviously, one should search for more information when buying an automobile or a stereo system than when buying a smoke detector or barbeque fuel or other relatively low-cost items which are difficult to rank qualitatively.

---

[17]For a paper on this subject and a comprehensive bibliography, see David R. Lambert, "Price as a Quality Signal: The Tip of the Iceberg," *Economic Inquiry*, 18 (January 1980), pp. 144–50.

This observation leads us to a consideration of the types of products for which the consumer might typically make a price-quality association. Highly technical items are an obvious candidate, since most of us don't understand why they work. Low-cost items that require high search costs to ascertain quality are another contender. Products for which quality is imperative are another.

- EXAMPLE: Medicines to correct ailments are often available as brand-name drugs or as generic drugs. Many people choose the higher-priced item, the brand-name drug, over the cheaper but chemically equivalent generic drug, presumably because they feel that their health is imperative and that any doubt they feel about the equivalence of the generics is easily erased by the expenditure of a few more cents or dollars. Cosmetic items to restore facial beauty, to stop the balding process, and to reverse inevitable consequences of aging are seen as quality-imperative to many of the consumers of these items. When one's self-esteem and ego is at stake, the marketing people do not expect the consumer to respond with caution and cost-consciousness.

New products are ideal candidates for the price-quality association, as long as price is the only real indicator of quality, simply because there will be no prior information for consumers even if they do conduct search. Rather than wait until information accumulates, consumers may prefer to pay the premium price now and avoid the search costs of waiting. We examine new-product pricing in the next chapter.

Finally, people who pay triple the price for designer jeans and sport shirts are doubtless getting superior quality and fit as compared to the mass-market jeans and shirts available at one third the price. But *three* times the quality? More likely, we are witnessing the *Veblen effect,* named after the classical economist Thorstein Veblen.[18]

- DEFINITION: The *Veblen effect* is defined as the tendency of some consumers to purchase more of an item when its price is higher because of the demonstration effect such a purchase has on others (namely, that the purchaser is sufficiently wealthy, exhibits good taste, and so on). This is also known as *conspicuous consumption,* since consumers may want to become conspicuous by their consumption of the more expensive, higher-quality product. It may alternatively be argued that the devotees of designer jeans, shirts, and other designer clothing simply feel that quality is imperative for their self-esteem, image, and lifestyle and that the extra cost is simply an insurance premium to make sure they get it.

Pricing Product Bundles

Product bundling is the practice of selling two or more products together as a package deal for a single price. A series of examples will indicate how widespread product bundling is. Computer software is often bundled with the hardware and sold as a package

---

[18]See H. Leibenstein, ''Bandwagon, Snob, and Veblen Effects in the Theory of Consumer Demand,'' *Quarterly Journal of Economics*, May 1950, pp. 183–207.

deal. Restaurants offer "fixed menus" which include soup, main course, dessert, and coffee for a single price. Automobiles offer luxury or sports packages that must be sold in conjunction with the basic vehicle. Retailers offer free parking if you buy something at their store. Gas stations offer free games when you buy gas. Professional sports teams and symphony orchestras offer season tickets that bundle together a variety of events for a single price.[19]

The theory of pricing product bundles has been examined by Stigler, Adams and Yellen, and Schmalensee.[20] Put simply, the firm has a profit incentive to bundle products together when doing so allows the extraction of a greater degree of consumer surplus from the potential customers. In general, it is optimal to offer the products both separately and in the bundle, since some consumers will only want one of the products and would not be willing to pay the bundle price. Offering both the bundle and the separate products is known as "mixed" bundling, as opposed to "pure" bundling, where the products are only available as a package deal.

Consumer surplus is measured in dollars by the excess of the consumer's reservation price over the actual price paid for an item. If the seller raises the price by a dollar, but the price remains less than or equal to the buyer's reservation price, the buyer will still buy the product but will receive one dollar less in consumer surplus. Instead, the extra dollar will be added to the producer's surplus, also known as profit. If the firm could treat each buyer separately, it would attempt to charge each buyer his or her reservation price, thus completely exhausting consumer surplus and maximizing producer surplus.[21]

In practice the seller will be unable to determine each buyer's reservation price and will simply assume that buyers have a range of reservation prices, such that there is a negatively sloping demand curve for both the products separately and collectively (the bundle). The seller will typically increase profit (over that available from pricing the products separately) by raising the prices of each product *if sold separately* and offering the bundle as a package deal at a price which is less than the sum of the prices of the components of the bundle. Thus buyers who only want one, or some subset, of the products in the bundle must pay more than they otherwise would have, and other buyers who would not have purchased all the products separately end up buying the bundle because it is the cheapest way to get the products that they do want. Raising the price of individual products will cause the firm to lose some sales, but the gain in sales resulting from the

---

[19]Note that there will be implications for product-line pricing here, since the bundle of goods may be a substitute for a product, or another bundle of products, in the firm's product line.

[20]George Stigler, "United States vs. Loew's Inc.: A Note on Block Booking," *Supreme Court Review*, 1963, pp. 153–157; William J. Adams and Janet L. Yellen, "Commodity Bundling and the Burden of Monopoly," *Quarterly Journal of Economics*, 90 (May 1976), pp. 475–98; Richard Schmalensee, "Commodity Bundling by Single-Product Monopolies," *Journal of Law and Business*, 25 (April 1982), pp. 67–71.

[21]In Appendix 9A we referred to this practice as first-degree price discrimination. In fact, product bundling is a technique by which the seller can practice price discrimination, since it divides potential buyers into groups based on their willingness to buy one or other of the products separately, or the bundle of products, and allows the seller to discriminate against those willing to buy only one or a subset of the products.

availability of the bundle typically outweighs that loss, such that the overall sales and profit are higher than if the products were priced separately.[22]

Quantity Discounts.   The theory of bundling explains why some firms offer a given product in several different sizes (such as small, medium, large, and jumbo bottles of Coke), and why some consumers buy only the small size and others pay more to buy larger sizes (but at a reduced price per unit, such as per ounce). The larger sizes can be viewed as bundles, or multiples, of the smallest size of the same product, and the buyer is given a discount for purchasing in quantity. Similarly, when a product is priced at, say, $3 each *or two for $5*, the buyer is essentially getting a discount on the second unit of the product if he or she chooses to buy that additional unit.

Why are some people induced to buy in quantity while others are not? A person will demand the extra units of the product bundled together in the larger size if the incremental cost to the consumer is less than the consumer's reservation price for those extra units.

- EXAMPLE: A consumer might be willing to pay a maximum of $1 for a 10 ounce bottle of cola, if she was very thirsty. The store price is, let us say, 70 cents. Since the asking price is less than the buyer's reservation price, the seller will make the sale. But suppose the seller also has a 20 ounce bottle of the same cola for $1.15. Will the consumer buy that one instead? Suppose that her reservation price on the 20 ounce size is $1.50, indicating she expects 50 cents worth of extra utility from the additional 10 ounces. Since the additional 10 ounces will cost her only 45 cents more, she will buy the larger size. Finally, suppose the store also has a 30 ounce size, priced at $1.75. The consumer's reservation price for the 30 ounce size is, say, $1.70, indicating her willingness to pay only another 20 cents for the additional 10 ounces. Since the additional quantity would cost her 60 cents, however, she chooses the 20 ounce size. The seller collects $1.15 from this customer, compared to only 70 cents that would have been collected if the cola had been priced uniformly per ounce regardless of bottle size. Assuming that the seller's marginal cost of the extra 10 ounces is always less than the price premium attached to the larger sizes, the seller will have increased both sales and profit. Of course, more thirsty customers, or someone buying the family groceries, is likely to buy the 30 ounce size, because their reservation prices are more likely to exceed the price asked.

In summary, the firm should consider offering its products in bundles as well as separately, because bundling may be expected to increase the firm's profits. Bundling includes the packaging together of different products, the offering of the same product in different-sized containers, and the offering of quantity discounts for multiple units of the

---

[22]Adams and Yellen, and Schmalensee, cited in footnote 20, determine the precise conditions under which mixed bundling will be a more profitable strategy than either pure bundling or individual prices only. The distribution of customers' reservation prices is critical, as is the relationship of marginal costs to the prices chosen. They conclude that mixed bundling is a more profitable pricing strategy under a wide variety of circumstances.

same product. Given the availability of bundles, the firm would then consider raising the prices of some or all of the individual products, of the smaller sizes, or of the single units, to extract more consumer surplus from those who want only part of the bundle. In practice, without full information on the distribution of consumers' reservation prices, the firm would need to conduct market research to estimate this distribution, or, if the search costs of that appear to be prohibitive, the firm would experiment by introducing product bundles and by changing the prices of individual units. If profit increases as a result of these changes, the firm may wish to fine-tune its pricing structure further until maximum profits appear to be attained.

In oligopoly markets a firm may be forced into bundling as a pricing strategy by the actions of its rivals. If the rivals offer product bundles, they will be capturing those consumers with relatively high reservation prices on the additional units included in the bundle, and the firm may feel it is necessary to seek its share of these customers. Note, however, that the existence of rivals constrains the oligopolist, to some degree, if it attempts to raise the prices of its separate products, its smaller sizes, or its single units. With the availability of substitutes, and consumer awareness of those substitutes, these price increases will meet a relatively elastic demand response. Thus the greater is the degree of similarity between the rivals' products, and the easier it is for consumers to evaluate the attributes of the products in the market, the less profitable one would expect product bundling to be.

Promotional Pricing

Promotional pricing, also known as "dealing," involves offering the consumer a temporary price reduction by placing the product "on sale" for a specified period. Several reasons for this practice are suggested. First, the firm may have excess inventories and wish to reduce its inventory costs. Second, the firm's supplier may have provided the goods at a discount from the usual wholesale price on condition that a promotional sale be held, in an attempt to broaden the producer's share of the final market. Third, a manufacturer wishing to expand its distributional network may offer an introductory discount to a retailer to induce the latter to handle the product. Fourth, the firm may reduce prices temporarily to avoid loss of market share when other firms have placed their products on sale or undertaken major advertising campaigns. Fifth, the firm may place some products on sale as "loss leaders" to attract buyers to the seller, with subsequent increases in the demand for other items. Finally, for many firms promotional pricing is simply part of their promotional strategy designed to keep customers aware of the seller's existence and the seller's commitment to low prices.

There may be some disadvantages associated with promotional pricing, from the firm's viewpoint, and these may include the following. First, sales revenue and profit from the product may fall if the demand is more inelastic than anticipated. This result could occur if a firm's price reduction triggered similar price reductions from its rivals. Second, some buyers may stop buying at the regular price and simply wait until the product is put on sale again, at which time they will buy several units to build a personal inventory of the item to tide them over until the product goes on sale again. Third, promotional pricing may increase the price consciousness of consumers, such that they more readily recall the price of the product and later react more elastically to price increases than they otherwise might. Fourth, it may damage the product's quality image, causing the quantity demanded at regular prices to fall as a result.

What kind of buyer is most likely to buy the product when it is priced promotionally? Blattberg[23] found that people with higher incomes, and couples with both spouses working, or with preschool children, tend to be less prone to such "deals". Furthermore, people who own their own houses and cars and consequently have relatively low storage and transportation costs tend to be more deal prone, other things being equal. Thus consumers who are prone to buying at promotional prices tend to have relatively low opportunity costs of their time, the ability to drive around to pick up a bargain, and a house in which to store personal inventories of these goods. The firm's advertising of their "sales" is thus more profitably aimed at low- to middle-income home and car owners. The myriad "flyers" that accompany the weekend newspapers delivered in the suburbs attest to the efficacy of that medium in reaching that kind of buyer.

Promotional pricing is frequently used on food and household convenience items that are bought frequently, such as aluminum foil, liquid detergent, headache remedies, facial tissues, and deodorant. It is also common for consumer durables that are bought infrequently, like stereo, video, and exercise equipment. What do these items have in common that makes them candidates for promotional pricing? Basic demand theory suggests that products for which demand is more elastic are better candidates for price reductions in general, since total revenue will increase more for a given price reduction. We saw in Chapter 4 that price elasticity depends on the number and availability of close substitutes, on the one hand, and the relationship of price to the consumer's income, on the other. Food and household convenience items typically have many close substitutes, causing the demand for any particular brand (or at any particular store) to be relatively elastic. Prices for stereo, video, and exercise equipment represent a relatively large proportion of the buyer's income, and thus these products also have relatively elastic demand.

Philip Nelson[24] has argued that more important than the number of substitutes is the number of substitutes of which the consumer is aware, and that the latter will vary with the type of product. That is, the more difficult it is to obtain information on a product and its attributes, the higher will be the search costs relative to the benefits, and the fewer substitutes the typical consumer will be informed about. Nelson categorized products into two types, those containing largely "search attributes" and those containing "experience attributes". The former can be easily evaluated prior to purchase; thus the consumer knows what he or she is getting for the price. Easily measurable or observable attributes, like size and weight of food items, design of clothing, and punctuality of airline depar-

[23]R. Blattberg, T. Buesing, P. Peacock, and S. Sen, "Identifying the Deal-Prone Segment," *Journal of Marketing Research*, 15 (August 1978), pp. 369–77.

[24]Philip Nelson, "Information and Consumer Behavior," *Journal of Political Economy*, 78 (March/April 1970), pp. 311–29. See also Louis Wilde, "The Economics of Consumer Information Acquisition," *Journal of Business*, 53 (July 1980), pp. S143–S158, and Nelson's comments following Wilde's paper.

tures fall into this category. Stereo and video equipment is similarly readily evaluated and compared on the basis of published specifications.

Experience goods contain attributes that can only be evaluated after purchase, but once evaluated will be purchased again on the basis of the consumer's recollection of the attributes. The taste of particular wines, the effectiveness of a detergent or deodorant, and the quality of paint are experience attributes. Darby and Karni[25] suggest a third category, "credence" goods, where the attributes are imperfectly evaluated even after repeated purchasing, such that the buyer tends to rely heavily on the product's projected image, brand name, and reputation. Professional services, like those of doctors, lawyers, and financial advisers, fall into this category. The quality of many goods, such as photographic film, is also difficult for many consumers to evaluate.[26]

Since it is more difficult to evaluate the products, it follows that the consumer's cost of information to evaluate a product increases as we move from search to experience to credence items. Thus we should expect consumers to seek less information about experience items than they do about search items, and to seek less information about credence items than they do about experience items. Thus credence items effectively have fewer substitutes *that the consumer is aware of*, as compared to experience goods, and experience goods similarly have fewer substitutes than search goods. Accordingly, we should expect to see promotional pricing used more frequently in markets for search products, where a price reduction will more likely lead to a highly elastic demand response.

More generally, price competition should be expected to be a more desirable competitive strategy, as compared to advertising, for example, if consumers can more easily evaluate the attributes (or relative quality) of the products. Price competition, including frequent-flyer programs, is particularly intense in the passenger airline markets, for example, where the attributes of each firm's product are easily ascertainable, including the time of departure, whether the flight is nonstop, whether meals and movie are provided, type of aircraft, and so on. (Nonprice competition, particularly advertising, is also quite intense among airlines, reflecting their desire to differentiate their services and thus reduce the price elasticity of demand.)

10.4   SUMMARY

In this chapter we have considered the firm's pricing problem in practical market situations. Firms typically lack full information concerning their cost and revenue functions and must make a decision whether or not to incur search costs to get the cost and demand information required to set prices that are optimal in light of their objectives. If the search costs involved are expected to be less than the value of information derived, the firm

---

[25]Michael Darby and Edi Karni, "Free Competition and the Optimal Amount of Fraud," *Journal of Law and Economics*, 16 (April 1973), pp. 67–88.

[26]This point, as well as several others made here, is attributable to Thomas Nagle, "Economic Foundations for Pricing," *Journal of Business*, 57 (January 1984), pp. S3–S26.

should first estimate its demand and cost curves and then set the short-run profit-maximizing price, the sales-maximizing price, or the limit price, as desired.

When search costs are expected to be prohibitive, the firm may earn greater profit by proceeding in ignorance, using some proxy pricing policy that may not give the "correct" price but that also does not require search costs for its implementation, such that the firm's objective may be better served if the revenues foregone because of the "incorrect" price are less than the search costs avoided. Markup pricing is typically used in practice, as is some form of price followership, including the following of "suggested" retail prices.

We showed that markup pricing can be profit maximizing if chosen at the level commensurate with the product's price elasticity of demand. If longer-term profit maximization is desired, the markup percentage is likely to be somewhat lower than for short-run profit maximization, since long-term price elasticities tend to be higher than short-term price elasticities. As well as saving information search costs, markup pricing acts to pass cost increases along to the customer and to maintain the purchasing power, or real value, of the firm's profits, and it assists in coordinating the pricing behavior of firms in oligopolistic markets.

We saw that there will be a range of acceptable markup rates if the firm does not incur search costs and that any one of these rates will allow higher profits or greater market share as compared to setting the optimal price *after* incurring search costs. The optimal markup rate remains optimal despite shifts in costs and demand curves, under certain conditions. Periodic search activity is recommended to ensure that the markup rate remains profit maximizing.

Choosing the appropriate price level in established product markets requires an evaluation of the attributes perceived to exist in your product vis-à-vis those in competing products. In these markets the general level of prices is established, and the problem is to ensure that each product is positioned in the existing price range such that the firm's objectives are best served. The price chosen should reflect the presence, absence, or degree of desirable attributes in each product, relative to the prices and attributes offered by competing products. Product-line pricing involves essentially the same problem, except that a particular firm produces several of the competing or complementary products and must, also consider the demand interdependencies. Again, attention must be paid to the relative price elasticities of demand, with allowances made for a basic product which has several complementary products, for the use of products as loss leaders, and for the entry-level and flagship products in a line of substitutes.

Prices may be set higher to infer higher product quality if price is the best indicator of quality available to the buyer. This method may be applicable to new products, to highly technical products which contain what we later called credence attributes, and to any product where the cost of information to the consumer is high relative to the price of the product.

Product bundling can allow a firm to increase its profit by raising individual product prices and setting the bundle price at less than the sum of the prices of the component products. Some consumers will be induced to buy the bundle and consequently spend more than they would have at the prices set for each of the products separately. At the same time this strategy discriminates against those buyers who want only one, or a subset, of the products in the bundle. Setting quantity discounts is also a bundle pricing problem. Larger sizes or multiples of the product are simply bundles of the same product, and the firm can increase profit by offering the buyers a choice of small sizes (or single units) at relatively high prices per unit and larger sizes (or multiple units) at lower prices per unit.

Promotional pricing, or putting an item temporarily on sale, is also expected to increase the firm's revenues and profit, although there are some problems to be wary of. Promotional pricing, as well as price competition in general, is likely to work better for products comprised of search attributes, namely attributes that are observable or measurable by the consumer at relatively low search costs. By way of corollary, products containing experience and credence attributes are less suitable for price competition, and their demand is probably better stimulated by advertising, which we consider in Chapter 13.

DISCUSSION QUESTIONS

10-1. When is it likely to be profit maximizing to use a rule-of-thumb price determination procedure rather than to determine price on the basis of estimated cost and revenue curves?

10-2. Can the markup formula linking price, average variable cost, and the price elasticity of demand be used to "plug in" the price elasticity and AVC figures to solve for the profit-maximizing price? Why or why not? What cost conditions are built into that formula?

10-3. Explain why there is a range of markup rates which make it preferable to avoid search costs. What does this range depend on?

10-4. Discuss the conditions under which a markup rate, if initially optimal in terms of the firm's objective, will remain optimal despite shifts in the cost and demand curves.

10-5. Explain why the presence or absence of desirable attributes in your product influences the optimal price positioning of that product in an established market.

10-6. Summarize the issues involved in product-line pricing strategy.

10-7. For what type of product is it feasible to infer higher product quality by setting a higher price? Under what circumstances, and for what objective, would it serve the firm's objective to set price *above* the short-run profit-maximizing level?

10-8. Explain how the firm may benefit from a product-bundling strategy, in the context of a computer manufacturer offering to sell the computer and various software programs separately, or the computer with several software programs as a package deal.

10-9. What considerations enter the firm's decision to offer a discount for quantity? How deep can its discount be? Explain your answer in terms of marginal costs and revenues.

10-10. Why would a firm place items temporarily "on sale"? What dangers are there in this practice? For what kind of products does promotional pricing work best? What kind of person responds to promotional pricing?

PROBLEMS AND SHORT CASES

10-1. The Ajzenkopf Company has been in operation for almost fifteen years and has enjoyed considerable success in the manufacture and sale of its glass vases.

The Ajzenkopf plant at present has a capacity of 35,000 units per year, and the facilities at the plant are highly specialized. Sales of vases are currently 29,000 units a year. The selling price is $7.00 per unit. Last month the average costs of production were determined to be as follows: average fixed costs, $1.03; average cost of labor, $1.98; and average cost of materials, $1.05. At those present price and cost levels the Ajzenkopf Company received a profit that management believed was quite acceptable.

This agreement situation came to an abrupt halt, however, when it was learned that the suppliers of raw materials were raising their prices and that there was a labor dispute which forced negotiations to begin. An agreement was reached, and the final settlement had the effect of increasing the average cost per unit of labor by 20%. A new contract has been signed with the suppliers of the raw materials, and the new prices of raw materials had the effect of increasing the average materials cost by 30%. This contract had been signed after other suppliers were contacted and no less expensive prices of raw materials could be found.

Faced with this situation, a meeting was called to determine what action should be undertaken to maintain an acceptable level of profit. It was agreed that a profit level of $75,000 was the minimum acceptable point. Two alternative suggestions were made. The first suggestion, made by the marketing manager, was to raise prices to $9.00 a unit, since he was fairly certain that this price level would reduce quantity demanded by only 8,500 units per annum. The marketing manager also offered an estimate of the average variable costs, stating that the average labor cost would be $3.10 and the average materials cost would be $1.39 at this level of output.

The plant manager proposed that the price should be reduced to $6.00. The plant manager was also fairly certain about the demand situation, stating that at this price level 32,500 vases would be demanded. He also offered his estimates of average variable costs, stating that at this level of output the average costs of labor and materials per unit would be $2.85 and $1.24, respectively. The plant manager further supported his proposal by stating that under this alternative, laborers need not be laid off and thus low labor morale would not reduce productivity of the workers.

(a) Using the information given above, derive graphical estimates of the firm's revenue and cost functions.

(b) Assuming that the firm wishes to maximize sales volume subject to obtaining a minimum profit of $75,000, what price do you suggest they charge? Discuss your answer fully. What qualifications do you wish to add to your analysis?

10-2. Regression analysis of the variations in prices and quantity demanded for Winton Garden Equipment's major product (conducted under controlled conditions in a consumer clinic by their marketing research department) provides the following results (where P is in dollars and Q represents thousands of units):

Regression equation	$Q = 49.147 - 2.941P$
Coefficient of determination	$R^2 = 0.96$
Standard error of estimate	$= 0.128$
Standard error of the coefficient	$= 0.086$

The production department has conducted its own study of weekly total variable costs and output levels over the past three months. Its results (with TVC in thousands of dollars and Q representing thousands of units) are as follows:

Regression equation	TVC $= 102.35 + 0.025Q^2$
Coefficient of determination	$R^2 = 0.92$
Standard error of estimate	$= 0.232$
Standard error of the coefficient	$= 0.003$

You are an executive assistant to the marketing manager, Derek Winton. Mr. Winton feels that the present price of $9.95 is fine. He argues that it positions the product in the upper part of the range of competitors' prices, and that the current sales level of approximately 20,000 units a week is fine in view of the company's capacity limit of only 25,000 units weekly. While he agrees that a price change of a dollar or so either way would go unchallenged by competitors, he does not think such a price change would improve the contribution made by this product.

(a) What is the contribution-maximizing price? Is the associated output level feasible?

(b) How confident are you that your prediction will in fact generate a greater contribution than the present price level? Explain in detail with supporting calculations.

(c) Are there any reservations you wish to attach to your recommendation?

10-3. The Pittsburgh Plastics Company introduced a new product in January which received strong initial support and has shown a steady growth of sales in subsequent months. The initial price was set somewhat arbitrarily as a 25% markup over average costs. The company's objective is to maximize the contribution to overheads and profits, and it is now anxious to know whether the $6.88 price is optimal. In light of the continual growth in sales and changes in certain cost components, it has commissioned a study by Market Researchers Incorporated, who report that the price elasticity of demand is approximately -2.5 at the current (March) price and output level.

The output and cost data for the past three months are as follows:

	January	February	March
Sales (units)	2,246	2,471	2,718
Direct materials	$1,415	$1,557	$1,712
Direct labor	3,369	4,077	4,933
Indirect factory labor	3,000	3,075	3,154
Office and administrative salaries	2,000	2,000	2,000
Light and heat	485	470	320
Other overheads	2,100	2,100	2,100

(a) Supposing that price can be varied each month, estimate the optimal price for the month of April.

(b) What output level could be sold at the optimal price level in April?

(c) What qualifications and other considerations do you wish to add to the above pricing and output decision?

10-4. The Laura Ann Boutique purchases a line of ladies dresses from a wholesaler and pays $30 per dress regardless of quantity purchased. These dresses are marked up 33.33% over their invoice cost and sell quite readily. The firm's objective is to maximize contribution to overheads and profits, and management is concerned whether or not 33.33% is the profit-maximizing markup rate.

(a) What would price elasticity of demand have to be for 33.33% to be the optimal markup rate?

(b) Suppose Laura Ann commissions a study, costing $500, that indicates that price elasticity of demand for these dresses is $\epsilon = -3.5$. Given the present price of $40 per dress and weekly sales averaging 300 dresses, was the present markup rate within the range of acceptable markups?

(c) Was the study worth it? Will it pay for itself in the future weeks?

10-5. The Archibald Truck Service (ATS) Company has been successfully servicing and repairing large trucks and tractor trailers for several years, specializing in Kenworth, Peterbilt, and Mack tractor service. Their pricing policy on each job is to charge $25 per hour labor and the "book price" for materials and replacement parts. The labor charge represents the actual cost to ATS plus 25%, and the "book prices" represent the invoice cost of the materials and parts plus 25%. Thus, ATS effectively sets price by marking up its direct costs by 25%. The founder and general manager, Mr. Joseph Archibald, reasons that this relatively low price structure is the best approach, since there is a lot of repeat business in service and repair work. He would rather have more work in the present period and maximize profits over the longer term.

For a typical service and repair job his cost is $600, and he charges $750. He does, on the average, 60 jobs per month. His overhead costs are $8,000 per month. Mr. Archibald is concerned that his monthly profits are too low; he wants at least $2,000 per month and is not earning that amount at present. He has asked all his customers over the past two months to complete a questionnaire, and from this he has been able to estimate that price elasticity for his service and repair job is approximately $\epsilon = -1.1$.

(a) Construct the demand, total revenue, and total cost curves for ATS from the data given.

(b) Advise Mr. Archibald of the price level and the implied markup rate on the average service and repair job which would maximize sales volume subject to the attainment of his profit target.

(c) Explain to Mr. Archibald the conditions under which that markup rate will remain optimal despite shifts in the cost and demand curves.

(d) Give him some guidance on how he should adjust the markup rate if the conditions referred to in part (c) do not hold.

10-6. The Napper Bag and Canvas Company, Ltd., is a specialist manufacturer of down-filled sleeping bags for sale in the camping equipment market. In this market there are several large companies with annual sales between $25 million and $30 million and many smaller companies with sales between $1 million and $5 million. Most of these companies have diversified product lines of camping equipment, including tents, cooking equipment, camping furniture, and sleeping bags with various types of filling. Napper's sales of $1.6 million last year came entirely from down-filled sleeping bags, however. Although more expensive than other materials, down has substantially more insulating value by weight and volume and commands the attention of a loyal segment of serious outdoorspeople. Only a few firms produce quality down-filled bags, but these firms face peripheral competition from other firms producing bags filled with other natural and artificial materials.

Last year Napper sold 21,000 bags directly to large department stores, catalog sales companies, and specialty sporting equipment stores. These clients typically require contracts guaranteeing prices for one year. The cost of manufacturing sleeping bags depends on the size of the bag, the materials used, and the amount of fill. A breakdown of Napper's latest manufacturing costs for a typical style is as follows:

Item	Cost per Unit
Down filling	$30.00
Other raw materials	14.40
Direct labor	8.12
Manufacturing overhead	6.09
Total unit cost	$58.61

A markup of 30% is added to total unit cost to provide for selling, administration, financial expenses, and profit.

During the past year the cost of down increased by between 80% and 95%, depending on the grade and blend. Napper was able to pass this on to its customers without any apparent loss of sales or share of the market. The suppliers of down are forecasting a minimum increase of 80% over the next year. For Napper the average price of down will increase from the current $12 per pound to $22 per pound. It is anticipated that the cost of other raw materials will rise by 8% and labor by 5% over the next year.

George Napper, the marketing manager, is concerned about the prospects for the coming year, and you are called on to advise him.

(a) What price level do you advise for Napper's typical style bag?

(b) Do you have any other advice for Mr. Napper concerning future marketing strategy?

10-7. The refrigerator market is characterized by a wide diversity of product offerings and a price range from less than $400 to more than $1,200, depending on the features of the specific refrigerator. Within this range, each manufacturer has a product line extending from the basic no-frills smaller refrigerators to the top-of-the-line luxury units.

A large chain of department stores buys various refrigerators from various manufacturers and sells them under its own brand name "Valhalla." Given the stores' reputation for quality products and after-sales service, this refrigerator line has achieved a substantial market share in the areas where it is sold. The marketing vice-president of the chain has been considering an addition to the Valhalla line. The new refrigerator, designated the Valhalla GE12456A, is made by General Electric and is similar to several sold by other major manufacturers, but it would fill a gap in the product line offered by the chain stores. The details of the Valhalla GE12456A are as follows: It is a 12-cubic-feet upright refrigerator/freezer, with two doors, a freezer at the top, and freezer capacity of 3.2 cubic feet, and it has four large aluminum trays for fresh meat and vegetables (taking up the lower two shelves), fully compartmentalized inner doors, butter and cheese compartments with individual temperature controls, and "easy-glide" wheels underneath. It comes in four colors and with door hinges on either side.

The refrigerators available that would seem most competitive with the Valhalla GE12456A are as follows (apart from the details shown, they are similar in all other respects to the Valhalla GE12456A):

Make/Model	Price ($)	Total Size (cu ft)	Freezer Size	Trays	Wheels
General Electric GE12456	525	12.0	3.2	4	Yes
Westinghouse WH11521	505	11.5	2.3	3	No
Store A house brand XY-4823	485	12.0	3.0	3	No
Store B house brand BK-7742	505	12.5	3.5	4	No
RCA RC-6821	515	11.8	2.8	4	Yes
Kelvinator K-7742	535	12.5	3.5	4	No

You are asked to assist in pricing the new addition to the Valhalla line.
(a) What price level would you recommend?
(b) Explain the basis for your recommendation in detail.
(c) Outline all qualifications you feel should be made to this recommendation.

10-8. Last fall, Peripherals conducted a three-month national mail-order campaign with its line of personal accessories relating to BMW automobiles. An advertisement, complete with photographs of the items, ran for three consecutive months in the BMW Owners Club magazine and generated orders over a six-month period. All of the items sold, including tiepins, key rings, caps, T-shirts, jackets, and umbrellas, carried the BMW logo and were designed to appeal to the pride of ownership felt by most BMW owners.

Peripherals' management is wondering whether the screen-printed T-shirts were priced at the contribution-maximizing level. The price charged was $8.95, and Peripherals sold 120 units during the period. The cost per unit of these shirts was $4, regardless of volume (once the initial costs, of design and of the screens, were paid for). The design was original, showing the colors of the BMW logo in a heart shape, and words which effectively said "I (love) my Bimmer." The shirts were high quality, 50% cotton and 50% polyester, and were advertised as such. Several other BMW T-shirts were available to buyers, being advertised in automobile magazines (including the club magazine) and typically priced at $9.50 or $9.95, as well as the T-shirt which is sold at the BMW dealerships for $11.50. Each of these shirts has a different design, ranging from the simple logo with the footnote "The Ultimate Driving Machine," sold by the dealerships, to a much more complex design including a car being driven at speed. Peripherals had pretested their design at a regional meeting of the club, and it was greeted favorably by virtually everyone who saw it. These respondents were told it would be priced "competitively."

The decision to price the shirt at $8.95 was made after consideration of the following factors. First, it did not seem fair to exploit fellow club members by pricing too much above direct cost. By pricing below the competition Peripherals felt they were giving very good value to club members. Second, Peripherals guessed that demand for the shirt would be somewhat elastic at prices below the competition, since all prices were stated in print, and the lead time necessary to change prices was at least three months. No estimates of quantity demanded were attempted, but a supplier was organized to produce the printed shirts in small batches as required. Third, it was recognized that demand for T-shirts would be somewhat softer in the fall, as compared to the spring or summer.

This summer, Peripherals plans to repeat their BMW campaign. Before choosing the price for T-shirts, however, Peripherals is considering taking several "experts" to lunch to find their views on the appropriate price of the shirts. These people are in the custom T-shirt business and seem to be quite successful. These lunches are expected to cost Peripherals $150 in total.

Based on the $8.95 price and the 120 units sold, Peripherals calculates that price elasticity would have had to be -1.80808 for the price to be contribution maximizing. This figure seems higher (in absolute terms) than Peripherals would have guessed. Their best estimate, considering that this will be a summer campaign, and given their experience last fall, is that price elasticity will be unitary at the $8.95 price level. They expect sales volume to be about 25% greater in the summer than in the fall.
(a) Given the estimated price elasticity and quantity demanded at $8.95 in the summer, estimate the demand curve which Peripherals thinks it will face.
(b) What is the contribution-maximizing price suggested by the estimated demand curve?
(c) Based on these estimates, should Peripherals spend the $150 finding out what the "experts" think?
(d) Outline all assumptions and qualifications which underlie your analysis.

10-9. Emerson Electric Corporation is considering the appropriate prices for two videocassette recorders that are being made in Japan and imported (as are all VCRs at this time) with

Emerson's brand name attached. These will be Emerson's first VCRs, although its name is well known in electric appliances generally. Model A being assembled for Emerson has four video heads, can record four programs in a fourteen-day period, has a varactor tuner capable of tuning ninety-nine channels, and has stereo with the Dolby feature. It does not have high fidelity, but it has multichannel television sound (MTS) capability. Model B has six heads, can record eight programs in twenty-one days, has a quartz tuner, stereo, Dolby, high-fidelity sound, and MTS capability. Emerson has asked you to recommend price levels which will appropriately position their products in the market. They supply you with the following information on VCR models available from Quasar and some other firms that they feel will be direct competitors. They tell you that the quartz tuner is superior to the varactor tuner, because it can pick up an unlimited number of channels and tune them in very finely. Varactor tuners must be preset to a given number of channels, and consumers typically prefer more than fourteen if they receive more than that number of channels on cable. Video quality is increased by having more heads. Both video and sound signals are derived from the two or four heads, except in the case of six-head systems, where the extra two heads are used exclusively for sound. In general, video and sound quality increase with the number of heads.

Brand and Model	Price	Heads	Programs	Tuner	Stereo	Dolby	Hi-fi	MTS
Quasar VH5154	$ 520	2	4/14	Var/14	No	No	No	No
Quasar VH5254	790	4	4/14	Var/99	Yes	Yes	No	No
Quasar VH5355	799	2	4/14	Var/99	No	No	Yes	Yes
Quasar VH5346	830	2	4/14	Var/14	Yes	Yes	Yes	No
Quasar VH5655	899	4	4/14	Var/99	No	No	Yes	Yes
Quasar VH5645	950	4	8/14	Quartz	Yes	Yes	No	No
Quasar VH5845	1,000	4	8/14	Quartz	Yes	Yes	Yes	No
Akai VS303U	600	2	4/28	Quartz	No	No	No	No
Akai VS603U	900	6	8/28	Quartz	Yes	No	Yes	No
Hitachi VT65A	750	4	4/14	Var/80	Yes	Yes	No	Yes
JVC HRD725U	1,199	6	8/14	Quartz	Yes	No	Yes	No
Magnavox VR8530	699	2	4/14	Var/99	Yes	No	Yes	Yes
Magnavox VR8544	750	4	4/14	Var/99	Yes	No	Yes	Yes

(a) Considering the quality of model A relative to these rival products, choose the price which you think appropriately positions it in this market. Outline the reasoning behind your decision.

(b) Now select a price for model B such that it is positioned appropriately in the VCR market, and explain your reasoning.

(c) What product-line pricing considerations entered your decisions?

(d) What qualifications and assumptions underlie your decisions?

10-10. Admiral Computer Company is planning to introduce a new version of its rather successful personal computer. The new model, designated the Personal Assistant, will have 128K bytes of RAM memory standard, with upgrades to 256K and 512K at extra cost. The Word Perfect word-processing software program will run on the 128K version, but Lotus 1-2-3 requires at least 256K memory, although some users will require 512K. Word Perfect is widely available for $695, and Lotus 1-2-3 now costs $495. Admiral could buy both programs on chips and bundle them with the computer, at half the retail price. The extra 128K memory chips cost Admiral $50 each, and $20 to install if bundled with the computer, or $100 to install if retrofitted to a customer's previously purchased computer. (To upgrade from 128K to 512K would require three additional 128 chips.)

Comparable personal computers (with 128K) are currently selling in the range $1,950 to $2,950, with IBM being the most expensive, and the IBM compatibles being in the upper half of that range. Admiral's Personal Assistant becomes IBM compatible if an extra wafer board is installed. This board has a direct cost to Admiral of $150, and, like the extra memory, can either be bundled in for $170 or installed later for $250. Admiral has asked you to advise them what price they should set for the 128K model, the 256K model, the 512K model, the IBM compatible version of each of these models, the 256K model with Lotus, Word Perfect, and IBM-compatibility bundled in, and the 512K model with these bundled in. Also, they want to know what price to set for the separate sale (and installation) of the Lotus and Word Perfect chips and IBM-compatibility board.

(a) Analyze this pricing problem on the basis of the information given here, and recommend prices for each product in Admiral's product line.

(b) Now suppose that IBM charges $400 for one extra 128K memory chip if it is bundled in and $750 if it is retrofitted, and its charges for the upgrade to 256K and 512K (from 128K) are $750 and $1,000, respectively. Others charge $200–300 less, citing the lower price as a positive feature in favor of their products. IBM's bundle prices tend to be about 95% of the sum of the prices of the products purchased separately, whereas the bundle prices of others tend to be between 70% and 80% of the sum of the products purchased separately. Does this factor change your recommended prices?

(c) What assumptions and qualifications underlie your analysis, and what further information would you seek, if any, before recommending the prices to Admiral?

SUGGESTED REFERENCES AND FURTHER READING

ADAMS, W. J., and J. YELLEN. "Commodity Bundling and the Burden of Monopoly," *Quarterly Journal of Economics*, 90 (May 1976), pp. 475–98.

ALPERT, M. I. *Pricing Decisions*. Glenview, Ill.: Scott, Foresman & Company, 1971.

BAGWELL, KYLE, and MICHAEL H. RIORDAN, "High and Declining Prices Signal Product Quality," *American Economic Review*, 81 (March 1991), pp. 224–39.

COHEN, M., and J. Y. JAFFRAY. "Rational Behavior under Complete Ignorance," *Econometrica*. 48 (July 1980), pp 1281–99.

CORR, A. V. "The Role of Cost in Pricing," *Management Accounting*, November 1974, pp 15–32.

CREADY, W. M. "Premium Bundling," *Economic Inquiry*, 29 (January 1991), pp. 173–9.

DANSBY, R. E., and C. CONRAD, "Commodity Bundling," *American Economic Review*, May 1984, pp. 377–80.

EARLEY, J. S. "Marginal Policies of 'Excellently Managed' Companies," *American Economic Review*, 46 (March 1956), pp. 46–70.

EICHNER, A. S. "A Theory of the Determination of the Mark-up under Oligopoly," *Economic Journal*, 83 (December 1973), pp. 1184–1200.

FERSHTMAN, C. "Price Dispersion in Oligopoly," *Journal of Economic Behavior in Organizations*, 3 (December 1982), pp. 389–401.

FRANKEL, M. "Pricing Decisions under Unknown Demand," *Kyklos*, 26. No. 1 (1973), pp. 1–24.

FRASER, R. W. "Uncertainty and the Theory of Mark-up Pricing," *Bulletin of Economic Research*, 37 (January 1985), pp. 55–64.

GREENE, D. L., "Short-Run Pricing Strategies to Increase Corporate Average Fuel Economy," *Economic Inquiry,* 29 (January 1991), pp. 101–14.

LANCASTER, K. "Competition and Product Variety," *Journal of Business,* 53 (July 1980), pp. S79–S103.

LIVESEY, F. *Pricing.* London: Macmillan, Inc., 1976.

NAGLE, T. "Economic Foundations for Pricing," *Journal of Business,* 57 (January 1984), pp. S3–S26.

OREN, S., S. SMITH, and R. WILSON. "Pricing a Product Line," *Journal of Business,* 57 (January 1984), pp. S73–S99.

PALDA, K. S. *Pricing Decisions and Marketing Policy.* Englewood Cliffs, N.J.: Prentice-Hall, Inc., 1971.

PALFREY, T. R. "Bundling Decisions by a Multiproduct Monopolist with Incomplete Information," *Econometrica,* 51 (March 1983), pp. 463–83.

NAISH, HOWARD F. "On the Near Optimality of Mark-up Pricing," *Economic Inquiry,* 28 (July 1990), pp. 555–85.

PETERSON, R. A. "The Price-Perceived Quality Relationship: Experimental Evidence," *Journal of Marketing Research,* 7 (November 1970), pp. 525–28.

SALOP, S., and J. E. STIGLITZ. "The Theory of Sales: A Simple Model of Equilibrium Price Dispersion with Identical Agents," *American Economic Review,* 72 (December 1982), pp. 1121–30.

SCHERER, F. M. *Industrial Market Structure and Industrial Performance* (2nd ed.) , chaps. 8, 11, and 12. Chicago: Rand McNally & Company, 1980.

SILBERSTON, A. "Price Behavior of Firms," *Economic Journal,* 80 (September 1970), pp. 511–82.

SIMON, J. L. "Unnecessary, Confusing, and Inadequate: The Marginal Analysis as a Tool for Decision Making," *American Economist,* 25 (Spring 1981), pp. 28–35.

WESTON, J. F. "Pricing Behavior of Large Firms," *Western Economic Journal,* 10 (March 1972), pp. 1–18.

Appendix 10A

ILLEGAL PRICING PRACTICES

EXECUTIVE SUMMARY

Every manager should be aware of the illegality of certain business practices. Since the passage of the Sherman Antitrust Act of 1890, business in the United States has been subject to **laws intended to promote competition between firms** in the best interests of the public. *The public* should be understood to mean both consumers and other firms, all of whom may be injured by anticompetitive actions on the part of one firm or a group of firms. The Sherman Act (1890), the Clayton Act (1914), The Federal Trade Commission Act (1914), the Robinson-Patman Act (1936), the Wheeler-Lea Act (1938), the Celler-Kefauver Act (1950), and other sundry pieces of legislation specify the restraints that are imposed on business practices. In this appendix we shall limit our purview to illegal pricing practices, and thus be largely concerned with **the Sherman and Robinson-Patman Acts.**

Penalties can be harsh for violation of these laws. General Electric, Westinghouse, and several other electrical companies were fined almost $2 million (in 1960 dollars) for their part in the **"Great Electrical Conspiracy"** to set prices collusively. Seven managers spent time in jail for their part in the conspiracy, and twenty-four others received suspended sentences. Treble damage suits brought by injured parties may have cost the conspirators more than $300 million over the next decade. More recent conspiracies uncovered have not been as wide ranging as this one (perhaps because of this one), but firms continue to find themselves in hot water for a variety of pricing practices not considered to be in the public interest. We shall discuss **price fixing, price discrimination, predatory pricing, and resale price maintenance.**

Price Fixing

The Sherman Act, 1890, section 1, states: "Every contract, combination . . . , or conspiracy, in restraint of trade or commerce . . . is declared to be illegal. . . . Every person who shall . . . engage in any combination or conspiracy . . . shall be deemed guilty of a felony, and . . . shall be punished by a fine not exceeding a million dollars if a corporation, or, if any other person, one hundred thousand dollars, or by imprisonment not exceeding three years, or by both said punishments, at the discretion of the court."

Price fixing, or the collusive agreement among firms as to the level of prices to be charged to customers, whether consumers or other firms, is one such "conspiracy in restraint of trade or commerce." These are known as horizontal price agreements, because all the firms involved are at the same level in the hierarchy between production and the final sale. For example, an agreement between manufacturers on the price to wholesalers, an agreement between wholesalers on the price to retailers, or an agreement between retailers on the price to consumers would each be a horizontal price agreement.[1]

A price agreement may involve an agreement with respect to either the price or the quantity, since limiting the quantity amounts to raising the price, because the market price will tend to rise to "clear the market," or to restrict demand to the available supply. Similarly, market-sharing agreements may constitute a price agreement in the eyes of the law. Markets may be shared by the agreement to assign territorial boundaries or individual buyers (or types of buyers) to individual sellers. Or the firms may agree simply to maintain their present market shares or to produce only some of the products that they might produce, leaving the markets for other products to other firms. In competitive bid markets, the firms might take turns to submit the lowest bid, or they might bid identically.

Price fixing is illegal per se, meaning there are no avenues of defense. To use the words of Chief Justice Earl Warren, "It has been held too often to require elaboration now that price fixing is contrary to the policy of competition underlying the Sherman Act and that its illegality does not depend on a showing of its unreasonableness, since it is conclusively presumed to be unreasonable. It makes no difference whether the motives of the participants are good or evil; whether the price fixing is accomplished by express contract or by some more subtle means; whether the participants possess market control;

---

[1] It would be irresponsible to ignore the other area of illegal business practices. In most economics departments a separate course will be offered, under the title Industrial Economics, or Industrial Organization, or Government and Business, that will give these matters the attention they deserve. Many books have been written on the subject, including Marshall C. Howard, *Antitrust and Trade Regulation: Selected Issues and Case Studies* (Englewood Cliffs, N.J.: Prentice-Hall, 1983); M. L. Erickson, T. W. Dunfee, and F. F. Gibson, *Antitrust and Trade Regulation: Cases and Materials* (New York: John Wiley & Sons, 1977); Peter Asch, *Industrial Organization and Antitrust Policy* (New York: John Wiley & Sons, 1983);and Frederic M. Scherer, *Industrial Market Structure and Economic Performance*, 2nd ed. (Boston: Houghton Mifflin Company, 1980). For details on the "Great Electrical Conspiracy" see John Herling, *The Great Price Conspiracy* (Washington, D.C.: Robert B. Luce, Inc., 1962); John G. Fuller, *The Gentlemen Conspirators* (New York: Grove Press, 1962); and Charles A. Bane, *The Electrical Equipment Conspiracies: The Treble Damage Actions* (New York: Federal Legal Publications, Inc., 1973).

whether the amount of interstate commerce affected is large or small; or whether the effect of the agreement is to raise or decrease prices."[2]

To obtain a conviction on price fixing, prosecutors must show evidence of a conspiracy to agree on the price level or market shares. Meetings of business leaders where prices are discussed, written and reported statements made by these people, and communications between them regarding prices or market sharing are admissible evidence. The existence of meetings, followed by identical or parallel pricing behavior, has been held to be evidence of a pricing conspiracy. The exchange of price lists or of information on prices charged to particular customers is illegal per se. "Signaling" practices, such as publicly speaking of the need for a price increase or making an advance announcement of a price increase, have recently been challenged as being indicative of a conspiracy to fix prices.[3]

What about price leadership and conscious parallelism? Are these conspiracies to set prices at the same level? Not if the firms independently exercise their own judgment, each deciding independently either to raise or lower its price to a new level in its own best interests. Parallel pricing behavior by itself does not indicate a conspiracy, but there had best not be any other evidence of meetings, discussions, communications, or announcements of prices which could invite prosecution. The risk-averse decision maker will avoid discussing prices with anyone outside the firm, other than customers.

Price Discrimination

The Robinson-Patman Act, 1936, section 2, states: "It shall be unlawful . . . to discriminate in price between different purchasers of commodities of like grade and quality, . . . where the effect of such discrimination may be to substantially lessen competition or tend to create a monopoly in any line of commerce, or to injure, destroy, or prevent competition."

There are four avenues of defense against a charge of price discrimination. First, price differentials that make due allowance for differences in the cost of manufacture and in the cost of serving particular customers are allowable. Such differentials would include quantity discounts to larger buyers and any differences in transport and service costs. Second, the practice may be allowable if there is no significant injury to competition, whether actual or potential. Third, price differences that result from a reduction made in good faith to match the prices previously set by competitors may be allowable. Finally, price reductions may be permitted in response to a deterioration in the marketability of the product, such as for perishable goods, goods rendered no longer fashionable or obsolete, end-of-season sales, and distress sales.

In Appendix 9A we considered economic price discrimination. Is that illegal? It is unless one or more of the defenses mentioned in the last paragraph can be claimed. The telephone company charges rates for daytime long-distance calls that are different from

---

[2]*U.S.* v. *McKesson & Robbins, Inc.*, 351 U.S. 305, 309–310 (1956). This passage is also found in Howard, *Antitrust and Trade Regulation,* pp. 56–57.

[3]See Howard, *Antitrust and Trade Regulation,* pp. 67–69.

the evening and weekend rates. Recall that the telephone industry was a regulated monopoly until recently, and thus there was no injury to competition. More recently, with the entry of several other suppliers of long-distance service, the new entrants have seen fit to generally follow the lead of AT&T and set higher prices for daytime use of their systems, although there have been price reductions offered in both markets. Thus we may conclude that if the firm is a monopoly it may practice price discrimination unless its actions serve to prevent the entry of a new firm. Next, if the firm is an oligopolist, it may practice price discrimination if all of its rivals similarly practice price discrimination by unspoken accord, such as through price leadership or conscious parallelism.

Predatory Pricing

Section 3 of the Robinson-Patman Act covers price discrimination "in particular localities . . . for the purpose of destroying competition, or eliminating a competitor." A large and financially secure firm might reduce prices in one region for the express purpose of impoverishing a smaller firm that contests only that regional market. Using its profits from other regional markets, it can support losses in one market until the rival firm is forced to leave the market or agree to a takeover. John D. Rockefeller is alleged to have used such tactics to eliminate competitors when he built the Standard Oil monopoly during the nineteenth century.[4]

More recently, Borden, Inc., was prosecuted for their pricing of ReaLemon, a processed lemon juice product. Although ReaLemon was priced 10 to 15 cents above rival firms' prices, it was alleged that Borden's prices were predatory. The value of the ReaLemon brand name required the other firms with less well-known brand names to set their prices 10 to 15 cents (about 25%) below ReaLemon's price to survive in the market, since at any lesser price difference consumers would prefer to pay a little extra for ReaLemon and be assured of the quality that they had come to expect from that product. The firms' costs were probably quite similar, although ReaLemon may have benefited from economies of plant and firm size. The resulting price-cost differentials meant that Borden could earn a reasonable profit while impoverishing rivals by reducing its price to the point that rivals' prices would be forced below costs. Thus the firm's price need not be set below rivals' prices to be considered predatory.[5]

The ReaLemon case is perplexing because it indicates that a firm need not cut its prices below costs to be guilty of predatory pricing. Economic analysis suggests that a firm, even if engaged in vigorous price competition, would not wish to set price below its average variable cost, and if observed doing so might be presumed to be engaging in predatory pricing.[6] The essential element lies in the words "for the purpose of destroying

---

[4]See John S. McGee, "Predatory Price Cutting: The Standard Oil (N.J.) Case," *Journal of Law and Economics,* 1 (October 1958), pp. 137–86.

[5]See Clement G. Krouse, "Brand Name as a Barrier to Entry: The ReaLemon Case," *Southern Economic Journal,* 51 (October 1984), pp. 495–502.

[6]See P. Areeda and D. F. Turner, "Predatory Pricing and Related Practices under Section 2 of the Sherman Act," *Harvard Law Review,* 88 (February 1974), pp. 697–733.

competition, or eliminating a competition.'' If the aggressor's intent can be shown to be the reduction of competition or the elimination of a competitor, an aggressive pricing strategy may be shown to be a predatory strategy. As in a competitive sport, the object is to win the game, not injure or kill the opponent.

Resale Price Maintenance

Fair-trade laws, which prevented retail prices from being reduced below a minimum specified by the manufacturer, were introduced during the 1930s and finally repealed in 1975. The Miller-Tydings Resale Price Maintenance Act (1937) and later the McGuire Act (1952) had exempted from prosecution (under the Sherman Act) such *vertical* price agreements between firms, ostensibly to protect small business from the ''cutthroat'' competition of larger firms. Between the late 1930s and 1975 the manufacturer of a brand name or trademarked product could specify the minimum resale price at the retail level, as long as manufacturers made no *horizontal* agreement with rival manufacturers.

Since 1976, however, when the repeal of the resale price maintenance (RPM) legislation became effective, it has been illegal to specify a price at which a product must be resold. Resale prices may be ''suggested'' but not enforced in any way, such as by threatening to stop supplying the reseller or by raising wholesale prices, for example. If a reseller, whether wholesaler or retailer, chooses to follow the suggested list price, at his or her own volition, no offense is committed, but there must be no implicit or explicit agreement that a minimum resale price is a condition of the manufacturer's sale of the goods. The abolition of RPM removes a barrier to competition among firms and is in the general best interest of both consumers and firms, although some manufacturers are no doubt disturbed (about a possible reduction of the product's quality image) when their product is used as a ''loss leader.''

That the abolition of RPM is in the general best interests of firms is evidenced by the fact that RPM almost died a natural death as many resellers ignored the minimum prices and manufacturers chose not to discipline them. By 1974 only 4% of retail trade was conducted using RPM, and enforcement of RPM persisted in only a few lines, such as stereo equipment, cosmetics, liquor, television sets, and prescription drugs.[7]

Summary

In this appendix we have briefly considered several pricing practices that may be held to be illegal by the Federal Trade Commission, which is empowered to investigate unfair methods of competition. Price fixing, meaning a horizontal price agreement among rivals, has been illegal under the Sherman Act since 1890. Vertical price agreements that involve resale price maintenance are also illegal under the Sherman Act, although these agreements were exempted for a protracted period. The decision maker's best defense is to stay away from any such agreements and abstain from discussions with other firms

---

[7]See Scherer, *Industrial Market Structure*, p. 594.

concerning prices. Pricing independently, even if in conscious parallelism or as a price leader or follower, will avoid the severe fines and the jail sentences that may follow prosecution on these charges.

The Robinson-Patman Act (1936) is the major problem for managers involved in pricing decisions, since it is not as clear as the Sherman Act as to which practices are forbidden and which are permissible. Many firms, such as Borden, Inc., with their ReaLemon product, have followed what may seem to be aggressive but fair competitive practices, only to receive unwelcome attention from the Federal Trade Commission. Familiarity with the Robinson-Patman Act and recent case history is a necessary attribute of a good corporate lawyer, and access to a good corporate lawyer is necessary for aggressive pricing decisions. A general knowledge of the laws governing the competitive behavior of business is important for all managers.

DISCUSSION QUESTIONS

10A-1. What is a horizontal price agreement, as distinct from a vertical price agreement?

10A-2. Why are market-sharing agreements tantamount to price fixing? What kind of market-sharing agreements may be construed as a price-fixing agreement?

10A-3. For a price-fixing conspiracy to be proven, must the Justice Department be able to produce a written and signed agreement?

10A-4. When is or is not conscious parallelism or price leadership and followership likely to be regarded as a pricing agreement?

10A-5. Under what conditions is price discrimination allowable?

10A-6. What is predatory pricing? How is predatory pricing to be distinguished from vigorous price competition?

10A-7. What is resale price maintenance? Can you think of reasons why a manufacturer would want to control the minimum price of its product at the retail level?

10A-8. What arguments, for or against resale price maintenance, can you imagine a reseller might voice in support of or in opposition to resale price maintenance?

SUGGESTED REFERENCES AND FURTHER READING

AREEDA, P. and D. F. TURNER. "Predatory Pricing and Related Practices under Section 2 of the Sherman Act," *Harvard Law Review,* 88 (February 1974), pp. 697–733.

ASCH, P. *Industrial Organization and Antitrust Policy,* esp. chaps. 11, 15, and 16. New York: John Wiley & Sons, 1983.

BANE, C. A. *The Electrical Equipment Conspiracies: The Treble Damage Actions.* New York: Federal Legal Publications, Inc., 1973.

CALVANI, T., et al. "Resale Price Maintenance: Theory and Policy in Turmoil," *Contemporary Policy Issues,* 3 (Spring 1985), pp. 1–58.

ERICKSON, M. L., T. W. DUNFEE, and F. F. GIBSON. *Antitrust and Trade Regulation: Cases and Materials.* New York: John Wiley & Sons, 1977.

FULLER, J. G. *The Gentlemen Conspirators.* New York: Grove Press, 1962.

HERLING, J. *The Great Price Conspiracy.* Washington, D.C.: Robert B. Luce, Inc., 1962.

HOWARD, M. C. *Antitrust and Trade Regulation: Selected Issues and Case Studies.* Englewood Cliffs, N.J.: Prentice-Hall, Inc., 1983.

ISSAC, R. M., and V. L. SMITH. "In Search of Predatory Pricing," *Journal of Political Economy,* 93 (April 1985), pp. 320–45.

KROUSE, C. G. "Brand Name as a Barrier to Entry: The ReaLemon Case," *Southern Economic Journal,* 51 (October 1984), pp. 495–502.

LOTT, J. R., JR. and R. D. ROBERTS. "A Guide to the Pitfalls of Identifying Price Discrimination," *Economic Inquiry,* 29 (January 1991), pp. 14–23.

MCGEE, J. "Compound Pricing," *Economic Inquiry,* April 1987, pp. 315–39.

MCGEE, J. S. "Predatory Price Cutting: The Standard Oil (N.J.) Case," *Journal of Law and Economics,* 1 (October 1958), pp. 137–86.

MILGROM, P., and J. ROBERTS. "Predation, Reputation, and Entry Deterrence," *Journal of Economic Theory,* 27 (August 1982), pp. 280–312.

ROSS, T. W. "Winners and Losers under the Robinson-Patman Act," *Journal of Law and Economics, 27* (October 1984), pp. 243–71.

SCHERER, F. M. *Industrial Market Structure and Economic Performance* (2nd ed.), esp. chaps. 19 and 21. Boston: Houghton Mifflin Company, 1980.

YAMEY, B. S. "Predatory Price Cutting: Notes and Comments," *Journal of Law and Economics,* 15 (April 1972), pp. 137–47.

WEISMETH, H. "Price Discrimination Based on Imperfect Information: Necessary and Sufficient Conditions," *Review of Economic Studies,* 49 (July 1982), pp. 391–402.

Chapter 11

NEW-PRODUCT PRICING

EXECUTIVE SUMMARY

Rapid technological advances over the past two decades have spawned an ever-increasing array of new products. Setting the appropriate price for a new product can present **a major challenge, because almost no information exists on the demand for new products**. Market research may be undertaken, but until the new product is properly understood, marketing research may be less reliable. Even the demand for the personal computer, which was no longer an unknown product to most people by the early 1980s, grew much faster than industry surveys had predicted (and allowed the penetration of the market by the IBM compatibles.)

New products cover a wide spectrum of newness. In the broadest sense, a product is new if it contains a different package of attributes compared to what was previously available, such as a "*new* lemon-scented dishwashing liquid" or the "*new* Chevrolet Corvette." These are simply **new versions of existing products** that basically serve the same consumer or producer needs, but with a few more bells and whistles added. As such, these products **can be priced in the context of the established markets**, by positioning their price with reference to the additional attributes they offer, relative to previous versions and competitors' current versions of the same product.

In this chapter we are concerned with **new products representing a quantum leap ahead** of the products that previously served the same need, or which serve a previously unsatisfied need. Examples include the television set, the hand calculator, jumbo jets, personal computers, electronic photography (using magnetic disks rather than film), hydroponic lettuce-growing machines, satellites, and so on. The demand curves for such products must be estimated virtually from scratch, as the value of the new attributes or the new service to potential consumers cannot easily be estimated with any accuracy.

We first consider setting the initial price and whether **price skimming** or **penetration pricing** is the appropriate strategy. We then examine the dynamic price path over time, considering **the impact of the learning curve, economies of scale, entry of new firms, the product life cycle, and first-mover advantages.**

11.1 SETTING THE INITIAL PRICE FOR A NEW PRODUCT

Traditionally, the appropriate initial price has been argued to be either the "skimming" price or the "penetration" price.[1] As the name implies, the skimming price skims the cream off the top of the market by initially setting a relatively high price. The penetration price, on the other hand, is set at a relatively low level, with the intent of achieving broad penetration of the market initially. We shall see that each strategy is appropriate in particular circumstances.

Price Skimming

- DEFINITION: *Price skimming* is the choice of a relatively high price for a new product when it is first introduced, with the intent of getting as much profit from the product as possible. At the skimming price, demand will be limited to those buyers willing to pay the relatively high price, but the contribution to overheads and profit per unit sold will be relatively high. In fact, price skimming may be none other than short-run profit maximization. We have said the price skimmer's intent is to get as much profit as possible from the product. If the firm's time horizon does not extend beyond the short run, then the skimming price will be the profit-maximizing price. Let us pursue this topic for a moment.

In Figure 11-1 we show the firm's profit-maximizing price for the new product. This graph is familiar, of course, but is repeated here to emphasize two important points. First, the innovating firm is essentially a monopolist in the market for the new product, since there is, at least initially, no other firm with a similar product. In subsequent periods the entry of competitors with similar products will turn the market into an oligopoly, unless this development is prevented by barriers to entry, such as a patent for the new product held by the innovating firm, the unavailability of resources to potential entrants, or the unavailability of technology. A second point is that the firm's initial output capacity may be small relative to the market demand, since the risk of new-product failure is notoriously high and the firm may be reluctant to commit resources to build a larger plant or may be unable to afford one until the extent of demand is demonstrated. The firm's capacity considerations are incorporated into the graph. In this case the firm is producing beyond full capacity, defined as the output level where average cost is minimized. In the long run this firm will surely consider increasing its plant size, and the relatively high contribution from the skimming price will help the firm afford this expansion.

Thus the skimming price is appropriate when the firm's objective is to maximize its short-run profits. Such a firm does not look beyond the short run, so the potential entry of rivals with competing versions of the product is of no concern to the firm in this case. A skimming price may also be appropriated if the firm's time horizon is longer than the short run and its objective is the maximization of long-term profit (or the EPV of net

---

[1]See Joel Dean, b "Pricing Policies for New Products," *Harvard Business Review*, 28 (November–December 1950).

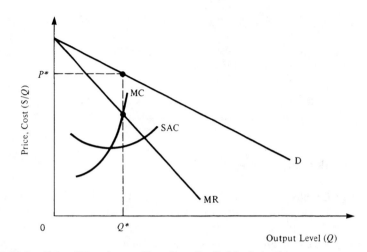

FIGURE 11-1. *Price Skimming as Short-Run Profit Maximization*

worth) over the horizon. There are essentially three situations in which the long-term profit (net worth) maximizer will choose a skimming price.

First, the long-term profit-maximizing firm will choose a skimming price if there are substantial barriers to the entry of new competitors with a similar product. If entry of new firms in subsequent periods is impossible, the firm will maximize the EPV of profit over its time horizon by setting the short-run profit-maximizing price. If the barriers to entry are not insurmountable but are nonetheless substantial, then the skimming price is the limit price, a price set just high enough to prevent the most likely entrant firm from being able to make a profit over its time horizon.

Second, if the firm expects a positive relationship between its chosen price and the quality of the product as perceived by buyers and potential buyers, it may be profit maximizing in the long term to set a relatively high (skimming) price initially. In this case the skimming price may be above or below the short-run profit-maximizing price, but it is high relative to the firm's average variable costs, or, equivalently, the markup rate is relatively high. In effect, the firm thinks that a higher price in the short run will cause the product to be perceived as a better product, and thus the quantity demanded will be higher at any given price than it would be if the product were perceived to be of lower quality. Put another way, the higher price is expected to cause an improved perception of the product; which operates to shift the demand curve for the product outward in the present and subsequent periods.

We noted in Chapter 10 that the price-quality association may be positive for new products, since there may be little alternative information on quality available to consumers, but the attributes of the product must be of the experience or credence type, rather than the search type that is easily ascertainable by consumers. Also, the more expensive the product is, the more search information consumers will rationally seek. Thus we might expect price skimming to be considered if the new product is a relatively inexpensive experience or credence good. We shall see below that there is a second reason why experience or credence goods may be candidates for price skimming.

Third, price skimming will be EPV-maximizing if the demand for the product is not expected to last beyond the short run, such that the question of entry of competitors is moot. Fad items catch the interest of the consumer briefly, and then interest fades away as the novelty value disappears. The "pet rock" enjoyed a very profitable few months before Christmas one year in the 1970s. It was reported at the time that the seller made $4 million dollars with this item, a novelty gift that was essentially a large pebble in a small cardboard box with a humorous set of instructions included. Other temporary markets, such as emergency situations where the need will soon pass, also indicate the profit-maximizing price as the best strategy for the EPV-maximizing firm (although this practice may be regarded as profiteering).

Price-skimming strategies usually result in the price being reduced in subsequent periods, as the number of buyers willing to pay the relatively high price dwindles, as the firm's cost of production falls because of the learning effect, or as rival firms enter the market with their own versions of the new product. We shall discuss the dynamic path of prices and their underlying causes later in this chapter.

Penetration Pricing

- DEFINITION: *Penetration pricing* is the practice of setting a relatively low price in the current period to achieve broad penetration of the market and ensure a larger market share in subsequent periods. Of course, the firm could achieve maximum penetration by giving the product away, but giving it away would cause losses, so a minimum profit constraint is implicit in penetration pricing. In fact, penetration pricing may be nothing more than short-run sales maximization subject to a profit target, a pricing model we introduced in Chapter 9.

Penetration pricing is undertaken when the firm is concerned about the entry of new firms with competing versions of the new product in subsequent periods. It is therefore appropriate for firms with a time horizon extending beyond the short run. We argued in Chapter 9 that sales maximization subject to a minimum profit constraint was a proxy policy for the maximization of the EPV of long-term profit or net worth. Greater sales in the short run lead to greater profit in the long term because of greater repeat sales, greater sales of complementary items, and a reduced probability of entry resulting from the lower price (when compared to the short-run profit-maximizing price).

Where the firm's EPV of long-term profit is best served by setting a price that will preclude the entry of new firms altogether, it must set the limit price. The limit price may be either a skimming price or a penetration price, depending on whether it is relatively high or relatively low. In turn, the height of the price level depends on the height of the barriers to entry. Entry barriers impose higher costs on the entrant firms. For example, the entrant may incur higher fixed costs per period because of advertising expenditures necessary to overcome consumer loyalty to the existing firm. It may incur higher average variable costs because of more expensive raw material sources, royalties payable to the patent holder, and so on. Recall that the limit price is set just below the minimum average cost of the potential entrant. If the barriers to entry are relatively high and entrants are thus expected to have relatively high costs of production, the limit price will be higher and may be regarded as a skimming price. Alternatively, if barriers are relatively low and the existing firm expects little or no cost advantage over entrant firms, then the limit price will be a penetration price. The limit-pricing models for high-cost entrants and low-cost entrants were discussed in Chapter 9.

The type of product is also a factor in the decision to set either a skimming or a penetration price. In Chapter 10 we noted that products may be classified as either search, experience, or credence products depending on how difficult it is for the consumer to obtain information about the attributes of the product. We now note that price skimming will more likely be the superior strategy if the product contains predominantly experience or credence attributes, whereas penetration pricing is more likely the best strategy if the product contains mostly search attributes. Let us see why.

Search attributes are relatively easy for the buyer to measure. It will be more difficult for the innovating firm to build and maintain product differentiation when the new product is a search good, since entrants will easily evaluate the new product and be able to produce their own versions which consumers will recognize as essentially similar. Thus, after the entry of new firms, demand will tend to be more price elastic for search goods than for experience or credence goods. If demand is more elastic after entry, the profit-maximizing markup will be lower, and the profit per period will be lower. This outcome is inevitable once entry takes place. To avoid this dilution of future profits, the innovating firm will more likely set the limit price and maximize the EPV of profit by earning a series of relatively moderate profits over its time horizon. The limit price is more likely to be a relatively low (penetration) price in the case of search goods, because the costs of the firms (after entry) are more likely to be similar, given the similarity of the products. Thus, if the new product is a search product, the EPV of profits following a penetration pricing strategy is more likely to exceed the EPV of the profits that would follow a skimming strategy.

With experience and credence products, on the other hand, it will be less difficult for the innovating firm to build and maintain product differentiation after the entry of rivals. Similarly, following their entry, rivals can more easily differentiate their products with their claims and brand names. Thus (after entry) the innovating firm's demand will be less elastic, its markups higher, and its business more profitable when the product is an experience or credence good rather than a search good. In this case the EPV of profits associated with price skimming is more likely to exceed the EPV of profits associated with the penetration price, and thus price skimming is more likely to be the strategy that best serves the firm's objective.

In summary, price skimming will be appropriate when the firm's objective is short-run profit maximization, when the objective is long-term profit maximization and entry barriers are insurmountable, or when demand for the product will be short-lived. If barriers to entry are not prohibitive but are relatively high, these barriers will impose relatively high additional costs on entrants, and thus the limit price may be regarded as a skimming price since it will be relatively high. Price skimming may also be appropriate if consumers draw price-quality inferences, which may happen with experience or credence goods. If the new product *is* an experience or credence good, post-entry profits will be higher than if the new product is a search good, again militating in favor of price skimming as the best initial strategy. Penetration pricing is indicated where the firm's time horizon falls in a future period, its objective is the maximization of long-term profit or net worth, and entry of new firms is relatively easy. Given all that, the firm might still choose price skimming initially if the nature of the product is such that it can develop and maintain a high degree of product differentiation in subsequent periods.

Choosing between the Skimming Price and the Penetration Price

The choice between the skimming price and the penetration price must be made if the firm's time horizon falls beyond the short run, demand continues beyond the short run, and the barriers to entry are not insurmountable. We shall now work through an example in which the innovating firm has estimated the market demand curve for the new product, has estimated the cost structure of potential entrants, and, finally, has estimated the probability of entry in the second and third periods following the introduction of the product in the first period.

The data on the entry probabilities and demand per firm are presented in Table 11-1. Note that the entry probabilities in the third period are conditional on what happened in period 2, reflecting the reactions of potential entrants to the number of firms already in the market. The demand per firm is based on the estimated market demand curve $P = 20 - 0.001\ Q$ and on the presumption that the firm will maximize profits as a monopoly initially, and as the low-cost price leader after entry takes place. Assuming that the firm's marginal cost is constant at $4 per unit regardless of output, the price will be $12 per unit both before and after entry, as shown in Figure 11-2. We also assume for simplicity that the firms will share the market equally when they all set the same price. Thus the innovating firm's profit-maximizing output is 8,000 units when the firm is a monopoly and is equal to $8,000/n$, where n is the number of firms, after entry has occurred.

In Figure 11-2 we show the innovating firm initially setting the profit-maximizing price and selling 8,000 units in the first period, period t. A new firm enters in period $t + 1$, causing the innovating firm's demand curve (which is now the *mutatis mutandis* curve of a price leader) to shift inward to represent exactly half the market demand at each price level. Referring to the new *mutatis mutandis* marginal revenue curve, the innovating firm finds that $12 is still the profit-maximizing price. This result follows only because we have assumed that MC is constant and that each firm's share of the market will be constant (in this case, one half) at various prices, as long as prices are equal. Note that the price leader's *mutatis mutandis* demand curve would continue to swing inward as progressively more firms enter. The price axis intercept remains the same but the slope becomes progressively steeper, equal to n times the slope of the market demand curve, where n is the number of firms. This inward swinging of the demand curve was called an iso-elastic demand shift in Chapter 10 in the context of markup pricing. The implicit markup here is 200% over AVC = MC, and this markup remains profit-maximizing despite entry of competitors, given the assumptions underlying this model.

TABLE 11-1.   Data for the Firm's New-Product Pricing Decision

| IN PERIOD 2 | | | IN PERIOD 3 | | |
New Entrants	Probability	Demand per Firm	New Entrants	Probability	Demand per Firm
No firms enter	0.2	8,000	No firms enter	0.1	8,000
			One firm enters	0.7	4,000
			Two firms enter	0.2	2,667
One firm enters	0.5	4,000	No firms enter	0.3	4,000
			One firm enters	0.5	2,667
			Two firms enter	0.2	2,000
Two firms enter	0.3	2,667	No firms enter	0.5	2,667
			One firm enters	0.4	2,000
			Two firms enter	0.1	1,600

Assuming away any price-quality association, the firm has a choice of setting either the profit-maximizing price or some lower price. For simplicity we shall reduce this problem to a simple dichotomy: The firm will set either the profit-maximizing (skimming) price or the limit (penetration) price. Setting the former, it risks attracting new entrants and having to share the market in future periods. Thus its profits will be relatively high during the first period, and profits may then be relatively low in subsequent periods following the probable entry of new firms. If, on the other hand, it sets the limit

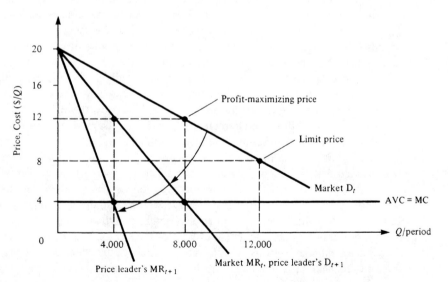

FIGURE 11-2.   Inward Shift of the Innovating Firm's Demand Curve after the Entry of One Firm

price, it is able to preserve its monopoly position while earning moderate profits in each period.[2]

As implied by the statement that the initial firm will assume the role of low-cost price leader if there is entry of new firms, the costs of the entrant firms are assumed to be higher than for the initial firm. In this example we assume that the entrants will each face marginal costs constant at $5 per unit and have total fixed costs per period of $12,000. The limit price is assumed to be equal to the average cost per unit of the first entrant, given that the first entrant would produce 4,000 units per period. Thus the limit price is $5 + $3 = $8. (In theory it should be fractionally less than the entrant's SAC, say, $7.99, but we shall use $8 for simplicity.) The limit price is set to prevent the entry of the first entrant, and thus no firms will enter. In markup terms, it represents a markup of 100% over the innovating firm's direct costs per unit.

At the limit price, $8, the innovating firm will sell 12,000 units each period, as indicated in Figure 11-2. Total contribution will be $48,000 per period, since per-unit contribution (the limit price less this firm's AVC) is $4. At the profit-maximizing price ($12), quantity demanded is 8,000 units when the firm is a monopoly, and the contribution per unit is $8, so profit is $64,000 in the first period. These profits must be discounted, however, since they are received on a more or less daily basis during the period. Assuming the period is a year and the opportunity discount rate is 10% and using the daily interest discount factors, we show the calculation of the EPVs of the alternate strategies in Table 11-2.

Note that after three years the EPV of the limit-pricing strategy exceeds the EPV of the profit-maximizing strategy, $125,241 compared to $113,323. If the firm has a three-year time horizon, the limit-pricing strategy is superior. If the firm has a shorter time horizon, however, the profit-maximizing strategy is superior, as can be seen by the summary results at the foot of the table. This result demonstrates quite forcefully the importance of the firm's time horizon in decision making. The longer it is, the more likely it is that the firm will be inclined to choose the limit price or any penetration price, rather than the profit-maximizing price or any skimming price, other things being equal. Similarly, the higher the probability of entry, the more likely it is that the limit price will be optimal, *ceteris paribus*.

Determining Price and Quality Jointly

In many cases the firm will face a choice concerning the level of quality that may be embodied in the new product. The new product may be introduced in a basic form or in a deluxe form, for example. It may be made of different materials (such as plastic or metal), which have different implications for the attributes that will enter the buyers' percep-

---

[2]To be complete, an analysis of the optimal initial price would include calculation of the EPV of contribution at a series of prices below the profit-maximizing price, with probabilities attached to the entry of one or more firms at each of these price levels. The firm might find it EPV maximizing to set the profit-maximizing price initially and induce the entry of one or more firms before switching to the limit price to inhibit the entry of any more firms.

TABLE 11-2. Calculating the EPV of the Skimming versus Limit-Price Strategy

Strategy A: Set profit-maximizing price, $12, in each period

PERIOD 1		PERIOD 2			PERIOD 3			ENPV CALCULATIONS		
Profit ($)	Present Value (0.9538)	Probability	Profit ($)	Present Value (0.8671)	Probability	Profit ($)	Present Value (0.7883)	NPV ($)	Joint Probability	ENPV ($)
64,000	61,043.	0.2	64,000	55,494.4	0.1	64,000	50,451.2	169,945.0	0.02	3,398.9
					0.7	32,000	25,225.6	144,720.0	0.14	20,260.0
					0.2	21,333	16,816.8	136,311.0	0.04	5,452.4
		0.5	32,000	27,747.2	0.3	32,000	25,225.6	116,972.0	0.15	17,545.0
					0.5	21,333	16,816.8	108,564.0	0.25	27,141.0
					0.2	16,000	12,612.8	104,360.0	0.10	10,436.0
		0.3	21,333	18,497.8	0.5	21,333	16,816.8	99,314.6	0.15	14,897.0
					0.4	16,000	12,612.8	95,110.6	0.12	11,413.0
					0.1	12,800	10,090.2	92,588.0	0.03	2,777.6
								Expected Net Present Value		113,323

Strategy B: Set the limit price, $8, in each period

PERIOD 1		PERIOD 2			PERIOD 3			ENPV CALCULATIONS		
Profit ($)	Present Value (0.9538)	Probability	Profit ($)	Present Value (0.8671)	Probability	Profit ($)	Present Value (0.7883)	NPV ($)	Joint Probability	ENPV ($)
48,000	45,782.	1	48,000	41,620.8	1	48,000	37,838.4	125,241	1	125,241

Summary

	Period 1 Present Value	Period 2 EPV	Period 3 EPV
Skimming	$61,043*	$91,565*	$113,323
Limit	$45,782	$87,403	$125,241*

*Optimal strategy if time horizon falls in the indicated period.

tion of product quality (such as weight and strength). It may be carefully polished by hand, or less carefully polished by machine, and so on. Higher quality typically costs more than lower quality, of course, and the firm must consider the cost of production in light of the demand for the product at each quality level.

Essentially, the firm should choose the price-quality combination that promises the maximum EPV of profit. The EPV of profit associated with each quality level should take into account the demand curve for the product *in that quality mode*, the cost curves associated with that quality level, and the probabilities of entry occurring in subsequent periods. For each quality mode the optimal (EPV-maximizing) initial price should be determined, as we did before. Then the maximum EPVs of each quality mode should be compared, and the firm should choose the quality mode with the largest EPV. Thus the joint price-quality decision is a relatively simple (although potentially laborious) extension of the new-product pricing problem.

Perhaps the skimming-versus-limit-pricing problem we examined did not seem very realistic to you. In practice, we see prices fall after the entry of new firms, but in the model the price level stayed at $12, and only the firms' sales decreased each time another new firm entered. This could well happen, of course, if the assumptions of the model fit the circumstances of the real-world situation. But it *is* a simple model. Market demand stays constant, rather than growing as we would expect in reality. The firms' costs remain constant, rather than falling because of the learning effect, as we expect in reality. Finally, the products were implicitly identical across firms, or at least symmetrically differentiated, such that the firms each had equal shares of the market when prices were equal. In reality, entrants are unlikely to win an equal share of the market immediately because of product differentiation advantages held by the first firm. (People still call copying machines Xerox machines, even if they are made by Canon or Toshiba.)

We shall now incorporate these complications into the new-product price model. In the next section we consider the impact of falling production costs, changes in the market demand, and asymmetric product differentiation.

11.2 ADJUSTING PRICE OVER TIME

The innovating firm will set its initial price based on its best estimates of the market demand situation, the probabilities of future entry of rival firms, and their probable cost structures. Once the new product is on the market and time passes, the firm's estimates are either supported or refuted by the data. Unexpected shifts in market demand, unexpected entry, unexpected cost increases or decreases, and unexpected product differentiation advantages may show the initial price to have been the incorrect price, necessitating unanticipated price adjustments. Anticipated changes in demand, costs, and the number of firms will also lead to price adjustments that were anticipated by the innovating firm. Thus there are likely to be a series of price adjustments in the market for the new product as time passes, and we can call the pattern of prices over time the *dynamic price path*.

The market for a new product will be immature initially, in the sense that the firms will be competing vigorously for market share and have no established rules or conventions to govern or guide their competitive behavior. As markets mature, the firms learn not to provoke vigorous competition without seriously considering the consequences. They develop patterns of behavior that the other firms come to recognize and expect, and thus uncertainty about rivals' reactions is reduced as the market matures. In mature oligopolies we expect to see more price and market share stability, whereas in new product markets we expect to see price and market share instability as the combatants struggle to maintain or achieve dominance. Underlying the instability of price are changes in costs and demand conditions, which we now investigate.

The Impact of the Learning Effect on Prices

We noted in Chapter 6 that the factors of production "learn" the production process as time passes and cumulative output grows. They become more efficient, producing more output per unit of input, as a result. This increased productivity is reflected in a downward shift of the firm's cost curves, other things (particularly input prices) remaining constant. As learning continues, the cost curves continue to shift downward. We noted that the major impact of the learning effect is felt early in the product's life, since cost reductions of a given percentage are expected every time the cumulative output *doubles*. Assuming a constant output level per period of 100 units and a learning rate of 20%, for example, average cost would decline by 20% in the second period and continue to decline by another 20% by the end of each of the 4th, 8th, 16th, 32nd, and 64th periods, and so on. As time passes, the cost decline in any given period would become less and less noticeable.

In Figure 11-3 we show the impact of the learning effect on the new product's price, with all other things remaining constant. Note that as the cost curves shift

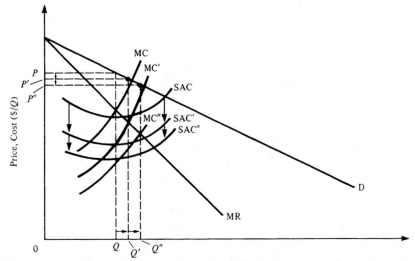

FIGURE 11-3. Impact of the Learning Curve on New Product Prices with No Changes in Demand or Plant Size

downward, the profit-maximizing price also falls, since the MC curve intersects the MR curve at progressively larger output levels. These quite substantial shifts of the cost curves must reflect either a very high rate of learning or large changes in the cumulative output level.

The Impact of Economies of Plant Size on Prices

If there are economies of plant size available to the innovating firm, it may have a profit incentive to expand plant size and subsequently set a lower price to expand sales to match its increased productive capacity. We noted that many innovating firms start with a relatively small plant size, perhaps because they are uncertain about the demand for the product and trade off potential profit for a reduced risk of bankruptcy. Alternatively, they may not be able to afford a larger plant initially, or they may not be able to raise a loan. Once demand for the product has been demonstrated, however, the innovating firm (and its banker) may foresee that greater profit will result from operation of a larger plant.

In Figure 11-4 we show the impact on price of a change in plant size involving economies of plant size, holding other influences on price constant. Note that the firm shifts from the plant size represented by the SAC and MC curves to that represented by the SAC' and MC' curves. It is subsequently profit-maximizing to reduce price from the level *P* to the level *P'* to induce expansion of quantity demanded from the level *Q* to the level *Q'*.

The Impact of Entry of New Firms on Prices

Earlier we saw that the entry of new firm(s) had no impact on the product's price; it merely forced the innovating firm to share the market quantity demanded (at that price)

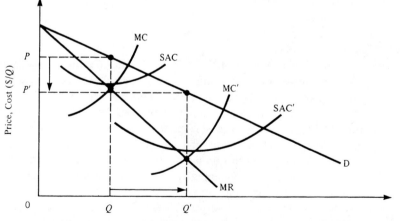

Output Level (*Q*)

FIGURE 11-4. The Impact of Economies of Plant Size on Product Price with No Changes in Demand or Learning

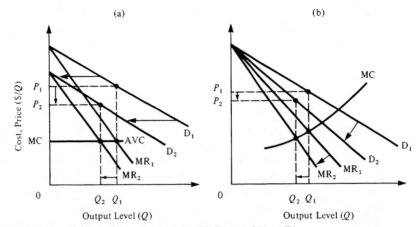

FIGURE 11-5. Falling Prices Caused by the Entry of New Firms

with the entrant firm(s). This result was due to two features of the model, however. First, the innovating firm's marginal cost was assumed to be constant, and second, the firms were assumed to maintain their market share at all price levels as long as they all set the same price (following the price leader, for example). Thus the innovating firm's demand curve suffered an iso-elastic shift each time a new firm entered.

    If entry causes a non-iso-elastic shift of the innovating firm's demand curve, how-ever, prices will change following entry. Suppose that rather than swing inward from the same intercept point, the innovating firm's demand curve shifts back in a more or less parallel fashion. This kind of shift would occur if the entrants refused to follow the innovating firm's price leadership, for example, such that the firm faces a *ceteris paribus* demand curve. Such a situation is shown in part (a) of Figure 11-5. Marginal costs are shown as constant, for comparability with the "no impact on price" case depicted in Figure 11-2 earlier.

    In part (b) of Figure 11-5 we show another possible combination—an iso-elastic demand shift caused by entry and a rising marginal cost curve (caused by diminishing returns in production). Again the profit-maximizing price is lower following the entry of the new firm(s). The remaining combination (namely a non-iso-elastic demand shift and a rising MC curve) will also cause a reduction in the innovating firm's profit-maximizing price. You may graph this case for yourself.

    Thus the initial conclusion that entry would not cause a price change was derived from a simplified model containing two restrictive assumptions, and one or the other of these may not fit a particular situation observed in the real world. Our purpose earlier was to abstract from price changes to show that the firm's profit per period would be reduced by entry even if prices stayed the same. Now we know that if the firms set prices independently rather than follow a price leader or if there are diminishing returns in production, then prices will fall following the entry of new firms.

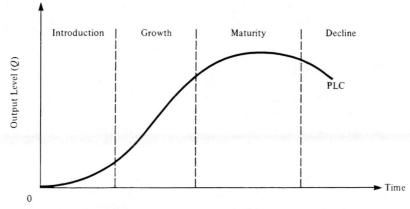

FIGURE 11-6. The Product Life Cycle

Shifts of the Market Demand Curve and the Product Life Cycle

Market demand for the new product is unlikely to remain static. More likely, the market demand curve will shift outward as the product becomes more widely known and appreciated. Eventually, market demand might be expected to shift inward when the tastes of consumers shift in favor of another new product that may become available and better serve their needs. The growth and eventual decline of the market demand for a new product is known as the product life cycle.

• DEFINITION: The *product-life-cycle* hypothesis stylizes the rate of demand for a product into three main phases, namely, the growth, maturity, and decline phases. In the growth phase, the quantity demanded per period (at a particular price level) increases rapidly. In the maturity phase the quantity demanded continues to increase and then begins to decrease. In the decline phase the quantity demanded per period falls progressively, and the product may eventually be withdrawn from the market. In Figure 11-6 the curve PLC represents a schematic representation of the product-life-cycle hypothesis.[3]

In terms of the market demand for the product, the product-life-cycle hypothesis says that the market demand curve will shift outward at an increasing rate at first, then continue to shift outward at a decreasing rate, and finally begin to shift back. In the context of new products, we are largely concerned with the growth phase, in which we

---

[3]For more on the product-life-cycle concept, see P. Kotler, *Marketing Management: Analysis, Planning, Implementation and Control*, Chapter 13 (Englewood Cliffs, N.J.: Prentice Hall, 7th edition, 1991); also T. Levitt, "Exploit the Product Life Cycle," *Harvard Business Review*, November–December 1976, pp. 81–94; and N. K. Dhalla and S. Yuspeh, "Forget the Product Life Cycle Concept!" *Harvard Business Review*, January–February 1976, pp. 102–12.

should expect to see entry of new firms. In the maturity phase the number of firms is more likely to have stabilized, and the price level is more likely to be relatively stable.

Given outward shifts of the market demand curve and the entry of new firms, the innovating firm might expect to garner a decreasing share of an increasing market. Whether this relationship translates to an increased quantity demanded or a reduced quantity demanded depends on the relative growth rates of market demand and the number of firms. If the market demand grows at a faster rate than the number of firms increases, the firms can expect to gain progressively larger sales volumes even if their market *shares* continue to fall with the entry of new firms. Thus the demand curve for each firm would tend to shift outward in subsequent periods, and this shift would have an upward impact on the price level.

Conversely, if the number of firms grows faster than the market demand grows, the firms will face demand curves that are shifting inward in successive periods. This kind of shift will have a depressing effect on the price of the product. This situation, with either iso-elastic or non-iso-elastic demand shifts, can be reviewed in Figure 11-5.

Thus prices are likely to fall as time passes following the introduction of a new product for any one or a combination of the following reasons: learning curve effects, economies of plant size, and entry of new firms at a rate greater than the rate of increase of market demand. Alternatively, the price of new products might increase over time if the cost reductions were small or absent and the market demand increased at a rate faster than the rate of growth of the number of firms.

First-Mover Advantages

- DEFINITION: *First-mover advantages* are the benefits accruing to the firm that first introduces a new product that turns out to be successful. These advantages include the monopoly profits it can earn while it is still the only firm in the market, as well as the additional profits it earns from the rapid cost reductions it will experience as a result of the learning curve.

The first firm to introduce the new product is able to start sliding down its learning curve immediately and have significantly lower costs per unit by the time the first competitor's product arrives in the marketplace. It takes time to design and manufacture a competing product, even if it is a relatively close copy of the original. The second and subsequent firms must start at the *top* of their learning curves, giving the first-mover a substantial cost advantage. Now, if prices decline because the imitator has to share the market, the first-mover is more likely to be profitable despite declining prices. In Figure 11-7 we show the dynamics of pricing and costs in a hypothetical situation. We suppose that the first-mover sets a price of $10, and it remains constant until time t_1, when entry of competing products occurs. Prices then decline over time as more firms enter and as the firms engage in price competition initially. Even if price leadership or conscious parallelism follows as the market matures, prices are likely to fall in response to falling costs for all firms.

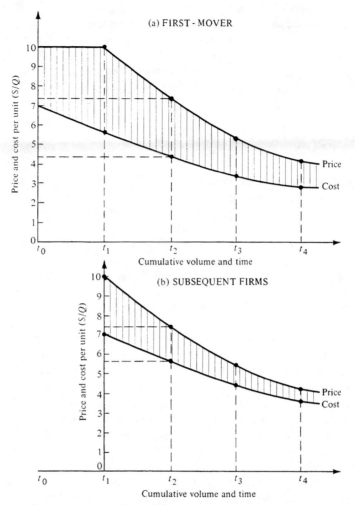

FIGURE 11-7. *Dynamic Price Paths and the First-Mover Advantage*[4]

Note that the first-mover maintains its higher profit margin through time despite the falling price level. At time t_2, for example, the price has fallen from its initial level of about \$10 to about \$7.40. The first-mover's costs have fallen to about \$4.40 while the subsequent entrants' costs are about \$5.60 per unit. Only if the subsequent entrants learn

[4]On the topic of first-mover advantages, see A. Michael Spence, "The Learning Curve and Competition," *Bell Journal of Economics*, 12 (Spring 1981), pp. 49–70; Richard Schmalensee, "Product Differentiation Advantages of Pioneering Brands," *American Economic Review*, 72 (June 1982), pp. 349–65; J. L. Guasch and A. Weiss, "Adverse Selection by Markets and the Advantage of Being Late," *Quarterly Journal of Economics*, 94 (May 1980), pp. 453–66; and A. Glazer, "The Advantages of Being First," *American Economic Review*, 75 (June 1985), pp. 473–80.

faster—that is, if they have a higher percentage of learning or if they can expand output faster—can they catch up with the first-mover firm.

Thus we see firms striving to discover and launch new products for the first-mover advantages and profits that result. Unfortunately, most new products are *not* major successes and the firm's profits as first-mover with one new product may easily be eroded by its losses with several other new products that did not sell well and were soon discontinued.[5]

11.3   SUMMARY

In this chapter we have examined the pricing of new products, meaning products that are radically different from what has gone before, rather than existing products that have simply been changed or improved. We noted that it is particularly difficult to collect reliable estimates of market demand for such products because of the lack of consumer awareness of the product and its usefulness. The innovating firm will search for information on the demand for the product initially, if it expects the value of this information to exceed the search cost. Given the high failure rate of new products, the value of information might be expected to be relatively high, and thus search activity should be seriously considered. Test marketing the new product in a limited area is a typical solution to this problem.

Price skimming will be the preferred pricing strategy if the firm's time horizon falls within the short run, if the demand for the new product will not extend beyond the short run, or if the barriers to entry are insurmountable. In these cases the skimming price will be the short-run profit-maximizing price. A skimming price is also indicated if the product is of the experience or credence type, since post-entry profit will be higher, and a higher initial price may favorably influence perceptions of the product's quality. The limit price to prevent the entry of a high-cost entrant may be viewed as a skimming price, since it will involve a relatively high markup over the innovating firm's (relatively low) unit costs.

Penetration pricing is appropriate when the innovating firm's time horizon falls beyond the short run and its EPV of profit is maximized by setting a relatively low price. This price may be the sales-maximizing price (subject to a minimum profit constraint) if the firm can tolerate entry of some firms and expects to earn greater profits in future periods through repeat sales of the item and sales of goods that are complementary to it. If the EPV of profit is maximized by preventing entry, and potential entrants would have little or no production cost disadvantages after entering, then the penetration price is the limit price. Search goods are more likely to be candidates for penetration pricing than are experience and credence goods, other things being equal.

---

[5]See R. G. Cooper, "The Dimensions of New Product Success and Failure," *Journal of Marketing*, 43 (Summer 1979), pp. 93–103; J. H. Davidson, "Why Most New Consumer Brands Fail," *Harvard Business Review*, 54 (March/April 1976), pp. 117–22; W. R. Dillon, R. Cantalore, and P. Worthing, "The New Product Problem: An Approach for Investigating Product Failures," *Management Science*, 25 (December 1979), pp. 1184–96.

After entry occurs, the resulting oligopoly may adopt low-cost price leadership if that is appropriate, or the innovating firm might initially be a dominant-firm price leader. Barometric price leadership, conscious parallelism, and independent pricing along *ceteris paribus* demand curves are also possible. The latter is more likely initially while the market is still immature, and some form of price leadership is more likely as the market attains maturity. We expect the price level to decline initially because of reductions in cost that result from learning effects and economies of plant size, as well as because of reduced demand for each firm that results from the entry of new firms at a rate faster than the rate of growth of the market demand. It is possible that prices would rise over time as a result of the inability of firms to enter as fast as the market grows, where there are few or no gains from learning or economies of plant size.

The innovating firm benefits from first-mover advantages, which are the initial monopoly profits and an ongoing unit-cost advantage which others will find difficult to overcome. Entrants may have a steeper learning curve because they may avoid some of the pitfalls and dead ends that the innovator encountered. This statement probably is particularly true for search products because these products are easier to evaluate and may therefore be easier to emulate. The innovating firm faces the risk that the new product will fail to be a market success and has typically incurred high developmental costs that may not be recouped if the new product is a failure.

DISCUSSION QUESTIONS

11-1. When is a "new" product best analyzed in the context of an established product market? Why?

11-2. Why is an estimate of the demand situation particularly important for new products?

11-3. Under what circumstances is the skimming price appropriately the short-run profit-maximizing price?

11-4. Under what circumstances could a skimming price higher than the short-run profit-maximizing price be EPV maximizing?

11-5. What pricing models can we use to select the penetration price? Why?

11-6. When is the limit price a skimming price, and when is it a penetration price? Why?

11-7. How does the type of product influence the new-product pricing decision?

11-8. What factors operate to cause the price of a new product to decline as time passes?

11-9. What is the product-life-cycle hypothesis? What determines whether the innovating firm's sales volume increases or decreases as entry takes place?

11-10. What are the first-mover advantages? What risks does the first-mover face?

PROBLEMS AND SHORT CASES

11-1. The Eastman Paint Company has developed a new paint which is unique in that it allows the user to turn ordinary glass windows and doors into one-way glass. Moreover, it prevents the transmission of ultraviolet rays, a major factor in the fading of furniture fabrics, carpets, and draperies. The production manager, Arthur Eastman, has estimated the following average variable cost levels (per gallon) for the product for this year and for the next two years. Note that costs decline over time as the production process becomes increasingly streamlined.

	OUTPUT LEVEL (gallons/month)				
	2,000	4,000	6,000	8,000	10,000
Year 1	$12.61	$11.82	$11.74	$11.84	$12.07
Year 2	10.05	9.76	9.60	9.56	9.82
Year 3	9.22	9.04	8.85	8.80	9.02

The advertising manager, Ms. Lois Eastman, is excited about the prospects of the new paint. She believes that the market has long felt the need for such a product, and she has prepared a large campaign to launch the product. Several television advertisements are being prepared and a brochure is in print, all referring to the extensive test results and benefits of the new paint. The focus of the campaign is on the increased privacy afforded by the new paint, with emphasis given to the protection it provides by filtering out the ultraviolet part of the sun's rays.

The price of the new product is to be determined. Market research suggests that the demand situation will be approximated by $Q = 16 - 0.67P$ in the first year (where Q represents thousands of gallons and P is in dollars); $Q = 20 - 0.77P$ in the second year; and $Q = 17.83 - 0.87P$ in the third year. Indications are that market demand will increase in each of the first three years, but the entry of competitors with substitute paints in year 3 will cause Eastman's demand curve to shift to the left, as implied by the above specifications.

The marketing manager, Ms. Margaret Turriff, is faced with the problem of plotting price strategy over the next three years. While year 2 and year 3 prices can be determined in due time, the president of the company wants to know what type of pricing strategy Ms. Turriff intends to employ, since she is concerned that returns from this product be maximized, given the extensive research and development program that gave rise to the new product.

(a) What is the profit-maximizing price in each of the first three years, as estimated from the data given?

(b) Under what conditions would you advise the Eastman Paint Company to pursue a penetration-pricing strategy?

11-2. Quick New Products, Inc., specializes in launching new products and uses intensive television advertising campaigns to encourage high-volume sales before any other firm can enter with a competing product. QNP has a new product ready to launch called the "tender trap," a mouse-trap which mice seem to love. Based on its experience, it expects to sell 20,000 units of this product in the first year at the introductory price of $9.95. Its initial cost (for the first 1,000 units) will be $14 per unit, but it expects costs to fall 20% for every doubling of output from that point forward. By the time it has sold 20,000 units, it expects two other rivals to be ready to imitate its product, and it expects that it will sell only 5,000 units per year in the following two years, with price gradually falling from $9.95 to $5.95. Total sales (QNP plus rivals') will be 15,000 in each of the second and third years. Its competitors will be subject to the same learning curve when they begin production as was QNP.

(a) Show graphically the dynamic price and average cost path over time for both QNP and one of its rivals (assume the rivals are similar).

(b) Explain the advantages which QNP can expect to derive as the result of being the first-mover in this market.

11-3. The Sharper Shirt Company has recently been formed by an aspiring young designer, Francine Stuart. Her first product will be a man's "budget" shirt. At this point, neither the price nor the quality decisions have been made. Francine knows that at the retail level, budget shirts typically are sold at certain fairly well defined "price points," notably $10, $13, $17, $23, and $30. Consumers have come to expect these price groupings and the salespeople prefer to deal with shirts that fit neatly into these price groups. Naturally, higher-quality shirts are expected at the higher price points.

Francine is trying to decide between going for the $17-shirt market or for the $30-shirt market. She has estimated her average costs to be $6 for the $17 shirt and $12 for the $30 shirt in the first year and approximately 80% of these figures in the second year. Note that Sharper Shirts would receive the wholesale price of only $12 for the $17 shirt and $20 for the $30 shirt. Market research activity in the form of tentative orders from retailers has resulted in the following probability distributions of demand for each shirt over the first two years.

Sales Level	$17 SHIRT Year 1	$17 SHIRT Year 2	$30 SHIRT Year 1	$30 SHIRT Year 2
10,000	0.25	0.10	0.30	0.20
20,000	0.50	0.60	0.60	0.65
30,000	0.25	0.30	0.10	0.15

   (a) Using decision-tree analysis and assuming an opportunity discount rate of 15%, calculate the expected net present value of each decision.
   (b) Is there much difference in the comparative risk associated with each strategy, based on the data provided?
   (c) Advise Ms. Stuart about which shirt she should produce and sell.
   (d) State any qualifications and assumptions which underlie your answer.

11-4. Boxem-Buddies, Inc., has developed a new exercise machine that will appeal to those who like to combine an exercise program with boxing practice. After a successful market-testing program they have estimated the demand curve for this machine to be $P = 188.2351 - 0.0023Q$. Their fixed costs are expected to be $200,000 per annum, and marginal costs rise with output as indicated by the expression $MC = 25.8634 + 0.0018Q$. The intercept of the market demand curve is expected to shift upward by 10% in the second year, with the slope term remaining the same. If Boxem-Buddies sets the profit-maximizing price in the first year, there will be entry of one firm at the start of the second year. Its cost curve is estimated to be $TC = 240,000 + 35Q + 0.002Q^2$. Because of its higher costs, it is expected to allow Boxem-Buddies to be the price leader. Moreover, because the innovating firm expects to gain a product differentiation advantage, the entrant will only get a third of the market when the prices are equal.
   (a) What are the short-run profit-maximizing price and output levels for the machine in year 1?
   (b) What is the limit price that would prevent the entry of the new firm? At that price what output would Boxem-Buddies sell?
   (c) Suppose BB sets the profit-maximizing price in year 1 and the new firm enters. What price will BB set as price leader? What are its output and profit levels in the second year?
   (d) In retrospect, should BB have set the limit price? Explain and defend your answer with any underlying assumptions.

11-5. Waltham Wallpaper Company has developed a new type of wallpaper that is easier to apply. WWC calls their product Magicpaper. It does not need glue, nor does it need to be immersed in water before application. Instead it is more like a contact paper that sticks by itself, but Magicpaper may be removed and readjusted very easily because the "glue" does not set permanently until twenty-four hours after exposure to air. Because of this ease of application WWC intends to supply Magicpaper in 40-inch widths, which is expected to be a major selling feature as well. Finally, the new type of backing used on Magicpaper allows all kinds of fabric and other materials to be bonded to the front side for a far superior finish, rendering all formerly available textured wallpapers inferior by comparison.

WWC's average variable cost of producing Magicpaper is expected to be $25.00 per linear yard (40 inches wide) the first month, and this cost is expected to fall by about 20% each time cumulative output doubles. The output rate is fixed at 2,000 yards per month. WWC's usual markup on wallpaper of 100% over AVC allows its prices to be quite competitive. With Magicpaper, however, it is considering setting the initial price using a 200% markup, since it expects demand to support this price given the limit on output per month. Also, it expects to be the only supplier for at least a year, and it would like to recoup its rather substantial developmental costs quickly. At this price, all five of the firm's rivals are likely to respond with similar versions of this new product by the second year, at which time prices will be forced downward until markups are more competitive, probably around the 100% level, since this is the conventional level in the wallpaper market. Eventually, market shares tend to come out equal in any particular product line, as well.

Alternatively, WWC could employ a strategy to limit entry to the only two other firms that could afford to incur the developmental costs. This strategy would involve using a markup of 150% initially and then reducing markups back toward 100% after the firms enter. At that price, demand is expected to be 2,500 yards per month, and WWC could produce this amount using a weekend shift. About half of the regular workers and several weekenders would work as long as it takes on Saturday to produce the extra 500 yards of Magicpaper. This Saturday session would initially have an incremental cost to WWC of $20,000, labor and materials included. Learning effects are expected to allow this figure to decline at the same rate as weekday production, however.

(a) Advise WWC what their EPV of contribution is likely to be if they follow the skimming-price strategy. (Assume an opportunity discount rate of 12% and make any other assumptions you need to, but consider the sensitivity of your answer to these assumptions.)

(b) Alternatively, what is the EPV of profits if WWC follows the moderate pricing strategy that will limit entry to just its two largest rivals?

(c) Should WWC simply start with a 100% markup and limit the entry of all rivals? Consider the issues involved.

(d) Summarize your recommendation to WWC.

11-6. The Knowlton Chemical Company plans to introduce its Bug Buster, a sex-lure trap that attracts all kinds of flying insects and beetles. The technology is simple—there is just one active ingredient, and this fact is public knowledge following a university researcher's publication of her research findings. Knowlton has the jump on competitors, however, since they funded the research and became privy to the findings at an earlier stage. Knowlton expects to have a monopoly on the new Bug Buster for the first year, but expects entry of two new firms in time for the second year's "bug season," and entry of three more in the third year. This entry is expected to take place because Knowlton's cost advantage over the entrants is expected to be minor, since the chemical ingredient is readily available at relatively low cost. Knowlton's estimated marginal cost of production is $4 per unit, constant across all foreseeable output rates.

On the demand side, Knowlton expects to sell 200,000 units in the first year at a proposed price of $9.99. Its marketing research team has estimated that this is the profit-maximizing price in the first year. At that price, market demand is expected to increase to 500,000 units in the second year and to approach 1 million units in the third year. (Note that there will be entry of new firms as well.) In the second and third years, the market price of the Bug Buster and its rival products would respond to supply and demand conditions, but it would tend to be fairly similar for all firms because of the limited scope for product differentiation.

(a) From the information given, deduce an expression for the market demand curve that apparently underlies the choice of the initial price.

(b) Assuming that the slope of the market demand curve stays the same, estimate the market demand curves for the second and third years.

(c) Specify the demand curve facing Knowlton in the second and third years, as your best estimation given the data supplied.

(d) Supposing that Knowlton assumes the role of low-cost price leader, what price would it wish to set in each of the second and third years, and what are its expected output levels in each of those years?

(e) What assumptions and qualifications underlie your analysis?

11-7. Hi-Techniks, Inc., has recently received a patent on a new product, an electronic cockroach deterrent. This device emits a high-frequency noise that drives cockroaches out of the user's house or apartment into neighboring dwellings. Hi-Techniks plans to produce and market the product themselves, as well as to allow production by any other company that is willing to pay a royalty of $10 per unit produced, under a licensing agreement.

Hi-Techniks estimates its total cost function will be $TC = 200,000 + 80Q$, up to a maximum output rate of 40,000 units per year. Because of learning effects, average variable costs are expected to decline 25% in each of the second and third years. The fixed costs of competitors are expected to be about 20% higher, and their variable costs will be similar to those of Hi-Techniks, except for the royalty payment to Hi-Techniks.

Market demand for the product, estimated on the basis of a market survey conducted in New York City, is expected to be represented by the expression $P = 300 - 0.005Q$ and is expected to remain steady at that level for several years as market awareness of the product spreads and continues to attract new customers. Hi-Techniks expects to be a monopoly for the first year. If entry occurs, each new entrant is expected to gain $1/(n + 1)$ of the market, and Hi-Techniks will end up with $2/(n + 1)$ of the market, where n is the number of firms. Hi-Techniks expects three other firms to seek licensing agreements and enter the market after the first year, if the price set by Hi-Techniks allows them to avoid losses. No further entry is expected after these firms enter. Hi-Techniks' time horizon is three years, and its cost of capital is 15% per annum.

(a) What is the profit-maximizing price that Hi-Techniks could set in the first year? How many units would be sold at that price?

(b) Assuming entry of three firms at the end of the first year and that Hi-Techniks will emerge as the low-cost price leader, what price will be profit-maximizing for Hi-Techniks in the second and third years? What sales volume should Hi-Techniks expect in these years?

(c) What is the limit price that would prevent any other firm from entering the market, presuming that the royalty remains at $10 per unit and that all three potential entrants would enter at the start of the second year if Hi-Techniks's price in the first year would allow the entrants to be profitable? (An approximate answer from a graph would suffice, or you may solve this problem algebraically.)

(d) Which is the EPV-maximizing strategy over the three-year time horizon, price skimming or penetration pricing?

(e) What assumptions and qualifications underlie your analysis?

11-8. Tropical Delights. Inc., is considering introducing a new fruit juice to the mainland market. This juice, to be called Tropic Morning, is a mixture of various tropical fruits, but TDI plans to keep the exact formulation secret. Consumer clinics conducted in Waikiki using tourists from mainland states indicate that the product will face a market demand curve in the first year of the venture specified by $P = 33.535 - 0.2828Q$, where Q represents cases and P is the price per case of twelve bottles. Market demand is expected to increase by 20% per year for the next five years. TDl's cost of production is expected to be TC = $300,000 + 6.25Q + 0.025Q^2$. The coefficients in this expression that determine the marginal cost are expected to decline by about 15% per year because of learning effects in the production process.

Other firms are expected to enter the market with competing tropical fruit juices if TDl's product proves to be a success in the first year (that is, if the demand estimates prove to be accurate). TDl will have no cost advantages over these potential entrants, and in fact will probably have higher costs than a large rival that currently specializes in pineapple fruit and juice production. TDl's cost disadvantage would be about 20%, it estimates. On the demand side, however, TDl expects to establish a strong brand name identity which will make rivals' products only imperfect substitutes for Tropic Morning, such that it will retain about half the market after the expected entry of three or four rival firms, when prices are roughly equal.

The management of TDl is deliberating whether to set a skimming price or a penetration price initially. Their time horizon is three years, and their opportunity discount rate is 10%. You are asked to advise them on the pricing strategy they should employ.

(a) What are the arguments that might be used in favor of the skimming price? What skimming price level would you recommend?

(b) What arguments militate in favor of the penetration price? What penetration price level would you recommend?

(c) What is likely to happen to TDl's price and output level in the second and subsequent years, (1) if a skimming price is set initially, and (2) if a penetration price is set initially?

(d) Advise TDl's management as to the strategy you feel they should pursue, with supporting arguments and qualifications.

11-9. Bowers Automotive Equipment is planning to launch its new product, a pair of miniature radio transmitters that would allow the owner to locate a car that was misplaced in a crowded parking lot, or even stolen and left somewhere else. One transmitter would be hidden in the car, and the owner would activate it by a hand-held transmitter/receiver that would be carried away from the car in a pocket or handbag. The owner would then zero in on the lost vehicle by moving in the direction of strongest signal. BAE calls this product the Car Finder. Test marketing of this product has resulted in the following initial demand curve being estimated: $P = 295.6 - 0.0852Q$, where Q is the number of Car Finders.

BAE has assembled 1,500 units in the past month and notes that average variable cost was $40 and average fixed cost was $60. They expect average variable costs to fall by 20% each time cumulative output doubles, however. They estimate that the quantity demanded initially will be 1,500 units per month at a price of $149.95, but that the demand curve will shift to the right by about 250 units every month following the product's launch. Their present plant can produce up to 3,000 units a month, with constant marginal cost, but that output is the absolute maximum. If sales exceed 3,000 units a month, a larger plant will be required. Larger facilities and automated assembly equipment would reduce the average variable costs by 30%, however, and marginal costs are expected to be constant at this new level. Overhead costs would increase by 50% with the larger plant, which would have a maximum output rate of 6,000 units a month.

Competition is expected in the market if demand increases at the suggested rate. BAE expects Eldridge Electronics to come up with their own version of the product within six months, and Abersen Digital Systems probably will also enter the market within a year. Based on their track records, both these firms are expected to come out with a product which is better in some way, and they would therefore reduce BAE's market share to 40% after six months and to 30% after twelve months. Of course, BAE's engineers will strive to improve the Car Finder as time passes, but the better research facilities at BAE's competitors mean that the new entrants' products will probably have a competitive edge. All firms would have similar initial cost structures and would experience similar rates of learning in production.

(a) Is the proposed price the profit-maximizing price for the first month? If not, why do you think BAE chose that particular price level?

(b) Calculate the expected monthly output rates and profits for each of the first six months, presuming that the price stays at $149.95 and that Eldridge will enter the market at the start of the seventh month. Should BAE plan to build the larger plant?

(c) Speculate what would happen if Eldridge were to enter the market after six months with a superior product priced at $169.95 and capture 60% of the market, which continued to grow. Should BAE change its price? Calculate the monthly output rates and profits that BAE might expect over months 7 through 12. If you haven't already recommended building the larger plant, would you recommend it now?

(d) Now speculate that Abersen will enter the market after twelve months with a product superior to Eldridge's but also priced at $169.95. What would you expect to happen to Eldridge's price? Should BAE change its price? Explain.

(e) Advise BAE as to the initial and subsequent prices they should set for their new product. Note all qualifications and underlying assumptions.

11-10. Yashoko Camera Company is the first to offer a new electronic camera that uses a magnetic disk to store visual images instead of film. After taking photographs in the usual way, the disk is transferred to a video player and the photographs may be viewed on the screen. Selected photographs may then be printed from this machine, in full color or in black and white.

Yashoko predicts that demand for this product will grow rapidly at first, then grow at a declining rate, and finally sales per month will begin to decline as other manufacturers bring out competing products and the market approaches saturation. The firm's demand function for the first year is expected to be $Q = 5146.7535 - 2.2584P$. The intercept term in this expression is expected to increase by 30% for the second year, then decrease by 10% for the third year, and finally decrease by another 30% in the fourth year.

The total variable cost function for this new product is estimated to be $TC = 100,000 + 480Q + 0.25Q^2$ for the first 2,000 units, and then the learning effect in production will cause the intercept term of this cost function to decline by 15% each time cumulative output doubles.

(a) Advise Yashoko as to the price level that is profit maximizing in each of the next four years.

(b) Considering the marketing benefits of having a stable price level over a period of time, and considering Yashoko's interest in establishing their brand name and reputation as a manufacturer of high-value products, recommend a pricing strategy that might be followed.

(c) Calculate the expected sales volume and profits for each year, given your choice of price(s) in part (b).

(d) Outline all qualifications and assumptions that underlie your analysis.

SUGGESTED REFERENCES AND FURTHER READING

COOPER, R. G. "The Dimensions of New Product Success and Failure," *Journal of Marketing*, 43 (Summer 1979), pp. 93–103.

DAVIDSON, J. H. "Why Most New Consumer Brands Fail," *Harvard Business Review*, 54 (March–April 1976), pp. 117–22.

DEAN, JOEL. "Pricing Pioneering Products," *Journal of Industrial Economics*, 17 (July 1969) pp. 165–79.

DEAN, JOEL. "Pricing Policies for New Products," *Harvard Business Review*, 28 (November–December 1950).

DHALLA, N. K., and S. YUSPEH. "Forget the Product Life Cycle Concept!" *Harvard Business Review*, January–February 1976, pp. 102–12.

DONNELLY, J. H., and M. J. ETZEL. "Degrees of Product Newness and Early Trial," *Journal of Marketing Research*, 10 (August 1973), pp. 295–300.

GABOR, A., and W. C. J. GRANGER. "The Pricing of New Products," *Scientific Business*, August 1965, pp. 141–50.

GLAZER, A. "The Advantages of Being First," *American Economic Review*, 75 (June 1985), pp. 473–80.

GUASCH, J. L., and A. WEISS. "Adverse Selection by Markets and the Advantages of Being Late," *Quarterly Journal of Economics*. 94 (May 1980), pp. 453–66.

KOTLER, P. and G. ARMSTRONG. *Principles of Marketing* (5th ed.), chap. 11. Englewood Cliffs, N.J.: Prentice Hall, 1991.

LAZEAR, EDWARD P. "Retail Pricing and Clearance Sales," *American Economic Review*, 76 (March 1986), pp. 14–32.

LEVITT, T. "Exploit the Product Life Cycle," *Harvard Business Review*, November–December 1976, pp. 81–94.

LIVESEY, F. *Pricing*, chap. 8. London: Macmillan, Inc., 1976.

SABEL, H. "On Pricing New Products," *German Economic Review*, 11, No. 4 (1973), pp. 292–311.

SCHMALENSEE, R. "Product Differentiation Advantages of Pioneering Brands," *American Economic Review*, 72 (June 1982), pp. 349–65.

SPENCE, A. M. "The Learning Curve and Competition," *Bell Journal of Economics*, 12 (Spring 1981), pp. 49–70.

Chapter 12

COMPETITIVE BIDS AND PRICE QUOTES

EXECUTIVE SUMMARY

Competive bidding occurs in any market where **a number of sellers compete for the business of a single buyer**. In most cases the buyer makes it known that a certain product or service is wanted, and the sellers tender their bids or price quotes. The buyer will then select the seller offering to complete the contract for the **lowest price, if the products are identical**, or select the seller offering the best combination of price and other features if the sellers are able to differentiate their products.

Competitive bid markets are really quite common. **Consumers** enter such a market every time they want their car fixed, teeth braced, house painted, and so on. **Firms** wanting stationery supplies, new machines, component parts, consulting advice, and so on, effectively call for competitive bids. **Governments** wanting roads and dams built, prisoners kept secure, fleets of cars supplied, and so on, similarly call for competitive bids from potential suppliers.

Each seller should expect the buyer to have quotes from another potential supplier, or at least to have a general idea of the appropriate price level. Each seller will recognize that if its **price is too high the business will go elsewhere**. If the price is too low, the seller will get the job but may end up losing money on the job. This is known as **the winner's curse**.

The pricing problem is that the seller must select a price high enough to provide a sufficient contribution to overheads and profit, yet low enough to ensure that a sufficient volume of work is actually obtained. Typically, the seller **must choose price in the face of considerable uncertainty**, not only with respect to what other sellers are simultaneously offering but with respect to what it may cost to complete the job as specified, since the job is typically slightly (and sometimes totally) different from what the firm has supplied before.

12.1   TYPES OF COMPETITIVE BIDS AND PRICE QUOTES

Competitive bid markets are usually characterized by one of three different types of bid or price quote, although mixed-bid markets may exist. When the supplier tenders a bid price, or makes a price quote, and undertakes to complete the job for that price regardless of any variation of costs from the expected level, the bid is known as a *fixed-price bid*. Note that the supplier must estimate the costs of fulfilling the contract and that there is uncertainty involved in these cost estimates because the bid price is tendered now and the costs will be incurred later. Input prices may change, the design may prove more difficult than expected, more labor and materials might be required, and so on. Thus there is a probability distribution of cost associated with the completion of the contract, and the expected value of this probability distribution is the supplier's estimated cost level. If costs will be incurred beyond the present period, they should be expressed in expected-present-value terms. In the fixed-price case the price is determined *ex ante*, before the contract is undertaken, and the supplier faces the entire risk of cost variability, which is measured by the standard deviation of the probability distribution of costs around the expected value of costs.

Cost-plus-fee bids are the opposite case, where the bid price is determined *ex post*, after the contract is completed, and is equal to the actual costs of the job plus a fee (or profit margin) for the supplier. In this case the entire risk of cost variability is borne by the buyer, who agrees to pay whatever the actual costs turn out to be plus a fee. The fee may be a fixed amount, or it may be based on the actual costs, in which case it is usually expressed as a markup over costs. The buyer retains the right to an audit of the supplier's costs, to assure the buyer that the actual costs are fair and reasonable. Cost-plus-fee bids are common where the degree of cost uncertainty is particularly high. Repair work to automobiles, household appliances, and industrial plant and equipment typically proceeds on this basis, because the actual labor time and parts required become known only as the repair work progresses. The main problem with cost-plus-fee bids, as any consumer will appreciate, is that the supplier has little incentive to control costs. Given that the buyer's audit of the costs is time-consuming and imperfect because of the asymmetry of information, the final price to the buyer is typically higher than it would have been if the supplier had had a greater incentive to keep costs to a minimum.

Incentive bids, also known as risk-sharing bids, are the intermediate case. Here the buyer and supplier agree beforehand on a bid price but agree to share any deviation from the expected cost level in a given way. The *ex ante* bid price is based on the expected costs plus a profit margin for the supplier. A deviation of the actual costs from the expected costs is known as a cost overrun or underrun. If there is a cost overrun, the buyer pays the *ex ante* bid price plus a share of the cost overrun, and the supplier's profit margin is reduced by its share of the cost overrun. Conversely, if there is a cost underrun, the buyer's *ex post* price is the *ex ante* price less the buyer's share of the cost underrun, and the supplier's profit margin is increased by its share of the cost underrun. This is easily summarized in symbols, as follows:

$$B = C_t + \pi_t + (1 - s)(C_t - C_a) \tag{12-1}$$

$$\pi_a = \pi_t + s(C_t - C_a) \tag{12-2}$$

where B is the *ex post* bid price paid by the buyer; C_t is the supplier's target costs (expected present value); C_a is the actual (*ex post*) costs; s is the supplier's share of the cost variation; π_a is the actual profit received by the supplier; and π_t is the target profit (expected present value) received by the supplier.

It can readily be seen that the risk-sharing case collapses to the fixed-price bid case when $s = 1$. In the fixed-price case,

$$B = C_t + \pi_t \tag{12-3}$$

$$\pi_a = \pi_t + (C_t - C_a) \tag{12-4}$$

Conversely, when $s = 0$, we have the cost-plus-fee case:

$$B = C_a + \pi_t \tag{12-5}$$

$$\pi_a = \pi_t \tag{12-6}$$

In what kinds of competitive bid markets should we expect fixed-price bids? Several possibilities suggest themselves. First, if suppliers are risk neutral, the risk of cost variability will mean nothing to them, and risk-averse buyers will prefer fixed-price bids. Second, if suppliers undertake many contracts of this type (incurring cost overruns on some and cost underruns on others), they can act as if they are risk neutral, because the law of averages will ensure that they will be better off using the expected-value decision criterion than any other. Third, if costs are relatively easy to control and there is consequently little or no cost uncertainty from the supplier's viewpoint, we should expect fixed-price bids. Fourth, if the supplier doesn't really care if there is a cost overrun or underrun, it may be willing to bid in this fashion. This might be the case where the value of the contract is trivial compared to the value of the supplying firm, and thus the marginal utility of the dollars involved in the cost variance is negligible. Alternatively, if the supplier is spending someone else's money and there is a principal-agent problem without proper incentives to cause the agent (manager) to act in the best interests of the principal (shareholder), the supplier may tender a fixed bid regardless of the risk of cost variability. Finally, if the buyer is extremely risk averse and will only accept fixed-price bids, the supplier will tender a fixed-price bid, even if it is also highly risk averse.

Cost-plus-fee bids will tend to predominate under the opposite conditions. If the buyer is risk neutral or can act as if it is risk neutral because it has many such contracts, suppliers will be happy to pass the risk of cost variability along to the buyer. If the buyer attaches low marginal utility to the dollars potentially involved in the cost variance, whether because of the relative triviality of the contract or because of a principal-agent problem, we should expect cost-plus-fee bids. Where there is extreme risk of cost variability, suppliers may refuse to bid in any other mode, since a cost overrun could be ruinous. Finally, if designs are speculative and quality is imperative to the buyer, such as in defense contracting, we should expect a preference for cost-plus-fee bids.

Risk-sharing, or incentive, contracts arise when cost uncertainty is relatively high but there is a perceived need to control the supplier's spending while ensuring that quality does not suffer. Defense contracting shifted to this mode, from the cost-plus-fee mode, for exactly these reasons. The share of the risk borne by each party will be determined by their relative risk aversions, the buyer's perception of the supplier's propensity to relax cost control, and competitive pressures from other suppliers willing to take a greater share of the risk at each *ex ante* bid level.[1]

The supplier's first problem is to ascertain the *ex ante* bid price that maximizes the expected present value of contribution (EPVC) to overheads and profit, assuming the supplier bears the entire risk of cost variability. Having ascertained that price, the risk-averse supplier will be willing to trade off some expected return for a reduced share of the cost variation. The supplier may wish to bid in the cost-plus-fee mode and will trade off some of the EPVC to reduce risk to zero. Thus the firm would tender a bid equal to the certainty equivalent of the EPVC-maximizing fixed-price bid, as we shall see. If the optimal strategy is a risk-sharing bid, the supplier will similarly trade off some expected profit in return for a reduced share of any cost variation and will submit a bid that is lower than the EPVC-maximizing bid level. We begin by finding the bid price level that maximizes the EPVC.

12.2   INCREMENTAL COSTS, INCREMENTAL REVENUES, AND THE OPTIMAL BID PRICE

We saw in Chapter 7 that there are three main categories of incremental costs and revenues, namely present-period explicit costs and revenues, opportunity costs and revenues, and future-period costs and revenues. Let us consider these in the context of the competitive bidding problem.

The Incremental Costs of the Contract

- DEFINITION: The *incremental costs of the contract* are all those costs, expressed in expected-present-value terms, which are expected to be incurred as a result of winning and completing the terms of the contract. Costs that have been incurred already (sunk costs) and costs that will be incurred whether this contract is won or lost (committed costs) are not incremental costs for the purpose of the pricing decision to be made.

Present-Period Explicit Costs.   This category of incremental costs consists of the direct and explicit costs associated with undertaking and completing the project. Included are

---

[1]See J. J. McCall, "The Simple Economics of Incentive Contracting," *American Economic Review*, 60 (September 1967), pp. 837–46; and F. M. Scherer, "The Theory of Contractual Incentives for Cost Reduction," *Quarterly Journal of Economics*, 78 (May 1964), pp. 257–80.

such cost categories as direct materials, direct labor, and variable overhead. For each of these cost categories we must be careful to include only those amounts that are expected to be paid for the purchases of materials, labor and supplies, and services required to complete production and delivery of the specified goods and services. These may be estimated on the basis of requirements for similar projects in the past, given present cost levels, plus a trend factor if one is apparent and the production will take an appreciable period of time.

In some cases an item of capital equipment must be purchased for a particular job and will have a useful life remaining after the completion of the present job. Incremental reasoning implies that the whole cost is applied to the present job and that the machine will not be part of the incremental cost on any subsequent jobs, if these in fact materialize. If ownership of the item will allow a stream of contributions to be earned in the future, the expected net present value of these contributions should enter the present decision, since they are incremental to this decision.[2]

Another consideration is the capacity utilization rate of the firm. When the firm is at or near full capacity, it must consider the additional incremental costs that will be incurred if it obtains the contract, such as overtime labor rates, outside contracting, penalty charges associated with existing contracts, and any other additional costs, and hence its minimum bid price must be higher to the extent that these costs are incurred.

Opportunity Costs. The opportunity cost of undertaking and completing a specific project is the value of the resources employed (that is, their contribution) in their best alternative usage. Hence, if plant, equipment, and personnel are lying idle, the opportunity cost of using them for a particular contract is zero. On the other hand, if these resources are currently employed in a project that will have to be set aside, delayed, or canceled, the contribution that would have been derived from this alternate project must enter the incremental costs as an opportunity cost. A firm may decide to submit a tender on a specific project and, if successful with that bid, may choose to defer completion of another project already in process. To the extent provided by the penalty clause in the earlier contract, this decision to defer completion will cost the firm money that is an incremental cost occasioned by receipt of the latter contract. To the extent that a project in process simply is delayed and is completed later, the opportunity cost is the interest income foregone as a result of the later receipt of payment for that job.

Future Costs. Future incremental costs may include the effects of ill will, deteriorating labor relations or supplier relations, and legal recourse by dissatisfied buyers or government prosecutors. Ill will is the EPVC of future contracts *lost* as a result of taking the present contract. There may be longer-term disadvantages, for example, in taking a con-

---

[2] The practice of apportioning the capital cost of an item over the present and future jobs implies a probability of unity that these future contracts will be gained. This may be an overstatement of the probabilities, of course, and may induce the firm to purchase an item, the cost of which may never be recouped. Moreover, the simple allocation of a cost over future jobs ignores the fact that a dollar received now is worth more than a dollar received in the future.

tract which breaks a strike or which takes advantage of the misfortune of a competitor or other party. Future labor problems may arise if the present contract would cause the firm to operate with congestion of work space and facilities. Hard work for employees and good profits for the firm may tip the balance in favor of a labor strike for a wage increase. Supplier relations may be exacerbated by the present contract if it requires very tight deadlines and unusually stringent quality control, leading to the firm's suppliers (or subcontractors) asking for a higher price for materials and supplies needed for future contracts. Finally there is always the possibility of future legal claims for damages associated with the present contract or of prosecution under the provisions of the antitrust laws or of other legislation. To the extent that these costs can be foreseen, their EPV should be estimated and included as an incremental cost.

- EXAMPLE: The city's garbage collectors have been on strike for several weeks, and the mayor calls for bids for a one-week contract with an outside firm to move the garbage. Your firm, which is engaged in the construction industry, has the trucks and the personnel necessary, and you calculate your incremental present-period explicit costs to be $100,000 for the week, composed of direct labor, fuel, repairs and maintenance, and so on.

  You are currently utilizing your equipment and work force on a day-to-day basis moving landfill to an area that will eventually be a new housing development. The contribution to overheads and profits from this job is $10,000 per week. If you win the contract to move the garbage, you must give up this contribution, and this is, therefore, the opportunity cost of winning the city's contract.

  If you win the job, you are afraid that there will be a backlash response from a company with whom you currently hold a contract for the annual removal of debris and waste products. Their labor force is strongly unionized and you feel that there is a fifty-fifty chance the firm may decide not to offer you the renewal of that contract. You reason that they may do this to avoid labor strife at their own plant, which they think may result if they renew the contract with the firm that helped break the city garbage workers' strike. Next year's contract with this firm is expected to contribute $20,000 to overheads and profits if it is renewed. Supposing your opportunity discount rate to be 15% and the cash flow to be one year away, the present value of next year's contract is $20,000 × 0.8696 = $17,392. Given your estimate of the probability of losing the contract at 0.5, the EPV of this future cost, or ill will, is $17,392 × 0.5 = $8,696.

  Thus the incremental cost of the job is estimated to be the sum of the present-period explicit costs, $100,000; plus the opportunity costs, $10,000; plus the EPV of the future costs, $8,696; or $118,696 in total. You would require incremental revenues to be at least this high before you would consider taking the job to avoid making an incremental loss on the job.

- NOTE: Incremental costs do not include any sunk costs or costs which would have been incured regardless of this particular pricing decision. As a result, *bid preparation costs* are technically *not* an incremental cost of the job but they are, instead, a cost of preparing to bid on the job. There are two separate decisions to be made: First, will the firm prepare and submit a bid at all; and, second, at what price level will this bid be? Bid preparation costs will include the search costs of generating information about costs, revenues, and probabilities of success at various price levels. On the basis of this information, the firm may decide not to bid at all. If it does decide to bid, the actual pricing decision will be taken after the bid preparation costs have been incurred. They are therefore *sunk* costs as far as the pricing decision is concerned and should not be included as incremental costs.[3]

The Incremental Revenues of the Contract

- DEFINITION: *The incremental revenues of the contract* are all those revenues, expressed in expected-present-value terms, which are expected to be received as a result of winning and completing the contract. These revenues may be considered under the same three categories—present period, opportunity, and future revenues.

Present-Period Incremental Revenues. If the contract will be completed and the bid price received during the present period, the bid price can be included in nominal dollars as an incremental revenue. In cases where payment will be received during a future period, the bid price should be discounted at the opportunity rate to find the present value of this cash flow. In some cases, the firm will have written into the contract that it will receive some portion of the bid price (for example, one half) when the job is one-half completed. In this case, part of the bid price may be treated in nominal dollars (if it is to be received in the present period) with the balance being discounted to present-value terms.

Opportunity Revenues. Costs which can be avoided if the contract is won are known as *opportunity revenues*.

- EXAMPLE: Opportunity revenues include severance pay and other costs of laying off personnel and the subsequent rehiring and retraining costs which would be incurred if the firm were forced to close down and wait until it won another contract before starting up again. Plant and equipment which will stand idle for a time must be "mothballed" to prevent their deterioration while idle. For example, machinery may need to be sprayed with oil to prevent rusting. Upon startup, there is an additional cost of cleaning and readying the plant for use again. Another possible opportunity revenue is the research and development costs which can be avoided as a result of the present contract. A firm may know it has to develop a particular electronic device, for example, for the improvement of one of its existing products. If the contract currently being considered involves the development of that technology as a by-product, then winning the present contract allows future research and development expenditure to be avoided. For example, Cubic

---

[3]At this point it is worth emphasizing that we are calculating incremental costs, not the actual bid price. To substantiate its chosen bid price, the firm may wish to include various sunk costs and exclude some of its incremental costs. This is effectively a promotional decision, to be taken *after* the pricing decision.

Corporation has found that some of its developments for the aerospace industry have been applicable to its products in other areas, notably elevators and fare-collection systems.

Future Revenues.   The present contract may give rise to future contracts and sales, which represent the *goodwill* to be generated by the present contract. Goodwill should be regarded as the expected present value of the contribution (EPVC) which is expected to be received from subsequent contracts won *as a result* of having won and successfully completed the current contract. Care must be taken to include only *incremental* goodwill; an established firm may foresee contracts which would have been won regardless of the current contract and therefore should not consider the current contract as contributing to goodwill. On the other hand, a firm trying to enter a market may need one or more initial contracts won and successfully completed to be considered for future contracts. Counting the EPVC of these future contracts as an incremental revenue of the current contract allows the firm to rationally submit a somewhat lower bid than its established rivals and thus increase the likelihood of its winning the contract.

• EXAMPLE: The Universal Lamp Company plans to bid on a contract to manufacture and supply energy-saving fluorescent-incandescent light bulbs for a government building. At present, Universal has no work to do and will have to lay off workers within a few weeks unless it wins this contract. Universal has never manufactured these new-generation light bulbs before and knows that it must establish its credibility by demonstrating that it can manufacture a high-quality product and that it can meet the delivery schedule proposed. Its proposed bid price is $278,500, which it expects will be at least $100,000 less than the next-lowest bid, given its knowledge of recent contracts awarded and publicized. Universal feels that it must bid this low to win the job—any lower price difference may cause the government purchaser to opt for a more expensive, but established, supplier. If it wins the job, it is confident that it will produce a high-quality product and, therefore, make itself eligible for future contracts at higher profit margins.

Suppose that Universal will avoid layoff, mothball, and other costs of $36,000 associated with closing down and later reopening this plant if they win this contract. Suppose further that if they win this contract, they expect a 75% chance of a follow-up contract, with contribution of $200,000, to be awarded next year. The present value of that contribution (at 15% opportunity discount rate, for example) is $173,920. The EPVC is, thus, $173,920 × 0.75 = $130,440.

This contract, therefore, promises incremental revenues of the bid price, $278,500; plus the opportunity revenues, $36,000; plus the EPVC of future sales foreseen, $130,440; or $444,940 in total. Thus the firm's incremental costs could be anything up to that figure, and it would still be incrementally profitable for Universal to complete the contract with its bid of $278,500.

The Optimal Bid Price

- DEFINITION: Given that the firm's objective is to maximize its net present worth, the *optimal bid price* will be the price level which maximizes the expected present value of contribution to overheads and profits.

    To find the expected present value of each bid price, we must multiply its EPVC by the probability of winning the contract at that price level. The higher the bid price, the lower the "success probability," or the likelihood that the firm will submit the lowest bid. (For simplicity here, we assume a completely specified contract where there are no design or quality differences between tenders.)

- EXAMPLE: Suppose that the firm has obtained a reliable set of success probabilities, after consideration of the past bidding behavior and current capacity utilization of all its rivals. In Table 12-1 we show an assumed incremental cost (in expected-present-value terms and net of any incremental revenues other than the bid price) of $50,000. Several arbitrarily chosen bid prices and the resultant contribution and success probability for each bid price are shown in columns 2, 3, and 4. The product of columns 3 and 4 is the EPVC for each bid price level. The bid price which appears to maximize EPVC is $70,000. But this price was chosen arbitrarily from a spectrum of possible bid prices. By plotting the EPVC against bid prices and interpolating between the points, we would find that the EPVC is maximized when the bid price is approximately $73,500, as indicated in Figure 12-1.

TABLE 12-1. Expected Present Value Analysis of a Bid-Pricing Problem

Net EPV Incremental Cost [1]	Bid Price [2]	Contribution [3]	Success Probability [4]	EPVC [5]
$50,000	$ 50,000	$ 0	0.90	$ 0
50,000	60,000	10,000	0.70	7,000
50,000	70,000	20,000	0.50	10,000
50,000	80,000	30,000	0.30	9,000
50,000	90,000	40,000	0.15	6,000
50,000	100,000	50,000	0.05	2,500

Thus the firm should bid at $73,500 to pursue the maximization of its net present worth. While it may not win this particular contract, if it bids for a large number of such contracts the present value of its total contribution to overheads and profits, and hence its net present worth, will be maximized by continually bidding at the price which maximizes EPVC for each particular contract. It wins some and loses some, but on average it comes out ahead, as compared to any other pattern of bidding.

Aesthetic, Political, and Risk Considerations. It is perhaps unreasonable to expect a decision maker to make a choice simply on the basis of quantifiable cost and revenue

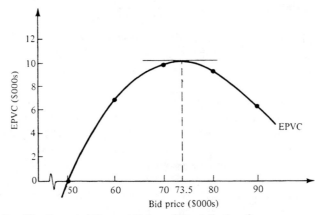

FIGURE 12-1. *The Expected Present Value of Contribution Curve*

considerations. In some cases certain aesthetic considerations enter the bidding process. Suppose the project alluded to in Table 12-1 was something other than a straightforward and normal project. On the one hand, it may appeal to the artistic tastes of the decision maker; on the other hand, it may involve considerable amounts of dirty and uncomfortable work. In the first case we might expect a decision maker to choose a bid price somewhat below the expected value, since the nonmonetary gratification received by the decision maker would offset some of the monetary compensation involved in the higher bid price. But if the job is expected to be dirty, uncomfortable, or inconvenient in some nonmonetary way, we might expect the decision maker's bid to be somewhat above the $73,500 indicated by the expected-value criterion, since the nonmonetary disutility attached to the job would need to be offset by some additional monetary compensation.

A further consideration that may cause the decision maker to choose a bid price different from the one with the maximum expected contribution is the possibility that the decision maker may see personal gain in bidding at a different price level. Thus individual decision makers within an organization may practice self-serving, or political, behavior. This may be functional political behavior in that it causes certain actions that at the same time promote the organization's objectives, or it may be dysfunctional in that it serves the decision maker's purposes but hinders the attainment of the organization's objectives. Since it is not unlikely that the objectives of the decision maker and the organization will differ on occasion, we should not expect all decisions to reflect single-minded pursuit of company goals. Hence, if the decision maker feels there is some personal gain likely to follow a bid price above or below that indicated by the expected-value criterion, the actual bid price may well deviate from that standard.

The personal gains to the decision maker may include a wide variety of tangible and intangible benefits which the decision maker may expect to receive as the result of a particular decision's being taken. Hence, a relatively low bid price may be chosen when the decision maker feels there is something to gain by winning the contract, and conversely, a relatively high bid price may be submitted when it is felt that the purchaser owes a favor to the supplier and the supplier expects the purchaser to settle this debt. Simple friendship between the supplier and the purchaser may also cause a lower bid price to be submitted, and the reduction from the expected-value bid price can be ascribed to political motivations, namely to the supplier's recognition of the personal value of the buyer's friendship. Note that these political considerations are separate from the goodwill considerations that we include in the incremental cost calculation.

Risk Considerations

Risk considerations should be addressed under two headings. First, there is the risk of not getting the contract. Note that the probability of winning at the $73,500 bid price is somewhere between 30% and 50%. (A simple interpolation indicates 43%.) If the firm bids on contracts like this frequently, it might expect to actually win a little more than four out of every ten it bids on. Consequently, the firm should bid on more contracts than it could possibly handle at any one time, recognizing that it will win only some proportion of those. If the firm bids on many different contracts, it can afford to be risk neutral with respect to any one contract, expecting the law of averages to work in its favor.

In many situations the firm will not wish to take its chances with the law of averages. If the firm has substantial excess capacity and is facing layoffs of its workers, or worse still, is facing bankruptcy, a 43% chance of winning will not be good enough. In effect, the firm's time horizon has shrunk back to the immediate future, and winning the next contract becomes very important to the firm. Thus the firm will be prepared to trade off some of the expected profit for a greater chance of winning the contract. Depending on how badly it needs the contract, it will reduce its bid price to increase the success probability. In the worst case, it would offer to do the job at a price which simply covers its net incremental costs (its incremental costs less the EPV of any incremental revenues other than the bid price).

The second category of risk to be considered is the risk of cost variability after the contract is awarded, as discussed at the beginning of this chapter. If there is a risk of cost variability and the supplying firm is risk averse, the firm may wish to bid at a lower level while transferring some of the risk of cost variability to the buyer.

Cost-plus-Fee Bids. As indicated earlier in this chapter, prices in some markets are typically set on the basis of *ex post* cost plus a fee or markup. In the automobile repair market this pricing convention is typical, although brake jobs, electrical tune-ups, and exhaust mufflers are often priced on a fixed-price basis, either as a temporary promotion or on a permanent basis to appeal to the risk-averse buyer. As a general rule, the greater the potential variability of cost, the greater the risk aversion of the seller relative to the buyer, and the greater the asymmetry of information regarding costs, the more likely it is that firms will wish to bid on a cost-plus-fee basis.

Having ascertained the EPVC-maximizing bid price, the firm wishing to tender a cost-plus-fee bid must decide how much EPVC (and equivalently, how much of the bid

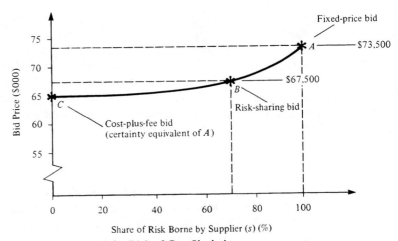

FIGURE 12-2.   The Bid Price and the Risk of Cost Variation

price) it is willing to give up to transfer the risk of cost variability to the buyer. In Figure 12-2 we show an indifference curve in bid-price–risk-share space as an illustration. Point *A* represents the EPVC-maximizing bid price, with all the risk of cost variability being borne by the supplier. The certainty equivalent of that bid price is shown as the point *C* on the vertical axis, where the risk share borne by the supplier is zero. Thus the cost-plus-fee bid the firm should tender is $65,000, which is indicated by the firm's certainty equivalent of the EPVC-maximizing price.

Note that if the firm were to tender a cost-plus-fee bid greater than this certainty equivalent value, it would not be pursuing its objective, which we have assumed to be the maximization of its (expected present) net worth subject to its attitude toward risk.

Incentive (Risk-Sharing) Bids.   In many cases the buyer will require that each tender state an *ex ante* price and also specify the share of any cost variation that the supplier will bear. The risk-averse supplier may arbitrarily select a value of the risk share, such as 70%, and tender the *ex ante* price that makes the supplier indifferent between that price and that risk share, and the EPVC-maximizing price with all the risk. In Figure 12-2 we show this tender as the point *B*, indicating an *ex ante* bid price of $67,500. An arbitrary choice of risk share is unlikely to be optimal, however. The firm must be guided by the recent experience in the market. What risk share is typical? What risk share did this buyer accept last time? Unless the firm chooses its risk share with an eye to these considerations, it is likely to lose the contract to a firm that does.

In general, the optimal tender will be the combination of *ex ante* price and risk share that best serves the buyer's objectives. If the buyer's objective is to maximize net worth without regard to risk, the optimal tender is the lowest bid price regardless of risk share offered. If the buyer considers both net worth and risk, the optimal tender is the one that maximizes the buyer's utility in risk-return space. We can show the buyer's indifference curves as in Figure 12-3, where they are superimposed on the seller's indifference

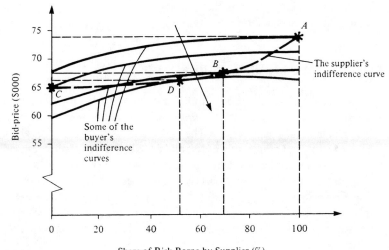

FIGURE 12-3.   The Buyer's Preferred Tender in Risk-Return Space

curve. The buyer's indifference curves must be positively sloped but convex from above, because the buyer will receive increasing marginal disutility from higher bid prices and diminishing marginal utility from larger shares of risk being assigned to the supplier. Thus the buyer's direction of preference is to the southeast, as indicated by the arrow.

Note that the buyer can rank the various tenders in terms of utility generated. Point A, representing the fixed-price bid of $73,500, is on the least-preferred indifference curve. The buyer prefers point C, the $65,000 cost-plus-fee bid, to the fixed-price bid, but ranks point B, the $67,500 bid with 70% (supplier's) risk share, over both of the other two. But a bid of about $66,250 with 50% risk share going to the supplier (point D) allows the buyer to attain the highest level of utility and is thus the optimal tender for the supplier to submit.

In practice, firms rarely use the theoretical guidelines outlined here. The search costs associated with obtaining the information are typically so great that the firm is better off using a simple decision rule like markup bid pricing, which we will discuss in a subsequent section. To utilize the EPVC approach, the firm must obtain estimates of all incremental costs and revenues that are likely to follow the pricing decision. This process would usually be difficult enough, but obtaining the probabilities of success for a variety of potential bid price levels may be even more difficult. Obtaining this information would involve an analysis of all rival suppliers culminating in estimates of the probability distribution of their potential bid prices, so the firm could deduce its success probability at each price level. Moreover, the buyer's degree of risk aversion must be estimated, and rivals' risk-share offers estimated, when the buyer requires or will accept risk-sharing tender offers. In perhaps most cases the firm will expect the search costs to be prohibitive and follow a more simple pricing decision rule. Nonetheless, the theoretical model of competitive bidding is valuable, since it identifies the concepts and variables which are important in the bid-pricing decision and allows the actual decision to be formulated in light of these considerations.

12.3   COMPETITIVE BIDDING IN PRACTICE

In practice most firms appear to choose their bid price by applying a markup to some measure of the costs associated with the job, rather than base their bid price on the incremental costs and revenues. The firm's cost base is typically calculated to include all explicit costs, bid preparation costs, and an allocation of other overhead costs. No explicit calculation is usually made to include opportunity costs or other incremental costs, and costs are usually considered only in nominal dollars rather than in present-value terms. The firm will typically choose the markup percentage with an eye to its past pricing practice, modifying this standard markup either up or down depending on current conditions in the market and the industry and with reference to longer-term considerations in some cases.

Markup Bid Pricing to Maximize EPVC

The firm's decision process described in the preceding paragraph may be a parallel but effectively equivalent means of arriving at the optimal bid price. Given that search costs are expected to exceed the value of the information derived, firms proceed using the markup-pricing rule of thumb and keep winning enough jobs to keep them in business and sufficiently profitable. Although they do not typically include all net incremental costs in their cost calculations, they typically allow for them in a crude way by varying the size of the markup applied.

- EXAMPLE: Suppose a job is expected to involve future goodwill effects or that getting this job would avoid costly layoffs and subsequent rehiring and retraining expenses; the decision maker would apply a *lower* markup than normally would be applied. Conversely, if lawsuits were likely to follow a particular job or if the firm were near full capacity and getting the contract might cause labor problems sometime in the future, the markup applied might be *higher* than the standard level. The markup approach incorporates the nonmonetary considerations in the same way: We would expect to see higher markups with consequently higher bid prices to compensate for nonmonetary costs and lower markups to compensate for nonmonetary benefits.

It is clear that the firm could stumble on the EPVC-maximizing price by using the markup approach. For example, suppose the firm calculates its cost base to be $61,250, comprised of direct costs and allocated overheads. A 20% markup on that cost base would result in a bid price of $73,500, the same as in the EPVC approach. Of course, this outcome would be sheer good luck. More likely, the firm using the simple (but inexpensive) markup pricing procedure will submit a bid which is either above or below the EPVC-maximizing price level.

How does the firm know if its markup is too high or too low? If it does not win enough contracts to keep its plant and employees operating within the desired range of capacity utilization, it will sooner or later determine that its markup rate (and hence its prices) is probably too high. Lowering the markup rate would be expected to bring improved capacity utilization with consequent larger total contribution to overheads and profits. Conversely, if the firm wins too many contracts, so its capacity is overutilized, with all the attendant costs and problems, it will sooner or later decide to raise its markup to reduce demand for its services and consequently increase the profits of the enterprise. Of course, in the latter case the firm should also be considering the possibility of expanding its plant size.

- NOTE: These capacity-utilization considerations entered the theoretical approach as well, but in the calculation of incremental costs. In the EPVC approach the potential costs of layoffs, rehiring, retraining, and so forth, which were associated with very low capacity utilization, operate to lower the total EPV of incremental costs of the potential job, and, given a structure of success probabilities, subsequently operate to lower the optimal bid price. Conversely, if the plant were near full capacity, the expected costs of future labor problems would be incorporated into incremental costs and cause the optimal bid price to be higher than it otherwise would be.

The Reconciliation of Theory and Practice

The first issue is that of information-search costs. In practice these are frequently expected to outweigh the benefits of the information derived, and the firm takes the completely rational decision to forego the information and proceed using a simple decision rule such as markup pricing. This behavior is rational in that it involves pursuit of the firm's objectives. Although the markup price might be $5,000 less than the maximum EPVC price, if this simple procedure obviates spending more than $5,000 on information-search costs, the firm comes out ahead using the simple decision rule.[4]

The second issue follows from the first. Having only an imprecise view of the longer-term incremental costs, opportunity costs, goodwill, and other costs and benefits not immediately calculable but indeed consequent on this pricing decision, the firm in practice tends to build these into a "cushion" in its markup. If these incalculable costs are larger, so too is the markup, to take into account in a rough way the probability that these incalculable costs will arise. Alternatively, if these incalculable costs are expected to be low, or if this contract will serve to enhance goodwill, the "cushion" in the firm's profit margin can be reduced by using a lower markup percentage.

Thus the markup price can be "wrong" to the extent of the information-search costs that were avoided, and the markup percentage, and hence the profit margin, must take into account all net incremental costs (in EPV terms) *not* considered and *not* calcu-

---

[4]We have no reason to believe this is the general case, however. In many cases firms would profit by seeking more information, but they abstain from search activity for reasons other than the costs involved, such as ignorance of the information source and the lack of personnel qualified to lead the search.

lated into the cost base for the markup calculation. To the extent that overhead costs, including bid preparation costs, are included in the cost base, the markup percentage will be lower, since the markup will be simply the profit margin, rather than the contribution to overheads and profits. By way of summary, Table 12-2 shows the alternate approaches to price determination in competitive bidding situations. Notice that the cost and revenue considerations which are not incorporated in the cost base should be incorporated in the choice of the markup percentage, if the markup is to lead to a price close to (within the search cost differential of) the EPVC-maximizing price.

- NOTE: After the firm's bid is submitted, the firm waits to learn the outcome. Suppose it loses this contract. No particular reaction is called for unless it loses "too many"contracts—that is, it finds that its probabilities were too high in the EPVC approach or that its markups were consistently too high in the markup approach. This feedback information calls for a change in the pricing level, as indicated in the bottom part of Table 12-2. Conversely, if the firm is successful "too often," it must revise its estimates of the success probabilities, revise its general price structure upward, and consider the expansion of its plant size.

Markup Bid Pricing for the Satisficing Firm

Often we notice that the practicing competitive bidder appears to exhibit the four basic features of a satisficing firm, as detailed in the behavioral theory of the firm.[5] First, the firm exhibits *bounded rationality*, calculating only its present costs and declining to search for future costs and probability distributions. Second, it practices *selectivity* by not bidding on all contracts offered but confining its attention, instead, to those it is most likely to win and for which it has the technology and capacity. Third, it establishes *decision rules*, like standard cost bases and markup pricing, to facilitate and expedite the decision process. Fourth, it establishes *targets* or satisfactory levels for its most important variables, and it uses feedback information to adjust these targets and decision rules when such action becomes necessary or desirable.

We argued in Chapter 9 that satisficing, or the pursuit of satisfactory targets, may be considered a proxy policy for the maximization of the firm's net present worth. If the targets are consistently achieved and upgraded, the firm should be expected to approach the bid price level which maximizes its EPVC without having to incur any major search costs.

Observation suggests that the main targets the bidding firm seeks to attain relate to the degree of capacity utilization and the rate of profitability. The capacity utilization target amounts to the same thing as a sales volume target and has implications for the firm's share of the market. It also has implications for the firm's cash flow and subsequent ability to meet its payroll obligations, interest expense, and other overhead costs.

---

[5]See R. M. Cyert and C. J. March, *A Behavioral Theory of the Firm* (Englewood Cliffs, N.J.: Prentice-Hall, 1963); and H. A. Simon, "Rational Decision Making in Business Organizations," *American Economic Review*, 69 (September 1979), pp. 493–513.

TABLE 12-2. *The EPVC Model and the Markup Model of Competitive Bidding*

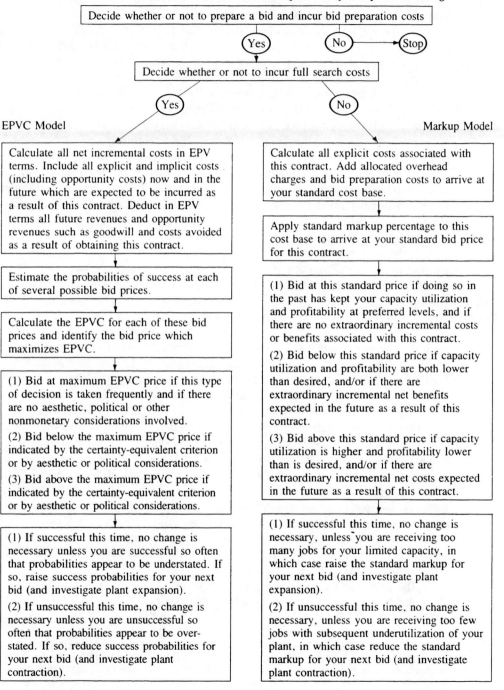

Decide whether or not to prepare a bid and incur bid preparation costs

Yes   No → Stop

Decide whether or not to incur full search costs

Yes   No

EPVC Model

Markup Model

Calculate all net incremental costs in EPV terms. Include all explicit and implicit costs (including opportunity costs) now and in the future which are expected to be incurred as a result of this contract. Deduct in EPV terms all future revenues and opportunity revenues such as goodwill and costs avoided as a result of obtaining this contract.

Calculate all explicit costs associated with this contract. Add allocated overhead charges and bid preparation costs to arrive at your standard cost base.

Apply standard markup percentage to this cost base to arrive at your standard bid price for this contract.

Estimate the probabilities of success at each of several possible bid prices.

Calculate the EPVC for each of these bid prices and identify the bid price which maximizes EPVC.

(1) Bid at maximum EPVC price if this type of decision is taken frequently and if there are no aesthetic, political or other nonmonetary considerations involved.

(2) Bid below the maximum EPVC price if indicated by the certainty-equivalent criterion or by aesthetic or political considerations.

(3) Bid above the maximum EPVC price if indicated by the certainty-equivalent criterion or by aesthetic or political considerations.

(1) Bid at this standard price if doing so in the past has kept your capacity utilization and profitability at preferred levels, and if there are no extraordinary incremental costs or benefits associated with this contract.

(2) Bid below this standard price if capacity utilization and profitability are both lower than desired, and/or if there are extraordinary incremental net benefits expected in the future as a result of this contract.

(3) Bid above this standard price if capacity utilization is higher and profitability lower than is desired, and/or if there are extraordinary incremental net costs expected in the future as a result of this contract.

(1) If successful this time, no change is necessary unless you are successful so often that probabilities appear to be understated. If so, raise success probabilities for your next bid (and investigate plant expansion).

(2) If unsuccessful this time, no change is necessary unless you are unsuccessful so often that probabilities appear to be over-stated. If so, reduce success probabilities for your next bid (and investigate plant contraction).

(1) If successful this time, no change is necessary, unless you are receiving too many jobs for your limited capacity, in which case raise the standard markup for your next bid (and investigate plant expansion).

(2) If unsuccessful this time, no change is necessary, unless you are receiving too few jobs with subsequent underutilization of your plant, in which case reduce the standard markup for your next bid (and investigate plant contraction).

By striving to keep capacity utilization at or above a particular target, the firm expects to avoid the costs of retrenchment, rehiring, and retraining that would follow a plant closure and subsequent reopening. It is often apparent that the capacity utilization target takes priority over the profitability target, since firms seem to sacrifice profitability to attain utilization targets, but then they price to obtain their required rate of return on contracts when they are at or above their target rate of capacity utilization.

The markup-bid-pricing model shown in Table 12-2 is easily modified to suit the satisficing firm. Table 12-3 shows schematically the decision process for the satisficing firm. When it first becomes aware of a call for bids on a particular contract, the firm does not immediately decide to prepare a bid. Rather, it first considers several factors of importance to the attainment of the firm's targets. Does it have the necessary technology, or could it obtain this through consultants or other subcontract work? Does it have sufficient capacity to handle this job, or could the job be partly or wholly given out to subcontractors without undue problems? Does it seem worthwhile to prepare a bid on this job, or alternatively, is there a strong enough chance that the firm will recoup its bid preparation costs by winning the contract?

If the answer is yes to these three basic questions, the firm should go ahead and prepare its bid on the contract. If the answer is no to any one question, the firm must consider four subsidiary questions which may induce it to prepare a bid in any case. First, is the firm desperate for work, or is it considering diversification into new lines of work? An affirmative response to these questions should cause the firm to reconsider preparing a bid despite not having the technology at the present time. Second, is it necessary to submit a bid to maintain goodwill with the buyer? If bids are requested privately, rather than being widely advertised, or if the firm feels that it should keep its name in front of the buyer, it may be important to submit a bid even without adequate capacity to do the job. Of course, this bid should be high enough to be profitable if the firm actually wins the contract.

Regarding the prior expectation of winning the contract, two subsidiary questions must be asked if it is not considered worthwhile to prepare a bid. Is the firm's capacity utilization target being achieved at present and for the duration of this proposed contract? If not, the firm should prepare a bid anyway, since it will perceive that the maintenance of capacity utilization levels is of primary importance. Even if capacity utilization is satisfactory, the firm should prepare a bid if its profitability target is not being met currently or may not be met in the foreseeable future. Thus the firm will prepare a bid, despite a low prior expectation of success, if either of its capacity or profitability targets are not met. Of course, its final decision on the bid price will reflect the circumstances; for example, it will be lower if the capacity target is not met and higher if the capacity target is met but the profitabilily target is not.

The firm will prepare its bid on the basis of a standardized cost base which is calculated by the application of several basic decision rules.[6] The bid price obtained by

---

[6]The satisficing firm may have developed a simple "costing sheet" which requires estimates of variable costs, variable overheads, bid preparation costs, and other fixed costs. The decision rules pertaining to variable overheads may be, for example, 50% of labor costs, and the overhead charges may be the proportion of the firm's work-year devoted to this job times the firm's total fixed costs.

TABLE 12-3. *Decision Sequence for the Satisficing Firm*

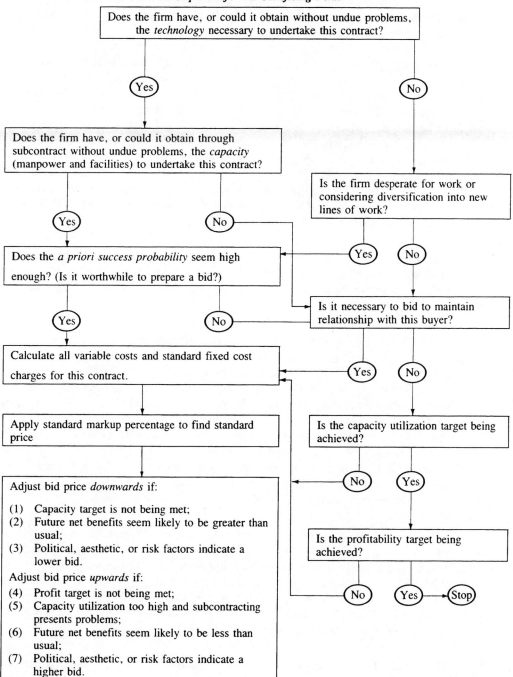

multiplying the standard cost base by the standard markup may be called the firm's standard price for the contract. It will bid at that level if its capacity and profitability targets are being met, and if the contract appears to have no extraordinary features about it. The firm will *lower* its markup percentage and hence its bid price if capacity utilization is below the target level, if it foresees abnormal longer-term benefits to be gained by winning this contract, or if political, aesthetic, or risk considerations require a monetary trade-off to increase the probability of success. Conversely, the firm will *raise* its markup percentage if the capacity target but not the profitability target is being attained, if future net benefits seem likely to be less than usual, or if political, aesthetic, or risk factors indicate a higher bid price. In addition, the firm would raise its markup if it did not have the capacity needed to complete the contract if won, but it was submitting a bid only to maintain the relationship currently enjoyed with the buyer. In each case the amount by which the bid price is raised or lowered from the standard price should be commensurate with the value to the firm of winning or losing the contract, as per the EPVC discussions earlier in this chapter.

The Targets.   What are the appropriate levels for the capacity utilization target and the profitability target? The desired rate of capacity utilization should be the same rate at which standard overhead charges are calculated and may be chosen, for example, to be 80% of full capacity.

- DEFINITION: *Full capacity* is defined as the total number of labor-days available per year, using a single shift and the optimal complement of manpower. The optimal complement of labor is construed as that quantity which allows average total cost to be minimized. Thus overfull capacity can be achieved by additional workers during the single shift, overtime operation, multiple-shift operation, or subcontracting. Notwithstanding the fact that average costs are minimized at full capacity, the firm may establish its target capacity utilization at something less than full capacity to leave a margin for error in the event of strikes or breakdowns and to avoid the frequent disruption of normal operations associated with overtime and extra-worker operation. Note also that if the target utilization rate is achieved, the firm's overheads are completely covered, and any extra work contributes directly to the firm's profits.

The profitability target, or the firm's required rate of return, will be determined by the firm's opportunity cost of capital. Suppose the firm feels that it could obtain 20% before taxes at comparable risk elsewhere: It will set this as its minimum, or target, level. While higher rates of profitability may seem desirable, managers will be inclined to trade off higher profits for reduced risk. They will be content to price somewhat lower than might be possible to better ensure the firm's future existence in the market, not to mention the continuation of their tenure as managers.

The Standard Costs, Markup, and Price.   The firm's standard cost-base calculations and its standard markup rate may be modified over time as a result of its bidding experience. The model outlined in Table 12-3 allows for adjustment in the markup rate if either of the targets is not met and for other reasons. If the firm wins virtually every contract it bids on, we would expect it to raise its markup on subsequent bids. Rather than make each bid a special case, the firm in this happy situation may simplify its subsequent pricing decisions by raising its standard markup to a higher level. Conversely, if the firm finds that it is consistently not winning enough contracts to attain its capacity utilization target, it may adjust its markup rate downward to a new, more appropriate, level.

In each case, the adjustment is made to cause the firm's bid to be slightly more or less desirable and should have a noticeable effect on the quantity of work obtained. The appropriate level of the markup, and hence the price, is that level which tends to keep the firm at or above its capacity utilization target. At this target level of output, the profitability target will also be attained, except for unforeseen costs associated with jobs in process and with unanticipated increases in overhead costs. The feedback to management from past contracts won or lost allows them to judge the most appropriate levels of the standard cost base and markup levels. As before, special circumstances surrounding any particular contract will justify a deviation from the standard price.

If over a prolonged series of contracts it becomes apparent that demand for the firm's services is either too strong or too weak for its present size of plant, the firm must consider adjustment of plant size. A reasonable presumption is that the firm would choose its new plant size such that the new plant's capacity utilization target is equal to the expected value of its annual demand at standard prices. Given the new plant size and potentially different technology, the firm would need to recalculate its standard cost base and may wish to adjust its standard markup percentage to bring its new standard price into line with the bid prices of other firms. It would make these readjustments in the normal process of winning or losing contracts: If it wins too few it will adjust its standard markup downward, and if it wins too many it will raise the level of its standard markup.

12.4 THE VIEW FROM THE OTHER SIDE: OPTIMAL PURCHASING

Before submitting its tender, the supplier should attempt to ascertain exacly what the buyer wants. Specifications will be provided by the buyer, of course, in either general or detailed terms, but even detailed specifications are unlikely to be complete, in the sense that there will remain room for discretion on the supplier's part in the design, quality, and other aspects of the work to be carried out. Knowledge of what the supplier expects to pay, how much quality is expected at that price, whether a risk-sharing bid would be entertained, and so on would allow the supplier to tailor its tender to fit the buyer's preferences exactly and thus increase the probability of winning the contract.

To achieve a better understanding of the buyer's choice problem and how the supplier's tender may better serve the buyer's objectives, we shall look at the competitive bid problem from the buyer's perspective. The purchasing agent responsible for selecting the winning bid must go through a decision process to arrive at that decision. One such decision process is known as value analysis.

Value Analysis for Optimal Purchasing

In general, the buyer's problem is to choose the tender that not only has an agreeable price attached to it but also includes the most desirable package of attributes in association with that price.

- EXAMPLE: Let us consider the purchasing decision of a householder who is contemplating having new windows installed in his somewhat older house. He receives three quotes, as shown in Table 12-4, after inviting representatives from each company to quote on the job. Notice that there is a difference not only in the prices quoted but in the qualitative aspects of the offers.

TABLE 12-4. Details of Price Quotes on Windows

	Company A	Company B	Company C
Price	$2,200	$1,280	$1,050
Frame	Baked enamel on steel	Baked enamel on aluminum	Anodized aluminum
Glass	Two separate 5-mm panes	Double 5-mm Thermopane	Double 3-mm Thermopane
Warranty	10 years, complete	5 years, complete	3 years, complete
Delivery	12 weeks	8 weeks	6 weeks

Which quote should the consumer accept? The answer obviously depends on a variety of considerations, including the consumer's financial liquidity, his aesthetic feelings and misgivings about the different types of materials and construction, the length of time he expects to own the house, and his attitude toward the risk and uncertainty associated with the different warranties. In the initial discussions with the buyer, the salesperson should attempt to find out exactly what the consumer wants and is prepared to pay for and should then tailor the bid accordingly. The essential consideration is whether the attributes involved in the different bids are worth as much (to the consumer) as the suppliers are asking. Clearly we cannot make the decision for this consumer, but we can say that if he chooses the bid made by company B, this decision indicates that he values the attributes provided by company B for that price more highly than he values the attributes provided by the others, relative to their prices.

Industrial purchasers are often required to rationalize their purchasing decisions in some objective manner to demonstrate that their purchasing policy is consistent with company objectives. A means of arriving at a purchasing decision (or for *post hoc* rationalization of a purchasing decision) is the technique known as value analysis. Using this approach, the decision maker identifies the attributes that are considered desirable and which may be present in each of the bids, applies weights to those attributes in order of importance to the decision maker, ranks and scales each bidder under each attribute, multiplies the weight by the scale, and chooses the bid that has the highest weighted score.

This procedure may be illustrated in terms of the window example. In Table 12-5 we indicate that the attributes of interest to this purchaser are price, quality, delivery lag, and warranty. We presume that the purchaser values these attributes in the proportions shown by the weights. The suppliers are then ranked in terms of their performance on each attribute on a scale of 0 to 10: the better the performance, the higher the scale. Note that for price, supplier A receives a value of 1, supplier B is assigned a value of 5, and supplier C is assigned a value of 8. This reflects the fact that supplier C has submitted the lowest price, followed by the price of supplier B, with supplier A's price a greater distance above. The scale values given to each of the suppliers need not be consecutive numbers if the attributes are different by different amounts.

TABLE 12-5. Value Analysis in Purchasing

Attribute	Weight	SUPPLIER A		SUPPLIER B		SUPPLIER C	
		Scale	Score	Scale	Score	Scale	Score
Price	7	1	7	5	35	8	56
Quality	4	8	32	7	28	1	4
Delivery	3	1	3	3	9	5	15
Warranty	2	10	20	7	14	4	8
Total score			62		86		83

The buyer then scales and scores each potential supplier on each of the other attributes, as indicated in Table 12-5. Multiplying the scales assigned by the weights for each attribute, we derive each supplier's score on each attribute, and these may be added up to find each supplier's total score over the attributes deemed desirable by the purchaser. Given this system of weighting and scaling the various attributes, supplier B has the most desirable bid, since the weighted sum of the scores is greatest.

- NOTE: The choice of the weights assigned to each attribute is essentially arbitrary, depending on the attitudes and judgment of the decision maker. Similarly, the ranking and then the scaling of the suppliers in terms of these attributes are at the discretion of the decision maker. Finally, other attributes may be included in the analysis, such as the supplier's previous experience with this type of project, financial stability, quality and reputation of personnel, provision of technical or consulting services, inventory charges, and shipping policy. A different decision maker may score the same three bids differently, such that supplier A or supplier C becomes the successful bidder.[7]

---

[7]The buyer is likely to set some minimum acceptable level or standard for each attribute which must be met for the seller's bid to be considered. For example, if the quality or delivery date was unacceptable or was expected to be unacceptable, the seller would be excluded from any further consideration.

The importance of value analysis in purchasing is its ability to force the decision maker to rationalize and scrutinize the purchasing decision. The choice of weights, value scales, and desirable attributes must be stated explicitly and is thus subject to argumentation by the decision maker's peers and superiors. Out of the discussion should arise a consensus of those weights, scales, and attributes that are considered consistent with the firm's objectives. Purchasing decisions may thus be justified on this relatively objective basis, rather than merely on the basis of unstated preferences and assumptions.[8]

From the supplier's point of view it would be immeasurably valuable to obtain the criteria on which the purchasing decision is made. With this information the supplier could tailor the bid price and other features such that the bid would score more highly and be more desirable to the buyer. In the previous case of the windows, the supplier should attempt to ascertain the likes and dislikes, willingness to pay for certain features, and other information about the prospective customer. In the industrial purchasing situation the potential supplier should attempt to judge which features the buyer regards as more or less important. In both cases the supplier will then be in a better position to supply exactly what is desired by the purchaser and will thus be more likely to be the successful bidder on the contract.

Collusive Bidding and Bid Disclosure

In the foregoing we have presumed that the firms bidding for a particular contract do so without benefit of any interaction or direct information flow between and among the potential suppliers. Where a small group of firms continually find themselves bidding against each other, it is not surprising that they will seek better information concerning each other's intended bids. Since retaliatory action cannot remove the immediate gains of a successful low bid, the firms will wish to eliminate the possibility of a rival's submitting an unexpectedly low bid. One means of achieving this purpose is to obtain prior agreement among firms about their bid prices or pricing procedures.

We might expect collusive practices to be more likely to exist in industries in which there is both the ability and the necessity to bid collusively. Regarding the ability to collude, where there are relatively few firms we expect firms to be able to communicate with all other firms more easily and effectively. Moreover, the fact that the actions of any one firm are more readily visible to the other firms assists in the policing of any agreement. Regarding the necessity to collude, where contracts are relatively few and far between and are of relatively high value, the incentive will be stronger for each firm to submit a relatively low bid to obtain the contract, even if doing so does not generate a profit above the fully allocated costs of operation. The longer-term result could be that all firms are pricing below full costs and that no firm earns a normal profit. As an alternative to some firms' being forced out of the industry, the firms may see collusive bidding as a necessity to avoid a degeneration of prices to unprofitable levels.

---

[8]Value analysis is implicit in any purchasing decision. It is done explicitly in many companies for the benefits stated above.

Identical Bids. The competing suppliers for a particular contract may agree to submit identical bid prices at a level that ensures that the business will be sufficiently profitable to the successful bidder. The purchaser is then forced to select the successful bidder on some criteria other than price level. This situation is akin to nonprice competition in established market situations. The suppliers will attempt to include those attributes in their bid that are desired by the purchaser, so at identical prices their bid appears to be the better deal. Suppliers may consider this nonprice competition to be a more ethical form of competition, since the successful bidder is rewarded for the expertise and efficiency involved in supplying a particular bundle of attributes at the given price, rather than for the simple ability to cut prices below what rivals are expected to bid.

Bid Rotation. Bid rotation is a method designed to allocate the available business among the competing suppliers in proportions agreeable to all. In effect, the firms take turns in submitting the lowest bid, so the available business is allocated around the industry. It is not necessarily allocated in equal shares among the competing suppliers, but more likely it will be allocated on the basis of historical market shares or current bargaining power.

As noted in Appendix 10A, however, collusive price fixing is illegal, and the firm may face prosecution for engaging in this practice. A second factor militating against the longer-term operation of collusive bidding in any particular industry is the profit incentive that individual firms may have to undercut the agreed price. Firms that are not getting sufficient work to obtain their desired degree of capacity utilization may break out of the agreement when an important contract is at stake. If the available business is not shared among the competing suppliers in a manner that is suitable to all, it is likely that a particular supplier will be motivated to undercut the agreed price to obtain the additional business.

While the exchange of information involved in collusive bidding operates to reduce the uncertainty involved in the pricing decision, the risk remains that one or more competing suppliers will operate at variance with their stated intentions. Thus it is still important to evaluate and form expectations about the probable behavior of competitors. To the extent that rivals are expected not to maintain their previous behavior pattern or are expected not to carry through with their stated intent, the decision maker may wish to adjust the bid price accordingly.[9]

Disclosure of Bids. After the contract is awarded to the successful bidder, the bid prices of other suppliers may be disclosed to all suppliers or to the public in general. The disclosure of the bid prices generates considerable information which may be valuable to the sellers in their future bidding policies. The unsuccessful bidders will obtain information about the amount they overbid, and the successful bidder will obtain information about the amount that this bid could have been increased without losing the contract. We

---

[9]Information concerning rival firms' bidding practices and intentions may be gleaned in conversation with rival decision makers at business and social gatherings or from industry gossip. Some people even believe in industrial espionage!

should expect, therefore, that disclosure of bid prices would lead to a compression of the range of bids over time, since the firms would gain an appreciation of the bid levels that are likely to be submitted by the other firms in the industry. Obviously, disclosure of bids provides information useful for the initiation and the policing of collusive bidding.

From the purchaser's point of view it may be a poor strategy to disclose the bid prices after the contract is awarded, since doing so may lead to a compression of the bid prices nearer the center of the range of bids and may facilitate collusive bidding. Such disclosure is likely to lead to an increased level of the lowest bid over time. From the purchaser's point of view it is surely better to keep the suppliers in the dark, since they are more likely to submit lower bids when they are in a greater state of uncertainty about the bids of the other firms. We should thus expect that purchasers would not wish to disclose the bids, and in some industries bid disclosure is considered an unethical procedure. Governments, which frequently purchase goods and services in this type of market, may be required to disclose bid prices, however, to show their constituents that the public funds involved have been spent wisely and without corruption.

12.5 SUMMARY

In this chapter we have applied the contribution approach to competitive bids and price quotes. The relevant cost concept is the incremental cost associated with the work involved in undertaking and completing the contract; and as long as the bid price exceeds this incremental cost less any other incremental revenues, some contribution will be made to overheads and profits by obtaining the contract. We considered the optimal bid price from the point of view of expected-value analysis, modifying this to the extent that aesthetic, political, and risk considerations were involved.

In practice many firms use cost-plus pricing procedures in their competitive bids and price quotes. These procedures can be equivalent to the expected-value approach, and they save time and expense in the decision-making procedure. However, it is important that the decision maker attempt to justify the bid price in terms of the theoretical procedures to ensure that the objectives of the company (or the individual decision maker) are being served. We saw that the satisficing firm may expect to approach the maximization of its EPVC by pursuing capacity utilization and profitability targets.

Both the expected-value approach and the markup approach involve an implicit or explicit estimation of the probability of success at each bid price level. The major factors involved in estimating these probabilities are the probabilities of competitors' bidding at various price levels and the appreciation that the buyer will have for price and quality differences. This latter aspect was examined from the buyer's side to show the factors likely to be considered in choosing the successful bid. Potential suppliers will benefit by an appreciation of the factors considered important by the buyer. The probable bid prices of rivals may be estimated on the basis of information obtained through a collusive exchange of pricing plans, by the disclosure of price levels on previous bid prices, or by knowledge of rival suppliers' capacity utilization levels and other factors.

DISCUSSION QUESTIONS

12-1. Outline three situations in which you have recently been the buyer in a competitive bidding or price quote situation (even if you received only one quote in each instance).

12-2. Make a list of those items that you would expect to enter the incremental cost calculation for a contract to remove the sea gulls from the vicinity of a major coastal airport.

12-3. In calculating the incremental costs of a particular project, how would you treat the possible future cost of a lawsuit that may occur as a result of this project, where the cost of such a lawsuit may range from $10,000 to $500,000 with an associated probability distribution?

12-4. How would you value the goodwill that is expected to be generated as a result of undertaking a particular contract? If there is expected goodwill, would you be prepared to bid lower than otherwise? Why?

12-5. Explain why the strategy of choosing the bid price with the highest expected value is likely to generate the greatest contribution to overheads and profits over a large number of successful and unsuccessful bids.

12-6. Outline the different types of bids that may be tendered. What is the relationship between the fixed-price bid and the other two types of bids?

12-7. Explain how the strategy of marking up incremental costs by a standard percentage (and subsequently winning some contracts and losing some contracts) may over a period of time give equivalent results as compared with the maximum-expected-value strategy.

12-8. Outline the factors that would cause you to use a lower markup on incremental costs (as compared with your usual markup) in a particular bidding situation.

12-9. Explain the logic behind value analysis. What is the relationship between value analysis and attribute analysis of consumer choice behavior?

12-10. Why is collusive bidding illegal? Does it hurt the customer? The competing firms? Other firms?

PROBLEMS AND SHORT CASES

12-1. The Billings Printing Company is preparing to bid for a contract to supply half a million brochures to a national mail-order company. The firm has calculated its incremental costs to be $50,000. Past experience with this type of contract has resulted in the following schedule, which shows the percentage of wins at each markup rate over incremental cost, for the past three years.

Markup Rate (%)	Contracts Won (%)
10	94
20	72
30	45
40	18
50	6

(a) Calculate the expected value of the contribution at each of the bid prices implied by the above markup rates.

(b) Interpolate between these rates to arrive at the markup rate, and bid price, that maximizes expected contribution from the contract.

(c) What assumptions and qualifications underlie your analysis?

12-2. Your company, Bright Paints, is one of several companies manufacturing a special reflecting paint used for traffic signs. Your two major customers are the state and the federal Departments of Transportation. The federal Department of Transportation has recently called for bids for 10,000 gallons of this special paint in a light blue, to be delivered within two months after signing the contract. You can foresee being able to fit in a production run of 10,000 gallons of the blue paint and have decided to bid on the job. This particular contract is absolutely standard, similar in all respects to hundreds of contracts you have bid on in the past two years.

Your pricing policy has always been to apply a markup to incremental cost to arrive at the bid price. Your markup has varied with the competitive situation perceived prior to each bid. You have assembled data on all past bids, relating the markup rate used to the percentage of times your bid was the winning one, as shown below. Incremental cost for this contract has been estimated to be $76,200.

Markup Rate (%)	Contracts Won (%)
0	95.9
10	84.8
15	65.4
20	41.3
25	15.7
30	3.0
35	0.2

(a) Why would your company have previously bid at zero markup over incremental costs? Why didn't it win all of those bids?

(b) What is the bid price that maximizes the expected contribution of the contract?

(c) Underlying your analysis is the assumption of *ceteris paribus*. Which things in particular must remain unchanged for your bid to be the optimal one?

(d) Why, or why not, is the fixed-price mode of bidding likely to be the best one to use for this contract?

12-3. The Esna Fabricating Company manufactures valves, faucets, and similar items under contract for various industrial and commercial clients. Whenever the company has no special jobs to do, it uses its labor force and plant to produce a line of faucets which it sells to a distributor for eventual sale in hardware stores. Esna can produce 5,000 of these faucets weekly, on average, and can sell them for $1.65 per unit, this representing a 50% markup over variable costs. This production is suspended whenever Esna wins a more lucrative contract, however. Esna is currently considering bidding for a contract to manufacture several very large pressure valves for use in the pulp-making industry. Esna has incurred $850 in expenses to acquire the detailed specifications for examination prior to submitting its bid. It has estimated the costs associated with this job as follows:

Direct labor (300 labor hours @ $20)	$6,000
Direct materials	8,650
Variable overhead expenses	4,270
Allocated overheads (150% of direct labor)	9,000

If the contract is won, Esna expects to incur another $2,500 for design costs before beginning manufacture of the valves, and the manufacturing process is expected to take 300 labor hours, or three weeks of the plant's time. No new direct labor will need to be hired for the job, since the regular labor force (diverted from faucet production) is expected to be sufficient to handle the job.

Esna's bidding policy is to mark up incremental costs of each job such that the expected value of contribution is maximized. An examination of the outcomes of over 300 jobs bid for in the past two years indicates that the probability of winning the contract is related to the ratio of the bid price to incremental cost, for each particular contract, in the following way:

$$P = 2.825 - 0.115R - 1.427R^2$$

where P is the success probability and R is the ratio of the bid price to the incremental costs of each job tendered for.

(a) What are the probabilities of winning the contract at markups of 10%, 15%, 20%, 25%, and 30%, respectively?

(b) What price should Esna submit?

(c) Outline any reservations or qualifications you may have concerning your recommended bid price.

12-4. Bids have been called for the fabrication of a steel watergate, and Stenson Steel is in the process of preparing to bid on this contract. The practice in your company has been to charge each contract with bid preparation costs of $2,000, which is actually about three times the actual value of time and office supplies spent on each bid but is costed this way because the company is the successful bidder only once in every three times it bids, on average. The bidding policy in the past has been to add a 15% margin to the incremental and allocated costs, and hence your colleague, a recent M.B.A. graduate from a rival university, insists that the appropriate bid price is $138,230, calculated as follows:

Bid preparation costs	$ 2,000
Direct materials	18,600
Direct labor	33,200
Variable overhead	14,400
Fixed overhead	52,000
Profit margin	18,030
Suggested bid price	$138,230

You are a little worried that conditions in the industry have deteriorated recently. You are aware that some of your competitors have been operating below capacity, and you suspect that demand for steel-fabricated products is likely to be depressed for the coming twelve months.

(a) What is the absolute minimum price you would bid on this contract? Explain and defend your answer.

(b) On the basis of the information given, what bid price would you recommend?

(c) What factors would you wish to investigate and evaluate before choosing the actual bid price?

12-5. Complete with newly-minted MBA in hand, you have joined Smithfield Re-Construction as Senior Pricing Analyst. Your first job is a bid-pricing problem. The Fitzwilliam Machinery Company has called for tenders on a contract to renovate one of their buildings. This job will involve gutting a building and reconfiguring the floor plan for new office space.

You have asked the accountant for the projected costs of completing the job. She has provided the following data, which she calls the "full costs" of the job:

Direct Labour	$320,000
Materials	480,000
Indirect Labour	160,000
Overhead allocation	320,000

Note that the contract should be signed within a month, and the winning bidder will begin construction within 2 months. The job should then take about 10 months to complete, and payment is made on completion. Your costs will be incurred more-or-less evenly over the 12 months, if you should win the contract. Your cost of capital is 14%.

You learn that your firm always bids on the basis of full costs plus a markup ranging from 10 to 30 per cent of full costs. Previous bidding on this basis has generated the following record:

Markup rate (%)	Contracts tendered for	Contracts won
10	14	10
15	10	6
20	11	5
25	10	3
30	10	1

(a) What is the present value of the incremental costs of this job?

(b) Calculate the expected present value of the contract at each markup rate.

(c) Choose the bid price that you believe will maximize the expected present value of the contribution to overheads and profit.

(d) Suppose that the above cost data are expected values representing a range of values in each case. Briefly argue the wisdom of bidding on a cost-plus or risk sharing basis.

(e) Outline all assumptions and qualifications that underlie your answer.

12-6. Your company, Canino Construction, has decided to bid on a government contract to build a bridge 50 miles from the city during the coming winter. The bridge is to be of standard government design and hence should contain no unexpected in-process costs. Your present capacity utilization rate allows sufficient scope to undertake the contract if awarded. You calculate your incremental costs to be $268,000 and your fully allocated costs to be $440,000. You expect three other companies to bid on this contract, and you have assembled the following information concerning these companies:

Consideration	Rival A	Rival B	Rival C
Capacity utilization	Near full	Sufficient slack	Very low
Goodwill consideration	Very concerned	Moderately concerned	Not concerned
Type of plant	Small and inefficient	Medium-sized and efficient	Large and efficient
Previous bidding pattern	Incremental cost plus 35–50%	Full cost plus 8–12%	Full cost plus 10–15%

Cost structure	Incremental costs exceed yours by about 10%	Similar cost structure to yours	Incremental costs 20% lower but full costs similar to yours
Aesthetic factors	Likes to utilize capacity fully	Doesn't like "dirty" jobs	Likes creative projects
Political factors	Decision maker has friends in government	Decision maker is seeking a new job	None known

Your usual bidding practice is to add between 60% and 80% to your incremental costs, depending on capacity utilization rate and other factors. What price will you bid (a) if you *must* win the contract or (b) if you wish to maximize the expected value of the contract? Defend your answers with discussion, making any assumptions you feel are supported by the information given or are otherwise reasonable.

12-7. Bids have been called for the construction of a turbine generator for the Milford Power Station. Your company accountant has examined the specifications and has established the following costs associated with the contract:

Bid preparation costs	$ 750
Direct materials	115,000
Direct labor	252,500
Specialized equipment required*	27,500
Variable overhead	42,000
Allocated overhead	86,750

*This equipment will not be purchased unless the contract is won. It will last for the fabrication of two more generators, should such contracts be forthcoming in the future, although there is no indication at this time that there will be a demand for any more generators like this one.

You are aware of three other companies that are likely to bid on this project. Relevant details are as follows:

Detail	Company A	Company B	Company C
Cost structure	Similar to yours	10% higher	10% lower
Previous bidding pattern	Incremental cost plus 60%	Full cost plus 15%	Full cost plus 40%
Current capacity utilization	Moderate	Very low	Near full

Your current capacity utilization is moderate, leaving sufficient capacity to handle this project. Your previous bidding practice has been to add 25% to full costs.

(a) What is the absolute *minimum* price you would bid on this contract?

(b) What is your *actual* bid price, on the basis of the information given?

(c) What other factors would you wish to consider or investigate before making your bid?

12-8. The City of Hudson has called for tenders for a private firm to supply toxic waste removal services. Your firm, Smalley Sanitation Services, already operates several household and industrial garbage routes under contract with Hudson and nearby cities, and is considering expansion into the toxic trucking business. The President of SSS has called for an internal study of the feasibility of tendering for this job. His sources indicate that the City expects to pay about $300,000 per annum for the service, since this was the value of a similar contract recently won by Garboli Transport, Inc. in a neighboring city.

Your accounting department has generated the following cost data relating to the Hudson contract for the 1987 year:

Direct Labor[1]	$ 50,000
Materials[2]	80,000
Indirect Labor[3]	10,000
Initial Training Program[4]	6,000
Modification of Vehicle[5]	30,000
Depreciation of Vehicle[6]	20,000
Insurance[7]	40,000
Repairs and Maintenance[8]	12,000
Allocated Overhead Expenses[9]	100,000

[1]Wage cost of two full-time driver/operators to be hired.

[2]Includes containers, safety clothing, neutralizing chemicals.

[3]The present manager's salary is apportioned 25% to this job.

[4]The two driver/operators and the manager must attend this program and become certified prior to bidding on the contract, since only "certified" firms are permitted to handle toxic waste, by state law.

[5]The truck must have these modifications made before the firm can be certified.

[6]The truck, now three years old, is being depreciated over five years at 20% each year.

[7]The firm's liability insurance premium will increase by this amount if the firm begins handling toxic waste.

[8]Projected expenses based on the past three years' experience.

[9]Allocated on the basis of 25% of the overhead burden, since the firm owns and operates four trucks.

SSS has one truck that is presently unutilized, since it recently lost contracts for several household garbage routes. (Several rival trash collectors have been expanding recently, and the bidding was considerably lower than SSS expected.) With only three trucks operating at the present time, SSS is just breaking even, and is looking for some way to become profitable again. For the Hudson contract, SSS expects Garboli and several other toxic waste disposers to bid. These firms are already certified to handle toxic waste, and their trucks are already modified to comply with state law.

(a) Which of the above cost items are incremental costs, and why?

(b) Should SSS go ahead and seek certification? Explain.

(c) After receiving certification, what price would you bid, if it was your decision? Why? How low could you go?

(d) What assumptions and qualifications underlie your decision?

12-9. The Primeau Prefabrication Company builds prefabricated cabins, homes, and industrial buildings for shipment and assembly at remote sites. They have enjoyed considerable success over the past several years as a result of their high-quality products and aggressive pricing strategy. Primeau has two main sources of its business. Private orders flow from its advertisements in Harrowsmith and other magazines for standard cabins and houses which are supplied from inventory. These are produced on a routine basis in the factory whenever more lucrative contracts are not forthcoming. Contracts are obtained from mining and construction companies, private parties requiring a non-standard cabin or house, and residential developers, who either call for tenders, or simply contact Primeau and ask for a quote on a particular job. Primeau's pricing policy is to ascertain the incremental costs of each job and apply a markup which is calculated to maximize the expected present value of contribution from each contract. The bidding record for the past three years is shown in Exhibit I.

EXHIBIT I   Bids Tendered and Won

Markup over incremental costs (%)	Bids tendered	Contracts won
0 - 10	18	18
11 - 20	32	30
21 - 30	68	53
31 - 40	46	25
41 - 50	22	6
51 - 60	8	1

Primeau's work force is currently engaged in the production of basic log cabins which sell for $12,000 at the factory door. This production will go to inventory and await orders. These cabins are being produced simply to keep the work force employed while waiting for more lucrative orders. The production costs of the basic log cabins are shown in Exhibit II. The figures refer to a four-week production period in which twenty (20) cabins would be prefabricated.

EXHIBIT II   Production Costs of Log Cabins

Materials	$ 23,500
Labor	118,000
Variable overhead	18,600
Fixed overhead	59,000

You have recently been hired as Assistant to the President, Mr. Primeau, as part of his reorganization of the company in response to its increasing size and success. Today he brings to your attention a call for tenders from Napier Mining. They want sixteen prefabricated buildings similar to those Primeau has supplied to various other mining and construction companies. Mr. Primeau says he is really interested in this contract because Napier has announced it will open another mining site within two years that will also require prefabricated buildings. He says that if you win this contract you have a 90% chance of being Napier's supplier for the second site as well, and this would bring a contribution of about $100,000, receivable about two years from now.

Your production department provides you with the cost estimates shown in Exhibit III and informs you that the Napier job will take about a month to complete. During this time production of the basic log cabins will be suspended while the plant's work force and equipment are utilized to finish the Napier job. The finance manager informs you that the firm's cost of capital is 12%. Mr. Primeau tells you that he has heard that rival prefabricators are also keenly eyeing the Napier job, but this is normal—the competition is no tougher or softer than it has ever been, he says. Your own information, gained from a friend working at Hilton Construction, is that Hilton is expecting Primeau to follow its usual bidding policy, and will choose its own bid price to just undercut the price it expects Primeau to set.

EXHIBIT III   Production Costs of Napier Job

Materials	$ 42,000
Labor	118,000
Variable overhead	36,000
Fixed overhead	59,000
New equipment required	12,800
Bid preparation costs	2,600

(a) What is the absolute minimum bid price you would consider for the Napier contract?

(b) What price would you bid if you must win this contract?

(c) What price would you bid to maximize the expected present value of contribution if you were unaware of Hilton's intentions?

(d) What price will you recommend to Mr. Primeau, all things considered?

(e) What assumptions and qualifications underlie your recommendations?

12-10. You are the newly hired vice-president of design and marketing at Bender Fender Automotive Design and Aerodynamics, Inc. Bender Fender has grown substantially in the past few years as a result of the quest by all automobile manufacturers for greater aerodynamic efficiency. Bender Fender is one of only about a dozen firms in the world with their own wind tunnels and the capability to design and build full-scale models for the world's automobile producers. These producers regularly contract out for new designs, and some of these designs eventually go into production.

The Ford Motor Company has called for tenders for a new design. The specifications are simple: the car must seat five passengers in comfort, use existing mechanical components for the most part, and have a coefficient of drag (C_x) less than 0.20. This is an exceptionally low C_x figure for a five-passenger car, and its design represents a real challenge. Undeterred by challenges, and with you as his right-hand person, Mr. Bender tells you to prepare a bid for the Ford contract. With the aid of the company accountant, you derive the following cost data:

EXHIBIT I   Costs Associated with the Ford Contract

Materials	$ 40,000
Direct labor	100,000
Variable overheads	60,000
Fixed overheads	40,000
New equipment	18,500
Bid preparation costs	5,000
Design costs	30,000

Design costs will only be incurred if the contract is won. These costs are uncertain and are shown in the table at their most likely value. Cost overruns or underruns are frequent, however, with the former being more likely. The accountant helps you construct the probability distribution of design costs from past experience, as follows:

**EXHIBIT II   Potential Variability
of Design Costs**

Costs	Probability
$50,000	0.10
40,000	0.20
30,000	0.50
20,000	0.15
10,000	0.05

The design and production of the model is expected to take a full year, with cost outlays being distributed more or less uniformly over the year. The firm's opportunity discount rate is 15%. Payment for the contract (the bid price) will be received in lump sum at the end of the first year. The firm's bidding practice over the past few years has been to mark up incremental costs by 30%, with adjustments to the markup rate to reflect current capacity utilization, profitability, foreseen future costs and revenues, opportunity costs, and so on. Mr. Bender says to bid at 30% over incremental costs this time because the situation is normal and there are no extraordinary features that are obvious to him.

You have been reading the trade association magazine, however, and know that if you win this contract and successfully design a car with C_x less than 0.20, you will be considered for the Automotive Designer of the Year award. To win this award would be a great boost to your career, and you think the probability of winning the award is 0.80 if you can achieve the specifications required by Ford. Moreover, if you win the award, you feel sure it will bring Bender Fender additional business in the following year, as indicated below. Assume that all cash flows relating to this future business are received and disbursed at the end of the second year.

**EXHIBIT III   Incremental Contribution
if Designer Award Is Won**

Incremental Contribution	Probability
$200,000	0.20
150,000	0.40
100,000	0.30
50,000	0.10

You ask Mr. Bender for the firm's records concerning past contracts tendered for. After weeding out those not related to automotive design, you have the following data:

EXHIBIT IV   Tenders Made and Contracts Won

Markup Rate (%)	Tenders Made	Contracts Won
10	20	16
20	60	45
30	160	96
40	80	32
50	50	4

(a) Calculate the minimum bid price, such that the expected present value of contribution from the contract would be zero, if won.

(b) Calculate the expected present value of contribution at each of the bid prices suggested by the markup rates shown above, and find the price which maximizes the EPVC.

(c) Consider all the issues, assumptions, and qualifications which underlie your analysis, and choose your bid price.

SUGGESTED REFERENCES AND FURTHER READING

ALPERT, M. I. *Pricing Decisions,* chap. 3. Glenview, Ill.: Scott, Foresman & Company, 1971.

EDELMAN, R. "Art and Science of Competitive Bidding," *Harvard Business Review,* 43 (1965), pp. 53–66.

EKELUND, R. B., JR., and R. F. HÉBERT. "Uncertainty, Contract Costs and Franchise Bidding," *Southern Economic Journal,* 47 (1980), pp. 517–21.

FRIEDMAN, L. "A Competitive Bidding Strategy," *Operations Research,* 4 (February 1956), pp. 104–12.

HOLT, C. A., JR. "Competitive Bidding for Contracts under Alternative Auction Procedures," *Journal of Political Economy,* 88 (June 1980), pp. 433–45.

KOTTAS, J. F., and B. M. KHUMAWALA. "Contract Bid Development for the Small Businessman," *Sloan Management Review,* 14 (Spring 1973), pp. 31–45.

KUHLMAN, J. M., and S. R. JOHNSON. "The Number of Competitors and Bid Prices," *Southern Economic Journal,* 50 (July 1983), pp. 213–20.

LIVESEY, F. *Pricing,* chap. 10. London: Macmillan, Inc., 1976.

MILLER, E. M. "Oral and Sealed Bidding: Efficiency versus Equity," *Natural Resources Journal,* 12 (July 1972), pp. 330–53.

OREN, M. E., and A. C. WILLIAMS. "On Competitive Bidding," *Operations Research,* 23 (November–December 1975), pp. 1072–79.

ROBERGE, M. D. "Pricing for Government Contractors," *Management Accounting* (June 1973), pp. 28–34.

ROERING, K. J., and R. J. PAUL. "An Appraisal of Competitive Bidding Models," *Marquette Business Review,* 21 (Summer 1977), pp. 57–66.

WALKER, A. W. "How to Price Industrial Products," *Harvard Business Review,* 45 (1967), pp. 125–32.

Chapter 13

ADVERTISING AND PROMOTIONAL DECISIONS

EXECUTIVE SUMMARY

In earlier chapters we considered price as the firm's strategic variable and considered the effectiveness of **price competition.** In some markets, however, we notice that the firms typically leave price alone and engage in **nonprice competition** through advertising and promotional expenditures.

Nonprice competition may be preferred over price competition for several reasons. First, price competition could deteriorate into a price war with losses for all or most firms. Second, nonprice competition may be preferred as a more suitable forum for competition because "any fool can cut prices, but it takes genius to conduct a successful promotional campaign." Third, firms may believe it is more difficult to raise prices again than it is to lower them in the first place, if they think they face a kinked demand curve. As we saw in Chapter 9, reducing prices may be expected to be a joint action along a relatively inelastic *mutatis mutandis* demand curve, whereas raising prices may be an independent action along a relatively elastic *ceteris paribus* demand curve, as rivals may have a profit incentive to hold price steady and gain market share.

Fourth, **some products are more suited to nonprice competition** than they are to price competition, and vice versa. Search goods, introduced in Chapter 10, are more likely candidates for price competition, while **experience and credence goods are best suited** to promotional competition, other things being equal, as the prospective buyer can less clearly see whether or not the quality claims made are indeed true until after purchase.

In this chapter we first examine **the advertising-sales relationship** under *ceteris paribus* conditions to see how sales might respond to advertising and promotional expenditures, given a price level. We subsequently **adjust price and advertising jointly** to find the optimal combination of these two strategic variables. We then consider the interdependence of advertising efforts, the prisoner's dilemma, the uncertainty of advertising's impact, and advertising as an investment.

13.1 OPTIMAL ADVERTISING EXPENDITURES UNDER *CETERIS PARIBUS* CONDITIONS

Throughout this chapter we shall, for simplicity of exposition, use the term *advertising* to include all elements of the promotional mix. The emphasis will be on the economics of the advertising and promotional decision, and we leave to the marketing practitioners the more specialized problems of media selection, message composition, promotional mix, timing, and pattern of promotional campaigns.

In Chapter 4 we saw that the firm's sales or demand level was a function of several controllable variables and a variety of uncontrollable variables. The controllable variables were later termed the firm's strategic variables and may be familiar to you as the marketing mix of price, promotion, product design, and distribution. Since the firm's sales are a function of these variables, it follows that the firm's profits are a function of these variables, and if the firm wishes to maximize profits it should adjust these controllable variables to the point where further adjustment would make no positive contribution to profits.

The Advertising-Sales Relationship

In Chapter 4 we held all other variables in the demand function constant while varying the level of price to find the influence on demand. Analogously, we shall now examine the effect of holding all other variables (including price) constant while varying the level of advertising. Thus demand will be equal to a constant (which represents the effect of all the other variables), plus some function of advertising expenditures. In the simple linear case:

$$Q = \alpha + \beta A \qquad (13\text{-}1)$$

where Q is the quantity demanded, α and β are parameters, and A is the level of advertising expenditure. Note that this equation implies that the marginal impact on sales for additional units of advertising expenditure (i.e., the parameter β) will be constant regardless of the level of advertising expenditure. More likely we would expect diminishing returns to advertising expenditures at higher advertising levels. Thus, the advertising function may be quadratic in form, such as

$$Q = \alpha + \beta_1 A + \beta_2 A^2 \qquad (13\text{-}2)$$

where β_2 would be a negative number if there are diminishing returns to advertising. Alternatively, it might be argued that initial levels of advertising may benefit from increasing returns, since certain threshold levels of advertising expenditure must be reached to afford certain types of media and to penetrate the buyer's consciousness. However, we would expect that these thresholds would be soon overcome and that diminishing returns would be expected to set in for higher levels of advertising expendi-

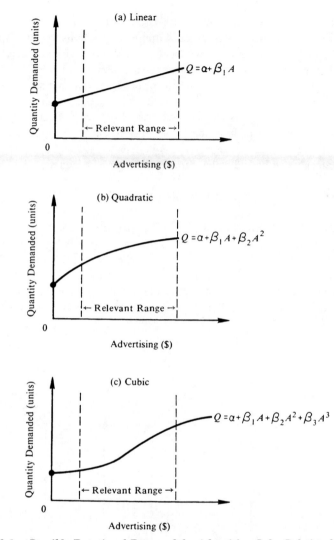

FIGURE 13-1. Possible Functional Forms of the Advertising-Sales Relationship

ture. Thus the general form of the advertising function for all levels of advertising might be expected to be cubic, such as

$$Q = \alpha + \beta_1 A + \beta_2 A^2 + \beta_3 A^3 \qquad (13\text{-}3)$$

where β_3 would be a negative number. These three types of advertising relationship are shown in Figure 13-1. Note that in all cases quantity demanded has some positive value (namely, the parameter α) when advertising is zero and that the general relationship between advertising and quantity demanded is positive. Clearly, we should not expect the relationship to be linear over a wide range of advertising levels, since this assumption neglects the probable occurrence of diminishing returns to advertising expenditures. Nevertheless, a linear advertising function may be a sufficient approximation of both the quadratic and the cubic functions over the relevant range of advertising expenditures.

The appropriate functional form of the advertising-sales relationship is of course the one that provides the best statistical fit to the data in a particular case. If a firm could be assured that *ceteris paribus* held for all other significant variables, or is able to observe the changes in these other determinants, and then varies its level of advertising over a period and observes the variations in demand, it could apply regression analysis to the data generated to find which form of the regression equation best fits the observed data.[1]

The Optimal Level of Advertising for a Given Price Level

You will recall from Chapter 4 that advertising expenditure is one of the variables that are held constant while a particular demand curve is being discussed. Changes in advertising expenditures cause a *shift* in the demand curve, causing it to move to the right when advertising expenditures are increased or to the left when expenditures are reduced. In Figure 13-2 we show the initial price and quantity coordinates as P_0 and Q_0 on demand curve D_0. Suppose now that advertising expenditures are increased

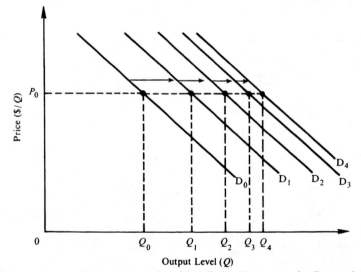

FIGURE 13-2.   *Impact of Increasing Advertising Expenditures on the Demand Curve*

[1]See, for example, V. R. Rao, "Alternative Econometric Models of Sales-Advertising Relationships," *Journal of Marketing Research*, 9 (May 1972), pp. 177–81; and V. K. Verma, "A Price Theoretic Approach to the Specification and Estimation of the Sales-Advertising Function," *Journal of Business*, 53 (July 1980), pp. S115–S137; and R. D. Carlson, "Advertising and Sales Relationships for Toothpaste," *Business Economics*, 16 (September 1981).

from their previous level by a given amount, causing the demand curve to shift to the right to that shown as D_1. Subsequent increases in advertising expenditures would be expected to shift the demand curve farther to the right, but if there are diminishing returns to advertising expenditures we should expect these subsequent shifts of the demand curve to become progressively smaller as advertising expenditures are increased by equal increments.

As advertising expenses are increased, total revenues derived are also increased, since at the given price level progressively larger quantities are demanded. If total revenues increase by more than the sum of the incremental cost of production and the increase in advertising expenditures, we must consider the increased advertising as beneficial if the firm's objective function is concerned with profits or sales levels. That is, increased profits will have been derived by virtue of the increased advertising expenditure, and the sales level will have been increased. Suppose the firm's objective is the maximization of contribution; the decision maker's problem is to increase advertising up to the point where the increase in total revenue just covers the increase in both the production and the selling costs that occasioned that increase in total revenues.

- EXAMPLE: To demonstrate this principle, let us suppose that the advertising function for a particular firm has been estimated as follows:

$$Q = 10,000 + 25.2A - 0.8A^2 \qquad (13\text{-}4)$$

where A represents advertising expenditures in thousands of dollars. The optimal level of advertising, using the marginalist approach, will be that level at which the last dollar spent on advertising contributes just one dollar toward overheads and profits. Thus the maximizing condition is

$$\frac{d\pi}{dA} = 1 \qquad (13\text{-}5)$$

where π represents contribution to overheads and profits. If we consider dA in one-dollar increments, the requirement for profit maximization, that is, $d\pi$, equals one dollar to cover the last dollar of advertising expenditure incurred. Note that to find $d\pi/dA$ we must first find how quantity demanded varies with advertising and then how profits vary with quantity demanded. That is, $d\pi/dA$ expands to

$$\frac{d\pi}{dA} = \frac{dQ}{dA} \cdot \frac{d\pi}{dQ} \qquad (13\text{-}6)$$

From equation (13-4) we can find dQ/dA by taking the first derivative of the estimated advertising function with respect to the level of advertising expenditures. Hence,

$$\frac{dQ}{dA} = 25.2 - 1.6A \qquad (13\text{-}7)$$

The second element on the right-hand side of equation (13-6), namely the change in contribution over the change in output, is in fact the contribution margin on the last unit produced. Thus we can express equation (13-6) as follows:

$$\frac{d\pi}{dA} = \frac{dQ}{dA} \cdot CM \tag{13-8}$$

Since the maximizing condition is to set $d\pi/dA$ equal to one, we may restate the maximization condition as

$$\frac{dQ}{dA} = \frac{1}{CM} \tag{13-9}$$

Supposing the contribution margin to be constant at \$6 per unit, by substitution from (13-7) into (13-9) we can solve for the optimal level of advertising as follows:

$$25.2 - 1.6A = \frac{1}{6}$$
$$151.2 - 9.6A = 1$$
$$-9.6A = -150.2$$
$$A = 15.646$$

Thus in the case where the advertising function is represented by equation (13-4) and the contribution margin is constant at \$6 per unit, the profit-maximizing level of advertising is 15.646 units, or \$15,646.

• NOTE: Where there are diminishing returns in production or a downward-sloping demand curve, we cannot expect the contribution margin per unit to remain constant regardless of output level, and hence we must specify the profit function in terms of total revenue and total costs such that we may accurately define the $d\pi/dQ$ term over all values of Q. A second problem arises where the advertising coefficient (dQ/dA) is estimated from a linear multiple-regression equation, in which case it will be the average of the marginal impact of advertising over the range of the data observations. Since we expect the marginal impact of advertising to decline as the level of advertising increases, the coefficient will overstate the effect of additional advertising at the upper end of the observations (where our interest will probably be) and should be used with caution for decision-making purposes.

Simultaneous Adjustment of Price and Advertising Levels

Where the firm is able to adjust both price and advertising, we should not expect the firm to wish to be constrained to a particular price level. The monopolistic competitor, for example, is able to adjust price without expecting retaliation from rival firms, and the

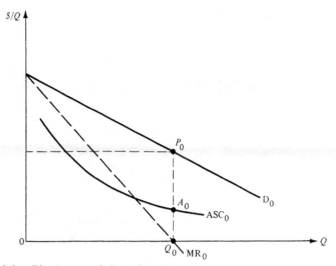

FIGURE 13-3. *The Average Selling Cost Curve*

monopolist has no rival firm's reactions to consider. Thus firms in these market situations may wish to adjust both prices and advertising levels simultaneously.

• NOTE: Advertising expenditures must be regarded as a fixed cost, since they are typically independent of the current level of output and sales. Thus the average advertising expenditures, or, more broadly, average selling costs, will be graphed as a rectangular hyperbola against the output level. In Figure 13-3 we show the average selling cost curve ASC_0 for a particular level of advertising expenditures, given a particular demand situation.[2] For simplicity we shall initially assume zero marginal costs. The intersection of the marginal revenue curve with the horizontal axis therefore indicates that the profit-maximizing or contribution-maximizing output level is Q_0, to be sold at price P_0. The relevant point on the average selling cost curve is the point labeled A_0, since this is the average selling cost level at output level Q_0. There is nothing in Figure 13-3 to indicate that ASC_0 is the *optimal* level of advertising expenditure. Larger advertising budgets will cause the demand curve to shift to the right but will also cause the average selling cost curve to move upward and to the right. To find the optimal level of advertising expenditure and the profit-maximizing price, we must know to what extent additional advertising expenditures will shift the demand curve.

In Figure 13-4 we show the results of increasing the level of advertising expenditure. Starting from the initial advertising level ASC_0, which gave rise to the optimal

[2]This analysis follows N. S. Buchanan, "Advertising Expenditures: A Suggested Treatment," *Journal of Political Economy*, August 1942, pp. 537–57. An alternate methodology is given by R. Dorfman and P. O. Steiner, "Optimal Advertising and Optimal Quality," *American Economic Review*, 44 (December 1954), pp. 826–36.

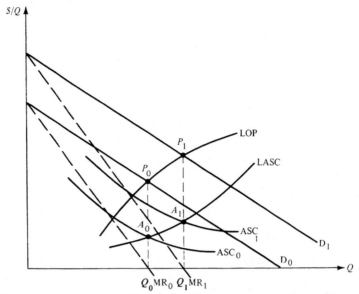

FIGURE 13-4. Optimal Prices for Successive Levels of Advertising Expenditure

quantity and price levels Q_0 and P_0, we suppose that advertising expenditure is increased to the level indicated by the curve ASC_1. This increase causes the demand curve to shift from D_0 to D_1. The new marginal revenue curve MR_1 cuts the horizontal axis at the output level Q_1, indicating a new profit-maximizing price level shown by the point P_1. At this output level, point A_1 indicates the average selling cost per unit.

By continuing this process we could trace a series, or locus, of optimal price points and a similar locus of average selling cost points. The locus of optimal prices for various levels of advertising expenditure is shown as the curve LOP in Figure 13-4, and the locus of the average selling costs for various advertising and demand levels is shown as the curve LASC. Each point on the LOP curve represents the optimal price-quantity combination on a demand curve relating to a particular level of advertising. (You have to imagine a series of demand curves, as in Figure 13-2 but not shown in Figure 13-4 for simplicity, that relate to a series of progressively higher advertising levels.) Similarly, each point on the LASC curve represents the advertising cost per unit of output at each optimal output level. Note that the assumption of diminishing returns to advertising expenditures is built into this model, and it is the reason for the LOP and LASC curves bending toward each other.

The LOP curve and the LASC curve in Figure 13-4 are both loci of a variable that represents an average—specifically, average revenue (or price) and average selling cost. Each of these average curves will have a curve that is marginal to it. In Figure 13-5 we show the LMR curve (locus of marginal revenue) as the curve that is marginal to the locus of optimal prices curve, and the LMSC curve (locus of marginal selling costs) as the curve that is marginal to the LASC curve. Note that the shape and placement of these marginal

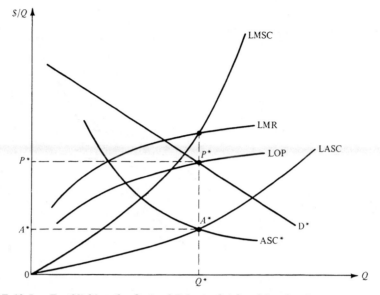

FIGURE 13-5. Establishing the Optimal Price and Advertising Levels

curves follow the general principles of the relationships between average and marginal curves. The decision maker's problem is to have the marginal increase in costs just equal to the marginal change in revenues. In this simple case, with zero marginal costs of production, the intersection of the LMSC curve with the LMR curve will indicate the output level at which the increment to revenues will be just equal to the increment to costs.

The optimal output level is shown as Q^* in Figure 13-5. There must be a demand curve crossing the LOP curve at that output level, and we show that demand curve as D^*. The optimal price level is thus P^*. Similarly, there must be an ASC curve crossing the LASC curve at output level Q^*, and we show this as ASC^*, which represents A^* dollars per unit of output at the optimal output level.

Having introduced this model in the simple context of zero production costs, let us now bring it closer to reality by incorporating positive levels of production costs. In Figure 13-6 the MC curve is added to indicate the marginal costs of production at all output levels. To maximize profits the firm must now expand the total of production and selling costs to the point where the change in these costs just equals the change in total revenues. To show the change in both production and selling costs for each unit of output we add vertically the MC and LMSC curves, and the resulting curve is shown as MC + LMSC in Figure 13-6. This combined marginal cost curve crosses the LMR curve at output level Q^*, indicating that the increment to total revenue is equal to the increment to *all* costs at this point. Thus the profit-maximizing price and advertising levels are P^* and A^* per unit, respectively.

- NOTE: The above approach assumes knowledge of the cost and revenue curves shown in the figures, as well as the underlying production, demand, and advertising functions. In

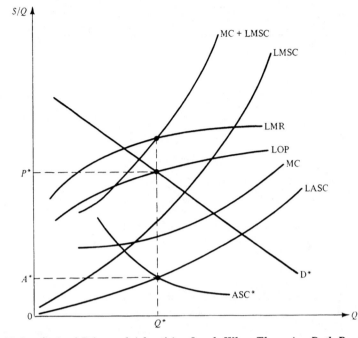

FIGURE 13-6.   Optimal Price and Advertising Levels When There Are Both Production and Selling Costs

practice, of course, it may be extremely difficult and expensive to ascertain the actual shape and placement of these curves. The model is nevertheless useful for its pedagogical and explanatory value, since it incorporates the notions of simultaneous adjustment of price and advertising levels, with the subsequent interaction of the "law" of demand and the "law" of diminishing returns to advertising. Note that in effect this model sets the same optimizing condition as in the earlier simple case where price was held constant; that is, the advertising is carried to the point where the increment to the total advertising cost is just covered by the increment to the total revenue derived from the sale of the marginal unit.

13.2   ADVERTISING AND PROMOTIONAL EXPENDITURES WHEN MUTUAL DEPENDENCE IS RECOGNIZED

In oligopoly markets the firm should recognize that its advertising and other marketing strategies will have a noticeable impact on the sales and profits of rivals, unless the other firms are simultaneously carrying out similar promotional campaigns. Unlike price adjustments, however, promotional campaigns require a significant lead time in which they must be planned and coordinated with the availability of time and space from the various advertising agencies and media channels. As a result, if a firm is caught napping by a competitor's new advertising campaign, there will be a significant lag before it can produce its own retaliatory campaign, during which time it may have lost a significant share of its market, which in turn may prove difficult or impossible to retrieve. The existence of this lag thus motivates firms to have an ongoing involvement in promotional activity. If there is always a new campaign in the pipeline, the firm does not expect to be caught napping to the extent that it would be if it waited until a competitor initiated a major new advertising or promotional campaign.

Advertising Interdependence

Given that firms tend to have continual advertising and promotional strategies, changes in market shares should be expected to occur only when the relative advertising and promotional effectiveness of firms is suddenly made different by an increase in the relative size of an individual firm's advertising budget or in the relative effectiveness of a firm's advertising expenditures.

- EXAMPLE: The advertising success story of 1984 was Wendy's hamburger restaurants' "Where's the Beef?" campaign. This campaign was so successful it helped increase the firm's fast-food sales revenues by 26% during that year. Prior to the campaign, the shares in the hamburger market were McDonald's, 41.5%; Burger King, 16.2%; Wendy's, 9.4%; and many others making up the remaining one third of the market. After the campaign Wendy's market share probably was about 12%, although the market may have expanded because of the barrage of competitive advertising that followed. A 26% increase in sales revenues translates into an extra $494 million over Wendy's 1983 sales of $1.9 billion. Wendy's spent $73.5 million on advertising during 1984, and of course their materials and labor costs were higher, but profit must have been enhanced considerably by that advertising campaign. Significantly, McDonald's spent about 3½ times as much on advertising, and Burger King nearly twice as much, yet these firms probably lost market share to Wendy's. (They may have held market share as a result of their counterpunching; that is, Wendy's gain in sales may have come largely at the expense of the smaller firms.) The point is that it is the *effectiveness* of the advertising, in addition to the magnitude of the expenditures, that translates into sales gains.[3]

The potential gains from a successful advertising campaign, and the benefits of larger advertising expenditures, may induce firms to continually increase their advertising budgets in search of competitive advantage. Suppose two large firms share the major part of a particular market and each budgets approximately $4 million toward promotional expenditures each year. In Table 13-1 we show the payoff matrix for the interaction of the firms' advertising strategies. When both firms spend $4 million, the net profits to each firm are $10 million. By convention, A's payoffs are shown first (followed by B's

---

[3]See "The Fast-Food War: Big Mac under Attack," *Business Week*, January 30, 1984, pp. 44–46; and *Wall Street Journal*, March 7, 1985, p. 35.

TABLE 13-1. *Payoff Matrix for Advertising Strategies*

		Firm B's Advertising Budget	
		$4 m.	$6 m.
Firm A's	$4 m.	10.0, 10.0	6.0, 12.0
Advertising Budget	$6 m.	12.0, 6.0	8.7, 8.7

payoffs) for each combination of promotional expenditure strategies. Suppose now that firm A contemplates increasing the promotional budget level to $6 million. If firm B maintains its promotional budget at $4 million, A's profits will rise to $12 million while B's profits will fall to $6 million. The result of A's additional $2 million promotional expenditures will be to cause a substantial proportion of the market to switch from firm B's products to firm A's products, with associated changes in the firms' relative profitabilities.

Conversely, if firm B considered increasing advertising levels to $6 million while firm A held its advertising constant at $4 million, it would be firm B that would benefit from the change in market share that resulted. Finally, if both firms increased advertising to the higher advertising levels, the result would be as shown in the lower-right-hand quadrant of the payoff matrix, namely that profits are reduced compared with the earlier levels of advertising expenditures. This result may be rationalized in terms of the market's becoming saturated by the products of the two firms, or we might conclude that the firms' competing messages to consumers tend to offset each other's effectiveness by creating "noise" in the communication process.

Given that the firms are likely to be risk averters and that there will be a significant lag before the firm can retaliate to an increase in advertising expenditures by the other firm, we might expect each firm to wish to avoid the worst possible outcome. Thus we may expect each firm to follow a maximin strategy. For each firm the worst outcome associated with the smaller advertising expenditure is $6 million profit, whereas the worst outcome associated with the larger promotional budget is $8.7 million profit. The best of these worst situations is the $8.7 million profit associated with the larger promotional expenditures. Thus the maximin strategy for each firm is to increase its promotional budget to the higher level.

In this example the firms have independently increased their expenditures in pursuit of private gain, but instead they find that the result is inferior to that which was enjoyed at the earlier promotional levels. The firms are subject to what has become known as the "prisoner's dilemma."

The Prisoner's Dilemma

• DEFINITION: The *prisoner's dilemma* situation arises when two or more parties are motivated to behave in a self-serving manner, and they assume that their rivals or adversaries will act similarly. The result is that the outcome to all parties is inferior to that which could have been attained if the parties had been able to assume that their rivals would not act in a way detrimental to them.[4]

- EXAMPLE: This situation is called the prisoner's dilemma after the supposed situation in which two bank robbers are caught with the proceeds of a robbery, but with no more than circumstantial evidence of their being involved in that robbery. Interrogated in two separate rooms, each is told that if he confesses and implicates the other he will go free as a "state's witness" while the accomplice will receive a substantial term in prison. Each prisoner knows that if they both refuse to confess they will receive a short prison term for possession of stolen goods, while if both prisoners confess, neither will be needed as a state's witness and both will receive relatively long jail sentences. Given the inability of the prisoners to communicate with each other (and since there is no honor among thieves), each will be motivated to avoid the worst possible outcome. Since the worst possible outcome is that of not confessing while the other does confess, the maximin strategy for each prisoner is to confess. Since each prisoner confesses, each ends up with a relatively long jail sentence, whereas if they had been able to communicate and coordinate their strategies they would have been sentenced to the relatively short prison term for possession of stolen goods.

The prisoner's dilemma thus applies to firms in situations of advertising rivalry. The lack of communication and coordination between parties with conflicting self-interest can lead to a situation in which both parties are worse off compared with the outcomes that would have been obtained had there been communication and coordination between those firms. Referring back to Table 13-1, had the firms agreed to limit their advertising expenditures to $4 million each, their net profits would have remained at the $10 million level. In pursuit of independent profit gains, however, and without knowing whether or not the other firm was simultaneously planning an increase in the promotional budget, both firms find themselves at a reduced level of profit.

Note that when both firms have increased their promotional budget to the $6 million level, there is no incentive for either firm to reduce the advertising budget independently, since doing so would lead to a loss of market share and net profits. Similarly, larger promotional budgets promise increases in net profit levels if they are undertaken independently. When each firm fears that the other may undertake a further increase in promotional expenditures, we have the prisoner's dilemma all over again, and both firms will be motivated to spend the additional amount on promotion so they will not be left standing still when the other's promotional campaign is launched.

Coordination of Advertising Expenditures

Is it reasonable to expect firms to coordinate their advertising and promotional expenditure levels? While firms may achieve an implicit agreement not to escalate advertising

---

[4]See R. D. Luce and H. Raiffa, *Games and Decisions* (New York: John Wiley & Sons, Inc., 1957), pp. 94–102; or F. M. Scherer, *Industrial Market Structure and Economic Performance* (Chicago: Rand McNally & Company, 1970), pp. 142–45 and 335–37.

budgets beyond present levels, it is unlikely that they will achieve agreement to reduce budget levels to a point that would seem to be more efficient in terms of total profitability. In part this reluctance is undoubtedly due to the distrust that a firm may feel about reducing its own advertising expenditures while rivals may not in fact reduce theirs. Given the lead time required to prepare additional promotional campaigns, a firm that double-crosses its rivals could gain a market share advantage that might be impossible to regain.

A second factor militating against the coordination of advertising and promotional competition is that these activities are seen as an appropriate forum for the competitive instincts of rival firms, an avenue for civilized competition that should not be closed to the firms. Promotional competition requires skill and planning and the services of talented people. Price competition, on the other hand, requires little planning and not much skill on the part of the instigator, yet the impact on the profitabilities of all firms may be significantly adverse. To avoid active competition shifting to the price arena, firms prefer to compete on a promotional level where gains in market shares and profits are the rewards for exceptional abilities on the promotional side.

13.3   UNCERTAINTY IN ADVERTISING

In the preceding section we have presumed that the firm can foresee the result of a given expenditure on advertising and promotion. In fact, $1,000 spent this month may be very effective in influencing the level of sales, whereas a similar amount spent next month may have virtually no impact. This outcome may be the result of differences in the qualitative aspects of the advertising campaign, a different media mix, autonomous changes in consumer tastes and preferences, or similar changes induced by concurrent advertising campaigns of rival firms.

The responsiveness of consumers to television advertisements has been linked to the weather. Research indicates that changes in the weather can reduce or boost consumer response to advertisements by 50 to 100%. Advertisements for Campbell's soups are strategically placed prior to and during winter storms. When a storm is predicted, Campbell's ads urge listeners to stock up on soup before the weather worsens. After the storm arrives, listeners are urged to stay inside and relax with a warm bowl of soup. Similarly, demand for breakfast cereal is more responsive to advertisements when there is cloudy weather, and demand for soda pop increases with wind velocity. (Don't ask me why.) Of course the demand for many goods is seasonal, but this variation in advertising effectiveness is on a day-to-day basis. In the summer, suntan oil advertisements are more effective on hot days than on cloudy days. Thus weather predictions have begun to determine the timing of advertisements, with media service firms monitoring weather predictions across the country and then advising their clients when and where to place their advertisements for maximum impact on sales.[5]

---

[5]See "Companies Look to Weather to Find Best Climate for Ads," *Wall Street Journal*, January 10, 1985, p. 29.

Predictability and Probabilities

Given the uncertainty surrounding the impact on sales of a particular advertisement, the firm may be able to estimate a probability distribution of outcomes that may be expected to follow the use of an advertisement in a particular region at a particular time. However, assigning the probabilities to the possible outcomes represents no small problem. The major issue is to predict the impact of the expenditures on the purchasing behavior of consumers, of course, but underlying this issue are the twin problems of understanding consumer needs and wants and predicting competitors' simultaneous offerings to satisfy these needs and wants.

To increase the probabilities of increased sales levels for a given level of advertising, the firm should have a sound knowledge, through market research, of what tangible and intangible features the buyers want to see involved in the product. The firm's advertising and promotional expenditures should then be directed to informing the buyers of the availability of these attributes in this particular product and to persuading the buyers that the desired attributes can be *best* obtained through purchase of this product. Similarly, if market research indicates that consumers are more receptive to the advertisements at some times than at others, this knowledge should influence the timing of the advertisement.

The existence of distinct market segments implies that products and promotion should be aimed at the appropriate segments of the overall market, where each segment is defined in terms of a common set of attributes desired by the buyers in that segment. The attributes that may be perceived and appreciated by consumers may be physically incorporated into the product (tangibles such as strength, durability, and other performance characteristics), or they may be intangibles that the consumer believes to exist (such as style, conferred status, and vicarious enjoyment of an agreeable life style). Different attributes will be stressed (or invented) in the advertising campaigns for different segments, and some part of the persuasive element of advertising may relate to those tangible attributes that cannot immediately be verified by the consumer, as well as to the intangibles.

Once the market research has been conducted to ascertain the attributes desired by consumers and the perception of these attributes in the product vis-à-vis the competitors' products, the choice of message, medium (or media mix), and timing will be selected by specialists in the advertising area and should be confirmed by pretesting and posttesting upon representative potential buyers. In summary, the better market research is able to identify the attributes desired by buyers, and the better the product and the advertising campaign conform to the desires of the target segment(s), the more confident the decision maker can be in assigning probabilities to the various possible outcomes of a given advertising expenditure.

Advertising as an Investment

The impact of an advertising campaign may not be felt simply in the period of that expenditure but should be expected to have a residual impact which gradually attenuates over subsequent periods. Potential buyers may be only partly convinced by a particular campaign, but the current campaign may build a necessary base for future persuasion. Alternatively, the campaign may convince consumers to switch to this product, but only after they deplete their personal inventories of rivals' products. Thus a dollar spent on advertising now may lead to revenues in the same period, plus a stream of revenues in future periods. In this respect advertising can be regarded as an investment project and should compete for funds within the firm on the same basis as other investment projects with multiperiod revenue streams.

The conditions for optimal advertising expenditure considered in the earlier sections of this chapter were generated under the implicit assumption that the total impact of the expenditure would be felt in the same period. This analysis remains sufficiently accurate if the residual impact of advertising expenditure is very low or if the time period used for analysis is long enough to include the greater part of the total impact. If there is a significant residual impact of advertising expenditures in subsequent periods, the present value of the future revenues generated must be included in the decision-making process. Current advertising expenditures may exceed the short-run profit-maximizing level to the extent of the present value of the future revenues generated, before we could say that the firm's longer-term objective of maximizing net worth was not being served.

Advertising to Raise Barriers to Entry

It is widely supposed that advertising and promotional efforts operate to raise or maintain barriers to the entry of potential competition.[6] Repeated messages concerning existing firms and their products are said to increase consumer loyalty to existing products and cause consumers to be reluctant to switch to the products of new entrant firms.[7] To convince consumers that their products have comparable quality, reliability, and other desirable features, the entrant firms may need to spend more on advertising and promotion at least over the first few years, as compared with the existing firms. It has been argued that the prospect of these additional expenses in an uncertain market for their products causes potential entrants to decide against entry because of the low or negative level of expected profits.

Thus high levels of advertising by existing firms in a particular industry might be expected to allow those firms to continue to earn higher than "normal" profits, since entry is not attempted (or successfully accomplished) because of the expectations (or actuality) of significantly higher cost structures for entrant firms. Various studies have been reported in which tests were made for the empirical relationship between levels of advertising and levels of profitability. The results of these tests tend to be ambiguous.[8]

---

[6]Following J. S. Bain, *Barriers to New Competition* (Cambridge: Harvard University Press, 1956), many economists have argued along these lines. For a comprehensive bibliography of earlier work, see D. Needham, "Entry Barriers and Non-Price Aspects of Firms' Behavior," *Journal of Industrial Economics*, 25 (September 1976), pp. 29–43.

[7]Notice that this argument involves the residual effects of past advertising and promotional efforts. It is the sum of these residual effects that operates to enhance consumer loyalty to existing firms' products.

[8]See the papers by Comanor and Wilson, Schmalensee, Peles, and Ayanian that are listed at the end of this chapter.

Another avenue of inquiry concerns advertising's function of imparting price and quality information which can be expected to increase competition rather than inhibit competition.[9]

13.4 SUMMARY

Advertising and promotional decisions within the firm are an important adjunct to the firm's pricing decision, and in some cases they become the firm's primary strategic variable. Advertising and promotional expenditures are expected to shift the demand curve outward and cause the price elasticity of demand to be reduced at any given price level. We expect diminishing returns to additional advertising expenditures as the marginal consumer becomes increasingly more difficult to convince and the market approaches saturation.

The optimal level of advertising expenditures is that level at which the incremental cost of advertising is just equal to the incremental net revenues associated with that expenditure. If these revenues extend beyond the current time period, they must be evaluated in present-value terms for comparability with the current advertising expenditures. The general (marginalist) rule for optimality expressed previously applies both to situations where price is held constant and to situations where price is adjusted simultaneously.

In practice, several problems inhibit the application of the marginalist rule for optimal advertising. First, *ceteris paribus* is not likely to hold in many market situations as rival firms simultaneously adjust their pricing and advertising strategies. Second, the impact of advertising expenditures cannot easily be predicted with any great degree of accuracy. This unpredictability in turn is due to the uncertainty as to what potential buyers want and whether or not the selected message and media will effectively inform and persuade the buyers that this particular product best provides the desired attributes.

In oligopoly situations the level of advertising and promotional expenditures may be taken to excess because of the uncertainty facing the decision maker concerning the simultaneous actions of rivals. Even when the future impact of advertising expenditues is taken into account, oligopolists unable or unwilling to coordinate their advertising strategies may be expected to spend beyond the point where profits (short- or long-term) are maximized. They must continue to run to stay in the same place, since any unilateral reduction in advertising expenditures would cause them to lose some part of their market share and would reduce the present value of their future profit stream.

Advertising and promotional expenditures tend to generate a stream of future revenues as new customers finally purchase the product and current customers return to purchase more units in the future. To the extent that advertising raises barriers to entry, it also helps to avoid loss of sales to potential entrants in future periods. Advertising and promotional expenditures may therefore be considered as an investment in future reve-

---

[9]See "A New View of Advertising's Economic Impact," *Business Week*, December 22, 1975, pp. 49 and 54.

nues, and they should therefore compete with other investment projects for the funds available.

DISCUSSION QUESTIONS

13-1. Under what conditions may a firm expect *ceteris paribus* conditions to hold for changes in its advertising and promotional expenditures?

13-2. Discuss the idea of a minimum threshold of advertising and promotional effectiveness. Is it reasonable to argue the existence of such a threshold?

13-3. Why should we expect diminishing returns to (eventually) apply to advertising and promotional efforts? Outline several reasons.

13-4. What is the rule for optimal advertising expenditure in the short run, given price and average variable cost levels? Explain.

13-5. Outline the process underlying the simultaneous selection of the optimal level of advertising and the optimal price.

13-6. Why do oligopolists face a prisoner's dilemma problem when it comes to deciding on the level of advertising expenditures?

13-7. If firms decided to limit their advertising expenditures to a given amount, would market shares then remain stable at the present levels? Why or why not?

13-8. Outline the issues involved in attempting to predict the impact of an advertising or promotional campaign.

13-9. If there are residual impacts in future periods from this period's advertising expenditure, is it necessarily excessive to spend beyond the point where short-run incremental cost of advertising exceeds short-run incremental revenue from advertising?

13-10. Outline the issues involved in the argument that advertising and promotional expenditures raise the product differentiation barriers to entry. Would these barriers exist without advertising? Why?

PROBLEMS AND SHORT CASES

13-1. The Thompson Textile Company has asked you for advice as to the optimality of its advertising policy with respect to one of its products, product X. The following data are supplied:

Sales (units)	282,500
Advertising elasticity of demand	2.50
Price per unit	$ 2.00
Marginal cost per unit is constant at	$ 1.00
Advertising budget for product X	$ 56,000

(a) Is Thompson's advertising budget for product X at the profit-maximizing level?

(b) If not, can you say how much more or less it should spend on advertising? Discuss all relevant issues and qualifications you think are important.

13-2. The McWilliams Bottling Company bottles and markets under license a major brand-name soft drink. Prices of soft drinks are virtually dictated by the market and the preponderance of dispensing machines that require a time-consuming adjustment in order to allow price changes to be effected. In the regional market that it serves, McWilliams has noticed that quantity demanded responds to variations in the level of advertising and promotional expenditures. The firm has kept the following records of sales (units) and advertising and promotional expenditures over the past two years:

Last Year	*Sales (units)*	*Advertising/ Promotion ($)*
1st quarter	96,000	3,400
2nd quarter	103,000	4,350
3rd quarter	93,000	3,750
4th quarter	111,000	5,900
Preceding Year		
1st quarter	90,000	2,600
2nd quarter	76,000	1,850
3rd quarter	104,000	5,200
4th quarter	120,000	7,300

McWilliams's present advertising and sales (units) levels are $4,000 and 99,500 units. Contribution margin (per unit) is considered to be constant at $0.22. The marketing department at McWilliams feels that there were no significant changes in any factors that would prevent the above data from being used to reliably estimate the firm's sales/advertising function.

(a) Plot the sales data against the advertising expenditures and sketch in what appears to be the line of best fit to the data.

(b) Please advise McWilliams as to the estimated optimal level of its advertising and promotional expenditures. Explain and defend your recommendation.

13-3. Flintrock Fixtures is a small partnership that produces and markets a variety of kitchen and bathroom fixtures in ceramics, metal, and marble. The market for these products in Flintrock's area is not highly competitive, since the rival firms tend to compete in separate market segments of the fixtures market. Over the past year, one of the major partners, Charles Flint, has been experimenting with advertising and promotional levels to ascertain the impact of this variable on sales. Regressing monthly sales revenue against monthly advertising and promotional expenditures, Mr. Flint has obtained the following regression equation: $TR = 110,482.5 + 2318.6A - 103.2A^2$, where TR represents sales revenue in dollars and A represents advertising and promotional expenditures in thousands of dollars. This equation was derived from data ranging from $1,000 to $8,500 spent per month on advertising and promotion. ($R^2 = 0.99$, significant at the 1% level.) The present level of advertising and promotional expenditure is $6,000 per month, and Mr. Flint, who wishes to maximize sales revenue, wishes to increase this expenditure to $7,500 per month, which is the maximum that Rocky Spinelli, the other major partner, will agree to.

A minor partner in the enterprise, Peter Pebble, is concerned with the short-term profits of the enterprise. He argues that given the firm's pricing policy of marking up average variable costs by 100%, monthly profits would be increased significantly by reducing advertising and promotional expenditures. Mr. Pebble argues that a reduction of at least $2,000 per month would augment profits considerably.

Another minor partner, John Stone, argues that the longer-term profitability of the enterprise is the appropriate objective to pursue and that he supports Mr. Flint.

(a) What level of expenditure on advertising and promotion would maximize monthly sales revenue, given no limit on this level? How confident are you about the accuracy of this prediction? Explain.

(b) What level of expenditure on advertising and promotion would maximize monthly profits? Explain.

(c) Make an argument to support Mr. Stone's position.

(d) Presuming Mr. Stone to be correct in his reasoning and Mr. Pebble to be outvoted, what do you suggest Flintrock do?

13-4. Record Breakers is a downtown store selling compact disks (CDs) and tapes. Its nearest competitor is about six blocks away, and its clientele is composed almost entirely of downtown office workers and other personnel from nearby buildings. Record Breakers has found that the sales of tapes vary with the number of tapes it places on special at $3.99 (compared with the regular price of $6.99) and with the space purchased in the city's morning newspaper for advertising these specials. The specials are intended to attract customers into the store where they will (it is hoped) also purchase one or more other tapes or CDs at the regular price. The greater the number of specials offered, the lower the total revenue per tape, or average price of the tapes sold. Given any specific number of tapes on special, the store finds that tape sales vary positively, but with diminishing returns, with the area devoted to advertising these particular tapes in the newspaper. Regression analysis indicates that

$$Q = 624.3 - 216.52P + 481.8S - 35.85S^2$$

where Q represents the weekly sales (units) of tapes; P is average price in dollars; and S is space units (100 square inches daily for five days) in the morning newspaper. This regression equation is highly significant and explains virtually all the variation in weekly record sales.

The average variable cost per tape is constant at $3 and space units in the newspaper cost $300, and this space is available in continuously variable fractions of a unit. The average situation is that Record Breakers will place six tapes on special and buy 2.5 units of advertising space each week. This combination causes the average price to be $5.75 over all tapes sold. The relationship between average price and number of tapes on special has been estimated as $P = 6.93 - 0.19 NS$ where NS is the number (of tapes) on special. This relationship holds independently of the units of advertising space purchased, although the latter does influence volume, as indicated by the earlier regression equation.

(a) Using graphical analysis, find the level of average price and the level of advertising space purchased that allow short-run profit contribution to be maximized.

(b) How many tapes should be put on special each week? Explain.

13-5. Vincenzo Pizzeria Limited operates the only pizza place in town although there are several other fast-food outlets in peripheral competition with Vincenzo. The manager, Vincenzo Fiorelli, feels that he has a virtual monopoly, since his clientele is largely comprised of fervent pizza lovers, and that selling more pizzas is just a matter of inducing people to eat out more often. Consequently Mr. Fiorelli holds prices constant and advertises in local newspapers and on a local television. His pizzas come in three sizes and with a variety of toppings, from plain (tomato paste and cheese) all the way up to deluxe (mushrooms, peppers, olives, ground beef, pepperoni, and heaps of mozzarella cheese).

Mr. Firorelli's son Paolo has recently obtained his business degree and has joined the family business as marketing manager. Paolo is interested in maximizing profits of the enterprise, since his father has promised him half of any extra profits generated as a bonus. Paolo decides to conduct an analysis of the cost and demand conditions facing the firm. First he examines the cost structure. Given the three different sizes of pizza and the various combinations of toppings, the firm is in effect offering a very broad product line. Paolo's first task is to convert all the product offerings into the terms of a common denominator, which he calls a medium-pizza equivalent (MPE). The weights attached to each product reflect the relative variable costs of that product. Thus a medium-deluxe pizza is equal to 1 MPE, a small-deluxe pizza is equal to 0.75 MPE, and a large-deluxe is equal to 1.5 MPEs, with lower weights given in each size category where the pizza is less than deluxe. The average variable cost of an MPE is $2.65, and Paolo finds this to be constant in the relevant output range. The first major decision Paolo makes is to standardize prices on all pizzas by marking up the average variable cost by 50%.

The marketing manager then undertakes a study of demand conditions. After examining past records and interviewing a random sample of 500 customers and potential customers, Paolo generates the following demand function for Vincenzo's pizzas:

$$Q = 28105.1 - 5842.2P + 1061.6A - 22.5A^2$$

where Q is the number of MPEs demanded per month; P is the price of an MPE in dollars; and A is the advertising and promotional expenditures per month in thousands of dollars.

At present, prices are as indicated by the above markup-pricing policy, and advertising and promotional expenditures are running at the rate of $8,000 per month.
(a) Using graphical analysis (with algebraic confirmation of results), find the optimal price and advertising/promotional levels.
(b) How much will Paolo's monthly bonus be? (State all qualifications and assumptions, if any, underlying your answers.)

13-6. The Silk Purse Cosmetics Company operates in close competition with several other major suppliers of cosmetics and toiletries. In this market, consumers do not seem to be very price conscious: If they believe a product will help them, they tend to buy that product as long as its price lies below a limit that the consumer considers intolerable. Consequently, Silk Purse and its rivals tend to compete through their advertising and promotional expenditures, which are typically aimed at informing consumers of the virtues of their new and established products. Silk Purse's advertising and promotion budget is $25 million for this year, and it estimates that its rivals will collectively spend about $100 million this year. Silk Purse's net profits are projected to be $2.8 million this year.

The vice-president of finance is worried that the expected profits this year will not be high enough to support the continuation of Silk Purse's research and development program, given that dividends, taxes, and managerial bonuses must be paid out of profits. He suggests that a reduction of advertising to around $20 million would cause the profit situation to improve.

The vice-president of marketing argues that a reduction in the advertising budget to $20 million would cause sales to drop by $10 million, meaning a $1.7 million dollar reduction in net profits. On the contrary, she says, Silk Purse should increase advertising and promotional expenditures to $30 million. This action will increase sales by $8.5 million and net profits by $1.2 million.

The president of Silk Purse, M. C. Hogg, fears that an increase in advertising and promotional expenditures of this magnitude will very likely cause a competitive reaction from the major rivals. You are called in to advise Mr. Hogg.
(a) With the aid of a payoff matrix, explain the vice-president of marketing's argument to Mr. Hogg .
(b) How does Mr. Hogg's assessment of the situation differ from that of the marketing vice-president?
(c) What information would you encourage Mr. Hogg to obtain for making his decision?

13-7. The automobile-manufacturing industry has three major domestic producers, one minor and several minuscule domestic producers, and several major foreign producers, each supplying vehicles to the North American market. Advertising and promotional expenditures constitute a large part of the competitive effort in this industry, once the product design and price levels have been determined for each model year. With a major purchase like an automobile, the potential purchaser must feel confident about the quality of the vehicle, the efficacy of after-sales service, and the future value of the automobile at trade-in time. Advertising campaigns typically stress these factors and are also aimed at reducing postpurchase dissonance and building brand loyalty.

Suppose you are the advertising manager of one of the very small domestic auto producers. Your company's sales have been hovering perilously around one-fortieth of one percent of the entire market. Your advertising budget is $1.5 million, and your projected net profits before taxes are less than $5 million. Your advertising budget represents 10% of sales revenue, compared with an industry average of 7.5%. Net profits are low, largely because of your relatively short production runs, which do not allow overheads to be amortized over large output levels.

(a) Prepare an argument to convince the marketing vice-president that your advertising budget should be increased. Include counterarguments to his probable objections in your proposal.

(b) Outline the information you would want the marketing research department to obtain before planning your major campaigns for this year.

13-8. Concord Microwave Systems, Inc., manufactures and markets radar detectors. Their original product, the Diplomat, had been the industry standard of excellence for several years, until their new miniaturized version, the Ambassador, was introduced three years ago. This smaller version now sets the standards that the other manufacturers try to meet. Sales have been strong from its introduction, but the management of Concord is considering whether or not the advertising budget should be increased. They currently spend only $180,000 per annum, mostly in auto magazines, on advertising and promotion. They prefer to keep a relatively low profile rather than stir up opposition to radar detectors. Nonetheless, they feel that they could increase their advertising budget by about a third without raising significant opposition to their product.

Based on monthly sales and advertising data collected over the past two years, Concord's marketing research department has estimated the sales-advertising function for its miniature radar detector to be $Q = 49{,}973.4 + 16.111A - 0.0115A^2$, where Q represents units of quantity demanded and A represents thousands of dollars spent on advertising. The price has been $295 ever since the introduction of the Ambassador model, and its average variable cost of production has stabilized at $200 per unit regardless of volume produced, within reasonable limits. Concord's total fixed costs amount to $2.5 million per annum, excluding advertising.

(a) Calculate the current output, total revenue, and total profit levels based on the sales-advertising function.

(b) What is the profit maximizing level of advertising?

(c) Calculate the output, revenue, and profit levels that Concord might expect if advertising expenditure was adjusted to the profit-maximizing level.

(d) State any assumptions and qualifications that underlie your analysis.

13-9. Meghan Alexandra Perfumes, Inc., manufactures a product line of exotic perfumes which are marketed worldwide. Sales of this perfume have been very strong, approaching a quarter of a million ounces in each of the first two years. Based on quarterly sales and advertising data, Meghan has estimated the dependence of sales volume on advertising expenditures as follows:

$$Q = 52{,}833.98 + 248.358A - 0.0491A^2$$

where Q is ounces of the perfume and A represents thousands of dollars spent annually on advertising. For the current year the advertising budget has been set at $950,000, over the objections of the marketing vice-president, who feels that it should be substantially higher than that. Meanwhile, others in the strategy group claim that it is already too high and simply wasteful. The wholesale price of the perfume is $9.99, and the marginal cost of production is constant at precisely one third of that. Overheads allocated to this product amount to $400,000 per annum, not including the advertising expenditure.

(a) At the planned level of advertising, and given the same price and cost situation, what will be the quantity demanded and the total profit for this line of perfumes?

(b) What is the profit-maximizing level of advertising expenditures?

(c) Is there a significant gain in revenues and profits available by adjusting advertising expenditures to a higher level?

(d) What assumptions and qualifications underlie your answers?

13-10. Andrew Evans, Inc., produces and sells toys for babies and toddlers, and the firm enjoyed considerable success in the past few years as the post-World War II "baby boomers" made their own baby boom in the late 1980s. Sales nationwide edged past the $4 million mark last year, and this year the president of Andrew Evans has set aside $1 million for advertising, up from $750,000 last year. The firm sells a variety of products, but it is a sufficient approximation to think in terms of an average product with an average price of $16 and marginal cost constant at $8 per average unit. The firm's overheads are $800,000 per annum, excluding advertising.

Market research has culminated in the following estimate of the firm's sales-advertising function:

$$Q = 110,386.3 + 298.674A - 0.10537A^2$$

where Q represents the units of the average product and A represents thousands of dollars spent on advertising.

(a) Calculate the expected sales volume and total profit given an advertising budget of $1 million.

(b) Calculate the profit-maximizing level of advertising expenditure.

(c) At that level, what would sales volume, revenue, and profit be?

(d) What reasons can you think of for supporting the president's decision to spend $1 million on advertising?

SUGGESTED REFERENCES AND FURTHER READING

AYANIAN, R. "Advertising and Rate of Return," *Journal of Law and Economics*, 18 (October 1975), pp. 479–506.

BRUSH, B. C. "The Influence of Market Structure on Industry Advertising Intensity," *Journal of Industrial Economics*, 25 (September 1976), pp. 55–67.

CLARKE, D. G. "Sales-Advertising Cross-Elasticities and Advertising Competition," *Journal of Marketing Research*, 10 (August 1973), pp. 250–61.

COMANOR, W. S., and T. A. WILSON. "The Effect of Advertising on Competition: A Survey," *Journal of Economic Literature*, 17 (June 1979), pp. 453–76.

CUBBIN, J. S. "Advertising and the Theory of Entry Barriers," *Economica*, 48 (August 1981), pp. 289–98.

DORFMAN, R., and P. O. STEINER. "Optimal Advertising and Optimal Quality," *American Economic Review*, 44 (December 1954), pp. 826–36.

ECKARD, E.W., JR., "Competition and the Cigarette TV Advertising Ban," *Economic Inquiry*, 29 (January 1991), pp. 119–33.

——— "Advertising, Competition, and Market Share Instability," *The Journal of Business* (October 1987), pp. 539–52.

FREIDMAN. J. W. "Advertising and Oligopolistic Equilibrium," *Bell Journal of Economics*, 14 (Autumn 1983), pp. 464–73.

GISSER, M. "Advertising, Concentration and Profitability in Manufacturing," *Economic Inquiry*, 29 (January 1991), pp. 148–65.

HOLT, CHARLES, and ROGER SHERMAN. "Advertising and Product Quality in Posted-Offer Experiments," *Economic Inquiry*, 28 (January 1990), pp. 39–56.

KOTLER. P. and G. ARMSTRONG. *Marketing Management* (5th ed.), chaps. 16–18. Englewood Cliffs. N.J.: Prentice-Hall, Inc., 1991.

LABAND, DAVID N. "The Durability of Informational Signals and the Content of Advertising," *Journal of Advertising*, 18 (March 1989), pp. 13–18.

LEFFLER, K. B. "Persuasion or Information? The Economics of Prescription Drug Advertising," *Journal of Law and Economics*, 24 (April 1981), pp. 45–74.

NEEDHAM, D. "Entry Barriers and Non-Price Aspects of Firms' Behavior," *Journal of Industrial Econonics*, 25 (September 1976), pp. 29–43.

NELSON, P. "The Economic Consequences of Advertising," *The Journal of Business* (April 1975), pp. 213–41.

NERLOVE, M., and K. J. ARROW. "Optimal Advertising Policy under Dynamic Conditions," *Economica* (May 1962), pp. 129–42.

PELES, Y. "Rates of Amortization of Advertising Expenditures," *Journal of Political Economy*, 79 (September–October 1971), pp. 1032–58.

PRIMEAUX, W. J., JR. "An Assessment of the Effect of Competition on Advertising Intensity," *Econonic Inquiry*, 19 (October 1981), pp. 613–25.

RAO, V. R. "Alternative Econometric Models of Sales-Advertising Relationships," *Journal of Marketing Research*, 9 (May 1972), pp. 177–81.

SCHERER, F. M. *Industrial Market Structure and Economic Performance* (2nd ed.), chap. 14. Chicago: Rand McNally Company, 1980.

SCHMALENSEE, R. "Advertising and Profitability: Further Implications of the Null Hypothesis," *Journal of Industrial Economics*, 25 (September 1976), pp. 45–54.

——— *The Economics of Advertising*. Amsterdam: North-Holland Publishing, 1972.

——— "Advertising and Entry Deterrence: An Exploratory Model," *Journal of Political Economy*, 91 (August 1983), pp. 636–53.

SIMON, J. L. *Applied Managerial Economics*, chap. 7. Englewood Cliffs, N.J.: Prentice-Hall, Inc., 1975.

SPENCE. A. M. "Notes on Advertising, Economies of Scale, and Entry Barriers," *Quarterly Journal of Economics*, 95 (November 1980), pp. 493–507.

TELSER, L. "Advertising and Competition," *Journal of Political Economy*, (December 1964), p. 537.

WIGGINS, S. N., and W.J. LANE. "Quality Uncertainty, Search, and Advertising," *American Economic Review*, 73 (December 1983), pp. 881–94.

Empirical Case 10

ESTIMATING THE ADVERTISING-SALES FUNCTION FOR PEPSI-COLA

Firms in the soft drink industry typically rely on nonprice strategies to gain market share. Few can forget the failure of New Coke—Coca Cola's decision to reformulate the popular soft drink it had successfully marketed for almost 100 years was met with a negative consumer reaction. Within the industry, this strategy appeared to intensify the so-called cola wars, in which the major players, Coca-Cola and PepsiCo, battle for top position in this multibillion-dollar industry. Advertising strategies are the main weapon in their arsenal, as they spend millions of dollars in an attempt to maintain or gain market dominance.

You decide to investigate the relationship between market share and advertising expenditures for PepsiCo from 1977 to 1987. In an attempt to explain this relationship accurately, you propose to test two alternative functional forms for your model. One functional form is linear, and the other is a quadratic, expressed as follows:

Linear: $\quad$ MKTSHR $= a_0 + a_1$ADEXP

Quadratic: $\quad$ MKTSHR $= a_0 + a_1$ADEXP $+ a_2$ADEXP^2

where MKTSHR represents PepsiCo's market share and ADEXP equals the firm's real advertising expenditure. The parameters a_0, a_1, and a_2 must be estimated with the aid of a statistical regression software package.

Table 1 presents the data you have collected. Estimate the above models and use your results to answer the following questions.

QUESTIONS

1. Given your statistical results, which functional form appears to best fit the data? Explain.

2. What are some of the assumptions necessary to support your conclusion to question 1?

3. Using the quadratic function, provide an estimate of PepsiCo's optimal level of advertising expenditures.

4. Given the optimal level of advertising expenditures, what does the model predict PepsiCo's market share will be? How confident are you with this prediction? Explain.

TABLE 1: *PepsiCo's Market Share and Advertising Data*

Year	Market Share (%)[a]	Real Advertising Expenditures ($ million)[b]
1977	22.3	41.41
1978	23.3	45.69
1979	24.2	58.02
1980	24.4	60.65
1981	26.1	53.54
1982	28.1	63.59
1983	28.3	71.24
1984	28.7	86.48
1985	29.8	132.45
1986	30.6	205.74
1987	30.8	216.95

[a]Percent of U.S. soft drink consumption.
[b]CPI-adjusted advertising expenditures.

Source: From Standard & Poor's *Industry Surveys for Food, Beverages & Tobacco*, various issues.

Chapter 14

PRODUCT QUALITY AND COMPETITIVE STRATEGY

EXECUTIVE SUMMARY

The four P's of marketing, namely price, promotion, product quality, and place of sale, are the firm's four main strategic variables. Having considered price and promotion in earlier chapters, we now consider **the firm's product quality decision.** Indeed, the place-of-sale decision can be analyzed in this context as well, since product quality refers to the presence or absence of desirable attributes in the product, and from the buyer's point of view place of sale translates to convenience of seller location, which is an attribute the buyer typically does consider in the purchasing decision.

In preceding chapters we took the design of the product for granted and considered its optimal price and advertising budget. We now step back and consider the design of the product and the quality that may or may not be incorporated into the product. **Quality should be seen as a vector of product attributes,** rather than a single-dimensional scale. Attributes such as durability, pleasing shape, functionality, and so on, can be **incorporated into a product at the design stage** to determine the quality of the product. Note that quality, like beauty, is in the eyes of the beholder. Unless potential buyers perceive the quality that is designed into the product, it might as well not exist—hence the scope for informative advertising.

Just as in the preceding chapter we were able to consider the joint determination of price and advertising, in this chapter we shall consider **the joint determination of quality, price, and advertising.** We do this in the context of Michael Porter's generic **competitive strategies,** known as *cost leadership* and *differentiation*. A competitive strategy must include decisions jointly taken as to the product's design, price, and promotion (and place of sale).

14.1 THE GENERIC COMPETITIVE STRATEGIES

We shall consider product quality, as well as the joint determination of quality, price, and advertising, within a framework introduced by Michael Porter in his two recent books *Competitive Strategy* and *Competitive Advantage*.[1] In short, Porter contends that the firm should choose a well-defined "competitive strategy" to achieve "competitive advantage." A competitive strategy will include a combination of values for the firm's strategic variables (in this case limited to quality, price, and advertising) that best serves the firm's objective.[2] The firm's objective, Porter contends, should be the attainment of a "competitive advantage." Competitive advantage is evidenced by the firm earning greater profit than others in its industry, not just momentarily or occasionally, but on a continuing basis. This superior and *sustained* profitability will, of course, serve to maximize the firm's net worth. Although these superior profits may attract the attention of potential entrants, Porter argues that achieving competitive advantage operates to inhibit entry of new firms, and if entry does occur, the firm is insulated from competition from entrants to a large degree, and in any case holds an advantage over the other firms in competing against any entrants.

Porter identifies three generic competitive strategies. (Generic means that they can be pursued in any market.) One is the "cost-leadership" strategy, where the firm strives to be the lowest-cost supplier and thus achieve superior profitability from an above-average price-cost margin. A second strategy is the "differentiation" strategy, where the firm strives to differentiate its product from rivals' products, such that it can raise price more than the cost of differentiating and thereby achieve superior profitability. Finally, there is the "focus" strategy, whereby the firm concentrates on a particular segment of the market and applies either a cost-leadership or a differentiation strategy. We shall consider each generic strategy in turn and examine the implications of each for product design, pricing, and advertising.

The cost of information to consumers (when they attempt to evaluate the quality of the product) is a major determinant of the optimal competitive strategy. This issue was introduced in Chapter 10 and was later discussed in the context of new products in Chap-

---

[1]Michael E. Porter, *Competitive Strategy: Techniques for Analyzing Industries and Competitors* (New York: The Free Press, 1980); and *Competitive Advantage: Creating and Sustaining Superior Performance* (New York: The Free Press, 1985).

[2]Marketers, who call this combination of strategic variables the "marketing mix," would go into much more detail than we do here. See Philip Kotler and Gary Armstrong, *Principles of Marketing* (fifth edition) (Englewood Cliffs, N.J.: Prentice Hall, 1991), esp. chaps. 1–18. At this point it is instructive to note the different roles of economists and marketers: Economists construct models to investigate the underlying principles and determining variables involved in the pricing, advertising, and quality choice decisions. By their nature these models are abstractions from reality, and the marketer will find them lacking as a tool for choosing the price, advertising, or quality level in a specific instance. But if the economist has provided guidance as to which variables are important and to the optimal relationships between those variables, then the marketer's task, of pricing a specific product in a specific market, will be made easier by the models of economists. See Thomas Nagle, "Economic Foundations for Pricing," *Journal of Business*, 57 (January 1984), pp. S3–S26. This paper from a symposium involving both economists and marketers indicates that rather than jealously protecting their turf, many economists and marketers are recognizing that they have much to learn from each other that will make them better economists and better marketers.

ter 11. Essentially, products can be categorized as search, experience, or credence products, based on the difficulty and expense that a typical consumer faces when attempting to evaluate the quality of the product. In a nutshell, search products are typically prime candidates for a cost-leadership strategy, whereas experience and credence goods are typically best marketed using a differentiation strategy.

Nevertheless, within any market the firm has a choice of a cost-leadership, differentiation, or focus strategy; its selection will also depend on the strategies already adopted by its rivals. For example, in a market for experience goods one or more firms may have significant product differentiation advantages, leaving cost leadership as the optimal strategy for the firm to pursue in that market to attain competitive advantage. Or, in a market for search products, one or more of the other firms may be competing vigorously for cost leadership, and the firm's best strategy may be to adopt a focus strategy, differentiating its product to best serve a particular segment, or niche, of the market, for example.

14.2 PRODUCT DESIGN FOR A COST-LEADERSHIP STRATEGY

The strategy of cost leadership requires the firm to seek the position as the lowest-cost firm in the market or, at least, one of the low-cost producers. It may achieve cost leadership by vigorously promoting sales to benefit from the learning effect in production, economies of plant size, or pecuniary economies (quantity discounts for buying materials in larger quantities). To keep costs at a minimum, the firm will also need to continually incorporate the latest technology into its production process. Sales can be promoted both by promotional pricing and by advertising, of course, so the cost-leadership strategy has implications for the price and advertising strategies of the firm. What implications does it have for the product design strategy, or quality decision, of the firm?

To answer this question, let us first consider the circumstances under which a cost-leadership strategy is likely to be the firm's optimal competitive strategy. We can discuss these under two main headings: when the product is a search product and when the role of cost leader is vacant or may be usurped, regardless of product type.

Search Products and the Cost-Leadership Strategy

- DEFINITION: *Search products* are products containing primarily attributes that are readily discernible by consumer information-search activity, and these *search attributes* form the basis for the consumer's purchasing decision. Weight, length, and color are search attributes, but so too are attributes that can be found out for the asking. For example, the attributes of stereo equipment, like the signal-to-noise ratio, the presence or absence of the Dolby noise reduction system, and the power per channel in watts, can be ascertained (and compared with rival products) given relatively little search cost on the part of the consumer. Similarly, the attributes of primary interest to a person wishing to take an airline flight, such as time of departure, type of aircraft, number of stops en route, meals, and movies, can be found out simply by asking a travel agent or the airline check-in person.[3]

Since search products are easily evaluated by consumers, they are easily *compared* by consumers. Consequently, if a firm's product does not measure up to the competition, it will not retain its market share at a similar price level. The firm must compensate for the lack of desired attributes by reducing the price, or it must proceed to redesign the product such that it is more competitive on the basis of quality. As a result, the firm will feel pressure to emulate the best-selling rival products to produce a product that has all the features other products have and does all the things that rivals' products do, since a product that is inferior will readily be identified as such by consumers and quickly lose sales to superior products.

If competition from rival firms forces suppliers to match each other's search attributes, differentiation may still take place on the basis of any experience or credence attributes that are also embodied in the products. Brand names, better service, longer warranties, more convenient locations, and so on will be used to differentiate the products, but these attributes are, by definition, not the major ones considered in the consumer's purchase decision in the case of search goods. Rather, they are minor but nonetheless significant considerations in the purchase decision. Typically, however, the opportunities for differentiating search goods are relatively limited or ineffective, since consumers' attention is directed mainly to the search attributes of the products. Thus search products will tend to be clustered closely together in attribute space, with relatively little product differentiation across competing brands.

In Chapter 9 we introduced the term *symmetric differentiation* to describe product differentiation when the firms' market shares are equal at equal prices. Essentially, each product is different, but so too are consumers' preferences. Some products have an advantage in one or more attribute dimensions, appealing to some consumers, and other products are superior in other attribute dimensions, appealing to other consumers, such that each seller attracts an equal number of the available buyers at a given price.

To the extent that the market for a search product approaches symmetric differentiation, we should expect the firm to find advertising relatively ineffective in persuading consumers that its product is substantially different from those of its rivals, because consumers can readily evaluate the differences for the most part, and the firms have a profit incentive to keep the quality of their products competitive. In general, the responsiveness of demand to changes in advertising will be relatively low. In other words, the advertising elasticity of demand is relatively low for search products.

Price elasticity of demand, on the other hand, will be relatively high for search products, since consumers know exactly what they are getting and leap at the chance to buy the product at a lower-than-normal price. A price reduction will distinguish the firm's product from rival products and will capture many consumers from rival sellers if

---

[3]See Philip Nelson, ''Information and Consumer Behavior,'' *Journal of Political Economy*, 78 (March–April 1978), pp. 311–29.

rivals do not react to the price reduction by similarly reducing prices. In Chapter 10 we saw that promotional pricing will work particularly well with search products.

If rivals do not match price reductions, demand will be more elastic than if they do, and even if they do match price cuts, demand will be more elastic for search goods than for experience or credence goods. When rivals match price reductions, they tend to do so with a lag, since time passes before the price cut is discovered, before the decision to match the price cut is made, and before this information is communicated to potential buyers, such that the firm initiating the price adjustment benefits from a relatively elastic demand response initially that may make the price cut worthwhile. Given the profit incentive to reduce prices, the general price level is likely to tumble downward to a level close to the firms' unit cost. We saw in Chapter 10 that the more price elastic demand is, the lower the profit-maximizing markup rate will be. Thus we expect to see relatively low markups (price-cost margins) in the market for search goods.

In such a market, where persuasive advertising is relatively ineffective and price competition keeps prices down near to the level of the firms' unit cost, competitive advantage (superior profitability) can be obtained only by having a lower cost structure than the other firms. If the firm has a cost advantage, it need not fear rivals cutting their prices below *its* costs, because its costs are lower than rivals' costs, and rivals will not wish to make a loss on any product (temporary "loss leader" situations aside). Thus a cost-leadership strategy is likely to be the best strategy for search products, other things being equal.

When the Cost Leader Position Is Vacant

If the cost leader role is vacant or if it may be wrested from the present cost leader, the firm's best competitive strategy may be to assume that role, even in markets for experience and credence goods. As discussed in Chapters 10 and 11, experience goods are those containing mainly attributes that the consumer can only evaluate after purchase, such as the taste of food or the musical quality of a concert. After experiencing the quality of the product, the buyer will store this information in memory and will use it as the basis for the purchasing decision the next time. Credence goods contain mainly attributes that are imperfectly evaluated even after purchase, so the credibility of the seller, the brand name, and the firm's public image and reputation become important elements in the consumer's purchasing decision.[4]

If all rival firms are pursuing a differentiation strategy, their products will tend to be spread out over attribute space, and the firm may foresee considerable difficulty in competing on the basis of experience or credence attributes. It may take years for the firm's brand name to acquire the intangible qualities held by rival firms' brand names. The best retail locations, such as in high-class shopping areas, may all be taken. The better taste of a certain food product may be due to an ingredient or a recipe that is

---

[4]Credence goods were suggested by Michael R. Darby and Edi Karni, "Free Competition and the Optimal Amount of Fraud," *Journal of Law and Economics*, 16 (April 1973), pp. 67–88.

unavailable to the other firms. (Note that Kentucky Fried Chicken and Coca-Cola each claim their "secret recipes" are responsible for their "better taste.")

Faced with these impediments to effective product differentiation, the firm should consider a cost-leadership strategy. If it can achieve significantly lower cost levels, the firm may then choose either to follow another firm's price leadership and quietly enjoy superior profitability or to assume the role of price leader itself. Because learning effects, economies of plant size, and pecuniary economies are related to increased sales volumes, it will typically serve the low-cost firm's objective to be one of the lower-priced firms if not the price leader.

Porter cautions that attempting to usurp the cost-leadership role is fraught with danger, since it may culminate in vigorous price competition with the established cost leader(s). Particularly in the markets for experience and credence products, which may be expected to exhibit less elastic demand responses to price reductions, an attempt to displace the cost leader may cause prices to fall well below the profit-maximizing level, and thus profit will be less than anticipated. Essentially, the firm should be cautious about attempting to be the cost leader, unless there is currently no relatively low-cost firm, or unless the existing cost leader is in a vulnerable position, assuming in both cases that cost reduction opportunities exist. The current cost leader may be vulnerable, for example, if it has not incorporated a major new cost-saving device and is prevented from doing so by its financial limitations.

The Implications of Cost Leadership for Product Design

A cost-leadership competitive strategy has three main implications for product design. First, the firm's product must "cover the bases" that are covered by other products offered for sale in the market at similar prices. To be considered to have similar quality for a similar price, the firm's first concern is that it at least emulate other products available to the consumer at each quality-price level. If the firm has a line of products, as discussed in Chapter 10, this consideration applies at each price-quality point it contests. We should expect a cost leader's product line to be confined to the basic, lower-priced, lesser-quality products, since we might expect more limited demand for the higher-price-and-quality products and thus fewer opportunities for cost reduction through learning, economies of plant size, and purchasing components in large quantities.

Second, to reduce costs the cost leader should "trim the fat" from its products. That is, it should trim each product down to the bare essentials required at each price-quality level and not oversupply the attributes at each quality level. For example, if consumers regard the acceptable minimum horsepower of a small car to be 75, then 75 horsepower is all the cost leader's product should have. Other firms, following differentiation strategies, may wish to incorporate more horsepower in their products, but the cost leader's competitive advantage is best served by simply meeting the minimum requirements.

Third, the cost leader may see fit to engage in product proliferation, which is the production of several competing products under different brand names. This strategy follows from the tendency of search products to be symmetrically differentiated. If they are, each brand name garners a $1/n$ share of the market at equal prices, where n is the number of competing brand names. If a firm brings out a second brand name its sales will be a $2/(n + 1)$ share of the market, which is larger than $1/n$ of the market. Even if product differentiation is not symmetric, there may be gains in overall market share from product proliferation.

• EXAMPLE: Proctor and Gamble has followed the product-proliferation strategy with laundry and kitchen detergents and soaps. General Motors has several different brand names of essentially the same product (Chevrolet, Buick, Oldsmobile, and Pontiac). Breweries produce rival brand-name beers, in anticipation of capturing a larger share of the market. Increasing its overall share of the market should allow the firm to benefit from economies of plant size, pecuniary economies (purchasing in greater quantity), and learning curve effects, culminating in lower unit costs of production and marketing, and hence superior profitability.

Pricing and Advertising Strategies to Complement Cost Leadership

In conjunction with a cost-leadership strategy we should expect to see the firm periodically use promotional-pricing and informative-advertising strategies. In between its promotional-pricing campaigns we might expect the firm to assume the role of price leader. Let us discuss each of these briefly.

Promotional pricing, introduced in Chapter 10, involves placing the product temporarily "on sale" to stimulate its sales. If the firm is the cost leader it can better afford this strategy, since its profit margins may still be acceptable at the "sale" prices. Higher-cost firms will be less inclined to use promotional pricing, since it may reduce their profit margins to less-than-acceptable levels. Thus they will tend to use it less often, and will less likely respond to the low-cost firm's "sale" with a matching price reduction. The low-cost firm may therefore expect a more elastic demand for its product than it would have if rivals' costs were similar.

Advertising will be necessary to inform potential buyers that the product is being placed on sale, to remind buyers of the quality features of the product, and to inform buyers where the product is available at the sale price. Such *informative* advertising is often little more than a picture of the item with a price attached, perhaps including the regular price for comparison, and perhaps also including a few words and numbers specifying features of the product.

Since search products tend to be more or less symmetrically differentiated, there is little to be gained from *persuasive* advertising—that is, attempting to persuade buyers to switch products on the basis of some feature that is only slightly better than that of competitors. Persuasive advertising that relates to experience and credence attributes would be more effective, but these attributes carry only a small weight in the buyer's purchasing decision for a search product. Thus the lack of important experience or credence attributes and the lack of strong differentiating features that can be advertised effectively mean that advertising messages for search goods are primarily informative, rather than persuasive. Since informative advertisements can be shorter and require only the facts (rather than the imagery, expensive art and camera work, and hired "celebrities" of persuasive advertising), advertising expenditures for search products will be less than for experience or credence products, other things being equal.

Finally, whether or not the cost leader periodically engages in promotional pricing, we should expect it to seek the price leadership role to set price at the level which best serves its own objectives. The low-cost-firm price leadership model, introduced in Chapter 9, is appropriate for the short-run profit maximizer. If the firm's time horizon extends beyond the short run, the sales-maximizing model (subject to a minimum profit constraint) or one of the limit-pricing models, also introduced in Chapter 9, may be appropriate, depending on the height of the barriers to entry, as discussed in Chapter 11.

14.3   PRODUCT DESIGN FOR A DIFFERENTIATION STRATEGY

Michael Porter speaks of the "value chain," the series of activities within a firm that serve to create value for the customer. Each link in this chain, from the technical excellence of the design to the courtesy of the people involved in after-sales service, must be nurtured, since weak links in the value chain operate to negate competitive advantage. Value for the customer may be achieved by means of a good basic product produced at low cost and sold at a low price (cost-leadership strategy) or by means of a more expensive product that more closely fits the customer's needs. In the latter case the firm's objective is to raise the value of the product to the consumer by more than the cost of production and selling is raised, and this objective is the essence of the differentiation strategy.[5]

Other popular authors have also advocated what may be construed as a differentiation strategy. Peters and Waterman's *In Search of Excellence* and the follow-up by Peters and Austin, *A Passion for Excellence*, contain elements of the same advice to managers.[6] In brief, they say that managers should pay particular attention to what consumers think and feel about the firm's product and strive to meet those needs. These authors contend that there are two essential ingredients in the firm's plan to create and sustain superior profit performance over the long term. First, it must take exceptional care of its customers, through superior service and superior quality. Second, it must constantly innovate to stay ahead of its rivals as they strive to emulate its successes. We shall find this advice to be particularly appropriate for the firm that follows a differentiation strategy.

Quality Leadership

The differentiation strategy effectively amounts to competition on the basis of quality, where *quality* is being used as a synonym for the presence of desirable attributes. To

---

[5]See Porter, *Competitive Advantage*, chap. 2.

[6]Thomas J. Peters and Robert H. Waterman, Jr., *In Search of Excellence: Lessons from America's Best-Run Companies* (New York: Warner Books, 1982); and Thomas J. Peters and Nancy Austin, *A Passion for Excellence: The Leadership Difference* (New York: Random House, 1985). For a summary report on the latter, see *Fortune*, May 13, 1985, pp. 20–32.

make the sale to any particular buyer, the product must offer the buyer greater quality relative to price than rivals' products offer, given that the buyer's reservation price is less than the asking price. Superior customer service, both point-of-sale and after-sale service (including warranty and repair work), noted by Peters, Waterman, and Austin, is simply another dimension (desirable attribute) of what we mean by quality. Innovation, which of course has implications for cost reduction, also has implications for quality, since new features must be discovered and incorporated in the firm's product to allow it to remain ahead of, or at least abreast of, its rivals.

In a sense, the firm adopting a differentiation strategy seeks to be the quality leader, at least in the eyes of its customers. It seeks to offer the target buyer the most quality for the price. Although a buyer might feel that another firm offers the best product (for example, Mercedes-Benz), the buyer may settle for something less than the best (for example, a Toyota) because of his or her reservation-price structure. In the buyer's price-quality range the product chosen is the one that offers the most quality for the price. Thus, although there may be an acknowledged quality leader in the market, each firm strives to be a quality leader in a more limited segment of the market. Recall that the relevant perception of quality is in the eyes of the beholder. This statement implies that marketing research—as well as listening to what customers say about the firm's product, its salespeople, its warranty service, and so on—should be the necessary first step for a differentiation strategy.[7]

Differentiation on the Basis of Search, Experience, and Credence Products

Differentiation is only effective if at least some buyers believe that there is a significant and desirable difference between the firm's product and the product offerings of rivals. These differences may be real or imagined, tangible or intangible. The differences and the similarities that exist will relate to the perception of attribute content in the firm's product, vis-à-vis the attribute content of rivals' products.

If consumer search costs (to evaluate the attributes that are of primary importance in the purchasing decision) are relatively low, we call the products search products. If the firm's product has a definite superiority over rivals' products in its search attributes, buyers will quickly recognize this fact, and many buyers will shift their allegiance to the quality leader. Rival firms will be motivated to match these attributes as soon as they can, and the gains will be relatively short-lived. Nonetheless, there are gains to quality leadership in search attributes, since the firm that is always one step ahead of the pack will be continually gaining sales at the expense of inferior substitutes.

Experience and credence products offer substantially more opportunities for the quality leader. Recall that these are products for which the consumer's purchasing decision is based largely on experience and credence attributes, respectively. Experience attributes, like taste, music quality, and product durability, cannot be evaluated before purchase, but having once purchased the item the consumer gains information that will form the basis for evaluating the product in the future. Credence attributes, like restau-

---

[7]See Peters and Waterman, *In Search of Excellence*, esp. chap. 6.

rant service, the taste of cat food, or the competence of doctors, lawyers, and other professionals, also cannot be evaluated prior to purchase, and even after repeated trials of the product the buyer is not sure about the product quality, either because it may vary next time (like restaurant service) or because it can be only imperfectly evaluated (like cat food and professional services).

Since consumers cannot completely evaluate these products prior to purchase, or even after repeated trials in the case of credence goods, there is more latitude for claims concerning the product's quality. Does Coke taste better than Pepsi? One thing is for sure, some people will prefer one, and others will prefer the other, since tastes differ. The producer's task is to engineer the taste in such a way as to enlarge the firm's market share.

- EXAMPLE: In 1984 the Coca-Cola Company was suffering sluggish growth for its main product, Coke. Pepsi's sales grew at more than 7% per annum, compared to a lackluster 3% for Coke, after Coca-Cola had decided to increase the amount of high-fructose corn sweetener and reduce the amount of sugar in Coke. (Sugar was selling for 31 cents per pound, compared to about 24 cents per pound for the corn sweeteners.) Pepsi had campaigned successfully on the basis of televised taste tests and had gained market share from Coca-Cola. On April 23, 1985, Coca-Cola announced the introduction of Cherry Coke and the replacement of regular Coke with a new Coke that had a ''smoother'' taste and had been overwhelmingly preferred in blind taste tests (involving 190,000 people) over the 99-year-old Coke. Turmoil followed. Pepsi issued a hastily produced advertisement implying that even Coca-Cola now agreed that Pepsi tasted better than Coke. People stockpiled the old Coke, while New Coke sales faltered. In July 1985, Coca-Cola announced it would bring back the old Coke, renamed Classic Coke, reversing its earlier decision in the face of unexpected pressure from consumers and bottlers. Whether it was a marketing blunder or not is debatable. The publicity surrounding the entire event was worth millions, and Coca-Cola had three products in the market competing against Pepsi where it previously had only one. In September 1985 the company announced that the combined sales volume of Cherry Coke, New Coke, and Classic Coke for July and August were 10% above the sales volume for Coke in the same months of 1984. This increase no doubt represented a market share gain at the expense of Pepsi, but analysts felt that both Coke and Pepsi will gain market share from smaller rivals, such as RC Cola and Dr. Pepper, as a result of the intensified advertising rivalry between the two larger firms.[8]

The soft drink market is a good example of competing firms each following differentiation strategies. Within the sugar-based cola segment, Classic Coke, Pepsi Cola, RC Cola, and other minor contenders battle for supremacy, each claiming better taste. Then there is the diet cola segment, the uncola segment (Sprite and Seven-Up), and the ''different'' tastes of Cherry Coke and Dr. Pepper. In the diet cola segment, claims and counterclaims are made concerning the taste and the possible health risks of the artificial

---

[8]See *Wall Street Journal,* December 13, 1984, p. 8; February 9, 1984; April 24, 1985; September 10, 1985, p. 8; and ''Coke's Man on the Spot,'' *Business Week,* July 29, 1985, pp. 56–61.

sweeteners used. The absence of caffeine is lauded as a superior feature. Note, however, that the type of sweetener and the absence of caffeine are search attributes, and the pioneering firms were quickly emulated by rivals after initially advertising these as distinguishing features of their product. Taste remains the pivotal issue in this market. Note also that celebrities (Bill Cosby for Coke and Michael Jackson for Pepsi) were instrumental in the advertising war between Coke and Pepsi, being used to confer credibility on the advertising claims that are not easily verifiable.

Brand-Name Advantages

When products contain experience or credence attributes that are important in the consumer's purchasing decision, consumers often look to the brand name of the item as an assurance of quality. A firm's brand name can be regarded as a "stock of information" that has been built up by the firm in the past. It includes information concerning the experience and credence attributes in products purchased under that brand name on previous occasions, information gleaned from advertisements as to current quality attributes, the image of the firm as community conscious or environment conscious, a benevolent employer, and so on. Some brand names are better than others, in terms of the level of quality that they imply will be found in a product, but all are the sum total of the firm's previous efforts to build up its brand-name recognition and quality image.

When a firm has an established brand name, it can introduce a new product or a new version of an existing product, and consumers will feel they already know something about the product's quality and will be more likely to purchase the product than if it were the same product introduced by a firm with a lesser brand name. This increased probability of purchase, which derives from the greater information stock embodied in the brand name, is what we mean by brand-name advantage. When a product has a brand-name advantage, other firms will have to offer a "compensating price differential," meaning a lower price, to compete effectively with that firm.

- EXAMPLE: ReaLemon, a well-known brand name for processed lemon juice, was priced 10 to 15 cents per quart above the prices of Golden Crown and other lesser-known brands of processed lemon juice in the late 1970s. Borden, Inc., producer of ReaLemon, was prosecuted by the Federal Trade Commission for conspiring to monopolize its market through predatory pricing. Borden had reduced the price of ReaLemon to a level that served to force its rivals' prices below their costs. (Rivals had to set their prices 10 to 15 cents lower to compete.) This practice was also argued to restrict new entry, since new firms would have an even greater brand-name disadvantage. Whether or not Borden was fairly treated by the courts is not the issue here. Rather, the point is that the information content of the ReaLemon brand name was apparently worth a price premium of about 25 percent. If Borden had avoided this predatory pricing charge, it might have been able to enjoy superior profitability on a sustained basis as a result of its differentiation strategy.[9]

---

[9]See Clement G. Krouse, "Brand Name as a Barrier to Entry: The ReaLemon Case," *Southern Economic Journal*, 51 (October 1984), pp. 495–502.

When buyers pay a price premium for a well-known brand, they are effectively paying an insurance premium to assure themselves of product quality. The consumer could avoid the premium by buying a lower-priced product with a lesser-known or unknown brand name, but at the same time the buyer would bear a greater risk of quality variation. As noted in Chapter 10, if the cost of information exceeds the price premium, the buyer may use the higher price as an indicator (or assurance) of higher quality.

Having established a brand-name advantage, the firm's asking price can be higher than its rivals', and its costs are likely to be higher as well, given that higher quality typically costs more than lower quality and that part of the brand-name advantage will derive from a relatively high level of advertising expenditures emphasizing experience and credence attributes. If the firm is able to raise price by a greater amount than cost per unit is raised by the expenses of differentiation, it will have gained a competitive advantage in the market.

The firm could conceivably cheat its customers by reducing its quality below what has come to be expected from that brand name. Thus its costs would be reduced but its price would remain at the premium level. This strategy would increase profit for only a short while, however, because the information content of the brand name will deteriorate, and it will no longer command a premium price. Firms have an incentive to maintain the quality of their brand-name products, since future sales depend on the quality of products sold today. The firm's brand name is, in effect, a forfeitable ''bond'' that the firm stands to lose if it does not follow through with its implicit promise to maintain the quality level of its products. Firms having the most invested in a brand name will have the most to lose by cheating on quality and thus will be less likely to cheat, other things being equal.[10]

Implications of Quality Leadership for Product Design

Several implications for product design arise from the preceding discussion. First, the differentiating firm must design products that *better serve the buyer,* in that buyer's price range. Thus research into the wants and needs of target consumers, as well as feedback from existing users of the product, should be sought and then incorporated into the product's design. Prototypes of the new product or new version of the product should be constructed, tested, and exposed to consumer clinics or market tests before being put into full-scale production. A differentiating firm must have an ongoing research and development program, from which product advancements will emanate for market testing and to which ideas for product improvements will be directed from the various sources within the firm that may collect information concerning consumer preferences. These would

---

[10]See Krouse, ''Brand Name as a Barrier,'' pp. 498–99. Conversely, the firm will have an incentive to dissipate the information content of its brand name if the firm's planning period is shorter than the time it takes for consumers to substantially depreciate the value of the brand name. Thus, if the firm or manager has a very short time horizon or if information transmission among consumers is relatively slow and repeat purchases are relatively infrequent, then dissipating the firm's brand-name advantage may be the EPV-maximizing strategy. Credence goods would be more likely than experience goods, and experience goods more likely than search goods, to suffer brand-name dissipation.

include market research, the service department, customer complaints, public relations departments, and so on.

There are two implications that follow from this first point. Since the tastes and quality demands of buyers differ, the firm should consider *offering a product line,* with products strategically placed at intervals along the price-quality spectrum. In this way the firm is more likely to offer exactly what a particular buyer is looking for and will gain sales that would otherwise go to a rival. The firm must ensure that the cost of adding and supporting any additional product in the line is less than the incremental revenue that this product is expected to generate. Also, the firm should consider offering one or more *product bundles.* A product bundle, as we saw in Chapter 10, is a collection of products that are complemenary to each other and might be purchased or as a package deal. For some buyers the bundle might offer additional convenience or some other advantage and thus allow increased sales volume at the expense of a rival firm.

Second, the quality leader must strive to be *first with new features* that allow it to differentiate its product from those of rivals. Being first is particularly important for search attributes, since these are easily evaluated by consumers, and thus differentiation is more readily established. If another firm is first with a search attribute that becomes a major determinant in the buyer's purchasing decision, the firm must also incorporate this attribute very quickly to avoid loss of market share. With experience and credence attributes, the advantage of being first and the urgency of emulating another firm's innovation are each probably less significant than for search goods, because the benefits of these features are not as readily apparent to potential buyers.

Third, there are longer-term benefits associated with the maintenance of quality at a particular standard, since the product's brand name becomes a stock of information about previous products that consumers will transfer to the firm's current products. Thus the *consistency of quality* is important—variations in quality from time to time tend to depreciate the brand-name advantage associated with the firm's products. A firm with a brand-name advantage has a longer-term profit incentive to at least maintain the standard of quality embodied in its products, because of repeat sales in future periods on the basis of the quality assurances provided by the brand name.

Pricing and Advertising Strategies to Complement Quality Leadership

If the product more closely satisfies the buyer's needs, one would expect the buyer's demand to be less elastic, or more inelastic, than it would be for a product that is not such a good match with the buyer's needs. A lower price elasticity means that the profit-maximizing markup will be higher, other things being the same. A less elastic demand means that these products will not be good candidates for promotional pricing or price competition in general. Thus the firm is likely to set the price at a relatively high level and compete on the basis of quality rather than price. If it is a quality leader, it can extract a price premium from those customers who believe that the product is worth the extra cost to them.

The firm's advertising strategy should be to reinforce the beliefs of current customers that its products are superior and to spread this belief to other potential buyers. Informative advertising is called for on all major search attributes, and persuasive advertising is called for on the major experience and credence attributes. Since experience and credence products are more amenable to the differentiation strategy, we should expect to see a preponderance of persuasive advertising associated with firms' attempts to differentiate their products. Such advertisements must be realistic to be believable, and they may involve exotic locales, well-known celebrities, and situations that are complex or humorous but above all are interesting. Because of these requirements, persuasive advertising tends to be expensive.

How much advertising should a firm do? We saw in Chapter 13 that this decision depends on the firm's sales-advertising function and its contribution margin. The rule given in Chapter 13 can be equivalently stated in terms of the firm's price and advertising elasticities of demand. Dorfman and Steiner first showed that the profit-maximizing ratio of advertising expenditure to sales revenue is given by the ratio of advertising elasticity to price elasticity. We can call this the "elasticities" rule for optimal advertising expenditures. Thus the higher the advertising elasticity, and the lower the price elasticity, the higher will be the profit-maximizing advertising budget as a proportion of sales revenue.[11]

We have argued that the price elasticity of demand will be relatively inelastic for experience and credence products, since consumers cannot easily ascertain whether or not they are close substitutes. On the other hand, we expect the advertising elasticity of demand for experience and credence goods to be relatively high, because consumers may be persuaded to try these products by advertisements that emphasize the product's brand name, the seller's reputation for quality, the assertions of famous people, and so on. Thus we see very large advertising expenditures by firms selling soft drinks and fast foods, by brewing companies, by pet-food companies, by automobile companies, and by accounting firms like H&R Block around tax return time. Firms selling goods or services which are largely composed of experience and credence attributes should be expected to have large advertising budgets relative to their total sales revenues, following the elasticities rule.

In conclusion, the appropriate advertising strategy to complement a differentiation strategy will require the firm to spend on advertising until it estimates that its advertising-to-sales ratio is equal to the ratio of its advertising elasticity to its price elasticity. This same prescription applies to firms following a cost-leadership strategy, of course. If their products are predominantly search products, however, we expect to see advertising as a

---

[11]See R. Dorfman and P. Steiner, "Optimal Advertising and Product Quality," *American Economic Review*, 44 (December 1954), pp. 826–36; or T. H. Naylor, J. M. Vernon, and K. L. Wertz, *Managerial Economics: Corporate Economics and Strategy* (New York: McGraw-Hill Book Company, Inc., 1983), pp. 230–32. In Chapter 13 we said profit would be maximized when $dQ/dA = 1/CM$, where the contribution margin, CM, equals $P - AVC$, and $AVC = MR$. Multiplying both sides by A/PQ we have $1/P[(dQ/dA)(A/Q)] = 1/(P - MC)(A/PQ)$. The term in the square brackets is the advertising elasticity of demand, which I shall call E_a. Thus $E_a = P/(P - MC)(A/PQ)$. From Chapter 10 we saw that when profit is maximized, $MC = MR = P[1 + (1/E_p)]$, where E_p signifies the price elasticity of demand. This expression can be rewritten as $E_p = P/(P - MC)$. Substituting for $P/(P - MC)$ in the expression for E_a we have $E_a = E_p(A/PQ)$. Hence $E_a/E_p = A/PQ$, or the ratio of the advertising elasticity to the price elasticity is equal to the ratio of advertising expenditure to total (sales) revenue, when P and A are each set at their profit-maximizing levels.

much smaller proportion of sales revenue, because for search products price elasticity is relatively high and advertising elasticity is relatively low.

14.4 PRODUCT DESIGN FOR A FOCUS STRATEGY

The third generic type of competitive strategy suggested by Michael Porter is the "focus" strategy, whereby the firm confines its attention to a particular segment or niche in the market and deliberately does not seek to serve the entire market. In its chosen market niche, the firm may adopt either a cost-leadership or a differentiation strategy. It may choose to be a cost leader in one niche, but follow a differentiation strategy in one or more other niches. Conceivably, the firm might be the cost leader in most of the market and yet follow a differentiation strategy in some segments. General Motors is no doubt a cost leader in most of the automobile market, yet its Cadillac Division seeks to differentiate its product to a limited target market. The major breweries have some brand-name beers for sale in the vast "economy beer" segment and simultaneously have premium beers that sell for two or three times as much and appeal to a more limited clientele.

The Cost-Focus Strategy

A firm may adopt a cost-focus strategy when it sees that by specializing in the service of a particular type of customer, it can serve these customers at a cost level significantly below the cost levels of rivals. In any market we expect to find a variety of buyers, whose quantity demanded ranges from one or a few units to thousands or even millions of units. Many, perhaps most, of the firms will seek the business of the larger buyers, since one sales agreement with a customer of that kind produces much more sales volume and profit than one sales agreement with a smaller customer. The smaller buyers with special orders may be neglected by the larger firms, or they may be charged a relatively high price. It is on these smaller buyers that a firm might focus its cost-leadership strategy, if it can supply its goods to them at a lower price than can the other firms, whether the other firms are larger firms (perhaps following a broad-based cost-leadership strategy or a broad-based differentiation strategy) or are other small firms (perhaps following a focused-differentiation strategy).

- EXAMPLE: Printing is a business in which orders come in all sizes and degrees of complexity. A large buyer might want millions of copies of a brochure, and a small buyer might want 250 business cards. Large printing firms will have large and relatively expensive plant and equipment, but small printing firms will have much smaller and perhaps much older printing equipment. The large firm may charge much more for an order of 250 business cards than a smaller firm would because it has much more substantial overhead costs and perhaps its setup cost is also higher. The smaller firm may be able to set a price that allows a superior profit and still quote a lower price than its larger rival.

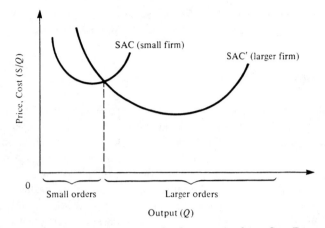

FIGURE 14-1.   Cost Curves to Demonstrate the Opportunity for a Cost-Focus Strategy

In Figure 14-1 we depict such a situation. The smaller plant, represented by the cost curve SAC, has lower costs per unit for small orders, whereas the larger plant, represented by the SAC' curve, has the lower costs per unit for larger orders. Undoubtedly the larger firm will quote lower prices on larger orders, and it may seek to be either a cost leader or a quality leader on those larger orders. For smaller orders, however, the smaller firm has a definite cost advantage over the larger firm. It can set a price substantially above its average costs and yet still be below the cost level of the larger firm.

Thus a cost-focus strategy involves selecting a small segment of the market and specializing in the production of the goods or services demanded by this group of customers. The firm's plant may then be limited to only that required to produce a limited range of goods, and thus costs may be kept to the lowest levels possible. If it is successful at this strategy there will be a tendency to expand productive capacity, but rather than grow larger the firm may prefer to open other small plants for cost-focus strategies in other market niches as well. This type of strategy may be appropriate if the smaller and more specialized demands of some customers are not being well served by the other firms. In markets where orders typically differ both in size and complexity, as in printing, clothing manufacture, automobile repair work, and home services (like landscaping, interior decorating, and carpet cleaning), the firm's best option for superior profitability may be to focus on the low-cost supply of goods and services to the smaller and more specialized buyers, rather than attempt to compete for the larger orders that will be hotly contested by the larger firms.

The Quality-Focus Strategy

In other markets the firm's best strategy might be to focus on a particular market segment or niche and compete on the basis of quality in that niche. If the other firms are preoccupied with the mass market, where orders are larger or there is a concentration of buyers wanting a rather standardized product (and there is already a strong cost leader) or where there are already several firms successfully differentiating their products, there might be a profitable opportunity to cater to the buyer who wants a distinctly different version of the product or service. People with special tastes, a desire to be distinguished from others, a desire to express themselves through their purchases, or a desire to flaunt their wealth may be willing to pay substantially more for a product that more closely mirrors their tastes. The firm following a quality-focus strategy must strive to produce this good for the customer at a price premium that exceeds the additional cost of differentiation, as compared with the standard fare.

- EXAMPLE: Rolls-Royce automobiles claim to be the best cars in the world, and in some respects they might be. They are hand built, and attention to detail is fastidious. They are very expensive, costing as much as three exotic sports cars, or as much as ten or fifteen compact or economy cars. Accordingly they are not very common, and a passing Rolls-Royce always attracts plenty of attention, both for itself and because it may be transporting a celebrity. The exclusiveness of owning a Rolls Royce probably attracts as many buyers as the mechanical specifications do. If wealthy people like to show their wealth, and if celebrities like to receive attention, this car is for them.

In any market there may be opportunities for the quality-focus strategy. Custom-tailored clothes, luxurious homes, exotic automobiles, higher-quality professional services, and "better" educations, for example, are sold in markets in which some firms follow quality-focus strategies alongside the more broadly based differentiation and cost leadership strategies of others. Several smaller breweries and wineries compete with the majors by limiting their output to premium brands and limited editions. Other examples abound, and they seem to illustrate that a firm can shield itself from direct competition from larger firms and from lower-cost firms by limiting its purview to a specialized niche in the overall market. In this niche it can earn above-average rates of profit if it is able to identify the wants and needs of its customers correctly, design a product to suit those customers, and attract their business at a relatively high price.

Product Design, Pricing, and Advertising for Focus Strategies

Most of the foregoing conclusions about product design, presented in the separate contexts of cost-leadership and quality-leadership strategies, apply here in the context of focused strategies of each type. Fundamental to a focus strategy is the clear and deliberate identification of the firm's target market, whereas a firm following a more broadly based cost-leadership or differentiation strategy may know less about its consumers and yet make above-average profit. The cost-focus strategist will design a product such that the costs of serving its target market are kept to a minimum, whereas the quality-focus strategist will add features to its product or service whenever it believes these features will allow price to be augmented by more than costs would be. We would expect search products to be better suited to the cost-focus firm, whereas experience and credence products are more likely optimal for the firm adopting a quality-focus strategy.

A focus strategy seems particularly appropriate for a firm attempting to enter a market for the first time. To gain a foothold and to avoid the direct competition of major firms, the new entrant might seriously consider focusing on a smaller, more specialized segment of the market that is relatively neglected at the present time. If successful in the chosen market segment, the new firm might later broaden its base, both to diversify its risk exposure and to allow it to expand beyond the confines of its initial clientele.

Pricing strategies for a cost-focus firm will be similar to those for the broadly based cost leader discussed previously. Price leadership (in the niche) to maximize short-run profit is possible, given the firm's lower costs, but it is appropriate only if the firm's planning period is short, if there are insurmountable barriers to entry, or if the EPV-maximizing strategy is to allow entry of some new firms at first and later restrict further entry. Pricing to maximize sales subject to a minimum profit constraint may be more appropriate if the firm expects a significant amount of repeat business and complementary sales in future periods and faces strong competition in the market niche. Limit pricing is indicated if the EPV of profits is best served by restricting the entry of new firms. Promotional pricing is indicated if the product is a search product.

Pricing strategy for the quality-focus firm will include product-line pricing, bundle pricing, and whatever short-run pricing rule best serves the firm's objective, taking into account the possibility of new entry, repeat and complementary sales, and so on.

Advertising strategy will tend to be informative if the product is a search product and to stress price if the firm follows a cost-focus strategy. In these cases, advertising expenditures will tend to be a relatively small proportion of sales revenue, following the elasticities rule. On the other hand, if the products are experience or credence goods and the firm follows a quality-focus strategy, advertising will tend to be optimal if it is mostly persuasive and if advertising expenditures are a relatively large proportion of sales revenue.

14.5 SUMMARY

In this chapter we have drawn together several threads to discuss the firm's competitive strategy in its market. A competitive strategy should include well-defined quality, pricing, and advertising policies. The firm's competitive strategy should be oriented to the firm's objective, which we presume to be the maximization of the EPV of profit over the firm's time horizon. Given the present participants in the market and the strategies they appear to be following, as well as consideration of its own strengths and weaknesses vis-à-vis those of the other firms, the firm should choose a particular type of strategy to pursue.

There are three generic strategy types—namely, cost-leadership, differentiation, and focus strategies. The two focus strategies are simply more narrowly targeted versions of the broad-based cost leadership and differentiation strategies. We called the firm following a differentiation strategy a quality leader, for simplicity of exposition and to emphasize the fact that such a firm essentially competes on a quality basis rather than a price basis.

The type of product, classified as a search, experience, or credence product depending on the cost to consumers of evaluating the quality attributes of the product, was seen to be of major importance. Search products are typically best marketed following a cost-leadership strategy, unless the firm's product has a unique (or far superior) search attribute that rivals cannot immediately emulate, in which case a differentiation strategy is appropriate (at least temporarily). Experience and credence goods are typically best suited to a differentiation strategy, since these are less easily emulated by rivals, as well as imperfectly evaluated by consumers.

Cost leaders should "cover the bases," "trim the fat," and practice product proliferation in the design of their products, particularly if their products are search products. Their products should contain all the necessary quality attributes for a target price-quality point but none in excess of consumer requirements unless these can be provided at no cost. Producing several brand names at once may allow the cost leader to gain a larger share of the market and subsequently reduce costs. Quality leaders should offer a broad product line, offer their products in bundles as well as separately, strive to be first with new features (or respond quickly to emulate rivals), and strive to maintain the consistency of quality to build up their brand-name advantages.

Pricing strategies to complement cost leadership include promotional pricing, profit-maximizing price leadership, pricing for sales maximization subject to a minimum profit constraint, and limit pricing, depending on which pricing strategy maximizes the EPV of the firm's profit over its time horizon. Quality leaders will be more likely to consider product-line pricing and bundle pricing, and they will use the short-run pricing rule that best serves the maximization of the EPV of the firm's profit.

Advertising will tend to be informative for search products and persuasive for experience and credence products. The larger is the ratio of the advertising elasticity to the price elasticity, the larger advertising budgets will be as a proportion of sales revenue. This elasticities rule explains why we see proportionately larger advertising budgets for experience and credence goods as opposed to search goods.

Finally, we noted that a firm considering entry might best gain a foothold, or a small firm attempting to make an above-average profit might more easily do so, if it adopts a focus strategy, serving only a subset of the market with a more specialized product.

DISCUSSION QUESTIONS

14-1. Distinguish between competitive strategy and competitive advantage in terms of means and ends. How does competitive advantage tie in with the objective of the firm?

14-2. What issues should the firm consider before deciding to follow a cost-leadership strategy?

14-3. Why is the price elasticity likely to be relatively high, and the advertising elasticity likely to be relatively low, for search goods?

14-4. What are the implications of cost leadership for product design?

14-5. What pricing and advertising strategies are likely to best complement a cost-leadership strategy?

14-6. How do Peters, Waterman, and Austin's "two essential ingredients" fit in with Porter's two main generic strategies approach?

14-7. What issues should the firm consider before deciding to follow a differentiation strategy?

14-8. What are the implications of quality leadership for product design?

14-9. When is a focus strategy likely to be the firm's best option?

14-10. Make up a list of firms and their brand-name products that appear to be following (a) a broad-based cost-leadership strategy; (b) a broad-based differentiation strategy; (c) a cost-focus strategy; and (d) a quality-focus strategy.

PROBLEMS AND SHORT CASES

14-1. Dixieland Ice Cream's profit rate has been declining over the past three years and is below average in the industry. Management has asked you to advise them as to ways that profitability may be raised. Your investigations reveal that although there is little inefficiency in production, employee productivity is relatively low, mainly because of Dixieland's reliance on relatively old equipment. In addition, product quality tends to vary perceptibly between batches as a result of the age of the equipment. Consumers think Dixieland's product is "just another ice cream," although brand-name recognition is quite high. Dixieland's ice cream is marketed in all major supermarkets and food stores, and it is priced in the middle of the range of prices found there. Their relatively low advertising budget is spent largely on joint promotions with supermarket chains when Dixieland's ice cream is one of the products used for promotional pricing.

Dixieland's competitors include several like itself, some small firms competing in only some of the regional markets, and a few others that specialize in higher-quality ice cream, with a creamier taste, more chunks of real fruit, and so on. These premium-price ice creams are marketed in ice cream parlors as well as in food stores generally. An ice cream parlor typically uses a single brand-name ice cream and is particularly concerned with high and consistent quality. Some ice cream parlors are owned by the manufacturers and are thus not able to use another manufacturer's product. The small firms, which market their products in only some of the food stores, accept a lower markup in an effort to achieve greater penetration of the market, but this approach causes the profit rates of most of the smaller firms to be relatively low, in turn limiting their ability to expand quickly.

(a) Discuss the competitive strategies that appear to be open to Dixieland.

(b) Based on the information given here, which strategy do you think they should adopt?

(c) What further information would you like to have before investing any money in Dixieland's stock, given that they will follow your advice?

14-2. The Kia Motor Company manufactures automobiles in Korea and has accumulated a great deal of experience supplying the home market. Recently it has been considering entering the United States market. It plans to test market some of its cars in Hawaii before expanding to the mainland states. The purpose of the test marketing program is to decide on the competitive strategy it will use in the mainland market.

Kia produces four different automobile lines for its home market. The smallest is its "City" commuter car, which is only seven feet long yet has adequate room for two adults and for groceries in the trunk. Interior trim is basic, the car's performance is moderate, and fuel economy is very high. Next is the "Rocker," a youth-oriented performance car that seats four without any room to spare. It has a peppier engine, is sold in several wild color schemes, and has a fairly good stereo system as standard. The "Family" model is somewhat larger, seats five adults, and has a larger engine and moderately comfortable interior trim. It is a look-alike version of the typical Japanese subcompact car. Finally, the "Executive'' model is larger and seats five adults in great comfort. Interior trim is luxurious, and performance is stately and comparable to the typical American compact.

Kia has incorporated the latest quality control techniques into their plant. The manufacturing process tends to be relatively labor intensive because of the high productivity of the workers and the relatively low wage structure. Everyone on the management team received an M.B.A. degree at an American university or college.

(a) Outline the alternative competitive strategies that Kia might adopt in the mainland market, and the pros and cons of each as you see it. Which seems like the best strategy to you?

(b) What do you think Kia should do in Hawaii to test your hunches about the receptiveness of the American market to their products? (Consider quality, pricing, and advertising decisions.)

(c) What other information would you seek before giving your final advice about their competitive strategy for the mainland market?

14-3. Richard Koster Legal Associates is a law firm in Boston that has special expertise in immigration law, since Richard worked for the Immigration and Naturalization Service (INS) for several years before completing his law degree. At the present time the firm is involved in all kinds of civil law prosecutions and defenses, including but by no means limited to immigration cases. Acknowledging that the law business is a jungle, Richard has retained your services to advise the firm as to their future competitive strategy.

Richard is fundamentally opposed to ''ambulance chasing,'' does not like dealing with criminals, and finds divorce proceedings unsettling. On the other hand, he does enjoy property transactions, antitrust proceedings, and dealing with immigrants who are seeking permanent resident status. In the latter area, particularly, Richard has an advantage over most other lawyers because of the knowledge he gained of immigration procedures while working for the INS and because of the contacts he still has there. In the Boston area many high-technology firms, as well as the various universities and colleges, seek Richard's assistance in getting work permits and resident alien papers for foreign nationals with special skills and expertise.

Currently, Richard feels he is being spread too thinly over several areas of law. He has to spend a great deal of time reading and conducting computerized searches whenever a case comes along that is in an area he has not considered for a while. His firm makes plenty of money, he says, but he feels that he could make at least as much and work shorter hours if he had a clearly defined competitive strategy.

(a) Which of the generic strategies do you think that this law firm should adopt, and why?

(b) What product, price, and promotion decisions should be considered in the execution of the strategy you have suggested above?

14-4. Upton College is a small liberal arts college located in upstate New York that has run into financial difficulties in recent years. The decline in the number of students since the passing of the baby boomers, the trend toward business education, and the revival of interest in science and engineering have left enrollments dwindling. Upton has lost many of its tenured faculty members because it refused to grant salary increases over the past few years in the face of this financial uncertainty. Consequently, many of the courses are covered by temporary and part-time instructors whose own education is lacking.

The president of Upton College, Imelda Greer, has hired you to investigate the options and recommend a competitive strategy that they would follow. Your investigations lead to the following information: Upton still has several very good liberal arts professors who could form the base for a revival of the college as a specialist in liberal arts education. The departure of some other tenured faculty members is actually a blessing in disguise, since it opens up tenure slots and gives the college more flexibility in hiring new professors. There is a local demand for business education, since the nearest business school is 60 miles away. And since Upton has dormitories on campus, the reach of a business school could extend well beyond the local area. Science and engineering are another option that could save Upton, but the cost of supplying this kind of education is much higher than for liberal arts and business degrees. The administration at Upton is top-heavy and ultraconservative, with the exception of Ms. Greer, who says she would willingly fire them all and start afresh in order to save the college. Finally, the town in which Upton is located. and the surrounding countryside, are pleasant almost to the point of being idyllic.

(a) Consider the alternative strategies that Upton might follow, listing the pros and cons of each one.

(b) Advise Ms. Greer which strategy you believe Upton should follow, and what product, price, and promotion decisions should be implemented in order to ensure survival and achieve competitive advantage.

14-5. Fisher Tools has developed a new product and has asked your advice as to the appropriate competitive strategy they should follow in order to earn a high and sustained profit from this product. The product is a paint applicator that continuously feeds paint under pressure to the roller, allowing painting to be done much more quickly and with less mess. The container could be pressurized either by an inexpensive hand pump that would need pumping regularly to maintain the desired pressure, or by a small bottle of compressed air that would maintain the correct pressure continuously through a (rather-expensive) valve. At present the competition for the new product consists of the conventional brushes and rollers, spray guns, and a few other continuous-feed roller systems that are not well developed and are messy to use.

(a) Discuss the type of product and its implications for competitive strategy.

(b) Outline the competitive strategies that are potentially usable here.

(c) What competitive strategy do you recommend that Fisher follow, and why?

(d) What do you recommend that they do?

14-6. Main Street Plumbing and Heating is a business owned and operated by Dick Watson and his wife Mary in a small Midwestern city. Dick has one full-time apprentice, and Mary works as secretary, receptionist, accountant, and public relations officer. Overhead costs are low because the business operates from the garage of the family home. Business is sporadic: There is too much work when a freezing spell bursts water pipes and too little work at other times, particularly in the summer, when the home handymen and women decide that they can do it themselves. Dick knows you are studying managerial economics and has asked for your advice on how to ensure a steady flow of work, preferably inside or summer work, with the potential of expanding the business and enjoying a greater income.

Your questions elicit the following information: There are literally dozens of general plumbing and heating firms in the area. Dick's costs and prices are as low as any of them. He does not advertise, except in the local yellow pages where he is listed under plumbing and heating contractors. He says that some plumbing and heating firms specialize in particular areas, such as solar-heating systems. Some work only in new construction, installing the heating, water, and sewer systems. There appear to be several opportunities open. There is no firm specializing in luxury bathroom design and installation, nor in in-ground lawn sprinkling systems, nor in fire-control systems for factories and other public buildings. Also, you perceive a need for a firm that sells plumbing tools and materials to the do-it-yourselfer where the proprietor knows plumbing and heating and is willing to dispense free advice to customers.

(a) Outline the generic strategies that are open to Dick and his wife.

(b) What strategy do you suggest, and why?

(c) Outline the product, price, and promotion decisions that must be made as part of this new strategy.

14-7. Getaway Island Tours operates a vacation planning and travel booking agency in the downtown area of a large northeastern city. They organize package tours and promote them in the local media. The winter is their busiest season, as people seek a week or two of sun and sand as a respite from the chilly winds and icy streets. A recent marketing survey indicates that the firm does not have very widespread brand-name recognition and is regarded as a supplier of cheap tours with a wide dispersion of quality across tours. Potential buyers fell into two categories: those who buy largely on the basis of lowest price for air fare, hotel, and transfers and those who choose on the basis of convenient times of departure and return, known high-quality hotels, and safe, interesting, and exciting locations. Special-interest groups, such as golfers, sailors, scuba divers, and surfers, could also be identified within the latter group more readily than within the former group.

Getaway has hired your consulting firm for advice on the choice of a competitive strategy. They are currently only marginally profitable and operate from day to day, taking whatever comes along. After years in the business, however, their personnel have been to virtually every hotel on every island in the Caribbean and they have had some experience with Europe as well. They have organized tours of virtually every type for any clientele, but they have tended to dissipate their efforts over too wide a front. The big discounts at the hotels are also not available to occasional users.

(a) Discuss the various strategies that are open to Getaway Island Tours.

(b) What strategy do you suggest they follow?

(c) What product, price, and promotion decisions do you suggest they implement as part of their competitive strategy?

14-8. Stephanie Ricardo has recently taken over her family's restaurant business. For twenty-five years the Ricardo Family Restaurant has served fine family fare—nothing exotic, just good basic American food. Business has been satisfactory, but it has never been heavy enough to justify an expansion of the facilities. Now the kitchen is somewhat antiquated, the tables and chairs need replacing, the interior needs renovating, and the outside needs sprucing up. The sign outside no longer lights up at night and cannot be repaired.

Now that Stephanie is in charge she is considering the various options open to her. Since the restaurant needs refurbishing it could be reborn as any kind of restaurant, catering to any kind of clientele. Her parents would be happy if she turned it into a fine Italian restaurant—this was always her father's dream. But she is also considering the lunch and supper business of business executives from local industry. A more restricted menu would hurt her chances of capturing a sizable share of that business. Rather than a linen-tablecloth restaurant, she could alternatively pursue the breakfast and fast-food market. A franchise from a national chain of family restaurants is currently available. This chain specializes in family dining at low prices. Other options abound, and therefore Stephanie has sought your help.

(a) Outline the various strategies that are available to Stephanie.

(b) What strategy do you suggest, and what product, price, and advertising decisions should be made in pursuit of this strategy?

(c) Outline the cost and revenue implications of your proposed strategy.

14-9. Whaleback Mountain Ski Resort is surrounded by other ski resorts and is barely making ends meet. The resorts closer to the city get more of the business, and the resorts that offer superior trails and artificial snow making also have an advantage over Whaleback. Whaleback's parking lot is relatively small and cannot be expanded. On busy days skiers must park and walk along the roads to get to the chair lifts, and of course the walk is uncomfortable and tiring in ski boots. Whaleback's trails are quite good by comparison with other resorts, although a little work and the services of a ski trail designer would transform them into very high-quality trails. The chalet at the base of the mountain is relatively small but very cosy and attractive. Whaleback is not set up for night skiing.

Next season will make it or break it for the present owners of Whaleback. They have a line of credit at their bank, and they are willing to spend the borrowed money to establish the resort as a viable competitor. They could simply advertise or make improvements, including snow-making equipment and trail design, and they could change their prices up or down. At present their ticket prices are lower than most other resorts.

(a) What strategies seem feasible for Whaleback Mountain?

(b) What do you advise concerning competitive strategy, and what does your advice imply for product, price, and advertising strategy?

14-10. The Billion Bytes Computer Company has grown from a startup venture in the early 1980s to become a multimillion-dollar-sales computer company in the early 1990s. But times are getting tougher for BBC, as the industry shakeout threatens to extend the list of victims. BBC currently has several personal and business computers on the market, but they are not compatible with the industry-standard operating systems and have fallen behind the frontier of hardware technology.

BBC is faced with a major strategic decision. Management feels that a cost-leadership strategy is out of the question, because of economies of plant size and pecuniary economies of its major competitors. A differentiation strategy seems to be indicated, but whether this should be focused or broad based is at issue. On the one hand, BBC could focus on developing special hardware and software for engineering and scientific applications, while on the other it could go into the general market and appeal to the users who value the light weight and easy portability of their machines. Other options exist, including adoption of MS-DOS, MicroSoft's Disk Operating System, which is now the industry standard. BBC already utilizes microdisks and is working on nanodisks (less than two inches in diameter) and miniaturized disk drives and printers that would be integrated into the same carrying case as the central processing unit.

(a) Consider the differentiation strategies that exist for BBC.

(b) Is the cost-focus strategy necessarily out of the question?

(c) What strategy do you think BBC should pursue?

(d) What product, price, and promotion decisions will be involved?

SELECTED REFERENCES AND FURTHER READING

ACKERLOF, G. "The Market for 'Lemons': Qualitative Uncertainty and the Market Mechanism," *Quarterly Journal of Economics,* 35 (August 1970), pp. 488–500.

CHAN, Y. S. and H. LELAND. "Prices and Qualities in Markets with Costly Information," *Review of Economic Studies,* 49 (October 1982), pp. 499–516.

DIXIT, A. K., and J. E. STIGLITZ. "Monopolistic Competition and Optimum Product Diversity," *American Economic Review,* 67 (June 1977), pp. 297–308.

DORFMAN, R., and P. STEINER. "Optimal Advertising and Product Quality," *American Economic Review,* 44 (December 1954), pp. 826–36.

DUDEY, MARC, "Competition by Choice: The Effect of Consumer Search on Firm Location Decisions," *American Economic Review,* 80 (December 1990), pp. 1092–1104.

GAL-OR, E. "Quality and Quantity Competition," *Bell Journal of Economics,* 14 (Autumn 1983), pp. 590–600.

GRILICHES, Z. *Price Indices and Quality Change.* Cambridge, Mass.: Harvard University Press, 1971.

KOTLER, P. *Principles of Marketing,* esp. chaps. 3, 8, 10, and 11-18. Englewood Cliffs. N.J.: Prentice-Hall, Inc., 1980.

KROUSE, CLEMENT G. "Brand Name as a Barrier to Entry: The ReaLemon Case," *Southern Economic Journal,* 51 (October 1984), pp. 495–502.

LABAND, DAVID N. "An Objective Measure of Search versus Experience Goods," *Economic Inquiry,* 29 (July 1991), pp. 497–509.

LANCASTER, K. "Socially Optimal Product Differentiation," *American Econontic Review*, 65 (September 1975), pp. 567–85.

LELAND, H. E. "Quality Choice and Competition," *American Economic Review*, 67 (March 1977), pp. 127–37.

LEVHARI, D., and Y. PELES. "Market Structure, Quality and Durability," *Bell Journal of Economics*, 4 (Spring 1973), pp. 235–48.

NAGLE, T. "Economic Foundations of Pricing," *Journal of Business*, 57 (January 1984), pp. S3–S26.

NAYLOR, T. H., J. M. VERNON, and K. L. WERTZ. *Managerial Economics: Corporate Economics and Strategy*, pp. 230–32 and 264–66. New York: McGraw-Hill Book Company. Inc., 1983.

ROSEN, S. "Hedonic Prices and Implicit Markets: Product Differentiation in Pure Competition," *Journal of Political Economy*, 82 (January–February 1974), pp. 34–55.

SCHMALENSEE, R. "Market Structure, Durability, and Quality: A Selective Survey," *Economic Inquiry*, 17 (April 1979), pp. 177–96.

SCHWARTZ, A., and L. L. WILDE. "Product Quality and Imperfect Information," *Review of Economic Studies*, 52 (April 1985), pp. 251–62.

SHAPIRO, C. "Premiums for High-Quality Products as Returns to Reputations," *Quarterly Journal of Economics*, 98 (November 1983), pp. 659–79.

SPENCE, A. M. "Product Selection, Fixed Costs, and Monopolistic Competition," *Review of Economic Studies*, 443 (June 1976), pp. 217–36.

STIGLER, G. J. "The Economics of Information," *Journal of Political Economy*, 69 (June 1961), pp. 213–25.

SWAN, P. L. "Durability of Consumer Goods," *American Economic Review*, 60 (December 1970), pp. 884–94.

VANDER WEIDE, J. H., and J. H. ZALKIND. "Deregulation and Oligopolistic Price-Quality Rivalry," *American Economic Review*, 71 (March 1981), pp. 144–54.

Chapter 15

CAPITAL BUDGETING AND INVESTMENT DECISIONS

EXECUTIVE SUMMARY

Capital budgeting is the decision making process concerned with **whether or not the firm should invest funds** in the purchase of assets or other resources in an attempt to make profit, and **how to choose among competing uses of funds** (or investment projects).

Investment projects may be to **replace or expand existing plant and equipment,** to **diversify the firm's activities**, to mount a major **advertising campaign**, and so on. In general, investment projects will involve revenue generation, cost reduction, or some combination of the two.

Where there are no limits on the availability of funds, the capital budgeting decision is simply whether to accept or reject each project that comes under scrutiny. In this chapter we consider a number of **decision criteria that allow the accept-reject decision to be made**. Where the investment projects are mutually exclusive (perhaps because they utilize the same funds, where funds are limited), we consider **decision criteria that allow the ranking of mutually exclusive projects** in terms of their desirability.

The basic structure of the capital budgeting decision process is already familiar to you, since it was introduced in Chapters 1 and 2. Here we reconsider the **expected-present-value decision criterion** in the context of the investment decision and consider new and related investment decision criteria. These include the **net-present-value** criterion, the **internal-rate-of-return** criterion, the **profitability index**, the **payback period**, and the **average-rate-of-return** criterion.

The simplistic payback-period criterion is reconciled with the net-present value criterion, and the net-present-value criterion is shown to be superior over both the internal-rate-of-return criterion and the profitability index when investments are mutually exclusive.

15.1 CAPITAL BUDGETING WITH UNLIMITED AVAILABILITY OF FUNDS

For ease of presentation, the analysis in this chapter will be presented, for the most part, in terms of the firm's having full information about future costs and revenues associated with each investment decision. Thus we speak of the net-present-value (NPV) criterion, for example, rather than the *expected*-net-present-value criterion. The analysis is easily modified for uncertainty—the single-point estimates of future costs and revenues can be designated to represent the expected values of the probability distributions surrounding each expected future cost and revenue. Rather than repeat all the analysis of Chapter 1 dealing with decision making under uncertainty, this chapter introduces new material and presumes that you will have little difficulty implementing it in the context of uncertainty.

When funds are unlimited, the capital budgeting decision is whether to accept or reject each available investment project. This decision must be based on whether or not each project contributes to the attainment of the firm's objectives. In the following paragraphs we shall take the standard view that the firm's objective is to maximize its long-term profitability, or its net worth in present-value terms. In some cases, of course, the firm's time horizon may be somewhat shorter because of cash flow or accounting profit considerations. In such cases a less profitable project may be undertaken if it promises a very short payback period or relatively large immediate gains, in preference to a more profitable project that generates its income over a longer period of time.

We shall consider five separate criteria for the accept/reject decision. We shall examine the relationships between these criteria and show why some of these criteria are superior to others.

The Net-Present-Value Criterion

You will recall from Chapter I that *net present value* refers to the sum of the discounted value of the future stream of costs and revenues associated with a particular project. If the net present value of a project is positive, this fact indicates that the project adds more to revenues in present-value terms than it adds to cost in present-value terms and should therefore be accepted. Symbolically, we can express the net present value as follows:

$$\text{NPV} = \sum_{t=1}^{n} \frac{R_t}{(1 + r)^t} - C_0$$

(15-1)

where R_t signifies the contribution to overheads and profits in each future period; C_0 represents the initial cost of the project, including installation charges and any other expenses such as increases in working capital required by the investment; r is the opportunity rate of interest; and $t = 1, 2, 3, \ldots, n$ is the number of periods over which the revenue stream is expected. Thus the revenue stream is discounted at the rate of interest that the firm could obtain in its next-best-alternative use of these investment funds at a similar level of risk. The revenue stream referred to in equation (15-1) by R_t should be regarded as the net cash flow after taxes.

• DEFINITION: *Net cash flow after taxes* can be defined as incremental revenues minus incremental costs, plus tax savings that result from depreciation charges that are deductible from taxable income, plus tax credits (if any) allowed against tax liability in connection with the particular investment project. If a tax credit (for example, 15% of the initial cost) is available for new investment, this credit will be deducted directly from the tax liability, and it thus avoids an outflow of a certain amount. Although this is not an actual inflow of cash, it is an opportunity revenue; the avoidance of what would otherwise be an outflow of cash in effect amounts to a cash inflow. Depreciation charges against revenues enter the cash flow picture only indirectly and as a result of the tax saving that can be obtained by subtracting the depreciation charges from the income of the firm.

• EXAMPLE: To demonstrate this definition, suppose an investment project involves an initial cash outlay of $10,000 and will generate revenues for three years, after which time it has a salvage value of $1,000. The value of the investment project to be depreciated over the three-year life of the project is thus $9,000, and for simplicity we use the straight-line method of depreciation to allocate $3,000 to each of the three years of the project's life. In Table 15-1 we show the calculation of the cash flow after taxes, given the contribution stream indicated.

We assume that the firm is subject to the tax rate of 48%: The tax saving shown as $1,440 in each of the three years represents 48% of the depreciation figure. The cash-flow-after-taxes column shows the sum of the contribution and tax saving for each year. The next column shows the discount factors at an assumed opportunity rate of 10%, and the final column shows the net present value of the cash flow after taxes in each year and in total.

Note that the sum of the net present value of the cash flow after taxes is positive, and hence this investment project adds to the net present value, or net worth, of the firm. It should therefore be accepted, and the firm should continue accepting projects for implementation until it is left with only those projects that have zero or negative net present value at the appropriate opportunity rate of discount.

Different Depreciation Methods.   The method of depreciation employed has important implications for the NPV of the investment project. In the example we used the *straight-line* method of depreciation, in which the difference between the initial cost of the asset

TABLE 15-1.   Calculation of NPV of Cash Flow after Taxes

Year	Contri-bution	Depre-ciation	Tax Saving	Cash Flow after Taxes	Discount Factors	Net Present Value
0	$ − 10,000	—	—	$ − 10,000	1.000	$ − 10,000.00
1	5,000	$3,000	$1,440	6,440	0.909	5,853.96
2	3,000	3,000	1,440	4,440	0.826	3,667.44
3	2,000	3,000	1,440	3,440	0.751	2,583.44
						$ 2,104.84

and its salvage value is allocated equally to each year of the asset's life. Alternatively, we might have used a method of depreciation that accelerates the recovery of the difference between the initial cost and the salvage value, so the depreciation expense is largest in the first year and declines each year until the asset is fully depreciated. Two such methods are the sum-of-years-digits method and the double-declining-balance method.

The *sum-of-years-digits* method, as implied by its name, adds up the digits of the years that the asset will last and each year depreciates a proportion of the amount to be recovered equal to the ratio of the number of years remaining to the sum of the digits. In the preceding example the asset is expected to last for three years, so the sum of the years' digits is $1 + 2 + 3 = 6$. Thus three sixths, or one half, of the total depreciation expense will be deducted in the first year; two sixths, or one third, will be deducted in the second year; and one sixth will be deducted in the final year.

The *double-declining-balance* method takes twice the depreciation rate implied by the straight-line method but applies it to the undepreciated balance remaining in each year. Thus, using this method, we would recover two thirds of $9,000 (that is, $6,000) in the first year; two thirds of the remaining $3,000 (that is, $2,000) in the second year; and the remainder ($1,000) in the third year. Notice that both of these accelerated depreciation methods shift forward in time part of the net cash flow after taxes and thus increase the NPV of these dollars, since they will be multiplied by a larger discount factor when received earlier.

- EXAMPLE: To demonstrate this effect, let us rework the above example using the sum-of-years-digits depreciation method. In Table 15-2 we show half of the depreciation (that is, $4,500) being deducted in the first year; one third being deducted in the second year; and one sixth being deducted in the third year. The tax saving is now weighted toward the earlier years, which in turn have larger discount factors. Hence, the net present value of the same project with an accelerated depreciation method can be shown to be significantly higher than it was as calculated using straight-line depreciation. In fact, the accelerated depreciation provisions of the tax laws exist primarily to encourage firms to invest in new plant and facilities for the employment multiplier impact of such investment on the economy.[1]

TABLE 15-2. *Impact of Depreciation Method upon Net Present Value*

Year	Contribution	Depreciation	Tax Saving	Cash Flow after Taxes	Discount Factors	Net Present Value
0	$-10,000	—	—	$-10,000	1.000	$-10,000.00
1	5,000	$4,500	$2,160	7,160	0.909	6,508.44
2	3,000	3,000	1,440	4,440	0.826	3,667.44
3	2,000	1,500	720	2,720	0.751	2,042.72
						$ 2,218.60

[1]See R. E. Hall and D. W. Jorgenson, "Tax Policy and Investment Behavior," *American Economic Review*, 57 (June 1967), pp. 391–414.

The Internal-Rate-of-Return Criterion

- DEFINITION: The *internal rate of return* (IRR) is the rate of discount that reduces the present value of the income stream to equality with the initial cost. It can be shown symbolically as

$$C_0 = \sum_{t=1}^{n} \frac{R_t}{(1 + i)^t}$$

(15-2)

where the only symbol different from equation (15-1) is i, which represents the internal rate of return.

Note that the internal rate of return will be that rate of discount which reduces the net present value of the income stream to zero. In the previous example we know that the internal rate of return exceeds 10%, since the net present value is positive at 10%. It will take a larger rate of discount to reduce the net present value to zero. We can calculate the internal rate of return for a given project by a process of trial and error. (This method beats attempting to solve a polynomial function of degree n.)

- EXAMPLE: In Table 15-3 we show the process of iteratively calculating the net present value at various discount rates, zeroing in on the rate of discount that reduces the net present value to zero. We start by testing for the value of net present value at the discount rate of 20%. this procedure leaves a net present value of $437.64, indicating that it requires a larger discount rate to reduce net present value to zero. We then try a discount rate of 25% and find that the net present value at that discount rate is negative. Thus the internal rate of return lies between 20 and 25%. We try 23% and find that the net present value is $17.84. Clearly, a slightly larger internal rate of return is indicated, and we try 23.2% in the last column of the table to find a net present value of a mere −$7.88. Further iterations would show the internal rate of return to be precisely 23.1415873%.[2]

TABLE 15-3. Calculation of the Internal Rate of Return

Year	CFAT	NPV @20%	NPV @25%	NPV @23%	NPV @23.2%
0	$−10,000	$−10,000.00	$−10,000.00	$−10,000.00	$−10,000.00
1	6,440	5,364.52	5,152.00	5,235.72	5,227.27
2	4,440	3,081.36	2,841.60	2,934.84	2,925.24
3	3,440	1,991.76	1,761.28	1,847.28	1,839.61
		$ 437.64	$ −245.12	$ 17.84	$ −7.88

---

[2] In case you are wondering how many iterations it took to find that answer, I must confess that my calculator is preprogrammed for the IRR calculation. Such calculators are becoming increasingly available at moderate cost and are, I think, an essential part of the business student's tool kit.

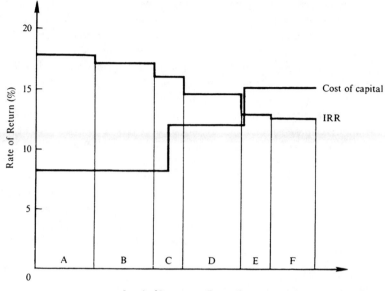

FIGURE 15-1. **Determining the Level of Investment Expenditure**

- RULE: The IRR *decision rule* is that projects with an internal rate of return greater than the opportunity rate of interest should be accepted and implemented by the firm. Given the availability of investment funds, investment in various projects should be taken to the point where the internal rate of return on the last project accepted just exceeds the cost of capital (the opportunity rate of interest for that project). Note that this decision rule is equivalent to the NPV rule that says to accept any project for which the NPV (when discounted at the opportunity rate) is above zero.

- EXAMPLE: In Figure 15-1 we show a series of investment projects as the blocks A, B, C, D, E, and F. These investment projects are ranked in order of their internal rate of return, which represents the height of each block, and the width of each block represents the amount of capital required for the implementation of each project. The top of these blocks, shown as the heavy stepped line, is the curve relating the IRR to the level of investment expenditure.

    The cost of capital to the firm is also likely to be a step function. Initially the firm will be able to utilize internal funds (undistributed profits), and the cost of these funds is their opportunity cost. That is, these could be invested elsewhere at a level of risk similar to that involved in holding the funds as undistributed profits, and the firm would wish to receive at least that rate by utilizing these funds in the proposed investment projects. After a point, however, the internal funds will be exhausted and the firm will need to borrow on the financial markets. We must expect the rate for such borrowing to exceed the opportunity cost of using internal funds, since the market will view the firm as involving at least some degree of risk. In Figure 15-1 we indicate that the firm's opportunity rate on internal funds is about 8% and that the firm can then borrow from the market (up to a point) at around 12%.

As the firm continues its borrowing in the financial market, however, the market will recognize the change in the financial structure of the firm and will at some point wish to impose a higher interest rate on loans to the firm. The greater debt-equity ratio (leverage) of the company as it continues to borrow in the market causes the firm to be a more risky proposition in the eyes of lenders. There is now a greater risk of default on the loans, and hence subsequent borrowing by the firm will take place only at a higher rate of interest. In Figure 15-1 we show the higher rate of interest demanded by borrowers to be in the vicinity of 15%. The top line of the blocks, which represents the availability of funds, may thus be regarded as the cost-of-capital line. It can be seen that projects A, B, C, and D promise an internal rate of return greater than the cost of capital, while projects E and F promise lower rates of return which do not compensate for the cost of capital. Thus the firm in this particular situation would be advised to undertake projects A to D only.

Relationship between NPV and IRR

It should be firmly understood that if the internal rate of return exceeds the opportunity rate of interest, the net present value of the proposed investment project will be positive. Using the example discussed earlier, we can plot the net present value of a project against all values that may be assigned to the rate of discount, as in Figure 15-2. To construct the net-present-value curve we have three points that are known to us. Point *A* in Figure 15-2 represents the net present value at a discount rate of zero. That is, when the future stream of profits is undiscounted (or discounted at zero percent), the project will have a net present value of $4,320, as we know from Table 15-1. The second point that is known to

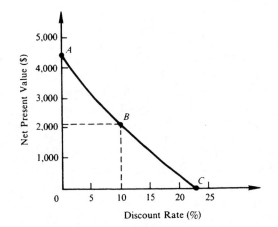

FIGURE 15-2.   *The Net-Present-Value Curve*

us, also from Table 15-1, is point *B*, which indicates the net present value of the project when discounted at an opportunity rate of 10%. The third point known to us is point *C*, which indicates the discount rate that reduces the net present value to zero. This is of course the internal rate of return, and we plot *C* at a discount rate of 23.14%.

- DEFINITION: Thus the *NPV curve* is a locus of the points representing the NPV of a project and the rate at which it was discounted, for all rates of discount between zero and the IRR. Note that the NPV curve is not a straight line but is slightly convex toward the origin. We shall return to the net-present-value curve later in this chapter.

The Profitability-Index Criterion

- DEFINITION: The *profitability index* is defined as the ratio of the present value of the future stream of net cash flows to the initial cost of the investment project. Symbolically, it may be represented as

$$PI = \frac{\displaystyle\sum_{t=1}^{n} \frac{R_t}{(1+r)^t}}{C_0} \tag{15-3}$$

Note the relationship of this criterion to the earlier formulas for the net present value and the internal rate of return. The profitability index is also called the *benefit/cost ratio* of an investment project or the *present value per dollar of outlay*. In the previous example with $r = 0.10$, the profitability index may be calculated as

$$PI = \frac{12,104.84}{10,000}$$
$$= 1.210484$$

- RULE: The decision rule using the profitabllity criterion is to implement any investment project that promises a profitability index exceeding unity. Any such project will thus add more to the present value of revenues than it will cost. It will therefore add to the present value, or the net worth, of the firm.

There is no conflict between the net-present-value, internal-rate-of-return, or profitability index for accept-reject decisions. If a project is acceptable under one criterion, it will be acceptable under all three. Thus any one of these criteria could be employed alone

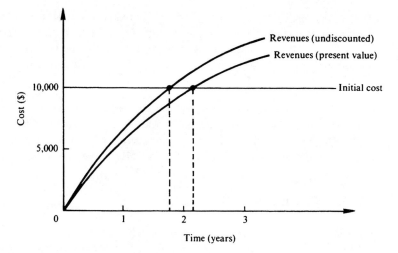

FIGURE 15-3.   The Payback-Period Investment Criterion

for accepting or rejecting investment projects when capital availability is unlimited. We now consider two investment criteria which are commonly used in practice.[3]

The Payback-Period Criterion

- DEFINITION: The *payback period* is defined as the period of time which elapses before an investment earns sufficient revenue to cover its initial cost.

- EXAMPLE: In Figure 15-3 we show graphically the determination of the payback period relating to the investment project we have been discussing. The initial cost of the project is shown at the $10,000 level and remains at that level over time. The undiscounted revenue stream reaches $6,440 at the end of the first year, $10,880 at the end of the second year, and $14,320 at the end of the third year. Interpolating between points, we are able to generate a curve showing the nominal-dollar inflow as a function of time. This curve crosses the initial cost line at approximately 1.8 years, which is therefore the payback period.

  Note that the payback-period criterion in this form ignores the time value of money. To avoid this fundamental shortcoming we could plot the present value of the revenue stream over time, and we have done so in Figure 15-3. In present-value terms, revenues amount to $5,853 in the first year, $9,521 in the second year, and $12,105 in the third year. The curve representing the present value of the revenue stream intersects the initial cost curve at approximately 2.18 years, and this is the payback period when determined by present values of the revenue stream. In either case the firm's decision rule will be to

---

[3]For empirical evidence of the capital budgeting techniques and criteria actually used in business practice, you are referred to the papers by Fremgen, Klammer, Mao, and others which are listed at the end of this chapter.

accept projects that have a payback period less than or equal to a specified period required by the firm.

A second problem is that the payback-period criterion ignores the revenues that occur after the payback period of that investment. A decision is made based simply on whether or not the investment pays back the initial cost before the elapse of a certain period. It would thus be unable to discriminate between two investment projects that had a payback period of, say, three years, but differed in that the net present value of one was substantially higher than the other because of a different or longer revenue stream.

• NOTE: The payback criterion may be appropriate for decision makers or firms with short time horizons, in which case managers are more concerned with short-term profitability. Projects that promise an early return of the outlay and hence will contribute well to accounting net income in the shorter term would be favored by decision makers under such an objective function. In a crude way the payback-period criterion also acts as a screen against risky projects. Since uncertainty increases with the length of time into the future that cash flows must be estimated, the payback period selects the less risky projects at the expense of those that have longer gestation periods and longer revenue streams.

Reconciliation of Payback-Period and IRR Criteria. It can be shown that the payback-period criterion may approximate the internal rate of return criterion under certain conditions.[4] If the original cost is the total cost, if projects are long-lived, and if the revenue stream is uniform, we can show that the internal rate of return and the payback criteria would rank projects identically. Where the revenue stream is expected to be uniform in nominal dollars, we can express the sum of this revenue stream as

$$\sum_{t=1}^{n} R_t = \frac{U}{1+i} + \frac{U}{(1+i)^2} + \cdots + \frac{U}{(1+i)^n} \tag{15-4}$$

where U is the uniform annual net cash flow after taxes. The sum of the geometric progression represented by equation (15-4) is

$$\sum_{t=1}^{n} R_t = \frac{U/1 + i[1 - (1/1 + i)^n}{1 - (1/1 + i)} \tag{15-5}$$

which simplifies to

$$\sum_{t=1}^{n} R_t = \frac{U}{i} - \frac{U}{i}\left(\frac{1}{1+i}\right)^n \tag{15-6}$$

[4]See M. H. Spencer, K. K. Seo, and M. G. Simkin, *Managerial Economics*, 4th ed. (Homewood, Ill.: Richard D. Irwin, Inc., 1975), pp. 449–56.

Or, in terms of the internal rate of return

$$i = \frac{U}{\Sigma R_t} - \frac{U}{\Sigma R_t}\left(\frac{1}{1+i}\right)^n \tag{15-7}$$

The first term in equation (15-7) is in fact the reciprocal of the payback period, since it is the uniform annual revenue stream divided by the total revenue stream. Where the project is long-lived the second term will approach zero, since the exponent n will be large. Hence, the internal rate of return will approach the reciprocal of the payback period when projects are long-lived and the revenue stream is uniform and when there are no other capital costs during the life of the investment project. Thus decision makers using the simple payback criterion may not be too far wrong in some cases.

The Average-Rate-of-Return Criterion

• DEFINITION: The *average rate of return* is defined as the average annual revenues (undiscounted) divided by the initial cost. Symbolically,

$$\text{ARR} = \frac{\left(\sum_{t=1}^{n} R_t\right)/n}{C_0} \tag{15-8}$$

• EXAMPLE: In the example we have been using, the total (undiscounted) revenues from the project are $14,320: The average annual revenues are, therefore, $4,773. Hence,

$$\text{ARR} = \frac{4,773}{10,000}$$
$$= 0.4773$$

Note that this criterion ignores the time value of money and would therefore be unable to discriminate between two projects with the same initial cost and revenue totals but with differing patterns of the receipts. If we modify the ARR criterion to include the discounted present value of the revenue stream, we have

$$\text{ARR} = \frac{(12,104.84)/3}{10,000}$$
$$= \frac{4,035}{10,000}$$
$$= 0.4035$$

Note that this result is exactly the profitability index divided by three, that is,

$$\frac{PI}{3} = \frac{1.210484}{3} = 0.4035$$

This result should be no surprise, for the only difference between the PI formula and the ARR formula (using the present value of the revenue stream) is that the latter is divided by the number of years of the project's life. The additional step of averaging the income stream may obscure important cash flow information, however. Thus the ARR criterion is seriously deficient in undiscounted form and can be regarded as inferior (or at least redundant) to the PI criterion even when the former is calculated using the present value of the revenue stream.[5]

15.2 MUTUALLY EXCLUSIVE INVESTMENTS

In many cases a firm will be considering investment projects that are mutually exclusive. For example, two or more projects may be able to perform the same function or will utilize the same space or other constrained resource, such as skilled labor within the firm. We defer discussion of investment projects that utilize the same funds to the next section, where limited availability of capital is discussed. Where investment projects are mutually exclusive, it is necessary for the firm to rank the investment projects in order of their desirability. It will then choose the project that contributes the most toward the firm's objective function.

- EXAMPLE: Suppose a firm is planning to introduce a new product and has called for bids for the construction of the plant and physical facilities to manufacture that product. Let us consider two bids, which we will call plant A and plant B. Plant A is more expensive but also more efficient in terms of cost per unit and maintenance requirements, as compared with plant B. The relevant cash flows and net present values are shown in Table 15-4.

 It can be seen that plant A offers the greater net present value when discounted at 15%. If the firm's objective is to maximize the present value of its longer-term profitability, it should thus choose plant A, since this alternative contributes more in present-value terms than does plant B.

---

[5]A variation of the ARR criterion is the accounting-return-on-investment (AROI) criterion. The latter is calculated as the ratio of accounting net income (undiscounted) to the initial cost of the project. This criterion is clearly inferior to those discussed above, since it ignores the time value of money, is subject to ambiguity resulting from the several acceptable accounting methods of calculating net income (for example, treatment of depreciation and allocation of overheads), and moreover allows sunk costs to enter the decision-making process.

TABLE 15-4.   Comparison of Costs and Revenues from Two Alternative Investment Projects

	PLANT A		PLANT B	
	Cash Flow ($)	NPV @15% ($)	Cash Flow ($)	NPV @15% ($)
Initial cost	− 100,000	− 100,000	− 60,000	− 60,000
Year 1	45,000	39,150	30,000	26,100
Year 2	55,000	41,580	37,000	27,972
Year 3	50,000	32,900	28,000	18,424
Net cash flow	50,000	13,630	35,000	12,496

The Superiority of NPV over IRR for Mutually Exclusive Investments

Let us now consider the relative internal rates of return of the two plants. Once again we need to find the internal rate of return by a trial-and-error procedure of zeroing in on the discount rate that reduces the net present value to zero. In Table 15-5 we perform this exercise for plant A and see that the internal rate of return is slightly more than 22.8%.

TABLE 15-5.   Calculation of Internal Rate of Return: Plant A

Year	CFAT	NPV @25%	NPV @20%	NPV @23%	NPV @22.8%
0	$ − 100,000	$ − 100,000	$ − 100,000	$ − 100,000	$ − 100,000
1	45,000	36,000	37,485	36,585	36,644
2	55,000	35,200	38,170	36,355	36,471
3	50,000	25,600	28,950	26,850	27,000
		$ − 3,200	$ 4,605	$ − 210	$ 114

In Table 15-6 we perform the search procedure for the internal rate of return to plant B and find that the rate of discount that reduces the net present value to zero is slightly more than 27.2%. Thus the internal-rate-of-return criterion would suggest that plant B is preferable to plant A, and it evidently conflicts with the judgment of the net-present-value criterion.

TABLE 15-6.   Calculation of Internal Rate of Return: Plant B

Year	CFAT	NPV @25%	NPV @28%	NPV @27%	NPV @27.2%
0	$ − 60,000	$ − 60,000	$ − 60,000	$ − 60,000	$ − 60,000
1	30,000	24,000	23,430	23,622	23,580
2	37,000	23,680	22,570	22,940	22,866
3	28,000	14,336	13,356	13,670	13,608
		$ 2,016	$ − 644	$ 232	$ 54

To see why this conflict arises, let us plot the net-present-value curves of both plant A and plant B, as shown in Figure 15-4. To plot the net-present-value curve for plant A,

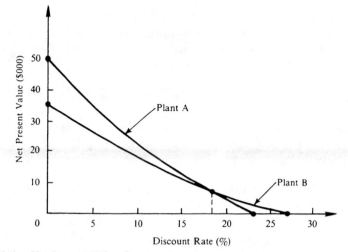

FIGURE 15-4. **Net-Present-Value Curves**

we know that at a zero rate of discount the net present value will be equal to the net cash inflow (in nominal dollars) of $50,000. From Table 15-4 we know that at a discount rate of 15%, the net present value of plant A is $13,630. Finally, we know that the rate of discount that reduces the net present value to zero is approximately 22.8%. Similarly, for plant B we can plot its present value curve, beginning at $35,000 when the discount rate is zero, passing through $12,496 when the discount rate is 15%, and terminating at 27.2% on the horizontal axis.

It is clear that the net present value curves for the two projects intersect at approximately the 18% rate of discount. For discount rates below 18%, the net-present-value criterion would suggest project A, but above 18% the net-present-value criterion would suggest project B. The internal-rate-of-return criterion, since it looks at only one point on the net-present-value-curve, would suggest project B under all opportunity rates of discount up to 27.2%. However, for actual opportunity rates of discount less than about 18%, the internal-rate-of-return criterion would suggest the investment project with the lower net present value and would thus lead decision makers to a suboptimal decision in terms of the addition to the firm's net worth, since plant A clearly has the greater net present value at these lower opportunity rates of discount.

- NOTE: Why does this conflict arise between the net-present-value and the internal-rate-of-return criteria? It arises because of the implicit assumption that the profit stream of each project could be reinvested at the internal rate of return. To see this, note that discounting a future stream of profits is the reverse of compounding a presently held sum over the same period of time at the same rate. At higher interest rates (namely, greater than 18%, the net present value of plant B would compound to a greater value over the three years than would the net present value of plant A at the same interest rates. The conflict with net present value arises because the calculation of net present value implicitly assumes the reinvestment of the profit stream at the opportunity discount rate rather than at the internal rate of return.

We need the decision criterion that will always indicate the project that adds the most toward the attainment of the firm's objective function. Hence, the net-present-value criterion is superior to the internal-rate-of-return criterion for situations where mutually exclusive projects must be evaluated.

The Superiority of NPV over the Profitability Index

Let us now calculate the profitability indices for each of the projects under consideration. According to the profitability-index criterion, the plant with the higher profitability index should be chosen for implementation. The calculations are as shown in Table 15-7.

TABLE 15-7.   *Calculation of Profitability Index*

	Plant A	Plant B
PV of revenues	113,363	72,496
Initial costs	100,000	60,000
Profitability index	1.13363	1.20826

Note that the profitability index supports the judgment of the internal-rate-of-return criterion, by indicating that project B is superior to project A in this situation. However, it is inferior to the net-present-value criterion for the same reason that the IRR criterion is: It would indicate acceptance of the project that contributes the lesser amount to the net worth of the firm in at least some cases and would therefore result in decisions that are not in accord with the objectives of the firm.

• NOTE: The conflict between the profitabilty-index criterion and the net-present-value criterion arises because of what is known as the "size disparity" problem. Where there is a difference in the size of the initial cost or in the magnitude and time pattern of the revenue streams, the profitability-index criterion and the net-present-value criterion may rank projects differently. If the firm's objective is to maximize its net worth, the net-present-value criterion must be used, since although the profitability index indicates which project is the most efficient at generating net present value, this is a relative consideration rather than the absolute consideration of maximizing the firm's net worth.

Thus, in general, it is preferable to use the net-present-value criterion for ranking mutually exclusive projects under situations of unlimited availability of capital. Both the internal rate of return and the profitability index may indicate the acceptance of projects that are not in the best interest of the firm's objective to maximize the present value of its longer-term earnings.

Capital Budgeting Given Limited Availability of Capital

The availability of investment funds should not, in theory, ever impose a constraint on the level of investments. We saw in Figure 15-1 that although the cost of capital may increase as the level of investment is increased, the level of investment will be carried to the point where the marginal investment project has an internal rate of return at least equal to the cost of capital. Thus, if the internal rate of return exceeds the cost of capital, if the net present value at the opportunity rate is positive, or if the profitability index exceeds unity, the project should be implemented since it will contribute to the enlargement of the firm's net present value. Where investment projects are mutually exclusive, the problem is to choose the one project of those available that would best serve the firm's objective function. The implicit assumption is that once this choice for this particular purpose is made, the firm would continue to consider other investment projects and groups of mutually exclusive investment projects and would implement those that met the acceptability criterion. In theory, the funds are always available, although at progressively higher rates of interest perhaps, and if the net present value is positive at this higher cost of capital, the investment project under consideration should be undertaken.

In practice, however, we often find the situation of a decision maker facing a constraint on investment funds. It is common business practice to set investment budgets for departments or divisions within the firm such that the decision-making unit faces a constraint on investment funds. Setting investment budgets for individual departments or decision-making units or for the firm as a whole may reflect the reluctance of top management to take on additional debt, with its subsequent impact on the leverage position and the market value of the firm's shares.

In such situations the decision maker faces an allocation problem and should proceed to select the investment projects which maximize the return from that limited supply of investment funds. The projects should be ranked in order of their NPV and implemented up to the point where the next project cannot be afforded. If any remaining projects (with positive NPV) farther down the list can be afforded, by virtue of their lower initial cost levels, the decision maker should skip over the unaffordable projects and implement the remaining projects which can be afforded before the capital budget is depleted. The remaining funds, if any, should then be invested at the opportunity rate of interest.

Some Qualifications

The estimation of the future cash flows associated with investment projects involves techniques discussed in Chapters 5 and 8. Initial costs should cause few estimation problems, since they are to be incurred in the very near future and thus should be determined with relative accuracy. Future costs and revenue streams, however, are subject to uncertainty and thus may be accompanied by a probability distribution. The preceding analysis would need to be modified by insertion of the expected values of the net cash flow after taxes for each project rather than the point estimates used in the examples.

Use of probability distributions and the resultant expected value of net cash flows after taxes for each year in the future involves the law of averages and could therefore cause the net-present-value criterion to be an unsuitable decision criterion for some investment decisions. "One-shot" investment decisions may expose the investor to the risk of a very low outcome, which cannot be averaged upward by other similar projects having outcomes above their expected values. Thus we might expect the firm with a one-shot decision involving capital budgeting to apply the certainty-equivalent criterion, which allows the decision maker to place his or her own evaluation upon the risk and other nonquantifiable aspects of the investment decision, as explained in Chapter 2.

Differing risks of differing investment projects are adjusted for by the use of differing opportunity rates of discount. Recall that the opportunity rate of discount for any project is what the investment funds involved in that project could earn elsewhere at a comparable degree of risk. Thus a firm considering a series of investment projects may discount these projects at differing opportunity discount rates if the degree of risk perceived to be associated with each project differs.[6]

15.3 SUMMARY

In this chapter we have considered the capital budgeting decision, which is the decision to invest in plant, equipment, and other projects expected to generate a future stream of net cash flows. Given unlimited availability of capital, but typically with an increasing cost of capital, the firm should invest up to the point where the marginal investment project implemented has an internal rate of return at least equal to the cost of capital. This will mean that the project has a net present value that is nonnegative, or a profitability index of at least unity. When investment projects are mutually exclusive, the three investment criteria mentioned may give conflicting results, and we found the net-present-value criterion to be the only reliable guide if the firm wishes to maximize its net worth. Where the investment funds available are constrained, the firm would implement the projects in order of their NPV ranking, up to the point where the next project cannot be afforded. It would then implement any other affordable projects and invest the remaining funds at the opportunity rate of interest.

The techniques introduced in Chapter 2 regarding the decision-making process under conditions of risk and uncertainty must be applied to the capital budgeting decision, since there will be a probability distribution surrounding the expected values of future cost and revenue streams. Similarly, the techniques outlined in Chapters 5 and 8 for demand and cost estimation and forecasting must be used to establish the future stream of net cash flow after taxes for each project under consideration. Finally, it should be noted that the appropriate decision criterion in any particular firm is the one that best pursues the firm's objective function. If the firm has a long time horizon and wishes to maximize the net present value of the firm, the net-present-value criterion is appropriate under most circumstances. On the other hand, if the firm's time horizon is relatively short and management is concerned with accounting profitability, market value of outstanding shares, and other considerations involving immediate or short-term cash flow, the payback criterion or the average-rate-of-return criterion may be the appropriate investment criterion in these cases.

---

[6]An alternate means of adjusting for differing risks is to reduce the period over which you will recognize the revenues from the more risky projects. See J. C. Van Horne, "Variation of Project Life as a Means of Adjusting for Risk," *Engineering Economist,* 21 (Spring 1976), pp. 151–58.

DISCUSSION QUESTIONS

15-1. Explain in three sentences why the NPV criterion and the IRR criterion must always agree on the accept/reject investment decision, given the availability of sufficient funds.

15-2. In calculating the expected net revenue stream associated with an investment project, what factors enter the calculation?

15-3. When comparing possible investment projects, why is it important to ensure that all projects have been evaluated using the same depreciation method?

15-4. Why is the cost of capital to the firm likely to be a step function of the amount of funds demanded for investment purposes?

15-5. Under what circumstances is the use of the payback-period investment criterion appropriate?

15-6. Why is the average-rate-of-return criterion inferior to the other investment criteria discussed?

15-7. Where projects are mutually exclusive, the IRR criterion may rank projects in conflict with their ranking by the NPV criterion. Why? Does this conflict invalidate the IRR criterion?

15-8. Under what circumstances might the profitability index disagree with the NPV criterion in the ranking of mutually exclusive projects? Explain.

15-9. Suppose investment projects are divisible, in the sense that any part of each project can be undertaken, with the return being proportionate to the investment. Does this factor change the analysis?

15-10. Why can the payback criteria be regarded as appropriate, in a crude way, for a risk-averse investor?

PROBLEMS AND SHORT CASES

15-1. The Omega Investment Corporation has more than half a million dollars to invest as the result of a recent windfall gain from the revaluation of a foreign currency it was holding. Failing all else, these funds can be invested in government bonds, which are considered to be risk free, at 8% per annum. Omega is evaluating four other investment projects as well. These projects seem to be equally risky, and Omega feels they should return at least 10% per annum in order to be considered an equivalent proposition to placing the funds in the risk-free bonds. The initial outlays and net cash flows after taxes (NCFAT) for each year of each project's life are as follows:

Project	A ($)	B ($)	C ($)	D ($)
Initial outlay	100,000	135,000	85,000	122,000
NCFAT				
Year 1	− 12,200	26,300	56,000	− 25,000
Year 2	− 8,500	34,400	32,000	10,600
Year 3	76,600	48,600	18,600	48,200
Year 4	62,400	56,500	12,400	96,500
Year 5	23,500	22,000	5,500	34,000
Year 6	9,500	10,000	0	18,700

You are asked to advise Omega about which of these projects, if any, it should undertake. Explain your reasoning.

15-2. The Anderson Electronics Company is considering investing $1 million in a major advertising campaign. This expenditure will be tax deductible at the end of the year in which it is incurred, and Anderson's tax rate is 48%. It will take a year to produce the campaign after the million dollars is spent, and the impact of the campaign on sales is expected to be felt over the following three years. The precise outcomes are uncertain, however. The marketing research department has generated the following estimates (and associated probabilities) of incremental net cash flows after taxes that will result from this campaign for each of the three years.

Incremental	PROBABILITIES		
NCFAT ($)	Year 2	Year 3	Year 4
50,000	0.05	0.10	0.25
150,000	0.10	0.20	0.35
250,000	0.15	0.40	0.25
350,000	0.35	0.15	0.10
450,000	0.25	0.10	0.05
650,000	0.10	0.05	0.00

The probability distributions should be treated as being independent from year to year (hence no conditional probabilities), and the NCFAT figures should be regarded as arriving at the end of each year. Anderson considers this project to be about as risky as investing the funds in the bonds of a large trust company which would currently pay 12% per annum. Assume that Anderson's tax assessment will be finalized one year after the million is spent.

(a) What is the net present value of this investment project?

(b) What is the internal rate of return of the project?

(c) Sketch the NPV curve against various opportunity discount rates and estimate from this the NPV if the appropriate discount rate is 10%.

15-3. Custy Canoe and Kayak, Inc., is considering investing in a facility that would allow it to manufacture lightweight fiberglass sports kayaks. The proposed plant would involve an initial investment of $212,500 and would have an expected life of four years, after which time its expected scrap value would be $12,500. The marketing manager, Maureen Custy, expects these kayaks to become increasingly popular in future years, although other firms are likely to begin supplying competitive canoes within two or three years. Extensive market research and cost estimation studies have established the following (independent) probability distributions of the level of contribution to overheads and profits in each of the four years.

Contributions	PROBABILITIES			
($)	Year 1	Year 2	Year 3	Year 4
10,000	0.05	0.05	0.10	0.20
25,000	0.20	0.15	0.20	0.30
50,000	0.40	0.20	0.35	0.25
75,000	0.25	0.35	0.20	0.15
100,000	0.10	0.15	0.10	0.10
125,000	0.00	0.10	0.05	0.00

Note that the contribution figures do not include consideration of the tax savings resulting from depreciation. For tax purposes, depreciation is calculated using the sum-of-years-digits method. The finance manager, Michael Gable, advises that the applicable tax rate is 48%, and that this project should be evaluated in terms of the alternative use of these funds to establish a camping resort area for canoe enthusiasts, which he considers to be of equal risk. The resort project has an expected internal rate of return of 15%.

Assume that the kayak plant can be purchased and installed at the start of this year, that tax payments or refunds are due at the end of each year, that the profit contributions are received continuously throughout each year, and that the expected scrap value is realized at the end of the fourth year.

(a) Calculate the expected net present value of the kayak project, taking care to use the appropriate discount factors.

(b) Find the approximate internal rate of return of the kayak project.

(c) Recalculate the expected net present value of the kayak project, assuming this time that all cash flows take place in lump sum at the start or end of each year.

(d) Explain why there is a difference between your answers to (a) and (c).

(e) In which project (kayak or resort) should Custy Canoe and Kayak invest the funds? Explain.

15-4. Marilyn Monibaggs is considering investing in a small shop in the downtown area of a large city. Ms. Monibaggs has not been lax in her investigations but has found that only two locations are feasible. Ms. Monibaggs is considering establishing either a sportswear boutique or a sporting equipment store, and she could put either type of store at either location. Location A is initially more suitable for the sportswear boutique, but the profitability of this venture will decline in the future because of the planned establishment of a major department store and other shops nearby. After this event the sporting equipment shop would be more profitable than the sportswear shop at this location. Location B, on the other hand, is close to several competitors in both types of merchandise but is frequented by a larger number of potential customers. The initial cash outlay will be $50,000 for the sportswear store versus $60,000 for the equipment store, and Ms. Monibaggs will pay a monthly lease on the location chosen. The cash flows after taxes for each of the four alternatives have been carefully estimated as follows:

| | LOCATION A | | LOCATION B | |
Year	Sportswear	Equipment	Sportswear	Equipment
1	$ − 18,000	$ − 24,000	$ − 24,000	$ − 30,000
2	37,400	26,000	32,000	28,600
3	26,200	28,400	33,500	30,800
4	22,400	29,800	34,300	36,400
5	20,800	30,200	35,000	38,900

These figures include the initial cash outlay for inventories that was incurred at the start of the first year. Treat the other net cash flows as arriving in a continuous stream throughout each year. Ms. Monibaggs is only interested in a time horizon of five years and considers the opportunity discount rates to be 14% and 15% for the sportswear and equipment stores, respectively, at location A; and 17% and 20% for the sportswear and equipment stores, respectively, at location B.

(a) What is the net present value of each of the four projects?

(b) Estimate the payback period for each of the four projects.

(c) Supposing Ms. Monibaggs is interested in maximizing her net worth, but at the same time wants to get her (undiscounted) money back quickly to be ready to invest elsewhere if an opportunity arises, which alternative should she choose? Explain.

15-5. A consortium of business professors at a city university are thinking of investing in the takeout food industry. A location has been found which is considered to be highly suitable because of its proximity to thousands of downtown offices and stores, a major stadium, and two very large high schools. The professors are in the process of deciding whether they should go with hamburgers, chicken, or tacos as their product line. Extensive studies have provided the following estimated probabilities for various levels of net cash flow after taxes in each of the first three years for each of the three projects.

| NCFAT | PROBABILITIES | | |
($)	Hamburgers	Chicken	Tacos
Year 1			
$ – 10,000	0.05	0.10	0.15
0	0.10	0.15	0.20
10,000	0.25	0.30	0.35
20,000	0.35	0.25	0.15
30,000	0.15	0.15	0.10
40,000	0.10	0.05	0.05
Year 2			
$ – 10,000	0.00	0.05	0.05
0	0.05	0.05	0.10
10,000	0.15	0.10	0.15
20,000	0.20	0.25	0.20
30,000	0.30	0.35	0.30
40,000	0.20	0.15	0.15
50,000	0.10	0.05	0.05
Year 3			
$ 0	0.00	0.05	0.00
10,000	0.15	0.10	0.05
20,000	0.20	0.30	0.10
30,000	0.30	0.35	0.40
40,000	0.20	0.15	0.25
50,000	0.10	0.05	0.15
60,000	0.05	0.00	0.05

The above net cash flows after taxes do not include the initial franchise fee of $50,000 for hamburgers; $40,000 for chicken; and $35,000 for tacos. They do allow for depreciation, however. The professors' time horizon is only three years, since they are all on three-year contracts at the university and expect their research and teaching efforts to suffer so badly that their contracts will not be renewed and they will have to go elsewhere for a job. Their collective judgment is that the opportunity discount rate is 15% for hamburgers, 13% for chicken, and 16% for tacos. Treat the expected net cash flows after taxes as arriving continuously throughout each year and the probability distributions as being independent of each other.

(a) Calculate the expected net present value of each alternative, assuming that the franchise fee cannot be recovered at the end of the period.

(b) Estimate the payback period for each project, using the undiscounted net cash flows after taxes.

(c) Advise the professors as to which project, if any, to undertake. Support your recommendation.

15-6. You have recently been hired as an assistant investment analyst in a small corporation which promotes new products and inventions. Your boss has asked you to evaluate and rank four potential investment projects. He tells you that the capital budget for the year is $105,000 and that anything left over can be invested in government bonds at 8.5% per annum. The details of the four projects are as shown in the following table.

Your boss tells you that it is company policy to consider the expected net cash flow stream up to and including the fourth year only. He says to treat flows as if they were to arrive in lump sum on the last day of each year.

(a) Calculate the expected net present value of each project, and rank the projects in descending order.
(b) Calculate the profitability index for each project and rank them in descending order.
(c) Which projects do you recommend should be implemented if your boss wishes to maximize the expected net present value of the capital budget?
(d) What is the maximum expected net present value of the capital budget? Explain.

| | PROJECT | | | |
	A	B	C	D
Initial cost	$35,000	$28,000	$16,000	$40,000
Expected NCFAT				
Year 1	12,681	9,650	8,480	22,680
Year 2	28,323	25,462	12,624	51,070
Year 3	36,084	31,836	28,970	28,218
Year 4	20,880	42,420	14,381	8,440
Salvage value	$10,000	$ 8,000	$ 2,000	$12,000
Opportunity discount rate	12%	10%	14%	15%

15-7. A large real estate firm has half a million dollars which it wishes to invest in urban housing development projects. The available opportunities have been carefully evaluated and the four most promising projects have been thoroughly examined, with cost and demand estimates being supplied by a reliable group of consultants at a cost of $10,000. The projects are known as North, South, East, and West because of their locations relative to the firm's main office. The relevant details are as follows:

| | PROJECT | | | |
	North	South	East	West
Initial cost	$120,000	$180,000	$250,000	$285,000
Expected NCFAT				
Year 1	40,000	62,000	90,000	115,000
Year 2	42,000	75,000	88,000	140,000
Year 3	45,000	81,000	84,000	132,000
Year 4	48,000	84,000	82,000	90,000
Year 5	51,000	80,000	80,000	75,000
Salvage value	$ 30,000	$ 20,000	$ 50,000	$70,000
Opportunity discount rate	10%	15%	12%	18%

Each project would be developed in five yearly stages, with all accounts being paid and all revenues being received from sales on the last day of each year. The initial costs shown refer to the cost of purchasing each tract of land, and this must be paid before any activity can begin.

(a) Calculate the expected net present value of each project and rank the projects in descending order.

(b) Calculate the profitability index for each project and rank them in descending order.

(c) Which projects should be undertaken to maximize the net present value of the funds available?

(d) What is the maximum net present value of the funds available? Explain.

15-8. Dimmock Dry Dock Services is considering installation of a new dry dock facility. There are two competing propositions. The first plan would cover two acres of waterfront land and be capable of servicing fifteen boats at the same time. This plan would require purchase of land adjacent to Dimmock's present facility. The second plan is more modest and involves replacing the present facility with a modernized dry dock capable of handling eight boats at a time. The initial outlays and net cash flows over the firm's planning period are as follows:

	First Plan	Second Plan
Initial costs	$1,580,000	$750,000
Expected NCFAT		
Year 1	350,000	200,000
Year 2	500,000	250,000
Year 3	600,000	300,000
Year 4	600,000	300,000
Year 5	600,000	300,000
Salvage value	500,000	250,000
Opportunity discount rate	18%	15%

(a) Calculate the expected net present value, the internal rate of return, and the profitability index for each plan.

(b) Advise Dimmock Dry Dock as to which plan they should implement, supporting your analysis with explicit recognition of the underlying assumptions.

15-9. Rasta Resorts, Inc., is planning to develop some beachfront land on an eastern Caribbean island. Plan A is to build a hotel-casino for short-stay guests (up to one week), whereas plan B is to build condominiums for a clientele who would typically stay longer than one week. The hotel-casino would need to be lavishly appointed with luxury rooms, and the condominiums would optimally be somewhat more spartan. Thus there is a substantial difference in the initial cost. Plan A will cost $EC20 million (Eastern Caribbean dollars) before a single guest arrives, whereas plan B will cost only $EC6 million. Revenues from the hotel-casino are likely to be four times those from the condominiums, and operating costs of the hotel-casino are likely to be only twice those of the condominiums. Rasta Resorts personnel tell you that the hotel-casino will reach payback in five years, whereas the condominiums will reach payback in three years (in nominal terms in both cases). The resale value of these resorts, once payback is reached, will be $EC30 million for the hotel-casino and $EC10 million for the condominiums, regardless of when they are sold after payback, because of the inevitable physical depreciation of the buildings.

(a) Assuming year-end cash flows, a time horizon of five years, and opportunity discount rates of 20% and 15% for the hotel-casino and the condominiums, respectively, calculate the expected present value of each plan.

(b) Would your answer be different if the time horizon was 10 years?

(c) Advise Rasta Resorts on this decision, making explicit all underlying assumptions and reservations you might have.

15-10. Hilltop Raceway Corporation has been formed to develop a 100-acre site into a motor-racing facility. At this point the final decision has not yet been made whether it will be an oval circuit with only four banked left-hand turns or a road circuit with about ten turns both to the left and the right. The HCR management knows there is more spectator support for oval racing and that a new circuit like this would get on the Indy-car schedule as well as the stock-car schedules organized by CART (Confederation of Auto Racing Teams), which have a tremendous following. But an oval circuit would involve much greater initial costs to level the hill and install the racetrack and spectator stands. A road circuit, on the other hand, would use the terrain to advantage and be considerably less expensive to set up. The road circuit would probably attract the Indy cars but not the CART stock cars; however, it would become a regular feature on the USAC (United States Automobile Club) calendar and might possibly attract the Formula One circus after two or three years of operation. USAC events have many more competitors but fewer spectators than CART events and thus are less profitable to the promoters. Formula One events are very profitable and involve a great deal of prestige for the racetrack owners, as well as reciprocal benefits at other race circuits around the world. The cash flow details (in millions) are as follows. Assume year-end cash flows.

	Oval Circuit	Road Circuit
Initial cost	$50	$40
Expected NCFAT		
Year 1	15	5
Year 2	20	8
Year 3	20	15
Year 4	20	20
Year 5	20	20

Expected resale value after five years (for condominium development) is $30 million if the landscape is modified for an oval track and $50 million if the land is used for a road-racing track. The firm's cost of capital will be 17% if it raises $50 million but only 14% if it only has to raise $40 million.

(a) Calculate the expected net present value of the two alternatives.

(b) Estimate the payback period for each alternative.

(c) Advise Hilltop Raceway as to what they should do.

(d) What assumptions and qualifications underlie your advice?

SUGGESTED REFERENCES AND FURTHER READING

AHMED, S. B. "Optimal Equipment Replacement Policy," *Journal of Transport Economics and Policy*, 7 (January 1973), pp. 71–79.

BAUMOL, W. J. *Economic Theory and Operations Analysis* (4th ed.), chap. 25. Englewood Cliffs, N.J.: Prentice-Hall, Inc., 1977.

CLARK, J. J., T. J. HINDELANG, and R. E. PRITCHARD. *Capital Budgeting*. Englewood Cliffs, N.J.: Prentice-Hall, Inc., 1979.

EISNER, R. "Components of Capital Expenditures: Replacement and Modernization versus Expansion," *Review of Economics and Statistics*, 54 (August 1972), pp. 297–305.

FELDSTEIN, M. S., and D. K. FOOT. "The Other Half of Gross Investment: Replacement and Modernization Expenditures," *Review of Economics and Statistics*, 53 (February 1971), pp. 49–58.

FREMGEN, J. M. "Capital Budgeting Practices: A Survey," *Management Accounting*, May 1973, pp. 19–25.

HALL, R. E., and D. W. JORGENSON. "Tax Policy and Investment Behavior," *American Economic Review*, 57 (June 1967), pp. 391–414.

HIRSHLEIFER, J. "Investment Decision under Uncertainty: Choice-Theoretic Approaches," *Quarterly Journal of Economics*, 79 (November 1965), pp. 509–36.

JORGENSON, D. W. "Econometric Studies of Investment Behavior: A Survey," *Journal of Economic Literature*, 9 (December 1971), pp. 1111–47.

KLAMMER, T. "Empirical Evidence of the Adoption of Sophisticated Capital Budgeting Techniques," *Journal of Business*, July 1972, pp. 387–97.

LORIE, J. H., AND L. J. SAVAGE. "Three Problems in Rationing Capital," *Journal of Business*, 28 (October 1955), pp. 229–39.

MAO, J. C. T. "Survey of Capital Budgeting: Theory and Practice," *Journal of Finance*, May 1970, pp. 349–60.

MILLER, E. "Decision-Making under Uncertainy for Capital Budgeting and Hiring," *Managerial Decisions in Economics*, 6 (March 1985), pp. 11–18.

PETTY, J. W., D. F. SCOTT, JR., and M. M. BIRD. "The Capital Expenditure Decision-Making Process of Large Corporations," *Engineering Economist*, 20 (Spring 1975), pp. 159–72.

VAN HORNE, J. C. "Capital Budgeting under Conditions of Uncertainty as to Project Life," *Engineering Economist*, 17 (Spring 1972), pp. 189–99.

———— *Financial Management and Policy* (6th ed.), chaps. 4–8. Englewood Cliffs, N.J.: Prentice-Hall, Inc., 1983.

———— "Variation of Project Life as a Means of Adjusting for Risk," *Engineering Economist*, 21 (Spring 1976), pp. 151–58.

WEINGARTNER H. M. *Mathematical Programming and Analysis of Capital Budgeting Problems*. Englewood Cliffs, N.J.: Prentice-Hall, Inc., 1963.

Appendix A

A REVIEW OF ANALYTIC GEOMETRY AND CALCULUS: FUNCTIONS, GRAPHS, AND DERIVATIVES

Functions and Graphs

A *function* is an expression of the dependence of one variable on one or more other variables. In *general* form we may write

$$Y = f(X) \qquad \text{(A-1)}$$

This expression is read, "The value of Y is a function of, or depends on, the value of X." Note that Y is known as the dependent variable, while X is the independent variable. The value of Y may depend on more than one independent variable, of course, such that we might express in general form the functional relationship as

$$Y = f(X_1, X_2, X_3, \ldots, X_n) \qquad \text{(A-2)}$$

In this multivariable function the value of Y is seen to depend on the value of several independent variables, where n is the number of these independent variables. For example, the sales of umbrellas may be a function of the price of umbrellas, the income of consumers, the rainfall levels, the advertising expenditures of umbrella manufacturers, and the price of taxi fares.

The form of the functional dependence of Y on the independent variables X_i, ($i = 1, 2, \ldots, n$), remains unspecified in the expressions shown. To find the exact nature of the dependence we must examine the specific form of the function. This may take a variety of mathematical forms: For example, Y may be a linear, quadratic, cubic, quartic, or higher-order function of X (or the X's), or it may be a power function, an exponential function, or a hyperbolic function, or it may take some other form. Let us examine these in turn.

Linear Functions. The general form of a linear function is

$$Y = a + bX \qquad \text{(A-3)}$$

- EXAMPLE: Suppose $Y = 4 + 0.5X$. In this example, $a = 4$ and $b = 0.5$. We can array the values for Y given the values for X, as shown in Table A-1. These values indicate the

TABLE A-1.   *Values of Y for Various Values of X.*

Values of X	0.0	1.0	2.0	3.0	4.0	5.0	6.0
Values of Y	4.0	4.5	5.0	5.5	6.0	6.5	7.0

specific dependence of the variable Y on the variable X. When X is zero, the second term in equation (A-3) drops out and Y is simply equal to the parameter a. Each time the variable X is increased by one unit, the value of Y increases to the extent of the parameter b.

Let us plot the above values on a graph that has X on the horizontal axis and Y on the vertical axis. Using the pairs of observations for X and Y as coordinates, we are able to plot the equation $Y = 4 + 0.5X$ as shown in Figure A-1. Strictly, the graph of this equation would extend into three of the four quadrants, but we show only the northeastern quadrant where both variables have positive values, since for most economic applications these are the only meaningful values of the function.

- NOTE: Notice that the graph intercepts the Y axis at the value of 4: Hence the parameter a is known as the *intercept* parameter. Similarly, the graph slopes upward and to the right at the rate of half of one unit of Y for each one-unit increase in X. The slope of the line (the vertical rise over the horizontal run) is thus equal to 0.5, precisely the value of the b parameter. Accordingly, b is often called the *slope* parameter. Thus by observing the values of the a and b terms in a simple linear function we are able to envisage the graphical form of that function.

For multivariable linear functions we simply extend the above analysis for the case of additional explanatory variables, such as

$$Y = a + b_1X_1 + b_2X_2 + b_3X_3 + \ldots + b_n X_n \tag{A-4}$$

where the X_i ($i = 1, 2, 3, \ldots, n$), represent several independent variables, and the b_i coefficients represent the influence that a one-unit change in the value of each independent varitable would have on the value of Y.

- EXAMPLE: A simple example of a multivariable linear equation is $Y = 2 - 0.4X_1 + 0.3X_2$. Substituting values for X_1 and X_2 into this expression allows us to obtain the values for Y, as shown in Table A-2. The values in the body of the table represent the value of Y for the values of X_1 and X_2 given by the coordinates of that value. Graphing the values of Y against the values of X_1 and X_2 we obtain Figure A-2, in which it can be seen that the above equation is that of a plane. Note that the parameter a is again an intercept value, or the value of Y when the values of the independent variables are zero, and that the b coefficients represent the slope of the function as we move one unit in the direction of a particular independent variable. Note too that the sign of b_1 is negative, indicating that the value of Y declines as additional units of X_1 are added.

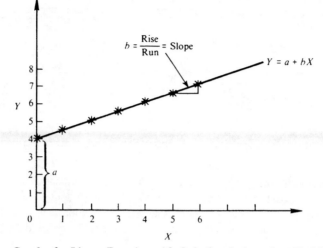

FIGURE A-1.　Graph of a Linear Function with Only One Independent Variable

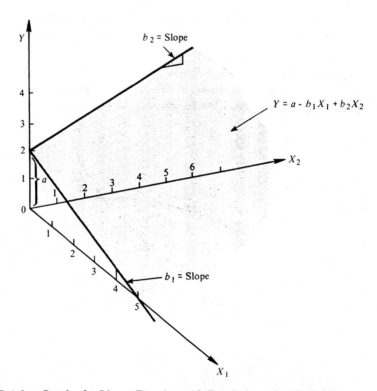

FIGURE A-2.　Graph of a Linear Function with Two Independent Variables

TABLE A-2.   *Values of Y for Various Values of X_1 and X_2*

		VALUES OF X_1					
		0	1	2	3	4	5
	0	2.0	1.6	1.2	0.8	0.4	0.0
	1	2.3	1.9	1.5	1.1	0.7	0.3
	2	2.6	2.2	1.8	1.4	1.0	0.6
Values of X_2	3	2.9	2.5	2.1	1.7	1.3	0.9
	4	3.2	2.8	2.4	2.0	1.6	1.2
	5	3.5	3.1	2.7	2.3	1.9	1.5

Quadratic Functions.   The preceding linear relationships represent what are known as first-degree functions, since each of the independent variables was raised to the first power only. We move now to quadratic, or second-degree, functions, in which one or more of the independent variables will be squared, or raised to the second power, such as

$$Y = a + bX + cX^2 \tag{A-5}$$

Hence Y is a function of the constant a plus the constant b times the independent variable X, plus the constant c times the square of that independent variable.

- EXAMPLE: Suppose we let $a = 5$; $b = 3$; and $c = 2$. We may calculate the values of Y for various values of X, as shown in Table A-3. Plotting these values as a graph, we obtain Figure A-3, in which it can be seen that the graphical representation of a quadratic

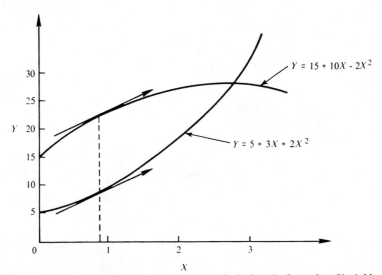

FIGURE A-3.   *Graph of Quadratic Functions with Only One Independent Variable*

TABLE A-3.   Values of Y for Various Values of X

Values of X	0	1	2	3	4	5
Values of Y	5	10	19	32	49	70

function is curvilinear, whereas linear functions are rectilinear. Notice that the parameter a remains the intercept term, but the slope depends not only on the value of X but also on the square of the value of X. In Figure A-3 we show a second quadratic function, $Y = 15 + 10X - 2X^2$, and it can be seen that the curvature of this function is concave from below, whereas the curvature of the first function was concave from above. This shape results from the negative sign in front of the second-degree term in the latter expression.

When there are multiple independent variables and the relationship between these variables and the independent variable is quadratic, we may express the function as follows:

$$Y = a + bX_1 - cX_1^2 + dX_2 - eX_2^2 \tag{A-6}$$

for the simple case in which there are only two independent variables, X_1 and X_2. This relationship is graphed in Figure A-4, where it can be seen that the negative signs preceding the second-degree terms indicate that the surface representing the function will be convex from above. Once again the parameter a is the intercept on the Y axis and takes a

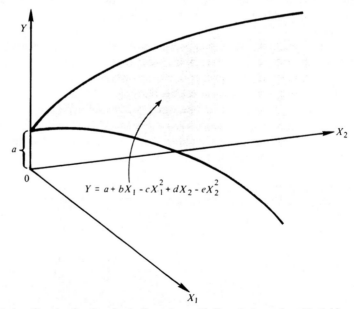

FIGURE A-4.   Graph of a Quadratic Function with Two Independent Variables

positive value. In other cases, of course, the parameter *a* may be zero or negative, just as the other coefficients may take values that are positive, zero, or negative.

Cubic Functions.   We turn now to the third-degree terms in the functional relationship. Cubic functions may have first-degree, second-degree, and third-degree terms such as the following:

$$Y = a + bX + cX^2 + dX^3 \qquad \text{(A-7)}$$

When all the coefficients have positive signs, it is clear that the values of *Y* will increase by progressively larger increments as the value of *X* increases. When the signs of the coefficients differ, the graph of *Y* may display both convex and concave sections, may have hills and valleys, or may simply exhibit a monotonically increasing or decreasing shape, depending on the values of the coefficients.

- EXAMPLE: Consider the function $Y = 25 + 10X - 5X^2 + 2X^3$. In Table A-4 we calculate the values of *Y* for several values of *X*. Plotting the values of *Y* against the value of *X* as in Figure A-5, we see that the function is monotonically increasing yet exhibits convexity from above at first, changing at the inflection point to concavity from above. In the same figure we show the graph of the equation $Y = 100 + 5X - 10X^2 + 2X^3$ and note that it has sections of both positive and negative slope. This result indicates that the values of the parameters are instrumental in determining the shape of the graphical relationship. The distinguishing feature of a cubic function as compared with a quadratic function is that the former may have an inflection point (where slope changes from convexity in one direction to concavity in that direction, or vice versa), whereas the latter does not.

    Cubic functions in two independent variables will produce a three-dimensional surface when graphed, as in Figure A-6. Again, the value of the parameters and the signs of these parameters and coefficients operate to determine the shape and placement of the surface depicting the functional relationship.

    We could continue the examination of functional relationships with fourth-degree and higher-degree terms influencing the value of the variable *Y*, but these are not necessary for an understanding of the material in this textbook. Instead we shall turn to some other types of functions that are useful to us.

TABLE A-4.   *Values of Y for Various Values of X*

Values of X			0	1	2	3	4	5
	25	=	25	25	25	25	25	25
	10X	=	0	10	20	30	40	50
Calculations	$-5X^2$	=	0	-5	-20	-45	-80	-125
	$2X^3$	=	0	2	16	54	128	250
Values of Y			25	32	41	64	113	200

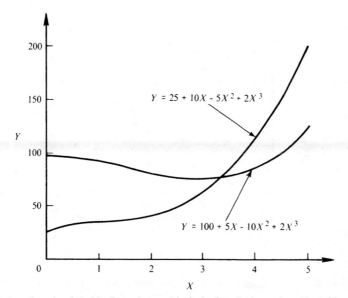

$$Y = 25 + 10X - 5X^2 + 2X^3$$

$$Y = 100 + 5X - 10X^2 + 2X^3$$

FIGURE A-5. **Graph of Cubic Functions with Only One Independent Variable**

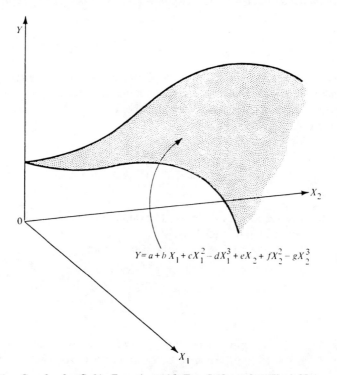

$$Y = a + bX_1 + cX_1^2 - dX_1^3 + eX_2 + fX_2^2 - gX_2^3$$

FIGURE A-6. **Graph of a Cubic Function with Two Independent Variables**

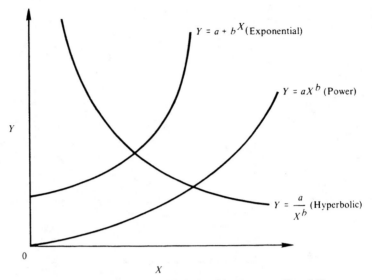

FIGURE A-7.   Graph of Other Functional Relationships between Y and X

Other Functional Forms.   *Exponential functions* take the form

$$Y = a + b^X \tag{A-8}$$

As you look at this specific form of the functional relationship, you should appreciate that the value of Y will increase monotonically as X increases, since the second term in the function assumes progressively higher degrees. An exponential function is shown in Figure A-7.

Power functions take the form

$$Y = aX^b \tag{A-9}$$

and can be seen from Figure A-7 to exhibit the general parabolic shape, as did the exponential and quadratic functions.

Hyperbolic functions take the general form

$$Y = \frac{a}{X^b} \tag{A-10}$$

In this case, as X grows larger the value of Y diminishes and approaches zero asymptotically, as shown in Figure A-7. You will note that hyperbolic functions are in fact power functions where the parameter b has a negative sign. That is, $Y = a/X^b = aX^{-b}$.

• NOTE: A special case of the hyperbolic function is the rectangular hyperbola $Y = a/X$, where the parameter b takes the value unity. Hence $YX = a$ at all points on the curve. In verbal terms the product of the two variables is a constant at all levels of the two variables indicated by points on the curve. The rectangular hyperbola has applications in managerial economics such as the representation of the average-fixed-costs curve, since total fixed costs are a constant equal to the product of the number of output units and the average fixed costs at each output level.

Derivatives and Slopes

The size of the coefficient to the independent variable indicates the extent to which a marginal change in that variable influences the dependent variable. Examination of the marginal impact of one variable on another is commonly referred to as *marginal analysis*. Economists make extensive use of marginal analysis when establishing normative rules for decision making. If Y is to be maximized, for example, the impact on the value of Y for a marginal change in the value of X is sought so we may decide to increase, decrease, or hold constant the value of the independent variable X. In general terms we would wish to know whether it was worthwhile in terms of the increment to Y to increase or decrease X. In terms of the graphical representations above, we are therefore interested in the slopes of the functions.

A mathematical technique that generates a slope of functions is one in which we take the first derivative (or differential) of the function. The derivative of a function shows the change in the value of the dependent variable Y given an infinitesimal change in the variable X, and is written as dY/dX, where d connotes the increment (or decrement) to each variable. For marginal analysis it is imperative that we consider small increases in the independent variable, since larger increases may incorrectly indicate the extent of change in the dependent variable. In Figure A-8 we depict a changing marginal relationship between Y and X. Suppose that the values of X and Y are as indicated by point A in that figure. The marginal relationship (or the slope of the function) is given by the slope of a tangent to the curve at point A. However, this is a correct representation of the slope of the function only for an infinitesimal change in the variable X. For larger changes such as to X_2 or X_3, the slopes of the arcs AB and AC are not accurate representations of the slopes of the function over those values of X and Y. They are in fact approximations or averages over the wider range of X and Y values. For decision-making purposes we are typically concerned with the incremental units of output (or some other variable) and hence require the more accurate marginal relationship between variables. It is therefore important that we understand the rules of derivation for use in optimization procedures.[1]

---

[1]These rules are stated without proof. See W. J. Baumol, *Economic Theory and Operations Analysis*, 4th ed., chap. 4 (Englewood Cliffs, N.J.: Prentice-Hall, 1976), or any good introductory calculus testbook, for formal proofs.

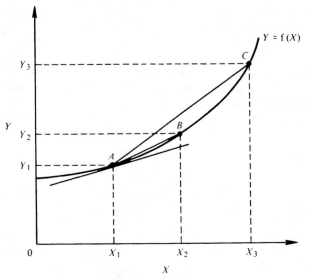

FIGURE A-8. *Change in Slope as ΔX is Increased*

Rules of Derivation

Constants. Since the derivative shows the amount by which the dependent variable changes for a change in an independent variable and since a constant by definition does not change, it is clear that the derivative of a constant must be zero. Therefore,

$$\text{If } Y = a, \text{ then } \frac{dY}{dX} = 0$$

The Power Rule. When the function includes a term that is raised to the first or higher degree, we use the power rule, which may be stated as follows:

$$\text{If } Y = aX^b, \text{ then } \frac{dY}{dX} = baX^{b-1}$$

- EXAMPLE: To illustrate this rule, let us begin with a first-degree function such as $Y = aX$. Since X is implicitly equal to X^1, it is clear that the application of the power rule reduces the X term to X^0. Since X^0 equals 1, the derivative of $Y = aX$ is simply the coefficient of the X term. Thus, if $Y = aX$, then

$$\frac{dY}{dX} = 1 \cdot a \cdot X^{1-1}$$
$$= 1 \cdot a \cdot X^0$$
$$= 1 \cdot a \cdot 1$$
$$= a$$

For higher-degree terms the power function is applied similarly. Suppose $Y = a + bX^2$, then

$$\frac{dY}{dX} = 2bX^{2-1}$$
$$= 2bX^1$$
$$= 2bX$$

To demonstrate the power rule in the context of terms of various degrees, consider the function $Y = 5 + 3X + 2X^2 + 5X^3$. Treating one term at a time, $dY/dX = 3 + 4X + 15X^2$. (Is that correct? Confirm it for yourself, using the above steps.)

The Function of a Function Rule.   In the case where Y and X are related through an intermediate variable Z, to find the change in Y caused by a variation in X we need first to ascertain the impact on Z of the change in X, and then multiply this by the impact of a variation in Z upon Y. Thus,

> If $Y = f(Z)$ and $Z = f(X)$,
>
> then $\dfrac{dY}{dX} = \dfrac{dY}{dZ} \cdot \dfrac{dZ}{dX}$

- EXAMPLE: If $Y = 4 + 6Z^2$ and $Z = 8 + 3X^3$, then

$$\frac{dY}{dX} = 12Z \cdot 9X^2$$
$$= 108ZX^2$$

The Chain Rule.   Where Y is the product of two variables X and Z which are themselves related, and we wish to find the derivative of Y with respect to X, we must consider both the "direct" influence on Y of a change in X and the "indirect" influence on Y of the change in Z that the change in X provokes. Thus,

> If $Y = ZX$ where $X = f(Z)$,
>
> then $\dfrac{dY}{dX} = Z + X\dfrac{dZ}{dX}$

Partial Derivatives

When a function has multiple independent variables and, consequently, each independent variable is only one of a number of variables that affect the value of the dependent variable Y, we take what is known as the partial derivative of the function for each independent variable. This is equivalent to the *ceteris paribus* assumption in economics; that is, we examine the influence of one of the independent variables on the dependent variable while holding all other variables constant. The partial derivative thus shows the impact on Y of an infinitesimal change in one of the independent variables while all other independent variables are held constant. By convention, and to distinguish it from the derivative of functions with only one independent variable, we depict the partial derivatives by the lowercase delta (δ), rather than the lowercase d as used above. Thus if Y is a function of several variables such as

$$Y = a + bX + cX^2 + dZ + eZ^2 + fQ^3$$

then

$$\frac{\delta Y}{\delta X} = b + 2cX$$

and

$$\frac{\delta Y}{\delta Z} = d + 2eZ$$

and

$$\frac{\delta Y}{\delta Q} = 3fQ^2$$

Each partial derivative shows the marginal impact of one of the independent variables upon the dependent variable while holding constant the impact of the other independent variables.

Maximum and Minimum Values of Functions

In the above we have been concerned with first derivatives, which show the slope of the function as the independent variable (or *one* of the independent variables) is varied by a small amount. The first derivative thus shows the rate of change of the dependent variable relative to the specified independent variable. With curvilinear functions that rate of change will vary for different starting points in the value of X. In Figure A-9 the quadratic function $Y = -10 + 30X - 3X^2$ is graphed, and it should be appreciated that the derivative of the function is positive initially where the graph is sloping upward and to

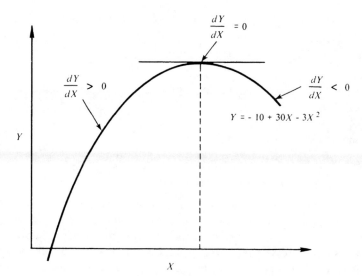

FIGURE A-9. *Changing Value of the First Derivative*

the right, but it is negative later where the value of Y decreases as additional increments of X are made. It is clear that the derivative is taking progressively declining values, being positive at first, falling to zero, and thereafter becoming increasingly negative. You may confirm this by taking the derivative of the function (that is, $dY/dX = 30 - 6X$) and substituting values for X into this expression. Clearly for values of X less than 5 the derivative is positive, but where X is equal to 5 the derivative is zero, and for values of X greater than 5 the derivative is negative.

- RULE: The above discussion allows us to establish a simple rule for finding the maximum of a function. To find the value of X for which Y is maximized, we simply set the derivative of the function equal to zero and solve for the value of X. Thus where we have

$$\frac{dY}{dX} = 30 - 6X = 0$$

Solving for X,

$$6X = 30$$
$$X = 5$$

Thus Y is at a maximum when X takes the value of 5.

- NOTE: A zero first derivative may indicate a *minimum* of a function rather than a maximum if the function is concave from above rather than concave from below. Suppose

$$Y = 100 - 16X + 2X^2$$

The first derivative of this function is

$$\frac{dY}{dX} = -16 + 4X$$

and is equal to zero when

$$X = 4$$

Inspection of the function should indicate to you that it is a parabola that is concave from above, since for small values of X it will be falling, reaching a minimum when X equals 4, and it will rise progressively more steeply for higher values of X. In more complex functions, however, the shape of the function may not be obvious from inspection, and thus we must check whether the zero first derivative implies a maximum or a minimum by means of taking the *second* derivative of the function.

Second Derivatives

- DEFINITION: The *second derivative* of a function is simply the derivative of the first derivative of that function. Since the first derivative indicates the rate of change of the function, the second derivative indicates the rate of change *of the rate of change* of the function. If the second derivative is negative, it indicates that the rate of change is falling. Referring to Figure A-9 we can see that the negative second derivative indicates that the curve is concave from below (or convex from above), since the first derivative at low values of X starts at a relatively high number and progressively falls to zero and then to negative values. Alternatively, if the curve was concave from above, the first derivative would be negative at first, rising to progressively smaller negative values, passing through zero and taking on progressively increasing positive values as X is increased. Thus we can say that the sign of the second derivative will be negative (when the first derivative is set equal to zero) if the function is concave from below, and that the sign of the second derivative will be positive (when the first derivative is set equal to zero) if the function is concave from above.

- RULE: The second-order condition for a maximum is that the second derivative must be negative, and the second-order condition for a minimum is that the second derivative must be positive.

Referring back to the function graphed in Figure A-9, where the first derivative was $dY/dX = 30 - 6X$, we may confirm that the sign of the second derivative is negative. The second derivative is equal to the derivative of the first derivative and is expressed as follows:

$$\frac{d^2Y}{dX^2} = -6$$

where the squared terms indicate that the value shown is the second derivative of the function. For the other function mentioned above, the first derivative was $dY/dX = -16 + 4X$. The second derivative of this derivative is equal to

$$\frac{d^2Y}{dX^2} = 4$$

The signs of these second derivatives confirm that the function of Y reaches a *maximum* in the first case when $dY/dX = 0$ and that it reaches a *minimum* in the second case when the first derivative is set equal to zero.

Use of Derivatives in Managerial Economics

Since one of the central aims of managerial economics is to establish rules and principles for achieving objectives, it is not surprising that derivatives may be helpful, since in many cases we are interested in maximizing profits, or minimizing costs, or optimizing some other variable.

• EXAMPLE: Suppose that a particular firm's cost and revenue functions are of quadratic form as follows:

$$TC = 1,500 + 50Q + 2Q^2 \tag{A-11}$$

$$TR = 250Q - 3Q^2 \tag{A-12}$$

where TC represents total costs; TR represents total revenues; and Q represents the output or sales level. Profits, represented by π, are the surplus of revenues over costs. Hence,

$$\begin{aligned} \pi &= TR - TC \\ &= 250Q - 3Q^2 - (1,500 + 50Q + 2Q^2) \\ &= 250Q - 3Q^2 - 1,500 - 50Q - 2Q^2 \\ \therefore \pi &= -1,500 + 200Q - 5Q^2 \end{aligned} \tag{A-13}$$

represents the profit function. Assuming that the firm wishes to choose the output level that maximizes profits, we may find that output level by setting the first derivative of the profit function equal to zero for solving for Q. Thus,

$$\frac{d\pi}{dQ} = 200 - 10Q = 0$$

$$10Q = 200$$

$$Q = 20$$

The output level that appears to maximize profits is thus 20 units (where the units may represent single units, thousands, or millions, depending on the initial specification of those units). To ensure that this output level represents the maximum profit rather than the minimum profit, we check the second-order condition. The second derivative of the profit function

$$\frac{d^2\pi}{d^2Q} = -10$$

is negative, indicating that profits are indeed maximized at the output level of 20 units.

An alternative approach to finding the profit-maximizing output level using derivatives is as follows. We know that profits will be maximized when the difference between revenues and costs is greatest. In terms of Figure A-10, where the cost and revenue functions are depicted, we wish to find the output level for which the vertical separation of the two curves is greatest.

Observe that the slope (or derivative) of the cost function takes increasingly larger values as output is increased, while the slope of the revenue function takes increasingly

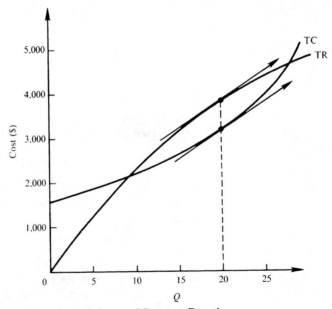

FIGURE A-10. Hypothetical Cost and Revenue Functions

reduced values. At some point the slopes of the two functions will be equal, and hence tangents to the two functions at that output level must be parallel lines, as shown in Figure A-10. Since a property of parallel lines is that they maintain a constant vertical separation, it must be true that as the slope of the cost function continues to increase and as the slope of the revenue function continues to decrease for larger output levels, the vertical distance between the two functions must be decreasing. Thus profits are maximized when the slopes (or first derivatives) of the functions are equal.

To solve for the output level where the slopes (first derivatives) are equal, let us restate the cost and revenue functions:

$$TC = 1,500 + 50Q + 2Q^2 \qquad \text{(A-11)}$$

$$TR = 250Q - 3Q^2 \qquad \text{(A-12)}$$

Finding the first derivatives of these functions, equating them, and solving for Q, we have

$$\frac{dTC}{dQ} = 50 + 4Q$$

$$\frac{dTR}{dQ} = 250 - 6Q$$

Set

$$\frac{dTC}{dQ} = \frac{dTR}{dQ}$$
$$50 + 4Q = 250 - 6Q$$
$$10Q = 200$$
$$Q = 20$$

Not surprisingly this alternate approach gives the same profit-maximizing output level as did the initial approach. The latter approach has received some fame (or notoriety) in economics as the marginalist principle, whereby marginal cost (the increment to total cost for a one-unit change in output level) is set equal to marginal revenue (the increment to total revenue for a one-unit increase in output or sales level). We discuss this topic in the context of different market situations in Chapter 9.

DISCUSSION QUESTIONS

A-1. Define the following terms:
   (a) function
   (b) independent variable

(c) dependent variable
(d) slope parameter
(e) constant
(f) intercept
(g) quadratic function
(h) exponent

A-2. Explain the logic of using the derivatives of a function to find the maximum or minimum of that function.

A-3. Explain the power rule of differentiation.

A-4. Explain the function-of-a-function rule of differentiation.

A-5. Explain the chain rule of differentiation.

PROBLEMS AND SHORT CASES

A-1. Rewrite $Y = f(X)$ in symbolic form as a function that is
(a) linear
(b) quadratic
(c) cubic
(d) exponential
(e) power
(f) hyperbolic

A-2. Find the first derivative, with respect to X, of the following functions:
(a) $Y = 36 + 4.5X^3$
(b) $Y = 8 - 3Z^2$, where $Z = 4 + 3X^3$
(c) $Y = 7KX$, where $X = 3 - 2K^2$
(d) $Y = -16 + 4J^2 - 6K^3$, where $J = 8 - 6X^2$ and $K = -3 + 4X^3$
(e) $Y = 3M(4N^2)$, where $M = -6 + 2X$ and $N = 4 - 2X^2$
(f) $Y = 4e^{2X}$

A-3. Solve for the maximum or minimum value of the following functions, using the second-order condition to specify whether it is a maximum or a minimum:
(a) $Y = -32 + 6X - 2X^2$
(b) $Y = 28 - 8X + X^2$
(c) $A = 4,285 - 625B + 5B^2$
(d) $K = 178 + 40J - 6J^2$

A-4. Suppose the monthly cost of maintaining a certain machine in operating order is a function of the time elapsed between shutdowns for servicing and maintenance as follows: $C = 1,400 - 30T + 0.7T^2$ where C represents cost in dollars and T represents time between services in hours. What is the optimal period between services?

SUGGESTED REFERENCES AND FURTHER READING

BAUMOL, W. J. *Economic Theory and Operations Analysis* (4th ed.), chaps. 2, 3, and 4. Englewood Cliffs, N.J.: Prentice-Hall, Inc., 1976.

CHILDRESS, R. L. *Calculus for Business and Economics* (2nd ed.). Englewood Cliffs, N.J.: Prentice-Hall, Inc., 1978.

KHOURY, S. J., and T. D. PARSONS. *Mathematical Methods in Finance and Economics.* New York: Elsevier-North Holland, Inc., 1981.

KOOROS, A. *Elements of Mathematical Economics*, chaps. 1, 2, 5, 6, and 7. Boston: Houghton Mifflin, 1965.

Appendix B

PRESENT-VALUE TABLES

622

TABLE B-1. Present Value of $1 Received at the End of *N* Years

Years Hence	1%	2%	3%	4%	5%	6%	7%	8%	9%	10%	11%	12%	13%	14%
							DISCOUNT RATE							
1	.9901	.9804	.9709	.9615	.9524	.9434	.9346	.9259	.9174	.9091	.9009	.8929	.8850	.8772
2	.9803	.9612	.9426	.9246	.9070	.8900	.8734	.8573	.8417	.8264	.8116	.7972	.7831	.7695
3	.9706	.9423	.9151	.8890	.8638	.8396	.8163	.7938	.7722	.7513	.7312	.7118	.6931	.6750
4	.9610	.9238	.8885	.8548	.8227	.7921	.7629	.7350	.7084	.6830	.6587	.6355	.6133	.5921
5	.9515	.9057	.8626	.8219	.7835	.7473	.7130	.6806	.6499	.6209	.5935	.5674	.5428	.5194
6	.9420	.8880	.8375	.7903	.7462	.7050	.6663	.6302	.5963	.5645	.5346	.5066	.4803	.4556
7	.9327	.8706	.8131	.7599	.7107	.6651	.6227	.5835	.5470	.5132	.4817	.4523	.4251	.3996
8	.9235	.8535	.7894	.7307	.6768	.6274	.5820	.5403	.5019	.4665	.4339	.4039	.3762	.3506
9	.9143	.8368	.7664	.7026	.6446	.5919	.5439	.5002	.4604	.4241	.3909	.3606	.3329	.3075
10	.9053	.8203	.7441	.6756	.6139	.5584	.5083	.4632	.4224	.3855	.3522	.3220	.2946	.2697
11	.8963	.8043	.7224	.6496	.5847	.5268	.4751	.4289	.3875	.3505	.3173	.2875	.2607	.2366
12	.8874	.7885	.7014	.6246	.5568	.4970	.4440	.3971	.3555	.3186	.2858	.2567	.2307	.2076
13	.8787	.7730	.6810	.6006	.5303	.4688	.4150	.3677	.3262	.2897	.2575	.2292	.2042	.1821
14	.8700	.7579	.6611	.5775	.5051	.4423	.3878	.3405	.2992	.2633	.2320	.2046	.1807	.1597
15	.8613	.7430	.6419	.5553	.4810	.4173	.3624	.3152	.2745	.2394	.2090	.1827	.1599	.1401
16	.8528	.7284	.6232	.5339	.4581	.3936	.3387	.2919	.2519	.2176	.1883	.1631	.1415	.1229
17	.8444	.7142	.6050	.5134	.4363	.3714	.3166	.2703	.2311	.1978	.1696	.1456	.1252	.1078
18	.8360	.7002	.5874	.4936	.4155	.3503	.2959	.2502	.2120	.1799	.1528	.1300	.1108	.0946
19	.8277	.6864	.5703	.4746	.3957	.3305	.2765	.2317	.1945	.1635	.1377	.1161	.0981	.0829
20	.8195	.6730	.5537	.4564	.3769	.3118	.2584	.2145	.1784	.1486	.1240	.1037	.0868	.0728
21	.8114	.6598	.5375	.4388	.3589	.2942	.2415	.1987	.1637	.1351	.1117	.0926	.0768	.0638
22	.8034	.6468	.5219	.4220	.3418	.2775	.2257	.1839	.1502	.1228	.1007	.0826	.0680	.0560
23	.7954	.6342	.5067	.4057	.3256	.2618	.2109	.1703	.1378	.1117	.0907	.0738	.0601	.0491
24	.7876	.6217	.4919	.3901	.3101	.2470	.1971	.1577	.1264	.1015	.0817	.0659	.0532	.0431
25	.7798	.6095	.4776	.3751	.2953	.2330	.1842	.1460	.1160	.0923	.0736	.0588	.0471	.0378

(Continued)

TABLE B-1. *Continued*

DISCOUNT RATE

Years Hence	15%	16%	17%	18%	19%	20%	21%	22%	23%	24%	25%	26%	27%	28%
1	.8696	.8621	.8547	.8475	.8403	.8333	.8264	.8197	.8130	.8065	.8000	.7937	.7874	.7813
2	.7561	.7432	.7305	.7182	.7062	.6944	.6830	.6719	.6610	.6504	.6400	.6299	.6200	.6104
3	.6575	.6407	.6244	.6086	.5934	.5787	.5645	.5507	.5374	.5245	.5120	.4999	.4882	.4768
4	.5718	.5523	.5337	.5158	.4987	.4823	.4665	.4514	.4369	.4230	.4096	.3968	.3844	.3725
5	.4972	.4761	.4561	.4371	.4190	.4019	.3855	.3700	.3552	.3411	.3277	.3149	.3027	.2910
6	.4323	.4104	.3898	.3704	.3521	.3349	.3186	.3033	.2888	.2751	.2621	.2499	.2383	.2274
7	.3759	.3538	.3332	.3139	.2959	.2791	.2633	.2486	.2348	.2218	.2097	.1983	.1877	.1776
8	.3269	.3050	.2848	.2660	.2487	.2326	.2176	.2038	.1909	.1789	.1678	.1574	.1478	.1388
9	.2843	.2630	.2434	.2255	.2090	.1938	.1799	.1670	.1552	.1443	.1342	.1249	.1164	.1084
10	.2472	.2267	.2080	.1911	.1756	.1615	.1486	.1369	.1262	.1164	.1074	.0992	.0916	.0847
11	.2149	.1954	.1778	.1619	.1476	.1346	.1228	.1122	.1026	.0938	.0859	.0787	.0721	.0662
12	.1869	.1685	.1520	.1372	.1240	.1122	.1015	.0920	.0834	.0757	.0687	.0625	.0568	.0517
13	.1625	.1452	.1299	.1163	.1042	.0935	.0839	.0754	.0678	.0610	.0550	.0496	.0447	.0404
14	.1413	.1252	.1110	.0985	.0876	.0779	.0693	.0618	.0551	.0492	.0440	.0393	.0352	.0316
15	.1229	.1079	.0949	.0835	.0736	.0649	.0573	.0507	.0448	.0397	.0352	.0312	.0277	.0247
16	.1069	.0930	.0811	.0708	.0618	.0541	.0474	.0415	.0364	.0320	.0281	.0248	.0218	.0193
17	.0929	.0802	.0693	.0600	.0520	.0451	.0391	.0340	.0296	.0258	.0225	.0197	.0172	.0150
18	.0808	.0691	.0592	.0508	.0437	.0376	.0323	.0279	.0241	.0208	.0180	.0156	.0135	.0118
19	.0703	.0596	.0506	.0431	.0367	.0313	.0267	.0229	.0196	.0168	.0144	.0124	.0107	.0092
20	.0611	.0514	.0433	.0365	.0308	.0261	.0221	.0187	.0159	.0135	.0115	.0098	.0084	.0072
21	.0531	.0443	.0370	.0309	.0259	.0217	.0183	.0154	.0129	.0109	.0092	.0078	.0066	.0056
22	.0462	.0382	.0316	.0262	.0218	.0181	.0151	.0126	.0105	.0088	.0074	.0062	.0052	.0044
23	.0402	.0329	.0270	.0222	.0183	.0151	.0125	.0103	.0086	.0071	.0059	.0049	.0041	.0034
24	.0349	.0284	.0231	.0188	.0154	.0126	.0103	.0085	.0070	.0057	.0047	.0039	.0032	.0027
25	.0304	.0245	.0197	.0160	.0129	.0105	.0085	.0069	.0057	.0046	.0038	.0031	.0025	.0021

TABLE B-2. Present Value of an Annuity of $1

Years Hence						DISCOUNT RATE							
	1%	2%	3%	4%	5%	6%	7%	8%	9%	10%	11%	12%	13%	14%
1	0.9901	0.9804	0.9709	0.9615	0.9524	0.9434	0.9346	0.9259	0.9174	0.9091	0.9009	0.8929	0.8850	0.8772
2	1.9704	1.9416	1.9135	1.8861	1.8594	1.8334	1.8080	1.7833	1.7591	1.7355	1.7125	1.6901	1.6681	1.6467
3	2.9410	2.8839	2.8286	2.7751	2.7232	2.6730	2.6243	2.5771	2.5313	2.4869	2.4437	2.4018	2.3612	2.3216
4	3.9020	3.8077	3.7171	3.6299	3.5460	3.4651	3.3872	3.3121	3.2397	3.1699	3.1024	3.0373	2.9745	2.9137
5	4.8534	4.7135	4.5797	4.4518	4.3295	4.2124	4.1002	3.9927	3.8897	3.7908	3.6959	3.6048	3.5172	3.4331
6	5.7955	5.6014	5.4172	5.2421	5.0757	4.9173	4.7665	4.6229	4.4859	4.3553	4.2305	4.1114	3.9976	3.8887
7	6.7282	6.4720	6.2303	6.0021	5.7864	5.5824	5.3893	5.2064	5.0330	4.8684	4.7122	4.5638	4.4226	4.2883
8	7.6517	7.3255	7.0197	6.7327	6.4632	6.2098	5.9713	5.7466	5.5348	5.3349	5.1461	4.9676	4.7988	4.6389
9	8.5660	8.1622	7.7861	7.4353	7.1078	6.8017	6.5152	6.2469	5.9952	5.7590	5.5370	5.3282	5.1317	4.9464
10	9.4713	8.9826	8.5302	8.1109	7.7217	7.3601	7.0236	6.7101	6.4177	6.1446	5.8892	5.6502	5.4262	5.2161
11	10.3676	9.7869	9.2526	8.7605	8.3064	7.8869	7.4987	7.1390	6.8052	6.4951	6.2065	5.9377	5.6869	5.4527
12	11.2551	10.5753	9.9540	9.3851	8.8633	8.3838	7.9427	7.5361	7.1607	6.8137	6.4924	6.1944	5.9176	5.6603
13	12.1337	11.3484	10.6350	9.9856	9.3936	8.8527	8.3577	7.9038	7.4869	7.1034	6.7499	6.4235	6.1218	5.8424
14	13.0037	12.1063	11.2961	10.5631	9.8986	9.2950	8.7455	8.2442	7.7862	7.3667	6.9819	6.6282	6.3025	6.0021
15	13.8651	12.8493	11.9379	11.1184	10.3797	9.7122	9.1079	8.5595	8.0607	7.6061	7.1909	6.8109	6.4624	6.1422
16	14.7179	13.5777	12.5611	11.6523	10.8378	10.1059	9.4466	8.8514	8.3126	7.8237	7.3792	6.9740	6.6039	6.2651
17	15.5623	14.2919	13.1661	12.1657	11.2741	10.4773	9.7632	9.1216	8.5436	8.0216	7.5488	7.1196	6.7291	6.3729
18	16.3983	14.9920	13.7535	12.6593	11.6896	10.8276	10.0591	9.3719	8.7556	8.2014	7.7016	7.2497	6.8399	6.4674
19	17.2260	15.6785	14.3238	13.1339	12.0853	11.1581	10.3356	9.6036	8.9501	8.3649	7.8393	7.3658	6.9380	6.5504
20	18.0456	16.3514	14.8775	13.5903	12.4622	11.4699	10.5940	9.8181	9.1285	8.5136	7.9633	7.4694	7.0248	6.6231
21	18.8570	17.0112	15.4150	14.0292	12.8212	11.7641	10.8355	10.0168	9.2922	8.6487	8.0751	7.5620	7.1016	6.6870
22	19.6604	17.6581	15.9369	14.4511	13.1630	12.0416	11.0612	10.2007	9.4424	8.7715	8.1757	7.6446	7.1695	6.7429
23	20.4558	18.2922	16.4436	14.8568	13.4886	12.3034	11.2722	10.3711	9.5802	8.8832	8.2664	7.7184	7.2297	6.7921
24	21.2434	18.9139	16.9355	15.2470	13.7986	12.5504	11.4693	10.5288	9.7066	8.9847	8.3481	7.7843	7.2829	6.8351
25	22.0232	19.5235	17.4131	15.6221	14.0939	12.7834	11.6536	10.6748	9.8226	9.0770	8.4217	7.8431	7.3300	6.8729

(Continued)

TABLE B-2. *Continued*

DISCOUNT RATE

Years Hence	15%	16%	17%	18%	19%	20%	21%	22%	23%	24%	25%	26%	27%	28%
1	0.8696	0.8621	0.8547	0.8475	0.8403	0.8333	0.8264	0.8197	0.8130	0.8065	0.8000	0.7937	0.7874	0.7813
2	1.6257	1.6052	1.5852	1.5656	1.5465	1.5278	1.5095	1.4915	1.4740	1.4568	1.4400	1.4235	1.4074	1.3916
3	2.2832	2.2459	2.2096	2.1743	2.1399	2.1065	2.0739	2.0422	2.0114	1.9813	1.9520	1.9234	1.8956	1.8684
4	2.8550	2.7982	2.7432	2.6901	2.6386	2.5887	2.5404	2.4936	2.4483	2.4043	2.3616	2.3202	2.2800	2.2410
5	3.3522	3.2743	3.1993	3.1272	3.0576	2.9906	2.9260	2.8636	2.8035	2.7454	2.6893	2.6351	2.5827	2.5320
6	3.7845	3.6847	3.5892	3.4976	3.4098	3.3255	3.2446	3.1669	3.0923	3.0205	2.9514	2.8850	2.8210	2.7594
7	4.1604	4.0386	3.9224	3.8115	3.7057	3.6046	3.5079	3.4155	3.3270	3.2423	3.1611	3.0833	3.0087	2.9370
8	4.4873	4.3436	4.2072	4.0776	3.9544	3.8372	3.7256	3.6193	3.5179	3.4212	3.3289	3.2407	3.1564	3.0758
9	4.7716	4.6065	4.4506	4.3030	4.1633	4.0310	3.9054	3.7863	3.6731	3.5655	3.4631	3.3657	3.2728	3.1842
10	5.0188	4.8332	4.6586	4.4941	4.3389	4.1925	4.0541	3.9232	3.7993	3.6819	3.5705	3.4648	3.3644	3.2689
11	5.2337	5.0286	4.8364	4.6560	4.4865	4.3271	4.1769	4.0354	3.9018	3.7757	3.6564	3.5435	3.4365	3.3351
12	5.4206	5.1971	4.9884	4.7932	4.6105	4.4392	4.2784	4.1274	3.9852	3.8514	3.7251	3.6059	3.4933	3.3868
13	5.5831	5.3423	5.1183	4.9095	4.7147	4.5327	4.3624	4.2028	4.0530	3.9124	3.7801	3.6555	3.5381	3.4272
14	5.7245	5.4675	5.2293	5.0081	4.8023	4.6106	4.4317	4.2646	4.1082	3.9616	3.8241	3.6949	3.5733	3.4587
15	5.8474	5.5755	5.3242	5.0916	4.8759	4.6755	4.4890	4.3152	4.1530	4.0013	3.8593	3.7261	3.6010	3.4834
16	5.9542	5.6685	5.4053	5.1624	4.9377	4.7296	4.5364	4.3567	4.1894	4.0333	3.8874	3.7509	3.6228	3.5026
17	6.0472	5.7487	5.4746	5.2223	4.9897	4.7746	4.5755	4.3908	4.2190	4.0591	3.9099	3.7705	3.6400	3.5177
18	6.1280	5.8178	5.5339	5.2732	5.0333	4.8122	4.6079	4.4187	4.2431	4.0799	3.9279	3.7861	3.6536	3.5294
19	6.1982	5.8775	5.5845	5.3162	5.0700	4.8435	4.6346	4.4415	4.2627	4.0967	3.9424	3.7985	3.6642	3.5386
20	6.2593	5.9288	5.6278	5.3527	5.1009	4.8696	4.6567	4.4603	4.2786	4.1103	3.9539	3.8083	3.6726	3.5458
21	6.3125	5.9731	5.6648	5.3837	5.1268	4.8913	4.6750	4.4756	4.2916	4.1212	3.9631	3.8161	3.6792	3.5514
22	6.3587	6.0113	5.6964	5.4099	5.1486	4.9094	4.6900	4.4882	4.3021	4.1300	3.9705	3.8223	3.6844	3.5558
23	6.3988	6.0442	5.7234	5.4321	5.1668	4.9245	4.7025	4.4985	4.3106	4.1371	3.9764	3.8273	3.6885	3.5592
24	6.4338	6.0726	5.7465	5.4509	5.1822	4.9371	4.7128	4.5070	4.3176	4.1428	3.9811	3.8312	3.6918	3.5619
25	6.4641	6.0971	5.7662	5.4669	5.1951	4.9476	4.7213	4.5139	4.3232	4.1474	3.9849	3.8342	3.6943	3.5640

TABLE B-3. Present Value of $1 Received throughout the Year on a Daily Basis

Years Hence	1%	2%	3%	4%	5%	6%	7%	8%	9%	10%	11%	12%	13%	14%
1	.9950	.9900	.9851	.9802	.9753	.9705	.9657	.9609	.9562	.9515	.9468	.9422	.9376	.9330
2	.9851	.9704	.9560	.9418	.9278	.9140	.9004	.8871	.8739	.8610	.8482	.8357	.8233	.8111
3	.9753	.9512	.9277	.9049	.8825	.8608	.8396	.8189	.7987	.7790	.7599	.7412	.7229	.7052
4	.9656	.9324	.9003	.8694	.8395	.8107	.7828	.7559	.7300	.7049	.6807	.6574	.6348	.6131
5	.9560	.9139	.8737	.8353	.7986	.7634	.7299	.6978	.6672	.6378	.6098	.5831	.5575	.5330
6	.9465	.8958	.8479	.8025	.7596	.7190	.6805	.6442	.6097	.5772	.5463	.5171	.4895	.4634
7	.9371	.8781	.8228	.7711	.7226	.6771	.6345	.5946	.5573	.5222	.4894	.4587	.4298	.4028
8	.9277	.8607	.7985	.7408	.6873	.6377	.5916	.5489	.5093	.4725	.4384	.4068	.3775	.3502
9	.9185	.8437	.7749	.7118	.6538	.6006	.5517	.5067	.4655	.4276	.3928	.3608	.3315	.3045
10	.9094	.8270	.7520	.6839	.6219	.5656	.5144	.4678	.4254	.3869	.3519	.3200	.2911	.2647
11	.9003	.8106	.7298	.6571	.5916	.5327	.4796	.4318	.3888	.3501	.3152	.2838	.2556	.2301
12	.8914	.7945	.7082	.6313	.5627	.5016	.4472	.3986	.3553	.3168	.2824	.2517	.2244	.2001
13	.8825	.7788	.6873	.6066	.5353	.4724	.4169	.3680	.3248	.2866	.2530	.2233	.1971	.1739
14	.8737	.7634	.6670	.5828	.5092	.4449	.3888	.3397	.2968	.2594	.2266	.1980	.1731	.1512
15	.8650	.7483	.6473	.5599	.4844	.4190	.3625	.3136	.2713	.2347	.2030	.1756	.1520	.1315
16	.8564	.7334	.6281	.5380	.4607	.3946	.3380	.2895	.2479	.2124	.1819	.1558	.1334	.1143
17	.8479	.7189	.6096	.5169	.4383	.3716	.3151	.2672	.2266	.1921	.1629	.1382	.1172	.0994
18	.8395	.7047	.5916	.4966	.4169	.3500	.2938	.2467	.2071	.1739	.1460	.1226	.1029	.0864
19	.8311	.6907	.5741	.4771	.3966	.3296	.2740	.2277	.1893	.1573	.1308	.1087	.0904	.0751
20	.8228	.6771	.5571	.4584	.3772	.3104	.2554	.2102	.1730	.1424	.1171	.0964	.0793	.0653
21	.8146	.6637	.5407	.4405	.3588	.2923	.2382	.1940	.1581	.1288	.1049	.0855	.0697	.0568
22	.8065	.6505	.5247	.4232	.3413	.2753	.2221	.1791	.1445	.1166	.0940	.0758	.0612	.0494
23	.7985	.6376	.5092	.4066	.3247	.2593	.2071	.1654	.1321	.1055	.0842	.0673	.0537	.0429
24	.7906	.6250	.4941	.3907	.3089	.2442	.1931	.1526	.1207	.0954	.0755	.0597	.0472	.0373
25	.7827	.6126	.4795	.3753	.2938	.2300	.1800	.1409	.1103	.0863	.0676	.0529	.0414	.0324

DISCOUNT RATE

(Continued)

TABLE B-3. *Continued*

							DISCOUNT RATE							
Years Hence	15%	16%	17%	18%	19%	20%	21%	22%	23%	24%	25%	26%	27%	28%
1	.9284	.9239	.9194	.9150	.9105	.9061	.9017	.8974	.8931	.8888	.8845	.8803	.8761	.8719
2	.7991	.7873	.7757	.7643	.7530	.7419	.7310	.7202	.7096	.6992	.6889	.6788	.6689	.6590
3	.6878	.6709	.6545	.6384	.6227	.6075	.5926	.5780	.5639	.5501	.5366	.5235	.5106	.4981
4	.5921	.5718	.5522	.5333	.5150	.4974	.4803	.4639	.4480	.4327	.4179	.4036	.3899	.3765
5	.5096	.4872	.4659	.4454	.4259	.4072	.3894	.3723	.3560	.3404	.3255	.3113	.2976	.2846
6	.4386	.4152	.3931	.3721	.3522	.3334	.3157	.2988	.2829	.2678	.2535	.2400	.2272	.2151
7	.3775	.3538	.3316	.3108	.2913	.2730	.2559	.2398	.2248	.2107	.1975	.1851	.1735	.1626
8	.3250	.3015	.2798	.2596	.2409	.2235	.2074	.1925	.1786	.1657	.1538	.1427	.1324	.1229
9	.2797	.2570	.2361	.2169	.1992	.1830	.1681	.1545	.1419	.1304	.1198	.1101	.1011	.0929
10	.2408	.2190	.1992	.1811	.1648	.1499	.1363	.1240	.1128	.1026	.0933	.0849	.0772	.0702
11	.2072	.1866	.1680	.1513	.1363	.1227	.1105	.0995	.0896	.0807	.0727	.0654	.0589	.0531
12	.1784	.1590	.1418	.1264	.1127	.1005	.0896	.0799	.0712	.0635	.0566	.0505	.0450	.0401
13	.1535	.1355	.1196	.1056	.0932	.0823	.0726	.0641	.0566	.0499	.0441	.0389	.0344	.0303
14	.1321	.1155	.1009	.0882	.0771	.0673	.0589	.0514	.0450	.0393	.0343	.0300	.0262	.0229
15	.1137	.0984	.0851	.0737	.0637	.0551	.0477	.0413	.0357	.0309	.0267	.0231	.0200	.0173
16	.0979	.0839	.0718	.0615	.0527	.0452	.0387	.0331	.0284	.0243	.0208	.0178	.0153	.0131
17	.0843	.0715	.0606	.0514	.0436	.0370	.0314	.0266	.0226	.0191	.0162	.0138	.0117	.0099
18	.0725	.0609	.0511	.0429	.0360	.0303	.0254	.0213	.0179	.0150	.0126	.0106	.0089	.0075
19	.0624	.0519	.0431	.0359	.0298	.0248	.0206	.0171	.0142	.0118	.0098	.0082	.0068	.0057
20	.0537	.0442	.0364	.0300	.0247	.0203	.0167	.0137	.0113	.0093	.0077	.0063	.0052	.0043
21	.0463	.0377	.0307	.0250	.0204	.0166	.0135	.0110	.0090	.0073	.0060	.0049	.0040	.0032
22	.0398	.0321	.0259	.0209	.0169	.0136	.0110	.0089	.0071	.0058	.0047	.0038	.0030	.0024
23	.0343	.0274	.0219	.0175	.0139	.0111	.0089	.0071	.0057	.0045	.0036	.0029	.0023	.0018
24	.0295	.0233	.0184	.0146	.0115	.0091	.0072	.0057	.0045	.0036	.0028	.0022	.0018	.0014
25	.0254	.0199	.0156	.0122	.0095	.0075	.0058	.0046	.0036	.0028	.0022	.0017	.0013	.0011

Appendix C

ANSWERS TO THE PROBLEMS

Following are brief answers to each of the end-of-chapter problems. These are typically numerical, to allow you to verify your methodology and calculations. Note that your answers may differ slightly due to rounding. In other cases, you may find that I have made a mistake. If so, please let me know, so that I can correct it as soon as possible. You can write to me at the School of Business, Bond University, Gold Coast, QLD, Australia, 4229. Your help will be greatly appreciated!

CHAPTER 1

1-1. (a) $9,856,300.
(b) $10,057,600 at 12%, $9,664,400 at 16%.

1-2. (a) $1,681.

1-3. (a) $273,115.

1-4. (a) Company A: $36,039; company B: $36,278.
(b) Company A: $35,286; company B: $35,122.

1-5. (a) $2,960 (using daily discount rates.)

1-6. (a) $75,108.
(b) $103,233.
(c) $278,125.
(d) Different ODR and/or time horizon?

1-7. (a) Project A: $67,736; project B: $75,727.

1-8. (a) Product A: $32,964; product B: $11,814.

1-9. (a) $39,500.
(b) $36,672.
(c) $36,523.

1-10. (a) Rebuild: $36,750; buy new: $37,600.
(b) Rebuild: $34,288; buy new: $33,128.

CHAPTER 2

2-1. (a) Minor face-lift: expected value is $34,000; standard deviation is 24,580; coefficient of variation is 0.723. New model: EV = $34,000; SD = 60,530; CV = 1.78.
(b) EV criterion ranks them equally; CV and maximin criteria both favor minor face-lift.
(c) Minor face-lift.

2-2. (a) Hot dogs: EV = $212.50, CV = 0.356; ice cream: EV = $213.75, CV = 0.583. Risk averters, unless only very slightly risk averse, will choose hot dogs. Your certainty equivalent will indicate your degree of risk aversion.

2-3. (a) Regular store: EPV = $327,650; super store: EPV = $137,150.

2-4. (a) Lease: EPV = $12,401; buy: EPV = $11,834.
   (b) Lease: SD = 7,185; buy: SD = 6,637.
   (c) EV favors lease; CV favors buy; maximin favors lease; CE is ambiguous, depending on risk return trade-off. Is management willing to accept $547 more risk along with $567 more expected return?

2-5. (a) Project A: EPV = $1,044,980, SD = 1,042,376; project B: EPV = $1,294,310, SD = $1,541,660.

2-6. (a) High: EPV = $1,505; medium: EPV = $3,806; low: EPV = $-292.
   (b) No, EPV of bond alternative is zero.
   (c) High, low, medium.
   (d) Medium, high, low.
   (e) Not for a risk averter.

2-7. (a) For plan A, ENPV = $1,070,950 with standard deviation $505,713. For plan B, ENPV = $1,045,026, with zero standard deviation (assuming payment is guaranteed).

(b) *Criterion*	*Favors*	*Reason*
ENPV	A	$1.07m > $1.045m
Coeff. of Var'n	B	0.0 < 0.47
Maximin	B	$1.045m > $0.372m
Cert'y Equiv.	Ambiguous	A has both greater risk and greater return.

2-8. (a) Product A: EPV = $38,316, SD = 27,757; product B: EPV = $68,713, SD = 126,313; product C: EPV = $54,411, SD = 44,036.

2-9. (a) Christmas trees: EPV = $173,915, SD = 249,519; fast food: EPV = $180,161, SD = 146,543.

2-10. (a) Plan A: EPV = $36,006; plan B: EPV = $61,672.
   (b) Plan A: SD = 32,874; plan B: SD = 49,162.

CHAPTER 3

3-1. (a) The budget line will swing inward, restricting the consumer to a lower indifference curve and fewer units of the product.

3-2. (a) *Ceteris paribus* allows us to isolate the impact of one variable at a time. First the budget line swings outward, then it shifts outward, and finally the indifference curves become flatter.

3-3. (a) An advertising campaign may improve consumer perceptions of the product, thus shifting the efficiency frontier outward, and may also change tastes in favor of the attributes embodied in product X, thus steepening indifference curves. Both effects will cause the consumer to buy more, prior to a price increase. A price increase would then cut sales back, but quantity demanded would be higher than it would have been without the prior advertising campaign.

3-4. (a) Mr. A's indifference curves will be flatter than Ms. B's, and his demand curve will be more elastic in the relevant range.

3-5. **(a)** The consumers' choices will depend on their marginal rates of substitution between power and economy.

3-6. **(a)** About 97 cents.

    (b) All consumers previously buying brand A, as well as some previously buying brand B, will switch to Norbert. Only those with MRS > 6.2 will continue to buy brand B.

3-7. **(b)** The market share data tells us something about the distribution of the slopes of consumers' indifference curves. Repositioning into a heavier part of this distribution will mean more customers are gained than lost. It is not clear that Snackers can do this without a price increase or a higher nutrient-calorie ratio.

3-8. **(a)** The efficiency frontier is linear across product rays B, D, and C. Plan 1 involves repositioning into a relatively crowded part of the market. Plan 2 looks more promising.

3-9. **(a)** Sportscar A. (Hint: Set the value of reliability equal to 1.)

    (b) Sportscar A.

    (c) Sportscar B, using the EV criterion, but sportscar A is favored by the minimax, CV, and CE criteria.

3-10. **(a)** More convenient Phoneshop.

    (b) Either the more convenient or the less convenient Phoneshop, depending on the curvature (MRS) of the consumer's indifference curve.

APPENDIX 3A

3A-1. If the price of a good increases, *ceteris paribus*, the CPI will rise, and rational consumers will substitute away from that good and in favor of other products. The income effect will reinforce, partially offset, or overwhelm the substitution effect, depending upon whether the good is a superior, inferior, or Giffen good.

3A-2. Your graph should show the budget line swinging inward, causing the consumer to buy less of both products, presuming non-Giffen goods. The income effect should be negative, offsetting the substitution effect to some degree.

3A-3. The indifference curves must be drawn close together at the top (small amounts of X) and far apart at the bottom (larger amounts of X) to reflect the rapid decline of the consumer's MU of the Giffen good as more is acquired. Following a price reduction, the point of tangency between the new budget line and the highest attainable indifference curve will occur at a lower level of product X. The income effect is negative and more than offsets the substitution effect.

CHAPTER 4

4-1. **(a)** Note that the choice of scale is critical.

    (b) Arc price elasticity varies from -3.03, for the price range $5 to $4.95, to -0.65 for the price range $4.55 to $4.60.

    (c) Demand is elastic for prices above $4.77, unitary at $4.77, and inelastic below $4.77.

4-2. **(a)** 116,415.6.

    (b) Point price elasticity is -0.437, cross-elasticity is 0.439, and advertising elasticity is 2.044.

    (c) Too low, since MR is negative (regardless of MC value).

4-3. (a) -1.74.
   (b) 1.05.
   (c) A price of $9.83 would maximize profits, assuming the rival leaves its price at $8.95.
   (d) $7.83.

4-4. (a) -0.99357. Demand is very near unitary elasticity, meaning that total revenue would change only very slightly for either a small increase or decrease in price.
   (b) $P = 1.585106 - 0.02649Q$.
   (c) $0.89.
   (d) $0.79.

4-5. (a) -1.21128. Demand is "elastic," meaning TR would rise if price were reduced, for example.
   (b) $P = 10.862 - 0.6789Q$.
   (c) No. $6.93.
   (d) $5.43.

4-6. (a) Arc price elasticity $= -3.0768$.
   (b) $4.17 and $17,210.

4-7. (a) No. $1.81.
   (b) $1.31.

4-8. (a) Sales are expected to decrease by about 18.5%.
   (b) Sales are expected to increase by about 4.5%.
   (c) Sales are expected to decrease by about 5.5%.

4-9. (a) $750 and 600,000.
   (b) $10,800,000.

4-10. (a) and **(b)** There are several price and advertising mixes that achieve both targets. I would suggest increasing advertising by 15% or a little less without any increase in price, but your answer is as good as mine.
   (c) 0.949, indicating that the product is a "necessity" and that its quantity demanded will change less than in proportion to changes in income.

CHAPTER 5

5-1. (b) $P = 12.838 - 0.00002063Q$.
   (c) $6.42.
   (d) -1.00. Demand is unitary elastic, meaning that for any small price change total revenue will remain constant.

5-2. (a) $P = 262.389 - 1.626Q$, for the sample, and $P = 262.389 - 0.00813Q$ for the market.
   (b) -2.183, -3.202, -5.183, and -10.693.
   (c) $206.19.

5-3. (a) $P = 41.9814 - 0.010965Q$.
   (b) $25.99 and 1,458 units.
   (c) -1.6257. This is "elastic" and indicates that TR and P will vary inversely.
   (d) 1,305 and 1,612 units.

5-4. (a) The cross elasticities are 0.945 and 0.774, respectively, indicating the goods are indeed substitutes. Price elasticity is -1.71, and income elasticity is 0.985, indicating a necessity good.
   (b) $88.30, at which 15,759 pairs would be sold.
   (c) 13,228 and 18,290 pairs.

5-5. (a) $2,980.
   (b) $2,230.
   (c) $-2.0134.$
   (d) 6,326 to 19,332.

5-6. (a) -3.83, 2.59, and 0.475, respectively.
   (b) $P = 239.55 - 0.000537Q$ and MR $= 239.55 - 0.001074Q$.
   (c) $186.
   (d) 86,826 to 112,557.

5-7. (a) $150.
   (b) $200.
   (c) $213.

5-8. (a) -1.08, 1.21, and 1.86, respectively.
   (b) $P = 94.16947 - 0.95465Q$ and MR $= 94.16947 - 1.9093Q$.
   (c) $47.08 (perhaps $46.99 would look better).

5-9. (a) The cross-elasticities are 1.666 between Hertz's compact car and the competitors' compact cars, and 1.111 between Hertz's compact cars and Hertz's subcompact cars. Thus, the competitors' compact cars are the stronger substitutes.
   (b) $P = 34.93528 - 0.2772Q$.
   (c) $17.47.
   (d) 57.78 to 68.22.

5-10. (a) Own price elasticity is -1.14; cross price elasticities are 4.198 with respect to Sudds and 1.638 with respect to the generic beer; and income elasticity is 1.0038.
   (b) $P = 14.9987 - 0.345Q$.
   (c) $7.50.
   (d) $8.50.
   (e) 17.338 to 20.338.

APPENDIX 5A

5A-1. (a) The intercept on the vertical axis (sales) should be about 5,300, and the line should slope upward at the rate of about 4 pails per household.
   (b) $S = 5,283.73 + 4.15H$.
   (c) About 11,500 pails.

5A-2. (a) Sales $= 0.06976 + 3.8398$ index.
   (b) Since $R^2 = 0.9992$, and the standard error of estimate (and the confidence intervals) are correspondingly very small, the index is a highly reliable indicator of sales.
   (c) 1,859, 1,977, 2,094, 2,211, and 2,329.
   (d) 7,139, 7,589, 8,040, 8,491, and 8,941.

5A-3. (a) They seem to be more than will be required.
   (b) 1,060, 1,044, and 1,028, based on assumptions I made. Your answers will depend on the assumptions you made but should also trend downward like this, following past patterns.

5A-4. (a) 34,732 units.
   (b) 32,254 to 37,210.

5A-5. (a) 52.33.
   (b) No change.
   (c) Yes, if one technician is fired.
   (d) Yes, if one technician is fired.

      (e) No.

5A-6. (a) 25,634.75.
      (b) 20,169 to 23,717.
      (c) 25,457.35 to 25,813.15.

5A-7. (a) $1.367 million.

CHAPTER 6

6-1. (a) Increasing MP up to about 5 divers; constant MP 6 to 12 divers; and diminishing MP after 12 divers.
      (b) 5 divers, where average product (Q/L) is maximized.
      (c) 14 divers, where TP is maximized.

6-2. (a) Size.
      (b) Economies of plant size, since SAC declines as number of production centers increases.
      (c) Mr. Panache and the other overheads were underutilized initially.

6-3. (a) For the existing plant:

Q (000s)	10	15	20	25	30	35	40	45
AVC ($)	0.63	0.50	0.46	0.51	0.62	0.77	1.01	1.70
SAC ($)	0.99	0.74	0.64	0.65	0.74	0.87	1.10	1.78

For the proposed plant:

Q (000s)	25	30	35	40	45	50
AVC ($)	0.60	0.51	0.44	0.39	0.51	0.71
SAC ($)	0.80	0.68	0.58	0.52	0.62	0.81

      (b) (i) $1,650   (ii) $-262.50   (iii) $5,277.50
      (c) $316,766 in ENPV terms.

6-4. (a) TP = 66.2, 85, 99.1, 103.6, 93.2, and 63, for $L = 1$ through 5.
      (b) After the first unit.
      (c) About 3.85 units, where TP is maximized.

6-5. (a) For plant 1, at output levels 30, 52, 80, and so on, SAC = $1,000.00, $769.24, $625.00, and so on.
      (b) Economies of plant size up to and including plant size 3, then diseconomies with plant size 4.
      (c) (1) Plant 1. (2) Plant 3. (3) Given equal likelihood of demand falling at any level within the range, plant 3 has both a lower expected value of average cost and a lower standard deviation, although plant 4 is favored by the maximin criteria.

6-6. (a) For example, with $K = 3$, and for $L = 1$ through 6, SAC = $85,000, $45,830, $34,650, $32,500, $34,170, and $36,550.
      (b) Economies of plant size are evident with $K = 3$ and 4, with diseconomies becoming evident with $K = 5$ and 6.
      (c) The expected value of SAC is lowest (at about $38,750) with plant 4, presuming that 250 cars can be produced at about $40,000 each. Otherwise, plant 5 can handle all output levels within the range 100 to 250 with a slightly higher EV of SAC (about $39,360) and has better potential if demand increases beyond 250.

6-7. (a) AVC at the output levels given are $9.23, $8.39, $8.91, $9.84, $10.79, and $12. SACs are $18.61, $12.59, $11.88, $12.30, $12.95, and $14.
      (c) Around 150 units of the variable inputs, or 10,000 units of output, where MC begins to rise.

(**d**) Around 20,000 units of output, where SAC is about $11.87.

6-8. (**a**) They sink downward. For example, at 20,200 units of output, AVC = $7.43 and SAC = $10.40.

(**b**) No, diminishing returns is a physical phenomenon that is independent of input costs.

(**c**) Again they sink downward. For example, at 22,220 units of output, AVC = $6.75 and SAC = $9.45.

(**d**) Each change increases the full capacity output level.

6-9. (**b**) $87.50, $82, and $84.50, for plants A, B, and C, respectively.

(**c**) Plant B, unless demand probability distribution underestimates demand situation.

(**d**) About 850 units, on average.

6-10. (**a**)

Output	500	600	700	800	900	1000	1100	1200	1300	1400	1500
Profit ($m)	0.498	0.617	0.707	0.766	0.795	0.795	0.765	0.704	0.614	0.493	0.343

(**b**)

Output	500	600	700	800	900	1000	1100	1200	1300	1400	1500
Profit ($m)	0.498	0.397	0.477	0.556	0.636	0.715	0.795	0.874	0.954	1.033	1.113

Plan A is preferable up to monthly outputs of 1000 units, beyond which level, plan B is more profitable. Is it necessary to reduce the backlist so quickly? Can the most-impatient buyers on the backlist be identified and served first to avoid losing them? Will quality standards be maintained from the outside supplier?

(**c**) Produce 700 units in-house and buy additional units from outside supplier.

APPENDIX 6A

6A-1. (**b**) About 127,000 units, using 4,500 labor hours and 1,400 machine hours.

(**c**) About 117,000 units, using 3,700 labor hours and 980 machine hours.

6A-2. (**b**) About 170 units.

(**c**) $300,000.

(**d**) $50,000.

6A-3. (**c**) About $112,500.

(**d**) Increase by $7,000 in the short run. In the long run the firm will increase K to about 1.05 and reduce L to reduce costs to about $118,500.

APPENDIX 6B

6B-1. (**a**) 2,833 pounds of fish cakes and 8,603 pounds of fish meal.

(**b**) $8,289.

(**c**) Shredding and packing processes.

6B-2. (**a**) 638.89 units of A, 388.89 units of B.

(**b**) $2.29.

(**c**) Sultanas and citrus are right at minimum limits. Munchies could buy these separately.

6B-3. (**a**) 90 sandy; 145 pebbly; 115 rocky.

(**b**) $868.75.

(**c**) All are binding.

6B-4. (**a**) Min. $0.00125A + 0.00085B + 0.0005C$, $A > 30$; $B > 15$; $C > 10$; $2A + B + 7C > 150$; $3.3A + 5B + 2C > 300$; $A + B + C > 100$.

(**b**) $0.0796 per bar.

(**c**) Yes, it is cheaper.

6B-5. **(a)** No; product A is not worthwhile.

(b) In the assembly process only.

CHAPTER 7

7-1. **(a)** Buy. (Incremental cost, including opportunity cost, is $4,930 versus $5,955.)

7-2. **(a)** Buy, subject to qualifications, since contribution of buy alternative is $40,000 versus $24,800 for make option.

7-3. **(a)** Accept the order, subject to qualifications, since contribution is $4,910.

7-4. **(a)** Probably not. Although the contribution is positive at $963 (assuming indirect factory labor is a variable cost), this is less than 1% of the firm's profits and involves several issues that are worrisome.

(b) Build inventory while investigating either plant expansion or a price increase.

7-5. **(a)** $3,105.67. Note that there is only a ⅔ probability that there would be opportunity costs.

7-6. **(a)** $P = 10 - 0.0006667Q$, and $MR = 10 - 0.001334Q$.

(b)

Q	SAC	AVC
2,000	$8.00	$5.50
4,000	4.85	3.60
6,000	3.93	3.10
8,000	4.63	4.00

(c) The MC and MR curves cross at approximately 5,500 units, implying a profit-maximizing price of $6.33. The sales (TR) maximizing price is $5.00, where quantity demanded will be 7,500 units.

(d) Data accuracy and *ceteris paribus* considerations.

7-7. **(a)** $8,745.

7-8. **(a)** Yes, subject to qualifications, since incremental revenues ($2,000) exceed incremental costs ($1,262).

7-9. **(a)** Strategy A: EPV = $125,142; strategy B: EPV = $102,457.

(b) Strategy B is favored by both the coefficient of variation and the maximin criteria. If Wyndham is only slightly risk averse, however, the CE criterion may favor strategy A.

7-10. **(a)** Wildlife farm: EPV = $77,670; amusement park: EPV = $87,906, assuming risk-free ODR = 9% in both cases.

(b) Decision is sensitive to ODR chosen. At ODRs of 17% and above, the wildlife farm has the greater EPV.

(c) This depends on the ODR and Yankee Jack's degree of risk aversion.

APPENDIX 7A

7A-1. **(a)** B/E volume is 3,692.

(b) For $P = 45, $Q = 3,500$, thus B/E volume is unattainable. Advise consideration of higher price, higher quality, or promotional activity.

7A-2. **(a)** 106,667, 138,196, and 142,248, respectively.

7A-3. **(a)** $42,100, $48,150, and $38,425, respectively.

(b) 18,563, 27,845, and 32,933, respectively.

(c) A, if highly risk averse; B, if less risk averse.

CHAPTER 8

8-1. (a) It should look like a cubic function.

(b) AVCs are approximately $9.83, $7.76, $6.83, $5.88, $5.31, $4.58, $4.15, $3.91, $3.72, $3.72, $3.89, and $3.99. MCs are approximately $5.48, $3.76, $2.87, $2.00, $1.58, $1.33, $1.54, $1.99, $3.50, $4.13, $6.40, and $7.24.

(c) About $5,484.

8-2. (a) AVCs are $19.17, $18.83, $18.70, $18.65, and $18.96. MCs (gradients) are $17.71, $18.12, $18.40, and $20.89.

(b) At about 920 units, where AVC is minimized.

(c) About 1,000 units, where MC = MR.

8-3. (a) $P = 9.24 - 1.09769Q$.

(b) SACs are $5.80, $4.40, and $5.30. Gradients are $3.23 and $7.50.

(c) $P = \$6.50$ and $Q = 2,500$, or thereabouts.

8-4. (a)

Q	AVC	SAC	MC
100	$20.78	40.78	21.56
200	21.56	31.56	23.13
300	22.35	29.01	24.69
400	23.13	28.13	26.26
500	23.91	27.91	27.82
600	24.69	28.03	29.38
700	25.47	28.33	30.95
800	26.26	28.76	32.51
900	27.04	29.26	34.08
1,000	27.82	29.82	35.64

(b) $37.05 and 328 pairs weekly.

(c) The contract would be marginally profitable if partially supplied from inventory. Also, the price increase should reduce quantity demanded from the regular buyers.

(d) Raise price to $37.05 and accept the store's offer (or make a counter offer above $28) and insist that the price to the store is an introductory offer only.

8-5. (a) 3 contracts, for 15,000 seats total, for contribution of $35,390.

8-6. (a) SACs are $31.52, $18.60, $13.78, $11.15, $9.47, $8.30, $7.48, $7, $6.85, $7.10, $7.63, and $8.32. Gradients are $5.68, $4.14, $3.26, $2.75, $2.45, $2.55, $3.65, $5.62, $9.38, $12.95, and $15.89.

(b) Leave it, since the expected contribution of the deal is $-2,384$, unless the buyer can be induced to pay the set-up cost or unless future business is expected to more than offset this deficit.

8-7. (a) Expected value of monthly profit from smaller plant is $13,625, compared to $28,043 from the larger plant. Standard deviations are 5,759 and 8,343, respectively. Coefficient of variation criterion indicates the larger plant, and the certainty equivalent criterion will support this unless the firm is extremely risk averse.

8-8. (a)

Q	1,000	2,000	3,000	4,000	5,000	6,000
SAC	$8.00	6.00	5.00	4.50	5.00	7.00
AVC	$5.00	4.50	4.00	3.75	4.40	6.50
MC		4.00	3.00	3.00	7.00	17.00

(b) Expected value of the Georgian order is about $11,050, depending on TVC interpolation, compared with $10,450 for the "leave it" alternative.

8-9. (a) $SAC = 6,669.68Q^{-0.32998}$.

(b) 20.45%.

(c) $475.03.

8-10. (a) $711.19 and $559.92, respectively.

(b) Very well. $R^2 = 0.9964$ and $S_e = 0.0101$. Thus the 95% confidence interval is a mere 2 cents each side of the predicted cost levels.

CHAPTER 9

9-1. (a) Market demand shifts back and price falls.

(b) Output is cut back such that MC equals the new price level.

9-2. (a) Presuming a kinked demand curve, the new MC curve remains within the MR gap.

(b) Traditionally these firms raise prices at the start of the new model year and might expect conscious parallelism at that time.

9-3. (a) New entrants undercut Prangle's price to retailers and gained market share as retailers pushed their products to gain the higher profit margin. Also, perhaps the number of competitors increased faster than the market did.

(b) Prangle believes that it faces a kinked demand curve.

(c) Contribution is maximized at $4.4 million at a price of $16 and output of 550,000 units.

9-4. (a) The firms' *mutatis mutandis* demand curves are coextensive, with the same intercept and three times the slope of the market demand curve.

9-5. (a) Struktatuff's demand curve is $P = 36,384 - 1.875Q$ and Steeldeal's is $P = 36,384 - 3.75Q$.

(b) $20,617.

(c) 12,613 total, 8,409 for Struktatuff and 4,204 for Steeldeal.

9-6. (a) The supply of the small firms is represented by $S = 15 + 1.125Q$, and the residual demand curve is $P = 55.26 - 0.592Q$.

(b) $P = $39.95 and $Q = 26,875$ units.

(c) $108,210 and $3,180, respectively.

9-7. (a) Author assumes demand is relatively elastic and wants to maximize TR, since royalties depend on TR.

(b) Publisher assumes that demand is relatively inelastic, and wants to maximize profits. Inelastic demand may reflect expectation that rivals would match a price reduction.

9-8. (a) About $30 per ton, depending on assumptions made.

(b) $106 per ton. This is only possible if all firms raise prices to this level and is only desirable if no further entry is feared within the firms' time horizons.

9-9. (a) $P = $30, $Q = 263,455$, and profits would be $1,174,685.

(b) $P = $19.95, $Q = 530,982$, and there would be a loss of $-2,615,491.

(c) $Q = 376,311$ and $P = $26.76.

9-10. (a) $P = $16.33 per dozen. Profits would be $17,778.

(b) $P = $14.94, $Q = 3,624$, and profits would be $16,414.

(c) Set price a safe margin below the limit price, at, say, $14.75 per dozen, in case the estimates of Popular's costs are inaccurate, for $Q = 3,700$ and profits of $16,091.

APPENDIX 9A

9A-1. Where the combined-MC curve cuts the combined-MR curve, project this level across to each of the MC curves to find the production in each plant, and across to each of the MR curves to find the allocation to each market.

9A-2. **(a)** 10,191.
   (b) 2,599 to the domestic market and 7,592 to the foreign market.
   (c) $61.02.
   (d) $41.02.

9A-3. **(a)** 4,886 pounds.
   (b) 3,073 pounds.
   (c) $44.07.
   (d) The contribution would decrease by $78.80.

9A-4. **(a)** $390,000.
   (b) $1,360.
   (c) $462,000.

9A-5. **(a)** $323.53.
   (b) 400 units, 314 transferred to the marketing division and 86 sold externally.
   (c) Transfer price is $465.33; 248 units will be transferred to the manufacturing division, and 459 units will be sold in the external market at $832.67 each.

9A-6. **(a)** (i) $6.85 per case (tomatoes)
           (ii) Total output 3,846 cases
           (iii) $14.88 per case (sauce)
       (b) (i) $6.00 per case (tomatoes)
           (ii) 3,000 cases (tomatoes)
           (iii) 1,114 cases (tomatoes)
           (iv) $14.53 and 4,114 cases (sauce)
       (c) (i) $9.92 per case (tomatoes)
           (ii) $12.96 per case (tomatoes)
           (iii) 6,923 cases split 4.051 cases to the external market and 2,872 cases to the internal market.
           (iv) $16.18 per case (sauce)

9A-7 **(a)** $P = 3,498.65 - 0.1647Q$ (western suburbs) and $P = 2,179.88 - 0.0325Q$ (eastern suburbs).
   (c) 7,553 units at $2,255 (western suburbs) and 17,987 units at $1,595 (eastern suburbs).
   (d) -1.813 and -2.729. The more elastic market gets the lower price.

CHAPTER 10

10-1. **(b)** $75,000 profits are unattainable at $7.95 profit-maximizing price. Maximum profits are $70,000 at output level of 24,600 units. Firm needs to shift demand curve, by promotion or product design, for example, or lower its costs, before it can achieve its objectives.

10-2. **(a)** $8.93.
   (b) Confident at 95% level. Profit at lower confidence boundary on sales volume exceeds profit at the old price.

10-3. **(a)** $7.15.

  (b) 2,720 units. (Hint: assume that the demand curve's slope remains the same as it shifts.)

10-4. (a) -4.0.

  (b) Yes, range of acceptable markups was from 21% to 50%.

  (c) No, at the profit-maximizing price of $P = \$40.71$ it will take years to recoup the search expenditure.

10-5. (a) $P = 1,431.82 - 11.3636Q$; TR $= 1,431.82Q - 11.3636Q^2$; TC $= 8,000 + 600Q$.

  (b) \$772.30, or a 28.72% markup.

10-6. (a) In the vicinity of \$110 to \$115.

  (b) Diversify product line, jointly promote down-filled products, develop effective substitute materials.

10-7. (a) \$499 or thereabouts.

10-8. (a) $P = 17.9 - 0.05593Q$.

  (b) \$10.95.

  (c) Probably not.

10-9. (a) \$775, or perhaps a little higher if Emerson's brand name and quality are considered equal to Quasar's.

  (b) \$1,199, or perhaps a little higher if Emerson's quality is considered equal to JVC's.

10-10. (a) Your answers will reflect your assumptions and strategy, of course. I decided to price the basic 128K model at \$2,195 and then add \$500 for IBM compatibility, \$150 for each extra 128K chip, \$600 for Word Perfect, and \$400 for Lotus, when these features are to be bundled in with the product. If sold later, I would add \$700 for IBM compatibility, \$300 for the first 128K chip, \$650 for the upgrade to 512K, \$650 for Word Perfect, and \$450 for Lotus.

CHAPTER 11

11-1. (a) \$17.75, \$17.50, and \$14.50.

11-2. (a) SAC falls from \$14 to \$11.20, \$8.96, \$7.17, \$5.73, and \$4.59 as output doubles from 1,000 to 2,000, 4,000, 8,000, and so on. Price is constant at \$9.95 up to 20,000 units, then declines smoothly to \$5.95 at 50,000 units.

11-3. (a) \$237,985 and \$295,747 using daily discount factors (or \$224,118 and \$278,559 using end-of-year discount factors, which probably understates the present value significantly).

  (b) Standard deviations are 52,375 and 66,226, using daily discount factors. Thus absolute risk is greater for the \$30 shirt. But relative risk, measured by the coefficients of variation, is virtually equal.

11-4. (a) \$129.88 and 25,370 units.

  (b) \$78.80.

  (c) \$135.20; 20,827 units; \$1,496,490.

  (d) No, it would suffer a loss of \$1.556 million in the first year.

11-5. (a) \$1,341,975 after 1 year, \$1,483,733 after 2 years, and \$1,542,880 after 3 years.

  (b) \$948,513 after 1 year, \$1,242,599 after 2 years, and \$1,378,573 after 3 years.

  (c) No, it would be unable to supply the demand, given the present plant.

11-6. (a) $P = 15.98 - 0.0000299Q$.

  (b) $P = 24.94 - 0.0000299Q$ and $P = 39.89 - 0.000029Q$.

  (c) $P = 24.92 - 0.000087Q$ and $P = 39.89 - 0.0001794Q$.

  (d) \$14.50 and \$21.95; 116,722 and 100,028 units.

11-7. (a) $190 and 22,000 units.
   (b) $180 and $172.50; 9,600 and 10,200 units.
   (c) $124.
   (d) The limit price strategy ($4,745,953 versus $3,845,925).

11-8. (a) $21 per case.
   (b) TR-maximizing price is $16.77, for profits only $70,000 less than profit-maximizing price.
   (c) 1) Entry will occur, price may fall to around $16.80. 2) Entry will occur, price may fall to perhaps $15.

11-9. (a) No. $167.80 per unit. BAE's lower price is presumably intended to increase production and allow benefit from learning effects before the entry of new firms.
   (b) Outputs will be 1,710, 1,960, 2,210, 2,460, 2,710, and 2,960 units. Profits will be $100,778, $145,058, $184,378, $222,168, $259,302, and $296,111, given the learning curve AVC $= 421.2432Q^{-0.32192}$, where Q represents cumulative volume. No, do not build larger plant.
   (c) No, assuming comparable quality/price ratio to consumer. Outputs are 1,284, 1,384, 1,484, and so on. Profits are $79,660, $93,440, $107,286, $121,193, $135,156, and $149,172. No.
   (d) Both would have to reduce price, by, say, $20.
   (e) Setting price at $167.80 for first six months allows higher profits. Then reduce price $20 each time there is entry.

11-10. (a) $1,704, $2,169, $1,968, and $1,423.
   (b) The product might be introduced at a nominal price of $2,169 but sold at a "special introductory price" of $1,699 for the first year, then priced at $2,169 in the second year, reduced to $1,968 in the third year, and reduced further to $1,423 in the fourth year.
   (c) Volumes are 1,310, 1,792, 1,577, and 1,000 units. Profits are $0.874 million, $2.05 million, $1.492 million, and $0.403 million in nominal terms, given SAC $= 1,091.81Q^{-0.00786}$, where Q represents cumulative volume.

CHAPTER 12

12-1. (a) $4,700, $7,200, $6,750, $3,600, and $1,500.
   (b) 23.25% markup, bid $61,625, EPVC $7,349.91.

12-2. (a) Desperation. Others firms' costs were lower.
   (b) $87,630.

12-3. (a) 0.972, 0.806, 0.632, 0.452, and 0.264.
   (b) $35,200.

12-4. (a) Incremental costs are $66,200.
   (b) Your answer will depend on your assessment of the situation and your degree of risk aversion, but it should be somewhat below normal bidding policy, such as $125,000, or about 5% above full costs.

12-5. (a) $895,968.
   (b)

Markup rate	10%	15%	20%	25%	30%
EPV(Profit)	$30,003	$57,969	$69,427	$62,669	$26,504

   (c) About 22% over nominal costs, or $1,561,600.

12-6. (a) About $396,500.
   (b) About $428,000.

12-7. (a) $437,000.

(b) Somewhat below normal practice, say $630,000, should win the contract.

12-8. (a) The incremental costs total $218,000.

(b) Yes, because expected contribution is $82,000.

(c) A bid significantly below $300,000, say $260,000, should win the contract. Bid no lower than $182,000.

12-9. (a) $216,952.

(b) About $270,000.

(c) About $280,000.

12-10. (a) $173,005.

(b) $206,857.

CHAPTER 13

13-1. (a) No, $dQ/dA = 12.62$.

(b) No, slope of the advertising function will decline as advertising increases. Thompson should make a series of increments to advertising and note sales reaction.

13-2. (a) Diminishing returns to advertising should be evident.

(b) About $7,000 per quarter.

13-3. (a) $11,233.53. Although R^2 is very high, this is an extrapolation outside the data base.

(b) About $1,625.

(c) Lagged impact of advertising on sales.

(d) Maintain advertising at current level while investigating lagged impacts.

13-4. (a) $P = \$6.56$ and $S = 5.5$.

(b) 2 tapes on sale per week.

13-5. (a) $P = \$4.50$ (for medium pizza) and $11,000 advertising.

(b) $563.26.

13-6. (a) V-P Finance is apparently assuming that rivals will also reduce their advertising outlays, while Marketing V-P expects *ceteris paribus* for reductions or increases in the advertising budget.

(b) Mr. Hogg expects rivals to match increases in advertising.

(c) Maintain current (maximin) advertising level while investigating rivals' attitudes toward advertising rivalry, their ability to increase advertising, and so on.

13-7. (a) Central to your argument would be that rivals will ignore your advertising increase and that sales would be responsive to increased advertising.

(b) Which attributes are desired by consumers and how much are they willing to pay for these? Will rivals react to your campaign?

13-8. (a) 52,501 units, TR = $15,487,730, and profit = $2,307,574.

(b) $242,812.30.

(c) 53,207 units, TR = $15,696,163, and profit = $2,311,884.

13-9. (a) 244,461 units and $278,112.40 profit.

(b) $1,000,079.

(c) No, only $820.20.

13-10. (a) 303,690 units and $629,522 profit.

(b) $824,115.

(c) 284,964 units, $4,559,429 revenue, and $655,600 profit.

CHAPTER 14

14-1. (a) Neither cost leadership nor quality leadership seems possible unless new equipment is purchased. New equipment should be chosen with a particular strategy in mind.

(b) Since the premium ice creams are higher priced, a quality leadership strategy, either focused to the ice cream parlors or more broadly oriented toward foodstores and the parlors, might be the best strategy. On the other hand, you might argue that given their quality reputation and proclivity for promotional pricing, they should pursue cost leadership.

(c) Cost of new equipment; relative costs of other firms; feasibility of repositioning their brand name in attribute space; feasibility of introducing a new brand name for a higher-quality ice cream; feasibility of opening one or more ice cream parlors; and so on.

14-2. (a) Focused cost leadership may be the best initial strategy.

(b) Introduce the City, Rocker, and Family models first, at relatively low prices, with promotion stressing their economy of purchase and operation, targeted at young adults.

(c) Other products available in each market segment; strategies being pursued by rivals; relative costs of rival firms; similarity of Hawaii and mainland markets; and so on.

14-3. (a) Focused differentiation strategy.

(b) Immigration law services, priced at a premium, promoted directly to colleges, universities, and high-technology companies who regularly hire foreign professionals.

14-4. (a) A focused differentiation strategy, offering a high-quality business program (with a strong liberal arts component) in an idyllic setting, or a focused cost leadership strategy as a new business school, would seem to be prime contenders.

(b) Establishing a new business school that specializes in liberally educated professionals seems promising. Fees should be relatively high, and the program should be promoted in business periodicals as well as through selected high schools in affluent suburbs of the major northeastern cities.

14-5. (a) The products are experience goods that may be learned through demonstration at the point of sale, rendering them virtual search goods. Thus, Fisher might consider either a cost-leadership or a differentiation strategy, perhaps focused on the professional painter.

(b) The major user benefits provided by the product (time saved and less mess) indicate a differentiation strategy, at least initially. There should be a considerable price premium for the "compressed air" model over the "hand pump" model, which in turn can be more expensive than other roller systems.

(c) Focus differentiation, targeting the professional painter with the "compressed air" model, and the 'do-it-yourself' painter with the "hand pump" model.

14-6. (a) Differentiation strategies seem most promising.

(b) Open a store catering to the do-it-yourselfer, incorporating a specialty service in luxury bathrooms.

(c) Products must include all those sought by the home handyperson, be priced slightly above hardware store prices due to the free advice available, and be promoted directly to the do-it-yourselfer in the local media. The luxury bathroom service would be featured in the advertisements and in the store itself.

14-7. (a) Cost focus strategies seem feasible, as do quality focus strategies. Broad-based cost leadership and differentiation strategies seem less promising.

(b) Reposition the firm as a supplier of high-quality, special-interest tours.

(c) The packages should be composed of direct flights with convenient departure times, quality hotels, quality recreation and sporting facilities, and so on. Prices should include a premium for this additional quality. Promotion should be targeted, by advertisements in special interest magazines, for example.

14-8. (a) The business lunch and dinner market and the fine Italian dining options are each quality focus strategies to a large degree. The family restaurant franchise and the breakfast and fast food market are more likely appropriate for a cost leadership strategy, since these markets tend to be more price conscious. Nonetheless, a broad-based differentiation strategy is also possible in these latter two types of restaurants.

(b) Your answer is as good as mine.

(c) Support your answer with an analysis of the cost and revenue implications.

14-9. (a) Cost leadership does not seem feasible, due to limited capacity. A focused differentiation strategy seems more promising.

(b) Upgrade the trails, install snow-making equipment, and focus on the more affluent, enthusiast skier. Product quality must be improved, prices increased, and promotion targeted on those who want the best and are willing to pay for it.

14-10. (a) Unless it adopts the industry standards, a broad-based differentiation strategy seems unwise. Even then, BBC may not be able to compete with the major players. A focus strategy, utilizing the nano-disks in a portable computer, seems like a good bet.

(b) No, a focused cost leadership strategy might be possible.

(c) Adopt MS-DOS and pursue miniaturization as a focused differentiation strategy.

(d) Small portable computers, with integral disk drives and printer, sold at a premium for those who value this combination and promoted to business professionals and the college market, might be a winning combination.

CHAPTER 15

15-1. (a) Undertake projects A, B, and C.

15-2. (a) $17,792.50.
(b) 12.995339%.
(c) About $57,000.

15-3. (a) $36,363.
(b) About 24.4%.
(c) $15,683.
(e) Kayak.

15-4. (a) $53,487, $46,767, $55,900, and $41,058.
(b) Using nominal cash flows, payback periods (in months) are 17.8, 23.1, 21, and 24. Using present-valued cash flows, they are 20, 27.5, 24.6, and 30.6.
(c) It is a tradeoff between Sportswear at either location A or location B.

15-5. (a) Tacos, $15,435; chicken, $11,624; hamburgers, $9,200.
(b) In months, 24.857, 24.923, and 26.
(c) Tacos.

15-6. (a) B: $60,172; D: $48,578; A: $44,210; C: $30,405.
(b) B: 3.15; C: 2.90; A: 2.26; D: 2.21.
(c) B, D, and A.
(d) $134,787.

15-7. (a) West: $103,145; east: $86,178; south: $81,628; north: $67,963.
(b) North: 1.57; south: 1.45; west: 1.36; east: 1.34.

    (c) West and south.

    (d) $184,772.

15-8. (a) EPVs are $231,174 and $255,177. IRRs are 23.26% and 26.47%. PIs are 2.15 and 2.34.

15-9. (a) Plan A EPV is $EC4.02m; plan B EPV is $EC5.68m.

    (b) No.

15-10. (a) Oval circuit EPV is $23.397m; Road circuit EPV is $28.864m.

    (b) Using nominal cash flows, 45 months and 55.2 months. Using present-valued cash flows, 59.3 months and 62.5 months.

    (c) Road circuit.

APPENDIX A

A-1. (a) $Y = a + bX$.

    (b) $Y = a + bX + cX^2$.

    (c) $Y = a + bX + cX^2 + cX^3$.

    (d) $Y = ae^{bx}$.

    (e) $Y = aX^b$.

    (f) $Y = a/X^b$, or $Y = aX^{-b}$.

A-2. (a) $dY/dX = 13.5X^2$.

    (b) $dX/dY = -6Z(9X^2) = -54X^2(4 + 3X^3)$.

    (c) $dY/dX = 21 - 42X^2$.

    (d) $dY/dX = 24(-32X + 27X^2 + 24X^3 - 36X^5)$.

    (e) $dY/dX = 24(4 - 2X^2)(4 + 24X - 10X^2)$.

    (f) $dY/dX = 8e^{2x}$.

A-3. (a) Y is maximized at -27.5 when $X = 1.5$.

    (b) Y is minimized at 12 when $X = 4$.

    (c) A is minimized at $-15,245.25$ when $B = 52.5$.

    (d) K is maximized at 244,667 when $J = 3.333$.

A-4. (a) 21.42357 hours.

AUTHOR INDEX

646

SUBJECT INDEX